Late Medieval Devotional Compilations in England

MEDIEVAL CHURCH STUDIES

*Editorial Board under the auspices of the
Department of History, University of Nottingham*

Ross Balzaretti, Peter Darby, Rob Lutton, Claire Taylor

Previously published volumes in this series are listed at the back of the book.
VOLUME 41

LATE MEDIEVAL DEVOTIONAL COMPILATIONS IN ENGLAND

Edited by

Marleen Cré, Diana Denissen, and Denis Renevey

BREPOLS

British Library Cataloguing in Publication Data

A catalogue record for this book is available from the British Library

© 2020, Brepols Publishers n.v., Turnhout, Belgium

All rights reserved. No part of this publication may be reproduced, stored in a retrieval system, or transmitted, in any form or by any means, electronic, mechanical, photocopying, recording, or otherwise, without the prior permission of the publisher.

ISBN: 978-2-503-57477-6
e-ISBN: 978-2-503-57478-3
DOI: 10.1484/M.MCS-EB.5.112874
ISSN: 1378-868X
e-ISSN: 2294-8449

Printed in the EU on acid-free paper

D/2020/0095/126

Contents

List of Illustrations — ix

Acknowledgements — xi

Introduction
MARLEEN CRÉ, DIANA DENISSEN, and DENIS RENEVEY — 1

Part I
The Dynamics of Devotional Compilations

Building a Bestseller: The Priest, the Pear Tree,
and the Compiler
    VINCENT GILLESPIE — 27

Compilation: The Gift that Keeps on Giving
    RALPH HANNA — 63

Theorizing the Miscellaneous and the Middle English
Biblical Paratext
    IAN JOHNSON — 83

A Talkyng of the Love of God: The Art of Compilation
and the Compiled Self
    ANNIE SUTHERLAND — 109

Reading Late Medieval Devotional Compilations in the
Fifteenth and Sixteenth Centuries
    MARGARET CONNOLLY — 131

Part II
Compiling the Compilation: Manuscript Transmission

Form and Fluidity: Reshaping the *Pore Caitif* and *Contemplations of the Dread and Love of God* in Oxford, Bodleian Library, MS Bodley 423 and Oxford, Bodleian Library, MS Bodley 938
    DIANA DENISSEN   157

Suffering for Love: Compilation and Asceticism in *Life of Soul*
    SARAH MACMILLAN   171

Compilers' Voices in Cambridge, University Library, MS Ii.6.40
    MARLEEN CRÉ   193

Part III
Compilation and Devotional Practice

A Hagiographic Compilation of Medieval Native Women in the *South English Legendaries*: Oxford, Bodleian Library, MS Bodley 779
    MAMI KANNO   215

Devotional Compilations and Lollard Sanctity in a Fifteenth-Century Anthology
    NICOLE R. RICE   231

'When is a man proude. When he wol not beknowen suche as he is': Knowing Oneself in London, British Library, MS Additional 37787
    SHERI SMITH   255

Resignation or Rebuttal? Three Biblical *Exempla* in Richard Whitford's *Dyuers Holy Instrucyons and Teachynges*
    BRANDON ALAKAS   271

Part IV
Mystics Compiled

'Desyrable is thi name': Fashioning the Name of Jesus in Some Devotional Compilations
    DENIS RENEVEY   291

The Scale of Perfection in Devotional Compilations
    MICHAEL G. SARGENT   309

The *Liber specialis gratiae* in a Devotional Anthology: London, British Library, MS Harley 494
    NAOË KUKITA YOSHIKAWA   341

Part V
Texts, Images, and Affect

The Living Book of Cambridge, Trinity College, MS B.15.42: Compilation, Meditation, and Vision
    LAURA SAETVEIT MILES   363

The Desert of Religion: A Textual and Visual Compilation
    ANNE MOURON   385

What Grace in Presence: Affective Literacies in *The Chastising of God's Children*
    A. S. LAZIKANI   411

Afterword

The Terminology and Ethos of Vernacular *Compilatio*
    NICHOLAS WATSON   435

Index of Manuscripts   457

General Index   459

Illustrations

Figure 1, p. 370. Richard Rolle, *The Commandment*, with side wounds marginalia (six total over page spread).

Figure 2, p. 372. Richard Rolle, *The Commandment*, with red marginal 'ihc' monogram noting the 'ihu' monogram with a red box around it in the text, for the Holy Name.

Figure 3, p. 372. *Meditaciones domini nostri* with parchment holes, through which the rubricated table of contents of *Contemplations of the Dread and Love of God* can be seen.

Acknowledgements

The way in which *Late Medieval Compilations in England* came into being is as the result of lively and academically stimulating exchanges within an international community of scholars over several years. The generous three-year grant from the *Swiss National Science Foundation*, supplemented with a half-year extension (2013–17), enabled the creation of the research team whose members are the co-editors of this volume. Compilers depend on networks for the success of their work, and we feel that, more than most other research projects, this one in general, and the ensuing volume in particular, immensely benefitted from the generosity of our academic colleagues during the official existence of the research project and beyond.

We would like to thank the institutions and colleagues who hosted us to present aspects of our research on the project. These early exchanges helped us define the volume as it stands now. We presented our first results at the *English Department Research Series* at the University of Lausanne. We also had the opportunity to present our work on the occasion of the *Research Days in Medieval English Studies* at Pázmány Péter Catholic University, Budapest, Hungary. We were also invited to present the project at the *Doctoral Workshop on Medieval and Early Modern English Studies* at the University of Geneva. Team members also developed a very strong and fruitful collaboration with members of the Cost-Action IS 1301 *New Communities of Interpretation: Contexts, Strategies and Processes of Religious Transformation in Late Medieval and Early Modern Europe*, directed by Professor Sabrina Corbellini. Marleen Cré benefited from a COST Short Term Scientific Mission Grant that enabled her to work in Oxford and Cambridge Libraries and as Academic Visitor in the English Faculty at Oxford. Team members also presented work at different COST venues, including Paris, Lisbon, and Tours. Diana Denissen received a SNSF six-month Mobility Grant which allowed her to study as a visiting student at the University of Oxford.

The SNSF team also organized three sessions at the Leeds International Medieval Congress (2015) and had the pleasure of benefitting from the stimulating responses of Ian Johnson. Our Leeds sessions speakers included Sarah Macmillan, Margaret Healy-Varley, Laura Saetveit Miles, and Ralph Hanna. The team was also invited to present their work at the *Medieval English Research Seminar* organized by the Faculty of English, University of Oxford (2015). Individual presentations by team members were offered at the Universities of Antwerp, Amsterdam, Belfast, Glasgow, and Salzburg. We also profited from interactions with members of the Leverhulme Trust, *Women's Literary Culture and the Medieval Canon*, directed by Diane Watt.

The 2016 Conference, *'This tretice, by me compiled': Late Medieval Devotional Compilations in Englan*, organised by the SNSF team, brought international scholars to the University of Lausanne to explore further areas of compilation activity. The conference was generously sponsored by the *Swiss National Science Foundation*, the Arts Faculty of the University of Lausanne, and the *Centre of Medieval and Post-medieval Studies* in the same faculty. Thanks are due to Eva Suarato, secretary of the English Department, and to the student-assistants, who helped us with practicalities. We were also privileged to hear the ensemble *Miroir de Musique* in a performance of music by Adam de la Halle and Philippe de Vitry. All these elements contributed greatly to the positive and constructive atmosphere of the conference.

The exceptional quality of both presentations and following exchanges incited us into submitting a volume that would leave a record of new discoveries in the field of religious compilations in late medieval England. We are therefore grateful to all the conference participants, including of course our plenary speakers, for making this event such a fruitful one. We would like to thank those who submitted their research for our volume. It has been a pleasure collaborating with you while preparing it for publication. We also would like to thank Brepols for the affable care they have shown in helping us with the production of the book. The anonymous reviewer provided excellent insights that helped us shape it to even better standards. Guy Carney has been a constant support from the early stages of the project onwards. Olena Danylovych and Simon Heller, who have both now completed their Master's studies at the University of Lausanne, were instrumental in providing an excellent version of the whole manuscript to our copyeditor, Deborah Oosterhouse, who has been the best one can dream of. Last but not least, we would like to thank members of the editorial board of *Medieval Church Studies* at Brepols for providing such a prestigious home to our volume.

Marleen Cré, Diana Denissen, and Denis Renevey

Introduction

Marleen Cré, Diana Denissen, and Denis Renevey

This book is a collection of essays with late medieval devotional compilations in Middle English as their common focus. The term 'devotional compilation' is a term we use to designate what Michael Sargent has termed 'minor devotional writings', 'works of religious devotion that cannot be attributed to such major writers as Rolle, Hilton, the author of *The Cloud of Unknowing*, Julian of Norwich, Nicholas Love, or Margery Kempe'.[1] These predominantly anonymous works, such as *Speculum christiani*, *The Three Arrows on Doomsday*, *Pore Caitif*, *A Talkyng of the Love of God*, *Þe Pater Noster of Richard Ermyte*, Edmund of Abingdon's *Speculum ecclesie*, *Life of Soul*, *Book to a Mother*, *Disce mori*, *The Chastising of God's Children*, and *The Desert of Religion*, all of which are discussed in this book, are in origin derivative. All of them incorporate fragments from existing texts that, in many cases, have been translated from a Latin original, yet, as compilations, they transcend '[their] limitation[s] as a collection of snippets from other works and took on an identity and a literary form of [their] own',[2] and thus became unique new texts. 'Devotional' is used here to refer to 'the entire range of piety from simple, affective prayer to works describing or inciting to contemplative union'.[3] These devotional compilations often also have ascetic, catechetic, penitential, and diagnostic characteristics.[4]

Because of the sheer numbers of copies in which some of these texts were transmitted — *Pore Caitif*, for instance, survives in full or in fragments in fifty-

---

[1] Sargent, 'Minor Devotional Writings', p. 147.

[2] Sargent, 'Minor Devotional Writings', p. 157.

[3] Sargent, 'Minor Devotional Writings', p. 147.

[4] Gillespie, 'Anonymous Devotional Writings', pp. 128–29.

four manuscripts — and the long list of texts that could be called devotional compilations, they make up an important part of literature in English and are intriguing objects of literary analysis in addition to the canonical religious as well as secular texts in English of the late medieval period. Yet strength does not only lie in numbers. Precisely because of their derivative nature, compilations help us understand medieval forms of authorship and of textual transmission, both of which are closely connected. Indeed, the evidence of compilatory agency (*compilatio*) that can be found in the selection, translation, and recontextualization of the fragments by compilers is similar to decisions made when texts are selected and ordered within a manuscript.[5] This shows in the frequent use of the word 'compilation' not only to designate derivative texts that developed into new, unique texts, but also to refer to multi-text manuscripts. We term these multi-text manuscripts anthologies, defined by Margaret Connolly as 'a collection of texts in which some organising principles can be observed', or miscellanies, which are manuscript books 'bringing together texts which do not present a coherent set of organising principles, among which one might find disparate, incomplete or jumbled notes of a personal nature alongside full-length texts'.[6] This is why nearly all essays in this volume also focus on the manuscript context of the compilations discussed: on variations between versions of a particular compilation in different manuscripts, or on the functioning of a compilation or text (fragment) within an anthology or miscellany, as can be seen in the descriptions of the essays below. In its focus on late medieval devotional compilations in England, this book maps another segment of late medieval religious literature and culture in England and is complementary to Vincent Gillespie and Kantik Ghosh's useful essay collection *After Arundel*, as well as Ian Johnson and Allan Westphall's *The Pseudo-Bonaventuran Lives of Christ*.

This book reflects a most crucial issue at the centre of our thinking about devotional compilations in the Swiss National Science Foundation project 'Late Medieval Religiosity in England: The Evidence of Late Fourteenth- and Fifteenth-Century Devotional Compilations', carried out at the University of Lausanne from 2013 to 2017: the intriguing relationship between the corpus texts and the various versions in the manuscripts in which they survive. The

---

[5] The theoretical side of medieval and scholarly thinking about *compilatio* has been laid out in detail in Parkes, 'The Influence of the Concepts of *Ordinatio* and *Compilatio*', Minnis, *Medieval Theories of Authorship*, Hathaway, 'Compilatio', and Minnis, '*Nolens auctor sed compilator reputari*'. Also see Gillespie's essay in this volume, and Renevey, 'The Choices of the Compiler'.

[6] Connolly, 'Understanding the Medieval Miscellany', p. 5.

focus in the project was on eight devotional compilations as texts with their own new identity and literary form, but that — though in some cases more so than in others — prove to be texts with identities less fixed than their presentation in edited form suggests.[7] *The Chastising of God's Children*, for instance, has been transmitted relatively stably from one manuscript to the next. Variations between manuscripts are minor, which might explain the fact that Joyce Bazire and Eric Colledge could choose as the base text for their 1957 edition of this compilation a version that in many instances has a reading different from any other manuscript in which the text survives.[8] The compilation known as *Þe Holy Boke Gratia Dei* survives in its longest form in one manuscript only, and in fragments and abbreviations in three others. Mary Luke Arntz's edition of this text is a plausible reconstruction of what could have been the full version of this text.[9]

The devotional compilations in our corpus or parts of them were often subject to recontextualization and recompilation. Fragments from *The Chastising*, a compilation itself built out of fragments from earlier texts, were recompiled in *Disce mori*, which shows that *The Chastising*'s integrity is not absolute.[10] In Lincoln, Lincoln Cathedral, MS 91, Robert Thornton has excerpted *Þe Holy Boke* and copied the fragments in a different order to how they figure in the longer, more complete version found in San Marino, Huntington Library, MS HM 148, and interspersed them with excerpts from texts by Richard Rolle to form a new whole that, arguably and effectively, functions as a new compilation within his family book.[11] *The Contemplations of the Dread and Love of God* survives in its full form in sixteen manuscripts, but fragments of this compilation, most often its final chapter, the AB chapter on prayer, occur on their own in a further fifteen manuscripts.[12] *Pore Caitif*, another compilation in the project corpus, survives in so many constellations that it is hard to tell whether its full version — a grouping of fourteen treatises in a fixed order attested in

---

[7] The devotional compilations in the project corpus were *The Chastising of God's Children, Þe Holy Boke Gratia Dei, Pore Caitif, The Tretyse of Loue*, Richard Rolle's *Oleum effusum* compilation, *A Talkyng of the Love of God, Contemplations of the Dread and Love of God*, and *Disce mori*.

[8] *The Chastising of God's Children*, ed. by Bazire and Colledge, and Cré and Rohrhofer, 'An Introduction', pp. 168–69.

[9] Rolle, *Þe Holy Boke Gratia Dei*, ed. by Arntz.

[10] *The 'Exhortacion'*, ed. by Jones, pp. xxxviii–xlii.

[11] Rolle, *Þe Holy Boke Gratia Dei*, ed. by Arntz, pp. vi–ix. Also see Cré, 'Miscellaneity, Compiling Strategies, and the Transmission', pp. 135–36.

[12] Connolly, 'Mapping Manuscripts and Readers', pp. 277–78.

twenty-nine manuscripts — is its initial form that the fragmentary attestations descended from in a process of selecting and borrowing, or whether the fragmentary attestations document earlier stages in the formation of the text that over time, with accretions and rewriting, was shaped into the fourteen-treatise form.[13]

Whatever the ad hoc character of the production stage of a compilation, anthology, or miscellany, the meaning of the text or multi-text manuscript for its intended reader(s) and its later, wider audience lies in 'its utility in context'.[14] The compilations and anthologies had a religious aim, which most of them express explicitly. As the *Disce mori* compiler spells it out in the prefatory poem addressed to 'my best beloued sustre Dame Alice',[15] the book teaches its reader how to live well by avoiding the vices and embracing the virtues:

> Þough *Disce mori* called be þe booke,
>
> Hit techeth wele to lyue, and to eschewe
> Vices, whiche hit declareth sufficiently
> The seuen capital; and also to sue
> Þe vertues contrarie to þe seuen, ...[16]

The prologue to the *Pore Caitif* points out the aim of the virtuous life it teaches: 'This tretyse [...] shal teche simple men and wymmen of gode wille the right way to hevene, yf they wille besye hem to have it in mynde and to worche therafter'.[17] *The Chastising of God's Children* teaches its addressee, a 'religious sister' about temptations, 'Of this matier ȝe han desired to knowe in comfort of ȝoure soule', adding how she should respond to them: 'medeful it were to ȝou, pacientli and gladli to suffre suche gostli chastisynges wiþ ful feiþ and sad hope, and abide his ordenance til he sende comfort bi grace and mercy'.[18] Often compilations and anthologies started from a compiler's specific focus or thematic concern, and this compiler would select and rearrange fragments from

---

[13] Denissen, 'Without the Multiplication of Many Books?', pp. 99–104. See also ch. 2 of Denissen, *Middle English Devotional Compilations*.

[14] Gillespie, 'Vernacular Books of Religion', p. 326.

[15] *The 'Exhortacion'*, ed. by Jones, p. ix. In Oxford, Jesus College, MS 39, 'Dame Alice' has been crossed out to accommodate another reader, in Bodl. Lib., MS Laud misc. 99, the name has been kept.

[16] *The 'Exhortacion'*, ed. by Jones, p. ix.

[17] See the Prologue to the *Pore Caitif*, in *The Idea of the Vernacular*, ed. by Wogan-Browne and others, p. 240, ll. 2–5. Also see '*The Pore Caitif*', ed. by Brady, p. 1, ll. 1–5.

[18] *The Chastising of God's Children*, ed. by Bazire and Colledge, p. 95, ll. 4–7.

existing texts in accordance to his aim. Many compilations and anthologies are confident of their readers' capacities; they 'rely on an informed and developed sense of self-awareness on the part of their readers, and an embracing by them of spiritual autonomy and responsibility'.[19]

In this book, as in the project that led to it, then, compilatory agency is approached both from the compilers' point of view, as an authorial activity, and from the audience's point of view, that is, in its effect on the readers of a compilation or anthology. Contributors investigate how compilers have dealt with their source texts, which can be compilations themselves, and how the new compilations have been transmitted in the manuscript tradition by looking at variation, co-texts, and marginal annotations. In addition, compilations and manuscripts are literary texts and artefacts that readers would have used as part of their religious lives. Thus, contributors also focus on readerly reception of the compilations, anthologies, and miscellanies. They investigate how variation between versions of the same compilation and its interaction with additional textual or visual material may have influenced the readers' understanding of the texts' religious message. As Jill C. Havens put it, devotional compilations 'invoke an immediate response and assume an interactive audience'.[20]

Part I. *The Dynamics of Devotional Compilations*

Techniques and strategies of compilatory composition are at the heart of Vincent Gillespie's essay. 'Building a Bestseller' bestows an accolade to Parkes, Minnis, and Richard and Mary Rouse for their pioneering work on compilatory composition. At the same time it shows the extent to which the field has been moving in the last three or four decades. Gillespie's discussion of the *narracio* of the priest and the pear tree in *The Book of Margery Kempe* elucidates the demands made by the laity to the Church for good quality teaching and preaching. The *narracio* overtly challenges the Church's failure to provide pastoral support to a well-educated laity, and in that respect it is perfectly in line with other Latinate texts sharing similar concerns. Indeed, the confident tone used by Margery in her rebuttal of Archbishop Bowet can be accounted for by the fact that it relies on the Latin pastoral and catechetical tradition that circulated similar requests for reformist and constructive teaching strategies which had been neglected by the official Church. Although the *Speculum christiani*

---

[19] Gillespie, 'Anonymous Devotional Writings', p. 129.
[20] Havens, 'A Narrative of Faith', p. 70.

was not translated before *The Book* was completed in the 1430s, Gillespie, on the basis of similar concerns and requests in both texts, argues for a knowledge of the *Speculum* by Margery by means of instant translation, a practice that was also possibly used by the priest who read aloud to her for seven or eight years. His reading included a Latin Bible with glosses, 'Hyltons boke, Boneventur, *Stimulus Amoris*, *Incendium Amoris*, and swech other'.[21] Despite the fact that the *Speculum christiani* was put together by trial and error — a process of compilatory composition one needs to keep in mind for some of our devotional compilations, it proved to be immensely successful, with sixty manuscripts of the complete text, a European circulation, and seven printed editions between 1484 and 1517. Although produced by initial haphazard experimentation, the success of the *Speculum* may have been due to its subtle blending of Latin and vernacular *pastoralia*.

Gillespie, together with Ralph Hanna, reminds us about the need to focus on Latin catechetical material in order to understand bilingual *pastoralia*. The *Speculum* itself is a tour de force of compilatory activity: it borrows its Latin material from a late fourteenth-century *summa* of pastoral proof texts known as the *Cibus anime*; but the complexity of compilatory activity does not stop here, as *tabula* 8 of the *Speculum* contains a sequence which is made up of a treatise on priestly duties (BL, MS Royal 5 A VI) which borrows both from a text called *Pupilla oculi* and from *Cibus anime*. It is impossible to argue for a descent from a single copy in the case of the *Cibus/Speculum* family of texts: the dynamics of transmission are marked, in the words of Gillespie, by restless compilatory experimentation, cross-fertilization, and dissemination. If the dissemination of the *Cibus/Speculum* family of texts may have been generated from a Carthusian centre, possibly the Beauvale and/or Axholme charterhouses, Gillespie does not exclude other, non-Carthusian centres more focused on *pastoralia*. The fact that the *Speculum* attracted the attention of priests associated with York Minster may offer a clue to further investigation. Gillespie returns to the *narracio* of the priest and the pear tree to suggest that it does not only function as a warning against priestly sloth, but that in fact it encapsulates the process of compilatory activity that may have been part of the reformist spirit of the Church up to 1430.

Trial-and-error method and restless creative compilatory activity also characterize the very brief (three printed pages long) but popular (thirty copies)

---

[21] See Kempe, *The Book*, ed. by Windeatt, p. 280. Bonaventure, the *Stimulus Amoris*, and *Incendium amoris*, like the Bible, could have been in Latin, and therefore requiring instant translation as part of the priest's reading process.

Three Arrows on Doomsday, a compilation with a tripartite sermon structure that Ralph Hanna defines as an original compilation ultimately derived from a Latin text whose version he has so far traced only in Alexander Carpenter's *Destructorium viciorum*, completed in 1429 and postdating the *Three Arrows* compilation. Originality is marked by substantial substitution, complementation, and insertion. The *Three Arrows* compiler uses a large variety of sources, for instance Robert of Basevorn's *Forma praedicandi*; he also deals intelligently with both Rolle's Latin and Middle English psalters when adding to the text. The suppression in the body and soul dialogue of the speech of the body modifies the tenor of the text importantly, with a substitute part that emphasizes forgiveness.

Hanna identifies five different versions of *The Three Arrows*. Some of these versions complement the 'original' version with additional citations. However, in Glasgow, University Library, MS Hunter 520, further compilatory activity takes place with the use of a translation from the Wycliffite Later Version of the Bible. Perhaps even more daringly, the compiler of Bodl. Lib., MS Tanner 336 inserts in his own translation a passage from Job (Job 3. 3, 11–13) which also appears in a similar context in another Middle English compilation, *Þe Holy Boke Gratia Dei*. Although the compiler had no need of this book as he had the full Latin source and a library, he seems to conform to the authority-giving of compilatory activity. As stated by Hanna in the case of the fifth version, compilers sometimes show a creative ease that compares well with their sources. However, when the compiler has a good text to fill his segments, he will use this text, rather than composing a new one. Evidence of compilatory activity in the middle of the fifteenth century suggests that it should not be regarded as the weaker descendant of original composition, but as an authority-giving activity preferred over original composition. Late medieval textual culture and activity are defined by their compilatory agency and should be assessed as such, against modern culture's affirmation of literary originality.

The last version of *The Three Arrows* explored by Hanna shows the text to be absorbed into *A Treatise of Ghostly Battle*, a text that is itself, for most of its parts, compiled as well. Indeed, the text is made up of 'The Horse or Armour of Heaven', one of the *Pore Caitif*'s tracts, an abbreviated version of *The Three Arrows*, and an extract from *The Prick of Conscience*. Compilation as the gift that keeps on giving is well attested in this case study. As a final demonstration, *The Three Arrows* joins with *The Mirror of Sinners* in sixteen manuscript occurrences, quite often next to it, thus possibly forming a new compilation in the eyes of the scribe, readers, and listeners. Even more intriguing, combined together, these two texts are sometimes found with the Middle English *Pore*

Caitif and identified as two additional tracts to the fourteen that make most of its versions. The many instances of compilatory activity linked to *The Three Arrows* show the extent to which the attempt to render coherent what may often be the result of serendipity or of forms of coherence restricted by practical and material circumstances that can no longer be unearthed is vain.

It is this ideological problem that Ian Johnson's contribution addresses: How can one grasp and conceive of miscellaneity without bending medieval reality and medieval literary production according to modern concepts? Although Johnson's starting point is the miscellaneous codex, his interest is in the investigation of miscellaneous textuality and miscellaneity as a concept, a 'force of consignificance'. As in the examples provided by Hanna, Johnson argues that randomness can be explained in some cases as a collateral consequence of exemplar poverty; and yet it should not be dismissed when scrutinizing textual productions. Although it escapes neat rational conformation, it is an essential element in the making of most manuscript textual productions. After a brief reference to the notions of the polythetic and dialogics, both of them shedding light on the structure of compilations and miscellanies, Johnson proposes 'heterarchy', more specifically heterarchic structures, as a way of conceptually understanding the way in which miscellanies and compilations function. Indeed, according to Johnson, the concept of heterarchy 'accommodate[s] the changing interrelations and variable groupings of textual items and perspectives in and across medieval manuscripts'. It makes possible the recognition of loose structural principles within miscellanies and compilations that therefore do not rely on hierarchical patterns in any significant way, even if these are not completely absent from miscellaneity.

The use of Middle English biblical paratexts makes for a powerful case study as it demonstrates the heterarchical structure of the ultimate Book, the Bible. Compilers and scribes producing biblical miscellanies are aware of the various functional modes of biblical books which make it possible for them to produce necessarily incomplete but profitable *sentence* as part of their biblical paratexts. Thinking heterarchically when dealing with medieval texts allows one to situate miscellaneity and compilatory modes at the heart of medieval culture, as part of a nexus of textual connections from which hierarchical structure has a very moderate role to play. Opening ourselves to the sensibility of the miscellaneous and the compilatory is one of the ways forward in medieval studies.

Annie Sutherland displays that particular sensibility in her reading of *A Talkyng of the Love of God*. As in the case of *The Three Arrows on Doomsday*, heterarchy structures the way by which the compiler of *A Talkyng* sorts out his segments, made up of antecedent texts in many cases, interwoven with new material. Whereas Hanna shows that *The Three Arrows* has different compilers in the five extant versions of the text, Sutherland is able to argue for a single compiler on the basis of textual evidence. Indeed, the degree of affective and intellectual cohesiveness in the way in which *A Talkyng* is compiled supports her hypothesis. Careful amplification of the material seems to be at the heart of his compilatory activity, with significant differences based on personal engagement with his thirteenth-century source texts, *On Wel Swuðe God Ureisun of God* and *Þe Wohunge of Ure Lauerd*. In the case of the latter, the compiler shows more personal, critical but ruminative engagement with the text, therefore sometimes appropriating hermeneutic and translation skills as part of his responses and re-rendering of the text. Occasionally giving in to aesthetic considerations at the cost of logical considerations, the compiler nevertheless seems to be under the influence of Anselmian rhetoric as part of his process of amplification, or when adding passages that are considered to be original contributions.

As in the case of the *Three Arrows* compiler who seems to have a library to work with, the compiler of *A Talkyng* equally has knowledge of, and possible access to, Anselmian treatises when producing original prose. This case of extensive borrowing from several Anselmian treatises, another compilatory act within compilation activity, displays the signs of heterarchic thinking as posited in Johnson's essay. Reading *A Talkyng* in the informed way suggested by Sutherland involves becoming a witness to heterarchy. That is, becoming aware of a compiler accommodating a variety of texts and rhetorical stances, as well as being aware of the changing and imperfect functions of the new sequences that he has created in a new manuscript context. In contrast to God's perfect act of creation 'ex nihilo', compilatory activity addresses the question of creativity and originality based on what already exists head-on and is by its very postlapsarian nature imperfect.

The dynamics of devotional compilations are approached from a readerly perspective in Margaret Connolly's essay. However specifically addressed intended readers can be in devotional compilations, such as 'suster, Dame Alice' in *Disce mori*, and however seemingly impossible it is to identify medieval readers by more than just a name, it often remains difficult to assess which was the compiler's priority: addressing the compilation to a specific reader or rather to a global, universal, audience. Connolly is able to identify sixteenth-century readers of the compilations *Pore Caitif* and *Contemplations of the Dread and Love of God*. The religious instability of the period would have triggered different ways of reading devotional writings, so the annotations by Thomas Roberts (d. 1542) in his personal copy of the *Pore Caitif* (BL, MS Harley 2322) offer useful information about devotional reading practices. His annotations, unevenly distributed among what he considers to be a treatise made up of twenty(!) tracts, show the attention paid to the tract on the Ten Commandments for instance; also, the addition of the Latin text to the articles of the Creed reflects a concern for the provision of the original Latin to this part of the treatise.

Glasgow, University Library, MS Hunter 520 contains extensive inscriptions, some of which have been identified as written by Henry Cobham (1537–1592), an Elizabethan diplomat. In several other cases mentioned by Connolly, annotations do not lead to a particular individual, but they nevertheless reveal that the compilation was actively read and in addition provide information about patterns of devotional reading.

The *Pore Caitif* and *Contemplations* are found together in eight manuscripts. They both address a 'simple' audience and are organized for selective reading as part of a heterarchy allowing a loose arrangement of texts that can be connected to one another in a multiplicity of ways. Although the dissemination of devotional compilations can be assessed by looking at the number of manuscript copies, annotations, and identification of a variety of hands, the ultimate circulation success of such works in the early modern period depends on their being selected or not for print. Although circulating together in manuscript form, the fate of these two texts took opposite directions with the advent of print. *Pore Caitif* manuscript fragments only served as binding material for an early printed book, while *Contemplations* went through two print runs in the sixteenth century.

Part II. Compiling the Compilation: Manuscript Transmission

Because they are often loosely structured, and because they have been transmitted in various manuscript contexts, many devotional compilations are dynamic texts, that is, they can be found in diverse attestations. Diana Denissen's essay extends Connolly's assessment of the transmission of *Pore Caitif* and *Contemplations* within two specific manuscript settings. She highlights the importance of distinguishing between textual and manuscript compilations. Her case study considers two manuscript compilations, Bodl. Lib., MS Bodley 423 and MS Bodley 938. As stated by Connolly, the common manuscript circulation of *Pore Caitif* and *Contemplations* can be attributed to their hospitable attitude towards an inexperienced audience, as well as by their loose structural configuration, which allows for either a faithful re-rendering of the compilation or an ad hoc selection of some of their parts according to the needs of a specific audience. While of course readerly needs are well attended to with the wish of the compiler to represent the social and co-dependent spiritual situatedness of his readers positively, Denissen also points to the spiritual benefits that the compilers accrue as part of the composition process.

Both *Pore Caitif* and *Contemplations* occur in MS Bodley 423, and belong to units B and C of this manuscript, which were copied by the Carthusian Stephen Dodesham (d. 1481/82). Interestingly, certain sections of *Contemplations* appear more than once in the manuscript. While Marleen Cré understands circular reading as a form of *ruminatio* which is physically inscribed in the manuscript context by the inclusion of the same text or themes within a manuscript book (*in casu* BL, MS Additional 37790),[22] Denissen suggests that the production context of sections B and C of MS Bodley 423 could also have been less intentional.

Compilation activity is carried on further in MS Bodley 423 with the addition of five unidentified tracts from *Pore Caitif* to the abbreviated chapters X-Y-Z of *Contemplations*. One is therefore witness to the making of yet another compilation from two combined compilations. Whether labelled 'recompilation' or 'the gift that keeps on giving', in late medieval culture compilatory composition is characterized by endless reshaping and recompiling as part of a dynamic compositional process. What takes place in MS Bodley 938 is, however, quite distinct from what has been described so far. Red ink annotations in MS Bodley 938 show awareness of the transformed structure of *Pore Caitif* in this manuscript, a phenomenon that can be expected from a compilation that invites non-sequential reading of some of its parts. And yet the red ink annotator seems to hesitate to let go of the original structure of *Pore Caitif* by offering readers the tools to reconfigure it, so that two forms of reading can be experienced: one that follows the 'original' fourteen-tract structure of *Pore Caitif*, and another one that integrates the non–*Pore Caitif* material. Denissen notes the paradox of the version found in MS Bodley 938, where the transformed structure is recognized and allowed to be disseminated, while an annotator points out what is and what is not *Pore Caitif* material.

If the examples of compilation activity so far seem to be marked by combination, addition, and expansion, some of the versions of *The Life of Soul* that Sarah Macmillan discusses are marked by abbreviation. *The Life of Soul* compiles a variety of material prescribed for instruction to the laity in a dialogic structure, inviting readers to take the part of the inquisitive interlocutor.

---

[22] Cré, *Vernacular Mysticism in the Charterhouse*, pp. 278–79 (quoted by Denissen).

Half of the compilation is made up of biblical quotations, so that one could align this compilation with the biblical paratexts discussed above by Johnson. Macmillan stresses the overall ascetic, non-affective characteristic of this compilation, with for example a reference to Christ not as object of love, but as exemplar of how to love. Additionally, spiritual experience is presented here in a non-visual form, with insistence upon the word of scripture, which invites comparison with the Wycliffite versions of the Bible as pre-Reformation texts as discussed by Johnson. The argument continues with an analysis of a version of *The Life of Soul* within its manuscript context. Macmillan argues that compilatory composition is in itself a form of ascesis, which is the main theme of *The Life*. The version of this compilation in BL, MS Arundel 286 represents an ultimate instance of textual ascesis: the text is stripped of the few remaining affective images and words that its longer version contained. This version is shorter by half than most of the other existing versions. What is more, the ascetic quality of *The Life* is shared by all the other devotional compilations found in BL, MS Arundel 286. Macmillan argues that suppression of excessive imagery and words serves to refine the readers' thoughts and is part and parcel of the ascetic practices of the scribe.

Compilatory agency seems to be fairly easy to identify in the case of *The Life of Soul*, although different levels and nuances occur in different manuscript contexts. This point is also raised by Marleen Cré's essay, which points to the loss of such nuances and fruitful instability when the compilations are fixed and read in modern editions. Cré suggests that reading compilations as part of the 'whole', that is, as part of all the textual items of any anthology and miscellany, offers a different experience and allows for a better understanding of compilatory agency. The unique versions of three compilations found in CUL, MS Ii.6.40 (C), which was at some point owned by Johanne Mouresleygh, a nun of Shaftesbury Abbey from 1441 to 1460, attest to the instability of compilations in general.

Indeed, *Contemplations of the Dread and Love of God*, 'A Tretis of Pater Noster', and 'A deuout meditacioun of Richard Hampole' as they occur in the Cambridge manuscript differ from all other attestations of these texts. Compiling activity seems to be motivated at times by the interest shown by the compiler in common sources, such as Birgitta's *Revelationes*, which is one of the source texts of *Contemplations*, and which is also a source of the text called *An Information* that the compiler adds to *Contemplations*. Elsewhere, compilatory agency and *intentio* are less easy to appreciate, as with the inversion of doublets in *Contemplations* or with abbreviations that have been made in both *Contemplations* and 'A Tretis'. The third idiosyncratic text, a translation of Edmund of Abingdon's *Speculum ecclesie*, is remarkable for its extensive expansions, which are closely dependent on the text and its biblical quotes.

Cré insists on reading compilations as part of a whole, while at the same time inviting an examination and understanding of compilatory activity that is in operation at various levels and at various times in a process of transmission that a single manuscript fixes in a temporality that conveys it only partially. She also points to the fact that our scholarly perspective, with access to multiple versions of a text, allows us to account for various compilers' voices that a medieval reader, in possession of a single textual version, would not necessarily hear.

Part III. Compilation and Devotional Practice

Although loose structure is guaranteed by *sanctorale* and *temporale* cycles, the genre of hagiography, which is intrinsically compilatory, allows hagiographers substantial freedom in the selection and organization of material. After showing the extent to which recent scholarship on the *South English Legendaries* confirms that its various manifestations are based on an organizational heterarchic principle and each form a unique anthology, Mami Kanno's essay focuses on Bodl. Lib., MS Bodley 779, itself unique in the way it includes five native female saints' lives not found in other manuscripts. A reading of the content of the 'whole book', as endorsed by Cré, allows Kanno to note the specific interest of this anthology in the condition of women in general, which it discusses with the text *Defence of Women*, women's religious lives in particular, and the inclusion of the largest collection of native female saints' lives in the whole of the *South English Legendaries*. The essay looks at *compilatio* and *ordinatio* and argues that more attention should be given to the latter, as Kanno notes that the liturgical calendar, although a significant structural principle, is not the only one to be considered. In the case of MS Bodley 779, nationality, gender, and the spiritual status of 'holy confessors' in part dictate the *ordinatio* of the manuscript. Indeed, even if at times groups of saints are placed in a random order, one can detect other organizational patterns shaped by saints' feast days and categories of saints.

The English identity of these female nuns turned saints begs the question of a possible readership of enclosed women for the manuscript. However, internal evidence indicates an intention to feminize the ideal reader, without narrowing this readership down to nuns. The provision of models of female piety would have appealed to a (female) religious and lay audience.

Audience and readers are also at the heart of Nicole R. Rice's investigation of BL, MS Additional 30897, which she considers to be a lollard production made from different texts with particular relationships to lollardy. Her concern is not so much with the identification of sources of the various compilations that make up this anthology, but with the devotional meanings these texts may have had for mid-fifteenth-century lollard readers. One of the themes carried over by the entire anthology is the launch of models or examples of sanctity for a lollard ideology, with the Virgin Mary present in the three compilations under investigation: the *Pore Caitif*, the commentary on the Ave Maria, and *Book to a Mother*.

Thirteen extant copies of *Pore Caitif* contain lollard comments on lollard topics such as images, oaths, and preaching. BL, MS Add. 30897 is one of them, but Rice points out that, in this manuscript, even sections with no lollard content, especially those insisting on meekness and self-sacrifice, as well as imitation of saints' patient suffering, would appeal to lollard readers. This particular appeal is not surprising, considering that *Pore Caitif*, if initially not a lollard text, as a reformist work would express concerns shared by orthodox and lollard readers. The essay offers evidence for the flexibility of compilations and their adaptability to suit different ideologies. As in the case of *The Life of Soul* discussed by Macmillan, *Pore Caitif* invites its readers not to look at Christ and his mother as objects of love, but as models of meekness and patient suffering, which would appeal to the lollard ideology and way of life. Like *Pore Caitif* and the Ave Maria commentary, the truncated version of *Book to a Mother*, near the end of the work, makes the Virgin Mary a more central figure. The Virgin Mary's characteristics of meekness and humility are blended with persecution and Saint Lucy's acts of generosity. The lollards as a persecuted minority would have been particularly receptive to such characteristics.

As with *The Life of Soul*, the texts considered here point to a form of devotion away from images and more strongly grounded in textuality, which again characterizes reformist and lollard textual productions in the mid-fifteenth century. The malleability of compilation as a form allows the transmission of new ideologies, sometimes distinct from and even clashing with those that their source texts initially conveyed.

Sheri Smith's essay focuses on BL, MS Additional 37787, a composite miscellany made up of devotional material in Latin, French, and English, with hierarchy suspended in relation to the supremacy of Latin over the two vernaculars. John Northewode, who was a Cistercian monk at St Mary's Abbey, Bordesley, near Worcester, initially owned the manuscript. Although the miscellany is often labelled as Northewode's prayer book, some of its components, especially the parts on confession, are written for the attention of a confessor persona, rather than the penitent. Indeed, the texts in this manuscript oscillate between instructional and devotional modes, while inviting the reader to ponder the self. Contrary to several other penitential manuals, the penitential part, explicitly stated to be based on compilatory composition, does not identify the self with the sins, but rather shows the self to be participating in them, which is a subtle but important nuance in the exploration of the language of subjectivity in this miscellany in particular, and late medieval penitential literature in general. The essay by Smith raises further questions about miscellaneity as a productive textual ground from which new explorations of subjectivity are made possible.

Brandon Alakas's analysis of Richard Whitford's *Dyuers Holy Instrucyons and Teachynges* brings us back to the turbulent religious world of the sixteenth century also explored by Connolly. *The Dyuers Holy Instrucyons* is an anthology made up of four texts written by Whitford. It is the only Syon text produced after the expulsion of the community and dissolution of the abbey, and as such Alakas argues for a reading of the anthology as a powerful boost to a beleaguered readership. As another form of biblical paratext, its anxious yet determined resolve to use medieval allegorical interpretation for its reading of the Old Testament figures of Job, Susanna, and Naboth exposes the change in reading modalities in the sixteenth century.

Whitford's anagogical reading of his chosen narratives has an autobiographical touch that would not have escaped the attentive eye of Thomas Cromwell's visitors and representatives who visited and then suppressed the monasteries. Job as a model of patience, Susanna as an exemplum of fortitude, Naboth as a model of patient resistance, all point to the complex political situation of Syon in 1541. The publication of the anthology in 1541 indicates Whitford's purposeful recommendation of patience and tenacity in the expectation of changing views towards Catholicism. The compilation of this anthology by Whitford, author of its four texts, shows the way in which ideological considerations can be funnelled and circulated in an anthology designed to be read as a 'whole book', as a powerful devotional as well as political tract carefully and purposefully organized.

Part IV. Mystics Compiled

The adaptability of compilations and miscellanies to suit different ideologies is also discussed in Denis Renevey's essay. The essay examines the compilatory composition of Richard Rolle's works and the complexity of the transmission of his authorial voice in texts and passages linked to the devotion to the Name of Jesus in the fifteenth century. The essay first looks at Rolle's *Expositio super primum versiculum Canticum Canticorum* and the Latin *Oleum effusum* compilation, which is made up of part four of *Super canticum* with a section of a letter by Saint Anselm as well as Chapters 12, 15, and the opening paragraph of Rolle's *Incendium amoris*. The role played by the practice of the devotion to the Name in the *Oleum effusum* compilation illustrates the importance of this devotion as part of Rolle's spiritual practice.

The essay then assesses the spread of the devotion to the Name of Jesus in two compilations that integrate it into their devotional programme: *The Chastising of God's Children* and *Disce mori*. These two compilations are connected to each other, because half of *The Chastising*, including Chapter 24 on patience, was selected as one of the source texts for *Disce mori*. Chapter 24 of *The Chastising* makes reference to the Name as a remedy against wicked spirits. The chapter, moreover, references Anselm and Bernard of Clairvaux as authorities, while references to Rolle are completely absent. Renevey suggests that the absence of Rollean passages in *The Chastising* could be read as a conscious effort to erase Rolle's most affective passages.

Disce mori, however, offers a different perspective on the authorial affiliations linked to the Name of Jesus. Although this compilation faithfully incorporates the Holy Name passage found in Chapter 24 of *The Chastising* with no reference to Rolle, the compilation's final treatise, 'Exhortacion', gives Rolle a significant authoritative position. Therefore, Renevey wonders whether the compiler of the 'Exhortacion' is the same as the compiler of the rest of *Disce mori*, or whether references to Rolle are more appropriate in a section of the compilation that encourages contemplative practice.

While Renevey connects the incorporation of affective Rollean material in compilations — or the absence of such passages — to the compilations' different devotional functions, Michael G. Sargent's essay enables a new perspective on the affective possibilities of Walter Hilton's *Scale of Perfection* II. By reading Hilton as a writer in the affective instead of the 'cognitive' tradition, the essay allows us to see Hilton's texts in a whole new light. A discussion of the critical limitations of the consideration of affect in late medieval devotional writing is followed by a characterization of what Sargent names 'Hilton's affective turn': Hilton's use of the terms 'affect', 'affection', 'devotion', and, most prominently, 'feeling'. The *Scale* II refers to 'feeling' a remarkable 213 times (as opposed to 42 occurrences of the word in *Scale* I), which signifies a major shift in the way Hilton describes the contemplative life.

The text of the *Scale* occurs in several devotional anthologies, and sentences or passages drawn from the *Scale* are included in a number of compilations. In the second part of his essay, Sargent offers a partial overview of the ways in which the *Scale* is embedded in these late medieval English devotional anthologies and compilations. The complete text of the *Scale* occurs in surviving medieval manuscripts together with other contents eleven times out of twenty-two originally complete examples. Another group of manuscripts of the *Scale* all share the characteristic that they read 'God' where the other manuscripts read 'Jesus' in more than a hundred instances. The 'theocentric' form of *Scale* I circulated in the north and west of England at the end of the fourteenth century in manuscripts in which it is compiled with other works, particularly those of Richard Rolle. The 'theocentric' form of *Scale* II occurs only in manuscripts already containing this version of *Scale* I, to which it was added in the fifteenth century in copies with more southerly connections. The small number of compilations comprising material drawn from the *Scale* also occur in manuscript anthologies of contemplative writings. One of these is the 'Westminster Compilation' (London, Westminster Cathedral Treasury, MS 4), which has been edited by Marleen Cré. The *Scale* is also one of the source texts in a pair of related short compilations: *Of Actyfe Lyfe and Contemplatyfe Declaration* in the anthology BL, MS Additional 37049, and *Via ad contemplacionem* in BL, MS Additional 37790.

By offering a partial overview of the ways in which the *Scale* is embedded in devotional compilations, anthologies, and miscellanies, Sargent illustrates that the *Scale* was transmitted in the company of other important late medieval devotional texts, such as Hilton's other English writings and the works of Richard Rolle. Sargent's essay therefore reinforces Cré's perspective on compilatory activity as occurring on various levels and various times in a process of manuscript transmission.

Naoë Kukita Yoshikawa's final essay in the 'Mystics Compiled' section discusses an anthology that contains passages of Mechtild of Hackeborn's *Liber specialis gratiae*: BL, MS Harley 494. In addition to short extracts, BL, MS Harley 494 contains three more substantial extracts from Mechtild's *Liber specialis gratiae*, which are abbreviated and modified from the Latin original texts. This manuscript, dated between 1532 and 1535, is an anthology of devotional texts written in a variety of late fifteenth- or early sixteenth-century hands and was owned by Anne Bulkeley, a Hampshire widow. It is very likely that Richard Whitford, the Syon monk we encountered in Brandon Alakas's essay, supervised the compiling process of BL, MS Harley 494. Yoshikawa's essay focuses on the three extracts from the *Liber* in the manuscript in order to illustrate how Mechtild's text was transformed to satisfy the needs of late medieval English audiences.

Yoshikawa asserts that BL, MS Harley 494 uniquely presents Mechtild as a familiar figure of orthodox piety and an expert on prayer, who will offer a good example of holy living to its readers. The compiler Richard Whitford was very familiar with the Latin *Liber* and probably also with its Middle English translation, the *Booke*, which was translated in a Carthusian/Birgittine milieu. Yoshikawa illustrates that, comparable to what we see in Renevey's discussion of *The Chastising of God's Children*, the Mechtildian materials contained in BL, MS Harley 494 reveal that Whitford (and other translators) concentrated on reducing the affective elements of the mystic's revelations. While this might undermine the uniqueness of Mechtild's revelatory experience, Yoshikawa shows that this form of compiling activity also made Mechtild an approachable devotional model for a wider readership.

Part V. Texts, Images, and Affect

'Compilations demonstrate how medieval literary traditions acutely challenge any modern notions of homogeneity or consistently hierarchized canon formation.' These are the opening words of Laura Saetveit Miles's essay in the final fifth part of the volume, and they interconnect with Johnson's notion of heterarchy. Miles focuses on the resonances between a little-studied Middle English compilation usually known as *Meditaciones domini nostri* and several other texts: Richard Rolle's *The Commandment*, the devotional compilation *Contemplations of the Dread and Love of God* (discussed earlier in this volume by Connolly, Denissen, and Cré), and the Latin literary visionary accounts of the Monk of Eynsham and Tnugdal in Cambridge, Trinity College, MS B.15.42.

In MS B.15.42, Richard Rolle's *The Commandment* is accompanied by graphic images representing Christ's side wounds. Miles states that these visual reminders of Christ's body set up a parallel between the book and Christ's body as a fundamental framework for approaching the rest of the codex. In this way, the manuscript invites access to Christ through visual and tactile engagement. This type of access to Christ as a lover, which also occurs in *A Talkyng of the Love of God*, discussed by Sutherland, is very different from the compilation *Life of Soul*, discussed by Macmillan, in which Christ is not represented as an object of love, but as an exemplar of how to love. In a related kind of participatory piety, two gaping holes in the vellum towards the end of *Meditaciones*, which focuses on Mary's role in Christ's life, resonate with the text itself. The words surrounding the 'parchment wounds' describe how Mary possessed a special understanding of the Incarnation of Christ, which the compilation connects to her (mothering) body and her heart. The red writing visible through the parchment holes, in turn, is what Miles names a 'special table of contents or calendar' for the devotional compilation *Contemplations of the Dread and Love of God*. Then, Miles notes that the two Latin purgatory visions that follow provide the kind of consequences that make the manuscript's spiritual guidance texts seem particularly urgent for its readers. The essay concludes that when reading MS B.15.42 as a whole, various visionary voices emerge as reminders of the thin boundaries between the past of Christ's life and the present of our material world. The manuscript facilitates a layered interlacing of vision and body, while at the same time reminding its readers that this body must be regulated.

The Desert of Religion, a 943-line poem of rhymed couplets that is richly illustrated in all its surviving manuscripts, is another example of a textual as well as a visual compilation. It survives in three British Library manuscripts: MS Additional 37049, MS Cotton Faustina B VI, pars ii, and MS Stowe 39, all of which are believed to have come from monastic houses in the north of England. Anne Mouron illustrates that the compiler of *The Desert of Religion* gathers catechetical doctrine into an allegory of a forest, which gives the poem its very shape. Moreover, the allegory of the forest is given a more literal interpretation in the manuscripts in that each section of the poem is accompanied by the illustration of a tree. While the tree-diagrams emphasize a conceptually progressive and hierarchical structure by repeating the information given in the text in an easily memorable form, providing extra information, or offering further subdivisions, the reader can also go from one tree to another, like wandering in a forest. Mouron therefore illustrates that the concepts of 'heterarchy' and 'hierarchy' are not always mutually exclusive. In addition to the tree-diagrams, *The Desert of Religion* offers its readers a second series of illustrations, mostly of saints and hermits. In the final section of her essay, Mouron suggests that *The Desert of Religion* can also be seen as a 'spiritual horticultural treatise', developing from garden treatises, which describe trees and their medicinal powers.

The final paper of the volume takes us back to the devotional compilation *The Chastising of God's Children*. Just like Hilton's *Scale of Perfection*, discussed by Sargent, *The Chastising* is another text that is often not considered to be part of the affective tradition. For instance, as Renevey has noted, any references to Rolle's affective writings are completely absent from *The Chastising*. However, Ayoush Lazikani sheds new light on *The Chastising* by examining the affective reading practices readers are invited to adopt when approaching this text, by focusing on the grace found in God's presence and the anguish felt in his absence. Lazikani argues that this hide-and-seek game of intimacy with the Lord, which functions as the basis of understanding temptation in the text, responds and contributes to the advanced 'affective literacies' of its readers.

With Miles and Mouron, Lazikani's essay shares a focus on the visual aspects of compilations. The second section of the essay turns to three church wall paintings with a *Virgo lactans* image and Doom scenes as examples of the kind of images that might have been available to the readers of *The Chastising*. Lazikani interprets text and image as inseparable components of devotional semiotics and describes how the game of absence and presence is also vivified for devotees on the painted walls.

* * *

Nicholas Watson's concluding afterword offers further reflections on devotional compilations, based on the distinction between the textual history of *compilatio* as a term and compilation as literary practice. Watson also identifies and comments on the challenges of studying these texts in their pastoral, devotional, and literary contexts and makes suggestions on how to approach *compilatio* and compilations in the vernacular. He suggests that the range of this long-standing 'strategy of mediation' is broader than the narrow use of the term *compilatio* in scholastic Latin, and that looking for coherence in compilations and anthologies, while also acknowledging the difficulties of that critical approach, advances our understanding of these derivative texts and the varied purposes they may have served.

It may be argued that the decision of whether a text (and in some cases a text with accompanying images) as it occurs in a manuscript is a compilation or whether a manuscript can be called an anthology or miscellany depends on the scholar's interpretation of the evidence. This interpretation itself depends on the scholar's assessment of the anthology as random or planned (unless there is enough material evidence to decide on either option), bearing in mind both Pearsall's caveat that to retrace and reconstruct the compiler's intentions is an exercise that should be carried out with great caution and Bahr's point that 'where traces of intentionality can be discerned, they are often interpretively valuable'.[23] It is worth pointing out here that Pearsall's essay does not deal with

---

[23] Pearsall, 'The Whole Book' and Bahr, 'Miscellaneity and Variance in the Medieval Book', p. 187.

religious anthologies or compilations,[24] but has as its main argument that 'it is possible, and all too possible, to overestimate the activity of the controlling or guiding intelligence of the scribe-compiler in the making of late medieval English *secular* miscellanies'.[25] Pearsall's observation that 'collections of religious writing made in monasteries' shared in some of the characteristics of Latin anthologies is borne out by the evidence of the anthologies and compilations discussed in the essays in this book.[26] Thus we can see that certain texts were transmitted together, and that compilers and scribes often seem to have had books at their disposal from which they could select related material to insert in the compilation or anthology, or against which they could compare the text they were copying. In addition, Pearsall points out that these practical conditions favoured the more careful organization of anthologies, and — we would add — compilations.[27]

The essays in this volume bear out that many late medieval religious anthologies and compilations indeed possess thematic coherence as a result of compilatory activity, whether as an act of authorial creation or as a response to the needs and demands of a very specific and concrete audience or of an envisaged wider readership beyond the compiler's immediate circle. They also show that readerships varied: compilations were owned and read by the literate laity, members of the secular and regular clergy, noblemen and women who wanted to lead better lives and sought out texts that could help them get closer to God.

However difficult it may be to categorize some of the manuscripts and texts produced for these readers, in order for scholars to discuss devotional compilations, anthologies, and miscellanies in a meaningful way, the working definitions of 'compilation', 'anthology', and 'miscellany' quoted at the beginning of this introduction are useful, and this is why they are used throughout this

---

[24] 'I shall make no further mention of [compilations of an exclusively religious nature] in this essay.' See Pearsall, 'The Whole Book', p. 22. Pearsall argues that it is not always possible to find a 'guiding intelligence' or a 'unifying set of principles' in a miscellaneous collection (p. 27), and 'speculations about compositorial intention' (p. 29) should not be confused with discussions of how an anthology or miscellany could have been read.

[25] Pearsall, 'The Whole Book', p. 29, italics ours.

[26] The characteristics of Latin anthologies are 'availability of a wider range of exemplars, circulation of exemplars, and the possibility of long-term borrowing from other houses, well trained scribes, and some measure of traditional agreement on what would constitute fixed canons, genres, periodizations, and forms for selection'. See Pearsall, 'The Whole Book', p. 27.

[27] Pearsall, 'The Whole Book', p. 26.

book.[28] Compilations indeed function as texts with their own identity and literary form. They are frequently signalled by their titles, introduced by prologues and tables of contents, and in many manuscripts rubrics also mark their subdivision into chapters as well as the end of the text. Yet, as many of the essays in this book make clear, the manuscript evidence also shows the flexibility with which compilations could be appropriated, recontextualized, and recompiled, how plans may have been changed during the production stage of a book, how certain texts tend to be transmitted together, and how omission of rubrics from one manuscript to the next could turn an anthology into a compilation. It is the very flexibility and pragmatism of compilatory agency (in compilations, anthologies, and miscellanies) that makes general conclusions about compilatory composition and agency difficult, and that necessitates case studies with a focus on the texts/compilations in their manuscript context, looking at both textual production and reception.

Works Cited

Manuscripts

Lincoln, Lincoln Cathedral, MS 91
Oxford, Bodleian Library [Bodl. Lib.], MS Laud misc. 99
Oxford, Jesus College, MS 39

Primary Sources

The Chastising of God's Children and the Treatise of Perfection of the Sons of God, ed. by Joyce Bazire and Eric Colledge (Oxford: Basil Blackwell, 1957)

The 'Exhortacion' from Disce mori: Edited from Oxford, Jesus College, MS 39, ed. by E. A. Jones, Middle English Texts, 36 (Heidelberg: Winter, 2006)

The Idea of the Vernacular: An Anthology of Middle English Literary Theory, 1280–1520, ed. by Jocelyn Wogan-Browne, Nicholas Watson, Andrew Taylor, and Ruth Evans, Exeter Medieval Texts and Studies (Exeter: University of Exeter Press, 1999)

---

[28] For the sake of convenience, the definitions are repeated and rephrased here. Compilations are texts that incorporate fragments from existing texts that, in many cases, have been translated from a Latin original, but that have taken on an identity and a literary form of their own. Anthologies are multi-text manuscripts in which there is evidence of organizing principles. Miscellanies are multi-text manuscripts in which few organizing principles can be seen at work; miscellanies contain disparate, incomplete material or personal notes.

Kempe, Margery, *The Book of Margery Kempe*, ed. by Barry Windeatt (Harlow: Longman, 2000)

'*The Pore Caitif*: Edited from MS. Harley 2336, with Introduction and Notes', ed. by Mary Teresa Brady (unpublished doctoral thesis, Fordham University, 1954)

Rolle, Richard, *Richard Rolle and Þe Holy Boke Gratia Dei: An Edition with Commentary*, ed. by Mary Luke Arntz, Salzburg Studies in English Literature, Elizabethan and Renaissance Studies, 92.2 (Salzburg: Institut für Anglistik und Amerikanistik, 1981)

Secondary Works

Bahr, Arthur, 'Miscellaneity and Variance in the Medieval Book', in *The Medieval Manuscript Book: Cultural Approaches*, ed. by Michael Johnston and Michael Van Dussen, Cambridge Studies in Medieval Literature, 94 (Cambridge: Cambridge University Press, 2015), pp. 181–98

Connolly, Margaret, 'Mapping Manuscripts and Readers of *Contemplations of the Dread and Love of God*', in *Design and Distribution of Late Medieval Manuscripts in England*, ed. by Margaret Connolly and Linne R. Mooney (York: York Medieval Press; Woodbridge: Boydell, 2008), pp. 261–78

—— , 'Understanding the Medieval Miscellany', in *Insular Books: Vernacular Manuscript Miscellanies in Late Medieval Britain*, ed. by Margaret Connolly and Raluca Radulescu, Proceedings of the British Academy, 201 (Oxford: Oxford University Press for the British Academy, 2015), pp. 3–15

Cré, Marleen, 'Miscellaneity, Compiling Strategies, and the Transmission of *The Chastising of God's Children* and *The Holy Boke Gratia Dei*', in *Late Medieval Personal Miscellanies*, ed. by S. Corbellini, G. Murano, and G. Signore, Bibliologia (Turnhout: Brepols, 2018), pp. 131–44

—— , *Vernacular Mysticism in the Charterhouse: A Study of London, British Library, MS Additional 37790*, The Medieval Translator/Traduire au Moyen Age, 9 (Turnhout: Brepols, 2006)

Cré, Marleen and Raphaela Rohrhofer, 'An Introduction to Oxford, Bodleian Library, MS Don. e. 247', *Journal of the Early Book Society*, 21 (2018), 137–208

Denissen, Diana, *Middle English Devotional Compilations: Composing Imaginative Variations in Late Medieval England*, Religion and Culture in the Middle Ages (Cardiff: Wales University Press, 2019)

—— , 'Without the Multiplication of Many Books? Compiling Styles and Strategies in *A Talkyng of the Love of God*, the *Pore Caitif*, and *The Tretyse of Love*' (unpublished doctoral thesis, University of Lausanne, 2017)

Gillespie, Vincent, 'Anonymous Devotional Writings', in *A Companion to Middle English Prose*, ed. by A. S. G. Edwards (Cambridge: Boydell and Brewer, 2004), pp. 127–49

—— , 'Vernacular Books of Religion', in *Book Production and Publishing in Britain, 1375–1475*, ed. by Jeremy Griffiths and Derek Pearsall, Cambridge Studies in Publishing and Printing History (Cambridge: Cambridge University Press, 1989; repr. 2007), pp. 317–44

Gillespie, Vincent, and Kantik Ghosh, eds, *After Arundel: Religious Writing in Fifteenth-Century England*, Medieval Church Studies, 21 (Turnhout: Brepols, 2011)

Hathaway, Neil, 'Compilatio: From Plagiarism to Compiling', *Viator*, 20 (1989), 19–44

Havens, Jill C., 'A Narrative of Faith: Middle English Devotional Anthologies and Religious Practice', *Journal of the Early Book Society*, 7 (2004), 67–84

Johnson, Ian, and Allan F. Westphall, eds, *The Pseudo-Bonaventuran Lives of Christ: Exploring the Middle English Tradition*, Medieval Church Studies, 24 (Turnhout: Brepols, 2013)

Johnston, Michael, and Michael Van Dussen, eds, *The Medieval Manuscript Book: Cultural Approaches*, Cambridge Studies in Medieval Literature (Cambridge: Cambridge University Press, 2015)

Minnis, A. J., *Medieval Theory of Authorship: Scholastic Literary Attitudes in the Later Middle Ages* (London: Scolar Press, 1984)

——, '*Nolens auctor sed compilator reputari*: The Late-Medieval Discourse of Compilation', in *La Méthode critique au Moyen Âge*, ed. by Mireille Chazan and Gilbert Dahan, Bibliothèque d'histoire culturelle du Moyen Âge, 3 (Turnhout: Brepols, 2006), pp. 47–63

Parkes, M. B., 'The Influence of the Concepts of *Ordinatio* and *Compilatio* on the Development of the Book', in *Medieval Learning and Literature: Essays Presented to Richard William Hunt*, ed. by J. J. G. Alexander and M. T. Gibson (Oxford: Clarendon Press, 1976), pp. 115–41

Pearsall, Derek, 'The Whole Book: Late Medieval English Manuscript Miscellanies and their Modern Interpreters', in *Imagining the Book*, ed. by Stephen Kelly and John J. Thompson, Medieval Texts and Cultures of Northern Europe, 7 (Turnhout: Brepols, 2005), pp. 17–29

Renevey, Denis, 'The Choices of the Compiler: Vernacular Hermeneutics in *A Talkyng of the Loue of God*', in *The Medieval Translator 6:* Proceedings of the International Conference of Göttingen (22–25 July 1996) / *Traduire au Moyen Age 6: actes du Colloque international de Göttingen (22–25 juillet 1996)*, ed. by Roger Ellis, René Tixier, and Bernd Weitemeier (Turnhout: Brepols, 1998), pp. 232–53

Sargent, Michael G., 'Minor Devotional Writings', in *Middle English Prose: A Critical Guide to Major Authors and Genres*, ed. by A. S. G. Edwards (New Brunswick, NJ: Rutgers University Press, 1984), pp. 147–63

Part I

The Dynamics of Devotional Compilations

Building a Bestseller: The Priest, the Pear Tree, and the Compiler

Vincent Gillespie

I seem inadvertently to have been a spectator at the birth of modern thinking about medieval compilations. In 1973 or early 1974, when I was a second-year undergraduate, at the end of a tutorial Malcolm Parkes threw me the proofs of what was to become the classic 1976 study of the influence of *ordinatio* and *compilatio*.[1] At the same time, Alastair Minnis was a Queen's University of Belfast graduate student working in Oxford, and his thinking about *compilatio* was taking shape under the guidance of Parkes, Beryl Smalley, and Richard Hunt.[2] Richard and Mary Rouse were often in Oxford in those days, and their augmentations and corrections to compilation theory were often talked about in the daily medievalist coffee breaks in the King's Arms.[3] What united those early discussions in the Oxford of the 1970s was their focus on Latin texts and

---

[1] Parkes, 'The Influence of the Concepts of *Ordinatio* and *Compilatio*', now reprinted in his *Scribes, Scripts and Readers*, pp. 35–70.

[2] Most famously in Minnis, *Medieval Theory of Authorship*, but adumbrated in Minnis, 'Late-Medieval Discussions of *Compilatio*', and, more recently, Minnis, '*Nolens auctor sed compilator reputari*'.

[3] As in Rouse and Rouse, *Preachers, Florilegia and Sermons*; Rouse and Rouse, '*Ordinatio* and *Compilatio* Revisited'. Important work has also been done on Vincent of Beauvais as a *compilator*: see, for example, Paulmier-Foucart, Lusignan, and Nadeau, *Vincent de Beauvais*; Lusignan, Paulmier-Foucart, and Duchenne, *Lector et compilator Vincent de Beauvais*.

Vincent Gillespie (vincent.gillespie@ell.ox.ac.uk) is J. R. R. Tolkien Professor of English Literature and Language, University of Oxford, and Fellow of Lady Margaret Hall.

their circulation. Since then a lot of energy has gone into looking at vernacular compiling and assemblage. My own essays on '*Lukynge in Haly Bukes*: *Lectio* in Some Late Medieval Spiritual Miscellanies' (1984), and 'Vernacular Books of Religion' (1989) were profoundly influenced by conversations with all these figures.[4] Reflections on vernacular compilations, *florilegia*, miscellanies, and anthologies have continued unabated since that time, and grown in frequency and intensity in the last few years.[5] But the time has come when the Latin and intralingual intertext of vernacular compilation practice needs to speak a little more audibly.[6] Nowhere is this more urgent than in the study of the many manuscripts of catechetic and devotional materials surviving from later medieval England.[7]

Reflecting once more on the role of catechetic and devotional compilations in the emergent and evolving devotional literacy of the laity in the fifteenth century, I started thinking about Margery Kempe's interrogation before Archbishop Henry Bowet in York in 1417, and her *narracio* (as a manuscript annotation calls it) of the priest and the pear tree, which sums up so many of the pastoral concerns and imperatives of those immediately post-Arundelian and post-schismatic years.[8]

---

[4] Gillespie, '*Lukynge in Haly Bukes*', Gillespie, 'Vernacular Books of Religion'. Both essays are now reprinted and updated in my *Looking in Holy Books*.

[5] For an important early essay, see Boffey and Thompson, 'Anthologies and Miscellanies'. More recently see, for example, Gillespie and Wakelin, *The Production of Books in England, 1350–1500*; Connolly and Mooney, *Design and Distribution of Late Medieval Manuscripts in England*; Johnston and Van Dussen, *The Medieval Manuscript Book*; Connolly and Radulescu, *Insular Books*; Rice, *Middle English Religious Writing in Practice*.

[6] The most sustained and cogent case for considering the multilingualism of English miscellanies has been made by Ralph Hanna in an important series of case studies of individual books over the last twenty years. For a taste of his many publications on this topic, see Hanna, 'Miscellaneity and Vernacularity', 'Producing Magdalen College MS lat. 93', 'Middle English Books and Middle English Literary History', 'Lambeth Palace Library, MS 260', 'Some North Yorkshire Scribes and their Context', and 'A Fifteenth-Century Vernacular Miscellany Revisited'.

[7] The huge range of Anglo-Norman catechetic and devotional texts remains far less visible to most medieval scholarship than is proper. For a snapshot of the range of texts, see the texts and discussion in Hunt, Bliss, and Leyser, *'Cher Alme'*, Meale, '"…Alle the Bokes That I Haue of Latyn, Englisch, and Frensch"'.

[8] Arnold, 'Margery's Trials'; Hudson, *The Premature Reformation*; Somerset, 'Wycliffite Spirituality'; Somerset, Havens, and Pitard, *Lollards and their Influence*.

Than seyd the Erchebischop to hir, 'thow schalt sweryn that thu schalt ne techyn ne chalengyn the pepil in my diocyse'. 'Nay, syr, I schal not sweryn', sche seyde, 'for I schal spekyn of God and undirnemyn hem that sweryn gret othys whersoevyr I go unto the tyme that the pope and holy chirche hath ordeynde that no man schal be so hardy to spekyn of God, for God almythy forbedith not, ser, that we schal speke of hym. And also the gospel makyth mencyon that, whan the woman had herd owr Lord prechyd, sche cam befron hym wyth a lowde voys and seyd, "Blyssed be the wombe that the bar and the tetys that gaf the sowkyn". Than owr Lord seyd agen to hir, "Forsothe so ar thei blissed that heryn the word of God and kepyn it". And therfor, sir, me thynkyth that the gospel gevyth me leve to spekyn of God'. 'A ser', seyd the clerkys, 'her wot we wel that sche hath a devyl wythinne hir, for sche spekyth of the gospel'. As swythe a gret clerke browt forth a boke and leyd Seynt Powyl for hys party ageyns hir that no woman schulde prechyn. Sche, answeryng therto, seyde, 'I preche not, ser, I come in no pulpytt. I use but comownycacyon and good wordys, and that wil I do whil I leve'. Than seyd a doctowr whech had examynd hir befortyme, 'Syr, sche telde me the werst talys of prestys that evyr I herde'. The bischop comawndyd hir to tellyn that tale. 'Sir, wyth yowr reverens, I spak but of o preste be the maner of exampyl, the whech as I have lernyd went wil in a wode thorw the sufferawns of God for the profite of hys sowle tyl the nygth cam upon hym. He, destytute of hys herborwe, fond a fayr erber in the whech he restyd that nygth, havyng a fayr pertre in the myddys al floreschyd wyth flowerys and belschyd, and blomys ful delectabil to hys syght, wher cam a bere, gret and boistows, hogely to beheldyn, schakyng the pertre and fellyng down the flowerys. Gredily this grevows best ete and devowryd tho fayr flowerys. And, whan he had etyn hem, turnyng his tayl ende in the prestys presens, voydyd hem owt ageyn at the hymyr party. The preste, havyng gret abhominacyon of that lothly syght, conceyvyng gret hevynes for dowte what it myth mene, on the next day he wandrid forth in hys wey al hevy and pensife, whom it fortunyd to metyn wyth a semly agydd man lych to a palmyr er a pilgrime, the whiche enqwiryd of the preste the cawse of hys hevynes. The preste, rehersyng the mater befron wretyn, seyd he conceyvyd gret drede and hevynes whan he beheld that lothly best defowlyn and devowryn so fayr flowerys and blomys and aftirward so horrybely to devoydyn hem befor hym at hys tayl ende, and he not undirstondyng what this myth mene. Than the palmyr, schewyng hymselfe the massanger of God, thus aresond hym, "Preste, thu thiself art the pertre, sumdel florischyng and floweryng thorw thi servyse seyyng and the sacramentys ministryng, thow thu do undevowtly, for thu takyst ful lytyl heede how thu seyst thi mateynes and thi servyse, so it be blaberyd to an ende. Than gost thu to thi messe wythowtyn devocyon, and for thi synne hast thu ful lityl contricyon. Thu receyvyst ther the frute of evyrlestyng lyfe, the sacrament of the awter, in ful febyl disposicyon. Sithyn al the day aftyr thu myssespendist thi tyme, thu gevist the to byng and sellyng, choppyng and chongyng, as it wer a man of the werld. Thu sittyst at the ale, gevyng the to glotonye and excesse, to lust of thy body, thorw letchery and unclennesse. Thu brekyst the comawndmentys of God thorw sweryng, lying, detraccyon, and bakbytyng, and swech other synnes usyng. Thus be thy mysgovernawns, lych onto the lothly ber, thu devowryst and destroist the flowerys and blomys of vertuows levyng to thyn endles dampnacyon and many mannys hyndryng lesse than thu have grace of repentawns and amending". Than the Erchebisshop likyd wel the tale and comendyd it, seying it was a good tale. And the clerk whech had examynd hir befortyme in the absens of the Erchebischop, seyd, 'Ser, this tale smytyth me to the hert'. The forseyd creatur seyd to the clerk, 'A, worschipful doctowr, ser, in place wher my dwellyng is most, is a worthy clerk, a good prechar, whech boldly spekyth ageyn the mysgovernawns of the pepil and wil flatyr no man. He seyth many tymes in the pulpit, "Yyf any man be evyl plesyd wyth my prechyng, note hym wel, for he is gylty". And ryth so, ser', seyd sche to the clerk, 'far ye be me, God forgeve it yow'. The clerk wist not wel what he myth sey to hir. Aftyrward the same clerk cam to hir and preyid hir of forgefnes that he had so ben ageyn hir.[9]

In Book I of her *Book*, which preserves the core of her ruminated experiences eventually written down in the 1430s after over twenty years of distillation and reflection, this repeated pattern of clerical correction places Margery firmly in the Latin tradition of women political prophets that runs from Hildegard through Birgitta of Sweden and Catherine of Siena.[10] The hard-edged visionary condemnation of failings in the institutional Church's provision of appropriate pastoral support and guidance for a pragmatically literate laity desperate for *soule-hele* and *Cibus anime* is a strand in Margery Kempe's *Book* that is often submerged by attention to her affective and defective responses to devotional stimuli.[11] But when put into the Latinate context of the lives of her antecedent political prophets (rather than viewed through the often softened and devotionally enhanced lens of their vernacular representations in translated epito-

---

[9] Kempe, *The Book*, ed. by Staley, I. 52. All subsequent citations by book and chapter to allow cross reference to other editions. See also Kempe, *The Book*, ed. by Meech and Allen, especially for Allen's notes. For a very perceptive reading of this passage, discussing Margery Kempe as 'the impeccable corrector' of clerical error, see Craun, *Ethics and Power*, pp. 132–42, esp. pp. 139–42. See also Rees Jones, '"A Peler of the Holy Cherch"'. I agree with these scholars in seeing Book I of Margery's text, in particular, to be addressing a particular crisis of pastoral and clerical leadership in the England of the post-Arundelian decades.

[10] Gillespie, 'Religious Writing'. Sahlin, *Birgitta of Sweden and the Voice of Prophecy*; Watt, *Secretaries of God*; Voaden, *Prophets Abroad*; Coote, *Prophecy and Public Affairs*.

[11] This aspect is well catered for in criticism. See, for example, Gibson, *The Theater of Devotion*, esp. pp. 47–65; Hirsh, *The Revelations of Margery Kempe*; Bhattacharji, *God Is an Earthquake*; Yoshikawa, *Margery Kempe's Meditations*. It is easily problematized: Beckwith, 'A Very Material Mysticism'; Beckwith, 'Problems of Authority in Late Medieval English Mysticism'; Renevey, 'Margery's Performing Body'.

mes), Margery emerges as a tough and demanding critic, and as a model for a kind of engaged lay spirituality for which the institutional Church seemed to struggle to cater.[12] Indeed the signs of struggle in the articulation of her text and its layered mediation through lay and clerical scribes, which has occupied so much critical energy in recent years, can be seen to be part of the same hegemonic dynamic of translation and selection that seeks to reduce the hard edges of a Birgitta or Catherine to the paradigmatically unchallenging devotionalism of institutionally 'approuyd wymmen' as they appear in texts like the *Speculum devotorum*.[13]

Margery's carefully canonical distinction between preaching and teaching at the start of this little narrative has often been said to echo the defensiveness of Julian of Norwich in her Short Text:

> Botte god for bede that ȝe schulde saye or take it so that I am a techere for I meene nouȝt so, no I mente nevere so; for I am a woman, leued, febille and freylle.[14]

But, to my ear, Margery's rebuttal of Bowet's requirement that she should forswear 'that thu schalt ne techyn ne chalengyn the pepil in my diocyse' (the verb *chalengyn* is particularly interesting there) is much sharper, more crisply articulated, and much more confident in its justification of her freedom to 'use but comownycacyon and good wordys'. Margery in such passages is more like the Latin Birgitta than the vernacular Julian in her hard-edged determination to fight for what she needs and to chastise those who fail to deliver it.[15] In fact

---

[12] See, for example, Pantin, 'Instructions for a Devout and Literate Layman'; Steele, *Towards a Spirituality for Lay-Folk*; Catto, 'Shaping the Mixed Life' and 'After Arundel'; Carey, 'Devout Literate Laypeople'; Somerset, *Clerical Discourse and Lay Audience*; Rice, 'Spiritual Ambition' and *Lay Piety and Religious Discipline*; Gillespie, 'Vernacular Theology'; Connolly, 'Books for the "Helpe of Euery Persoone That Thenkith to Be Saued"'. Yoshikawa, *Margery Kempe's Meditations*, pp. 120–33, has recently discussed the influence of 'mixed' life theology on Margery Kempe's life and thought.

[13] *A Mirror to Devout People*, ed. by Patterson, p. 6; on this work and its context, see the essays in Mann and Nolan, *The Text in the Community*. I explore this in more detail in *'Approuyd Wymmen'*, the 2016 Etienne Gilson Lecture, forthcoming from the Pontifical Institute of Mediaeval Studies, Toronto.

[14] The Short Text is cited from Julian of Norwich, *A Book of Showings*, ed. by Colledge and Walsh, 1. 222; see also Julian of Norwich, *The Writings*, ed. by Watson and Jenkins, p. 75, Section 6.

[15] On Birgitta's influence on Margery, see, for example, the early discussion by Cleve, 'Margery Kempe'; Watt, 'Political Prophecy', which revises some of her arguments in *Secretaries of God*; Dillon, 'Holy Women and their Confessors', Johnson, '*Auctricitas?*'. I would argue that the sharply prophetic Latin Birgitta of the *Revelationes* is more like Margery in Book I than

her distinction between preaching and teaching has a contemporary parallel in one of the most successful compilations of catechetical and pastoral material in fifteenth-century England, a compilation which is strikingly Latinate and clerical in its focus and target audience.[16]

The *Speculum christiani* opens assertively with an orthodox canonical distinction between preaching and teaching:[17]

> Magna differencia est inter predicacionem et doctrinam. Predicacio est, ubi est convocacio sive populi invitacio in diebus festivis in ecclesiis seu in aliis certis locis et temporibus ad hoc deputatis, et pertinet ad eos qui ordinati sunt ad hoc et iurisdictionem et auctoritatem habent, et non ad alios. Informare autem et docere potest unusquisque fratrem suum in omni loco et tempore oportuno, si videatur sibi expedire, quia hoc est elemosina, ad quam quilibet tenetur.[18]

This is rendered by the later (mid-fifteenth-century) Middle English translation of the whole work as:

> A grete differens es be-twene prechynge and techynge. Prechynge es in a place where es clepynge to-gedyr or foluynge of pepyl in holy dayes in chyrches or other[r] certeyn places and tymes ordeyned ther-to. And it longeth to hem that been ordeynede ther-to, the whych haue iurediccion and auctorite, and to noon othyr. Techynge es that eche body may enforme and teche hys brothyr in euery place and in conable tyme, os he seeth that it be spedful. For this es a gostly almesdede, to whych euery man es bounde that hath cunnynge.[19]

That distinction was something of a commonplace in preacher's guides. Alan of Lille says:

> Preaching must be public, because it is not done for the benefit of one but of many: if it were offered to one person only, it would not be preaching but teaching [...]. Preaching is an instruction for many, given openly to teach them about their way

---

the more devotional vernacular versions of Birgitta in popular circulation; Ellis, "'Flores ad Fabricandum ... Coronam'".

[16] On this popular but still under-studied text, see Gillespie, 'The Literary Form of the Middle English Pastoral Manual'. For subsequent publications, see Gillespie, '*Doctrina* and *Predicacio*', 'The Evolution of the *Speculum christiani*', and 'Chapter and Worse'.

[17] All citations are from *Speculum christiani*, ed. by Holmstedt. Subsequent references are to page and line number of this edition. Gillespie, 'The Evolution of the *Speculum christiani*', contains an updated list of manuscripts and printed editions of the work, including at least fourteen manuscripts and several printed texts not known to Holmstedt.

[18] *Speculum christiani*, ed. by Holmstedt, 3.4–11.

[19] *Speculum christiani*, ed. by Holmstedt, 2.5–13.

of life; teaching is offered to one person or to a group for the purpose of adding to their knowledge.[20]

Robert of Basevorn similarly distinguishes between teaching many (*predicatio*) and few (*monitio/collatio*).[21] But, more pointedly, Margery's questioning by Archbishop Bowet, and her hyper-cautious and canonically accurate responses, reflect the heat surrounding the issue of women's preaching, a topic which at this time in England had become particularly associated with the Lollards, but which had a long and poisonous prehistory in the wider Church.[22] But it is most likely that Margery gets her awareness of the distinction from the *Speculum christiani*, a work probably not fully translated into Middle English until sometime after her book was written down in the 1430s, and certainly long after the reported exchanges with Bowet in 1417.[23] So, like many of her other books, Margery may have encountered the text through instant translation from the Latin by one of her clerical supporters.[24]

Margery Kempe's subversive little story of the priest and the pear tree shadows the concerns of *Speculum christiani*, an artfully compiled collection of Latin and vernacular *pastoralia* for use by parish priests charged with the cure of souls.[25] Margery Kempe's embedded tale is treated by several later annotators of the unique manuscript as a standalone story comparable to homiletic *exempla*. It is marked in the margin as a *narracio* by Annotator 2, and further signalled in the margin by Annotator 3 with the reddish brown title '*of the prest*

---

[20] Alan of the Isles, *A Compendium*, trans. by Miller, p. 230.

[21] Robert of Basevorn, *Forma Praedicandi*, p. 238.

[22] On the contentious topic of women preaching, see Gertz-Robinson, 'Stepping into the Pulpit?'; Somerset, '*Eciam mulier*'; Kerby-Fulton, 'When Women Preached'; Spencer, *English Preaching in the Late Middle Ages*, pp. 51–54; Minnis, *Fallible Authors*, pp. 170–245, has a comprehensive overview of the extensive previous scholarship on this subject; for the continental tradition of women offering *admonitiones*, see Kerby-Fulton, *Books under Suspicion*, pp. 247–60.

[23] The complete translation into Middle English survives uniquely in BL, MS Harley 6580 (s. xv med).

[24] See note 34, below. Most works referred to in *The Book of Margery Kempe* as having been read to Margery or read by her clerical scribe either retain their Latin title (*Stimulus amoris*; *Incendium amoris*) or would have been unlikely to be available in Middle English versions at the dates they were said to be read to Margery. Ellis, 'Margery Kempe's Scribe'.

[25] Margery Kempe's apparent echoing of this distinction in *Speculum christiani* has been noted by various previous scholars, including Kempe, *The Book*, ed. by Staley; Lochrie, *Margery Kempe*, pp. 111–12; Kempe, *The Book*, ed. by Windeatt, p. 253; Gertz-Robinson, 'Stepping into the Pulpit?', p. 463.

and the pertre.²⁶ This attention from later readers is hardly surprising: the story is striking, indeed scatologically shocking. But her *exemplum* also describes rather precisely the pastoral crisis in the English Church in the early fifteenth century. The finished form of the *Speculum christiani* was an attempt to address that same pastoral crisis. The success it enjoyed in subsequent decades suggests that it reached an audience that appreciated its resources and responded to the pastoral judgement and skill that has been shown in selecting materials from a range of Latin and vernacular catechetic and didactic sources, in order to build a responsive and comprehensive pastoral resource.

Immediately after the distinction between preaching and teaching echoed by Margery Kempe, the *Speculum christiani* moves directly into a lament for the state of the institutional Church, a lament that uses similarly strong imagery to Margery's parable:

> Quomodo potest quis ueraciter dicere se deum diligere & eius amorem appetere, si eius ymaginem uideat denigrari & in sterquilinio peccatorum iacere, preciosissimum sanguinem Christi sub pedibus conculcari, spiritus sancti habitaculum pollui, sponsam Christi prostitui, fidem catholicam deici, preceptum dominicum et totam eius beatitudinem pro uilibus uoluptatibus & uiciis contempni & ipse non curat, nec clamat, sed dissumulans solum suam quietem requirit.²⁷

> How may any man sey truly hym-self to loue god and desyr hys loue if he see the ymage of god be defoulede and ly in the dounge-hepe of synnes and the moste precyus blode of Criste to be troden vndyr fote, the dwellynge place of the holy gooste to be defoulede, Cristes spouse to be a strompet, alle-holy feyth to be caste doun, our lordes commaundment and al hys blyssyd hede to be dyspysede or forsake for vyle lustys and vices, and he rekkyth not ther-of, ne cryes ther aȝens bot as a fenynge man sekyth only his owne quiete?²⁸

However conventional, and indeed patristic, such laments may be (and the institutional Church has been lamenting its deviation from apostolic ideals since the time of the Acts of the Apostles), the *Speculum christiani* is addressing these concerns with a new urgency that reflects the pressures felt in the *Ecclesia Anglicana* not only from the Great Schism, and the scandal of multiple popes (a time indeed when the question 'Is the Pope Catholic?' might very precisely have been applied to an *exemplum* like Margery's about what bears do in the

---

²⁶ On the layers of annotation in the *Book of Margery Kempe*, see the notes to Meech and Allen's EETS edition; Kempe, *The Book*, ed. by Windeatt, pp. 439–52; Parsons, 'The Red Ink Annotator'; Fredell, 'Design and Authorship'.

²⁷ *Speculum christiani*, ed. by Holmstedt, 3.14–21.

²⁸ *Speculum christiani*, ed. by Holmstedt, 2.16–24.

woods), but also from the attacks on the priesthood and the sacraments from the Wycliffite critique of the bloated functionalities of the Church in those days.[29] In tone and content it aligns itself with the vein of orthodox reform that emerges in English pastoral writing from the 1380s onwards.[30] This orthodox reform movement, closely associated with Salisbury and Oxford, overlaps in many respects (and even in some personnel) with the Wycliffite critique, but differs from it in its more positive view of the Church's ability to reform itself. This reformist zeal is a distinctive feature of the conciliar movement of these years, where the councils of Pisa, Constance, Pavia-Sienna, and Basel pursued 'reformation in head and members' of the Church until the steam gradually went out of the movement in the 1430s.[31]

It is absolutely not accidental that those sections of *The Book of Margery Kempe* describing events that are broadly dateable to the years 1414 to 1418 — that is, the precise years in which the Council of Constance sat and during which she told Bowet her parable — are full of references to Margery's obsessive exercise of sacramental confession, her hunger for good preaching, her praise for traditional clerical values and ideals, and her sorrow at being excluded from some sermons:

> On a tyme, as the forseyd creatur was in hir contemplacyon, sche hungryd ryth sor aftyr Goddys word and seyd, 'Alas, Lord, as many clerkys as thu hast in this world, that thu ne woldyst sendyn me on of hem that myth fulfillyn my sowle wyth thi word and wyth redyng of Holy Scriptur, for alle the clerkys that prechyn may not fulfillyn, for me thynkyth that my sowle is evyr alych hungry. Yyf I had gold inow, I wolde gevyn every day a nobyl for to have every day a sermown, for thi word is mor worthy to me than alle the good in this world.' (I. 58)

Margery visited Constance on her 1414 pilgrimage to the Holy Land, when the city would have been in the throes of preparations for the opening of the council

---

[29] Craun, *Ethics and Power*; Haines, *Ecclesia Anglicana*; Harvey, *Solutions to the Schism*; Harvey, *England, Rome, and the Papacy*; Crowder, *Unity, Heresy and Reform*; Hudson, *The Premature Reformation*.

[30] On the topic of orthodox reform, the best introductory resource is the essays collected in Gillespie and Ghosh, *After Arundel*. Some of the discussions there get continued in the volumes recently produced by the Geographies of Orthodoxy project: Johnson and Westphall, *The Pseudo-Bonaventuran Lives of Christ*; and Kelly and Perry, *Devotional Culture in Late Medieval England and Europe*.

[31] See now especially the essays by Catto, Gillespie, Lepine, Lindenbaum, and others in Gillespie and Ghosh, *After Arundel*; Brandmüller, *Das Konzil von Konstanz*; Brandmüller, *Das Konzil von Pavia-Siena*; Burns and Izbicki, *Conciliarism and Papalism*.

in the autumn of that year, and claims to have talked to an unidentified English papal legate there. Structurally the two sections dealing particularly with her need for good quality pastoral care (Chapters 23–25 and, particularly, 56–60 of Book I) are pivotal in establishing her own orthodox teaching authority and demonstrating her struggle against disruptive elements in the Church (particularly friars, whose status as preachers and confessors remained a hot topic of debate during this period).[32] Chapters 56–60 follow on immediately after her receipt from Henry Chichele, Arundel's successor as Archbishop of Canterbury, of a letter authorizing her to be confessed and to receive communion at will, which must have happened late in 1417 or early in 1418, exactly when the English hierarchy was restating the ideals of the priestly office so strikingly and challengingly articulated by Margery Kempe.[33] Central to this was the exercise of the ministry of preaching, something that Margery returns to frequently:

> The seyd creatur beyng present, and, beheldyng how fast the pepyl cam rennyng to heryn the sermown, sche had gret joy in hir sowle, thynkyng in hir mende, 'A, Lord Jhesu, I trowe, and thu wer here to prechyn thin owyn persone, the pepyl schulde han gret joy to heryn the. I prey the, Lorde, make thi holy word to sattelyn in her sowlys as I wolde that it schulde don in myn, and as many mict be turnyd be hys voys as schulde ben be thy voys yyf thu prechedist thyselfe.' (I. 61)

These same pastorally orientated sections of Book I report her delight in being read to by her priest, and the great worth he drew from those books when he moved into 'gret cur of sowle' (I. 58) later in his career. 'Thus, thorw heryng of holy bokes & thorw heryng of holy sermonys, sche euyr encresyd in contemplacyon & holy meditacyon' (I. 59).[34] Margery is a paradigm of the new, orally instructed laity envisaged by the English episcopacy at this period.[35] She

---

[32] For an important recent debate about the nature of the text in *The Book of Margery Kempe*, see the spirited exchange between Nicholas Watson and Felicity Riddy in Olson and Kerby-Fulton, *Voices in Dialogue*: Watson, 'The Making of *The Book of Margery Kempe*'; Riddy, 'Text and Self in *The Book of Margery Kempe*'; and Watson and Riddy, 'Afterwords'.

[33] I have developed this argument in more detail and with fuller bibliography in Gillespie, 'Chichele's Church'.

[34] Ellis, 'Margery Kempe's Scribe'. Jenkins, 'Reading and *The Book of Margery Kempe*' assumes that she was being read vernacular versions of the books she mentions. On Kempe's literacy and intellectual ability, see, for example, Lawton, 'Voice, Authority, and Blasphemy'; Furrow, 'Unscholarly Latin and Margery Kempe'; Tarvers, 'The Alleged Literacy of Margery Kempe'. For a similar debate about the literacy and learning of Julian of Norwich, see the bibliography in Gillespie, '"[S]he Do the Police in Different Voices"'.

[35] Gillespie, 'Vernacular Books of Religion' addresses this; it is striking that the Birgittine

often encounters severe shortcomings in the local implementation of that pastoral policy and is an important diagnostic witness of the problems facing the Chichelean campaign to improve pastoral care. But, judging by its circulation and surviving copies, the *Speculum christiani* is one of the most popular tools developed to encourage greater clerical efficiency in the *cura animarum*, a successful exercise in compilation, blending Latin and vernacular *pastoralia*.

The *Speculum christiani* survives in at least sixty manuscript copies of the complete text, and many more extracts and fragments. It enjoyed a limited but real circulation in continental Europe and was printed at least seven times between 1484 (from the press of William de Machlinia, probably from a continental manuscript copy) and 1517.[36] Dr Margaret Laing's linguistic analysis of surviving copies of the *Speculum christiani* has established that most members of the very important transitional C^3 group reflect dialectal features from the East Midlands area, particularly Lincolnshire. Copies assigned to this group cluster particularly in southern Lincolnshire. As Richard Beadle comments in his brief summary of the linguistic evidence, 'the centre of origin for the text would appear to have lain in the Lincolnshire-Nottingham area'.[37] BL, MS Lansdowne 344, the base text for Holmstedt's edition, contains tables for finding the dominical letter, bissextile, and golden number for 1425 and appears on palaeographical grounds to have been written around then. Interestingly it has been profiled as revealing Norfolk dialectal features in its vernacular elements, supporting the idea that the text could have been known to Margery Kempe before she began to compose her book in the 1430s. BL, MS Harley 6580, where the text has all been translated into the vernacular, displays linguistic features from Leicestershire.[38] So this is a non-metropolitan text, produced and largely circulating in the East Midlands, offering a regional insight

---

Simon Wynter's life of St Jerome translated from the Latin for Margaret, Duchess of Clarence, envisages it to be freely disseminated among her lay contacts: Keiser, 'Patronage and Piety in Fifteenth-Century England'; for a new edition, with extensive commentary, see *Virgins and Scholars*, ed. by Waters; Riddy, '"Women Talking about the Things of God"'; Erler, *Women, Reading, and Piety*; Krug, *Reading Families*.

[36] For a full list, see Gillespie 'The Evolution of the *Speculum christiani*', and for further discussion, see Gillespie, 'Chapter and Worse'.

[37] Laing, 'Studies in the Dialect Material of Mediaeval Lincolnshire', I, 258–61: her findings were incorporated into *A Linguistic Atlas of Late Mediaeval English*; Beadle, 'Middle English Texts and their Transmission' (including helpful synoptic maps), p. 89.

[38] For both manuscripts, see Meg Laing's dissertation and the data archived in Benskin and others, *An Electronic Version of a Linguistic Atlas of Late Mediaeval English*. Neither has a full linguistic profile in *eLALME*, but both are listed and discussed.

into provincial attempts to address the pastoral problems of the late fourteenth and early fifteenth centuries.

The *Speculum* is divided into eight loosely articulated sections, or *tabulae* (this term perhaps deriving from the fashion for displaying schematic representations of catechetic materials on boards in churches).[39] Most of these *tabulae* address the orthodox catechetic teaching syllabus (covering the Creed, Commandments, works of mercy, seven deadly sins, and other moral waymarkers, but not the sacraments) through the medium of Middle English verse summaries and moral poems supported by patristic Latin authorities and proof texts. These vernacular verses could easily have been used as sermon *distinctiones*, providing the mnemonic framework for the quarterly public exposition of the syllabus required by most English episcopal legislation.[40] And the *Speculum* includes at the end of its opening section a citation of the 1282 Lambeth decree *Ignorantia sacerdotum* of John Pecham that formed the basic skeleton of catechetic instruction in England and was given further force by its reissue by John Thoresby for the Northern Province in 1357 and its inclusion by Thomas Arundel in his 1409 Oxford decrees for Canterbury. These legislative citations of Pecham, and their various initiatives to improve education and pastoral aids, reflect serious intent by several generations of English bishops to address issues around the quality and quantity of pastoral care.[41] The archdiocese of York under John Thoresby (1353–73), Thomas Arundel (1388–96), and their successors, including Margery Kempe's inquisitor, Henry Bowet (1407–23), had an established track record of concern for the quality of its pastoral care, the orthodoxy of its teaching, and the spiritual development of its clergy.[42] Similarly, the diocese of

---

[39] On *tabulae*, see Gillespie, 'Medieval Hypertext' and references there; Van Dussen, 'Tourists and Tabulae'.

[40] The legislation itself is available in *Councils and Synods*, ed. by Powicke and Cheney. On the framework for the legislation, see Gibbs and Lang, *Bishops and Reform*; Cheney, *English Synodalia*, 'The Earliest English Diocesan Statutes', 'Some Aspects of Diocesan Legislation'; Haines, 'Education in English Ecclesiastical Legislation'. On the impact of the legislation on English pastoral handbooks, see Gillespie, '*Doctrina* and *Predicacio*'; Shaw, 'The Influence of Canonical and Episcopal Reform'; Boyle, 'The Fourth Lateran Council'; Martin, 'Middle English Manuals of Religious Instruction'; Gillespie, 'Vernacular Books of Religion'.

[41] Pantin, *The English Church*, and the essays collected in Boyle, *Pastoral Care*; Burgess and Duffy, *The Parish in Late Medieval England*; Barr, *The Pastoral Care of Women*; Gunn and Innes-Parker, *Text and Traditions of Medieval Pastoral Care*. See also the important recent discussions in Somerset, *Clerical Discourse and Lay Audience*; Rice, *Lay Piety and Religious Discipline*; and Rice, *Middle English Religious Writing in Practice*.

[42] For all its errors, and overstatements, the account in Hughes, *Pastors and Visionaries*

Lincoln during the episcopate of the orthodox reformer (and recanted mild Wycliffite) Philip Repingdon (1405–19) was also engaged in a campaign to improve the standard of parochial clergy.[43]

In addition to supporting preaching, the *Speculum*'s distinctive blending of short sections of schematic vernacular verse and prose with Latin *auctoritates* might have been useful in confessional catechesis and other forms of mnemonic instruction, especially in paraliturgical and devotional contexts where Latin remained the language of most prayers. The verse comes from a variety of pre-existing sources, including the *Pricke of Conscience*, popular mnemonic formulations of the Commandments, and prayers to the Virgin, while there are prose lists of sins that may come from Richard Rolle's vernacular epistle *The Form of Living*, and other hortatory vernacular prose, all interspersed with and supported by Latin patristic and scriptural proof texts.[44] Many years ago I established that most of the Latin materials come from an antecedent late fourteenth-century *summa* of pastoral proof texts known as the *Cibus anime*, which survives in two- and three-book recensions, and whose copies often contain other short texts that eventually found their way into the rather flexible and hospitable textual boundaries of the *Speculum*.[45] The *Cibus anime* also shared

---

remains suggestive and spasmodically informative. See also his thesis, Hughes, 'Religion in the Diocese of York'.

[43] Repingdon was an Augustinian canon, and that order traditionally had a commitment to high-quality *cura animarum*. He granted many licences for priests to study at a *studium generale*, at a time when the system was in general decline. *The Register of Bishop Philip Repingdon*, ed. by Archer. On the state of the Church in Lincolnshire, see Owen, *Church and Society*, esp. chs 8 and 9.

[44] Gillespie, 'The Evolution of the *Speculum christiani*', tabulates sources for some of the work; Gillespie, 'Chapter and Worse' adds some identifications. For a full analysis, see Gillespie 'The Literary Form of the Middle English Pastoral Manual'. On extracts from the *Pricke of Conscience* in *Speculum christiani*, see now Morris, *Prick of Conscience*, ed. by Hanna and Wood, pp. lvii. I am indebted to Professor Hanna who commented to me (personal communication, 22 October 2011), that 'Holmstedt 151/11–14, 153/1–2 are approximately the same (three verses pretty much identical) with *Prick of Cons* 1178–79, 1176–77, 1169–70. It's perfectly plausible that this is accident and that both of them have stumbled into the same passage in Bartholomaeus anglicus and happen to have hit on similar renditions. But I wonder whether this whole bit on *mundus* isn't just a paraphrase of the other poem, eventually extended well beyond *Prick*, and with a change in metrical form'.

[45] Copies of the original two-book recension of *Cibus anime* are contained in Oxford, Balliol College MS 239; Manchester, John Rylands Library, MS Latin 341; Cambridge, Trinity Hall, MS 16; BL, MS Harley 2379. Copies containing the three-book recension (which adds an exhortation to the contemplative life) are Bodl. Lib., MS Rawlinson C. 19; Oxford, University College, MS 60; CUL, MS Additional 6315 (II); BL, MS Harley 237; BL, MS Harley 407;

an engagement with high-quality pastoral care: the copy in London, Lambeth Palace Library, MS 460, for example, is headed by Pecham's decrees, added 'pro uberiori intellectu' (for more abundant understanding), and has a colophon describing itself as 'sana doctrina super illo capitulo ignorantia sacerdotum' (sound teaching upon the same topic/chapter of *Ignorantia sacerdotum*) explicitly articulating its utility in exploring the Pecham syllabus. That utility was further exploited in the construction of the *Speculum christiani* by the blending of vernacular material to Latin proof texts.

The earliest surviving copies of the *Cibus anime* (Manchester, John Rylands Library, MS Latin 341, and Cambridge, Trinity Hall, MS 16, both copies of the original two-book recension) can be dated palaeographically to the first decade of the fifteenth century. A supplementary reference to Part 5 of John de Burgh's *Pupilla oculi* (composed *c*. 1384 and in circulation before 1389) in all complete copies of *Cibus anime* except Trinity Hall offers a possible terminus post quem for the work, which therefore may not have been in circulation much before 1400.[46] This would push the compilation and initial circulation of the *Speculum christiani* firmly into the early years of the fifteenth century. The *Pupilla oculi*, a pastoral reworking of the popular but more canonically complex early fourteenth-century (1320s) *Oculus sacerdotis* of William of Pagula, provides a lot of catechetic material and a few Latin *auctoritates* that are ingested into the *Cibus anime*.[47] The *Pupilla oculi*, compiled in Cambridge 'pro simplicium sacerdotum' (for simple priests), comments in its *prohemium* that 'our predecessors, moved by *zelus animarum*, collected sentences and treatises from various places which related to the *regimen animarum*'.[48] Singling out the *Oculus sacerdotis*, it comments that, because of the way that the earlier book

London, Lambeth Palace Library, MS 460. Two copies are incomplete and are impossible to assign to a recension: Cambridge, King's College, MS Salt 47; BL, MS Harley 3363. One copy (BL, MS Royal 5 A VI) contains only the contemplative Book III. There are extracts from Book III in BL, MS Harley 3820. On the (very interesting) contemplative third book of *Cibus anime*, see Gillespie, 'The *Cibus anime* Book 3'.

[46] *Cibus anime*, Book I, cap. 26 (*contra detractores*), as part of the discussion of the fifth commandment (prohibiting 'murder by the tongue', that is gossip and detraction). Part 5 of *Pupilla oculi* deals with the sacrament of penance.

[47] On William of Pagula's *Oculus sacerdotis*, see the definitive survey by Boyle, 'A Study of the Works Attributed to William of Pagula'; Boyle, *Pastoral Care*, pp. 81–110, 415–56. For the *Pupilla oculi* and the general context of these Latin works of *pastoralia*, see Pantin, *The English Church*, pp. 189–209.

[48] All quotations from the early printed text *Pupilla oculi omnibus presbyteris precipue Anglicanis summe necessaria* (*STC* 143693), fol. ii^r.

had been laid out and organized, and on account of its size and prolixity, it has been neglected by curates who are indiscreet or cannot afford the price of purchasing it. Because contemporary taste is for brevity ('quia brevitate gaudent moderni'), the *Pupilla oculi* instead offers a 'brevis compendium de his qui sacerdotibus curatis ignorare non licet ex variis sentenciis et scripturis quedam de constitutionibus provincialibus utilia similiter adiciens' (a brief compendium of those things of which a priest with the cure of souls must not be ignorant, gathered from various *sententiae* and certain other writings, likewise adding useful provincial constitutions). That is a pretty accurate description of what the *Cibus anime* is also trying to achieve: both it and the *Pupilla* are witnesses to a pastoral initiative in the last quarter of the fourteenth century to make pertinent material covering the catechetic syllabus and the sacraments available in accessible formats to minimally Latinate clergy with the cure of souls. The insertion of vernacular materials in the *Speculum christiani* is a further stage in that process. But all these texts draw on the rich inheritance of Latin *pastoralia*.

The catechetic Section 10 of *Pupilla oculi* provides the raw material for some of the broader sacerdotal teachings in the *Speculum*'s *tabula* 8. Much of this material from *Pupilla oculi* comes via texts associated with the *Cibus anime* rather than through independent direct borrowings by the compiler of *Speculum christiani*.[49] In particular, a treatise on the priestly office preserved in BL, MS Royal 5 A VI, which borrows heavily from *Pupilla oculi* and *Cibus anime*, has extracts from twelve of its seventeen chapters included in a sequence on priestly duties in *tabula* 8 of the *Speculum christiani*,[50] with some of the Latin *auctoritates* also found in Book III of *Cibus anime*.[51] The Royal treatise

---

[49] Ralph Hanna suggested that these borrowings were from *Pupilla* direct to the *Speculum* in a personal communication (22 October 2011): 'A great deal of stuff in the first four tables (and the very end of prologue) is straight from John de Burg's *Pupilla*. Spec Xiani p. 27: the versus with the distinctio at the top is from *Pupilla*, and 27/29–29/4 are verbatim Pupilla (this is fol. 127ra in the 1510 EEBO version). A second would be 47/22–49/5 on the cardinal virtues, all from *Pupilla* (fol. 128rb). But the entire argument of SpecChris is divided between tabulae to match the way Burgh divides his chapters in Part 10 (and not to reproduce the citation from Peckham at head, which appears in same position and same wording in Burgh).' Some of these indebtednesses are already noted in Gillespie, 'The Literary Form of the Middle English Pastoral Manual', where the citation of *Pupilla oculi* as a cross-reference is used as a dating criterion. On closer investigation, I am confident that the *Pupilla* materials all come via the broader *Cibus anime* textual network, and not independently into *Speculum*.

[50] *Speculum christiani*, ed. by Holmstedt, 171.1–185.15.

[51] The Royal MS also contains Book III of *Cibus anime* (which may have circulated independently as an exhortation to contemplative life) and a few extracts from *Speculum christiani*. But it has its own integrity as a text and was drawn on by the *Speculum* rather than from it.

on the priestly life is part of an independent but related second-tier family of texts circulating with, closely related to, or textually dependent on the *Cibus anime*. All share a common *modus agendi*: they use Latin authorities, usually drawn from *Cibus anime*, and several use those *auctoritates* to support vernacular devotional and didactic materials. Most similar to the structure of the *Speculum christiani* are the three linked *tabulae* with *auctoritates* in Oxford, Corpus Christi College, MS 132, which contain extracts on the examination of conscience from the second book of Walter Hilton's *Scale of Perfection* (also found in copies of *Cibus anime*), a couplet moralization of the idol in the Dream of Nebuchadnezzar, also drawing on Hilton, and a description of a proposed scheme of decoration in the Lady Chapel at York Minster.[52]

In addition to the stand-alone texts (*Speculum* and *Cibus anime*), a broader constellation of brief pastoral and hortatory texts that circulates in various permutations alongside the *Cibus anime* is often also reflected in the textual tradition of the *Speculum christiani*.[53] These additional texts, usually short paragraphs of thematically clustered patristic proof texts, or listings of diagnostic signs of moral decline, are sometimes assimilated into the 'standard' form of the *Speculum* (as edited by Holmstedt), but are often added to it at the end of the eighth *tabula*. This section shows the most fluidity in its contents in surviving copies, being added to rather in the manner of a commonplace book: the list of *tabulae* at the start of the *Speculum* comments that this section contains 'plura alia notabilia bona', so it seems to have been deliberately designed to allow for new material to be easily subsumed, in effect to allow for bespoking of the book by individual users.[54]

> **Peccata Britonum & causa deposicionis eorum**. Necgligencia prelatorum, rapina potentum, cupiditas iudicum, rabies periuriorum, inordinatus cultus uestimentorum, detestanda luxuria. Omne peccatum publicum est notorium clamat uin-

---

A copy seems to have been in the library of the brethren at Syon Abbey. For more details, see Gillespie, 'A Syon Manuscript Reconsidered' and 'The Literary Form of the Middle English Pastoral Manual', pp. 287–94.

[52] For editions and analysis of the second-tier texts in the Corpus manuscript, see Gillespie, 'Idols and Images' for the two Hilton adaptations; Gillespie, 'Medieval Hypertext' for the York Minster text, which uses Latin verses from the thirteenth-century English Cistercian guide to church decoration *Pictor in carmine*, but its *modus agendi* is the same as the other texts in the group.

[53] These additional materials in *Cibus anime* and *Speculum christiani* manuscripts are analysed and edited in Gillespie, 'The Literary Form of the Middle English Pastoral Manual'; for one particularly unusual reworking of additional materials, see Gillespie, 'Chapter and Worse'.

[54] *Speculum christiani*, ed. by Holmstedt, 9.31–32.

dictam ad deum set precipue quatuor: merces mercenarii, peccatum sodomiticum, homicidium, oppressio innocencium. Heu! heu! heu! Quot clamantes uindicte sunt nunc ante deum.[55]

Peccata Britonum & causa deposicionis eorum. Negligence of prelates. Raueyne or extorsyon of grete men. Couetyse of iuges. False wodnes of for-sworne men, disgysede and lewde. Out of reule araymente of clothynge, of tyres and of other vnthrifty aray, both of men and wymen. A-cursede and vn-spekable lechery. Al maner opyn synne and knowen crye3 veniaunce to god bot namly foure: Fals wyth-holdynge of wages or dew dettes of seruantes or of eny other, the synne of sod-omyte, manslaughter, fals extorsion and oppressyon of innocente folke. Allas! allas! How many veniaunce be crynge now be-for god![56]

Because the additional materials in *Cibus anime* manuscripts often vary from copy to copy, but nearly all of them are to some extent reflected in the surviving copies of the *Speculum christiani* or in other members of the family, it is probable that these various permutations of texts from the *Cibus/Speculum* family all come from a centre that exerted fairly tight control on the production and initial circulation of those texts. The texts are so ramified throughout the family that it is impossible to argue that there is descent from a single copy containing all the source materials: the story is one of restless compilatory experimentation, cross-fertilization, and dissemination. One copy of the *Cibus anime* is actually called *Speculum christiani*, and one copy of the *Speculum*, Takamiya (*olim* Foyle), was copied by the same scribe who wrote the Trinity Hall copy of *Cibus anime*, whose elegant hand has been dated by Malcolm Parkes to the first decade of the fifteenth century.[57] There are other shared scribal hands between parts of the textual community, suggesting the possibility of organized copying at one or more centres.[58] This seems to be a case of recurrent use of a network

---

[55] *Speculum christiani*, ed. by Holmstedt, 221.1–8. The *Peccata Britonum* schema is widely found added to copies of *Cibus anime*.

[56] *Speculum christiani*, ed. by Holmstedt, 220.1–11.

[57] Now on deposit at New Haven, Yale University, Beinecke Library, as MS Takamiya 96. I am grateful to Professor Toshiyuki Takamiya and Professor Ray Clemens for facilitating recent access to digital surrogates of this manuscript, which I first consulted in the late 1970s in Beeleigh Abbey, Essex, home of Miss Christina Foyle. Other early copies may include Bodl. Lib., MS Bodley 89 (dialect: ?S.E. Notts. or S.W. Lincs.), MS Hatton 97 (S.E. Lincs), MS Laud misc. 104 (not studied); CUL, MS Ff.1.14 (Lincs); Manchester, John Rylands Library, MS Latin 201 (not studied). All linguistic characterizations are from *eLALME*.

[58] *Cibus anime*: BL, MS Harley 407 and Cambridge, King's College, MS Salt 47 are written by the same scribe. *Crossover*: Cambridge, Trinity Hall, MS 16 and Takamiya; Hand 2 of Trinity

of texts that share a common *modus agendi* and persistently experimental redeployment of materials from that network in a variety of different forms, genres, and pastoral modalities.

The *Cibus anime/Speculum christiani* family of texts is strikingly labile, and its core materials are subjected to frequent recombinative pressures and deployments. Even the apparently more settled members of the family, like the *Cibus anime* and the *Speculum*, seem to have evolved through several generations of compilatory experimentation, rather than to have achieved immediate stability. When dealing with such large text *corpora*, with a lot of surviving witnesses showing significant variation in form, it is essential to pay close attention to any evolutionary stages of those texts that may be glimpsed in the surviving textual archive: this one shows that compilations can evolve or adapt form and linguistic medium in order to address or interpellate changed needs or circumstances.[59] (In Middle English, the variability of the textual witnesses to the *Pore Caitif*, much the most important vernacular compilation still without a modern edition, is a clear illustration of this mutability, which is probably one of the reasons it remains unedited.) There is evidence to suggest that the *Speculum christiani* did not spring fully formed from the mind of its compiler, or that it was not the only attempt made at rearranging material present in manuscripts of the *Cibus anime* into a more practical and pastorally useful form. In particular, the complicated textual group identified by Holmstedt as C^3 contains manuscripts which, although containing material also found in the *Speculum*, preserve that material in strikingly different *ordinationes*.[60] (It will be

---

Hall 16 is the main hand in CUL, MS Dd.14.26 (III). *Speculum christiani*: BL, MSS Additional 10052 and 21202, and San Marino, Huntington Library, MS HM 124 are all by the same scribe. For more, see Gillespie, 'The Literary Form of the Middle English Pastoral Manual', 1.228–29.

[59] For an overview of recent thinking on some of these topics, see the essays in Gillespie and Hudson, *Probable Truth*.

[60] On the C^3 group, see *Speculum christiani*, ed. by Holmstedt, pp. clxv–clxxi. The manuscripts in the group, with Holmstedt's sigils, are BL, MS Additional 15237 (Ad^1); MS Royal 8 E V (Ro^2); MS Additional 37049 (Ad^5); MS Harley 2388 (Har^7); CUL, MS Dd.14.26 (III) (Dd); Rylands MS Lat. 341 (Sal); and Oxford, Balliol College, MS 239 (Bal). Of the relationship between them, Holmstedt comments: 'Only two of the seven above mentioned MSS are comparatively complete, namely Ad^1 [Add. 15237] and Ro^2 [Royal 8 E V]. Most of the others contain only very short portions, but still two distinctly separate sub groups can be discerned: on one side Ad^1, Ro^2, Ad^5 [Add. 37049], Har^7 [Harley 2388], Dd [Dd.14.26 III] and on the other Sal [JRL Lat.341] and Bal [Balliol 239]' (p. clxv). Sample collations show that two of the copies unknown to Holmstedt (Takamiya (*olim* Foyle) and CUL, MS Dd.4.51) also belong to this group, in the same sub-group that contains Dd 14.26 (III).

recalled that Meg Laing argued that the C³ group represented copies close to the dialectal point of origin of the ordinary form of the *Speculum christiani*.) One particularly significant feature of the C³ group (as expanded to include the copies unknown to Holmstedt) is that it contains two closely related copies of the *Cibus anime* (Rylands MS Lat. 341 and Oxford, Balliol College, MS 239). Given that the same scribe was copying the Trinity Hall *Cibus anime* and the C³ version of *Speculum* materials in Takamiya, this suggests that the C³ group may be textually, chronologically, and geographically close to the point when the authorities in the *Cibus anime* began to be exploited and deployed in new ways, primarily through the addition of vernacular materials. I analysed in particular CUL, MS Dd.14.26 (III), which I showed had a distinctive *ordinatio*, retaining the ordering into formal chapters found in the *Cibus anime*, rather than the looser division of material into *tabulae* in the *Speculum*.[61] Like the *Speculum*, all these C³ manuscripts are intimately related to the *Cibus anime*, and it is possible that they were products of the same milieu, perhaps even the same centre that produced the 'ordinary' form of the *Speculum*. It is even possible that they, or the earlier work they may represent, are the work of the same man, although there can be no firm evidence of this. They are either parallel attempts to present material from the *Speculum* tradition which failed to find the popularity of the more widely circulated form, or experiments in structuring the material which were later supplanted by what became the 'finished' version of the *Speculum christiani*. Either way, the various experimental presentations of materials from the *Cibus anime* tradition in the C³ group, in particular in regularly partnering them with vernacular materials, along with the similar procedures employed in other compilations in the group, shows the process of trial and error that went into building the work now known as the *Speculum christiani*. This is a messy but fascinating textual maelstrom, and one that appears to be seeking to achieve a macaronic blend of the best of the Latin tradition of pastoral catechetics with the best of the vernacular tradition of instructional catechetic verse. That is a pastoral, catechetic, and linguistic synthesis very typical of the English Church in the early decades of the fifteenth century. But it is important not to underestimate its ongoing Latinity.

The *Pupilla oculi* is a possible model for and an important part of the pastoral toolkit and reference library of those responsible for compiling both the *Cibus anime* and the *Speculum christiani*. Indeed the *Speculum christiani* might be thought of as a continuation of the process of popularization at work in

[61] For detailed analysis of this claim, see Gillespie, 'Chapter and Worse'.

the *Pupilla oculi*, in particular through the addition of vernacular verse and prose as the mnemonic vehicle for much of the teaching, replacing the traditional Latin mnemonic verses found in the *Pupilla* and other Latin pastoral aids. Chronologically this would place the work of compilation as taking place between 1385 and 1420, and most probably in the years between 1385 and 1410. The *Speculum* stands as a compilatory bridge between the world of the vernacular verse *summae* such as *Pricke of Conscience* and *Speculum vitae* and the older Latin tradition of ad hoc pastoral manuals.[62] Despite important, indeed pioneering work by W. A. Pantin and Leonard Boyle, this liminal space of bilingual *pastoralia* has not been as fully studied as it deserves. Just as it is impossible fully to understand the late-career vernacular writings of Richard Rolle without a proper engagement with the Latin texts that form the bulk of his output, so too it is unsafe to discuss vernacular catechetic and devotional compilations without a detailed familiarity with the Latin and macaronic textual foundations on which they rest.

If the *Cibus anime* is indeed originally a Carthusian text, as I have argued elsewhere, and if the dialectal evidence that early prototypes of the *Speculum* emerged in the Lincolnshire area is correct, then it may be that the earliest version of the *Cibus anime* was originally composed in a charterhouse in Lincolnshire or Nottinghamshire (the candidates are Beauvale in Nottinghamshire (founded 1343) and Axholme in Lincolnshire (founded 1397)) before being reworked, expanded, and copied by scribes with these regional linguistic characteristics, with the intention of producing more directly pastoral and catechetic treatments of the Latin materials.[63] That may have been but need not have been in a charterhouse: the early form of *Cibus anime* is more suited to monastic use than its later more developed versions, which have more sophisticated reference aids. But there is no inherent impediment to a charterhouse wishing to assist in the provision of Latin pastoral materials for parochial clergy.[64] Many Carthusians entered the order after careers as priests with the cure of souls and may have brought their books and their pastoral interests with them. But, given their well-documented caution about their materials reaching the hands of the laity, it is perhaps less likely that they would have been interested in linking those Latin materials to vernacular verse and prose, even in formulations such as *Speculum christiani* that are obviously aimed primarily at priests with the

[62] For *Speculum vitae*, now see the new edition *Speculum Vitae*, ed. by Hanna.

[63] Gillespie, 'Cura Pastoralis in Deserto'. See also Gillespie, 'The Evolution of the *Speculum Christiani*' and 'Chapter and Worse'.

[64] On this topic, see Gillespie, 'Cura Pastoralis in Deserto'.

cure of souls. So perhaps there was a second, more pastorally oriented, centre that took up these materials and was responsible for the flurry of textual reworking and reconfigurations that characterize the *Cibus anime/Speculum christiani* family of texts. It seems subsequently (and quite quickly) to have achieved popularity and circulation among priests attached to York Minster and might have been further circulated from there. But I would hesitate to exclude the possibility that the text was mainly copied and circulated inside Lincoln diocese. Its East Midland provenance and circulation certainly help to explain why Margery Kempe and her priestly advisers and readers might have been aware of it.

Margery's apparently highly developed aural memory for catechetic and theological instruction might explain why she recalls elements of it (the *Speculum christiani*'s teachings on tears also resonate with Margery's thoughts on that charism),[65] although there is almost no evidence of it circulating in lay ownership (which is hardly surprising given its sacerdotal focus and heavy use of Latin *auctoritates*). She models for us an important synapse between materials targeted at priests charged with the *ars artium*, the *regimen animarum*, and the penetration of those materials into wider circulation. Christ's words to Margery about the career development of a vicar who came to her for advice could have been drawn from any number of English Episcopal documents from John Pecham through to John Thoresby and beyond to Thomas Arundel and to Henry Chichele:

> 'Bydde the vykary kepyn stylle hys cure and hys benefyce and don hys diligence in prechyng and techyng of hem hys owyn persone and sumtyme procuryn other to teche hem my lawys and my comawndmentys so that ther be no defawte in hys parte, and, yyf thei do nevyr the bettyr, hys mede schal nevyr be the lesse.' And so sche dede hir massage as sche was comawndyd, and the vykary kept stylle hys cur. (I. 23)

Such admonitions can also be found in texts like the *Oculus sacerdotis* and *Pupilla oculi*, or Rolle's *Judica me Deus* (much of which pretty fiercely plagiarizes the *Oculus sacerdotis*, and which is probably William Langland's route to awareness of the *Oculus*).[66] It is interesting to note the expectation expressed here that catechesis might sometimes be subcontracted ('sumtyme procuryn

---

[65] See I. 57, and the note in Windeatt's edition, p. 277.

[66] The second major section of the *Judica me deus* (*Judica* B1–3) is heavily dependent on *Oculus sacerdotis*. Rolle, *An Edition of the Judica Me Deus*, ed. by Daly; Watson, 'Richard Rolle as Elitist and as Popularist'; Hanna, 'The Transmission'.

other to teche hem'), which would widen the pool of those in need of training and guidance in such matters. Indeed I have argued that the vernacular verse and lyric in the *Speculum christiani* is probably designed very precisely to act as a mnemonic nodal point around which the wider Latin teaching of the text might cluster, and to serve as a vector of delivery of those teachings into formal and less formal parochial and confessional teaching environments.

There is, therefore, something distinctly timely as well as pastorally timeless about the diligence in preaching and teaching, the *zelus animarum*, that characterizes the pastoral objectives of the *Speculum christiani*. The work is not a guide to confession, but would have assisted a priest with the broader *cura animarum* in the daily execution of his pastoral rather than sacramental duties. At the beginning of *tabula* 8, there is a long rumination on the nature of the priestly calling and the moral responsibility of neglecting pastoral instruction through preaching and teaching that again reflects the urgency of Margery Kempe's message:

> Subtracio uictus anime est omissio predicacionis uerbi dei [...]. Mercenarii sunt qui curam animarum suscipiunt non quia cupiunt regere & custodire ecclesiam in iusticia & sanctitate sed quia uolunt diuites fieri & in altitudine mundana pre aliis honorari; & ideo incidunt in laquem & in temptacionem diaboli. De salute ouium non curant nisi ut lac & manam habeant. [...] De temporalibus lucris pascuntur, impensa ab hominibus reuerencia letantur. Isti enim sunt mercedes mercenariorum, pro quibus principaliter laborant.[67]

> Defaute or lettynge of prechyng or techynge of goddes worde when any man be holden ther-to, it es wyth-drawynge of the soules fode [...]. Thei be marchaunt3 that taken cure of soule not for thei couete to gouerne and kepe the chirche in ri3twysnes and holynes, bot for thei couete to be made rych and be honourde in worldly worschipe be-for other. Ther-for thei fallen in-to the trappe and temptacion of the deuyl. Marchuant3 recke not of helth of the schepe bot that thei haue mylke and wolle. Thei gapen aftur erthly profites, thei ioyen of honour of prelacy, their be fede with temperalle lucrys, thei reioycen of hye reuerence that men do to hem. These ben the medes of marchaunt3 for whiche thei laboure principally.[68]

The following sections outline an ideal of clerical life, including a long quotation from Robert Grosseteste, the reforming thirteenth-century Bishop of Lincoln, within whose diocese the *Cibus anime/Speculum christiani* textual nexus seems to have developed. Grosseteste's critiques of clerical indolence and venality had been co-opted by Wycliffite polemic and were then assidu-

---

[67] *Speculum christiani*, ed. by Holmstedt, 171.1–173.2, omitting Latin *auctoritates*.
[68] *Speculum christiani*, ed. by Holmstedt, 170.1–172.2, omitting the Latin *auctoritates*.

ously reclaimed by the orthodox reformers as part of their own lexis of reform. Here, Grosseteste, whose Latin handbook of the *cura pastoralis*, the *Templum dei* or *Templum domini*, provides some schematic materials elsewhere in the *Speculum*, lays out very clearly the duties of the pastoral care, using the corporal works of mercy to stress the human dimension of the priestly role:[69]

> ***Lincolniensis***: Opus cure pastoralis non solum consistit in sacramentorum adminstracione & in horarum canonicarum dictione & missarum celebracione, sed eciam in ueraci doctrina ueritatis uite & uiciorum terrifica dampnacione, in uiciosorum, cum necesse est, dura & imperiosa correpcione & rigida castigacione. Consistit insuper in pastione esuriencium, in potacione sitiencium & coopersione nudorum, in suscepcione hospitum, in uisitacione infirmorum & incarceratorum & maxime propriorum parochianorum, quorum sunt bona temporalia ecclesiastica; quarum operacionum exemplis instruendus est populus.[70]

> ***Lincolniensis***: The dede of charge of curates es not oonly in mynistracion of sacramentes and in seynges of houres and syngynge of masses, bot also in verrey doctrine of truth of lyfe and in ferful dampnacion of vices and in herde correpcion of viciouse men and scharpe and streyte chastysmente when it es nede. Also the werke of curates es in fedynge of hungry, in drynke ȝeuynge to thursty, in couerynge of naked men, in herberynge of pore gestes, in visitacion of seke men and of presoners and moste of her oune paryschenges, whose temperalle gudes ben of the chyrch. Be ensaumple of suche werkes the peple aweȝ to be taught.[71]

This broader based definition of the priestly role spreads beyond the purely sacramental and into an exemplary stress on 'verrey doctrine of truth of lyfe' ('ueraci doctrina ueritatis uite'). Geoffrey Chaucer's Parson, under such a definition of the parochial role, would not be suspected of Lollard leanings, but would merely be seen to be enacting an apostolic form of the clerical idea to which the institutional Church of the conciliar period was seeking to return, in its public pronouncements and formal decrees at least.

The *Speculum christiani* is a missionary text, aware of the dangers of demoralization in the priests who will use it, but urging them to embrace the high ideals of clerical life and pastoral zeal characteristic of English reform orthodoxy

---

[69] *Templum Dei*, ed. by Goering and Mantello. Its schematic listing of prohibited degrees of marriage is cited at *Speculum christiani*, ed. by Holmstedt, 229.1–14, and the listing of the clauses of the Apostle's Creed also derive from there: for analysis, see Kemmler, *'Exempla' in Context*, Appendix II (The Influence of Robert Grosseteste's *Templum Domini* on the *Speculum christiani*), pp. 197–99. In each case, supporting Latin *auctoritates* are provided from *Cibus anime*.

[70] *Speculum christiani*, ed. by Holmstedt, 173.27–175.6.

[71] *Speculum christiani*, ed. by Holmstedt, 172.33–174.7.

of the early fifteenth century. It became one of the catechetic bestsellers of the fifteenth century precisely because it was so carefully constructed and deliberately targeted. By a process of rigorous Darwinian testing and selection, the broad textual resource provided by the *Cibus anime* and the texts that typically circulated with it was winnowed and sorted until the *Speculum* emerged into a form that remained more or less stable until it appeared in print in London and in Paris. That careful compilatorial work of trial and error is unusually fully available for inspection in the *Cibus/Speculum* textual tradition. And the exploitation of Latin and vernacular resources in the same text reminds us of the need to attend to the intralingual and multilingual modalities of English *pastoralia* in this period.

In a final act of self-justification, the *Speculum* argues that the production and circulation of such pastoral texts is an act of charity and spiritual almsgiving:

> Magnum enim meritum est illi & multum premium habebit in futuro, qui scribit uel scribere facit doctrinam sanam ea intencione ut ipse querat in ea quomodo sancte uiuat & ut alii eam habeant ut per eam edificentur. Hoc certissime scito quod tot premia pre aliis habebis quot anime per te salue fiant.[72]

> Grete meryte is to hym, and he schal haue myche mede in tyme to come, that wryteȝ or dooȝ to write holsom doctrine for that entente that he may lyue holily ther-by, and also that other men mowe be edifyede ther-by. Knowe that certenly that thou schalt haue so many medes bi-forne other as many soules as be sauede by the.[73]

How successful this pastoral agenda was is harder to assess. Despite the large number of surviving copies, there are slight suggestions at the end of the *Speculum christiani* that the compiler might not have had complete confidence in a positive outcome. A citation from the fashionable (if still at this date contestable) revelations of Saint Birgitta of Sweden, one of the 'approuyd wymmen' of English reform orthodoxy, calls prophetically in the voice of the Virgin Mary for the conversion of others as one of the primary responsibilities of all Christians:

> Legitur in libro beate Brigide quod amici dei non debent attediari in seruicio dei, set laborare ut homo malus sit melior & homo bonus ueniat ad perfectiora. Nam quicumque uoluntatem haberet sibilandi in aures omnium transiencium quod Iesus Christus esset uere dei filius & faciendo conaretur quantum posset ad aliorum conuersionem licet nulli uel pauci conuerterentur nihilominus eandem mer-

---

[72] *Speculum christiani*, ed. by Holmstedt, 241.1–5.
[73] *Speculum christiani*, ed. by Holmstedt, 240.1–6.

cedem optineret ac si omnes conuertentur. Propterea non est cessandum, quamuis uel pauci uel nulli recipiant verbum dei. *Gregorius*: Nullum sacrificium ita placet deo sicut zelus animarum.[74]

It is red in the lyfe of seynt bride that frendes of god owen not to be wery in godes seruice; bot labours that the wicked man be amendede and the gude may come to more perfyte thynges. For who-so-euer haȝ wil to soune in al mennes eerys that Criste Ihesus wer truly goddes sone and desyre wyth gud seele in doynge what he may to true conuersyon of other, althoue none or fewe be conuertede, nertheles he schal haue the same mede as if al were turnede and conuertede to god. Ther-for it is not to be cessed althoue feue or non receyuen the worde of god. *Gregorius*: No sacrifise pleseȝ so god as seele or loue of soules.[75]

Not for the first time, the language and reform agendas of Birgitta and Margery Kempe reflect each other. Given that both are responding prophetically to instructions from Christ, this is perhaps unsurprising. But the inclusion of this Birgittine quotation in *Speculum christiani* reminds us that Birgitta and Margery Kempe both thought of themselves as participants in a process of pastoral and clerical renewal. This sort of citation from Birgitta could have helped create both Margery's sense of mission, and perhaps also the clerical taste by which Margery Kempe's own teachings might have come to have been appreciated.

My father-in-law used to claim that the archetypal story had three decisive elements to its narrative arc: Algy met a bear; the bear got bulgy; the bulge was Algy.[76] Margery's bear is more fortunate in its diet:

[The priest], destytute of hys herborwe, fond a fayr erber in the whech he restyd that nyght, havyng a fayr pertre in the myddys al floreschyd wyth flowerys and belschyd, and blomys ful delectabil to hys syght, wher cam a bere, gret and boistows, hogely to beheldyn, schakyng the pertre and fellyng down the flowerys. Gredily this grevows best ete and devowryd tho fayr flowerys. And, whan he had etyn hem, turnyng his tayl ende in the prestys presens, voydyd hem owt ageyn at the hymyr party.[77]

---

[74] *Speculum christiani*, ed. by Holmstedt, 241.7–18. The quotation from Birgitta comes not from her *Life*, but from her *Revelationes*, Book IV, cap. 21, par 11–13, 16.

[75] *Speculum christiani*, ed. by Holmstedt, 240.7–17.

[76] This is a family variant of a familiar ditty. The more usual form of the verse is: 'Algy met a bear. The bear met Algy. The bear was bulgy. The bulge was Algy'. It is sometimes attributed to Ogden Nash.

[77] Kempe, *The Book*, ed. by Staley, I. 52.

I find myself wondering if this *narracio* is more than just a critique of clerical sloth. Is it also perhaps a cunning integumental allegory of the process of florilegial compilation, such as we observe in the *Cibus/Speculum* tradition? Flowers (*flores*) are shaken from the pear tree (the flourishing and fruitful textual tradition of Latin and vernacular *pastoralia*); these *flores* are devoured by the compiler; they are digested and broken down and are finally expelled in a differently synthesized form at the end of the process, the reshaped end products being very deliberately aimed in the direction of the parochial clergy for whom these texts were intended. (I am absolutely sure that Thomas Hoccleve would have had no problem in coming up with such a moralization if he had included this story in his *Series*.) The textual history of the *Speculum christiani*, with expansive resources to choose from in both Latin and vernacular catechesis, shows that the production of hybrid compilations of this kind could be a messy and laborious process, with dead ends, failures, and abandoned experiments. But in this case, when it clicked into place, the sustained popularity of the text in later decades and into print demonstrates that the compilers finally succeeded in building a bestseller. Perhaps its popularity was because of rather than despite its rich interactions with the Latin tradition of *pastoralia*. If so, that Latin tradition deserves closer attention.

Works Cited

Manuscripts

Cambridge, King's College, MS Salt 47
Cambridge, Trinity Hall, MS 16
Cambridge, University Library [CUL], MS Additional 6315 (II)
Cambridge, University Library [CUL], MS Dd.4.51
Cambridge, University Library [CUL], MS Dd.14.26 (III)
Cambridge, University Library [CUL], MS Ff.1.14
London, British Library [BL], MS Additional 10052
London, British Library [BL], MS Additional 15237
London, British Library [BL], MS Additional 21202
London, British Library [BL], MS Additional 37049
London, British Library [BL], MS Harley 237
London, British Library [BL], MS Harley 407
London, British Library [BL], MS Harley 2379
London, British Library [BL], MS Harley 2388
London, British Library [BL], MS Harley 3363
London, British Library [BL], MS Harley 3820
London, British Library [BL], MS Harley 6580
London, British Library [BL], MS Lansdowne 344
London, British Library [BL], MS Royal 5 A VI
London, British Library [BL], MS Royal 8 E V
London, Lambeth Palace Library, MS 460
Manchester, John Rylands Library, MS Latin 201
Manchester, John Rylands Library, MS Latin 341
New Haven, Yale University Library, Beinecke Library, MS Takamiya 96
Oxford, Balliol College, MS 239
Oxford, Bodleian Library [Bodl. Lib.], MS Bodley 89
Oxford, Bodleian Library [Bodl. Lib.], MS Hatton 97
Oxford, Bodleian Library [Bodl. Lib.], MS Laud misc. 104
Oxford, Bodleian Library [Bodl. Lib.], MS Rawlinson C. 19
Oxford, Corpus Christi College, MS 132
Oxford, University College, MS 60
San Marino, California, Huntington Library, MS HM 124

Primary Sources

Alan of the Isles, *A Compendium on the Art of Preaching* (Preface and Selected Chapters), trans. by J. M. Miller, in *Readings in Medieval Rhetoric*, ed. by J. M. Miller, M. H. Prosser, and T. W. Benson (Bloomington: Indiana University Press, 1973), pp. 228–39

Councils and Synods with Other Documents Relating to the English Church, vol. II: A.D. 1205–1313, ed. by F. M. Powicke and C. R. Cheney, 2 parts (Oxford: Oxford University Press, 1964)

Julian of Norwich, *A Book of Showings to the Anchoress Julian of Norwich*, ed. by Edmund Colledge and James Walsh, 2 vols (Toronto: Pontifical Institute of Mediaeval Studies, 1978)

——, *The Writings of Julian of Norwich: 'A Vision Showed to a Devout Woman' and 'A Revelation of Love'*, ed. by Nicholas Watson and Jacqueline Jenkins, Medieval Women (University Park: Pennsylvania State University Press, 2006)

Kempe, Margery, *The Book of Margery Kempe*, ed. by Sanford Brown Meech and Hope Emily Allen, Early English Text Society, o.s., 212 (Oxford: Oxford University Press, 1940 for 1939)

——, *The Book of Margery Kempe*, ed. by Lynn Staley, TEAMS (Kalamazoo: Medieval Institute Publications, 1996)

——, *The Book of Margery Kempe*, ed. by Barry Windeatt (Harlow: Longman, 2000)

A Mirror to Devout People (Speculum Devotorum), ed. by Paul J. Patterson, Early English Text Society, o.s., 346 (Oxford: Oxford University Press, 2016)

Morris, Richard, *Richard Morris's Prick of Conscience: A Corrected and Amplified Reading Text*, ed. by Ralph Hanna and Sarah Wood, Early English Text Society, o.s., 342 (Oxford: Oxford University Press, 2013)

Pupilla oculi omnibus presbyteris precipue Anglicanis summe necessaria (Paris: William Hopyl per impensis William Breton, 1510)

The Register of Bishop Philip Repingdon, 1405–1419, ed. by M. Archer, Lincoln Record Society, 57–58 (Lincoln: Lincoln Record Society, 1963)

Robert of Basevorn, *Forma Praedicandi*, in Th. Charland, *Artes Praedicandi: Contribution à l'histoire de la rhétorique au moyen âge*, Publications de l'Institut d'études médiévales d'Ottawa, 7 (Paris: Vrin; Montreal: Institut d'études médiévales, 1936)

Rolle, Richard, *An Edition of the Judica Me Deus of Richard Rolle*, ed. by John Philip Daly (Salzburg: Institut fur Anglistik und Amerikanistik, Universitat Salzburg, 1984)

Speculum christiani, ed. by Gustaf Holmstedt, ed., Early English Text Society, o.s., 182 (Oxford: Oxford University Press, 1933)

Speculum vitae: A Reading Edition, ed. by Ralph Hanna, Early English Text Society, o.s., 331–32, 2 vols (Oxford: Oxford University Press, 2008)

Templum Dei, ed. by Joseph Ward Goering and F. A. C. Mantello (Toronto: Pontifical Institute of Mediaeval Studies, 1984)

Virgins and Scholars: A Fifteenth-Century Compilation of the Lives of John the Baptist, John the Evangelist, Jerome, and Katherine of Alexandria, ed. by Claire M. Waters (Turnhout: Brepols, 2008)

Secondary Works

Arnold, John H., 'Margery's Trials: Heresy, Lollardy and Dissent', in *A Companion to the Book of Margery Kempe*, ed. by John H. Arnold and Katherine J. Lewis (Cambridge: D. S. Brewer, 2004), pp. 75–93

Barr, Beth Allison, *The Pastoral Care of Women in Late Medieval England*, Gender in the Middle Ages (Woodbridge: Boydell, 2008)

Beadle, Richard, 'Middle English Texts and their Transmission, 1350–1500: Some Geographical Criteria', in *Speaking in our Tongues: Proceedings of a Colloquium on Medieval Dialectology and Related Disciplines*, ed. by Margaret Laing and K. Williamson (Cambridge: D. S. Brewer, 1994), pp. 69–91

Beckwith, Sarah, 'Problems of Authority in Late Medieval English Mysticism: Language, Agency, and Authority in the Book of Margery Kempe', *Exemplaria*, 4 (1992), 171–200

——, 'A Very Material Mysticism: The Medieval Mysticism of Margery Kempe', in *Medieval Literature: Criticism, Ideology and History*, ed. by David Aers (Brighton: Palgrave, 1986), pp. 34–57

Bhattacharji, Santha, *God Is an Earthquake: The Spirituality of Margery Kempe* (London: Darton, Longman and Todd, 1997)

Boffey, Julia, and John J. Thompson, 'Anthologies and Miscellanies: Production and Choice of Texts', in *Book Production and Publishing in Britain, 1375–1475*, ed. by Jeremy Griffiths and Derek Pearsall, Cambridge Studies in Publishing and Printing History (Cambridge: Cambridge University Press, 1989; repr. 2007), pp. 279–315

Boyle, Leonard E., 'The Fourth Lateran Council and Manuals of Popular Theology', in *The Popular Literature of Medieval England*, ed. by Thomas J. Heffernan, Tennessee Studies in Literature, 28 (Knoxville: University of Tennessee Press, 1985), pp. 30–43

——, *Pastoral Care, Clerical Education and Canon Law, 1200–1400* (London: Variorum Reprints, 1981)

——, 'A Study of the Works Attributed to William of Pagula: With Special Reference to the *Oculus Sacerdotis* and *Summa Summarum*' (unpublished doctoral thesis, University of Oxford, 1956)

Brandmüller, Walter, *Das Konzil von Konstanz, 1414–1418*, 2 vols, Konziliengeschichte. Reihe a: Darstellungen (Paderborn: Ferdinand Schöningh, 1991)

——, *Das Konzil von Pavia-Siena, 1423–1424* (Paderborn: Ferdinand Schöningh, 2002)

Burgess, Clive, and Eamon Duffy, eds, *The Parish in Late Medieval England: Proceedings of the 2002 Harlaxton Symposium*, Harlaxton Medieval Studies, 14 (Donington: Shaun Tyas, 2006)

Burns, J. H., and Thomas M. Izbicki, eds, *Conciliarism and Papalism* (Cambridge: Cambridge University Press, 1997)

Carey, Hilary M., 'Devout Literate Laypeople and the Pursuit of the Mixed Life in Later Medieval England', *Journal of Religious History*, 14 (1987), 361–81

Catto, Jeremy, 'After Arundel: The Closing or the Opening of the English Mind', in *After Arundel: Religious Writing in Fifteenth-Century England*, ed. by Vincent Gillespie and Kantik Ghosh, Medieval Church Studies, 21 (Turnhout: Brepols, 2011), pp. 43–54

——, 'Shaping the Mixed Life: Thomas Arundel's Reformation', in *Image, Text and Church: Essays for Margaret Aston*, ed. by Linda Clark, Maureen Jurkowski, and Colin Richmond (Toronto: Pontifical Institute of Mediaeval Studies, 2009), pp. 94–108

Cheney, Christopher R., 'The Earliest English Diocesan Statutes', *English Historical Review*, 75 (1960), 1–29

——, *English Synodalia of the Thirteenth Century* (Oxford: Oxford University Press, 1941; repr. with a new introduction, 1968)

——, 'Some Aspects of Diocesan Legislation in England in the Thirteenth Century', in Christopher R. Cheney, *Medieval Texts and Studies* (Oxford: Oxford University Press, 1973), pp. 185–202

Cleve, Gunnel, 'Margery Kempe: A Scandinavian Influence in Medieval England', in *The Medieval Mystical Tradition in England: Exeter Symposium V*, ed. by Marion Glasscoe (Cambridge: D. S. Brewer, 1992), pp. 163–79

Connolly, Margaret, 'Books for the "helpe of euery persoone þat þenkiþ to be saued": Six Devotional Anthologies from Fifteenth-Century London', *Yearbook of English Studies*, 33 (2003), 170–81

Connolly, Margaret, and Linne R. Mooney, eds, *Design and Distribution of Late Medieval Manuscripts in England* (York: York Medieval Press; Woodbridge: Boydell, 2008)

Connolly, Margaret, and Raluca Radulescu, eds, *Insular Books: Vernacular Manuscript Miscellanies in Late Medieval Britain*, Proceedings of the British Academy, 201 (Oxford: Oxford University Press for the British Academy, 2015)

Coote, Lesley A., *Prophecy and Public Affairs in Later Medieval England* (Woodbridge: York Medieval Press, 2000)

Craun, Edwin D., *Ethics and Power in Medieval English Reformist Writing* (Cambridge: Cambridge University Press, 2010)

Crowder, C. M. D., *Unity, Heresy and Reform, 1378–1460: The Conciliar Response to the Great Schism* (London: Edward Arnold, 1977)

Dillon, Janette, 'Holy Women and their Confessors or Confessors and their Holy Women? Margery Kempe and Continental Tradition', in *Prophets Abroad: The Reception of Continental Holy Women in Late Medieval England*, ed. by Rosalynn Voaden (Cambridge: D. S. Brewer, 1996), pp. 115–40

Ellis, Roger, '"Flores ad Fabricandum … Coronam": An Investigation into the Uses of the Revelations of St Bridget of Sweden in Fifteenth-Century England', *Medium Aevum*, 51 (1982), 163–86

——, 'Margery Kempe's Scribe and the Miraculous Books', in *Langland, the Mystics and the Medieval English Religious Tradition: Essays in Honour of S. S. Hussey*, ed. by Helen Phillips (Cambridge: D. S. Brewer, 1990), pp. 161–75

Erler, Mary C., *Women, Reading, and Piety in Late Medieval England* (Cambridge: Cambridge University Press, 2002)

Fredell, Joel, 'Design and Authorship in *The Book of Margery Kempe*', *Journal of the Early Book Society*, 12 (2009), 1–28

Furrow, Melissa, 'Unscholarly Latin and Margery Kempe', in *'Doubt Wisely': Papers in Honour of E. G. Stanley*, ed. by M. Jane Toswell (London: Routledge, 1996), pp. 240–51

Gertz-Robinson, Genelle, 'Stepping into the Pulpit? Women's Preaching in *The Book of Margery Kempe* and *The Examination of Anne Askew*', in *Voices in Dialogue: Reading Women in the Middle Ages*, ed. by Linda Olson and Kathryn Kerby-Fulton (Notre Dame: University of Notre Dame Press, 2005), pp. 459–82

Gibbs, Margaret, and Jane Lang, *Bishops and Reform, 1215–1272, with Special Reference to the Lateran Council of 1215* (London: Oxford University Press, 1934)

Gibson, Gail McMurray, *The Theater of Devotion: East Anglian Drama and Society in the Late Middle Ages* (Chicago: University of Chicago Press, 1989)

Gillespie, Alexandra, and Daniel Wakelin, eds, *The Production of Books in England, 1350–1500*, Cambridge Studies in Codicology and Palaeography, 14 (Cambridge: Cambridge University Press, 2011)

Gillespie, Vincent, '*Approuyd Wymmen*': Birgitta of Sweden and the Politics of Late Medieval English Spirituality, The 2016 Etienne Gilson Lecture (Toronto: Pontifical Institute of Mediaeval Studies, forthcoming)

——, 'Chapter and Worse: An Episode in the Regional Transmission of the *Speculum Christiani*', in *English Manuscript Studies 1100–1700*, vol. XIV, ed. by A. S. G. Edwards (London: British Library, 2008), pp. 86–111

——, 'Chichele's Church: Vernacular Theology in England after Thomas Arundel', in *After Arundel: Religious Writing in Fifteenth-Century England*, ed. by Vincent Gillespie and Kantik Ghosh, Medieval Church Studies, 21 (Turnhout: Brepols, 2011), pp. 3–42

——, 'The *Cibus Anime* Book 3: A Guide for Contemplatives?', in *Spiritualität Heute und Gestern*, vol. III, Analecta Cartusiana, 35.3 (Salzburg: Institut für Anglistik und Amerikanistik, Universität Salzburg, 1983), pp. 90–119

——, '*Cura Pastoralis in Deserto*', in *De Cella in Seculum: Religious and Secular Life and Devotion in Late Medieval England*, ed. by Michael G. Sargent (Cambridge: D. S. Brewer, 1988), pp. 161–81; repr. in Gillespie, *Looking in Holy Books*, ch. 2, pp. 21–47

——, '*Doctrina* and *Predicacio*: The Design and Function of Some Pastoral Manuals', *Leeds Studies in English*, n.s., 11 (1980 for 1979), 36–50

——, 'The Evolution of the *Speculum Christiani*', in *Latin and Vernacular: Studies in Late-Medieval Texts and Manuscripts*, ed. by Alastair J. Minnis (Cambridge: D. S. Brewer, 1989), pp. 39–62

——, 'Idols and Images: Pastoral Adaptations of *The Scale of Perfection*', in *Langland, the Mystics and the Medieval English Religious Tradition: Essays in Honour of S. S. Hussey*, ed. by Helen Phillips (Cambridge: D. S. Brewer, 1990), pp. 97–123

——, 'The Literary Form of the Middle English Pastoral Manual with Particular Reference to the *Speculum Christiani* and Some Related Texts' (unpublished doctoral thesis, University of Oxford, 1981)

——, *Looking in Holy Books: Essays on Late Medieval Religious Writing in England*, Brepols Collected Essays in European Culture, 3 (Turnhout: Brepols, 2011)

——, '*Lukynge in Haly Bukes*: *Lectio* in Some Late Medieval Spiritual Miscellanies', in *Spätmittelalterliche Geistliche Literatur in der Nationalsprache*, ed. by James Hogg (Salzburg: Institut für Anglistik und Amerikanistik, 1984), pp. 1–27

——, 'Medieval Hypertext: Image and Text from York Minster', in *Of the Making of Books: Medieval Manuscripts, their Scribes and Readers. Essays Presented to M. B. Parkes*, ed. by P. R. Robinson and Rivkah Zim (Aldershot: Scolar Press, 1997), pp. 206–29

——, 'Religious Writing', in *The History of Literary Translation in English*, vol. I: *To 1500*, ed. by Roger Ellis (Oxford: Oxford University Press, 2008), pp. 234–83

——, '"[S]he Do the Police in Different Voices": Pastiche, Ventriloquism and Parody in Julian of Norwich', in *A Companion to Julian of Norwich*, ed. by Liz Herbert McAvoy (Cambridge: D. S. Brewer, 2008), pp. 192–207

——, 'A Syon Manuscript Reconsidered', *Notes and Queries*, n.s., 30 (1983), 203–05

—— , 'Vernacular Books of Religion', in *Book Production and Publishing in Britain, 1375–1475*, ed. by Jeremy Griffiths and Derek Pearsall, Cambridge Studies in Publishing and Printing History (Cambridge: Cambridge University Press, 1989; repr. 2007), pp. 317–44

—— , 'Vernacular Theology', in *Middle English*, ed. by Paul Strohm (Oxford: Oxford University Press, 2007), pp. 401–20

Gillespie, Vincent, and Kantik Ghosh, eds, *After Arundel: Religious Writing in Fifteenth-Century England*, Medieval Church Studies, 21 (Turnhout: Brepols, 2011)

Gillespie, Vincent, and Anne Hudson, eds, *Probable Truth: Editing Medieval Texts from Britain in the Twenty-First Century* (Turnhout: Brepols, 2013)

Gunn, Cate, and Catherine Innes-Parker, eds, *Text and Traditions of Medieval Pastoral Care: Essays in Honour of Bella Millett* (Woodbridge: York Medieval Press, 2009)

Haines, Roy Martin, *Ecclesia Anglicana: Studies in the English Church of the Later Middle Ages* (Toronto: University of Toronto Press, 1989)

—— , 'Education in English Ecclesiastical Legislation of the Later Middle Ages', in *Councils and Assemblies*, ed. by G. J. Cuming and Derek Baker, Studies in Church History, 7 (Cambridge: Cambridge University Press, 1971), pp. 161–75

Hanna, Ralph, 'A Fifteenth-Century Vernacular Miscellany Revisited', *Bodleian Library Record*, 27 (2013), 188–207

—— , 'Lambeth Palace Library, MS 260 and the Problem of English Vernacularity', *Studies in Medieval and Renaissance History*, 3rd ser., 5 (2008), 131–99

—— , 'Middle English Books and Middle English Literary History', *Modern Philology*, 102 (2004), 157–78

—— , 'Miscellaneity and Vernacularity: Conditions of Literary Production in Late Medieval England', in *The Whole Book: Cultural Perspectives on the Medieval Miscellany*, ed. by Stephen G. Nichols and Siegfried Wenzel (Ann Arbor: University. of Michigan Press, 1996), pp. 37–52

—— , 'Producing Magdalen College MS lat. 93', *Yearbook of English Studies*, 33 (2003), 142–55

—— , 'Some North Yorkshire Scribes and their Context', in *Medieval Texts in Context*, ed. by Denis Renevey and Graham D. Caie (London: Routledge, 2008), pp. 167–91

—— , 'The Transmission of Richard Rolle's Latin Works', *The Library*, 7th ser., 14 (2013), 313–33

Harvey, Margaret, *England, Rome, and the Papacy, 1417–1464: The Study of a Relationship* (Manchester: Manchester University Press, 1993)

—— , *Solutions to the Schism: A Study of Some English Attitudes 1378 to 1409*, Kirchengeschichtliche Quellen und Studien (St. Ottilien: EOS Verlag, 1983)

Hirsh, John C., *The Revelations of Margery Kempe*, Medieval and Renaissance Authors (Leiden: E. J. Brill, 1989)

Hudson, Anne, *The Premature Reformation: Wycliffite Texts and Lollard History* (Oxford: Clarendon Press, 1988)

Hughes, Jonathan, *Pastors and Visionaries: Religion and Secular Life in Late Medieval Yorkshire* (Woodbridge: D. S. Brewer, 1988)

―――, 'Religion in the Diocese of York, 1350–1450' (unpublished doctoral thesis, University of Oxford, 1985)
Hunt, Tony, Jane Bliss, and Henrietta Leyser, eds, *'Cher Alme': Texts of Anglo-Norman Piety* (Tempe: Arizona Center for Medieval and Renaissance Studies, 2010)
Jenkins, Jacqueline, 'Reading and *The Book of Margery Kempe*', in *A Companion to the Book of Margery Kempe*, ed. by John H. Arnold and Katherine J. Lewis (Cambridge: D. S. Brewer, 2004), pp. 113–28
Johnson, Ian, '*Auctricitas? Holy Women and their Middle English Texts', in *Prophets Abroad: The Reception of Continental Holy Women in Late Medieval England*, ed. by Rosalynn Voaden (Cambridge: D. S. Brewer, 1996), pp. 177–97
Johnson, Ian, and Allan F. Westphall, eds, *The Pseudo-Bonaventuran Lives of Christ: Exploring the Middle English Tradition*, Medieval Church Studies, 24 (Turnhout: Brepols, 2013)
Johnston, Michael, and Michael Van Dussen, eds, *The Medieval Manuscript Book: Cultural Approaches*, Cambridge Studies in Medieval Literature (Cambridge: Cambridge University Press, 2015)
Keiser, George, 'Patronage and Piety in Fifteenth-Century England: Margaret, Duchess of Clarence, Symon Wynter and Beinecke Ms 317', *Yale University Library Gazette*, 60 (1985), 32–46
Kelly, Stephen, and Ryan Perry, eds, *Devotional Culture in Late Medieval England and Europe: Diverse Imaginations of Christ's Life* (Turnhout: Brepols, 2014)
Kemmler, Fritz, *'Exempla' in Context: A Historical and Critical Study of Robert Mannyng of Brunne's 'Handlyng Synne'* (Tubingen: Gunter Narr Verlag, 1984)
Kerby-Fulton, Kathryn, *Books under Suspicion: Censorship and Tolerance of Revelatory Writing in Late Medieval England* (Notre Dame: University of Notre Dame Press, 2006)
―――, 'When Women Preached: An Introduction to Female Homiletic, Sacramental and Liturgical Roles in the Later Middle Ages', in *Voices in Dialogue: Reading Women in the Middle Ages*, ed. by Linda Olson and Kathryn Kerby-Fulton (Notre Dame: University of Notre Dame Press, 2005), pp. 31–55
Krug, Rebecca, *Reading Families: Women's Literate Practice in Late Medieval England* (Ithaca: Cornell University Press, 2002)
Laing, Margaret, 'Studies in the Dialect Material of Mediaeval Lincolnshire' (unpublished doctoral thesis, University of Edinburgh, 1978)
Lawton, David, 'Voice, Authority, and Blasphemy in *The Book of Margery Kempe*', in *Margery Kempe: A Book of Essays*, ed. by Sandra J. McEntire (New York: Garland, 1992), pp. 93–115
Lepine, David, '"Let Them Praise Him in Church": Orthodox Reform at Salisbury Cathedral in the First Half of the Fifteenth Century', in *After Arundel: Religious Writing in Fifteenth-Century England*, ed. by Vincent Gillespie and Kantik Ghosh, Medieval Church Studies, 21 (Turnhout: Brepols, 2011), pp. 167–86
Lindenbaum, Sheila, 'London after Arundel: Learned Rectors and the Strategies of Orthodox Reform', in *After Arundel: Religious Writing in Fifteenth-Century England*,

ed. by Vincent Gillespie and Kantik Ghosh, Medieval Church Studies, 21 (Turnhout: Brepols, 2011), pp. 187–208

Lochrie, Karma, *Margery Kempe and Translations of the Flesh* (Philadelphia: University of Pennsylvania Press, 1991)

Lusignan, Serge, Monique Paulmier-Foucart, and Marie-Christine Duchenne, *Lector et compilator Vincent de Beauvais, frère prêcheur: Un intellectuel et son milieu au XIIIe siècle* (Grâne: Créaphis, 1997)

Mann, Jill, and Maura Nolan, eds, *The Text in the Community: Essays on Medieval Works, Manuscripts, Authors, and Readers* (Notre Dame: University of Notre Dame Press, 2006)

Martin, Clarence A., 'Middle English Manuals of Religious Instruction', in *So Meny People Longages and Tonges: Philological Essays in Scots and Mediaeval English Presented to Angus McIntosh*, ed. by M. Benskin and M. L. Samuels (Edinburgh: Middle English Dialect Project, 1981), pp. 283–98

Meale, Carol M. '"…Alle the Bokes That I Haue of Latyn, Englisch, and Frensch": Laywomen and their Books in Late Medieval England', in *Women and Literature in Britain, 1150–1500*, ed. by Carol M. Meale (Cambridge: Cambridge University Press, 1993), pp. 128–58

Minnis, Alastair J., *Fallible Authors: Chaucer's Pardoner and Wife of Bath* (Philadelphia: University of Pennsylvania Press, 2008)

——, 'Late-Medieval Discussions of *Compilatio* and the Role of the *Compilator*', *Beiträge zur Geschichte der deutschen Sprache und Literatur*, 101 (1979), 385–421

——, *Medieval Theory of Authorship: Scholastic Literary Attitudes in the Later Middle Ages* (London: Scolar Press, 1984)

——, '*Nolens auctor sed compilator reputari*: The Late-Medieval Discourse of Compilation', in *La Méthode critique au moyen âge*, ed. by Mireille Chazan and Gilbert Dahan, Bibliothèque d'histoire culturelle du Moyen Âge, 3 (Turnhout: Brepols, 2006), pp. 47–63

Olson, Linda, and Kathryn Kerby-Fulton, eds, *Voices in Dialogue: Reading Women in the Middle Ages* (Notre Dame: University of Notre Dame Press, 2005)

Owen, Dorothy M., *Church and Society in Medieval Lincolnshire*, History of Lincolnshire, 5 (Lincoln: Broadview Press, 1971)

Pantin, W. A., *The English Church in the Fourteenth Century* (Cambridge: Cambridge University Press, 1955)

—— , 'Instructions for a Devout and Literate Layman', in *Medieval Learning and Literature: Essays Presented to Richard William Hunt*, ed. by J. J. G. Alexander and M. T. Gibson (Oxford: Clarendon Press, 1976), pp. 398–422

Parkes, Malcolm B., 'The Influence of the Concepts of *Ordinatio* and *Compilatio* on the Development of the Book', in *Medieval Learning and Literature: Essays Presented to Richard William Hunt*, ed. by J. J. G. Alexander and M. T. Gibson (Oxford: Clarendon Press, 1976), pp. 115–41

——, *Scribes, Scripts and Readers: Studies in the Communication, Presentation and Dissemination of Medieval Texts* (London: Hambledon, 1991)

Parsons, Kelly, 'The Red Ink Annotator of the Book of Margery Kempe and his Lay Audience', in *The Medieval Professional Reader at Work: Evidence from Manuscripts of Chaucer, Langland, Kempe, and Gower*, ed. by Kathryn Kerby-Fulton and Maidie Hilmo (Victoria: University of Victoria, 2001), pp. 143–216

Paulmier-Foucart, Monique, Serge Lusignan, and Alain Nadeau, eds, *Vincent de Beauvais: Intentions et réceptions d'une œuvre encyclopédique au moyen-age. Actes du XIVe colloque de l'Institut d'études médiévales* (Paris: Vrin, 1990)

Rees Jones, Sarah, '"A Peler of the Holy Cherch": Margery Kempe and the Bishops', in *Medieval Women: Texts and Contexts in Late Medieval Britain. Essays in Honour of Felicity Riddy*, ed. by Jocelyn Wogan-Browne and others, Medieval Women: Texts and Contexts, 3 (Turnhout: Brepols, 2000), pp. 377–91

Renevey, Denis, 'Margery's Performing Body: The Translation of Late Medieval Discursive Religious Practices', in *Writing Religious Women: Female Spiritual and Textual Practices in Late Medieval England*, ed. by Denis Renevey and C. Whitehead (Cardiff: University of Wales Press, 2000), pp. 197–216

Rice, Nicole, *Lay Piety and Religious Discipline in Middle English Literature*, Cambridge Studies in Medieval Literature (Cambridge: Cambridge University Press, 2009)

——, ed., *Middle English Religious Writing in Practice: Texts, Readers, and Transformations*, Late Medieval and Early Modern Studies, 21 (Turnhout: Brepols, 2013)

——, 'Spiritual Ambition and the Translation of the Cloister: The *Abbey* and *Charter of the Holy Ghost*', *Viator*, 33 (2002), 221–60

Riddy, Felicity, 'Text and Self in *The Book of Margery Kempe*', in *Voices in Dialogue: Reading Women in the Middle Ages*, ed. by Linda Olson and Kathryn Kerby-Fulton (Notre Dame: University of Notre Dame Press, 2005), pp. 435–53

——, '"Women Talking about the Things of God": A Late Medieval Sub-Culture', in *Women and Literature in Britain, 1150–1500*, ed. by Carol M. Meale (Cambridge: Cambridge University Press, 1993), pp. 104–27

Rouse, Richard H., and Mary A. Rouse, '*Ordinatio* and *Compilatio* Revisited', in *Ad litteram: Authoritative Texts and their Medieval Readers*, ed. by Mark D. Jordan and Kent Emery (Notre Dame: University of Notre Dame Press, 1992), pp. 113–34

——, *Preachers, Florilegia and Sermons: Studies on the 'Manipulus florum' of Thomas of Ireland*, Studies and Texts, 47 (Toronto: Pontifical Institute of Mediaeval Studies, 1979)

Sahlin, Claire L., *Birgitta of Sweden and the Voice of Prophecy* (Woodbridge: Boydell, 2001)

Shaw, Jane, 'The Influence of Canonical and Episcopal Reform on Popular Books of Instruction', in *The Popular Literature of Medieval England*, ed. by Thomas J. Heffernan, Tennessee Studies in Literature, 28 (Knoxville: University of Tennessee Press, 1985), pp. 44–60

Somerset, Fiona, *Clerical Discourse and Lay Audience in Late Medieval England* (Cambridge: Cambridge University Press, 1998)

——, '*Eciam mulier*: Women in Lollardy and the Problem of Sources', in *Voices in Dialogue: Reading Women in the Middle Ages*, ed. by Linda Olson and Kathryn Kerby-Fulton (Notre Dame: University of Notre Dame Press, 2005), pp. 245–60

——, 'Wycliffite Spirituality', in *Text and Controversy from Wyclif to Bale: Essays in Honour of Anne Hudson*, ed. by Helen Barr and Ann M. Hutchison, Medieval Church Studies, 4 (Turnhout: Brepols, 2005), pp. 375–86

Somerset, Fiona, Jill C. Havens, and Derrick G. Pitard, eds, *Lollards and their Influence in Late Medieval England* (Woodbridge: Boydell, 2003)

Spencer, H. Leith, *English Preaching in the Late Middle Ages* (Oxford: Clarendon Press, 1993)

Steele, F. J., *Towards a Spirituality for Lay-Folk: The Active Life in Middle English Religious Literature from the Thirteenth Century to the Fifteenth* (Lewiston: Edwin Mellen, 1995)

Tarvers, Josephine K., 'The Alleged Literacy of Margery Kempe: A Reconsideration of the Evidence', *Medieval Perspectives*, 11 (1996), 113–24

Van Dussen, Michael, 'Tourists and Tabulae in Late-Medieval England', in *Truth and Tales: Cultural Mobility and Medieval Media*, ed. by Fiona Somerset and Nicholas Watson (Columbus: Ohio State University Press, 2015), pp. 238–54

Voaden, Rosalynn, ed., *Prophets Abroad: The Reception of Continental Holy Women in Late Medieval England* (Cambridge: D. S. Brewer, 1996)

Watson, Nicholas, 'The 81Making of *The Book of Margery Kempe*', in *Voices in Dialogue: Reading Women in the Middle Ages*, ed. by Linda Olson and Kathryn Kerby-Fulton (Notre Dame: University of Notre Dame Press, 2005), pp. 395–434

——, 'Richard Rolle as Elitist and as Popularist: The Case of *Judica Me*', in *De Cella in Seculum: Religious and Secular Life and Devotion in Late Medieval England*, ed. by Michael G. Sargent (Cambridge: D. S. Brewer, 1988), pp. 123–43

Watson, Nicholas, and Felicity Riddy, 'Afterwords', in *Voices in Dialogue: Reading Women in the Middle Ages*, ed. by Linda Olson and Kathryn Kerby-Fulton (Notre Dame: University of Notre Dame Press, 2005), pp. 454–57

Watt, Diane, 'Political Prophecy in *The Book of Margery Kempe*', in *A Companion to the Book of Margery Kempe*, ed. by John H. Arnold and Katherine J. Lewis (Cambridge: D. S. Brewer, 2004), pp. 145–60

——, *Secretaries of God: Women Prophets in Late Medieval and Early Modern England* (Woodbridge: D. S. Brewer, 1997)

Yoshikawa, Naoë Kukita, *Margery Kempe's Meditations: The Context of Medieval Devotional Literature, Liturgy, and Iconography* (Cardiff: University of Wales Press, 2007)

Online Publications

Benskin, Michael, Margaret Laing, Vasilis Karaiskos, and Keith Williamson, *An Electronic Version of a Linguistic Atlas of Late Mediaeval English* (Edinburgh, © 2013) <http://www.lel.ed.ac.uk/ihd/elalme/elalme.html> [accessed 24 July 2016]

STC = Universal Short Title Catalogue, <https://www.ustc.ac.uk/>

Compilation: The Gift that Keeps on Giving

Ralph Hanna

The text customarily known as *The Three Arrows on Doomsday* is one of those peculiarities endemic in Middle English prose. Quite in contrast to verse circulation, which privileges mega-texts like *The Canterbury Tales*, this is an extraordinarily brief and apparently ephemeral piece, under three printed pages long, but with a very wide circulation in manuscript, around thirty copies in all.[1] All but one of these occur in a devotional compilation of some stripe, and the text is worth an attention it has never received.

In form, *The Three Arrows* is a sermon. It has a distinct protheme, and it has the conventional tripartite structure recommended to preachers for sermon development, the *tres principales*. This generic identification extends even down to the rhyming mnemonic tags conventional in such productions: 'an arrow of cleping' (to the Doom), 'an arrow of sharp reproving', and 'an arrow of endless damning'. It will then come as no surprise that most of the text presents nearly completely the body, the tripartite argument, of an extant Latin sermon.

This I have as yet not found independently in manuscript. I know it only from a compilation of preachers' commonplaces that clearly postdates the

---

[1] The text appears in Lewis and others, *Index of Printed Middle English Prose*, as number 842. (I henceforth refer to this source as *IPMEP*.) The account there includes one ghost (there is no copy of *The Three Arrows* in BL, MS Harley 2385), and I will add an overlooked version below. As *IPMEP* indicates, the only published version is *Yorkshire Writers*, ed. by Horstman, II, 446–48 (but see further note 11 below).

Ralph Hanna (Ralph.Hanna@keble.ox.ac.uk) is Professor of Palaeography emeritus, University of Oxford, and Fellow of Keble College.

Middle English text, itself a product of the late fourteenth century. The Latin appears in Alexander Carpenter's *Destructorium viciorum*, completed in 1429 — a thoroughly unoriginal encyclopaedic compilation (absolutely everything in it represents utter commonplace and has been gathered from elsewhere).[2]

Neither Carpenter nor *The Three Arrows* gives any indication of a specific occasion for this pulpit effusion, nor does either indicate its 'theme', the specific biblical text addressed. Much of the Latin protheme, as Carpenter reports it (and to which I will briefly return), appears as part of the protheme of a Middle English sermon unique to Bodl. Lib., MS Bodley 806; this addresses 'And there shall be signs in the sun/Erunt signa in sole' (Lk 21. 25) and is designed for delivery on the second Sunday in Advent, an occasion, as we will see, that would be appropriate for the Latin.[3] In contrast, insofar as *The Three Arrows* responds to a biblical text, it is apparently a verse from a familiar ferial canticle, sung once a week in churches, Deut 32. 23: 'I will heap evils upon them, and I will spend my arrows among them/Congregabo super eos mala, et sagittas meas complebo in eis'.

Although the body of the Latin sermon appears here mostly intact, *The Three Arrows* is, if one will excuse the paradox, an original compilation. For example, the first segment of its argumentative portion, 'cleping', has been bloated with original importations. At this point, the Latin presents a dialogue between the Soul and the Body, each rebuking the other for its contribution to damnation. This the compiler of *The Three Arrows* cuts roughly in half; only the Soul gets to speak in the Middle English text.

Instead of the response of Corpus, the author here makes two reasonably learned insertions. First, he offers a brief reference to the damned reading from 'the books of their consciences'; at least the guts of this has been lifted verbatim from William Peraldus's *Summa aurea*, where it is the nineteenth reason to fear the Last Judgement (and has been inspired by Apoc 20. 12).[4]

---

[2] See Carpenter, *Destructorium* 6.80, fols [D v]$^{ra-vb}$. The sermon appears as the climax of a discussion of the Last Judgement as a remedy against pride and other sins.

[3] The parallel materials, a bit of which I cite below, appear at fols 4–5^v. For a description of the manuscript, and this sermon in particular, see O'Mara and Paul, *A Repertorium*, III, 1703–05.An edition of the full set of sermons is forthcoming; see Sasu, 'Les Sermons moyen-anglais'.

[4] See Peraldus, *Summa aurea*, 'De viciis' 1.9.6, fol. x [j]^{vb}: 'Item ad certitudinem [reatus] faciet quod ipsi peccatores habebunt litteras propria manu scriptas in conscientijs suis, que testificabuntur contra eos' (As a verification of their guilt, these sinners will have letters, written with their own hands in their consciences, that will provide witness against them), with cited proof-texts from Dan 7. 10 ('opened books') and Apoc 20. 12 ('the dead were judged by those things that were written in the books, according to their works'). A similar moralization appears

This interpolated bit is succeeded by what one might construe a displaced substitute for the speech of the Body that the compiler has suppressed. This is an extensive discussion — nearly a quarter of the full text of *The Three Arrows* — of Psalm 6. 2, 'O Lord, rebuke me not in thy indignation, nor chastise me in thy wrath/Domine, ne in furore tuo arguas me, neque in ira tua corripias me'.

This material, rather than the *altercatio* of Soul and Body, here of God and sinner, invites a more moderated dialogue that leads to forgiveness. It explicates the first penitential psalm, conventionally read as asking God to send worldly tribulation so that the sinner, by penitential endurance, might avoid the wrath of Doomsday. The *Three Arrows* author here recycles and expands upon Rolle's reading in his Psalter commentary, and he is thorough. Rolle routinely offers differing explanations in his Latin and English Psalters, and the compiler has used, and carried over citations, from both versions:

arguynge, as clerkes knowen wel, is to ouercome anoothere with skiles [...]

[Dauid] in persoone of alle synneres, felyng him vnmy3ty to bere euer either, first asketh to be delyuered of helle, and sitthen of purgatorie = Vox est poenitentis, dolentis pro peccatis et timentis poenam inferni et purgatorij (He speaks in the voice of a penitent person, lamenting his sins and fearing the torment of hell and purgatory).[5]

Elsewhere the author of *The Three Arrows* shows himself similarly knowledgeable. Like many Latin sermons, the source-text rather runs out of gas near its end; the development of the second and third points, 'sharp reproving' and 'endless damning', is treated rather perfunctorily there. These blank slots, as it were, the compiler fills out, mainly with biblical materials from the description of Doomsday in Matthew 25, citations additional to those already present in the Latin. But he also adds several patristic citations in Latin, including one ascribed to Eusebius Gallicanus, not exactly your household name. Some of these fathers he found by looking under 'sagitta' in a topical diction-

---

at Bromyard, *Summa praedicantium* I.ii.19, in vol. I (unsigned). Bromyard cites Isaiah 11. 3 ('the rod shall not judge according to sight or hearing') as a proof-text for the book of conscience, 'nanque quilibet damnandus literas portabit Vrie, id est proprie mortis et damnationis' (for everyone who is to be damned will carry Uriah's letters, that is ones indicating his own death and damnation; in allusion to II Reg 11. 14–18). Although Bromyard's subsequent moralization proceeds in another, more commonplace direction (the steward's accounts from Luke 16), it concludes with another citation of Apoc 20. 12.

[5] For the first, a direct quotation, see Rolle, *The Psalter*, ed. by Bramley, p. 22; for the second, I cite the material paraphrased in the Middle English from *D. Richardi Pampolitani Anglosaxonis Eremitæ ... in Psalterium Davidicum*, fol. 3ᵛ.

ary or anthology (about all I can say on this score is that it's not William de Montibus);[6] the Eusebius appears elsewhere in a Middle English text, in its Latin form (although that may be derived from the citation here),[7] and must have been lifted from a similar collection of *flores*, an example of what I hope to show as an almost endemic compositional feature, a compilation existing to generate more of its kind.

The compiler, however, worked most extensively on the protheme of the Latin sermon. This, unlike the preacher of MS Bodley 806, he rejected *in toto*. The original had provided a quite conventional moralization, but one presented as the development of a pun that really works only in Latin. God's relationship with man, the argument runs, is like an *arcus*: as a rainbow, the sign of the covenant with Noah, it reflects God's ongoing interest in and merciful intentions for man; as a sign of wrath, it is a bow that shoots out God's destructive judgement. At least the initial formulation in the Latin, which provides moral readings for the colours of the rainbow, goes back to Gregory the Great's homilies on Ezechiel:

> Est notandum quod Cristus significatur per arcum celi, scilicet per yridem de quo dicitur Genesis 9, *Arcum meum ponam in nubibus celi*. In quo arcu tres colores apparent, scilicet color mixtus, color ceruleus, et color igneus. Per quos quidem colores significatur triplex nostri creatoris et saluatoris aduentus, scilicet aduentus eius ad hominis creationem, aduentus eius ad hominis redemptionem, et aduentus ad hominis iudicationem.

> [Notice that the heavenly bow is a sign for Christ — the rainbow, about which see Gen 9[. 13], *I will set my bow in the clouds*. In this bow, three colours appear, one mixed, one blueish, and one fiery. For these colours indicate our creator and saviour's threefold advent, namely his comings to create man, to redeem man, and to judge man.]

In the Bodley sermon, analogous materials appear:

> Criste is bitokened by þe reynebowe in whiche apperen þre colours, a medelid coloure, bryȝt, and fyren, by þe which is signified þre comynges of Criste. For in his first comynge schewed þe medelid coloure, whanne he of verry riȝtwisnesse puttide

---

[6] For this influential early thirteenth-century teacher, see Goering, *William de Montibus (c. 1140–1213)*.

[7] In a sermon delivered in 1406 by one Richard Alkerton. *A Study and Edition of Selected Middle English Sermons*, ed. by O'Mara, p. 66, lines 278–80. See also O'Mara's discussion in her introduction, pp. 48–50, which seems to me to exaggerate the connection with *The Three Arrows*.

or punisched penaunce to oure formefadris — and ȝhut non fully as þei hadden disserued with, bot medeled hit with mersy so þat fynaly he dampned hem not. In þe secounde comynge he was as wete watir for þorouȝ myldenesse and mekenesse of takynge of mannekynde, he was made vnto vs watur abul to be drounke. In þe þridde comynge he schalle deme þe quicke and þe dede and þe worlde also by fyer he schal deme. þere is þe fyren colowre.[8]

Although the rainbow/bow is initially presented as only double, either God's support or his wrath, the sermon is following Gregory's moralization. This intrudes a third, mediate stage in the relationship, concording the discussion with 'Christ's three advents' (as is evident in the Bodley sermon's appropriation). In the third, divine wrath is balanced by potential mercy for reformed sinners.

The compiler of *The Three Arrows* was clearly stimulated by that rainbow in the sky, but saw a better way to present substantially the same moral reading of God's changing relations with man through salvation history. He chose to associate the three stages of the relationship with Christ as sun, and with the sun's passage through a quarter of its ecliptic path, from Leo, through Virgo, to the end, Libra, the sign of judgement. Horstman, in a note to his presentation of *The Three Arrows*, thought that the compiler had been inspired by a pseudo-Rollean discussion appended to the Passion meditation from *Þe Holy Boke Gratia Dei*. So far as I can see, the two passages only resemble one another in citing 'Congregabo', the verse in Deut 32, and in including three arrows, which they do identify in identical language. In *Gratia Dei*, the first of these is connected with a lion. But the argument is developed differently in each work, their exemplary citations/proof-texts differ, and *Gratia Dei*'s lion has been derived from a bestiary, not the heavens.[9]

One might offer at least a couple of suggestions about this development, rather inspired independent innovation. The *Three Arrows* author might have been stimulated, as is the Bodley homilist, by Luke's account of the last days and concorded it with the commonplace association of Christ as sun (of justice). But a more elegant background reveals further compilational aspects of the text, the author's recourse to sophisticated books.

Here he has probably been drawn to this material from a *distinctio* he could have found in Robert of Basevorn's *Forma praedicandi*, perhaps the most elabo-

---

[8] The citations are from Carpenter, *Destructorium*, fol. [D v]^{ra}; and MS Bodley 806, fol. 4^r. Cf. Gregory, *Homeliae in Ezechielem* 1.8.29, on Ez 1. 28 (ed. by Migne, cols 867–68).

[9] The text, an excerpt from *The Holy Boke Gracia Dei* (*IPMEP* 502), appears as *IPMEP* 480. For editions, see *Yorkshire Writers*, ed. by Horstman, I, 116–21; and, considerably more authoritatively, Rolle, *Þe Holy Boke Gratia Dei*, ed. by Arntz, 90/10–98/6.

rate (and yet not very widely disseminated) of *artes praedicandi*, rhetorical manuals for preachers. There Basevorn offers a sample development for a sermon, predicated upon the three zodiac signs. It appears there as a reading of Ezech 32. 7, 'solem nube tegam' (I will cover the sun with a cloud). But Basevorn provides the material to illustrate how to divide a sermon theme, that is, how to generate a tripartite argument from a single verse, and thus gives only an outline, a *distinctio*.[10] Just as in the author's dextrous weaving of detail from Rolle's Psalters into a consecutive argument, the development here — 'the lyoun is a strong beest and a fel' (not what *Gratia Dei* says at all) — is his own.

Now this is probably compilation enough for anyone. Except that it does not stop. As I have said, there are about thirty copies of *The Three Arrows*, but only with suffrance can one see them as reflecting a single comparable text. There are at least five different versions circulating under this title (and I have not yet examined all the manuscripts).

At the most benign, in two instances the producers of these quasi-independent textual versions merely perform as did the original compiler. Where he found insufficient material, or material he thought inappropriately pointed in his Latin source, he simply augmented it, supplied additional citations. Likewise, in these instances, his inheritor compilers, in addition to a good deal of fussy local verbal revision, simply augmented the citations they found in the original.

In the simplest version of such procedures, not very demanding, the reviser took one of the original compiler's citations and extended it.

> The original text: seyenge þe woorde of þe wise man, *Hii sunt quos aliquando habuimus in derisum etc. Nos insensati etc.*, þat is, 'Thise ben þoo þe whiche sumtyme we hadden in scorn and despit. We vnwitty wrecches heelden here lif woodnesse and here eende withouten honour, but lo now, how þei been acounted amonges þe sones of God'.
>
> * * *
>
> The extended 'version 2': seyinge þe word of þe wise man, *Hij sunt quos aliquando in derisum habuimus et in similitudinem improperij. Nos insensati uitam eorum estimabamus insaniam et finem illorum sine honore. Quomodo ergo computati sunt inter filios Dei et inter sanctos sors illorum est. Ergo errauimus a via veritatis, et iusticie lumen non luxit nobis, et sol intelligencie non est ortus nobis. Lassati sumus in via iniquitatis et perdicionis et ambulauimus vias difficiles; viam autem domini ignorauimus. Quid nobis profuit superbia, aut diuiciarum iactancia quid nobis contulit? Transierunt omnia illa tanquam vmbra, et virtutis quidem nullum signum valemus ostendere; in malignitate autem nostra consumpti sumus.* Þat is, 'These ben þo þe

---

[10] See the edition, Charland, *Artes Praedicandi*, ch. 34, p. 276.

whiche sumtyme we hadden into scorn and into liknes of schenschip. We vnwitti wrecchis helden her lyf woodnes and her eende wiþouten honour, but lo now, how þei ben acountid amonge þe sones of God and amonge þe seyntis of God þe lott of hem is. Þerfore we han errid fro þe weie of truþe, and þe liȝt of riȝtwisnes haþ not schyned to us, and þe sunne of vndirstondyng haþ not sprong to vs. We been maad wery in þe weie of wickidnes and of perdicioun and we han goone harde weies, for þe weie of þe Lord we knewe not. What haþ pride profitid to vs, or þe boost of riches what haþ it brouȝte to vs? Alle þese þingis han passid as a schadowe, and we forsoþe mown schewe no tokene of holines, for we ben wastid in oure wickidnes'.

In the original, this quotation does, it must be said, end with 'etc.', and that might be taken as an open invitation to add more. At this point, the original *The Three Arrows* offers tag citations, the incipits only, of Sap 5. 3 and 4; this expanded version includes nine verses, Sap 5. 3–9 and 13, in full (and is at least thoughtfully selective in ignoring, *inter alia*, Sap 5. 12, where an arrow's flight is, inappositely for this new context, taken as a mark of transience).

In a further secondary act of compiling, the redactor expanded the provided Middle English translation (the original is always bilingual). However, unlike the original author, he did not produce the translation himself, but appears to have derived it by a further act of compilational consultation, from the Wycliffite Later Version as the comparable translation illustrates:

And her part is among seyntis? Therfor we erriden fro the weie of treuthe, and the liȝt of riȝtfulnesse schynede not to us, and the sunne of vndurstondyng roos not vp to us. We weren maad weri in the weie of wickidnesse and of perdicioun, and we yeden hard weies, but we knewen not the weie of the Lord. What profitide pride to vs, ethir what brouȝte the boost of richessis to vs? All tho thingis passiden as schadewe [...], and sotheli we myȝten schewe no signe of vertu; but we weren wastid in oure malice.

One could take Glasgow, University Library, MS Hunter 520 as an exemplary copy of the text in this form, and I know at this point at least five similar manuscripts.[11]

---

[11] Of the manuscripts I have seen, the original appears in Cambridge, Magdalene College, MS Pepys 2125; Bodl. Lib., Laud misc. MSS 23 and 174; Oxford, University College, MS 97 (the source of Horstman's accurate text); BL, MSS Add. 22283 ('the Simeon MS') and Harley 1706 (II); CUL, MS Ff.2.38; and 'The Coughton Court MS'/Lambeth Palace Library, MS 3597. Manuscripts of version 2 include: *Hunter 520; Bodl. Lib., MS Bodley 3 (conflated with the original); BL, MSS Add. 10036, Arundel 197 (conflated with the original), and *Harley 2388; and CUL MS *Ff.6.55. This version has been edited from the books starred above by Martin, 'Edinburgh University Library Manuscript 93', pp. 497–533.

A little more original is the behaviour of another compiler, that of Bodl. Lib., MS Tanner 336 and three additional copies. Taking a clue from the original compiler's citation of Job 26. 14 under his second point, 'sharp reproving', he intruded comparable materials near the end of the third point, 'endless damning'. At this juncture, where the damned are described as lamenting their fate, he supplied them with a script, Job 3. 3, 11–13, here in his own translation. While I doubt that the author of *The Three Arrows*, in possession of a full Latin source and a library, needed inspiration from *Gratia Dei*, it is possible that this redactor knew and borrowed from that text, where the same citation appears at a comparable point.[12]

The Tanner version is, on the whole, a good deal less heavily edited than the Glasgow, but for one feature. Like the original, version 2 is routinely bilingual in citations; the Tanner version, number 3, never gives the Latin *originalia*, but only English. One might consider it an effort at appealing to a somewhat less sophisticated audience than the original, a view that may receive some confirmation from additional compilatory acts, for this version is typified by two further major intrusions.

Both of these, running maybe ten–twelve typescript lines each, are clearly original and not exceptionally inspired. The first, intruded into the Rollean materials pleading for penitential tribulation in this world, rather than eternal punishment, projects a life of humble abnegation:

> The original text: þat I may hertly forthenke hem and cleerly confesse hem and lawefully amende hem by ensample of newe cleene lyuyng to men, feruent preier to God, and by discreet chastisement of myself heere whiles I lyue so þat þou haue no wil to chastise me in þi wratthe after þis life in purgatorie. And þat it be þus, *Miserere mei domine quoniam infirmus sum*.
>
> * * *
>
> Version 3 (Tanner, fol. 136ʳ⁻ᵛ): þat I verily forþinke alle my wickidnesses, truly confessynge hem to þee and to hem þat ben wiser þan I in weiȝynge and tellynge to me my defautis, whiche oþerwise neiþir I knowe ne can amende, neiþir to þee Lord, ne to hem whom I haue offendid. For bi new clene lyuynge bifore hem to whom I haue trespassid, it bihoueþ me to lyue in mekenesse withouten veyne glorie, feruentli preyynge to God for myself and for hem whom I haue offendid wityngly or vnwityngli, alwei scharpli punisschynge my synne here þe whils I lyue, so þat I ascape here and after þis lijf þi vengeaunce. And þat it þus be, I preie þe, 'Lord haue

---

[12] Manuscripts of this version (#3) include Bodl. Lib., MSS Tanner 336 and Douce 13; Glasgow, University Library, MS Hunter 496; and Manchester, John Rylands Library, MS English 85. For the parallel Job citation, see *Yorkshire Writers*, ed. by Horstman, I, 120–21, and Rolle, Þe Holy Boke Gratia Dei, ed. by Arntz, 96/6–12, respectively.

mercie of me'. Forþi merciful Lord, for þin hooli name helpe me now in þis lijf and schewe to me here þi greet mercie, puyrgynge me here with diuerse tribulaciouns aftir my diuerse trespassyngis, þat þereþorou I be made clene bifore þi dome, passynge forþ fro þens into þi blisse wiþ þe. For I knowleche, Lord, þat neiþer in þi dome I may beire þi arguyng, ne bifore þat tyme þi chastisyng, but if þou upbeire me with þi mercie, boþe here and þere.

One might especially note the intrusions into the first sentence. These presuppose an audience incapable of self-examination, indeed of recognizing the difference between sinful and other acts (cf. the later 'offendid wityngly or vnwityngli'). Such individuals, powerless except in their faith in the power of 'þin hooli name', require direction from 'hem þat ben wiser þan I', presumably an actively confessing parish priest — or the redactor of this version.

The second intrusion, again like the Job material fleshing out the brief third principal of the sermon, 'endless damning', lamely expands on Mt 25's 'Ite maledicti'; it explains 'ignem qui preparatus est diabolo et angelis suis' (the fire prepared for the devil and his angels) through the observation that:

> The original text: 'euerlastynge fuyre þe whiche is ordeyned to þe feend and to þe aungelis of him'. This arwe schal wounde hem þat it falleth on so greuously þat alle þe lechis, phisiciens, and surgiens ne ȝet alle þe creatures in heuene and in eerthe schullen not mowe heele þe wounde of it.
>
> * * *
>
> Version 3 (Tanner, fol. 139^{r-v}): 'euerlastynge fire, þe which is bifore ordeined to þe deuil and to hise aungels'. Lucifer is þe prince of deuils, and he haþ a greet oost of aungels þat fellen wiþ him, and of men and of wymmen þat schulen be dampnid. And ich of þese is an aungel of Lucifer to tempte men to yuel, for as ich good man and womman is þe aungel of God sente of him to drawe oþir fro vice to vertu bi her gode ensaumple of kepyng of Goddis heestis, so ich wickid man and womman is þe aungel of þe deuil sente of him to drawe men fro vertu to vice bi here yuel ensaumple of brekyng of Goddis heestis. For wheþir man or womman sue god or þe deuil, in effecte þei clepen ech oþir man and womman aftir hem, and þereaftir schulen þei be rewardid ioie or peyne, wheþir many, fewe, or noon suen hem. Forþi whanne Crist schal sitt domisman, departynge with his word proude stynkynge gete fro meke lombis, þanne so fers vengeaunce schal anoon sue his word as moost scharpe arowe, woundynge hem so greuously upon whom it falliþ þat alle þe lechis, fisiciens, or surgiens ne alle þe creaturis in heuene or in erþe schal not hele þe wounde of him or of hir þat schal be dampnid.

Just the kind of superstitious claptrap that only an Eamon Duffy might value.[13] But of course, were one to believe the first description of the audience's

---

[13] Eamon Duffy's various writings, including the influential *The Stripping of the Altars*, seem

incapacity to recognize sin, one might well be perplexed as to exactly how this argument might logically follow. If one cannot see how to govern one's own behaviour in accord with 'kepyng of Goddis heestis', how is one to distinguish the 'gode' and the 'yuel ensaumple'? Just as intruding additional verses from Job and as in requesting a life of penitential torment, the redactor here seems simply to terrify his audience into an approximation of Christian virtue.

One might pause for a moment over such textual behaviour (even though the intellectual capacities of the version 3's compiler do not merit it). Compiling here specifically involves a 'reader-oriented' text, for consultation by a specific audience. For the hand behind version 3, some things are apparently too difficult for his target group and may be considered otiose (the biblical Latin); some require excessively extended pedestrian explication. All works of this type are similarly audience aware, a fact perhaps most (surprisingly?) explicit in the Latin tradition.

In that linguistic context, there are a very large number of compilations, usually (like Carpenter, in his frequent reliance on materials originally Peraldan) displaying very similar, if not identical materials. But new additions to the stock always explain their appearance by appealing to user friendliness and/or ease of consultation. For example, there is a lively late medieval trade in alphabetical *libri distionccionum*. Works of this stripe group their manifold citations under topic-headings, easy to consult because arranged in an order that typically runs something like *Abstinencia* to *Xpus* ('Christus'). Frequently, they offer additional aid to readers through systems of cross-reference, perhaps the most elaborate in Thomas of Ireland's popular *Manipulus florum*.[14]

But other systems, although often lacking such clarity, occur equally frequently. The international success, Fr Laurent's *Somme le roi*, is organized around the popular instructional septenary. It thus, after an opening devoted to basic catechetical lore, performs much the same job as Peraldus's *Summa aurea* (Vices and Virtues), but, unlike this source, arranges its argument in a schematic sequence of parallels that outline an ascendant pattern leading from sin to beatitude. In contrast, Peter of Limoges's *De oculo morali* (Moralized Eye) offers a modulated variety of topics associated with vision, from specifically scientific information to discussions of differing social *statūs*. Peter clearly imagines an audience well versed in 'concordance thinking', one that seeks materials

---

to me unduly engaged in their applause of 'popular piety'. Too often Duffy echoes John the Carpenter's 'Blessed be alwey a lewed man', and in ignoring the absence of any beatitude 'Blessed be the stupid/ignorant', he debases the grand Catholic tradition.

[14] Extant in more than 175 manuscripts and innumerable early prints; see Rouse and Rouse, *Preachers, Florilegia and Sermons*.

to explain one of the several thousand uses of *oculus* or *videre* (and their derivatives) in the Vulgate.¹⁵ Different forms of entrée allow diverse readerly audiences specifically useful access to often similar or identical materials.

This leads me to suggest that one term one hears frequently about compilatory production, 'mouvance', probably should be avoided. Insofar as it describes textual variousness, it merely states the obvious, true across a range of texts and of all eras: all texts are mediated, medieval ones neither more nor less than those of other periods.¹⁶ Moreover, suggesting 'mouvance' as 'the property of the medieval text' or 'the medieval textual condition' manages to overlook the active human agency involved in this procedure. Just as Latin *compilatores*, seeking to facilitate a new audience or purloin one from its established favourites, productions like this might be construed as overt 'niche-marketing'. The text has been designed or emended to appeal to those whom similar materials have not reached previously — and probably in a Middle English situation, a known audience. The compilation is not, in essence, in competition with the original *qua* text, not *en mouvance*, as it were, but deliberately venturing into (and hoping to open out) new territory.

I will say very little about the fourth effort with *The Three Arrows*, largely because it is generically recuperative in a way the others are not. A late fifteenth-century Cheshire preacher recycled a paraphrased version of the text as a formal Advent sermon. This appears in a book overlooked in *IPMEP*, Shrewsbury School, MS 3.¹⁷

But most interesting of all is the fifth and most widely disseminated of these versional redactions/compilations, *A Treatise of Ghostly Battle*.¹⁸ This appears in seven manuscripts; the text is usually taken as typified by the well-known Douce 322, although I suspect that other manuscripts actually convey versions more proximate to the original. In this instance, *The Three Arrows* has been absorbed, in an abbreviated form,¹⁹ into a text for the most part compiled

---

¹⁵ See respectively, *La Somme le roi*, ed. by Brayer and Leurquin-Labie, and Peter of Limoges, *The Moral Treatise*, trans. by Newhauser.

¹⁶ The form of mediation, however, remains potentially subject to further historical specification. For example, the medieval sense of 'accurate reproduction' is a good deal looser than our own, and thus any *nomen divinum* might be construed in context as good as any other.

¹⁷ For this manuscript and sermon, see O'Mara and Paul, *A Repertorium*, IV, 2468–70 (sermon 7); and for a full scholarly description, Ker, *Medieval Manuscripts*, vol. IV, ed. by Piper, pp. 290–92.

¹⁸ Indexed as *IPMEP* number 120. For editions, see *Yorkshire Writers*, ed. by Horstman, II, 420–36; and with full collations, Murray, 'An Edition of *A treatyse of gostly batayle*'. Murray presents the portions derived from *The Three Arrows* at II, 26/18–33/17.

¹⁹ The text lacks a substantial chunk from the centre of the imported Rolle materials.

— through joining in sequence pre-existing Middle English materials. *Ghostly Battle* presents successively the allegorical tract 'Horse or armour of heaven', one of the constituent segments of *Pore Caitif*; next its abbreviated *Three Arrows*; and finally what probably represents a *dérimage* from the ubiquitous *Prick of Conscience*. Its author is skilful at writing connective material to join his three selections — they show, in order, how to resist sin actively in the world, the horrors that await one at Last Judgement if one does not, and the differently inspiring pains of purgatory and joys of heaven to drive one on. One might initially wonder some about why this person felt so dependent on earlier materials, since he writes an original conclusion that displays no mean homilist at work:

> [Youre erthely moder] fareth as the nykar or meremayden, that cast opon the waterside dyuerse thyngis whyche semen fayre and gloryous to man, bot anone as he taketh hit and weneth to be sure theroff, anon she taketh hym and deuoureth hym.[20]

Indeed.

All these variously derivative examples show the text of *The Three Arrows* as persistently subjected to the very act that had created it in the first place, compilation, the rather impersonal gathering and citation of diverse materials deemed authoritative. But with *The Three Arrows* the process has got no brakes on it. As all rhetorical manuals ceaselessly reminded their users, authorship is expressed through individualized amplification. Or put otherwise, were it good to have done it once, doing it more fully is even better. In this kind of writing, citation of biblical authority provides the best evidence for the truth of any statement. The simplest intruders on the original text of *The Three Arrows* follow this imperative. For the compiler behind the Glasgow manuscript, if a brief citation is good, the fuller one exceeds it. Similarly, but perhaps a little more constructively, the compiler behind Tanner sees that if one downer citation from Job strikes a note of efficacious fear, a second, longer one will do the job yet more thoroughly.

In this context, the author of *Ghostly Battle* might be seen as an exemplary 'vernacular theologian', not to coin a phrase. He imagines an outline argument — from custody of the self in its battle against the world all the way to the reward of heavenly bliss. He also sees the plan as logically capable of division into segments, and he is well-read enough to know where to find widely transmitted English materials that adequately fill each of his segmented slots. I have

---

However, given that this omission begins at a point involving repetition in the original, it may equally reflect the compiler's or an archetypal scribe's error (returning to copy too far along), rather than specifically an authorial/editorial decision.

[20] *Yorkshire Writers*, ed. by Horstman, II, 435.

already commented on the fact that this seems to me an unusual act, since the compiler's original peroration shows that he was probably capable of writing something every bit as good as, if not better than, what he borrowed. But it may be — the text cannot have been composed much before 1450, I would think — that compilation was preferable to original composition because it attached his work to writings by this point deemed classic enough to have an authority all their own, some of which would rub off on his own contribution.

Yet one might defer this conclusion, since *The Three Arrows* routinely engages with a further form of compilation. This introduces no copies of the text additional to those I have mentioned, and requires no further re-editing or augmentative recompiling of it. This gesture is largely associational and involves (as the segmented composition of *Ghostly Battle* does) bringing the text into collocation with others deemed appropriate. The property of bookmen and not authors, this compilatory act reveals itself in repeated textual collocations and associations. Such activity obviously reconfigures what has been received, but in a considerably more open fashion than the compiler of *Ghostly Battle* essentially telling his reader, 'Here's *The Three Arrows*, the best English discussion I could find on horrors of Last Judgement'.

The most prominent of these junctures is between *The Three Arrows* and the text called *The Mirror of Sinners*.[21] The *Mirror* is an abbreviated translation of the Latin *Speculum peccatoris* usually attributed to Augustine. However, *Speculum* is, at the very best, a late twelfth-century concoction (and may be early thirteenth-century), and the transmissional evidence suggests that it may have been produced by an insular author, or at least someone from the Anglo-Norman ambit. I think there are twenty-two copies of its Englishing; in sixteen instances, it appears in the same manuscript with *The Three Arrows*, and they quite frequently sit cheek by jowl.

Although their rhetorical mien is very different, their connection is broadly thematic. *The Mirror*, if rhetorically flamboyant, is fairly standard-issue contempt of the world, learn-to-die material. But one powerful reason for its association with *The Three Arrows* is that it explicates a relevant biblical text, 'Vtinam saperent et intelligerent ac nouissima prouiderent' (O that they would be wise and would understand, and would provide for their last end) (Deut 32. 29).

---

[21] *IPMEP* number 213. From this entry, delete BL, MS Additional 60577, which has no copy. Add *olim* 'Buckland House' (like 'The Coughton Court MS', owned by the Throckmorton family); it was sold at Christie's, 20 December 1972, among lots 204–11. The *Historical Manuscripts Commission*, 10th Report, Appendix 4:171 (1885), describes an apparently small manuscript, containing only this single text. The only edition is *Yorkshire Writers*, ed. by Horstman, ii, 436–40 (the full original is ed. by Migne, cols 983–92).

This, like *The Three Arrows*'s 'Congregabo', is derived from Moses's ferial canticle, 'Audite celi'; errant Israel will be destroyed, unless it wises up, as it were. *The Three Arrows* is likewise a powerful effort at *nouissima*/Last Things, and it cites at the head of its independent protheme the more conventional *Memorare nouissima* from Sir 7. 40. In this conjunction, *The Mirror* rather moderates the effect of the text I have been considering by offering more or less practical advice in how to avoid the end that *The Three Arrows* compellingly imagines.

However, the two texts are often not simply seen as companion pieces offering differently instructive fragments of the same narrative. They also are frequently aligned with (or perhaps potentially absorbed into?) one of the great Middle English compilational texts, the *Pore Caitif*. Both appear together in nine manuscripts with *Pore Caitif* materials, often the full text; another *Pore Caitif* manuscript has *The Three Arrows* only, and four more *The Mirror* only. Particularly in copies with the full *Pore Caitif*, *Arrows* and *Mirror* usually sit at the end of the book, as if they were two further tracts, added to the fourteen that comprise that work. While from the standpoint of the *Pore Caitif*, this circulation represents rather a drop in the bucket, a feature common to maybe a quarter of the manuscripts, this collocation affects just over half the total copies of both *Arrows* and *Mirror*.[22]

The two tend to appear in such positions for reasons of comparability and complementarity. On the one hand, they look rather like the shorter (and most frequently excerpted) portions of the *Pore Caitif*, for example 'The Charter of Heaven'. But they are also compensatory or complementary; they offer an antidote to the rather sunnier positive teaching of the work to which they are appended. And their inclusion in this context may be designed to offset or obscure the rather awkward conclusion to the *Pore Caitif*. Chastity is certainly a high state, but a rather limited one, particularly if, as the *Pore Caitif*'s circulation would suggest is the case, one is seeking to engage a broad lay audience (and not simply inclaustrated holy women). For a more general group, a final exhortation to penitential self-examination and self-awareness might be considered a more effective conclusion.

These thoughts, however, would suggest a distinction between this kind of compiling and the kinds of textual adjustments I have examined previously,

---

[22] For the relevant examples, see the list of 'Caitif' manuscripts at Jolliffe, *Check-List*, B (pp. 65–67). The juxtaposition of the two texts with the *Pore Caitif* occurs irrespective of what version of *The Three Arrows* is on offer; e.g. in the 'original version' Lambeth MS (see further below), but also in my favoured copies of both versions 2 and 3 (in the latter only a[n extensive] selection of tracts).

both that of redactors and of persons joining *The Three Arrows* and *The Mirror of Sinners*. I have heretofore discussed fairly clear instances of 'like for like'; *Three Arrows* versions 2 and 3 simply duplicate the activities that had constructed the text in the first place; similarly, the two juxtaposed texts, *Three Arrows* and *Mirror*, resemble one another generically. But in this instance, there is a certain disconnect between the *Pore Caitif* and these appended texts, what I have genially tried to pass off as 'complementarity'.

This situation broaches an issue where 'compilation (or devotional) studies' might especially heed the widely held views of scholars who investigate manuscript 'miscellaneity'. In general, studies of miscellaneous books have always found a superfluity in such productions, a lingering sense that miscellaneous books challenge, rather than foster, one's sense of coherence.[23] Quite simply, such books are not univocal — there are nearly invariably texts that do not easily show congruence with the remainder — and efforts to render them so are these days rather generally suspect.

The effects of this non-communication between the two disciplines — devotional literary studies and codicology — have been particularly baneful in post–Anne Hudson Wycliffite studies.[24] That a manuscript contains one or several Wycliffite texts scarcely means that all its texts are to be so characterized (or that the volume actually represents 'Lollard book-production/consumption'). Indeed, given that heretical Wycliffism was in the Middle Ages frequently recognized on the basis of a numerically small set of propositions, the proper presupposition might well be that in broad areas of devotional practice, Wycliffites were no different from anyone else. Consequently, compilers of any stripe may have been just as willing to put orthodox materials beside sectarian ones as the compilers of some *Pore Caitif* manuscripts to copy alien, if not contradictory, materials. And the logic underlying such mixtures, barring explicit marginal statements, may resist any totalizing urge; it is perfectly plausible to imagine that texts in apparently alien contexts have been reproduced on the basis of a selective interest in one focus of the discussion (not a full 'literary' reading) — and one not necessarily obvious to a modern scholar.

But it is worth considering whether there is not some symbiosis between differently compilatory gestures, actively redacting texts and communicating

---

[23] See Pearsall, 'The Whole Book', or my comments in a review of Bahr's *Fragments and Assemblages* in *Medium Ævum*.

[24] Largely stimulated by Somerset, *Feeling Like Saints*. In manuscript studies, this kind of thinking, which underlies Horstman's ebullient sense of the Rolle canon in *Yorkshire Writers*, was long ago dispelled by the more disciplined efforts of Hope E. Allen.

them, albeit unchanged, as clumps or clusters. I am particularly struck by one presentation of *The Three Arrows* with extras, that in 'the Coughton Court MS'/Lambeth Palace Library, MS 3597. There *The Mirror* and *The Three Arrows* appear together in reasonable proximity to two tracts extracted from the *Pore Caitif*, 'Horse' and 'The Charter of Heaven':

> fols 2rb–4va *Mirror*;
> fols 4va–6rb *Three Arrows* (succeeded by Jolliffe's I.31 and G.19);
> fols 9rb–11vb 'Horse' (here called 'A tretyse of goostely batayle');
> fols 11vb–13vb 'The Charter of Heaven'.

This collocation might imply a different view of *Ghostly Battle*, that transmission, customarily considered secondary, is itself generative or faciliatory. Something like the situation in the Lambeth MS might be what initially inspired the accomplished preacher of *Ghostly Battle*. He is clearly excited by the prospect of replacing his audience's evil 'natural mother', the world; he preaches as their 'foster-mother', the true, friendly, and consolatory voice of the Church. The materials he compiles allow him to get on with his real task, powerful homiletic exhortation, rather than mess with instructional basics, already done perfectly adequately elsewhere. (Here the late date of composition may be revelatory; manuscript evidence would indicate that the need for basic catechesis, the so-called 'Pecham programme', probably diminished during the century after its 1281 promulgation.) These appropriated texts are enabling, but enabling only; they underwrite a more powerful suasion only this author can give, one that focuses and situates their teaching. There would seem to be an unstoppable force and continuum that joins authors, redactors (sometimes puttering and sometimes a good deal less so), and book-producers (who may be identical with members of both the previous groups).

One sees here a reprise of what is almost a *de rigueur* presentation at conferences on Middle English romance. Is there only one 'Guy of Warwick' or 'Bevis of Hamtoun'? How would one go about presenting such a textual object to readers? (In my computer, there is a very tentative version of *The Three Arrows*, ignoring the mainly paraphrased version 4, in four quadrants, displayed across a page-opening.) But perhaps devotional compilation provides the most telling instances of what Alastair Minnis discussed out long ago in a more idealizing mode, the rather slippery dividing lines between different species of medieval 'authorship'.[25]

---

[25] See Minnis, *Medieval Theory of Authorship*, e.g. Bonaventura's famous definition of four relations between writing and its creator, at pp. 94–95.

Works Cited

Manuscripts

Cambridge, Magdalene College, MS Pepys 2125
Cambridge, University Library [CUL], MS Ff.2.38
Cambridge, University Library [CUL], MS Ff.6.55
Glasgow, University Library, MS Hunter 496
Glasgow, University Library, MS Hunter 520
London, British Library [BL], MS Additional 10036
London, British Library [BL], MS Additional 22283
London, British Library [BL], MS Additional 60577
London, British Library [BL], MS Arundel 197
London, British Library [BL], MS Harley 1706
London, British Library [BL], MS Harley 2385
London, British Library [BL], MS Harley 2388
London, Lambeth Palace Library, MS 3597 (the Coughton Court Manuscript)
Manchester, John Rylands Library, MS English 85
Oxford, Bodleian Library [Bodl. Lib.], MS Bodley 3
Oxford, Bodleian Library [Bodl. Lib.], MS Bodley 806
Oxford, Bodleian Library [Bodl. Lib.], MS Douce 13
Oxford, Bodleian Library [Bodl. Lib.], MS Douce 322
Oxford, Bodleian Library [Bodl. Lib.], MS Laud misc. 23
Oxford, Bodleian Library [Bodl. Lib.], MS Laud misc. 174
Oxford, Bodleian Library [Bodl. Lib.], MS Tanner 336
Oxford, University College, MS 97
Shrewsbury School, MS 3
Olim Buckland (Berks.), The Buckland House Manuscript

Primary Sources

Augustine, *Speculum peccatoris*, in *Patrologiae cursus completus: series Latina*, ed. by J.-P. Migne, 221 vols (Paris: Migne, 1844--65), XL, cols 983–92
Bromyard, John, *Summa praedicantium* (Lyons, 1522)
Carpenter, Alexander, *Destructorium viciorum* (Paris, 1516)
Gregory, *Homeliae in Ezechielem*, in *Patrologiae cursus completus: series Latina*, ed. by J.-P. Migne, 221 vols (Paris: Migne, 1844–65), LXXVI, cols 867–68
Martin, C. A., 'Edinburgh University Library Manuscript 93: An Annotated Edition of Selected Devotional Treatises with a Survey of Parallel Versions' (unpublished doctoral thesis, University of Edinburgh, 1978)
Murray, Valerie, 'An Edition of *A treatyse of gostly batayle* and *Milicia Christi*', 2 vols (unpublished doctoral dissertation, University of Oxford, 1970) [Bodleian, MS D. Phil. d.5158]

Peraldus, Gulielmus, *Summa aurea de virtutibus et vitijs* (Venice, 1497)
Peter of Limoges, *The Moral Treatise on the Eye*, trans. by Richard Newhauser, Medieval Sources in Translation, 51 (Toronto: Pontifical Institute of Mediaeval Studies, 2012)
Rolle, Richard, *Richard Rolle and Þe Holy Boke Gratia Dei: An Edition with Commentary*, ed. by Mary L Arntz, Salzburg Studies in English Literature, Elizabethan and Renaissance Studies, 92.2 (Salzburg: Institut für Anglistik und Amerikanistik, Universität Salzburg, 1981)
——, *The Psalter or Psalms of David and Certain Canticles, with a Translation and Exposition in English by Richard Rolle of Hampole*, ed. by H. R. Bramley (Oxford: Clarendon Press, 1884)
——, *D. Richardi Pampolitani Anglosaxonis Eremitæ ... in Psalterium Davidicum* (Cologne, 1536)
La Somme le roi par frère Laurent, ed. by Édith Brayer and Anne-Françoise Leurquin-Labie, SATF (Abbeville: Paillart, 2008)
A Study and Edition of Selected Middle English Sermons, ed. by V. O'Mara, Leeds Texts and Monographs, n.s., 13 (Leeds: University of Leeds School of English, 1994)
Yorkshire Writers: Richard Rolle of Hampole, an English Father of the Church, and his Followers, ed. by C. Horstman, 2 vols (London: Swan Sonnenschein, 1895–96)

Secondary Works

Charland, Th. M., *Artes Praedicandi: Contribution à l'histoire de la rhétorique au moyen âge*, Publications de l'Institut d'Études Médiévales d'Ottawa, 7 (Paris: Vrin; Montreal: Institut d'études médiévales, 1936)
Duffy, Eamon, *The Stripping of the Altars: Traditional Religion in England, 1400–1580*, 2nd edn (New Haven: Yale University Press, 2005)
Goering, Joseph, *William de Montibus (c. 1140–1213): The Schools and the Literature of Pastoral Care*, Studies and Texts, 108 (Toronto: Pontifical Institute of Mediaeval Studies, 1992)
Hanna, Ralph, Review of Arthur Bahr, *Fragments and Assemblages*, *Medium Aevum*, 83 (2014), 329–31
Jolliffe, P. S., *A Check-List of Middle English Prose Writings of Spiritual Guidance*, Subsidia mediaevalia, 2 (Toronto: Pontifical Institute of Mediaeval Studies, 1974)
Ker, Neil, *Medieval Manuscripts in British Libraries*, 4 vols (Oxford: Clarendon Press, 1969–92)
Lewis, R. E., and others, *Index of Printed Middle English Prose* (New York: Garland, 1985)
Minnis, Alastair J., *Medieval Theory of Authorship: Scholastic Literary Attitudes in the Later Middle Ages*, 2nd edn (Philadelphia: University of Pennsylvania Press, 1988)
O'Mara, V., and S. Paul, *A Repertorium of Middle English Prose Sermons*, 4 vols (Turnhout: Brepols, 2007)
Pearsall, Derek, 'The Whole Book: Late Medieval English Manuscript Miscellanies and their Modern Interpreters', in *Imagining the Book*, ed. by Stephen Kelly and John J. Thompson, Medieval Texts and Cultures of Northern Europe, 7 (Turnhout: Brepols, 2005), pp. 17–29

Rouse, Richard H., and Mary A. Rouse, *Preachers, Florilegia and Sermons: Studies on the 'Manipulus florum' of Thomas of Ireland*, Studies and Texts, 47 (Toronto: Pontifical Institute of Mediaeval Studies, 1979)

Sasu, Elena, 'Les Sermons moyen-anglais du manuscrit Bodley 806: Édition et étude' (unpublished doctoral thesis, Université de Poitiers, 2014)

Somerset, Fiona, *Feeling Like Saints: Lollard Writings after Wyclif* (Ithaca: Cornell University Press, 2014)

Theorizing the Miscellaneous and the Middle English Biblical Paratext

Ian Johnson

Miscellaneous Theoretical Candidates

Valuable scholarly work has been done, and continues to be done, on medieval compilations and miscellanies. This has been conducted predominantly at the codicological level, with something of a concentration on the material production of books and on the circumstances of their demand or use — whether these are institutional, personal, or more informally social. Common considerations inform such scholarship: evident changes of plan in the making of a compilation; the calibration of random versus planned elements; issues of texts travelling together from codex to codex; circumstances of availability of sources, and 'exemplar poverty'.[1]

The consideration of such factors is all well and good. Ralph Hanna's tellingly important reminder, however, made in the essay in which exemplar poverty features so centrally and so influentially — that literary production in

---

[1] For a broad and illuminating range of approaches to miscellanies on a European scale, see Doležalová and Rivers, *Medieval Manuscript Miscellanies*, and especially the Introduction, pp. 1–12. See also Nichols and Wenzel, *The Whole Book*; Boffey and Thompson, 'Anthologies and Miscellanies'; Connolly, 'Compiling the Book'; Connolly and Radulescu, *Insular Books*; and Bahr, 'Miscellaneity and Variance in the Medieval Book'. A classic treatment of the idea of exemplar poverty with regard to English materials is to be found in Hanna, 'Miscellaneity and Vernacularity'.

Ian Johnson (irj@st-andrews.ac.uk) is Professor of Medieval Literature at the University of St Andrews and a member of the St Andrews Institute of Mediaeval Studies.

Middle English was most typically miscellaneous — has not been followed up as energetically as the codicological aspects of miscellanies have been. Miscellaneity, for Hanna, applies not only to Geoffrey Chaucer's *Canterbury Tales*, John Gower's *Confessio amantis*, and William Langland's *Piers Plowman*, but also to 'the great range of popular spiritual classics', which 'meld shortish discrete materials, ultimately of diverse sources, and hold them together through mechanical thematic devices'.[2] Indeed, 'within Middle English literary production generally, miscellaneity forms a model procedure for creative work — as well as for its presentation in books'.[3] This essay is accordingly an attempt to think about compilations, miscellanies, and the miscellaneous from a somewhat theoretical and literary point of view, and to consider how miscellaneous textuality may have had implications beyond the miscellaneous codex.

This essay will try to look at miscellaneity in formal textual terms and to think about a textual and/or cultural repertoire or possibilities attaching to the miscellaneous. This is not an entirely straightforward business, especially as it is by no means clear that there was, in the first place, such a phenomenon as miscellaneity. I would rather imagine the miscellaneous, then, as a condition, an aspect, a matter, or a force of consignificance rather than as an entity of outright existence and of autonomous significance. It is the purpose of this study, therefore, by looking at some examples in Middle English biblical paratextuality, to ruminate some terms and ideas to see if they are suggestive in shedding light or in offering an interesting perspective on this topic of the miscellaneous. This is inevitably a bittily — indeed miscellaneous — business, and entails digging around in terms and texts.[4]

As a starting point, however, it can be said with a certain degree of historical confidence that in late medieval England it was believed to be desirable, possible, and permissible to treat miscellaneous or compiled materials fruitfully. This was meant to be accomplished with behaviour fit for the task. At the freewheeling end of the spectrum, the nuns of Syon are free to wander piously at will in the seven-by-five alleys of *The Orchard of Syon*: this is *lectoris arbitrium* at large, then.[5] But there is more to this than a walk in the park: reader free-

---

[2] Hanna, 'Miscellaneity and Vernacularity', p. 49.

[3] Hanna, 'Miscellaneity and Vernacularity', p. 50.

[4] This essay complements Johnson, 'A Sensibility of the Miscellaneous?', which proceeds on the same premises for going beyond the codicological, but which focuses instead on formal and theoretical considerations with regard to Chaucer's *Canterbury Tales* and Reginald Pecock's works.

[5] *The Orchard of Syon*, ed. by Hodgson and Liegey.

dom and responsibility are enormously important; they take their power and burdensomeness from the inescapability of free will and of absolute spiritual obligation. Such duteous freedom in negotiating compilatory *divisiones* was incontestably a factor in how compilations might be used, and in how a reader could or must move around within and amongst textual items or, less concretely, amongst their nodes and strands of *sententia* and sentiment.

Sometimes, be it to a greater or lesser degree, items fall into an educative or thematic sequence — as is the case in *The Contemplations of the Dread and Love of God*.[6] The component texts of a manuscript like Vernon or Simeon possess both relative autonomy and a degree of supertextual interdependency by virtue of being collocated in one codex and being therefore negotiable variously, in terms of each other or in terms of a sequence of edification.[7] For readers, textual items may become coloured by the company they keep in a manuscript, but it may also be open to them on various occasions to weigh differently or even to set aside or ignore the multi-textual surroundings of a particular textual item. In the light of this, then, modern scholars may draw a variety of interpretative conclusions, on a case-by-case basis, as to how individual miscellanies might conceivably have been used. Moreover, an enhanced appreciation of the pragmatic workings of miscellanies may also help to shed new light on textual items that would not be shed on them if they were merely observed on their own.

So much for individual manuscripts and textual items. Can, however, the miscellany and the miscellaneous be theorized to any useful extent? A potent binary with sticky implications, before one even starts to theorize the miscellany, is, unavoidably, the issue of randomness versus order. In itself, randomness, by its very nature, is not easily theorizable, especially as a feature of cultural phenomena. What makes things more difficult still is that modern scholars must face the perils of mistakenly miscalibrating the balance of randomness and order in a manuscript in the absence of knowing the design intentions of the original arranger of materials. Most English manuscripts were miscellanies, and it is often hard to fathom the relationships (or lack thereof) amongst their textual items. Their apparent randomness may be due to some extent, however, to one thing that can, thankfully, be understood readily enough: 'exemplar poverty'. By the term, 'exemplar poverty', I refer to the now-common scholarly conception according to which the combination of materials making up an individual manuscript (or indeed a text) may owe itself in different degrees and in

---

[6] *Contemplations*, ed. by Connolly.

[7] For the notion of the supertextuality, in which a number of otherwise autonomous texts combine serially to form a 'supertext', see Müller, 'Non-autonomous Texts', pp. 100–101.

various ways to the restricted choice of manuscript sources available to whoever was engaged in the writing process. Although Hanna is careful not to describe the random or unstructured appearance of texts as universally being attributable to exemplar poverty, he nevertheless states an important truth that 'difficulties of textual supply, as numerous studies indicate, contribute to the miscellaneous, not just say random, appearance of many Middle English books'.[8] The utility of the notion of exemplar poverty is in no way reduced by our awareness of manuscripts in which apparent variations and miscellaneousness otherwise attributable (in whatever degree) to exemplar poverty can instead (or also) be credibly explained in terms of the needs, agendas, or desires of commissioners or users. Exemplar poverty, then, may significantly contribute to helping to explain the recurrent presence and distribution of certain items and features of order in a number of manuscripts. In being able to account both dynamically and structurally, though by no means exclusively, for key features of miscellanies, this term without pretensions to being fancy theory is in fact a powerful modern theoretical tool. May we look, however, to any other modern theoretical notions to see if they shed some light on the structure, function, and behaviours of the medieval miscellany and the miscellaneous?

Is there, first of all, anything to be said for assessing the structures of compilations and miscellanies in terms of the 'polythetic'? This term has a certain currency in the social sciences and is used for describing complex and uncertain social or cultural structures characterized by a multiplicity of features whose order is hard to detect or define. A 'polythetic group' (in Rob Lutton's handy restatement of the term) is a 'group of representations that collectively share a set of features in such a way that no one feature is necessary but any large enough subset of features is sufficient for a representation to fall within the group'.[9] Miscellanies are certainly polythetic. It is not, however, clear that this loose, limited, and rather bland notion is of much use for our purposes. The term runs into particular difficulty if we take into account that it is unclear (to me at least) when and how the category of the polythetic is primarily a matter of measurement and of sorting, and is therefore numbly data-derived, or when and how it can be made to be genuinely conceptual or typological as an

---

[8] Hanna, 'Miscellaneity and Vernacularity', p. 47. Connolly, 'Books for the "helpe of euery persoone þat þenkiþ to be saued"', is in effect similarly nuanced in accounting for surprising variation amongst comparable manuscripts by distinguishing between occasions on which 'compilers were unable to get hold of the exact material they wanted' and occasions on which 'such differences must also surely sometimes arise by design as well as by accident' (p. 171).

[9] Lutton, '"Love this Name that is IHC"', p. 121.

explanatory metaphor for the nature and operation of the textual items and interrelations of miscellanies.[10]

More familiar to medievalists than the polythetic is dialogics. To treat a compilation dialogically, with reference to the persons, actants, and authorial voices in its text and paratext, seems straightforward and sensible. For instance, in the case of a devotional compilation such as Nicholas Love's *Mirror of the Blessed Life of Jesus Christ*, one can imagine easily enough an assortment of relationships being dialogically articulated in various moments and situations of text and paratext — amongst Love, his readerships/hearerships real or imagined, the Poor Clare of the Latin original, contemporary Carthusian lay brothers, pious aristocrats, or a broader national audience of less exalted *simple soules*, Archbishop Arundel, Bonaventura, Pseudo-Bonaventura, Christ, Mary, Saint Cecilia, and God.[11] One can also posit productive and critically significant cross-currents amongst discourses in the *Mirror*: the Bible, commentary, narrative, moral exposition, meditation, prayer, translatorly insertions and instructions, and so on. Being transactional and dynamic, a dialogic approach is thus capable of considering not only the modes, levels, and materials that are compiled, translated, and authored/authorized in a composite work like a compilation or a miscellany, it can also encompass various interrelations of items and features not only within such multi-textual works and codices but also across their boundaries.

Dialogics is therefore fruitful. Indeed, one could cite examples of modern scholars working dialogically on miscellanies and compilations, even though

---

[10] See Bailey, 'Monothetic and Polythetic Typologies', for discussion of this.

[11] Love, *Mirror*, ed. by Sargent. While Love's *Mirror* is derived from a single source rather than being a multi-textual assemblage, it is indubitably a compilation, as disclosed in the memorandum attached to many manuscripts, which refers to Love as 'compilator eiusdem' (p. 7). As the product of an age in which many translators regarded themselves as compilers, the *Mirror* exhibits several hallmarks of *compilatio*: it works by a mode of excerption, self-consciously taking liberties with redividing, selecting, reordering, combining, and abbreviating materials, even going so far as to distinguish, in classic compiling fashion, between materials rendered from the Latin source (which are marked with a 'B' for Bonaventura, to whom the *Meditationes vitae Christi* was then attributed) and those of Love's own, which are initialled in the margin with an 'N'. Typical also of the genre is the manner in which Love observes the compiler's repertoire in features of layout, by, for example, providing citations of sources, indicating divisions of materials by theme, and deploying *capitula* at the head of each chapter. In similar compilatory vein, he produces a meticulously packaged *ordinatio* according to the days of the week and is also happy to let readers exercise their *lectoris arbitrium* (as with other compilations) by reading the work according to times of the church year or in line with their individual changing preferences and needs (p. 220). For a study of Nicholas Love in terms of dialogics, see Johnson, 'Theoretical and Pragmatic Dialogics'.

they may not cite, let alone be enthusiasts of, dialogic theory or terms as they do so. Beyond the relative familiarity of dialogics there is another approach, another term. It is hitherto unknown to medieval textual studies, but suggests itself as a candidate for theorizing the miscellany. This approach has been employed in a number of different ways in disciplines as varied as biophysics, archaeology, anthropology, sociology, philosophy, management studies, and computing science. The term/concept in question is that of 'heterarchy' and the 'heterarchic'. Uncannily, heterarchic structures, as described in disciplines beyond medieval textual studies, do, to a significant extent, look and behave rather like miscellanies in their organizational diversity. Variously orderable, they seem to be able to accommodate miscellaneously contingent varieties of thought, discourse, and perspective. They even thrive on the ambiguities and inconsistencies that seem to typify the miscellany: 'A heterarchy is a system of organization replete with overlap, multiplicity, mixed ascendancy, and/or divergent-but-coexistent patterns of relation. [...] A heterarchy usually requires ambivalent thought [...] a willingness to ambulate freely between unrelated perspectives.'[12]

The idea of heterarchy is worth exploring because, as we shall see, it seems to accommodate the changing interrelations and variable groupings of textual items and perspectives in and across medieval manuscripts. It also encompasses the derivation of items, human motivation, and evaluation, and allows for protean mixes of randomness and order. It even gives space for hierarchy, which is of course at the heart of authoritative medieval textuality, however miscellaneous.

It may be said at this point that although it is not the primary purpose of this essay to focus on manuscripts themselves, it is conceivable that aspects of the heterarchical could be harnessed in the study of miscellaneous collections. The case of the psalms springs to mind: Psalter manuscripts — be they complete, abbreviated, or in the forms of primers or other liturgical, catechetic, or devotional manifestations — certainly maintained a rich diversity of forms, utilities, perspectives, *formae tractatus*, palaeographical features, thematics, and textual selectivities in this period. Annie Sutherland's *English Psalms in the Middle Ages, 1300–1450* shows repeatedly just how heterarchical this variegated manuscript tradition was, identifying it 'in terms of a creative, non-

---

[12] 'Heterarchy', *Wikipedia*. The definitions of heterarchy on this indubitably heterarchic site have been subject to interesting discussion and change. The first sentence quoted has since been deleted, and access on 18 July 2016 showed that it had not returned. Nevertheless, it is useful for our purposes. It is notable that standard reference works of sociology and anthropology — dictionaries, guides, and companions — do not have 'heterarchy' as an entry. The *OED* entry for the term labels it obsolete and contains a single quotation from the seventeenth century somewhat irrelevant to this study, 'the rule of an alien' (accessed 18 July 2016).

ancestral, nexus of vernacularization'.[13] Heterarchically enough, manuscripts of the Wycliffite psalms — conceived by their Lollard translators as the epitome of the dissident vernacular Psalter — very often include the full Latin Vulgate and had orthodox readers; and primers, with 'little to suggest anything other than orthodox intentions on the part of their compilers', relied on Wycliffite versions of the psalms.[14] Further heterarchic ambivalence attaches to manuscripts of Richard Rolle's Psalter, whose absence of Latin may indicate either that the audience was non-Latinate or, on the contrary, that it included readers of considerable Latinity who had access to the Vulgate or who had ingested the Latin text. It could also mean such manuscripts could accommodate both types of user.[15] Productive heterarchic incohesiveness can be seen too in other miscellaneous manuscripts. For instance, Vincent Gillespie points to Bodl. Lib., MS Laud misc. 210 'as a collection of "forms of living"' and other devotional works that, given its palpable lack of *ordinatio* and apparatus, would have been 'difficult to use casually', despite the evident care and high spiritual seriousness with which the book was produced.[16]

Other examples of manuscriptal heterarchicality could be cited, but this essay is more concerned with introducing the concept of heterarchy to the medieval literary and cultural field more generally. A standard and rudimentary definition of heterarchy, as formulated by the archaeologist Carole L. Crumley, is as follows: 'Heterarchy may be defined as the relation of elements to one another when they are unranked or when they possess the potential for being ranked in a number of different ways.'[17] This description fits miscellanies — their structures and their mutabilities. Dmitri Bondarenko provides a matching definition of heterarchy's opposite, termed by him neologistically as 'homoarchy': 'we can define homoarchy as "the relation of elements to one another when they are rigidly ranked only in a single way, and thus possess no (or not more than very limited) potential for being unranked or ranked in another or a number of different ways"'.[18]

---

[13] Sutherland, *English Psalms in the Middle Ages*, p. 275. See in particular pp. 230–72 for discussion of manuscripts variously housing psalms.

[14] Sutherland, *English Psalms in the Middle Ages*, pp. 265, 157.

[15] Sutherland, *English Psalms in the Middle Ages*, p. 259.

[16] Gillespie, 'Vernacular Books of Religion', p. 326. See also, on the orthodox/heterodox hybridity of readers and manuscripts, Johnson, 'Vernacular Theology/Theological Vernacular', pp. 86–88.

[17] Crumley, 'Heterarchy and the Analysis of Complex Societies', p. 3.

[18] Bondarenko, 'Homoarchy as a Principle of Sociopolitical Organization', p. 187.

A homoarchic text or codex would therefore be monolithic and monovocal — unlike a miscellany. Bondarenko does not posit hierarchy as the antithesis of heterarchy.[19] It is important more generally to understand that hierarchy is not the opposite of heterarchy, despite the fact that a number of social scientists and others apparently misuse the term as if it were the natural anti-hierarchical bedfellow of equality, tolerance, democracy, and the like. Hierarchy, it must be stressed, may be contained and even sustained within and by heterarchy. Indeed, no hierarchical society — or text — is likely to be without heterarchic elements and potentials. (A dictatorship, after all, may be accompanied by a relatively toothless parliament or advisory council.) Medieval miscellanies, then, for all their network-like heterarchicality, also inevitably accommodate, or are governed by, or are accountable to, pyramidally hierarchical absolutes of faith, *auctoritas*, and other ideological directives and structures flowing from and to divine and secular order.[20]

The sociologist of the firm, David Stark, suggestively complicates the notion of heterarchy by folding into it features of the dynamic, the cognitive, and the transactional, which for him are to do with the structures and behaviours of people and of commercial organizations, but which for our purposes may conceivably be translated cautiously and reunderstood in terms of the dialogical interactions and structures of the multi-textual discourses, human agencies, and contexts characteristic of miscellanies.[21] For Stark, heterarchies accommodate and generate 'co-existing logics and frames of action':[22] this could be a description of the multiple *ordinationes*, thematic directives, and overlapping imperatives with which not only meaning but also readerly and writerly conduct may be fashioned in a miscellany. Fascinatingly too, the open-ended but motivated complexity that medievalists find in the miscellany has a corollary in Stark's formulation of a heterarchic structure as not being 'consistent or elegant or coherent' but as nevertheless having an open-ended capacity to optimize, in that 'the complexity that it promotes and the lack of simple coherence that it tolerates increase the diversity of options'.[23] One might note here Vincent Gillespie's comments concerning the option-generating transformation and 'liberation of purpose' observable of the highly structured *Cibus anime* when

---

[19] Bondarenko, 'Homoarchy as a Principle of Sociopolitical Organization', p. 190.

[20] Bondarenko, 'Homoarchy as a Principle of Sociopolitical Organization', p. 187.

[21] See Stark, 'Heterarchy' and especially the first chapter of his monograph, *The Sense of Dissonance*, 'Heterarchy: The Organization of Dissonance', pp. 1–34.

[22] Stark, 'Heterarchy', p. 24.

[23] Stark, 'Heterarchy', p. 24.

rendered anew as the looser-limbed *Speculum christiani*. This work is no longer to 'be regarded as an organic unity [...] but as a series of loosely articulated units having no causal relationship with each other — [...] an instant miscellany'. Indeed, 'this new compilation could serve well in any didactic context'.[24] Moreover, whereas the miscellany and the compilation rechannel meaning and discursive power, and adjudicate their priorities by dividing and devolving portions of repotentiated significance and meaning to their chosen parts, with variously repurposed reader-usability, the heterarchy works on a comparable principle of subsidiarity in distributing understanding and cognition amongst human users and their social structures in new, situationally contingent ways. Or, as Stark puts it: 'Heterarchies are about distributed intelligence and the organization of diversity'.[25] Miscellanies may thus be seen as motivated and remotivatable forms that preserve, transmit, and add cultural value, enhancing and reinvesting cultural capital by distributing diverse understanding diversely, and they are not unorganized in doing so.

Middle English Biblical Paratexts and the Challenge of the Miscellaneous

In the *Speculum maius*, Vincent of Beauvais ordered his encyclopaedic materials according to an *ordinatio* embodying the authority of the Creator and Creation and attempting to assist the restoration of knowledge lost or obscured at the Fall. His desire, to order disparate topics rationally and in terms of an orthodox hierarchic ideology, was strong indeed, as it was throughout mainstream learned culture.[26] This was particularly the case with the mid-fifteenth-century reforming bishop, Reginald Pecock. His new repackaging of Christian knowledge and doctrine in a massive programme of interrelated texts was prepared at different levels of difficulty for various audiences. It aimed to give reasoned structure to such knowledge and doctrine. In high scholastic fashion, Pecock reordered and recodified the Church's traditional discourses of catechesis and belief, such as the Ten Commandments and the seven deadly sins, rearticulating them in his four hyper-rationalistic *meenal* and *eendal* tables; he even referred to them as 'a heep', and, worse, 'lose gibilettis'.[27] The Latin term

---

[24] Gillespie, '*Doctrina* and *Predicacio*', p. 14.

[25] Stark, 'Heterarchy', p. 24.

[26] Minnis, *Medieval Theory of Authorship*, pp. 154–55, 157–59; Parkes, 'The Influence of the Concepts of *Ordinatio* and *Compilatio*', pp. 59–60; Paulmier-Foucart, 'L'*Actor* et les *Auctores*'.

[27] Pecock, *The Donet*, ed. by Hitchcock, pp. 146–47. See also Johnson, 'Loose Giblets',

miscellanea means, tellingly for our purposes, 'broken meats'.²⁸ Here, doubtless, Pecock is sniping at the disordered miscellaneousness of official ecclesiastical discourse. For him, this was miscellaneity *in malo*, though for those happy enough to hang onto traditional forms of catechesis, it was, doubtless, *in bono*. Even so, for all his belief in hierarchical reason, his oeuvre is cross-cut with different schemes and orders. Pecock shaped it heterarchically in order to negotiate a shifting and asymmetrical array of arguments, themes, polemical exigencies, and audiences. It is undoubtedly as heterarchical in structure and temper as it is hierarchical. Bearing in mind, then, what we were saying a little earlier about how the accommodation of hierarchy within the heterarchical does not mean that the heterarchical is the opposite of hierarchy, we may then, perhaps, imagine the miscellaneous, in its heterarchicality, as an Other which hierarchy habitually has to accommodate in various ways.

For medieval textual culture, the Word of God itself was at times miscellaneous, for the hierarchic and the heterarchic vied with each other in conceptions of the workings of the Bible. Indeed, the Bible is the ultimate and original miscellany (and a devotional one at that) — 'not a book but a collection of texts'.²⁹ The books of the Bible are all authoritative and of divine origin, but they are also all filtered variously through human authors in generically different ways in a heterarchic *collectio* of biblical books. Throughout history the problematic miscellaneity of the Bible has exercised those who would understand it, and the Middle Ages was no exception. The Bible required and encouraged medieval academe to come up with habits and strategies for finding authentic meaning, teaching, and value in a uniquely and bewilderingly heterarchic manifestation of the absolute. In the Middle Ages, the proliferation of different styles and of *modi* in Holy Scripture was celebrated and attracted profuse comment (as did the complex interrelations not only amongst the books of the Bible but also between the Old Testament and the New Testament).³⁰ In the prologue to his *Breviloquium* Bonaventure, for example, accordingly embedded a heterarchic array of discursive modes within the all-empowering hierarchic mode of divine authority:

---

pp. 335–42. For general studies on Pecock, see Scase, *Reginald Pecock*; Green, *Bishop Reginald Pecock*; Brockwell, *Bishop Reginald Pecock and the Lancastrian Church*, and Campbell, *The Call to Read*.

²⁸ For a discussion of the etymology and linguistic history of *miscellaneus*, see Murano, 'Zibaldoni', p. 394.

²⁹ Lawton, 'The Bible', p. 198.

³⁰ For discussion of this, see Minnis, *Medieval Theory of Authorship*, pp. 118–45.

> In tanta igitur multiformitate sapientiae, quae continetur in ipsius sacrae Scripturae latitudine, longitudine, altitudine et profundo, unus est communis modus procedendi authenticus; videlicet intra quem continetur modus narrativus, praeceptorius, prohibitivus, exhortativus, praedicativus, comminatorius, promissivus, deprecatorius et laudativus. Et omnes hi modi sub uno modo authentico reponuntur, et hoc quidem satis recte.[31]

> [Among all the many kinds of wisdom which are contained in the width, length, height, and depth of Holy Scripture, there is one common way of proceeding: by authority. Grouped within it are the narrative, preceptive, prohibitive, exhortatory, instructive, threatening, promising, supplicating, and laudatory modes. All these modes come within the scope of that one mode, proceeding by authority, and quite rightly so.][32]

Authority may seem to be a reassuring container for whatever readers encounter in the Bible, but it does not help readers to understand difficult scriptural texts. In itself, authority does not shed light on the confusingly diverse features of the Bible that challenge those who would understand how they work separately and together. Medieval commentators and adaptors, nevertheless, did not duck the heterarchic difficulties of biblical hermeneutics. On the contrary, they often came up with approaches and concepts making sense not just as theory but also as readerly pragmatics, and nowhere else did they perform more impressively than they did with the Psalter.

For the Middle Ages, the miscellaneous poems of the Psalter, with their centrifugal medley of themes and personae, constituted a special test for exegetes, not least because it was thought that the Psalter distilled the entirety of the Bible. The greatest late medieval Bible commentator, the Franciscan Nicholas of Lyra, was eloquent in providing an analysis of the structure and workings of the book of Psalms. He made a key distinction between, on the one hand, relatively unordered *collectio* and, on the other, more explicitly ordered *compilatio*. The Psalter, for him, is undoubtedly a *collectio*:

> Non potest diuidi secundum ordinem auctorum nec et temporum, vt patet ex dictis: nec et materiarum, quia in diursis psalmis & diuersorum auctorum & distanter scriptis eadem materia frequenter tangitur, & econuerso aliquando in eodem psalmum de diuersis materijs agitur. propter quod non video bene qualiter artificiose potest diuidi liber iste nisi in quodam generali.[33]

---

[31] Bonaventure, *Breviloquium, prologus*, 5, p. 206.

[32] Bonaventure, *Breviloquium*, trans. by Scott, p. 235.

[33] *Postilla literalis*, in *Biblia Sacra cum Glossa ordinaria*, III, cols 433–34.

[Neither can it [the Psalter] be divided according to the order of the authors or of temporal sequence, as appears from what has been said. For the same matter is often touched on in different psalms, and in psalms by different authors, and psalms widely separated from each other. Conversely, on occasions various subjects are treated in one and the same psalm. Thus I cannot very well see how this book could be divided artificially (*artificiose*), except in some general way.][34]

As a heterarchically organized assembly, the Psalter has no single principle of order. It entertains a co-existing diversity of logics, themes, subject-positions, and divisions of matter. To put it in the latter-day terms of heterarchy, the Psalter's looseness of structure promotes a complexity and a diversity of options propitious for its function of compendiously comporting the entire Bible. Moreover, the Psalter's ability to recombine various properties conduces to the fruitful management and extraction of value from its ambiguous, and therefore reusable, textual capital.[35] It is in the cases of the Psalter — to say nothing of the rest of the Bible — that the most telling challenges of miscellaneous textuality lie, so it is appropriate to examine some important Middle English biblical paratexts to see how they variously meet such challenges.

A variety of suggestive approaches to authoritative heterarchic textuality is to be found in some culturally central Middle English biblical paratexts. These, as we shall see, provide a serviceable range of different ways of tackling the lack of explicit structure in the bewildering yet compelling multiplicity of books in which biblical textuality miscellaneously presents itself.[36] We start with the description of the Psalter in the General Prologue to the Middle English (Wycliffite) Bible, which lays on the line what the Book of Psalms does so variously:

> Þe Sauter comprehendiþ al þe elde and newe testament and techiþ pleynli þe mysteries of þe Trinite and of Cristis incarnacioun, passioun, rising aȝen, and stiyng into heuene and sendyng doun of þe Hooli Goost and prechyng of þe gospel, and þe comyng of antecrist, and þe general doom of Crist, and þe glorie of chosun men to blisse and þe peynes of hem þat shulen be dampned in helle; and ofte rehersiþ þe

---

[34] Nicholas of Lyre, *Literal Postill*, ed. and trans. by Scott, p. 275. I have altered this translation to bring it into accord with the Latin of the Venice edition. See Minnis's discussion of such features of the Psalter in *Medieval Theory of Authorship*, pp. 85–94, 151–53.

[35] Stark, 'Heterarchy', pp. 24–29.

[36] This is not to say that the difficulty of interpreting the Bible is solely to do with structure, for the sheer obscurity of passages makes up much that is hard to understand in Holy Writ. Nevertheless, part of that very obscurity is often to do with the challenge to connect various parts of the Bible with each other, especially when it comes to the interrelations of Old and New Testament.

stories of þe elde testament, and bryngeþ in þe kepyng of Goddis heestis and loue of enemyes.[37]

Clearly, the Psalter is a distillation of the whole Bible. Here, the Psalter's key narrative and doctrinal elements are summarily inventoried. These elements, however, are not just discrete items of subject matter; they constitute a comprehensive repertoire of *sentence*, a scriptural competence tied to hermeneutic possibility and readerly performability. The Psalter is not just a collection *in* the Bible; it is a collection and recollection *of* the Bible. The totality of Scripture and the Psalter are multiply complex sibling glosses of each other, refracting each other unendingly. A reader's or commentator's ability to look in one and understand what is in the other invites sophisticated interpretative engagement — an appreciation of persona, voice, style, genre, thematics, and the episodic or narrative context informing them. (The less capable reader or hearer can acquire a degree of spiritual profit from this process too.) The take-home point here is that anyone acquainted with, or simply aware of, the complex formal and thematic mutualities and the sensible heterarchies between Scripture and the Psalter is likely to be agile enough and adequately equipped to negotiate, to some advantage, the ad hoc synapses and variously far-fetched and contingent interrelations within and amongst other vernacular codices and compilations beyond the Bible.

As for the Psalter's *ordinatio*, it is multiple and heterarchic indeed. Amongst other schemata, it may be divided by eighties and seventies; by eights and sevens; or by three fifties, in which each fifty represents spiritual progress from penance to righteousness to praising the life hereafter: 'This boc forsothe is deuydid bi thre fifties; bi the whiche thre statis of cristene religioun ben betocned. Of whiche the firste is in penaunce, the secounde in riȝtwisnesse, the thridde in preising of the euere lastende lif.'[38] Richard Rolle makes much of the same division in the prologue to his own Psalter translation-commentary. (Let us not forget here, either, the grouping of psalms into the Seven Penitential Psalms (which were not overlooked by makers of medieval devotional collections), to say nothing of the complex sequences in the tradition of the recitation of the liturgical Psalter.)

The Psalter is governed by another principle: it is Christocentric. And even though it is part of the Old Testament, it would be no poetic licence and no false perspective, says the Lollard Psalter prologue, to see David as evangelizing rather than prophesying:

[37] 'The Prologue to the Wycliffite Bible', ed. by Dove, p. 58, ch. 11. 2007–14.
[38] Prologue to the Psalter in *The Holy Bible*, ed. by Forshall and Madden, p. 737.

Forsothe wee beholden Dauid, a man sleere and auoutrer, bi penaunce maad a doctour and a profete, [...] and therfore this profecie is oftene had in vse, for among othere profecies it passith in openyng of sawys; tho forsothe thingus that othere profetis dercly and as bi figure seiden of the passion and the resureccioun of Crist, and of the euerlastende geteng, and of othere mysterijs, Dauid of profetis most excellent so euydentli openede, that more he be seen to euangelisen than to profecien.[39]

The transformational shift in genre from prophecy to evangelization is heralded by David's transformation, through penance, from sinner to 'doctour and a profete', and thus to his symbolization as proto-Christ. This generic and personal shift, however, from prophecy to evangelization (though never leaving prophecy behind), not only views genre as malleable but also reminds the reader that, in distilling the whole Bible, the Psalter is capable of yet more: a scripturally perfect Christological hybridity — the conflation of prophecy with an evangelizing realization of prophecy, a conflation of Old Testament and New Testament proper to its function of encompassing the whole Bible.[40] Rolle is in accord with this in appraising the Psalter as the 'perfeccioun of dyuyne pagyne' and as the compendious bearer of all Holy Writ:

> This boke of all haly writ is mast oysed in halykyrke seruys, forthi that in it is perfeccioun of dyuyne pagyne. for it contenys all that other bokes draghes langly. that is, the lare of the ald testament. & of the new.[41]

The Psalter, as the 'perfeccioun of dyuyne pagyne', redistributes divine meaning and cognition heterarchically without compromising its completeness, divine authority, or the perfection of truth. The idea that God's truth may be manifested in multiple ways and remanifested in different articulations is not

---

[39] Prologue to the Psalter in *The Holy Bible*, ed. by Forshall and Madden, pp. 737–38.

[40] Intriguingly, Hanna, 'Miscellaneity and Vernacularity', pp. 46–47 n. 35, observes that the alliterative *Siege of Jerusalem* was apparently viewed trans-generically in different manuscripts as 'biblical history (Bodl. Lib., MS Laud misc. 656), a romance (Caligula A.ii), specifically a crusader romance (British Library, MS Additional 31042), or learned secular history (Cambridge University Library, MS Mm.5.14)'. Evidently, in late medieval England genres were a matter of malleability not just from the point of view of those who produced texts but also from the point of view of those who copied or read them. With regard to the question of a biblical source for this work, Michael Livingston, the TEAMS editor of the *Siege of Jerusalem*, points out that the work does indeed have a French scriptural source, being 'in the main, a compilation from three primary sources: *Vindicta salvatoris* (the basis for lines 1–200 and 1297–1340), Roger d'Argenteuil's *Bible en François* (for lines 201–788), and Ranulf Higden's *Polychronicon* (for lines 789–1296)'.

[41] Rolle, *The Psalter*, ed. by Bramley, p. 4.

uncommon elsewhere. Often, across medieval devotional literature, one passage of text may also do the work of another passage or work, and some passages may mutually revisit related topics in different *loci*.

In his next sentence, Rolle proceeds to identify the *materia* and the *modus agendi* of the work he expounds:

> The matere of this boke is crist & his spouse, that is, haly kyrke, or ilk ryghtwise mannys saule. the entent is; to confourme men that ere filyd in adam til crist in newnes of lyf. the maner of lare is swilke. vmstunt (*sometimes*) he spekis of crist in his godhed. vmstunt (*sometimes*) in his manhed. vmstunt (*sometimes*) in that at he oises the voice of his seruauntes. Alswa he spekis of haly kyrke in thre maners. vmwhile (*sometimes*) in the person of perfite men. somtyme of vnperfite men. som tyme of ill men, whilk er in halikyrke. by body noght by thoght; by name noght by ded, in noumbire noght in merit.[42]

There is more to be said at this point, however, than merely to observe that Rolle is working from the Latin *accessus* tradition.[43] Here, at the commanding heights of literate devotional culture, Rolle asserts and combines comprehensiveness of *sentence* with heterarchically (un)ordered occasionality: three *vmstunt*s containing the voices and personae, respectively, of Christ in his divinity, Christ in his manhood, and the voices of God's servants. All divine and human voices are thus accounted for. This formulation strategically combines the contingent and the totalizing. Rolle then repeats the same kind of move, mixing the all-encompassing with ad hoc occasionality by means of the temporal adverbs, 'vmwhile [...], somtyme [...], and som tyme', in a sequence of perfect, imperfect, and sinful humans. This is another totalizing and progressive series of categories, refracted paratactically through the non-sequentialism of unordered temporality. The sensibility informing Rolle's Psalter is, it would seem, commensurate with that of relatively ordered *compilatio*, but it has more in common with the less ordered, or variously ordered, miscellany.

That this should be so is theoretically significant. Rolle discloses a model of the Psalter as a heterarchic catch-all and as polythetically capacious, albeit bounded and driven by the Christology which is its authorizing matter, its motivation, and its end. The various voices, persons, plights, and lessons of the Psalter are for readers and hearers to observe, reimagine, mark, learn, ruminate, and digest. For them, situational variety, redistributed perspectives, and contingency

---

[42] Rolle, *The Psalter*, ed. by Bramley, p. 4.

[43] See Minnis's discussion of the tradition of the *accessus* and prologues more generally in *Medieval Theory of Authorship*, pp. 9–72.

are accommodated in a form and with a performability in which miscellaneous elements and forces work connectedly and coherently with an overarching Christology and divine authority. Even though the Psalter is extraordinarily open-ended and heterarchic in terms of its reading pragmatics, it is ultimately totalizing and hierarchical in terms of its underpinning ideology and *telos*. Here, heterarchic human discourse serves an absolute and transcendent divine end.

Turning now to Middle English paratextual treatment of the Bible as an otherwise uncontainably heterarchic whole, where better to head for than the General Prologue to the Middle English (i.e. Wycliffite) Bible, which for all the dissidence of some of its translators and paratextual polemicists, was, methodologically, highly conventional in the best manner of the age? Here we may look for an assortment of normative types of hermeneutic agility responding to the challenge of Scripture.

We start with what looks like a plain enough statement about the authority of the Bible:

> But soþeli alle þe bookis of þe newe testament […] ben fulli of autorite of bileue. Þerfore cristen men and wymmen, elde and ȝonge, shulden studie fast in the newe testament, for it is of ful autorite, and opene to vndurstonde of symple men as to þe poyntis þat ben moost nedeful to saluacioun, and þe same sentence is in þe derkest places of hooli writ which sentence is in þe open places.[44]

This, however, is not merely an advertisement that the Bible is fully authoritative and open to all; it is an instruction and an encouragement to engage in an ad hoc method which operates without recourse to a palpable orientating structure and which takes the self-definingly open places of Scripture as a resource and tool to bring to bear on all dark places, none of which is without *sentence*. Likewise, outside the Bible, a reader may flit around a compilation or miscellany with little regard to structure and find mutual illumination or fruitful consanguinity amongst various passages.

The extensive summary of the whole Bible that takes up much of the General Prologue taxonomizes a *divisio* — an *ordinatio*. It enumerates and generically identifies the biblical books, discusses their various interconnections, and identifies their functions in the larger whole. This is not, however, a neat *ordinatio*, but it is powerful, authorized, and designed to be reassuring in offering repeated and varied orientation in a complex and asymmetrical textual landscape. The following, however, is one of its more overarching divisions: 'The elde testament is departid in to þre partis, into moral comaundementis, iudicials, and

---

[44] 'The Prologue to the Wycliffite Bible', ed. by Dove, p. 5, ch. 1. 72–79.

cerymonyals.'⁴⁵ Each Old Testament book is, moreover, more than an archive of themes and lessons; it also has a function (or functions) in the overall design of the Bible, as with Deuteronomy, which is accorded a multiplicity not so much of subject matter but of roles relating to other parts of the Holy Writ and to the duties of humans to their maker: 'The fyfeþe book, clepid Deutronomy, is a rehersyng and confermyng of al þe lawe bifor-going, and stiriþ men gretli to kepe and teche Goddis heestis, and adde noþing to þo neþer drawe awei onyþing from þo.'⁴⁶

This book, enumerated as the fifth in the sequence, faithfully deploys a triad of hermeneutically and rhetorically valorizing modes of all previous God-given law, for it reruns, confirms, and adjudicates/authenticates previous items in the canonical sequence. It also canonically fixes an upper and a lower limit — no more, no less — on God's commandments, making their canonicity and its parameters fascinatingly dependent on an affective appeal to humanity (in that it 'stiriþ men gretli to kepe and teche Goddis heestis') to take responsibility for this final form and to apply it accordingly elsewhere as a spiritual *forma tractandi*. 'Deutronomy' is thus preparatory, internally paratextual, and disposes to a proper belief in Christ and to a proper Christian *habitus*, understanding, and application of the *sentence* of the Old (and thus the New) Testament: 'Cristen men shulden myche rede and here and kunne þis book of Deutronomy, þat comprehendiþ al þe lawe of Moises and disposiþ men for to bileue in Crist and here and kepe his wordis.'⁴⁷ These various functional modes found in and exercised by 'Deutronomy' — rerunning, confirming, adjudicating, authenticating, preparing, and so on — are all modes that could be replayed (as a matter of habit rather than of direct textual influence) by a reasonably educated and adept compiler or reader when negotiating a multi-textual compilation or miscellany.

Like Deuteronomy, Paralipomenon (I and II Chronicles) provides a precedent for texts variously contextualizing other textual items. For example, it not only gives context for the understanding of other books of the Old Testament, it also distinctively raises and addresses numerous issues subsequently addressed in the Gospels: 'The bookis of Paralipomenon ben ful nescessarie to vndurstonde þe stories of þe elde testament [...], and vnnoumbrable questiouns of þe gospel ben declarid bi þese bookis.'⁴⁸ Likewise, in a compilation or

---

⁴⁵ 'The Prologue to the Wycliffite Bible', ed. by Dove, p. 6, ch. 2. 95–96.
⁴⁶ 'The Prologue to the Wycliffite Bible', ed. by Dove, p. 10, ch. 3. 239–41.
⁴⁷ 'The Prologue to the Wycliffite Bible', ed. by Dove, pp. 13–14, ch. 3. 383–85.
⁴⁸ 'The Prologue to the Wycliffite Bible', ed. by Dove, p. 34, ch. 8. 1121–27.

miscellany, issues raised in one part of a collection may be addressed elsewhere in it.⁴⁹

As far as the General Prologue is concerned, a kind of exemplar poverty occurs in the Bible itself. Old Testament kings, we are told, lacked access to many scriptural books. After all, most of these books had not been written yet. But although, as with Middle English devotional miscellanies and compilations, there may have been a dearth of texts, there was nevertheless more than enough content in the books that were available to provide the kings with sufficient edification and moral guidance in the ways of the Lord:

> And þouȝ kingis and lordis knewen neuere more of hooli scripture þan þre stories of the ij. bookis of Paralipomenon and of Regum, þat is, the stori of kyng Iosaphat, þe storie of king Eȝechie and þe storie of kyng Iosie, þei myȝten lerne sufficientli to lyue wel and gouerne wel hire puple bi Goddis lawe.⁵⁰

Exemplar poverty doubles here with exemplar sufficiency. Here too, perhaps, is an early exemplar (in another sense) of the 'Advice to Princes' tradition. Here, rulers have to be good and diligent enough readers to apply the lessons of the books they have. In an oddly reflexive moment, these Old Testament kings are not only obliged to be good kings in line with biblical standards, they are, in order to be so, obliged to be good Bible readers too. Following the Lollard archetype, these good Bible readers must be good livers, and these good livers must be good Bible readers.

Later in the same prologue, in another famously Ralphian moment evidencing exemplar poverty, attention is drawn to unavailable books in an attempt to elaborate the various rules for interpreting Holy Writ:

> Isidere in þe firste book of *Souereyn Good* touchiþ þese reulis schortliere, but I haue hym not now, and Lire, in þe bigynnyng of þe Bible touchiþ more openli þese reulis, but I haue him not now, and Ardmacan in þe bigynnyng of his book *De Questionibus Armenorum* ȝyueþ many good groundis to vndurstonde hooli scripture to þe lettre, and gostli vndurstonding also, but I haue him not now.⁵¹

Not having books to hand for the meanwhile may not, however, entirely hinder the project, but it does provide a salutary reminder that one can only work with what one has in the textual format (be it physical or memorial) in which one has it. Moreover, exemplar poverty does not exactly prevent this writer of the

---

⁴⁹ For similar issues in other compilations, see the essays by Cré and Denissen in this volume.

⁵⁰ 'The Prologue to the Wycliffite Bible', ed. by Dove, p. 47, ch. 10. 1577–81.

⁵¹ 'The Prologue to the Wycliffite Bible', ed. by Dove, p. 68, ch. 12. 2359–64.

General Prologue asserting the underpinning principles of guidance to negotiating the Bible.

When it came to interpreting the Bible, medieval biblical commentators were, then, able to take many approaches. Indeed, medieval exegesis constituted a heterarchic tradition or repertoire of approaches (which modern heterarchic theory might label as 'rival logics') that could all be used separately or concurrently. The General Prologue invokes the most common principles — the advice of Saint Augustine in *De doctrina christiana*, fourfold exegesis, figurative speech, and so on:

> Bi these reulis of Austin and bi foure vndurstondingis of hooli scripture and bi wiys knowing of figuratif spechis, wiþ good lyuyng and mekenes and studiyng of þe Bible, symple men moun sumdel vndurstonde þe text of hooli writ and edefie myche hemsilf and oþere men.[52]

Here is a mighty miscellany of approaches fit for the task. They are not restricted to academic techniques, for they include good moral living, meekness of spirit, and sheer hard work. Given all these, it might be of interest to look across at what Stark has to say about heterarchies' success depending on nurturing a diversity of operative rationales and procedures: 'Heterarchies are *complex* adaptive systems because they interweave a multiplicity of organizing principles.'[53] This statement would also be an apposite comment on the efficacity of the organizational diversity of approaches entertained by biblical exegetical tradition and of the allied behaviours invoked here in the General Prologue. Moreover, Stark's judgement, that 'heterarchies create wealth by inviting more than one way of evaluating worth', also holds up when one considers the multiple ways in which biblical textuality was, and indeed had to be, approached in order to do justice to its protean superabundance of forms and *sentence*.[54]

The standard vernacularized hermeneutic armoury (a take-home exegetical kit for proper Bible reading), as articulated here in the General Prologue, gives ammunition and encouragement to Christians to take on the otherwise overwhelming and sprawling miscellaneity of Scripture, and to find edifying sufficiency and fruitfulness therein; or, as the writer of the General Prologue puts it so measuredly: 'symple men moun *sumdel* vndurstonde þe text of hooli writ and edefie myche hemsilf and oþere men'. The word 'sumdel' indicates a part-share, an incomplete but nevertheless profitable portion of *sentence*. It is also

[52] 'The Prologue to the Wycliffite Bible', ed. by Dove, p. 69, ch. 12. 2403–06.
[53] Stark, 'Heterarchy', p. 26.
[54] Stark, 'Heterarchy', p. 26.

an indefinite quantity: any given rendering can only express so much *sentence*. Likewise, different readers will diversely get more or less from their individual reading capabilities and performances. Here, exemplar poverty has a corollary in limited supplies of apprehensible/articulable *sentence* and reader performance. Even so, 'sumdel' is desirable, and is enough — just as a compilation may be 'enough', by dint of being profitable enough, for all its shortcomings, and because it might address what other translations might not. A fitting accompaniment to this part-share *in bono* is the prologue's accompanying refrain, so common to medieval translation culture, that multiple renderings of authoritative, and especially biblical, works can only be a good and illuminating thing: 'Þerfor Grosted seiþ þat it was Goddis wille þat dyuerse men translatiden and þat dyuerse translaciouns be in þe chirche, for where oon seid derkli, oon or mo seiden openli.'[55] Note how there is diversity not just in texts and in matter treated, but also in actors, that is, in translators. Robert Grosseteste's position on repetition and variation, whereby one rendering sheds light where another could not, is commensurate with the repetition and variation one finds in the extractive and adaptational flexibility within and amongst compilations and miscellanies.

Our final example expresses economically a profound and transparent principle concerning figurative language in Scripture. This principle has wider application beyond the Bible: 'Whateuere þing in Goddis word mai not be referrid propirli to honeste of vertues ne to þe treuþe of feiþ þat is figuratif speche.'[56] When the open literal sense does not present an obvious lesson of charity or openly apprehensible doctrine, it is to be interpreted figuratively. In addition, the figurativeness of things and not just of words is explained and exemplified — when 'þe same word or þe same þing in scripture is takun sumtyme in good and sumtyme in yuele'.[57] Here, the reader has a duty to be aware, as far as is reasonable, of how things may, in the tradition of the *distinctio*, have *in bono* and *in malo* meanings, be they leaven or lion. All these examples shift from the literal to the spiritual and/or the symbolic. Heterarchies, too, sustain themselves by finding and manipulating ambiguity and by shifting criteria of evaluation *improprie* without regard to original literal understanding or to order.[58] Commensurately, across Middle English literature, writers such as the *Pearl*-poet, William Langland, Thomas Usk, Julian of Norwich, and countless others move, however seamlessly or self-advertisingly, from the *proprie* to the

---

[55] 'The Prologue to the Wycliffite Bible', ed. by Dove, p. 84, ch. 15. 2929–31.

[56] 'The Prologue to the Wycliffite Bible', ed. by Dove, p. 64, ch. 12. 2200–2202.

[57] 'The Prologue to the Wycliffite Bible', ed. by Dove, p. 65, ch. 12. 2237–39.

[58] Stark, 'Heterarchy', pp. 24–26, 29, 39.

improprie, from the literal to the symbolic, and even mix or merge symbolic and literal representation. A reader of a compilation or a miscellany may in turn move variously amongst symbolic and literal meanings in an ad hoc manner and with different degrees of inventiveness, with or without regard to internal or external textual borders or to the discreteness of textual items. Likewise, a user of a devotional compilation may interconnect words and things in the loose manner of the *distinctio*. This associative move, being lexically or conceptually based, is a dynamic move unbounded by the linearity of language, syntax, *ordinatio*, or textual structure — a somewhat extreme and mobile form of heterarchic signifying and resignifying.

If we look beyond the Middle English Bible, and even beyond the Lausanne project's corpus of devotional compilations, what signs or examples are there in Middle English textual culture of a sensibility of the heterarchic/miscellaneous? It is easy enough to see that Chaucer's *Canterbury Tales* undermines and remakes its *(dis)ordinatio* heterarchically in a radically open-ended manner, through 'co-existing logics and frames of action' — through organized diversity and diverse organization. Its relativism is marked by a remarkable distribution of cognition and perspectives amongst its tellers and amongst its experientially protean generic discourses.[59] One would be going a bit further out on a limb, however, to discern something akin to miscellaneity in the visions of Julian of Norwich.[60] It would, however, be true to say that before she packaged her showings and controlled them within layers of ruminative commentary, thereby according them a measure of partial order of *sentence*, her visions must have seemed somewhat miscellaneous. Perhaps one might say that Julian's work is 'ex-miscellaneous'. It is certainly heterarchic. One might also perhaps say that there is something happenstance, but hardly ex-miscellaneous, in the episodic criss-crossing, centrifugality, and cyclical collectiveness of Margery Kempe's *Book*, at the heart of which are life events looking for a structure and a divine order.[61] Reginald Pecock designed his totalizing scheme of books to replace the *miscellanea* of official Church discourse, and in so doing he gave it hierarchic-cum-heterarchic shape and function.[62] And, finally, the hapless Thomas Usk, in

---

[59] Chaucer, *Canterbury Tales*, ed. by Benson. See Johnson, 'A Sensibility of the Miscellaneous?' for discussion of the miscellaneity of this work.

[60] Julian of Norwich, *The Writings*, ed. by Watson and Jenkins.

[61] Kempe, *The Book*, ed. by Meech and Allen.

[62] Pecock, *The Repressor of Over Much of Blaming the Clergy*, ed. by Babington; Pecock, *Book of Faith*, ed. by Morison; Pecock, *The Donet*, ed. by Hitchcock; Pecock, *The Folewer to the Donet*, ed. by Hitchcock; Pecock, *The Reule of Crysten Religioun*, ed. by Greet.

his *Testament of Love*, assembles, from fragments of authoritative works, a self-shaped miscellaneous work and a miscellaneously formed self, struggling to follow a variety of unresolved principles of order and desire that run anxiously through and across a heterarchically textualized soulscape.[63]

Conclusion

The modern notion of heterarchy and the heterarchic does seem to have some intriguing corollaries with a surprising range of key characteristics of medieval miscellaneous textuality. Middle English biblical paratexts, and in particular the paratext of the Psalter, have some particularly interesting resonances with heterarchies as conceived in recent academe. It is also fruitful, without detriment to its hierarchicality and authority, to consider the Bible, for the purposes of broader literary and cultural history, in terms of the miscellaneous. Some of the most hermeneutically challenging instances and sophisticated conceptions of the miscellaneous in Middle English involve, as we have seen, biblical paratexts. In an age when miscellanies were so central to Middle English textual culture, attitudes and practices typical of the miscellany and of the miscellaneous were not, so it would seem, restricted to miscellanies alone.

The parabiblical passages discussed in this essay make for a substantial array of pointers to a sensibility of the miscellaneous or compilatory. Nor are they irrelevant to a modern understanding of how various medieval composite texts and books could be made to work. As representative of common moves and attitudes working routinely in vernacular biblical hermeneutics and in wider literary tradition, such paratexts may be entertained as part and parcel of a *habitus* of no little pragmatic authority, familiarity, and portability. Their lessons are neither universally present nor all-solving, but they do seem to shed some light, albeit miscellaneously.

In an essay about the recycling of the words of others, it is fitting to close with a quotation, for once not from a medieval text. Carole Crumley's suggestive point, on sophisticated self-organizing structures as typically operating at the very juncture of order and randomness, seems uncannily true also of the fertile adaptability, the intelligence, the functional autonomy, and the robustness of medieval miscellaneous textuality: 'One of the most interesting findings is that self-organizing systems are able to perform the most sophisticated computations when operating at the boundary between order and randomness.'[64]

[63] Usk, *Testament of Love*, ed. by Shawver.
[64] Crumley, 'Heterarchy and the Analysis of Complex Societies', p. 3.

Miscellanies and the miscellaneous were not necessarily the poor relations of highly 'ordinated' works — although commonly they were. Moreover, the paratexts of the Middle English Bible, let alone *The Canterbury Tales* and of a whole host of multi-textual devotional works, give credence to the idea that often, in late medieval England, the most sophisticated and challenging of human articulations of experience and of authority required and enjoyed the miscellaneous as their best possible form.

Works Cited

Manuscripts

Oxford, Bodleian Library [Bodl. Lib.], MS Laud misc. 210
Oxford, Bodleian Library [Bodl. Lib.], MS Laud misc. 656

Primary Sources

Biblia Sacra cum Glossa ordinaria, 6 vols (Venice, 1603), also available on the Lollard Society web site, <http://lollardsociety.org>

Bonaventure, *Breviloquium*, in *Opera Omnia*, vol. v (Quaracchi: Collegium S. Bonaventurae, 1891)

—— , *Breviloquium*, trans. by A. B. Scott, in *Medieval Literary Theory and Criticism, c. 1100–c. 1375: The Commentary-Tradition*, ed. by A. J. Minnis and A. B. Scott, with the assistance of David Wallace (Oxford: Clarendon Press, 1989), pp. 233–38

Chaucer, Geoffrey, *The Canterbury Tales*, in *The Riverside Chaucer*, gen. ed. by Larry D. Benson (Oxford: Oxford University Press, 1988), pp. 3–328

Contemplations of the Dread and Love of God, ed. by Margaret Connolly, Early English Text Society, o.s., 303 (Oxford: Oxford University Press, 1993)

The Holy Bible, Containing the Old and New Testaments, ed. by Josiah Forshall and Frederick Madden, 4 vols (Oxford: Oxford University Press, 1850)

Julian of Norwich, *The Writings of Julian of Norwich: 'A Vision Showed to a Devout Woman' and 'A Revelation of Love'*, ed. by Nicholas Watson and Jacqueline Jenkins, Medieval Women (University Park: Pennsylvania State University Press, 2006)

Kempe, Margery, *The Book of Margery Kempe*, ed. by Sanford Brown Meech and Hope Emily Allen, Early English Text Society, o.s., 212 (Oxford: Oxford University Press, 1940)

Love, Nicholas, The Mirror of the Blessed Life of Jesus Christ: A Full Critical Edition, ed. by Michael G. Sargent (Exeter: University of Exeter Press, 2005)

Nicholas of Lyre, *Literal Postill*, ed. and trans. by A. B. Scott, in *Medieval Literary Theory and Criticism, c. 1100–c. 1375: The Commentary-Tradition*, ed. by A. J. Minnis and

A. B. Scott, with the assistance of David Wallace (Oxford: Clarendon Press, 1989), pp. 266–76

The Orcherd of Syon, ed. by Phyllis Hodgson and Gabriel M. Liegey, Early English Text Society, o.s., 258 (London: Oxford University Press, 1966)

Pecock, Reginald, *Reginald Pecock's Book of Faith*, ed. by J. L. Morison (Glasgow: J. Maclehose and Sons, 1909)

——, *The Donet … with the Poore Mennis Myrrour*, ed. by Elsie Vaughan Hitchcock, Early English Text Society, o.s., 156 (London: Oxford University Press, 1921 [for 1918])

——, *The Folewer to the Donet*, ed. by Elsie Vaughan Hitchcock, Early English Text Society, o.s., 164 (London: Oxford University Press, 1924 [for 1923])

——, *The Repressor of Over Much Blaming of the Clergy by Reginald Pecock, D. D., Sometime Lord Bishop of Chichester*, ed. by Churchill Babington, Rolls Series, 19.1, 19.2, 2 vols (London: Longman, Green, Longman, and Roberts, 1860)

——, *The Reule of Crysten Religioun*, ed. by William Cabell Greet, Early English Text Society, o.s., 171 (London: Oxford University Press, 1927)

'The Prologue to the Wycliffite Bible', in *The Earliest Advocates of the English Bible: The Texts of the Medieval Debate*, ed. by Mary Dove (Exeter: University of Exeter Press, 2010), pp. 3–85

Rolle, Richard, *The Psalter, or Psalms of David and Certain Canticles, with a Translation and Exposition in English by Richard Rolle of Hampole*, ed. by H. R. Bramley (Oxford: Clarendon Press, 1884)

Siege of Jerusalem, ed. by Michael Livingston (Kalamazoo: Medieval Institute Publications, 2004), available at <http://d.lib.rochester.edu/teams/publication/livingston-siege-of-jerusalem>

Usk, Thomas, *Testament of Love*, ed. by Gary W. Shawver, based on the edition of John F. Leyerle, Toronto Medieval Texts and Translations, 13 (Toronto: University of Toronto Press, 2002)

Secondary Works

Bahr, Arthur, 'Miscellaneity and Variance in the Medieval Book', in *The Medieval Manuscript Book: Cultural Approaches*, ed. by Michael Johnston and Michael Van Dussen, Cambridge Studies in Medieval Literature, 94 (Cambridge: Cambridge University Press, 2015), pp. 181–98

Bailey, Kenneth D., 'Monothetic and Polythetic Typologies and their Relation to Conceptualization, Measurement and Scaling', *American Sociological Review*, 31 (1973), 18–33

Boffey, Julia, and John J. Thompson, 'Anthologies and Miscellanies: Production and Choice of Texts', in *Book Production and Publishing in Britain, 1375–1475*, ed. by Jeremy Griffiths and Derek Pearsall, Cambridge Studies in Publishing and Printing History (Cambridge: Cambridge University Press, 1989), pp. 279–315

Bondarenko, Dmitri, 'Homoarchy as a Principle of Sociopolitical Organization: An Introduction', *Anthropos*, 102 (2007), 187–99

Brockwell, Charles W., Jr, *Bishop Reginald Pecock and the Lancastrian Church: Securing the Foundations of Cultural Authority*, Texts and Studies in Religion, 25 (Lewiston: Edwin Mellen Press, 1985)

Campbell, Kirsty, *The Call to Read: Reginald Pecock's Books and Textual Communities* (Notre Dame: University of Notre Dame Press, 2010)

Connolly, Margaret, 'Books for the "helpe of euery persoone þat þenkiþ to be saued": Six Devotional Anthologies from Fifteenth-Century London', *Yearbook of English Studies*, 33 (2003), 170–81

——, 'Compiling the Book', in *The Production of Books in England, 1350–1500*, ed. by Alexandra Gillespie and Daniel Wakelin, Cambridge Studies in Codicology and Palaeography, 14 (Cambridge: Cambridge University Press, 2011), pp. 129–49

Connolly, Margaret, and Raluca Radulescu, eds, *Insular Books: Vernacular Manuscript Miscellanies in Late Medieval Britain*, Proceedings of the British Academy, 201 (Oxford: Oxford University Press for the British Academy, 2015)

Crumley, Carole L., 'Heterarchy and the Analysis of Complex Societies', *Archeological Papers of the American Anthropological Association*, 6 (1995), 1–5

Doležalová, Lucie, and Kimberly Rivers, eds, *Medieval Manuscript Miscellanies: Composition, Authorship, Use* (Krems: Medium Aevum Quotidianum, 2013)

Hanna, Ralph, 'Miscellaneity and Vernacularity: Conditions of Literary Production in Late Medieval England', in *The Whole Book: Cultural Perspectives on the Medieval Miscellany*, ed. by Stephen G. Nichols and Siegfried Wenzel (Ann Arbor: University of Michigan Press, 1996), pp. 37–52

Gillespie, Vincent, '*Doctrina* and *Predicacio*: The Design and Function of Some Pastoral Manuals', in *Looking in Holy Books: Essays on Late Medieval Religious Writing in England*, Brepols Collected Essays in European Culture, 3 (Turnhout: Brepols, 2011), 3–20

——, 'Vernacular Books of Religion', in *Book Production and Publishing in Britain, 1375–1475*, ed. by Jeremy Griffiths and Derek Pearsall, Cambridge Studies in Publishing and Printing History (Cambridge: Cambridge University Press, 1989), pp. 317–44

Green, V. H. H., *Bishop Reginald Pecock: A Study in Ecclesiastical History and Thought* (Cambridge: Cambridge University Press, 1945)

Johnson, Ian, 'Loose Giblets: Encyclopaedic Sensibilities of *Ordinatio* and *Compilatio* in Later Medieval English Literary Culture and the Sad Case of Reginald Pecock', in *Encyclopaedism from Antiquity to the Renaissance*, ed. by Jason König and Greg Woolf (Cambridge: Cambridge University Press, 2013), pp. 325–42

——, 'A Sensibility of the Miscellaneous? The *Canterbury Tales* of Geoffrey Chaucer and the Works of Reginald Pecock', in *Collecting, Organizing and Transmitting Knowledge: Miscellanies in Late Medieval Europe*, ed. by Sabrina Corbellini, Giovanna Murano, and Giacomo Signore, Bibliologia, 49 (Turnhout: Brepols, 2018), pp. 23–38

——, 'Theoretical and Pragmatic Dialogics in and through Nicholas Love's *Mirror of the Blessed Life of Jesus Christ*', *English*, 67 (2018), 97–118

——, 'Vernacular Theology/Theological Vernacular: A Game of Two Halves?', in *After Arundel: Religious Writing in Fifteenth-Century England*, ed. by Vincent Gillespie and Kantik Ghosh, Medieval Church Studies, 21 (Turnhout: Brepols, 2011), pp. 73–88

Lawton, David, 'The Bible', in *The Oxford History of Literary Translation in English*, vol. I: *To 1550*, ed. by Roger Ellis (Oxford: Oxford University Press, 2008), pp. 193–233

Lutton, Robert, '"Love this Name that is IHC": Vernacular Prayers, Hymns and Lyrics to the Holy Name of Jesus in Pre-Reformation England', in *Vernacularity in England and Wales, c. 1300–1550*, ed. by Elisabeth Salter and Helen Wicker, Utrecht Studies in Medieval Literacy, 17 (Turnhout: Brepols, 2011), pp. 119–45

Minnis, A. J., *Medieval Theory of Authorship: Scholastic Literary Attitudes in the Later Middle Ages* (London: Scolar Press, 1984)

Müller, Diana, 'Non-autonomous Texts: On a Fifteenth-Century German "Gregorius" Manuscript (Constance, City Archive, Ms A I 1)', in *Medieval Manuscript Miscellanies: Composition, Authorship, Use*, ed. by Lucie Doležalová and Kimberly Rivers (Krems: Medium Aevum Quotidianum, 2013), pp. 84–101

Murano, Giovanna, '*Zibaldoni* (Commonplace Books)', *Scriptorium*, 67 (2013), 394–406

Nichols, Stephen G., and Siegfried Wenzel, eds, *The Whole Book: Cultural Perspectives on the Medieval Miscellany* (Ann Arbor: University of Michigan Press, 1996)

Parkes, Malcolm B., 'The Influence of the Concepts of *Ordinatio* and *Compilatio* on the Development of the Book', in M. B. Parkes, *Scribes, Scripts and Readers: Studies in the Communication, Presentation and Dissemination of Medieval Texts* (London: Hambledon, 1991), pp. 35–69

Paulmier-Foucart, 'L'*Actor* et les *Auctores*: Vincent de Beauvais et l'écriture du *Speculum maius*', in *Auctor et Auctoritas: Invention et conformisme dans l'ecriture medievale. Actes du colloque de Saint-Quentin-en Yvelines (14–16 juin 1999)*, ed. by Michel Zimmerman, Memoires et documents de l'École des chartes, 59 (Paris: École des chartes, 2001), pp. 145–60

Scase, Wendy, *Reginald Pecock*, Authors of the Middle Ages, 8 (Aldershot: Variorum, 1996)

Stark, David, 'Heterarchy: Exploiting Ambiguity and Organizing Diversity', *Brazilian Journal of Political Economy*, 21 (2001), 21–39

——, *The Sense of Dissonance: Accounts of Worth in Economic Life* (Princeton, NJ: Princeton University Press, 2009)

Sutherland, Annie, *English Psalms in the Middle Ages, 1300–1450* (Oxford: Oxford University Press, 2015)

Online Publications

'Heterarchy', *Wikipedia*, <https://en.wikipedia.org/wiki/Heterarchy> [accessed 18 July 2016]

'Heterarchy', *Oxford English Dictionary*, <http://www.oed.com/view/Entry/86423?redirectedFrom=heterarchy#eid1788958> [accessed 18 July 2016]

A TALKYNG OF THE LOVE OF GOD: THE ART OF COMPILATION AND THE COMPILED SELF

Annie Sutherland

An extraordinary meditation on Christ's nature and Passion, marked by an acute awareness of the crippling effects of sin, *A Talkyng of the Love of God* is extant in full in the late fourteenth-century Vernon manuscript (Bodl. Lib., MS Eng. poet. a. 1) and in part in the roughly contemporary Simeon (BL, MS Additional 22283).[1] Its composition date remains a subject of discussion, and although there can be little doubt that it was written by a man and aimed, originally, at a predominantly male audience, its survival in Vernon suggests that it circulated widely among a variety of readers.[2] It has been long recognized that *A Talkyng* borrows substantially from two thirteenth-century English prayers, *On wel swuðe God Ureisun of God Almihti* (extant in full in BL, MS Cotton Nero A XIV and in part in London, Lambeth Palace Library, MS 487) and *Þe Wohunge of Ure Lauerd* (extant in BL, MS Cotton Titus D XVIII). *A Talkyng* combines these borrowings with material for which no immediate source has been found, though much of it is strongly reminiscent of the writings of Anselm, Archbishop of Canterbury (*c.* 1033–1109). In fact,

---

[1] All references to *A Talkyng* are to *A Talkyng of þe Loue of God*, ed. and trans. by Westra and are given in the format page number(s)/line number(s).

[2] For discussion of date and audience, see Renevey, 'The Choices of the Compiler', p. 233 and pp. 242–43. See also *A Talkyng*, pp. xxx–xxxi.

Annie Sutherland (annie.sutherland@ell.ox.ac.uk) is Associate Professor, University of Oxford, and the Rosemary Woolf Fellow in Old and Middle English, Somerville College.

A Talkyng's Anselmian affiliations are apparent from its very beginning. It is prefaced with an introduction which recommends a mode of reading closely affiliated with that recommended by Anselm in the prologue to his *Liber meditationum et orationum*:

> Hit falleþ for to reden hit. esyliche and softe. So as men may mest in Inward felyng. and deplich þenkyng. sauour fynden. And þat not beo dene. But bi ginnen and leten in what paas. so men seoþ. þat may for þe tyme ȝiuen mest lykynge.[3]

The introduction's concern that *A Talkyng*'s rhythmical prose should be carefully punctuated ('Men schal fyden lihtliche þis tretys in Cadence. After þe bigynnynge. ȝif hit beo riht poynted') is also redolent of Anselm.[4] As G. R. Evans notes, his early manuscript tradition 'shows that he was extremely vigilant about the copying of [his writings], apparently supervising even the punctuation'.[5] The unusually precise and varied repertoire of punctuation in Vernon's *A Talkyng* (including the *punctus*, the *punctus elevatus*, the *punctus interrogativus*, and the *paragraphus*) recalls something of Anselm's fastidious attention to such details.[6]

After its introduction, *A Talkyng* proceeds immediately to an expansive rendering of the *Ureisun* and follows this with 'Anselmian' material for which no single source has been located.[7] The next section is largely indebted to the *Wohunge*, with a prayer to Mary taken from the *Ureisun*.[8] After this, *A Talkyng*

---

[3] *A Talkyng*, 2/3–6. For Anselm's preface, see Anselm of Canterbury, *Opera omnia*, ed. by Schmitt, III, 'Orationes sive Meditationes', p. 3: 'Orationes sive meditationes quae subscriptae sunt, quoniam ad excitandam legentis mentem ad dei amorem vel timorem, seu ad suimet discussionem editae sunt, non sunt legendae in tumultu, sed in quiete, nec cursim et velociter, sed paulatim cum intenta et morosa meditatione. Nec debet intendere lector ut quamlibet earum totam perlegat, sed quantum sentit sibi deo adiuvante valere ad accendendum affectum orandi, vel quantum illum delectat. Nec necesse habet aliquam semper a principio incipere, sed ubi magis illi placuerit'. For a translation, see Anselm of Canterbury, *The Prayers and Meditations*, ed. and trans. by Ward, p. 159: 'The purpose of the prayers and meditations that follow is to stir up the mind of the reader to the love or fear of God, or to self-examination. They are not to be read in a turmoil, but quietly, not skimmed or hurried through, but taken a little at a time, with deep and thoughtful meditation. The reader should not trouble about reading the whole of any of them, but only as much as, by God's help, he finds useful in stirring up his spirit to pray or as much as he likes. Nor is it necessary for him always to begin at the beginning, but wherever he pleases'.

[4] *A Talkyng*, 2/16–17.

[5] See Evans, 'Anselm's Life, Works and Immediate Influence', p. 11.

[6] For discussion of *A Talkyng*'s punctuation, see Morgan, 'A Treatise in Cadence'.

[7] *A Talkyng*, 2/21–10/14 and 10/15–26/13.

[8] *A Talkyng*, 26/14–62/24; prayer at 56/1–28.

concludes with an apparently independent ending.⁹ At no point in the treatise does the *Talkyng* author (hereafter referred to as compiler in recognition of the fact that his text combines borrowed elements with apparently original prose) make any reference to the fact that what he is producing is largely a compilation of antecedent texts, interwoven with some new material. Although its status as compilation opens a tantalizing window onto the circulation of thirteenth-century anchoritic literature among fourteenth-century readers, speculation in this area cannot form part of this chapter. I will focus instead on what *A Talkyng*'s borrowings might tell us about the art of compilation, looking first at the *Ureisun* and the *Wohunge* and then at the apparent debt to Anselm.

Directly after the aforementioned introduction, the *Talkyng* compiler turns to the *Ureisun*, reprising its opening invocation with considerable accuracy. While the thirteenth-century prayer begins 'Iesu soð god <soð> godes sune. Iesu soð god. soð mon. & soð meidenes bern. Iesu min holi luue. Mi sikere spetnesse. Iesu min heorte. mine soule hele'¹⁰ (Jesus true God, <true> God's son. Jesus true God, true man, and true son of a virgin. Jesus my holy love. My sure sweetness. Jesus my heart, health of my soul),¹¹ in *A Talkyng*, we find 'Ihesu soþ God. Godes sone. Ihesu. soþ God.' soþ mon. Mon Maydenes child.» Ihesu myn holy loue. Mi siker swetnesse. ¶ Ihesu myn herte. my sele. my soule hele'.¹²

---

⁹ *A Talkyng*, 62/24–69/18.

¹⁰ *Ureisun*, 5/1–4. All references to the *Ureisun* and the *Wohunge* are to *Þe Wohunge of Ure Lauerd*, ed. by Thompson and are given in the format page number(s)/line number(s). The bracketed <soð> is reproduced from Thompson's edition and indicates an interlinear addition made by the original Nero scribe. Nero and Titus's abbreviations, retained by Thompson, have been silently expanded throughout.

¹¹ All translations of the *Ureisun* and the *Wohunge* in this chapter are my own.

¹² *A Talkyng*, 2/21–23. The Lambeth *Ureisun* begins: 'Iesu soð god. godes sune. Iesu soð god. soð mon. Mon Meidene bern. Iesu min hali loue min sikere spetnesse. Iesu min heorte. Misel. misaule hele' (1/1–3) (Jesus, true God. God's son. Jesus true God. True man. Man, son of a virgin. Jesus my holy love, my sure sweetness. Jesus my heart. My joy. Health of my soul). We might note that while the Lambeth *Ureisun* and *A Talkyng* address Christ as 'Mon Meidene bern / Mon Maydenes child', the Nero *Ureisun* calls him 'soð meidenes bern'. And both Lambeth and the *Talkyng* refer to Christ as 'Misel/my sele', a descriptor lacking in Nero. Although the *Talkyng* compiler cannot have been directly reliant on Lambeth's incomplete *Ureisun*, these are not the only occasions on which he seems to be drawing on a version of the earlier text which has more lexical similarities with Lambeth than it does with Nero. For example, where the Nero *Ureisun* addresses Christ as 'liuiinde louerd' (5/20) (living lord), Lambeth calls him 'louende louerd' (1/17) (loving lord), as does *A Talkyng* ('louynde lord', 4/17). And where the speaker of the Nero *Ureisun* tells us 'ich wot' (5/26) (I know) that one cannot love both the earthly and spiritual realms, the Lambeth speaker claims to know this 'wel' (1/22), as does *A Talkyng* ('wel ichot', 4/23).

However, the fourteenth-century compiler immediately follows this invocation with a passage in which he richly embellishes the rhetoric of the earlier prayer. The *Ureisun* reads:

> Swete iesu mi leof. mi lif. mi leome. min healewi. min huni ter. þu ert al þet ich hopie. Iesu mi weole. mi wunne. mi bliðe breostes blisse. Iesu teke þet þu ert so softe. & so swete. ȝet þerto þu ert so leoflich. so louelich. & so lufsum. þet te engles euer biholdeð þe. ne ne beoð heo neuer ful. forto logen on þe.[13]

> [Sweet Jesus my love, my life, my light, my balm, my honey-drop, you are all that I hope for. Jesus my happiness, my joy, happy bliss of my breast. As well as that, Jesus, you are so soft and so sweet. Still, in addition, you are so dear, so lovely and so loveable that the angels always behold you and are never satisfied with looking on you.]

This becomes in *A Talkyng*:

> [S]wete Ihesu. *Ihesu.' deore Ihesu. Ihesu.' Almihti Ihesu. Ihesu mi lord*. my leof. my lyf. *myn holy wey*. Myn hony ter. *Ihesu.' al weldinde Ihesu. Ihesu* þou art al þat I.hope. ¶ *Ihesu mi makere. þat me madest of nouȝt. And al þat is in heuene. and in eorþe.* ¶ *Ihesu my Buggere. þou bouȝtest me so deore. wiþ þi stronge passion. wiþ þi precious blod and wiþ þi pyneful deþ on Roode.* ¶ *Ihesu my saueour. þat me schalt sauen. þorw þi muchel Merci. & þi muchele miȝt* Ihesu mi weole. & *al* my wynne.' *Ihesu þat al my blisse is inne.* ¶ Ihesu al so. þat þou art. so *feir* and so swete. ȝit art þou so louelich. Louelich and louesum. þat þe *holy* Angeles. þat euere þi bi holden.' ben neuere folle. to loken on *þi face*.[14]

The additions here are characteristic of the compiler's approach to the *Ureisun* throughout this section of *A Talkyng*. His goal is, in part, the amplification of the speaker's affective engagement with Christ. So, Jesus is not only 'swete'; he is also 'deore' and 'Almihti'. And he is no longer simply 'mi wunne', but has become 'al my wynne.' Ihesu þat al my blisse is inne'. Here, the rhyme of 'wynne/inne', its effect intensified by the positioning of the *punctus elevatus*, requiring a pause after 'wynne', is also characteristic of the compiler's own markedly rhythmical prose. And the outlining of Christ's past and future redemptive achievements (he 'made [...] bouȝt' and 'schalt sauen' the speaker) is typical of *A Talkyng*'s tendency to sharpen the doctrinal implications of the *Ureisun*'s affective proclamations.[15]

---

[13] *Ureisun*, 5/4–9.

[14] *A Talkyng*, 3/23–4/9. Italics are mine and are used throughout this chapter to indicate *A Talkyng*'s additions to its sources.

[15] For further evidence of the *Talkyng* compiler's predilection for supplementing the

This tendency to sharpen doctrinal implications is also perceptible in the compiler's response to the *Ureisun*'s one quotation from the Bible (Galatians 2. 20). In the earlier text, we read:

> [M]akien me liuien to þe ðet ich muwe seggen wið seinte powel ðet seið. Ich liuiee nout ich.' auh crist liueð in me. ðet is to seggen. ich liuie nout ine liue þet ich liuede . auh crist liueð in me. þuruh his wuniinde grace.' ðet a cwikeð me. wel was he ibeoren þet mei iesu þis baldeliche seggen to þe.[16]
>
> [Make me live to you so that I might speak with St. Paul who said, 'I live, not I, but Christ lives in me'. That is to say, 'I live, not in the life that I lived, but Christ lives in me through his dwelling grace that always enlivens me'. Blessed was he, Jesus, who might boldly say this to you'.]

In *A Talkyng*, however, the vernacular translation of Paul's words has been prefaced by a quotation from the Vulgate (Galatians 2.20):

> [M]ake me lyuen in þe *liuinde lord. þat I. be to þe world ded. and a lyue to þe.* so þat I. mai *verrreyliche.* sigge wiþ *þe apostle.* Paulus. *viuo ego. iam non ego. viuit autem in me Christus.* I. liue not Ich. but crist lyueþ in me. *þat is poules wordes.*

But more than this, the gloss has been expanded to emphasize that Christ has saved the speaker from the death that results from sin:

> And þus for to siggen. In liue not in lyue þat I. liuede .' but crist liueþ in me þorw wonyinde grace. Þat *from deþ of sunne. me torneþ and* quikneþ *to lyf þat is blisful. of gostliche hele. From alle worldliche loue. & fleschliche lustes. al one forto lyuen. in likyng of crist.*[17]

This is followed by:

> ¶ *A. deore lord þin ore.* wel weore him bi gon. *þat feled in his soule.* Þat *seli word* to siggen. *To goderhele weore he boren. & to muche blisse .' for eueri grome were him gome. & eueri wo. winne.*[18]

Ureisun with basic doctrinal truths, see the earlier text's 'a.' iesu louerd. þi grið. hwi habbe ich eni licunge. in oðer þinge.' þeni þe' (6/44–46) (A, Jesus Lord, your protection. Why do I take any pleasure in anything other than in you). In *A Talkyng*, this becomes 'A. Ihesu þin ore.whi haue I.likyng in oþer þing þen in þe. *þat bou3test me so deore*' (6/5–6).

[16] *Ureisun*, 8/121–27.

[17] For further evidence of the compiler's pronounced awareness of sin and its effects, note the alteration made to the *Ureisun*'s plea that Christ should 'brihtte mine soule þet is suti' (5/16–17) (brighten my soul that is filthy). In *A Talkyng*, this becomes: 'Graunte þat þi brihtnesse clanse my soule.' þat is vnseliche. *wiþ sunne foule I. fuiled*.' (4/13–14).

[18] *A Talkyng*, 10/8–18.

It is worth noting that the neat, alliterating transformations of 'grome' to 'gome' and 'wo' to 'winne' are original to *A Talkyng* and again emphasize that the later treatise is a consciously crafted elaboration on the earlier material.

A Talkyng is also marked by a particular anxiety to distinguish between the realms of the physical and the spiritual. So, while the *Ureisun*'s speaker laments that she does not 'behold […] hu [Christ] streihtest þe for me on þe rode' (behold […] how Christ stretches himself out for me on the cross), *A Talkyng* emphasizes that such a sight would be witnessed only 'wiþ eȝe of myn herte'.[19] And while the *Ureisun* recognizes that Christ's outspread arms on the cross have the 'gostliche' (spiritual) significance of a mother embracing her child, *A Talkyng* is more thoroughgoing in its negotiation of the distinction between physical action and spiritual meaning.[20] Its speaker notes that Christ spread his arms 'bodiliche on Roode' and that this was a 'toknyng' of his grace which 'open is and redi to alle þat in synne beoþ gostliche storuen'.[21] Although not exclusively characteristic of fourteenth-century devotional literature, such policing of the boundaries between the physical and spiritual is a recurrent concern for writers such as Walter Hilton and the *Cloud* author.[22] That it features in *A Talkyng* might provide support for those who read the treatise as a fourteenth-century compilation of thirteenth-century material, rather than as itself originally dateable to the 1200s.[23] The compiler's characterization of the means by which we engage with Christ's Passion as 'holy meditacion' might also be seen as indicative of a fourteenth-century tendency to schematize the life of prayer.[24]

There are some similarities between the compiler's approach to the *Ureisun* and his dealings with the *Wohunge*. With the latter, as with the former, he is keen to intensify the speaker's affective engagement with Christ. So, for example, the *Wohunge*'s introductory invocation reads:

---

[19] *Ureisun*, 6/47–48, and *A Talkyng*, 6/7. Renevey, 'The Choices of the Compiler', pp. 236–38, also comments on this.

[20] *Ureisun*, 6/52.

[21] *A Talkyng*, 6/13–15.

[22] For discussion of the characteristics of fourteenth-century spirituality in England, see Catto, '1349–1412: Culture and History' and Ellis and Fanous, '1349–1412: Texts'.

[23] For further evidence of the compiler's anxiety to distinguish between physical and spiritual sight, note the *Wohunge* speaker's claim that she sees the crucified Christ: 'forhwen þat iseo o þe þat henges me biside' (36/599–600) (for when I look on you who hangs beside me). At the same moment in *A Talkyng*, the compiler is rather more circumspect: 'For whon I. *in my soule. wiþ al hol muynde.* seo þe *so reuply.* hongen on Rode' (60/8–9).

[24] *A Talkyng*, 6/26–27. See Ellis and Fanous, '1349–1412: Texts'.

Iesu swete Iesu. mi druð. mi derling. mi drihtin. mi healend mi huniter. mi haliwei. Swetter is munegunge of þe þen mildeu o muðe. Hwa ne mei luue þi luueli leor? Hwat herte is swa hard þat ne mei to melte iþe munegunge of þe?[25]

[Jesus, sweet Jesus, my dearest, my darling, my lord, my saviour, my honey-drop, my balm. Sweeter is the memory of you than honey in the mouth. Who may not love your lovely face? What heart is so hard that it may not melt in the memory of you?]

This is considerably expanded in *A Talkyng*:

Ihesu *my derworþe lord. Ihesu myn oune Fader.* Swete Ihesu *heuene kyng.* Mi druri my derling. *Mi deoring Mi louyng. Myn hony brid. My sweting.* Myn hele. & myn hony ter. *Min hony lyf.* Min halewy. Swettore art þou. þen hony *or Milk* in Mouþe.» *Meode Meþ or piȝement.* maad wiþ spices swete. Or eny lykinde licour.' þat ouȝwher may be founden.» Ho ne may loue lord.' þi leoue lofsom leore.» what herte is so ouer hard. þat ne may to melte in þe monyg of þe.' *loueliche lord*.[26]

Without fundamentally altering the original, the compiler has amplified its already extravagant praise of 'Iesu', imitating its dense alliteration with its own alliterative additions. Such amplification can also be heard in *A Talkyng*'s rewording of the response to the sight of Christ journeying towards Calvary. While the *Wohunge* reads 'A hwat schal i nu don? Nu min herte mai to breke. min ehne flowen al o water' (A, what shall I do now? Now may my heart break. My eyes flow with many tears),[27] in the later text, we find 'A *derworþe lord.* what schal I. nou don.» *Nou mai I liue no more. for serwe. and forsore. now my dere lemmon. schal vnderfonge deþ.»* Nou mai I Murne strongly. nou mai I. wepe bitterli. nou mai I. syke sore.' & serwen euer more'.[28] The repeated pattern of verb followed by adverb ('murne strongly'; 'wepe bitterly'; 'syke sore'), culminating in the final '& serwen euer more', functions for the reader as a prompt to performance. The compiler is modelling an appropriate response to Christ's suffering, with the aforementioned punctuation (here including the *punctus*, the *punctus elevatus*, and the *punctus interrogativus*) working to encourage measured, ruminative enunciation. That the response concludes with the pairing of 'sore/more', their effect intensified by the *punctus elevatus* after 'sore', emphasizes the scripted nature of the utterance and recalls the rhyming additions that also feature in the compiler's reworking of the *Ureisun*.

[25] *Wohunge*, 20/1–5.
[26] *A Talkyng*, 26/14–21.
[27] *Wohunge*, 33/488–90.
[28] *A Talkyng*, 48/23–26.

A Talkyng's status as a carefully crafted elaboration of earlier material is also demonstrated by the changes that the compiler makes to the refrain which punctuates the narrative of the *Wohunge*. In the original text, the refrain reads 'A iesu mi swete iesu leue þat te luue of þe beo almi likinge' (A Jesus, my sweet Jesus, grant that the love of you might be all my delight), but in *A Talkyng*, this has become (with occasional variations):

> ¶ A swete Ihesu gode leof. *let me beo þi seruaunt. And lere me for to loue þe. louynde lord. þat onliche* þe loue of þe. be euer al my likyng. *Mi ȝeornyng Mi longyng. Mi þouȝt and al mi worching Amen.*¶[29]

Not only does the speaker supplement 'likyng' with the fourfold 'ȝeornyng [...] longyng [...] þouȝt and [...] worching', but he also asks Christ to 'lere' (teach) him 'for to loue þe'. The idea that one can 'learn' to love Christ and that this involves 'worch' is a striking addition to the original, emphasizing that the individual affect cannot be cultivated without a disciplined mind and will. Further, the desire to become Christ's 'seruaunt', expressed throughout *A Talkyng* in a series of additions to both the *Ureisun* and the *Wohunge*, hints at a decorous distance between the divine and the human in keeping with the compilation's previously noted emphasis on the alienating effects of sin.

Such similarities in approach to the *Ureisun* and the *Wohunge* suggest strongly that what we have in *A Talkyng* (including the 'Anselmian' middle section and the apparently original ending, both to be discussed below) is the work of one individual. Nonetheless, there are some notable ways in which the treatment of the *Wohunge* differs from that of the *Ureisun*. Broadly speaking, the compiler is less loyal to the letter of the *Wohunge*; not only is his response more ruminative and expansive, but he also appears to hold the original at arm's length, engaging with it as critically as he does deferentially.[30] Most strikingly, on occasion he handles the *Wohunge* in the manner of a commentator or translator, whose job it is to gloss obscurities of meaning in the original. So, for example, in its

---

[29] *Wohunge*, 21/55–57, and *A Talkyng*, 28/15–18.

[30] For evidence of the compiler's ruminative response to both the *Ureisun* and the *Wohunge*, see his treatment of the latter's address to Christ, 'Poure þu born was of þe meiden þi moder' (*Wohunge*, 28/321–22) (Poor, you were born of the virgin, your mother). In *A Talkyng*, this has become 'Pore were þou *furst* boren. of þi *leue* mooder.' *þat mayden is and moder. of þe þat art hire fader*' (42/2–3). Such delight in the profoundly paradoxical relationship between Mary and Christ is not, however, original to *A Talkyng*. Rather, it would seem to have been inspired by an address to Mary found in the *Ureisun*: 'Meiden. & moder. Meiden. hwas. moder dohtor þu ert his þet wroht & welt. al þet ischeapen is' (9/138–40) (Virgin. And mother. Virgin who is mother and daughter of he who created and rules all that is made). This *Ureisun* address to Mary is also recalled later in *A Talkyng* (56/10–12).

account of Christ's nativity, the *Wohunge* tells us that he was born 'in a waheles hus imiddes þe strete' (in a wall-less house in the middle of the street).[31] However, with the glossing 'þat was' so characteristic of the medieval commentator/translator (in practice, there was considerable overlap between the two roles), the *Talkyng* compiler offers the following explanation: 'in a wouhless hous. amidde þe street.' *þat was a symple refuit. in so cold a tyme*'.[32] And again, while the *Wohunge* tells us that Christ was 'caldeliche dennet in a beastes cribbe' (coldly lodged in an animal's crib), the later text is careful to explain the spiritual significance of this physical location:

> Þer weore þou [...] coldliche i leyd. in a beestes crubbe.' *so woldest þou be conuersaunt. and comuyn wiþ bestes. To maken vs caytyues. þat beestlich liuen here.' wiþ þi self conuersaunt in heuene riche blisse.*[33]

Providing further evidence that this compiler was practised in the techniques of the commentator/translator is his tendency to replace single words in the original text with 'synonymous variants'.[34] This is a habit at its most obvious in the compiler's reproduction of the list of Christ's desirable attributes. For example, the *Wohunge* speaker's 'And hwa is frerre þen þu?' (And who is more generous than you?), addressed to Christ, becomes '[a]nd ho is freore þen þou. *or largore of ʒifte*'.[35] Similarly, the earlier text's reflection on Christ's gift of his own self and blood, '[d]erre druri ne ʒef neauer na lefmon to oðer' (a more precious gift was never given by one lover to another), is expanded to become '[s]o derworþe dreweri *ne so deore ʒifte.*' ne ʒaf neuer *in þis world*. lemmon to oþer'.[36] And in its response to the *Wohunge*'s remark that a suitor's 'largesce is lutel wurð þer wisdom wontes' (generosity is worth little where wisdom is lacking), *A Talkyng* supplies variants for both 'lutel wurð' and 'wisdom': 'But largesse is luyte worþ. *And luyte loue worþi. Þat riht rulynde wit. and* wisdam wonteþ'.[37] Here, we are provided with a glimpse of the compiler's artistry in the

---

[31] *Wohunge*, 29/326–27.

[32] *A Talkyng*, 42/5–6.

[33] *Wohunge*, 29/328–29, and *A Talkyng*, 42/6–10.

[34] For discussion of the use of synonymous variants in biblical translation, see Sutherland, *English Psalms in the Middle Ages*, p. 110. See also Dove, *The First English Bible*, p. 154.

[35] *Wohunge*, 22/81–82, and *A Talkyng*, 32/2–3.

[36] *Wohunge*, 22/96–98, and *A Talkyng*, 32/12–15.

[37] *Wohunge*, 23/107–09, and *A Talkyng*, 32/23–24. For an example of threefold variation on the original in *A Talkyng*, note that the *Wohunge*'s question (addressed to Christ) 'And is ani swa hardi swa ar tu?' (23/122–23) (And is anyone as brave as you are?) becomes 'And is eny so

chiastic arrangement of the variants (original (luyte worþ) — variant (luyt loue worþi) — variant (riht rulynde wit) — original (wisdam)). The resulting phrase visually enacts the shaping role played by the original; the compiler's elaborations remain bordered and contained by the wording of the source.

Something of the difference in approach to the *Ureisun* and the *Wohunge* can also be observed in the compiler's treatment of the biblical quotations and allusions found in the earlier texts. We have already seen that in his response to the *Ureisun*, he reproduces the vernacular translation of Galatians 2. 20, supplementing it with the Vulgate original. He sometimes follows this model in his approach to the rather more extensive biblical material in the *Wohunge*. For example, Psalm 24. 1 (23. 1), quoted in English in the *Wohunge*, 'for as te hali prophete dauid cwiddes. drihtines is te eorðe. & al þat hit fulles werld & al þat trin wuneð' (For as the holy prophet David says, the earth is the Lord's and all that fills it, the world and all that dwells therein),[38] is given in Latin in *A Talkyng*: 'For as þe prophete seiþ.' Dauid *in his psalme. Domini est terra & plenitudo eius.»* Þin is þe eorþe.' and al þat þer in woneþ'.[39] Similarly, in recounting Christ's agony in the garden of Gethsemane, the *Wohunge* provides a vernacular rendition of Luke 22. 44 ('as. seint luk seið i þe god spel. þu was i swa strong a swing þat te swat as blodes dropes eorn dune to þe eorðe'; As Saint Luke said in the gospel, you were in such severe hardship that the sweat ran down to the earth like drops of blood).[40] *A Talkyng*, however, prefaces its translation with the Vulgate original ('Factus est sudor eius sicut gutte sanguinis in terram decurrens').[41]

But the compiler does not only supplement vernacular translations of the Bible with their Vulgate original. He seems also to reflect on the implications and associations of the earlier treatise, supplementing it with biblical citations when needed. For example, while the *Wohunge* notes that Mary, at the foot of the cross, was 'wið inne martird iþi moderliche herte' (martyred within in your motherly heart), at the same moment the *Talkyng* compiler recalls Simeon's prophecy over Mary (Luke 2. 35), stating that: 'þe chaungyng of his cheere. þin herte stongen þorw out þi deþ als hit weore. Animam tuam pertransyuit

---

hardi. *so bold. and so douhti*. as þou art *my leue lyf founden in a say*' (34/8–10). The compiler does not always replace single words with synonymous variants, however. For example, where the *Wohunge* refers to the devil who is 'lest laðeliche *& grureful*' (23/128) (least loathsome and horrible), *A Talkyng* describes him as simply 'lest lodlich' (34/12).

[38] *Wohunge*, 21/63–22/67.

[39] *A Talkyng*, 30/20–22.

[40] *Wohunge*, 32/454–58.

[41] *A Talkyng*, 46/20–21.

gladius'.⁴² Unlike the *Ureisun*, in which all biblical citations are in English, the *Wohunge* contains two quotations from the Vulgate. Given his predilection for Latin material, we might expect the *Talkyng* compiler to reproduce both these Latin quotations. This is certainly the case with Psalm 69. 7 (68. 8); in both the *Wohunge* and *A Talkyng*, the crucified Christ addresses the reader with the Psalmist's words ('Because for thy sake I have borne reproach; shame hath covered my face'), although the wording of the Latin differs slightly between the two.⁴³ But Psalm 116. 12 (115. 3) ('What shall I render to the Lord, for all the things he hath rendered unto me?') is also quoted in Latin in the *Wohunge*:

> Bote nu mai i seggen wið þe salmewrihte. *Quid retribuam domino pro omnibus quæ retribuit mihi.* Lauerd hwat mai i ȝelde þe for al þat tu haues ȝiuen me. Hwat mai þole for þe for al þat tu þoledes for me?⁴⁴

> [But now may I speak with the Psalmist: *Quid retribuam domino pro omnibus quae retribuit mihi*. Lord, what can I give in return for all that you have given to me? What can I suffer for all that you have suffered for me?]

However, in *A Talkyng* it is paraphrased in the vernacular, with no reference to its biblical origin:

> what may I þenke.» what may I speke.» what may I.worþly don.' for þe loue of þe.» what may I ȝelde þe.» what may I. þole for ȝe aȝeyn. þat þou hast þoled for me.⁴⁵

This inconsistency of approach to the *Wohunge*'s biblical references is also witnessed elsewhere. For example, in its reproduction of the *Wohunge*'s citation of Colossians 2. 3 ('Inwið þe mi leue lif is hord of alle wisedom hid as te bok witnesses'; Within you my dear life is hidden the treasure of all wisdom, as the book bears witness), *A Talkyng* makes no reference to 'te bok' as the source of the words ('In wiþ þe my leue lyf. is welle of alle wisdam').⁴⁶ And in its enu-

---

⁴² *Wohunge*, 35/556–58, and *A Talkyng*, 54/22–23. This same quotation appears earlier in *A Talkyng*, in the 'Anselmian' middle section (20/23–25).

⁴³ The *Wohunge* reads '[s]cito quoniam propter te sustinui opprobrium operuit confusio faciem meam' (31/403–05), while *A Talkyng* has '[s]cito quoniam proper te mortificamur tota die. obprobium. operuit confusio faciem meam' (44/21–23). This may well suggest that the compiler was working from, or was familiar with, a different version of the Latin Bible.

⁴⁴ *Wohunge*, 35/580–36/585.

⁴⁵ *A Talkyng*, 58/28–30.

⁴⁶ *Wohunge*, 23/115–17, and *A Talkyng*, 32/30. Note also that while the *Wohunge* tells us that crowds called out for Christ to be crucified 'as i þe godspel is writen' (30/382) (as is written in the gospel), *A Talkyng* makes no reference to the gospel at the same point.

meration of Christ's loveworthy qualities, *A Talkyng* does not reproduce the *Wohunge*'s quotation from Psalm 24. 8 (23. 8) ('for þi of þe mi lefmon was soðliche quiddet. Drihti[n] is mahti strong & kene ifihte'; Therefore of you, my lover, it was truly said: The Lord is mighty, strong, and brave in battle).[47]

The compiler does, however, introduce some biblical references of his own. For example, while the *Wohunge*'s likening of Christ to a lamb who 'neauer neh opnedes [his] muð to grucchen' (did not ever open his mouth to complain) is clearly inspired by Isaiah 53. 7, it is only in *A Talkyng* that the Old Testament link is made explicit ('for þi muchele Mekenesse. as witnesseþ holi writ.' to lomb were þou euenet').[48] And *A Talkyng*'s account of the aftermath of Christ's death, not borrowed from the *Wohunge*, seems to invoke the authority of Matthew 27. 51–53:

> A.' Ihesu.' nou deskeþ þe sonne. Nou þe eorþe trembleþ.' and þe stones bersten. Nou þe temple cloueþ. for serwe of my lemon. Nou risen vp þe ded. In witnesse of þi godhede.' & walken in Ierusalem. *as writen was bi foren*.[49]

Much of the time, *A Talkyng*'s additions are in keeping with the tone of the *Wohunge*. On occasion, however, the compiler's inventive interaction with his source produces a text so extravagantly elaborated as to lose something of the original's subtle restraint. For example, while the *Wohunge*'s speaker tells us that her enemies were 'grennende for gladschipe euchan toward oðer as wode wulues þat fainen of hare praie' (smiling for gladness, each one towards the other, like mad wolves eager for their prey), in *A Talkyng* this becomes:

> [They] *maden me mony a res*. wiþ grennynde beere. *ful grimme and ful grisly. as wolues as hit weore*. wenden in heore wyse. wiþ sum kunnes ginne.' wiþ a poynt of chekmat. comen me wiþ inne.[50]

The 'wode wulues' of the *Wohunge* are now the rather incongruous chess-playing wolves of *A Talkyng*. The neat rhyme of 'ginne/inne', once again emphasized by the positioning of the *punctus elevatus*, is aurally pleasing, but it is difficult not to feel that aesthetic considerations have overwhelmed a concern for logic at this point. This is a sense compounded by the compiler's elaboration of the *Wohunge* speaker's account of her near-defeat at the hands of her enemies, saved only by Christ: 'Bot neh hefde i fulliche buhed til alle mine þre fan. þu com me to helpe. feng to fihte for me' (But when I had almost completely yielded to all

---

[47] *Wohunge*, 24/148–51.
[48] *Wohunge*, 25/202–04, and *A Talkyng*, 36/14–15.
[49] *A Talkyng*, 52/14–18.
[50] *Wohunge*, 28/288–91, and *A Talkyng*, 38/1–4.

my three enemies, you came to help me, undertook to fight for me).[51] In the *Talkyng*, this imagery of the spiritual life as battle is juxtaposed with imagery of the spiritual life as sea voyage:

> Þer art þou redilich. and stondest bi sydes.' wiþ alle þat beþ so bi set. and troubled in care. Or in anguisse. or wandreþ wawes.' of þis worldly séé. seilen and faren.» Þi self steerest þe schip. & ledest to þe hauene. of euer lastynde pes. þer alle weoles aren.' and art in vch a such fiht. in þe vauwarde.' & makest scheld of þi self. þi lemmon to sparen.[52]

While it is entirely conventional in homiletic prose, such a seafaring metaphor, in which Christ assumes the role of pilot, jostles very awkwardly with the metaphor of Christ as 'scheld'. Once again, an abundance of images threatens the logical coherence of the meditation.[53]

More often, however, the compiler's additions to the *Wohunge* are coherent developments of theme and image, marked by restraint rather than excess.[54] Even if they take *A Talkyng* in directions not envisaged by the *Wohunge* author, they can be read as legitimate repurposings of earlier material for a later, different audience. This is most obvious in the compiler's adaptation of the *Wohunge* speaker's proclamation:

> Mi bodi henge wið þi bodi neiled o rode. sperred querfaste wið inne fowr wahes & henge i wile wið þe and neauer mare of mi rode cume til þat i deie. For þenne schal i lepen fra rode in to reste. fra wa to wele & to eche blisse. A. iesu swa swet hit is wið þe to henge.[55]

> [May my body hang with your body, nailed on the cross, enclosed on all sides within four walls. And I will hang with you and never more come down from my cross until I die. For then shall I leap from the cross into rest, from woe into happiness and into endless bliss. A Jesus, it is so sweet to hang with you.]

In his response to this extraordinarily vivid sequence, *A Talkyng*'s compiler dispenses with the 'fowr wahes' (presumably of the anchoritic cell) of the *Wohunge* and

---

[51] *Wohunge*, 28/303–06.

[52] *A Talkyng*, 40/3–6.

[53] In *A Talkyng*, the *Wohunge*'s 'bur' (35/573) (bower) or 'chaumbre' (35/574–5) (chamber) into which Christ has brought the speaker has become a 'cage' (66/23) in which he, as Christ's 'owne brid' (58/12), 'sing[s] swetely' (66/23). The disturbingly claustrophobic, not to mention voyeuristic, associations of the cage again sit rather uncomfortably with the intimate privacy envisaged in the original *Wohunge*.

[54] Note, however, the increased gore in *A Talkyng*'s descriptions of the crucified Christ (47/32–48/18).

[55] *Wohunge*, 36/590–99.

carefully distinguishes between 'my roode', which he equates with 'þis holy ordre', and 'þin harde roode' on which Christ alone hangs.⁵⁶ The earlier speaker's 'henge i wil wið þe' is replaced by the rather more decorous 'here wol I. dwellen. wiþ þe my swete lemmon'.⁵⁷ And the *Wohunge*'s extravagant imagined leap 'fra rode in to reste' becomes the resolutely mundane 'þen wol I. beo grauen heer vnder þe eorþe'; only after this burial will he rise 'aȝeynes þe. and wenden þenne al hom wiþ þe':

> But ȝit such as (my 'wrecche bodi') is. I ȝiue it *enterlyche*. to þi seruise.' nayled *and spred faste* in *my* roode. *in þis holy ordre*. as þou were nayled for me. *in þin harde roode*. ¶ And here wol I. dwellen. *wiþ þe my swete lemmon*.' and neuer more wol I. of my Roode comen. neuer whil þat I lyue.' *for þe loue of þe.»* þen wol I. beo grauen heer vnder þe eorþe. as þou weore grauen for me. And on domes day. wol I. risen aȝeynes þe. and wenden þenne al hom wiþ þe.⁵⁸

As the preceding discussion has demonstrated, tracing the compiler's interactions with the *Ureisun* and the *Wohunge* is relatively straightforward. Even if we cannot know precisely the form in which he encountered these thirteenth-century texts, comparative analysis of the versions that we have gives us a keen sense of his priorities and preoccupations.

Considerations of the 'Anselmian' middle section are rather more challenging. Westra was of the opinion that it drew on an 'originally independent treatise' which was 'probably [...] inserted in full'.⁵⁹ Yet while it is the only part of the treatise to name an external *auctor* ('Anselmus'), no single source has been located, so straightforward comparative analysis is not possible.⁶⁰ There is, in fact, no way of knowing whether the compiler is drawing on some unidentified work, or whether (inspired by Anselm) he is writing original meditative prose. However, leaving aside this question (which we cannot hope to answer here), it is worth pausing over the section's affiliations with Anselm. Although Westra's sense was that its Anselmian links were of a loosely ruminative nature, the existence of some striking verbal parallels in fact suggests a rather closer relationship. For example, of the aforementioned invocation of Anselm, 'Anselmus. A.' serwe and sikyng. criȝing. & gronyng. wher be ye ryue.' ȝif ȝe here faylen.¶ Wher be ȝe feruent.' ȝif ȝe heere slaken',⁶¹ Westra states that

---

[56] *A Talkyng*, 58/35–37.
[57] *A Talkyng*, 58/37.
[58] *A Talkyng*, 58/34–60/4.
[59] *A Talkyng*, p. xx.
[60] *A Talkyng*, 20/5.
[61] *A Talkyng*, 20/5–6.

there is no 'direct borrowing'.[62] But close comparative reading of Anselm indicates that *A Talkyng* is here actually reproducing a vivid moment in his *Oratio ad Sanctum Iohannem Evangelistam hominis timentis damnari*: 'Maerores, dolores, gemitus, rugitus: ubi adestis, si hic deestis? Ubi fervetis, si hic tepetis?' ('Grief, sorrow, groans, sighs, where are you present if here you are absent? Where are you fervent if here you are tepid?').[63] And what is most striking about this vernacular rendition of Anselm is the way in which it closely imitates the careful rhetorical patterning of the Latin. In both, a fourfold iteration of vocal grief is followed by two questioning clauses, each balanced between 'ubi/wher' and 'si/ʒif'.

Another close echo of Anselm (this time, of his *Oratio ad Sanctam Mariam cum mens est sollicita timore*) can be heard a few lines later. Lamenting his distance from God, who 'stured is to wraþþe', the speaker asks:

> ʒif I ha wraþþed þe sone. nis þe moder erred.' And ʒif þe Mooder be wroþ. hou is þe sone quemed?» who schal pese me wiþ þe sone. ʒif þe Moder beo my fo? ¶ Or who schal me geten þe Moderloue ʒif þe sone me hate?[64]

Without precisely replicating Anselm's terminology, *A Talkyng* here carefully imitates his chiastic positioning of mother and son ('sone [...] moder' / 'filium [...] matrem'): 'Cum enim peccavi in filium, irritavi matrem, nec offendi matrem sine iniuria filii' ('When I have sinned against the son, I have alienated the mother, nor can I offend the mother without hurting the son').[65] Omitting Anselm's address to himself as 'peccator' ('Quid ergo facies, peccator? Quo igitur fugies, peccator?'; 'What will you do, then, sinner? Where will you flee, sinner?'),[66] *A Talkyng* then reproduces his second chiasmus ('Mooder [...] sone' / 'matrem [...] filii'): 'Quis enim me reconciliabit filio inimica matre? Quis mihi placabit matrem irato filio?' ('Who can reconcile me to the son if the mother

---

[62] *A Talkyng*, p. 76 n. 50. This borrowing was first noted by Nancy Jiang in her unpublished Oxford master's thesis. Jiang, 'Encountering Anselm's *Prayers* and *Meditations* in *A Talkyng of the Loue of God*', p. 22 and p. 42.

[63] The Latin is taken from Anselm of Canterbury, *Opera omnia*, ed. by Schmitt, III, 43. The English translation is taken from Anselm of Canterbury, *The Prayers and Meditations*, ed. and trans. by Ward, p. 159.

[64] *A Talkyng*, 20/9–14.

[65] Anselm of Canterbury, *Opera omnia*, ed. by Schmitt, III, 16; Anselm of Canterbury, *The Prayers and Meditations*, ed. and trans. by Ward, p. 112.

[66] At this point, Ward's translation omits the second 'peccator' (sinner). I have, however, inserted it here in order to provide a more precise replication of Anselm's Latin.

is my enemy, or who will make my peace with the mother if I have angered the son?').[67] Once again, it appears that Anselm's tightly patterned rhetoric has provided an unmistakeable framework for our English text to adopt.

Proceeding to reflect on the possibility of God's mercy, the *Talkyng* speaker then enquires:

> Wher is þenne þat word. of cumfort & blisse.' þat þou seidest þiself. derworþe lord. Nolo mortem peccatoris. I.nul not þou seist. þe deþ of þe synful.' but I wole he torne.' and stunte of his sunne. And ryse to my grace.' in lyf wiþ outen ende. (Ezechiel 33. 11)[68]

That Anselm should quote the same verse in his *Deploratio Virginitatis male Amissae* is, in itself, unremarkable. But that he should preface it with the rhetorical question 'ubi est' ('Ubi est, o verax deus, ubi est: "vivo ego, nolo mortem peccatoris, sed ut convertatur et vivat?"'; 'God of truth, where is it written that "as I live I do not desire the death of a sinner but rather that he be converted and live"?') is more striking.[69] For it suggests that, in its introduction of the verse with 'wher is', *A Talkyng* is once again inspired by Anselm's mode of expression.

Such recollections of Anselm's rhetoric and terminology are not isolated to the lines following *A Talkyng*'s invocation of his name, but can also be found in the preceding material, where the *Oratio ad sanctum Iohannem Baptistam* features strongly. The speaker's acute sense of himself as having disfigured God's own reflection in himself, '[H]e prented in my soule.' þe ymage of him selue. And I. enprented a boue.' þe liknesse of helle. Allas my deore ladi. Allas what haue I. don',[70] draws on Anselm's related lament, 'Reformasti in me amabilem imaginem tuam, et ego superimpressi odibilem imaginem, heu, heu. (*Oratio ad sanctum Iohannem Baptistam*) ('You refashioned your gracious image in me, and I superimposed upon it the image that is hateful. Alas, alas, how could I?'),[71] rendering his 'superimpressi' as 'enprented' and replicating his repeated 'heu' with 'Allas […] Allas'. *A Talkyng*'s subsequent comparison of the sinful self to Satan is modelled on the same prayer, the speaker's '[h]e fel […] aȝeyn his makere. and I aȝeyn my

---

[67] Anselm of Canterbury, *Opera omnia*, ed. by Schmitt, III, 16; Anselm of Canterbury, *The Prayers and Meditations*, ed. and trans. by Ward, p. 112.

[68] *A Talkyng*, 20/30–34.

[69] Anselm of Canterbury, *Opera omnia*, ed. by Schmitt, III, 83; Anselm of Canterbury, *The Prayers and Meditations*, ed. and trans. by Ward, p. 228.

[70] *A Talkyng*, 12/16–17.

[71] Anselm of Canterbury, *Opera omnia*, ed. by Schmitt, III, 27; Anselm of Canterbury, *The Prayers and Meditations*, ed. and trans. by Ward, p. 129.

makere. and myn eft makere' reproducing the Latin '[i]lle contra eum qui se fecit, ego contra eum qui me fecit et refecit' ('He sinned against his maker; I against him who made me, and re-made me').[72] And *A Talkyng*'s agonized fear of introspection, 'Allas ȝif I. seo my self.' Ine may soffre my self. And ȝif i ne seo my self nouȝt.' þenne gyle I. my self',[73] is modelled on the same prayer's 'Si me inspicio, non tolero me ipsum; si non inspicio, nescio me ipsum' ('If I look within myself, I cannot bear myself; if I do not look within myself, I do not know myself'),[74] with the English treatise once again mirroring Anselm's careful rhetorical balance ('ȝif I [...] I ne [...] ȝif I ne [...] I' / 'Si me [...] non me [...] si non [...] me').

However, in the lines which immediately follow this in *A Talkyng*, we move away from the *Oratio ad sanctum Iohannem Baptistam*. The speaker likens himself, in his state of sin, to 'stynkinde careyne. and muche more wlatsum. bi fore godes face.' þen eny fulþe so foul. Þat eny mon may þenken'.[75] And in so doing, he appears to have in mind the opening of Anselm's *Meditatio ad concitandum timorem* in which the sinful man is described as 'foetentem peccatis' ('a foul-smelling sinner'), before the speaker goes on to lament '[q]uam tolerabilius canis putris foetet hominibus quam anima peccatrix deo!' ('The rotting corpse of a dog smells more tolerable than the soul of a sinful man to God, it is less displeasing to men than that other is to God').[76]

Yet by no means all of the material in this middle section of *A Talkyng* is obviously derived from Anselm. For example, the striking description of the 'deueles Mirour' which distorts perceptions of reality for those who turn their back on God is not traceable in this way.[77] Nor is the chilling depiction of the 'deueles Maumet' (devil's puppet) as 'more eorþly. þen euer was eorþe. fikelore þen þe wynt More veyn þen is þe eir. Hattore in his lustes.' þen is þe fuir þat brenneþ. Hardore þen eny ston [...] Caldore of charite.' þen forst in his kuynde'.[78] Such apparently original material is interwoven with Anselmian borrowings in an accomplished, assured manner.

---

[72] *A Talkyng*, 12/29–30. Anselm of Canterbury, *Opera omnia*, ed. by Schmitt, III, 27; Anselm of Canterbury, *The Prayers and Meditations*, ed. and trans. by Ward, p. 129.

[73] *A Talkyng*, 14/6–7.

[74] Anselm of Canterbury, *Opera omnia*, ed. by Schmitt, III, 28. Anselm of Canterbury, *The Prayers and Meditations*, ed. and trans. by Ward, p. 130.

[75] *A Talkyng*, 14/8–9.

[76] Anselm of Canterbury, *Opera omnia*, ed. by Schmitt, III, 76; Anselm of Canterbury, *The Prayers and Meditations*, ed. and trans. by Ward, p. 221.

[77] *A Talkyng*, 16/25–26.

[78] *A Talkyng*, 18/4–8.

In drawing on Anselm, then, the compiler of *A Talkyng* does not appear to follow a specific treatise or treatises from beginning to end. Rather, he borrows elements from a number of treatises, apparently combining them with non-Anselmian prose, reading in the selective manner encouraged by Anselm in the preface to his collection of prayers for Matilda, Countess of Tuscany.[79] The compiler's detailed familiarity with a range of Anselm's writing is striking, but we cannot know whether he was inspired by the Latin originals or whether he was drawing on vernacular translations of the same. The possibility of the latter is indicated by the circulation of translations of Anselm (including his *Deploratio Virginitatis male Amissae* and *Meditatio ad concitandum timorem*) in late medieval England; according to its table of contents, Vernon itself originally contained a vernacular version of Anselm's *Orisons off seynt anselmes meditaciouns*.[80] Given the *Ureisun*'s and *Wohunge*'s well-attested links with Anselmian devotion, it is tempting to speculate that our compiler may have encountered Anselm in translation in a manuscript which also contained these vernacular prayers; such a situation would go some way towards explaining *A Talkyng*'s somewhat puzzling combination of material. Yet it remains no more than hypothesis and does not, in any case, account for the closing section of *A Talkyng*, for which there is no obvious single source, Anselmian or otherwise.

Westra was scathing in her analysis of the final part of *A Talkyng*, dismissing it as composed by 'a pious but not highly gifted person'.[81] It is certainly the case that the treatise verges on the excitable in its closing moments, most notably in the speaker's likening of himself to a greyhound:

> I. lepe on him [i.e., Christ] raply. as grehound on herte. al out of my self. wiþ loueliche leete. And cluppe in myn armes. þe cros bi þe sterte. þe blood I.souke of his feet. þat sok is ful swete. ¶ I. cusse and I. cluppe and stunte oþerwhile. as mon þat is loue mad. and seek of loue sore.[82]

In fact, it is tempting to read the *Cloud of Unknowing* author's advice that one should 'abide curtesly and meekly þe wil of oure Lorde & lache not ouer-hastely, as it were a gredy grehounde' as a reaction against the extravagant sensuality of

---

[79] Anselm of Canterbury, *Opera omnia*, ed. by Schmitt, III, 4: 'Nec debet intendere lector quamlibet earum totam legere, sed tantum quantum ad excitandum affectum orandi, ad quod factae sunt, sentit sibi sufficere'. Anselm of Canterbury, *The Prayers and Meditations*, ed. and trans. by Ward, p. 90: 'It is not intended that the reader should feel impelled to read the whole, but only as much as will stir up the affections to prayer; so much as it does that, think it to be sufficient for you'.

[80] See Serjeantson, 'The Index of the Vernon Manuscript', p. 237.

[81] *A Talkyng*, p. xxii.

[82] *A Talkyng*, 60/22–26.

utterances such as this, if not as a pointed criticism of *A Talkyng* in particular; after all, no other English devotional text of the period deploys the 'grehound' simile in this way.[83] Yet to dismiss the entire conclusion to *A Talkyng* as somehow inferior to the rest of the compilation misses the fact that, for all its discordant excesses, it also manages to preserve and develop important themes that have run through the treatise as a whole. Most notably, a strongly Anselmian preoccupation with man as created by God and recreated by Christ unites *A Talkyng* as a whole and is pursued in this closing section, in which the speaker marvels repeatedly that God not only made him but also 'deore bouȝtest' him on the cross.[84]

Towards the end of *A Talkyng*, the speaker appears particularly preoccupied with the fact that God created him from nothing, marvelling that 'lord whon I. nas nouȝt. þenne þou me maadest' and that 'þou me formedest furst. and madest lyk þi self of nouȝt'.[85] This is a mystery referenced in the *Wohunge*, but it is also a repeated theme for Anselm, for whom God 'potuit omnia de nihilo facere' ('was able to make all things out of nothing').[86] For the *Talkyng* compiler, as for Anselm, God's ex nihilo creation of man is astonishing:

> And for þou madest me lord al þat I. am.' I. am al þat I.am. holden to þe one.» For in þat ilke makyng. þou madest me so clanly. so feir and enterly. wiþ outen lac of eny lyme.' lyk þi self al one.[87]

In contrast with God, the compiler, by definition, does not create from nothing, but assembles pre-existing material. And while the *Talkyng* compiler does

---

[83] See *The Cloud of Unknowing*, ed. by Hodgson, ch. 46, 48/28–29. For discussion of the hunting motif, see Rooney, *Hunting in Middle English Literature*. Rooney registers the 'infrequent appearance' of the motif of Christ as prey in English texts, and notes that the greyhound simile appears in only the *Ayenbite of Inwyt* (where the 'gentyl hond' behaves in a rather more decorous manner), *A Talkyng*, and the *Cloud* (pp. 133–35). She also notes that the *Cloud* author's call for moderation was justified in light of the words of the German mystic Elsbeth Hainburg, who 'compares her ardour in devotion to the eagerness of a hound which will run itself to death rather than lose its prey' (p. 136). But *A Talkyng*'s blood-sucking greyhound provides us with a justification rather closer to home. Both Riehle and Bryan note that the greyhound is mentioned by Elsbeth and the *Cloud* author, but neither notes that the latter author might have been aware — and critical — of the *Talkyng* similitude. See Riehle, *The Secret Within*, p. 318, n. 11, and Bryan, *Looking Inward*, p. 230, n. 35. 60.

[84] *A Talkyng*, 64/22.

[85] *A Talkyng*, 62/23–24 and 66/13.

[86] 'Oratio ad Sanctam Mariam pro Impetrando eius et Christi' in Anselm of Canterbury, *Opera omnia*, ed. by Schmitt, III, 22; Anselm of Canterbury, *The Prayers and Meditations*, ed. and trans. by Ward, p. 121.

[87] *A Talkyng*, 62/24–27.

not at any point remark on the fact that his treatise is a compilation, and thus not wholly original, it is striking that he should reflect on God's unique status as originating author towards the end of his own, compiled text. He, as human creature, can never create from nothing, but must always work with that which already exists and is imperfect.

Returning to the notion of sinful man as recreated by Christ in his Incarnation, one might argue that God here plays a part akin to that of the compiler, generating a new creation from an old, marred original. Yet even here, God outdoes man; for unlike us, God has the capacity to create something entirely new and unspoilt from something which already exists and is imperfect. Of course, literary compilation does not work in quite this way; the compiler is not aiming to produce a 'perfect' text from an 'imperfect' original, but to reconfigure material in a way which makes it accessible to a new audience. Nonetheless, the compiler of *A Talkyng* is alert to the fact that Christ offers him (and his readers) a chance to be rewritten or recompiled as new creations, using the old materials of the sinful self. In the *Wohunge*, the speaker notes that the crucified Christ 'oppnes me þin herte for to cnawe witerliche & in to reden trewe luue lettres' (opens your heart for me, to know truly and to read therein true love letters).[88] But in *A Talkyng*, the act of reading has become one of writing:

> A.' Ihesu swete lemmon. hou kuyndeliche openest þou me. þi derworþe herte. lyues. and deþes. Forte knowen witerli. al þi loue þer inne. and writen hit dernely. in myn herte trewely. wiþ trewe loue lettres.' of þin herte blood.[89]

Here, the self is presented as having been wholly rewritten with Christ's 'herte blood'; the resulting individual is a 'clan[] [...] feir and enter[]' creation.[90] While *A Talkyng* itself cannot claim an equivalent perfection, it functions as an inventive response to earlier material, providing a forum in which questions of compilation and creativity can be considered and reconsidered.

---

[88] *Wohunge*, 35/546–48.
[89] *A Talkyng*, 52/35–54/3.
[90] *A Talkyng*, 62/26.

Works Cited

Manuscripts

London, British Library [BL], MS Additional 22283
London, British Library [BL], MS Cotton Nero A XIV
London, British Library [BL], MS Cotton Titus D XVIII
London, Lambeth Palace Library, MS 487
Oxford, Bodleian Library [Bodl. Lib.], MS Eng. poet. a. 1

Primary Sources

Anselm of Canterbury, *S. Anselmi Cantuariensis archiepiscopi opera omnia*, ed. by Franciscus Salesius Schmitt, 6 vols (Edinburgh: Thomas Nelson and Sons, 1940–61)
——, *The Prayers and Meditations of St Anselm, with the Proslogion*, ed. and trans. by Benedicta Ward (London: Penguin, 1973)
The Cloud of Unknowing and Related Treatises, ed. by Phyllis Hodgson, Analecta Cartusiana, 3 (Exeter: Catholic Records Press, 1982)
A Talkyng of þe Loue of God, ed. and trans. by Sister M. Salvina Westra (The Hague: Martinus Nijhoff, 1950)
Þe Wohunge of Ure Lauerd, ed. by W. Meredith Thompson, Early English Text Society, o.s., 241 (Oxford: Oxford University Press, 1958)

Secondary Works

Bryan, Jennifer, *Looking Inward: Devotional Reading and the Private Self in Late Medieval England* (Philadelphia: University of Pennsylvania Press, 2008)
Catto, Jeremy, '1349–1412: Culture and History', in *The Cambridge Companion to Medieval English Mysticism*, ed. by Samuel Fanous and Vincent Gillespie (Cambridge: Cambridge University Press, 2011), pp. 113–32
Dove, Mary, *The First English Bible: The Texts and Contexts of the Wycliffite Versions*, Cambridge Studies in Medieval Literature, 66 (Cambridge: Cambridge University Press, 2007)
Ellis, Roger, and Samuel Fanous, '1349–1412: Texts', in *The Cambridge Companion to Medieval English Mysticism*, ed. by Samuel Fanous and Vincent Gillespie (Cambridge: Cambridge University Press, 2011), pp. 133–62
Evans, G. R., 'Anselm's Life, Works and Immediate Influence', in *The Cambridge Companion to Anselm*, ed. by Brian Davies and Brian Leftow (Cambridge: Cambridge University Press, 2004), pp. 5–31
Jiang, Nancy, 'Encountering Anselm's *Prayers* and *Meditations* in *A Talkyng of the Loue of God*' (unpublished masters' thesis, University of Oxford, 2006)
Morgan, M. M., 'A Treatise in Cadence', *Modern Language Review*, 47 (1952), 156–62

Renevey, Denis, 'The Choices of the Compiler: Vernacular Hermeneutics in *A Talkyng of þe Love of God*', in *The Medieval Translator 6:* Proceedings of the International Conference of Göttingen (22–25 July 1996) / *Traduire au Moyen Age 6: actes du Colloque international de Göttingen (22–25 juillet 1996)*, ed. by Roger Ellis, René Tixier, and Bernd Weitemeier (Turnhout: Brepols, 1998), pp. 232–53

Riehle, Wolfgang, *The Secret Within: Hermits, Recluses, and Spiritual Outsiders in Medieval England* (Ithaca: Cornell University Press, 2014)

Rooney, Anne, *Hunting in Middle English Literature* (Woodbridge: Boydell and Brewer, 1993)

Serjeantson, Mary S., 'The Index of the Vernon Manuscript', *Modern Language Review*, 32 (1937), 222–61

Sutherland, Annie, *English Psalms in the Middle Ages, 1300–1450* (Oxford: Oxford University Press, 2015)

Reading Late Medieval Devotional Compilations in the Fifteenth and Sixteenth Centuries

Margaret Connolly

The question of the audience for a late-medieval devotional text is rarely simple.[1]

In the context of the audience anticipated by the author of *Disce mori*, E. A. Jones notes that a singular recipient, addressed as 'best-beloued sustre Dame Alice', is identified in the envoy, three stanzas of rhyme royal that describe the work's contents and purpose, and which preface the text in its two extant manuscripts.[2] Despite this specific address, the compilation as a whole shows every sign of having been originally written with a general readership in mind, with only the concluding section, the 'Exhortacion', tailored to a woman of religious status; even then, as Jones points out, the use of appropriate pronouns is not maintained consistently, and the various slippages in language lead him to wonder in which direction the text may have been pointed first: gendered and personalized, or generic and universal.

In assessing what audience may have been intended or imagined for a work by its author, weight may be given to various forms of internal textual evidence. These include the overt statements made by authors and compilers in prologues,

---

[1] *The 'Exhortation'*, ed. by Jones, p. xxix.
[2] *The 'Exhortation'*, ed. by Jones, p. ix.

Margaret Connolly (mc29@st-andrews.ac.uk) is Senior Lecturer in Medieval Studies at the University of St Andrews.

envoys, *incipits*, and *explicits*, and in the prefaces and colophons of printed books; other clues may come in direct forms of address or comments made within the text; and there is also the linguistic register chosen by the author. There may be some external evidence too, such as the existence of known patrons or presentation copies. Yet beyond the question of a work's *intended* audience lies the more complex issue of the *actual* readership that it achieved. To assess this aspect, attention must be directed to more material forms of evidence. This largely means looking closely at any marks that readers left in their copies of a text, such as marginal notes and comments, and other annotations including the use of signs, symbols, pointing hands, and underlining. For the book historian it is ideal if such material traces of readership occur in conjunction with inscriptions of ownership and dates of use, because this allows the profiling of *types* of actual reader — by gender, social class, and so on. And this may be supplemented by the information offered in various forms of historical record, principally wills, and sometimes also booklists and other inventories of property.

A further complicating factor is that this question of *actual* rather than *intended* readership is not restricted to the text's era of production. Textual reception is a more open-ended affair than scribal production, and works continued to be read long after their own day by readers who may have been different from those expected by the texts' authors. And even if the constituency reached by a work remained essentially the same as that intended by its author, the work's *reception* might be affected by changed social and political circumstances. The reading environment in sixteenth-century England for religious texts in particular was transformed by Henry VIII's break with Rome, and successive changes in official religion during the reigns of Edward VI, Mary Tudor, and Elizabeth I created an uncertain intellectual climate. Those who read medieval devotional compilations in this period had a more complicated experience of religion and a less stable outlook than could ever have been imagined by the original producers of those works.

One such reader was Thomas Roberts, a London lawyer who died in 1542 at the height of the Henrician reformation. Amongst several other English and Latin books Thomas Roberts had a manuscript copy of the *Pore Caitif*, a late fourteenth-century compendium of vernacular religious instruction that consists of a prologue and fourteen tracts. The first three tracts explain the central teachings embodied in the Creed, Decalogue, and Pater Noster, after which ten shorter tracts cover related aspects of Christian devotion, and the work then concludes with a lengthier piece on the topics of virginity and chastity.[3]

---

[3] The usual ordering of the fourteen tracts, as established in Brady, 'The Pore Caitif', p. 532,

Thomas Roberts's copy of the *Pore Caitif* is now BL, MS Harley 2322, a small fifteenth-century volume, professionally prepared and written, with some gold initials marking the beginnings of major sections.[4] Thomas Roberts annotated this volume in various ways, adding his name in formal statements of ownership at the beginning and end of the book, and in a number of other places too, typically setting his characteristic 'Robertz' inscription at the top corner of recto leaves. He sometimes wrote his name lower down in the margins too, in all of these places at the starts of new texts (not new fascicles), thus indicating an interest in marking textual content rather than just insistently proclaiming his ownership of the volume.

Thomas was concerned to quantify the length of each individual tract in the compilation, adding at the start of each a note of just how many leaves it comprised: the Creed, for example, consisted of fourteen leaves, 'The Charter of our Heavenly Heritage' of eight leaves, and so on. Thomas then transferred this total to the list of the volume's contents that he had compiled at the beginning of the manuscript, providing a rudimentary apparatus that made consultation of the contents more efficient. In another of his books, a collection of medical recipes that is now Bodl. Lib., MS Rawlinson C. 299, Thomas devised a more sophisticated finding aid, with page numbers and marginal headings keyed to an index at the back of the book, perhaps employing indexing techniques that he had learned as a lawyer.[5] In both instances the effort involved is an indication of use: no one would go to such trouble to customize a volume if they did not use it on a regular basis. The list in BL, MS Harley 2322 also reveals something about Thomas's understanding of the *Pore Caitif* because it enumerates twenty separate texts, not the usual fourteen. The discrepancy arises partly because this is one of the copies of the *Pore Caitif* that has additional contents — the tract on the Ave Maria and the 'Answeris to hem þat seien þat we schulde not speke of holy writt' are interlopers in the compilation — and partly because Thomas habitually listed the constituent parts of individual tracts as separate items: he recorded the prologue to the Pater Noster and the prologue and epilogue to the Ten Commandments as items in their own right. Clearly he also just misunderstood the nature of the final

is Creed, Ten Commandments, Pater Noster, 'The Counsel of Christ', 'Of Virtuous Patience', 'Of Temptation', 'The Charter of Our Heavenly Heritage', 'The Horse or Armour of Heaven', 'The Name of Jesus', 'Desire of Jesus', 'Of Meekness', 'Of Man's Will', 'Of Active Life and Contemplative Life', 'The Mirror of Chastity'.

[4] For Thomas Roberts's ownership of this and other fifteenth-century manuscripts, see Connolly, *Sixteenth-Century Readers, Fifteenth-Century Books*.

[5] See Connolly, 'Evidence for the Continued Use of Medieval Medical Prescriptions in the Sixteenth Century'.

tract, 'The Mirror of Chastity', taking its first chapter to be the whole work, and identifying Chapters 2–5 as a separate work on 'Virgynete'.

A preoccupation with numbering characterizes Thomas's approach to the compilation's individual components. In the tract on the Pater Noster Thomas marked the prayer's individual clauses by setting small roman numerals in the margins alongside, even though these sentences had already been underlined with red ink by the rubricator so that additional emphasis was unnecessary. Thomas numbered the clauses of the Creed in the same way, and also various lists of features mentioned in the text. This persistent numbering makes particular sections easier to retrieve and shows signs of attentive reading, perhaps even an attempt to learn or memorize the content. In the tract on the Ten Commandments Thomas gave brief marginal summaries of each in English: 'worship fadir & mother' (fol. 59^r); 'slee no man' (fol. 61^v); 'do no lecherie' (fol. 67^r); and so on.[6] In the Creed he also provided marginal translations into Latin, linking the vernacularized statements of the Creed back to their Vulgate equivalents. In some manuscripts of the *Pore Caitif* the articles of the Creed are given in the text in both Latin and English, and in others the Latin is given as a marginal gloss (by the original scribes), but this is the only instance I know of where a reader rather than a scribe has provided the Latin text.[7]

In some of Thomas Roberts's other books, including his book of hours, CUL, MS Ii.6.2, his additions are more substantial, consisting of the contribution of many prayers, some in English but most in Latin, a language with which, as a lawyer, he would have been perfectly familiar. In BL, MS Harley 2322 his interactions with the text remain at a more simplistic level. He may have been customizing the volume for use by his children or other members of his household who had less learning, or perhaps he used this book at an early period in his life, when he was himself a schoolboy, practising his Latin and learning his catechism: indeed these different uses are not necessarily exclusive. A recent study of the reception of the *Pore Caitif* that focuses on marks made by fifteenth-century readers finds that the tract on the Ten Commandments is consistently the one that is the most heavily annotated.[8] Gabriel Hill argues

---

[6] In all quotations from manuscript, abbreviations have been silently expanded in this essay.

[7] Other manuscripts that include Latin are Bodl. Lib., MS Additional B. 66; CUL, MS Ff.6.55; Cambridge, Trinity College, MS B.14.53; Glasgow, University Library, MS Hunter 496 and MS Hunter 520; and London, Lambeth Palace Library, MS 484; these are discussed by Trivedi, '"Trewe techyng and false heritikys"', p. 139. Latin marginal glosses occur in BL, MS Stowe 38 and MS Harley 2335.

[8] Hill, 'Pedagogy, Devotion, and Marginalia'.

that this and other parts of the compilation were used as educational primers as well as devotional readers, and that literacy and basic religious values were thus taught simultaneously. There is no reason to suppose that such practices faded away quickly or completely in the sixteenth century. Two sets of injunctions issued in the 1530s stressed the need for good knowledge of the fundamental tenets of the Christian faith (that is, of the Pater Noster, the articles of the Creed, and the Ten Commandments), and the injunctions of 1536 even stipulated that parents were to teach these basics to their children.[9]

Hill's study lists a number of manuscripts with users' annotations but cannot identify many fifteenth-century readers of the *Pore Caitif* by name, citing only two, both of whom were London-based: Thomas Eborall, clerk and master of Whittington College 1444–64, and John Gamalin, probably a merchant.[10] Eborall owned London, Lambeth Palace Library, MS 541, and may have been responsible for the copious 'nota' and 'nota bene' marks in its margins. Gamalin is credited with the financing of BL, MS Harley 2336, a common-profit book, and whilst he cannot himself have been a reader of this actual book, which was produced after his death from monies he bequeathed for that purpose, the impetus suggests a familiarity at least with the type of contents to be furnished for other readers within his own circle.[11] Another fifteenth-century owner was John Graunge, who added the inscription 'Johannes Graunge me possidet' on the flyleaf of Cambridge, St John's College, MS G. 28, and who was presumably also responsible for the Latin prayer on fol. 1^r: 'O pater omnipotens qui verbo cuncta creasti / Orat Graungeus des sibi regna poli' (O father almighty who created everything by the word, Graungeus prays that you give him the kingdom of heaven).[12] Other additions on the flyleaves and in the margins are by sixteenth-century hands, and include various English verses of a pious or aphoristic nature: 'Honor thyn god and pitty the poor / repent & amend & sinn no more'; 'Mans fletinge lyffe fyndes surest staye / Wher sacred vertue

[9] *Visitation Articles and Injunctions*, ed. by Frere and Kennedy, pp. 1–11.

[10] On Eborall, see Emden, *A Biographical Register of the University of Oxford*, I, 622–23; Gamalin was named with John Colop in the settlement of the property of a London grocer in 1439, as noted by Scase, 'Reginald Pecock, John Carpenter, and John Colop's "Common Profit" Books', p. 262.

[11] The common profit inscription is on fol. 137^{r-v}, with another name 'Phillip?Sherr' written beneath by a different (sixteenth- or seventeenth-century) hand.

[12] John Graunge also owned Cambridge, St John's College, MS G. 11, a collection of Latin theological and canonistic materials; see *The Works of a Lollard Preacher*, ed. by Hudson, pp. xix–xx.

bearethe swaye'. These and other similar verses that note the brevity of man's life, the need for repentance, and advice for good living (and dying), are set in the lower margins of the first few leaves of the *Pore Caitif*; the content of the verses reveals something of the preoccupations of the annotators, and their presence clearly demonstrates that the volume continued to be read and used in the sixteenth century.[13]

It is well known that the *Pore Caitif* circulated in the capital in the fifteenth century and that this was also a centre for its production, so it is not surprising to find that it continued to be read there in the following century.[14] Another manuscript which has provenance information that connects it with London in the last quarter of the fifteenth century is London, Westminster School, MS 3. This volume has the inscription 'Amen per Ricardo Cloos the wiche is owner of this bouke anno 1472' (fol. 231ʳ), allowing it to be linked with the draper and merchant adventurer Richard Cloos (or Close) who was churchwarden at St Mary at Hill between 1483 and 1502, although there are two men of this name and it is not always possible to distinguish between them.[15] This manuscript contains only two tracts from the *Pore Caitif*, 'The Charter of Heaven' and 'The Mirror of Chastity', but its other contents cover ground that is cognate with the compilation, offering expositions of the Pater Noster and Decalogue (in fact it has two commentaries on the Ten Commandments). Its readers were therefore exposed to the same kind of texts, and the same kind of combinations of religious instructional materials, as readers of the *Pore Caitif* itself. Another copy of the *Pore Caitif* that bears evidence of much handling in the early modern period is Glasgow, University Library, MS Hunter 520.[16] A plethora of inscriptions on its flyleaves provides a corpus of data that might be mined to yield a clearer picture of this volume's history as it passed through the hands of 'Johannes Ruxton', 'Gnatisiauton Foster', 'Henry Cobham', and 'Master Grymston'; another sixteenth-century note suggests a connection with mercantile operations in Ipswich, naming 'Robertus Canndy' and 'Thomas Marsshe', and a ship called 'le christofer'. Of these only Henry Cobham (1537–1592) has so far been identified: he was an Elizabethan diplomat, much travelled, and much involved

---

[13] Cambridge, St John's College, MS G. 28, pp. 1, 5–7, 10–19, 22–26; the verses are listed individually in this manuscript's entry in *DIMEV*.

[14] On the text's metropolitan production, see Trivedi, 'The "Pore Caitif"'.

[15] The manuscript's production has been discussed by Hanna, 'The Origins and Production'; more information about its owner has been uncovered by Moss, 'A Merchant's Tales'.

[16] This manuscript also contains a copy of Ralph Hanna's version 2 of *Three Arrows on Doomsday*. See also Ralph Hanna's essay in this volume.

with local government administration in Kent.[17] This book was still being used in the seventeenth century too, with other names and inscriptions in hands of this period; most telling, in terms of continued reading, is the addition of a table of the volume's contents on a front flyleaf, written by a clear italic hand and signed 'Mi: Wigmor'. Beyond inscribed names, reports of book possession may also reveal something about circulation and reception, and in this regard it is appropriate to note John Foxe's account of the case of 'Maistres Smith widdowe of Couentry' who was burned in 1519 for possessing a 'skrol' that contained 'the Lords praier, þe articles of þe faith & x commaundments in English' (a conjunction of texts that sounds very like the first part of the *Pore Caitif*).[18]

In those instances where it may not be possible to discover much about particular owners, either because no names are provided, or where inscribed names resist identification, annotations alone may provide the key to understanding how the compilation was used by individual anonymous readers. And where the *Pore Caitif* survives in full or in part in conjunction with other works, those different textual combinations may be fruitful aspects to explore. The 'whole book' approach to the investigation of manuscripts, sometimes overzealously pursued in attempts to determine unified design in textual production, may turn out to be more naturally suited to investigations of textual reception because except in the case of composite manuscripts we can at least be sure of the combinations of texts that readers would have found in particular codices, and of the order in which they encountered them (though not of course the order in which they may have chosen to *read* them).[19]

One other devotional compilation with which the *Pore Caitif* keeps company, in various forms, is *Contemplations of the Dread and Love of God*. To see these two works circulating together is not surprising. Returning for a moment to the question of a text's *intended* readers, it is clear that both these compilations positioned themselves for very much the same audience. The *Pore Caitif* aims to teach 'symple men & wymmen of good will' (Brady, p. 1, lines 3–4), and *Contemplations* articulates a mixed audience, 'religious and seculer' (Connolly, p. 8, B/99), of similar nature and intent: 'men and women of þat good wil'

---

[17] For details of his career, see Lock, 'Brooke, Sir Henry (1537–1592)'. Cobham's inscription, with the date 1573, is set on an otherwise blank leaf facing the start of the *Pore Caitif* on p. 1 (the manuscript is paginated); traces of another inscription, now damaged by cropping and tearing, may be seen at the top of p. 1.

[18] Foxe, *Actes and Monuments*, pp. 420–21.

[19] Pearsall, 'The Whole Book', criticizes the tendency to overemphasize coherence and intentionality in the understanding of medieval manuscripts.

(Connolly, p. 5, A/27), 'to oþere of simple knowyng' (Connolly, p. 5, A/33), 'to suche simple folk' (Connolly, p. 41, Z/65).[20] Both works overtly advertise their own structures: the *Pore Caitif* through its prologue that links its core catechetical elements and the 'short sentencis' that follow into a 'laddir of dyuerse rongis' by which the reader can 'stie up' to heaven (Brady, p. 2, lines 2–3, 4–5); and *Contemplations* by its subdivisions of degrees and points that the reader may 'eisliche come to, on aftur anoþer' (Connolly, p. 11, D/71). *Contemplations* also allows for selective reading through its provision of a table of contents; this is in most copies, and so would appear to be an authorially designed strategy, whereas it might be remembered that in the case of the *Pore Caitif* Thomas Roberts had to provide his own.

There are eight instances where these two works occur (or originally occurred) together, either wholly or in part, a codicological conjunction that is discussed elsewhere in this volume by Diana Denissen.[21] These are:

- Cambridge, University Library, MS Hh.1.12
- Cambridge, University Library, MS Ii.6.40[22]
- Glasgow, University Library, MS Hunter 520
- London, British Library, MS Harley 1706
- Manchester, John Rylands Library, MS English 85
- Oxford, Bodleian Library, MS Ashmole 1286
- Oxford, Bodleian Library, MS Bodley 423
- Oxford, Bodleian Library, MS Douce 322

Amongst these eight manuscripts only one contains both texts in full rather than in extract form: this is Bodl. Lib., MS Ashmole 1286, in which *Contemplations* (fols 4ʳ–32ᵛ) is followed immediately by the *Pore Caitif* (fols 32ᵛ–108ᵛ). Reading sequentially was not the only choice; as the preface to the table of contents in *Contemplations* articulates, free ranging was also possible: 'þat þou mowe sone finde what mater þe pleseþ' (Connolly, p. 3, CL/2–3). Nevertheless, any reader of this manuscript who approached the task of reading its contents sequentially

---

[20] Quotations from the texts are from '*The Pore Caitif*', ed. by Brady, and *Contemplations*, ed. by Connolly. Quotations from manuscript versions of the texts are linked to the equivalent passages in these editions.

[21] See Diana Denissen's essay in this volume.

[22] This manuscript is discussed in Marleen Cré's essay in this volume.

would have been led first through the highly organized system delineated by *Contemplations*, comprising four degrees of love (ordained, clean, steadfast, and perfect) and five special virtues (good will, devotion in praying, resistance to temptation, patience in tribulation, perseverance in good deeds), before reaching the starting point offered by the *Pore Caitif* which was the statement of faith enshrined in the Creed. *Contemplations* ends with a chapter that contains a meditation and various forms of prayer, and in some manuscripts additional prayers are appended, but in Bodl. Lib., MS Ashmole 1286 there was no need to provide extra prayers because the reader would quickly encounter the words of the Pater Noster within the third tract of the *Pore Caitif*. Manuals of religious instruction, of which there are numerous surviving examples, put forward a clear hierarchy of elements to be learned, beginning with the key Christian prayers of the Pater Noster and Ave, followed by the Creed and the Ten Commandments; these were preceded by the true basics — the sign of the cross and the alphabet.[23] With its alphabetized arrangement of chapters which features prominently in the work's design in the majority of its manuscripts, as here, *Contemplations* might be seen as organizationally inspired by that most basic of required elements, the ABC, offering through its twenty thousand words the most extensive possible expansion of the ABC imaginable. The reader of Bodl. Lib., MS Ashmole 1286 could — if he or she chose — experience the work in this way, learning the ABC of *devotion* before progressing to the next required elements of the Peckamite syllabus via the contents of the *Pore Caitif*.

A series of annotations in the margins of Bodl. Lib., MS Ashmole 1286 allows the activity and engagement of a number of early readers of its texts to be traced. Several different hands may be observed in the margins of *Contemplations* and the *Pore Caitif*, one of which, a sloping cursive sixteenth-century secretary, is responsible for a sustained series of annotations in both texts. In *Contemplations* this hand does not become active until the later, more substantial, chapters that outline the five special virtues and models of prayer (chapters T, V, X, Y, Z, and AB), suggesting that this reader found the earlier parts of the text easy to understand. The nature of the annotations to the final six chapters is largely explanatory, with statements that occur in the text repeated or summarized in the margins. Thus, for example, in Chapter V, on prayer, the following additions in the left margin of fol. 21ᵛ — 'prey generally for all', 'Eache beare one an others burthen', 'pray for all' — are drawn from

---

[23] Manchester, John Rylands Library, MS English 85 offers a typical example of such a devotional manual on fols 2ʳ–19ʳ; see Connolly, 'Books for the "helpe of euery persoone þat þenkiþ to be saued"', pp. 172–73.

statements within the text: 'þou schalt preye generally', 'Eche of ȝou bere oþeres burþen', 'For who so preyeþ for alle oþur as for hym silf' (Connolly, p. 31, V/71, V/77, V/79–80). These marginal repetitions are either part of a process of active reading, added to aid the process of comprehension, or intended to function as markers for future rereadings of the text. Similar signposting is evident in the margins of 'The Creed', the first text of the *Pore Caitif*, where the start of each of the twelve articles has been signalled with a marginal note. Unlike Thomas Roberts's copy of the text, the version in Bodl. Lib., MS Ashmole 1286 attributes the individual statements of the Creed to Christ's twelve Apostles, a feature consistently repeated by the marginal notes, usually in the format 'Art: 7. St Philip' (fol. 36^r).[24] Other points that are enumerated in the text, such as the listing of the four parts of the cross of penance in the fourth article or the classification of four degrees of mankind at the last judgment in the seventh article, are marked collectively in the margins: '4 partes of penance' (fol. 35^v; Brady, p. 9, lines 4–5), '4 seuerall soules of men att the day of iudgment' (fol. 36^v; Brady, p. 11, lines 10–11). This reader does not routinely attach further numbers to each individual point, though marginal numbers are added to the list of the seven sacraments on fol. 40^v (Brady, p. 21, lines 17–24).

In the *Pore Caitif*, as in *Contemplations*, many of the annotations by this cursive sixteenth-century secretary hand summarize points articulated in the text. A note in the right margin of fol. 37^r, 'wicked speeches', draws attention to the more specific discussion of 'bacbitynge, sclaundrynge, scornynge, false auisynge, liynge, swerynge' (Brady, p. 13, lines 8–9) that may be found on that leaf; 'sinnes of omission' (Brady, p. 13, lines 16–19) in the left margin of fol. 37^v both notes and paraphrases the content of the text at that point. The topics that elicited responses from this reader in both texts are largely eschatological: the final judgment, life after death, and purgatory seem to have been major preoccupations. Annotations in the margins of the Creed note 'how wee should rise from deathe' (fol. 36^r) by means of the spiritual medicine of contrition, confession, and satisfaction (Brady, p. 10, lines 16–18), and that Christ 'with the same wounds that he had att the passion shal come to iudgment' (fol. 36^v; Brady, p. 11, lines 6–9). The types of men who will be saved are noted, as is the searching nature of the final reckoning: 'The least euill thoughts iudged att the last doome' (fol. 37^r; Brady, p. 13, lines 15–16); what will happen to sinners is paraphrased on fol. 38^v: 'The deuill att the day of iudgment layeth claime

---

[24] Brady, 'The Apostles and the Creed' discusses this feature with reference to the *Pore Caitif*. For other Middle English texts that responded to the ancient belief that the Apostles composed the Creed, see Raymo, 'Works of Religious and Philosophical Instruction', p. 2283.

to the wicked' (Brady, p. 16, lines 11–15). A textual reference to purgatory in the ninth article of the Creed (on fol. 40ᵛ) has been marked with a truncated 'Pur:' in the margin (Brady, p. 20, lines 24–25). The responsibility of praying for those in purgatory is specified in the final lines of *Contemplations*: 'Graunte parte to þe soulis whiche ben departyd from þe body in peynes of purgatorye abydynge ȝoure mercy', noted by the annotator as 'prayer for them in purgatory' (fol. 32ʳ; Connolly, p. 44, AB/122–23). On fol. 31ʳ the final three words of the phrase 'and for alle oþur quike and deede' (Connolly, p. 43, AB/62) have been emphatically underlined, and some words are written alongside in the left margin; the annotation now disappears into the central gutter and is hard to decipher, but it is clear what point is being noted. Other advice about praying for the dead which occurs in an earlier chapter has also been marked: 'Prayers for dampned soules not accepted' is the annotator's *précis* of 'As if þou preye for soulis þe which ben dampned þi preyere is not acceptyd' (fol. 21ʳ; Connolly, p. 30, V/54–55).

Although most of the annotations contributed by the cursive sixteenth-century hand are in English, a few are written in Latin. In the ninth article of the Creed descriptions of 'þe fyȝttynge churche' (fol. 40ʳ; Brady, p. 20, line 20), 'þe churche ouercomynge', and the Church that 'haþ fully ouercome alle enemyes' (fol. 40ᵛ; Brady, p. 21, lines 4–5, 7) are marked in the margins as, respectively, 'Ecclesia militens', 'Vincens Ecclesie', and 'Triumphors'. Statements about the immaculate conception of Christ in the third article of the Creed on fol. 35ʳ — 'sche beynge as clene mayde aftir as bifore' (Brady, p. 8, lines 12–13) and 'so sche chylded hym wiþouten synne and bodili peyne' (Brady p. 8, lines 14–15) — attract the marginal notes 'ante et post' (signifying that Mary was a virgin before and after Christ's birth) and 'sine dolore peperit' (signifying that his birth was without pain). Other Latin annotations by this hand include quotation from the Bible, as in the description of faith at the bottom of fol. 33ʳ: 'super lapidos hunc adificabo ecclesia' added alongside 'For upon þis stoon þat is sadde feiþ [fol. 33ᵛ] criste seyde þat he wolde bylde his churche' (Brady, p. 3, lines 19–21).[25] But not all of the Latin annotations are by this cursive secretary hand. An earlier more open and upright hand, probably fifteenth- rather than sixteenth-century, has written two quotations from Luke's gospel on fol. 33ʳ, the first in the top margin: 'fides tua te saluam fecit vade in pace luc 7', and the second in the right margin: 'nec inueni tantam fidem in israel'.[26] The second annotation responds to the example and citation alongside within the text:

---

[25] Matthew 16. 18.

[26] Luke 7. 50 and 7. 7 respectively.

'And centurio was myche preysyd of crist for þe stidfaste bileeue þat he hadde to the power of his godhede as the gospel of luc vij seiþ' (Brady, p. 3, lines 7–9). The other example of faith offered earlier in this passage is that of the Canaanite woman whose daughter is tormented by devils, 'Feiþ was þe pryncipal ground þat made þe womman of Canane to purchase helþe of soule and of body to hir douȝttir of crist þat was yuel trauayled wiþ a deuel as þe gospel witnessiþ Mᶜ xxv' (Brady, p. 3, lines 3–7), but this is not the episode invoked by the first annotation which refers to the prostitute who washed Jesus's feet with her tears, although both women were applauded for their faith by Christ.[27] The same open upright hand has provided a marginal source reference 'ad hebreos 11' on fol. 33ᵛ where this epistle is cited in the text: 'Seyntis as seynt poule seiþ þorouȝ stydfastnesse if verrey feiþ ouercamen kyngdomes' (Brady, p. 4, lines 3–4), writing the same reference on the previous leaf in the interlinear space between lines 6 and 7 of column b, again locating a quotation from the same epistle: 'For wiþouten bileeue it is inpossible as seynt poule seiþ þat eny man plese god' (Brady, p. 1, lines 10–12).[28] These demonstrations of scriptural knowledge might be taken as evidence of a reader who had clerical training, but we should not reach this conclusion too hastily. The use of Latin in general need not imply a hard distinction between religious and lay since some types of lay users — lawyers in particular — would also be proficient in Latin. Furthermore, some manuscripts of the *Pore Caitif* had a system of marginal glosses that detailed the sources of quotations; the open, upright hand which supplied these annotations in Bodl. Lib., MS Ashmole 1286 may simply have belonged to a reader who had access to another more informative copy of the text.[29]

In Bodl. Lib., MS Ashmole 1286 the attentive sixteenth-century reader whose cursive secretary script is so apparent in the margins of the Creed seems to have found little that was worthy of comment in the rest of the *Pore Caitif*. There are one or two annotations in the opening leaves of the tract on the Ten Commandments, and these leaves are worn and dirty, as if well read, but the rest of this text remains unmarked, as is the tract on the Pater Noster. In the later parts of this copy of the *Pore Caitif* there are very few annotations. Exceptionally, the start of the tract 'On Meekness' on fol. 95ʳ is marked with the addition of the word 'meknes' in the right margin, but this was written by the clear, upright hand (probably fifteenth-century in date) that added a few

---

[27] Matthew 15. 22–28.

[28] Hebrews 11. 33 and 11. 6 respectively.

[29] BL, MS Harley 2336, the manuscript used by Brady as the basis for her edition, has this system of original marginal glosses.

notes elsewhere.[30] If the sixteenth-century reader and contributor of the cursive secretary annotations found this tract interesting he left no indication of that, and in fact this and the other short tracts of the *Pore Caitif*, like the shorter chapters of *Contemplations*, do not seem to have engaged his interest at all.

Two manuscripts, Bodl. Lib., MS Bodley 423 and CUL, MS Ii.6.40, contain substantially complete versions of *Contemplations* and extracts from the *Pore Caitif*, along with other texts. Bodl. Lib., MS Bodley 423, a composite codex made up from four originally separate parts, has the full text of *Contemplations* as well as — separately — its final chapter (AB), and a derivative text on temptation based on chapters X-Y-Z.[31] The extracts from the *Pore Caitif* comprise five of the 'short sentences' ('The Counsel of Christ', 'Of Virtuous Patience', 'Of Temptation', 'The Charter of Heaven', and 'The Horse or Armour of Heaven').[32] These sections from the *Pore Caitif* are copied immediately after the X-Y-Z text from *Contemplations*, meaning that here, as in Bodl. Lib., MS Ashmole 1286, readers would have encountered material from both compilations in close conjunction.[33] One such reader was Alin Kyes, a London pewterer, who was apprenticed to William Richmond in 1503–04 and recorded as a member of the pewterers' company throughout the 1520s.[34] His name occurs (on fol. 227^r) with that of Robert Cuttynge, who is designated as 'master governor of SG'. Cuttynge himself does not seem to have been a pewterer; he may have had a connection with the shipwrights' guild because the other name on this leaf, the mysterious 'Peter Pungyarnar-', is actually the name of a ship, the *Peter Powngarnerd*, variously spelt, or 'Peter Pomegranate'. The *Peter Pomegranate* was built along with the *Mary Rose* in 1510, and named in honour of Katherine of Aragon (the pomegranate was part of the arms of Granada); when it was rebuilt in 1536 it was renamed simply the *Peter*.[35] This is an important reminder that personal names in manuscripts may not always be what they seem. Additionally, these facts help to narrow down the date of Kyes's inscription, and thus his reading of these particular texts, to between 1510 and 1536,

---

[30] 'On Meekness' is the compilation's twelfth tract according to Brady, 'The Pore Caitif', p. 532.

[31] See Connolly, 'A New Tract on Temptation'.

[32] Tracts 5–9 according to Brady, 'The Pore Caitif', p. 532.

[33] The X-Y-Z text is on fols 167^r–168^v; the extracts from *Pore Caitif* are on fols 168^v–178^r.

[34] More information about Kyes has been uncovered by Rice, 'Profitable Devotions'.

[35] Colledge, *Ships of the Royal Navy*, I, 417, gives details of the rebuilding; the ship is illustrated in the Anthony Roll of 1546, see Knighton and Loades, *The Anthony Roll of Henry VIII's Navy*, pp. 42–43.

whilst his use of the formula *Ego sum bonus puer quem deus amatt* ('I am a good boy whom God loves') suggests that he may have inscribed the book closer to the beginning of that period.

Conversely, Glasgow, Univ. Lib., MS Hunter 520 contains a complete copy of the *Pore Caitif* in conjunction with a single extract from *Contemplations*. In this manuscript, in contrast to the other annotated copies of the *Pore Caitif* discussed here, the opening tracts on the Pater Noster, Creed, and Ten Commandments have been left almost entirely unmarked, and most readerly activity occurs in the later 'short sentences'. An unpractised secretary hand has written a variety of notes in the margins of the 'Love of Jesus', 'On Meekness', and 'The Mirror of Chastity', though mostly only enumerating or reiterating points that are already listed in the text.[36] Where the text reads 'Throgh twey þingis principali may a man knowe wher he be meke' (p. 223: Brady, p. 165, lines 4–5), the annotator repeats: 'throgh ij thynges princypaly' and then adds the numbers '1' and '2' beside the relevant points. Alongside the mention of 'þre degrees of goddis loue' (p. 215; Brady, p. 158, lines 8–9) the annotator repeats: 'thur be thre degrees of þe treu loue of gode'. Occasionally, as is apparent from the use of identical ink, this hand employs a distinctive square symbol as a non-verbal marker of text, as for instance further down this leaf beside the penultimate line where the text reads 'whanne man suffriþ gladly & mekely for crist alle anguischis and is not ouercomen wiþ no delectaciouns' (Brady, p. 158, lines 18–20), and again on p. 225 beside a comment on covetousness: 'For where couetise is þere is not þe loue of crist' (Brady, p. 166, lines 5–6). This square mark recurs several times in the final tract of the *Pore Caitif*, 'The Mirror of Chastity', where it is used to draw attention to various statements such as: 'Crist seide alle moun not but not alle wolen take' (p. 255; Brady, p. 188, line 27 — p. 189, line 1), and 'Crist seiþ in þe gospel aske ȝe & it shal be ȝeuen to ȝou' (p. 256; Brady, p. 189, lines 13–14). The same hand is also active in the extract from *Contemplations*, the much-reproduced final chapter (AB) on the topic of prayer, here given the rubricated title *Bona Oratio* ('Good Prayer', p. 357). Here the marginal reiterations of text (partly lost due to cropping) may have been conceived as devotional prompts '<t>o get comp<un>tion behold with þi goostly yȝe hys pytous passyens' (p. 358; Connolly, p. 42, AB/19–20); 'deuocyon cast dou<n> thy bod<y> to þe gr<o>und' (p. 361; Connolly, p. 43, AB/63). A different hand characterized by hooked not looped ascenders, a double compartment 'a', and an almost circular 'e' with a vertical bar has noted points that relate to the afterlife in 'The Horse or Armour of Heaven', contrib-

---

[36] Tracts 11, 12, and 15 according to Brady, 'The Pore Caitif', p. 532.

uting marginal summaries 'of þe peynes of helle' (p. 196; Brady, p. 143 lines 8–12) and 'of purgatorye' (p. 198; Brady, p. 144, lines 17–19). The latter annotation drew the attention of a Protestant sympathizer who deleted both it and the reference to purgatory in the text at the top of p. 199: 'Thanne sende hem to [pur... *3 or 4 words erased*] passynge eiþer lastyng for a tyme and loke hou þei schulen fare' (p. 199).[37] A much less accomplished hand that struggles to achieve a cursive format has written 'remember' in large shakily formed letters in the bottom margin of p. 193 where the discussion of the allegory concerns the saddle (equivalent to Brady, p. 140, line 27 – p. 141, line 10), but in this instance the annotation may not relate to the text: the same hand tries the same word several times throughout the manuscript, most fully on p. 264 'remembere me bel', and abortively 'Re' on p. 268 at the very end of the *Pore Caitif*.

The multiple sixteenth-century users of Glasgow, Univ. Lib., MS Hunter 520 found points of interest in parts of the *Pore Caitif* that did not attract the attention of the early sixteenth-century lawyer Thomas Roberts, and if other members of Thomas's family read his copy of the text in BL, MS Harley 2322, they left no sign of their reading. One of his sons, Edmund Roberts (1520–1585), had a devotional anthology of his own, Bodl. Lib., MS Rawlinson C. 894, a late fifteenth-century collection of short English prose texts that includes no part of the *Pore Caitif* itself, but which does offer a text that resembles one of its tracts: *A Treatise of Ghostly Battle* is very similar to the *Pore Caitif*'s spiritual allegory 'The Horse or Armour of Heaven'. *A Treatise of Ghostly Battle* was one of the items in the collection that Edmund Roberts read most diligently: he annotated it carefully, underlining key allegorical terms and condensing their meaning into marginal notes. Edmund did not annotate all of the texts in this anthology, but one other that he clearly valued was its copy of the final chapter from *Contemplations*. On fol. 57ʳ he picked out the start of its embedded prayer, 'A lord god allmy3ty blessid mot þou be' (Connolly, p. 43, AB/65), which had no distinguishing rubric or paraph, and made it easier to spot by underlining its opening words; further, he also added an approving comment in the margin alongside: 'here begnnethe a vere good praer'.[38]

Edmund Roberts was not alone in his regard for this fifteenth-century devotion. The sixteenth-century reader whose cursive secretary hand supplied so many

---

[37] Equivalent to Brady, p. 144, lines 19–20, but her text omits the words erased here, reading simply: 'þanne sende him to purgatorie & loke hou þei shulen fare'.

[38] For more detailed discussion of Edmund Roberts's reading, see Connolly, 'Sixteenth-Century Readers Reading Fifteenth-Century Religious Books' and Connolly, *Sixteenth-Century Readers, Fifteenth-Century Books*.

annotations to the leaves of Bodl. Lib., MS Ashmole 1286 added more notes to this final part of *Contemplations* than to any of its other chapters, marking the line 'God of þi grete mercy haue mercy on me' (fol. 31ʳ; Connolly, p. 43, AB/81) with the opening words of Psalm 51, 'Miserere mei deus', and adding pointers to emphasize the requirement to pray for the dead, as noted above.³⁹ In the chapter's earlier description of Christ's Passion this annotator picked out some graphic details which suggest a meditative style of reading that dwelt repeatedly on aspects of Christ's suffering. Thus the text's lengthier account of the flogging of Christ and the breaking of his body is condensed in the margins of fol. 30ʳ⁻ᵛ into a series of sharp summaries: 'Christ whipt till he voyded so much blood of that he stod vp to the oncles there in'; 'his flesh raced to the bone'; 'Christs sinewes & ioynts all burst vpon the Crosse' (Connolly, p. 42, AB/28–30, 31, 44–45). This final chapter of *Contemplations* was the part of the work that was most often reproduced, extant in seventeen copies independently from the full text. In five of these instances the chapter occurs in conjunction with the *Pore Caitif*: in addition to Glasgow, Univ. Lib., MS Hunter 520 and Bodl. Lib., MS Bodley 423 discussed above, chapter AB occurs in BL, MS Harley 1706, fols 83ʳ–84ʳ a few leaves before the variant version of the 'Charter of Heaven', as it does also in that manuscript's congener, Bodl. Lib., MS Douce 322, fol. 97ʳ⁻ᵛ. In CUL, MS Hh.1.12, which has lost its opening leaves, chapter AB originally stood at the head of an anthology which had as its next item the tract on the Pater Noster from the *Pore Caitif*, and which borrows eleven tracts in total from the compilation.

Material from both compilations, in either full or extracted forms, was copied in similar manuscript contexts, meaning that until the end of the fifteenth century users of religious anthologies were equally likely to encounter either text in their devotional reading. Thereafter the fates of the two texts began to diverge. One difference between *Contemplations* and the *Pore Caitif*, and a crucial difference in terms of their reception, is the fact that the *Pore Caitif* was never printed: its circulation was wholly dependent on manuscript format. It was certainly extensively copied. In their bibliography of English mystical writings Valerie Lagorio and Michael Sargent recorded a total number of fifty-six manuscript witnesses; these comprise thirty-two complete or originally complete copies, and twenty-four copies that consist of extracts or fragments, and to these may now be added two more manuscripts: Durham, University Library, MS Additional 754 and New Haven, Yale University, Beinecke Library, MS Takamiya 110.⁴⁰ With a total of witnesses approaching sixty, the *Pore Caitif*

---

³⁹ See p. 141 above.
⁴⁰ Lagorio and Sargent, 'English Mystical Writings', pp. 3135–36 and 3470–71.

is comparable in the size of its corpus to Nicholas Love's *Mirror of the Blessed Life of Jesus Christ* and Walter Hilton's *Scale of Perfection*, both texts that survive in full and extracted forms. Michael Sargent has considered what such numbers of manuscripts might mean in terms of the production, transmission, and availability of texts in the later medieval period.[41] Yet despite such a comparatively large number of manuscripts the *Pore Caitif* could never achieve the kind of expansive circulation that printing allowed and that *Contemplations* enjoyed.

Contemplations was printed by Wynkyn de Worde, first in 1506 and then again in 1519(?). The effect of these two successive print-runs would have been to push a significant number of extra copies of the text onto the market, though it is hard to be sure just how many. The most useful comparisons come from the study of law books, where J. H. Baker suggests 'print-runs well into three figures in respect of books which now survive only in a handful of copies', based on a lawsuit that quantified the stock of a book-seller.[42] These of course are books intended for a discrete set of users, but similar figures — between three hundred and five hundred — are suggested by Mary Erler for printed books of hours, a type of text aimed at a wider market.[43] From Wynkyn de Worde's two printings of *Contemplations* only nine copies are recorded by the online *STC*, comprising six of the later, undated, printing and three of the first edition of 1506.[44] Recently a further copy has come to light in the Russell Library at St Patrick's College, Maynooth, Republic of Ireland, where it had gone unnoticed because it is bound at the back of a collection of late seventeenth- and early eighteenth-century forms of prayer.[45] This copy of *Contemplations* has no contemporary readers' annotations or marks. Its clean margins are typical of most of the other printed copies of this text, with the result that we know almost nothing about those who owned or read the work in printed format. Exceptionally one early owner of the printed version may be identified: this was James Morice, the Tudor administrator who was clerk of works to Lady Margaret Beaufort and who held various positions in the reigns of Henry VIII and Edward VI; he died in the reign of Mary Tudor.[46] In the list of the books that Morice compiled as being in his possession in 1508 the eleventh of twenty-

---

[41] Sargent, 'What Do the Numbers Mean?'.

[42] Baker, 'The Books of the Common Law', p. 427.

[43] Erler, 'Devotional Literature', p. 496.

[44] *STC* 21259, 21260.

[45] See Connolly, 'An Unrecorded Copy'.

[46] On Morice's career, see Oates, 'English Bokes Concernyng to James Morice' and Erler, 'The Laity', pp. 145–48.

three items is described only as 'Richard Rolle', but since none of Rolle's works had been printed by this date this reference must signify the 1506 edition of *Contemplations*, whose full title was *Richard Rolle hermyte of Hampull in his Contemplacyons of the drede and love of God*.

Wynkyn de Worde's choice to print *Contemplations* demonstrates a perceived readership for the compilation shortly after the turn of the sixteenth century and throughout its first two decades; printers printed what they believed would sell, and de Worde's decision to issue a second edition is further proof of the work's market appeal. By the third decade of the century there might therefore have been between six hundred and one thousand printed copies of the text in circulation.[47] In addition there were at least seventeen manuscript copies: sixteen extant manuscripts and one more, because none of the surviving manuscripts was the copy text used by de Worde. And *Contemplations*, just like the *Pore Caitif*, was also subject to extraction and anthologization. If the manuscripts that contain individual chapters of the text are counted amongst its circulation, then a total of about thirty-five manuscript copies may be reached, and this is doubtless a lower number than actually existed. Whilst this total does not match the number of manuscript copies of the *Pore Caitif*, once the printed copies are added in it is clear that the reach of *Contemplations* in the sixteenth century must have greatly exceeded that of its companion compilation.

Printed copies did not wholly displace manuscripts in the sixteenth century as the continued annotation of manuscript copies shows. Yet at the same time that the various sixteenth-century readers of Bodl. Lib., MS Ashmole 1286 and Glasgow, Univ. Lib., MS Hunter 520 were diligently annotating their copies of the *Pore Caitif*, elsewhere other manuscripts of that same text were being discarded and making their way into the workshops of bookbinders to be recycled as wrappers and spine guards. This was doubtless the way in which innumerable medieval manuscripts met their ends, thereby vanishing without trace, but clear evidence that this was the precise fate of two copies of *Pore Caitif* may be presented here.

In the first instance, two single leaves from the same manuscript were used in the binding of the same late sixteenth-century printed book. Both the book and the manuscript leaves are now in the Bodleian Library, where the leaves have two separate manuscript pressmarks.[48] The book is a copy of

---

[47] I base these figures on Mary Erler's most conservative estimate and a more generous one suggested by Andrew Pettegree, private communication.

[48] The printed book is Bodl. Lib., 8° I 5. Th.; the leaves are Bodl. Lib., MSS Bodl. Eng. th. c. 50 and Bodl. Eng. th. e. 1.

Doctrinae Iesuiticae praecipua capita, which was printed in France, at Rupellae (La Rochelle) between 1585 and 1588, but bound in England. The manuscript leaves contain parts of 'The Charter of Heaven' and 'The Horse or Armour of Heaven'.[49]

The second instance where a copy of the *Pore Caitif* was chopped up and transformed into manuscript waste survives in the form of four bifolia that were used as pastedowns in the binding of a sixteenth-century book. The book, previously part of the library of the Earls of Macclesfield at Shirburn Castle, was sold at Sotheby's on 2 October 2008, lot no. 4810, and is now in the Takamiya collection.[50] It actually comprises two works: *Commentarii in librum Demetrii Phalerei de elocutione*, by Pietro Vettori (1499–1585), printed in Florence in 1562, and *Poetica Horatiana*, by Giovanni Battista Pigna (*c*. 1530–1575), printed in Venice in 1561. The two works were bound together in a contemporary English blind-tooled calf binding, probably at the behest of its first known owner, Thomas Byng, whose inscription 'Tho Bingus' is on the first title-page. Byng was Master of Clare College Cambridge and Regius Professor of Civil Law; he died in 1599 and was buried in Hackney Church in Middlesex.[51] He was the owner of this book, but cannot be regarded as a *reader* of the *Pore Caitif*: his interest undoubtedly lay in the volume's printed contents and not its vellum covers. The contents of the bifolia, not identified at the time of the Sotheby's sale, are parts of the texts on the Ten Commandments and the Pater Noster, some of the most frequently annotated tracts in the *Pore Caitif*, and amongst those which had caught the attention of another lawyer, Thomas Roberts, a few decades earlier.[52]

In contrast to these two occasions where the *Pore Caitif* was dismembered, there is no equivalent instance of the reuse of *Contemplations* in the binding of an early printed book. It may just be a matter of time before one comes to light, since there are many discoveries still to be made in the retrieval and identification of binding fragments, but the current absence of such evidence makes it possible to point to the late sixteenth century as the moment when the afterlives of these two late medieval devotional compilations took very different turns.

---

[49] Tracts 8 and 9 according to Brady, 'The Pore Caitif', p. 532. For information about the content of the leaves, see Hanna, *The Index of Middle English Prose, Handlist XII*, p. 9 and p. 11.

[50] New Haven, Yale University, Beinecke Library, MS Takamiya 110; for a brief description, see Takamiya, 'A Handlist', p. 440.

[51] On Byng's career as a civil lawyer, academic, and public orator, see Stein, 'Byng, Thomas (d. 1599)'.

[52] I thank A. S. G. Edwards for drawing my attention to these bifolia.

Contemplations was given renewed vigour by the printed editions issued by Wynkyn de Worde, and a reputational boost by his ascription of its authorship to Richard Rolle; these factors allowed the text to enjoy an active and expansive readership in the sixteenth century. The association with Rolle later prompted the text's inclusion in Horstman's *Yorkshire Writers*, essentially a reprint of de Worde's 1506 edition for a new generation of late Victorian readers, and the text is now widely accessible through the modern edition prepared for the Early English Text Society.[53] By contrast the only editions of the *Pore Caitif* that have been undertaken presently remain in less accessible formats.[54] Scholarly attention to these two texts from the late nineteenth century onwards has deepened the divergence in their fortunes, but the key to their contrasting post-medieval fates lies in their very different encounters with early modern printing. Lacking the advantage of print circulation, and labouring under the disadvantage of a negative association with Wycliffe and Lollardy, the *Pore Caitif* fell gradually into disuse during the sixteenth century.[55] Its perceived value in terms of early modern book production was as *waste*, and in the codicological contexts cited above it is no more than a passive element that has ceased to enjoy an active function in the books in which it is housed. It is no longer a text to be read and ruminated and responded to; instead it has been reduced to its own very materiality, transformed into passive components of the physical construction of other books. The compilation now finds itself part of most unexpected assemblages, which were contexts definitely not anticipated by its author; indeed, in unforeseen ways these copies of the *Pore Caitif* have become participants in the very 'multiplicacioun of manye bookis' (Brady, p. 1, line 6) against which its author had counselled.

---

[53] *Yorkshire Writers*, ed. by Horstman, II, 72–105; *Contemplations*, ed. by Connolly.
[54] 'The Pore Caitif', ed. by Brady; 'Le Pore Caitif', ed. by Moreau-Guibert.
[55] See Nicole Rice's essay in this volume.

Works Cited

Manuscripts

Cambridge, University Library [CUL], MS Ff.6.55
Cambridge, University Library [CUL], MS Hh.1.12
Cambridge, University Library [CUL], MS Ii.6.2
Cambridge, University Library [CUL], MS Ii.6.40
Cambridge, St John's College, MS G. 11
Cambridge, St John's College, MS G. 28
Cambridge, Trinity College, MS B.14.53
Durham, University Library, MS Additional 754
Glasgow, University Library, MS Hunter 496
Glasgow, University Library, MS Hunter 520
London, British Library [BL], MS Harley 1706
London, British Library [BL], MS Harley 2322
London, British Library [BL], MS Harley 2335
London, British Library [BL], MS Harley 2336
London, British Library [BL], MS Stowe 38
London, Lambeth Palace Library, MS 484
London, Lambeth Palace Library, MS 541
London, Westminster School, MS 3
Manchester, John Rylands Library, MS English 85
New Haven, Yale University, Beinecke Library, MS Takamiya 110
Oxford, Bodleian Library [Bodl. Lib.], MS Additional B. 66
Oxford, Bodleian Library [Bodl. Lib.], MS Ashmole 1286
Oxford, Bodleian Library [Bodl. Lib.], MS Bodley 423
Oxford, Bodleian Library [Bodl. Lib.], MS Douce 322
Oxford, Bodleian Library [Bodl. Lib.], MS Eng. th.c.50
Oxford, Bodleian Library [Bodl. Lib.], MS Eng. th.e.1
Oxford, Bodleian Library [Bodl. Lib.], MS Rawlinson C. 299
Oxford, Bodleian Library [Bodl. Lib.], MS Rawlinson C. 894

Primary Sources

Contemplations of the Dread and Love of God, ed. by Margaret Connolly, Early English Text Society, o.s., 303 (Oxford: Oxford University Press, 1994)

The 'Exhortacion' from Disce mori: Edited from Oxford, Jesus College, MS 39, ed. by E. A. Jones, Middle English Texts, 36 (Heidelberg: Winter, 2006)

Foxe, John, *Actes and Monuments* (London, 1563)

'*The Pore Caitif*: Edited from MS. Harley 2336 with Introduction and Notes', ed. by Mary Teresa Brady (unpublished doctoral dissertation, Fordham University, 1954)

'Le Pore Caitif: Editions critique et diplomatique d'après le manuscrit de la Bibliothèque Nationale de Paris, anglais 41, avec introduction, notes et glossaire', ed. by Karine Moreau-Guibert (unpublished doctoral thesis, University of Poitiers, 1999)

Visitation Articles and Injunctions, vol. II, ed. by W. H. Frere and W. P. M. Kennedy (London: Longmans Green, 1910)

The Works of a Lollard Preacher, ed. by Anne Hudson, Early English Text Society, o.s., 317 (Oxford: Oxford University Press, 2001)

Yorkshire Writers: Richard Rolle of Hampole, an English Father of the Church, and his Followers, ed. by C. Horstman, 2 vols (London: Swan Sonnenschein, 1895–96)

Secondary Works

Baker, J. H., 'The Books of the Common Law', in *The Cambridge History of the Book in Britain*, vol. III: *1400–1557*, ed. by Lotte Hellinga and J. B. Trapp (Cambridge: Cambridge University Press, 1999), pp. 411–32

Brady, Mary Teresa, 'The Apostles and the Creed in Manuscripts of *The Pore Caitif*', *Speculum*, 32 (1957), 323–25

——, 'The Pore Caitif: An Introductory Study', *Traditio*, 10 (1954), 529–48

Colledge, James Joseph, *Ships of the Royal Navy: An Historical Index*, 2 vols (Newton Abbot: David and Charles, 1969–70)

Connolly, Margaret, 'Books for the "helpe of euery persoone þat þenkiþ to be saued": Six Devotional Anthologies from Fifteenth-Century London', *Yearbook of English Studies*, 33 (2003), 170–81

——, 'Evidence for the Continued Use of Medieval Medical Prescriptions in the Sixteenth Century: A Fifteenth-Century Remedy Book and its Later Owner', *Medical History*, 60 (2016), 133–54

——, 'A New Tract on Temptation: Extracts from *Contemplations of the Dread and Love of God* in MS Bodley 423', *Notes and Queries*, 237 (1992), 280–81

——, *Sixteenth-Century Readers, Fifteenth-Century Books: Continuities of Reading in the English Reformation* (Cambridge: Cambridge University Press, 2019)

——, 'Sixteenth-Century Readers Reading Fifteenth-Century Religious Books: The Roberts Family of Middlesex', in *Middle English Religious Writing in Practice: Texts, Readers, and Transformations*, ed. by Nicole R. Rice, Late Medieval and Early Modern Studies, 21 (Turnhout: Brepols, 2013), pp. 239–62

——, 'An Unrecorded Copy of Wynkyn de Worde's 1506 Edition of *Contemplations of the Dread and Love of God*', *Notes and Queries*, 64 (2017), 228

Emden, A. B., ed., *A Biographical Register of the University of Oxford to AD 1500*, 3 vols (Oxford: Clarendon Press, 1958)

Erler, Mary C., 'Devotional Literature', in *The Cambridge History of the Book in Britain*, vol. III: *1400–1557*, ed. by Lotte Hellinga and J. B. Trapp (Cambridge: Cambridge University Press, 1999), pp. 495–525

——, 'The Laity', in *A Companion to the Early Printed Book in Britain, 1476–1558*, ed. by Vincent Gillespie and Susan Powell (Cambridge: D. S. Brewer, 2014), pp. 134–49

Hanna, Ralph, *The Index of Middle English Prose, Handlist XII: Manuscripts in Smaller Bodleian Collections* (Cambridge: D. S. Brewer, 1997)

——, 'The Origins and Production of Westminster School 3', *Studies in Bibliography*, 41 (1988), 197–218

Hill, Gabriel, 'Pedagogy, Devotion, and Marginalia: Using the *Pore Caitif* in Fifteenth-Century England', *Journal of Medieval Religious Cultures*, 41 (2015), 187–207

Knighton, C. S., and D. M. Loades, eds, *The Anthony Roll of Henry VIII's Navy: Pepys Library 2991 and British Library Additional MS 22047 with Related Documents*, Occasional Publications of the Navy Records Society, 2 (Aldershot: Ashgate, 2000)

Lagorio, Valerie M., and Michael G. Sargent (with Ritamary Bradley), 'English Mystical Writings', in *A Manual of the Writings in Middle English, 1050–1500*, vol. IX, ed. by Albert E. Hartung (New Haven: Connecticut Academy of Arts and Sciences, 1993), pp. 3049–3137 and 3405–71

Moss, Amanda, 'A Merchant's Tales: A London Fifteenth-Century Household Miscellany', *Yearbook of English Studies*, 33 (2003), 156–69

Oates, J. C. T., 'English Bokes Concernyng to James Morice', *Transactions of the Cambridge Bibliographical Society*, 3.2 (1960), 124–32

Pearsall, Derek, 'The Whole Book: Late Medieval English Manuscript Miscellanies and their Modern Interpreters', in *Imagining the Book*, ed. by Stephen Kelly and John J. Thompson, Medieval Texts and Cultures of Northern Europe, 7 (Turnhout: Brepols, 2005), pp. 17–29

Raymo, Robert R, 'Works of Religious and Philosophical Instruction', in *A Manual of the Writings in Middle English, 1050–1500*, vol. VII, ed. by Albert E. Hartung (New Haven: Connecticut Academy of Arts and Sciences, 1986), pp. 2255–2378 and 2467–2582

Rice, Nicole, 'Profitable Devotions: Bodley MS 423, Guildhall MS 7114, and a Sixteenth-Century London Pewterer', *Journal of the Early Book Society*, 10 (2007), 175–83

Sargent, Michael G., 'What Do the Numbers Mean? A Textual Critic's Observations on Some Patterns of Middle English Manuscript Transmission', in *Design and Distribution of Late Medieval Manuscripts in England*, ed. by Margaret Connolly and Linne R. Mooney (York: York Medieval Press, 2008), pp. 205–44

Scase, Wendy, 'Reginald Pecock, John Carpenter, and John Colop's "Common Profit" Books: Aspects of Book Ownership and Circulation in Fifteenth-Century London', *Medium Aevum*, 61 (1992), 261–74

Takamiya, Toshiyuki, 'A Handlist of Western Medieval Manuscripts in the Takamiya Collection', in *The Medieval Book: Essays in Honour of Christopher de Hamel*, ed. by James H. Morrow, Richard A. Linenthal, and William Noel (Netherlands: Hes en De Graaf Publishers, 2010), pp. 421–40

Trivedi, Kalpen, 'The "Pore Caitif": *Lectio* Through *Compilatio*: Some Manuscript Contexts', *Mediaevalia*, 20 (2001), 129–52

——, '"Trewe techyng and false heritikys": Some "Lollard" Manuscripts of the *Pore Caitif*', in *In Strange Countries: Middle English Literature and its Afterlife. Essays in Memory of J. J. Anderson*, ed. by David Matthews (Manchester: Manchester University Press, 2011), pp. 132–58

Online Publications

The DIMEV: An Open-Access, Digital Edition of the 'Index of Middle English Verse', comp. by Linne R. Mooney, Daniel W. Mosser, and Elizabeth Solopova, <http://www.dimev.net>

Lock, Julian, 'Brooke, Sir Henry (1537–1592)', in *Oxford Dictionary of National Biography* (Oxford: Oxford University Press, 2004), <http://www.oxforddnb.com/view/article/5743> [accessed 4 August 2016]

STC = Universal Short Title Catalogue, <https://www.ustc.ac.uk/>

Stein, Peter, 'Byng, Thomas (d. 1599)', in *Oxford Dictionary of National Biography* (Oxford: Oxford University Press, 2004), <http://www.oxforddnb.com/view/article/4265> [accessed 5 August 2016]

Part II

Compiling the Compilation: Manuscript Transmission

Form and Fluidity: Reshaping the *Pore Caitif* and *Contemplations of the Dread and Love of God* in Oxford, Bodleian Library, MS Bodley 423 and Oxford, Bodleian Library, MS Bodley 938

Diana Denissen

The late medieval devotional compilations the *Pore Caitif* and *Contemplations of the Dread and Love of God* (also known as *Fervor amoris*) both consist of a series of (partly similar) texts and extracts of texts that have intentionally been put together to constitute a new single and unified text.[1] The *Pore Caitif* is a manual for lay religious instruction, supplemented by borrowings from, among others, Richard Rolle's *Form of Living* (Chapters 10 and 12) and his *Emendatio vitae* (Chapters 1, 5, 6, and 7). Rolle's *Form of Living* was also an important source text for *Contemplations*. This compilation opens with an explanation on why each man should desire to love and dread God, and then elaborately discusses four degrees of love — (1) 'ordeigne love', (2) 'clene loue', (3) 'stedefaste love', (4) 'parfit love' — largely based on Rolle's *Form of Living*.[2] The exact wording used in *Contemplations* to describe these four forms

---

[1] This paper is based on research as part of the Swiss National Science Foundation project 'Late Medieval Religiosity in England: The Evidence of Late Fourteenth- and Fifteenth-Century Devotional Compilations', carried out at the University of Lausanne from 2013 to 2017.

[2] For further discussion of the differences between the discussion of the four degrees of

---

Diana Denissen (dianadenissen@gmail.com) received her PhD from the University of Lausanne, where she was a project member of the Swiss National Science Foundation project 'Late Medieval Religiosity in England: The Evidence of Late Fourteenth- and Fifteenth-Century Devotional Compilations'.

of love could, however, also find its source in Saint Bridget's *Revelations* (1370). The Middle English version of the text by this Swedish mystic describes how the 'city of joy' may only be entered by people who 'haue a iiii-fold cherite: þat is to sey ordinat, clene, trewe, and perfite'.³

Both compilations must have been widely read. The *Pore Caitif* is extant in thirty-two complete (or substantially complete) versions, sixteen extract versions, and six manuscripts with only the variant version of one of the compilation's tracts ('The Charter of Heaven').⁴ In its fullest form, the *Pore Caitif* consists of fourteen different tracts. These tracts are entitled: (1) The Bileeue, (2) The Heestis, (3) Pater Noster, (4) The Councel of Crist, (5) Of Vertuous Pacience, (6) Off Temptacioun, (7) The Chartre of oure Heuenli Eritage, (8) Of Goostli Batel, (9) The Name of Ihesu, (10) Desiir of Ihesu, (11) Off Mekenes, (12) Off Mannes Will, (13) Of Actif Liif and Contemplatif Liif, (14) The Myrour off Chastite.⁵ However, the exact number of tracts as well as their order differs in the extant manuscripts, and some manuscripts also combine two or three tracts under one rubric. Moreover, tracts from the *Pore Caitif* were often incorporated in new manuscript contexts and (parts of) the compilation often appeared in miscellaneous manuscripts alongside other texts. Like the *Pore Caitif*, the *Contemplations* compilation also survives in both a full form (sixteen manuscripts) and in extract forms (twenty manuscripts), which only contain a selection of the text's twenty-four chapters.⁶

---

love in Rolle's *Form of Living* (who could have borrowed his system of degrees of love from Richard of St Victor's *Four Degrees of Violent Charity*) and *Contemplations*, see Rice, *Lay Piety and Religious Discipline*, pp. 28–30.

³ Bridget of Sweden, *Liber Celestis*, ed. by Ellis, ll. 15–16 (p. 240).

⁴ Fundamental groundwork on the *Pore Caitif* manuscripts has been done by Ian Doyle in his unpublished PhD thesis (1953), by Mary Teresa Brady in the introduction of her unpublished *Pore Caitif* edition (1954), and by Kalpen Trivedi in his unpublished PhD thesis (2001), in addition to Lagorio and Sargent. See Doyle, 'A Survey of the Origins and Circulation'; '*The Pore Caitif*', ed. by Brady; Trivedi, 'Traditionality and Difference'; and Lagorio and Sargent, 'English Mystical Writings', pp. 3049–3137. All quotations from and references to the *Pore Caitif* will be taken from Brady's 1954 edition (based on BL, MS Harley 2336), unless otherwise specified. For a list of the *Pore Caitif* manuscripts, see Jolliffe, *Check-List*, pp. 65–67.

⁵ The fourteen tracts correspond to the following lines, given in the format page number(s)/line number(s): '*The Pore Caitif*', ed. by Brady, 3/1–23/16; 24/1–91/26; 92/1–116/27; 117/1–121/22; 122/1–125/21; 126/1–127/16; 128/1–137/9; 138/1–150/4; 151/1–156/9; 157/1–163/10; 164/1–167/21; 168/1–170/10; 171/1–174/18; 175/1–199/14.

⁶ The text is edited by Connolly, *Contemplations*. All quotations will be taken from this edition. Connolly based her edition of the text on the Maidstone manuscript (Maidstone Museum,

Apart from their form, and some similar source material, the *Pore Caitif* and *Contemplations* have more in common. Both texts are addressed to the same kind of readership. Although the *Contemplations* compiler also aims to reach the higher ranks of society, 'lordis and ladies', and believes that his text is suitable for 'eche Cristen man, religious and seculer', he specifically addresses the compilation to 'suche þat be nat knowinge [...] in what maner þei schul drede and loue' and 'neuer herd speke of suche degres of loue bifore time'.[7] This is comparable to the *Pore Caitif* compiler's characterization of his audience as 'a child willynge to be a clerk', because both compilers describe their mixed-gender audience as inexperienced.[8] Furthermore, this reveals a sense of both spiritual and pedagogical ambition.

The compilers of the *Pore Caitif* and *Contemplations* suggest that compiling activity is beneficial to themselves as well as to their audience. When the *Pore Caitif* compiler writes that 'This tretis compilid of a pore caitif & nedi of goostli help of al cristen peple' he refers to why he took on the task in addition to teaching his audience 'þe riȝt weie to heuene'.[9] The same occurs in *Contemplations* when the compiler explains:

> Now þan goode God of his endeles miȝt and plenteuous goodnes graunte me grace to þinke sumwhat of his dure love and how he scholde be loud; of þat same loue sum wordis to write, whiche mowe be to him worschipe, to þe writer mede, and profitable to þe reder. Amen.[10]

The *Contemplations* compiler indicates that he wrote his text as an activity of worship, the result of which is also beneficial ('profitable') to the reader. The same mode of thinking can be found in the *Pore Caitif*, whose compiler presents himself as equally needy as his audience.

The *Contemplations* compiler is somewhat more cautious about the ability of laymen and women to reach high degrees of contemplation than the *Pore Caitif* compiler. One could read the comments of the *Contemplations* compiler that his readers 'moue nat come to suche hie contemplatif lif' as a deliberate attempt to perpetuate a hierarchy between the compiler and his audience, and

---

MS 6). For an overview of all the *Contemplations* manuscripts, see the appendix of Connolly, 'Mapping Manuscripts and Readers'.

[7] *Contemplations*, ed. by Connolly, l. 85 (p. 7), ll. 98–99 (p. 8), ll. 95–96 (p. 8), and l. 26 (p. 6).

[8] '*The Pore Caitif*, ed. by Brady, ll. 6–7 (p. 1).

[9] '*The Pore Caitif*, ed. by Brady, ll. 1–4 (p. 1).

[10] *Contemplations*, ed. by Connolly, ll. 50–54 (p. 4).

to reaffirm his authority over his readers.[11] Contrary to this, Nicholas Watson argues that the *Pore Caitif* 'sees its authority over the reader as temporary. It is necessary only as specific processes of education are in progress after which they can be replaced by internalized images of Christ himself'.[12] The phrasing in *Contemplations* about the contemplative life could, however, also be read as a reassurance. The compiler might want to stress that when one lives a worldly existence and is occupied most of the day by other necessary, but non-religious tasks, reaching higher degrees of love is not possible, but also not desirable. The *Contemplations* compiler reassures his readers that

> for þay þou be a lord or a laidi, housbond-man or wif, þou maist haue as stable an herte and wil as some religious for alle mowe not be men or women of religion þat sitteþ in þe cloistre. But soþ it is þat þe most seker wey is to fle as religious don; but for alle mowe not be men or women of religion, þerfore of eche degre in þe world God haþ ichose his seruantis.[13]

Although the *Contemplations* compiler stresses that the 'most seker way' to reach a 'stable heart' is an enclosed life, he also states that God has his chosen ones among all ranks of life. This even seems to imply that people who live a worldly existence and also have a 'stable heart' are to be admired, because even though they are not in the ideal position to maintain such a spiritual state, they are taught that leading a good life as a layperson is equivalent to the religious life. This presents the lay readers of *Contemplations* with a positive outlook on their way of life.

From a pragmatic point of view, there was of course a certain danger to lay retreat from the world. Nicole Rice defines this as the mediation between 'desire and discipline'. She describes how texts like *Contemplations*

> translate monastic models of regulation, stability, and enclosure for their anticipated lay readers, while carefully discouraging the detachment from the world that actual cloistered life (at least in its ideal form) would entail. The authors of these works posit lay spiritual enthusiasm as a potentially disruptive force. Thus, texts must mediate between desire and discipline.[14]

It is precisely this mediation between desire and discipline that makes devotional compilations like *Contemplations* and the *Pore Caitif* interesting as

---

[11] *Contemplations*, ed. by Connolly, ll. 86–87 (p. 7).

[12] Watson, 'Conceptions of the Word', p. 110.

[13] *Contemplations*, ed. by Connolly, ll. 36–41 (p. 40).

[14] Rice, *Lay Piety and Religious Discipline*, p. 17.

reflections of the challenges and opportunities presented to their compilers. Compared to the *Pore Caitif*, the *Contemplations* compiler is more strict and structured in his approach, and his work is less of a mixed or plural collection (with Rolle's *Form of Living* at its core) than the *Pore Caitif*. However, in the end both compilers share the same purpose to provide their lay audience with Middle English devotional texts that would fulfil some of their pious aspirations by using a textual and spiritual model of ascent, and they employed the same method for this: compiling.

Pore Caitif and Contemplations in MS Bodley 423

Contemplations and the *Pore Caitif* appear together in a group of eight manuscripts, but there is only one manuscript — Bodl. Lib., MS Ashmole 1286 — in which both compilations appear in their complete versions.[15] One of the most striking of the manuscripts in which the *Pore Caitif* and *Contemplations* occur together is Bodl. Lib., MS Bodley 423 (hereafter MS Bodley 423). This manuscript originally consisted of five sections, bound together as follows: A fols 1–127^v; B fols 128^r–226^v; C fols 228^r–242^v; D fols 244^r–345^v; E fols 346^r–416^v. Sections B and C were written between 1430 and 1480 by the Carthusian Stephen Dodesham and appear to have circulated as a single unit. Twenty manuscripts have now been identified as written by Dodesham. On the basis of the bulk of some of his tasks, Ian Doyle concludes that it is likely that Dodesham had links with the commercial book trade.[16] The *Pore Caitif* and *Contemplations* were both copied by Dodesham in unit B of MS Bodley 423, which suggests that the two compilations shared a similar transmission context.

One of the things that stand out in the organization of sections B and C of MS Bodley 423 is the repetition of certain parts of *Contemplations*. The compi-

---

[15] Manuscripts with both *Contemplations* and *Pore Caitif* are (1) CUL, MS Hh.1.12: *Pore Catitif* (10 tracts) – *Contemplations* (AB chapter: wanting due to loss of first folios), (2) Bodl. Lib., MS Ashmole 1286: *Pore Caitif* (complete) – *Contemplations* (complete), (3) Bodl. Lib., MS Bodley 423: *Pore Caitif* (5 tracts) – *Contemplations* (complete + summary chapters 'XYZ' + AB chapter lines 4–17), (4) Manchester, John Rylands Library, MS English 85: *Pore Catitif* (1 tract) – *Contemplations* (chapters D–M), (5) Bodl. Lib., MS Douce 322: *Pore Catitif* (1 tract) – *Contemplations* (AB chapter), (6) BL, MS Harley 1706: *Pore Catitif* (2 tracts) – *Contemplations* (AB chapter), (7) Glasgow, University Library, MS Hunter 520: *Pore Catitif* (complete) – *Contemplations* (AB chapter), (8) CUL, MS Ii.6.40: *Pore Catitif* (1 tract) – *Contemplations* (without table of contents, shortened version). For more on this, see also the essays by Margaret Connolly and Marleen Cré in this volume.

[16] Doyle, 'Stephen Dodesham of Witham and Sheen'.

lation is first copied as a whole (although the beginning of the text is missing) on fols 128–50, but this is followed by an abbreviated version of Chapter X on fol. 167ʳ and an incomplete version (lines 4–17 only) of the AB chapter on fol. 241ᵛ in section C of the manuscript. Marleen Cré identifies this feature of compiled texts as a 'circular' movement. A repetition of what has already been mentioned makes the reader pause, and 'rumination' is thus built into the text.[17] However, the production context of sections B and C of MS Bodley 423 could also have been less organized and intentional than this. Dodesham could for instance also have acquired the different versions and extracts of *Contemplations* in a more haphazard manner during the copying process.

The abbreviated version of Chapter X that follows the full version of the *Contemplations* in MS Bodley 423 is not only a selection of Chapter X, but it also adds a small amount of material from Chapters Y and Z, for instance the key passage of Chapter Z discussed earlier that not everyone needs to lead an enclosed religious life and God has chosen his servants among all ranks of worldly life (fol. 168ᵛ). As Connolly has noted, the length of this version of Chapter X is reduced by at least a third. Moreover, Connolly remarks that whereas the *Contemplations* compiler mostly refers to his sources in an elliptical way — saying only 'I rede' or 'I rede that' whilst usually noting the source in a marginal gloss — the version in MS Bodley 423 makes reference to the source within the text itself. Connolly asserts that what the author-compiler of the treatise is definitely not doing is making a summary of the last part (Chapters X-Y-Z) of *Contemplations*. Instead, the author-compiler is 'using his own predetermined principles of selection to extract relevant material from different locations, in order to form a new treatise from the existing material before him. His theme is temptation and from this he never deviates'.[18] The example of MS Bodley 423 illustrates that *Contemplations* could take on different shapes, even with the full version of the text and the compiled extracts within close proximity in the same manuscript.

In addition, the abbreviated version of *Contemplations* Chapters X-Y-Z is immediately followed by a selection of five tracts from the *Pore Caitif*. The *Pore Caitif* is not identified as a separate text in MS Bodley 423, although the different titles of the five tracts included in the manuscript are rubricated. Therefore, the five *Pore Caitif* tracts blend together with the three preceding short texts in the manuscript — including the abbreviated *Contemplations* chapters — to form a new section of the manuscript. One could therefore view this section

---

[17] Cré, *Vernacular Mysticism in the Charterhouse*, pp. 278–79.

[18] Connolly, 'A New Tract on Temptation', p. 281.

as a second compilational layer in which extracts from *Contemplations* and the *Pore Caitif* are combined. Some selections from *Contemplations* and the *Pore Caitif* on fols 164–74 resonate with each other in this part of MS Bodley 423. *Contemplations* Chapter X, 'How thou shalt be war and withstande temptaciouns bothe slepynge and wakynge' (fol. 167ʳ), can for instance be connected to the *Pore Caitif* tract on the same subject, entitled 'Of Temptacyon' (fol. 171ʳ).

The structure of both the *Pore Caitif* and *Contemplations* perhaps invited the type of fragmented transmission that is visible in MS Bodley 423, because while the two compilations are a unified whole in their fullest form, the different chapters of both texts also had the potential to function on their own, that is, in an altered manuscript context and/or altered form. Additional evidence for such a mode of transmission is a text on charity (not included in MS Bodley 423), which seems to be a derivative of nine chapters of *Contemplations*. Comparable to the abbreviated version of Chapters X-Y-Z in MS Bodley 423, this text, which Connolly entitled *Eight Points on Charity*, is a selection and abbreviation of *Contemplations* Chapters D-E-F-G-H-I/K-L-M with some rewritten passages.[19] Connolly argues that *Contemplations* and *Eight Points* are interdependent, while Vincent Gillespie suggests that both texts derive from a common ancestor treatise.[20] The end of the *Eight Points* is especially interesting, because the text is defined as a 'short compilation':

> Now in þe eende of þis short tretijs þou shalt vndirstonde þat al Goddis lawe and al declaracioun þerof as in þis short co[m]pilacioun and alle oþir tretijs, is not ellis but to brynge mankynde to two þingis. Oon is to loue God and drede God and his lawe aboue alle oþir þingis, in heuene and in erþe; and þe secunde is to brynge man to loue his euene cristen in goodnesse as himsilf, and for-to come herto þou mostist loue vertues and hate vicis.[21]

While the compiler of the *Pore Caitif* writes in the compilation's prologue that the text makes the 'multiplication of many books' unnecessary because everything is contained in this one text ('without multiplicacioun of manye bookis'),[22] compilations like the *Pore Caitif* and *Contemplations* were in fact

---

[19] This text survives in four full and one partial manuscript copies: (1) Rylands MS English 85; (2) Durham, Cathedral Library, MS A. iv. 22; (3) Cambridge, Trinity College, MS R.3.21; (4) Cambridge, Trinity College, MS O.1.74; (5) Cambridge, Corpus Christi College, MS 385 (only introductory section).

[20] Connolly, 'The "Eight Points of Charity"', p. 202, and Gillespie, 'Review'.

[21] Connolly, 'The "Eight Points of Charity"', ll. 227–33 (p. 215).

[22] '*The Pore Caitif*', ed. by Brady, l. 6 (p. 1).

important sources for textual multiplications in the form of recompilation, but also through the occurrence (and even repetition) of fragments from a compilation within an anthology or miscellany.

Annotating the Pore Caitif: The Example of MS Bodley 938

The devotional anthology Bodl. Lib., MS Bodley 938 (hereafter MS Bodley 938) provides evidence of a different perspective on the form and fluidity of the *Pore Caitif*. Contrary to the less strictly defined form of the compilation in MS Bodley 423 discussed earlier, the annotations in MS Bodley 938 point to a different process of transmission. From what has been discussed in the previous two sections of this article, one might get the impression that the transmission process of the *Pore Caitif* was completely free and fluid, or in other words, that while the *Pore Caitif* compiler composed his text as a unity, this got lost for the most part in the manuscript transmission. This was not the case. About half of the extant *Pore Caitif* manuscripts were more or less standardized manuscript copies with complete or substantially complete versions of the compilation in a fixed fourteen-tract order.[23] MS Bodley 938 moves between the standardized and fluid forms of the *Pore Caitif*'s transmission.

MS Bodley 938 was produced in or around London in the first half of the fifteenth century. The manuscript is made up of three booklets, and it consists of 283 folios in total. This section focuses on the organization of the *Pore Caitif* in booklet two and the beginning of booklet three of MS Bodley 938. The different booklets in MS Bodley 938 illustrate that the entire codex was presumably not planned or executed as a whole volume. The *Pore Caitif* tract on virginity is not included in booklet two, but opens the third booklet of MS Bodley 938. Ryan Perry suggests that perhaps the scribe decided to put booklets two and three together as he was in the process of copying the *Pore Caitif*.[24] The *Pore Caitif* is incorporated in the manuscript design of MS Bodley 938 as follows:

---

[23] Gillespie, 'Vernacular Books of Religion'. Gillespie notes that these 'typical' copies are BL, MSS Harley 953, 2322, and 2336; London, Lambeth Place Library, MSS 484 and 541; Bodl. Lib., MSS Bodley 3 and 288, Lyel 29, and Rawlinson C. 69; CUL, MS Ff.6.34; Cambridge, St John's College, MS G. 28; and Cambridge, Trinity College, MS B.14.53.

[24] See the detailed description of Bodl. Lib., MS Bodley 938 by Ryan Perry (2010) on the 'Geographies of Orthodoxy' website, <http://www.qub.ac.uk/geographies-of-orthodoxy/resources/?section=manuscript&id=91> [accessed 23 August 2017].

- fols 24ʳ–35ᵛ: Pater Noster commentary
- fols 35ᵛ–39ᵛ: Ave Maria commentary
- fols 39ᵛ–50ʳ: The Creed (**PC 1**)
- fols 50ʳ–56ʳ: 'þre þingis distrien þis world. fals confessours. fals men of lawe. & fals marchantȝ'
- fols 56ʳ–59ᵛ: '16 conditions of charite'
- fols 60ᵛ–62ʳ: Short treatise on the Ten Commandments
- fols 62ʳ–73ᵛ: 'Of weddid men & wemmen & of her children'
- fols 73ᵛ–117ʳ: Long exposition of the seven deadly sins
- fols 117ᵛ–153ᵛ: Treatise on the ten 'Heestis' (**PC 2**)
- fols 153ᵛ–166ᵛ: Treatise on the Pater Noster (**PC 3**)
- fols 167ʳ–169ᵛ: Conceil of Crist (**PC 4**)
- fols 169ᵛ–171ᵛ: On Virtuous Patience (**PC 5**)
- fol. 172ʳ⁻ᵛ: Off temptacioun (**PC 6**)
- fols 172ᵛ–178ʳ: Chartere of heuene (**PC 7**)
- fols 178ʳ–184ᵛ: Hors ether armer of heuene (**PC 8**)
- fols 184ᵛ–187ʳ: The Loue of Ihesu (**PC 9**)
- fols 187ᵛ–190ᵛ: The Desire of Ihesu (**PC 10**)
- fols 190ᵛ–192ᵛ: Of Verry Mekeness (**PC 11**)
- fols 192ᵛ–194ʳ: The effect of wille (**PC 12**)
- fols 194ᵛ–196ʳ: Of actif liif and contemplatif (**PC 13**)
- fols 196ʳ–209ʳ: The tretys of viriginite (**PC 14**)
- fols 209ᵛ–236ᵛ: Richard Rolle, *Form of Living*

The first *Pore Caitif* tract on the Creed in MS Bodley 938 opens with an annotation in red ink:

> Here begynneþ þe Crede þᵗ is þᵉ begynninge of þᵉ pore caytyf & because þᵗ þᵉ materes of þᵉ forseyd book pore caytiif sto[n]dyn not here in ordre y haue markyd þᵉ materes be numbrarye . oon . ij . iij & and so forþ. (fol. 39ᵛ)

This is actually a mix between a rubric and a marginal annotation. The regular rubrics in the manuscript are marked differently with red underlining, whereas this text is written in red in a small hand. There is not enough space between the end of the Ave Maria commentary and the beginning of the Creed, and therefore part of the annotation is written in the margin. It is hard to say whether the annotation is written in the same hand as the main text, because of the difference in size between the two scripts.

The note that marks both the beginning of the Creed and the *Pore Caitif* compilation is not the only annotation to the text in the manuscript. The Creed in MS Bodley 938 ends with the rubric (underlined in red) 'Here endiþ þe crede' (fol. 50ʳ) and then continues (still underlined in red) 'þre þinges distrien þis world. fals confessours. fals men of lawe. And fals marchantȝ', to mark the beginning of the following text. Next to this rubric, the annotator adds (two letters in black ink and the rest in red): 'þis longeþ to þe pore ca[y]tyf'. However, there is some confusion about this in the manuscript, because someone has in turn added the word 'not' in superscript between 'longeþ' and 'to' in black ink. Perhaps this was done because it is not entirely clear if the annotation 'þis longeþ ^not^ to þe pore ca[y]tyf' refers to the first half of the rubric on this folio ('Here endiþ þe crede') or to the introduction of the next tract — which indeed does not form part of the *Pore Caitif*.[25] This indicates that the *Pore Caitif* was read by active and involved readers, and regardless of whether they were 'right' in their annotations or not, the title *Pore Caitif* had important referential value to them. More annotations continue throughout MS Bodley 938 to introduce the different tracts of the compilation.[26] They end on fol. 209ʳ with the remark 'Here endiþ þe mater of þe pore caytyf which is a book so clepid'. Therefore, there are two somewhat contradictory things going

---

[25] Comparable to this is the annotation in a hand different to the hand of the principal annotator on the bottom of fol. 55ᵛ of BL, MS Harley 1197: 'Here endith the booke caulid the poore Caytife which lacketh the begineth'. However, two *Pore Caitif* tracts, 'Hors and Armor of Heaven' (PC 8) and the tract on the Name of Jesus (PC 9) follow tract PC 1 (incomplete), PC 5, PC 6, and PC 7.

[26] Bodl. Lib., MS Bodley 938, fol. 117ᵛ: 'ij . þis is þe secunde mater of þe pore caytif' (PC 2); fol. 153ᵛ: 'þis is þe iij mater of þᵉ pore caitif . iij' (PC 3); fol. 167ʳ: 'þis is þe iiij mater of þᵉ pore caitif . iiij' (PC 4); fol. 169ᵛ: 'þis is þe v mater of þᵉ pore caitiff' (PC 5); fol. 172ʳ: 'þis is þe vi mater of þᵉ pore caitiff' (PC 6); fol. 172ᵛ: 'þis is þe vii mater of þᵉ pore caitiff' (PC 7); fol. 178ʳ: 'þis is þe viii mater of þᵉ pore caitiff' (PC 8); fol. 184ᵛ: 'þis is þe IX mater of þᵉ pore caitiff' (PC 9); fol. 187ᵛ: 'þis is þe X mater of þᵉ pore caitiff' (PC 10); fol. 190ᵛ: 'þis is þe XI mater of þᵉ pore caitiff' (PC 11); fol. 192ᵛ: 'þis is þe XIJ mater of þᵉ pore caitiff' (PC 12); fol. 194ᵛ: 'þis is þe XIIJ mater of þᵉ pore caitiff' (PC 13); fol. 196ʳ: 'þis prolog wit V chapters of virginite folwynge is þe xiiij mater & þe last of þe pore caitiff' (PC 14).

on in this manuscript. On the one hand there is the transformed structure of this adapted version of the *Pore Caitif*, and on the other hand there is someone who wants to make sure that future readers know which tracts belong to the *Pore Caitif* and in which order they are supposed to read them.

The annotator of this section in MS Bodley 938 conceives of the *Pore Caitif* in its entirety as 'a book', which could refer to another version of the text, perhaps one of the more standardized single-text *Pore Caitif* manuscripts. There is a certain tension in MS Bodley 938 in the way the *Pore Caitif* is perceived either as a coherent treatise or as a text that could be partitioned into different parts and used in new contexts. In its hybridity, the compilation might have catered for a broad variety of devotional needs in the fourteenth and fifteenth centuries. In its simplest and 'standardized' version, the *Pore Caitif* was a step-by-step guide that would have been relatively easily available in small, pocket-sized volumes in single columns. The fact that the *Pore Caitif* could be partitioned into different parts, however, also meant that certain selections of the compilation could function in collections of a more specialized or specific nature.

The annotations in MS Bodley 938 that refer to the text as the 'Pore Caitif' are later additions, either by the scribe at a later stage in the copying process or by somebody else. Perhaps an annotator recognized the *Pore Caitif*, because s/he knew another version of the text, while the scribe did not. There are two things about the organization of the different tracts in this section of MS Bodley 938 that are striking. First of all, the *Pore Caitif* tract on the Creed is the only tract that is isolated from the rest of the compilation and placed between other kinds of source material in the manuscript's organization. Secondly, MS Bodley 938 now contains two different versions of the Pater Noster. Thus, it is also possible that the scribe of MS Bodley 938 in the first instance only had an exemplar of the *Pore Caitif* tract on the Creed and at a later stage came across the full version of the compilation. He then added the rest of the *Pore Caitif* (including the compilation's Pater Noster tract) and explained himself in the annotations.

The annotations in MS Bodley 938 added interesting possibilities for the readers of the *Pore Caitif*, because these notes enabled them to read the text in different ways. Either the readers could go through the text sequentially and include the interpolated pieces in their reading, or they could extract just the *Pore Caitif* tracts and read those in isolation. The later annotations of this section in MS Bodley 938 may therefore bear witness to the needs of devotional readers who wanted to be directed more quickly to specific texts, but they could also have been intended to act as a 'safety device' to avoid any more interpolations or piecemeal transmission. In other words: the annotations to the *Pore Caitif* in MS Bodley 938 added a form of 'stability' to the text.

* * *

The transmission of the *Pore Caitif* and *Contemplations* in MS Bodley 423 and MS Bodley 938 illustrates how in fact the compiling process was never fully finished. Compiled texts could be broken down to form the basis of new compilations or anthologies in an open-ended process. It is interesting that the annotations in MS Bodley 938, which reconstruct the *Pore Caitif* as the annotator knew it, counter this transmission process of compiling and recompiling. Therefore, as Steven Nichols has noted, the — what he names — 'manuscript matrix' often is 'a place of radical contingencies: of chronology, of anachronism, of conflicting subjects of representation'.[27] This also means that *Pore Caitif* and *Contemplations* allow and create space for plurality, both within the compilations themselves and through their compilation and recompilation in various anthologies and miscellanies.

---

[27] Nichols, 'Introduction', p. 8.

Works Cited

Manuscripts

Cambridge, Corpus Christi College, MS 385
Cambridge, Trinity College, MS B.14.53
Cambridge, Trinity College, MS O.1.74
Cambridge, Trinity College, MS R.3.21
Cambridge, University Library [CUL], MS Ff.6.34
Cambridge, University Library [CUL], MS Hh.1.12
Cambridge, University Library [CUL], MS Ii.6.40
Durham, Cathedral Library, MS A. iv. 22
Glasgow, University Library, MS Hunter 520
London, British Library [BL], MS Harley 953
London, British Library [BL], MS Harley 1197
London, British Library [BL], MS Harley 1706
London, British Library [BL], MS Harley 2322
London, British Library [BL], MS Harley 2336
London, Lambeth Palace Library, MS 484
London, Lambeth Palace Library, MS 541
Maidstone Museum, MS 6
Manchester, John Rylands Library, MS English 85
Oxford, Bodleian Library [Bodl. Lib.], MS Ashmole 1286
Oxford, Bodleian Library [Bodl. Lib.], MS Bodley 3
Oxford, Bodleian Library [Bodl. Lib.], MS Bodley 288
Oxford, Bodleian Library [Bodl. Lib.], MS Bodley 423
Oxford, Bodleian Library [Bodl. Lib.], MS Bodley 938
Oxford, Bodleian Library [Bodl. Lib.], MS Douce 322
Oxford, Bodleian Library [Bodl. Lib.], MS Lyel 29
Oxford, Bodleian Library [Bodl. Lib.], MS Rawlinson C. 69

Primary Sources

Bridget of Sweden, *The Liber Celestis of St Bridget of Sweden: The Middle English Version in British Library MS Claudius B I, Together with a Life of the Saint from the Same Manuscript*, ed. by Roger Ellis, Early English Text Society, 291 (Oxford: Oxford University Press, 1987)

Contemplations of the Dread and Love of God, ed. by Margaret Connolly, Early English Text Society, o.s., 303 (Oxford: Oxford University Press, 1993)

'*The Pore Caitif*: Edited from MS. Harley 2336 with Introduction and Notes', ed. by Mary Teresa Brady (unpublished doctoral dissertation, Fordham University, 1954)

Secondary Works

Cré, Marleen, *Vernacular Mysticism in the Charterhouse: A Study of London, British Library, MS Additional 37790*, The Medieval Translator/Traduire au Moyen Age, 9 (Turnhout: Brepols, 2006)

Connolly, Margaret, 'The "Eight Points of Charity" in John Rylands University Library MS English 85', in *And Gladly Wolde He Lerne and Gladly Teche: Essays of Medieval English Presented to Professor Matsuji Tajima on his Sixtieth Birthday*, ed. by Yoko Iyerli and Margaret Connolly (Tokyo: Kaibunsha, 2002), pp. 195–215

——, 'Mapping Manuscripts and Readers of *Contemplations of the Dread and Love of God*', in *Design and Distribution of Late Medieval Manuscripts in England*, ed. by Margaret Connolly and Linne R. Mooney (York: York Medieval Press; Woodbridge: Boydell, 2008), pp. 261–78

——, 'A New Tract on Temptation: Extracts from *Contemplations of the Dread and Love of God* in MS Bodley 423', *Notes and Queries*, 237 (1992), 280–81

Doyle, Ian, 'Stephen Dodesham of Witham and Sheen', in *Of the Making of Books: Medieval Manuscripts, their Scribes and Readers. Essays Presented to M. B. Parkes*, ed. by P. R. Robinson and Rivkah Zim (Aldershot: Scolar Press, 1997), pp. 94–115

——, 'A Survey of the Origins and Circulation of Theological Writings in English in the 14th, 15th and Early 16th Centuries with Special Consideration of the part of the Clergy Therein', 2 vols (unpublished doctoral dissertation, University of Cambridge, 1953)

Gillespie, Vincent, 'Review of the *Index of Middle English Prose, Handlist II: John Ryland's and Chetham's Libraries, Manchester*', *Medium Aevum*, 57 (1988), pp. 111–12

——, 'Vernacular Books of Religion', in *Book Production and Publishing in Britain, 1375–1475*, ed. by Jeremy Griffiths and Derek Pearsall, Cambridge Studies in Publishing and Printing History (Cambridge: Cambridge University Press, 1989), pp. 317–44

Jolliffe, P. S., *A Check-List of Middle English Prose Writings of Spiritual Guidance*, Subsidia mediaevalia, 2 (Toronto: Pontifical Institute of Mediaeval Studies, 1974)

Lagorio, Valerie M., and Michael G. Sargent (with Ritamary Bradley), 'English Mystical Writings', in *A Manual of the Writings in Middle English, 1050–1500*, vol. IX, ed. by Albert E. Hartung (New Haven: Connecticut Academy of Arts and Sciences, 1993), pp. 3049–3137

Nichols, Stephen, 'Introduction: Philology in a Manuscript Culture', *Speculum*, 65 (1990), 1–10

Rice, Nicole, *Lay Piety and Religious Discipline in Middle English Literature*, Cambridge Studies in Medieval Literature (Cambridge: Cambridge University Press, 2008)

Trivedi, Kalpen, 'Traditionality and Difference: A Study of the Textual Traditions of the *Pore Caitif*' (unpublished doctoral thesis, University of Manchester, 2001)

Watson, Nicholas, 'Conceptions of the Word: The Mother Tongue and the Incarnation of God', in *New Medieval Literatures*, ed. by Wendy Scase, Rita Copeland, and David Lawton (Turnhout: Brepols, 1997), pp. 85–124

Suffering for Love: Compilation and Asceticism in *Life of Soul*

Sarah Macmillan

In the devotional literature of late medieval England asceticism and textuality are increasingly related concepts. For instance, in a recent article, Amy Appleford draws attention to the underlying asceticism of the works of Julian of Norwich and Thomas Hoccleve. She argues that their religious discourse centres on the materiality of the body as text and demonstrates how the practice of writing is directly connected to the development of an ascetic identity. Moreover, she suggests that both Julian and Hoccleve's understanding of authorship transcends traditional concepts of 'masculine *auctoritas* and female *experientia*', and instead offers an image of the writer as an exemplary ascetic figure and the act of writing as ascetic.[1] Central to Appleford's argument is the important idea that both writers' sense of ascetic identity is 'neither penitential nor affective'.[2] This movement away from the penitential and the affective can be found elsewhere in ascetically inclined Middle English writing. Indeed, various devotional works offer ascetic models for their readers that are not based on penitence or affectivity but on imitation of the example set by Christ in an explicitly textual form. Drawing on Appleford's work we can think not only about authorial self-construction in terms of asceticism but also about two other important forms of text-based asceticism: firstly, the ways in which tex-

---

[1] Appleford, 'The Sea Ground and the London Street', p. 67.
[2] Appleford, 'The Sea Ground and the London Street', p. 49.

Sarah Macmillan (S.M.Macmillan@bham.ac.uk) is a Research Officer at the University of Birmingham.

tual representations of Christ are intended to shape the responses of readers and foster the development of their own ascetic identities; and secondly, the ways in which the compiling and editing of texts constituted a form of asceticism. These two elements of textual asceticism form the focus of this essay, which argues that compilers of devotional manuals not only envisioned ascetic responses in their readers but engaged in a form of textual asceticism themselves.

Numerous late medieval devotional compilations seek to transform their readers' performance of piety from the affective and penitential into an ideal of continuous asceticism based on scriptural example. For instance, the version of the late fourteenth-century treatise *Life of Soul* extant in Bodl. Lib., MS Laud misc. 210 opens with an invocation of Hebrews 13. 14: 'Frend in Crist, as Seynt Poule seiþ, we ne hauen here no Cyte þat is dwelling, but we sechen on þat is to come hereafter'.[3] This immediately emphasizes the text's intention to orientate its readers' thought away from the concerns of the world towards those of the spirit, and it directly authorizes this vision through scriptural quotation. *Life of Soul* then goes on to invoke one of the most important scriptural passages for ascetical theology, Matthew 10. 37 (echoed in Luke 14. 26):

> þou shalt loue þi Lord God abouen alle oþer þinges. For Crist seiþ: Who þat loueþ fader or moder, broþer or syster, wif or child abouen hym, he ne is not worþi to hym. And who þat hatiþ not his owne lif for me, he ne is not worþi to me.[4]

This is an explicit assertion of the life of the spirit over that of the body and its worldly associations. Inclinations such as these have clear ascetic overtones and suggest that an impulse to asceticism in the pursuit of spiritual perfection underlies much devotional literature of the late Middle Ages.[5] Indeed, Gavin Flood suggests that asceticism acts out 'the narrative of tradition',[6] and this essay argues that an ascetic ideology underpins many of the spiritual practices advocated in several late medieval devotional compilations, especially in *Life of Soul*, and that this can be linked to an explicit interest in textuality, in particular that of the Bible.

---

[3] *Þe Lyfe of Soule*, ed. by Moon, p. 1, ll. 1–3. All quotations, unless otherwise stated, come from this edition, which is based on the version extant in Bodl. Lib., MS Laud misc. 210. There is also a partial translation of the Laud text of *Life of Soul* by Schaffner.

[4] *Þe Lyfe of Soule*, ed. by Moon, p. 28, ll. 16–21.

[5] For Middle English literature and asceticism, see Hughes-Edwards, *Reading Medieval Anchoritism*, ch. 4 (religious context), and Appleford, *Learning to Die in London*, ch. 3 (secular context). Harpham, *Ascetic Imperative*, p. 23, notes that Luke 14. 26 presumes a 'total disjunction between the social and the divine' on the part of the ascetic follower of Christ.

[6] Flood, *The Ascetic Self*, p. 2.

Before examining *Life of Soul* it is helpful to establish the relationship between asceticism and textuality. In general terms asceticism refers to 'a range of habits or bodily regimes designed to resist or reverse the instinctual impulse of the body and to an ideology that maintains in so doing a greater good or happiness can be achieved'.[7] In Christian tradition such happiness consists of the restoration of the link between the human and the divine, a link that is deeply connected to love.[8] One particularly relevant way of conceptualizing asceticism is that offered by Alexander Elchaninov, who asserts that 'asceticism is necessary first of all for creative action of any kind, for prayer, for love: in other words, it is needed by each of us throughout our entire life [...]. *Every Christian is an ascetic*'.[9] Creativity, especially the creation and translation of narrative, is central to asceticism. Indeed, Geoffrey Galt Harpham argues that asceticism is 'an ideology of narrative' and the writing of ascetic exemplars enables both closure and continuation (through imitation).[10] Thus it is possible for individual selves to both engage in the narrative performance of ascetic tradition and to transcend it via ascetic imitation. This is as applicable to writers as it is to readers. In the accounts of the desert fathers, hagiographers often 'figured the author in the image of the ascetic and represented the act of composition as formative spiritual practice', especially by drawing examples from the scriptures as models of self-control.[11] Like Appleford, Derek Krueger argues that literary creation is itself an act of asceticism.[12] What follows is therefore an exploration of how asceticism is treated as a textual practice related to the development and expression of love in late medieval devotional compilations. It suggests that a goal of *Life of Soul*, and related texts such as *The Book of Tribulation*, is to foster an inward-looking love of God which simultaneously realigns one's love of the world in an ascetic ideology based not on penitence but on a continual state of contrition grounded in textuality.

It is important to note here that contrition can be understood as an inward ascetic state — as a constant awareness of the temptation to sin, resistance

---

[7] Flood, *The Ascetic Self*, p. 4.

[8] Flood, *The Ascetic Self*, pp. 145–46. Love, for instance, is central to the asceticism of Peter Damian; see Flood, *The Ascetic Self*, p. 185.

[9] Elchaninov, *The Diary of a Russian Priest*, pp. 177 and 188, cited in Ware, 'The Way of the Ascetics', p. 13, italics in original.

[10] Harpham, *Ascetic Imperative*, p. 85.

[11] Krueger, *Writing and Holiness*, p. 95. Appleford argues that the ascetic identities of both Hoccleve and Julian of Norwich are based on the example set by Job and mediated through the Office of the Dead; see Appleford, 'The Sea Ground and the London Street', pp. 50 and 54–55.

[12] Krueger, *Writing and Holiness*, p. 95.

to it, and sorrow for it — rather than penance for sins committed. As David Jasper argues, 'Contrition, regret, error — this is the language of the ascetic'.[13] Moreover, that love and asceticism (desire and denial) should be paired is not a contradiction.[14] Even John Cassian asserts that desire is necessary to enter the ascetic life, and he appeals to affective imagery in his denial of the body. Pleasure too (of self-mastery, of serving God, and of ultimate union with the divine) is considered a necessity for the ascetic.[15] *Life of Soul*, an important but little-studied text, encourages its reader to embrace tribulation as an active choice for the pleasurable reward it entails and the love it fosters, for a 'man is iblessed þat abydeþ temptacioun, for whan he is ipreuid he schal vndurfong a crowne of lif þat god hath behote to þilk þat louen hym'.[16] Patient suffering (the endurance of temptation) is understood to directly evidence love and is rewarded accordingly. Thus through the textual examples of patience offered in *Life of Soul* the reader is encouraged to take part in the narrative of Christian tradition, interweaving biblical exemplars with present lived experience.

Life of Soul is a devotional manual which compiles a variety of material prescribed for the instruction of the laity in Archbishop Peckham's syllabus of 1281 on the Ten Commandments, seven deadly sins, works of mercy, and Christian virtues. In this it is comparable to both the *Lay Folks' Catechism* (the English translation of John Thoresby's 1357 Latin catechism) and to the catechetical *Book to a Mother* (*c.* 1370–80).[17] Its principle focus is the two Evangelical Precepts — the commandments to love God and one's neighbour as oneself — and its structure is that of a catechetical dialogue in which questions about how to attain heaven lead into an exposition of the necessary sustenance of the soul, whose bread is faith in Christ and whose drink is devotion to his words. *Life of Soul* is extant in three fifteenth-century manuscripts where it is accompanied solely by religious works: Bodl. Lib., MS Laud misc. 210 (where the dialogue is between 'Friend' and 'Sir'); San Marino, Huntington Library, MS HM 502

---

[13] Jasper, *The Sacred Body*, p. 173.

[14] Jasper, *The Sacred Body*, ch. 5, pp. 63–86.

[15] Humphries, *Ascetic Pneumatology*, p. 35; Milhaven, 'Asceticism and the Moral Good', p. 376.

[16] *Þe Lyfe of Soule*, ed. by Moon, p. 6, ll. 12–15.

[17] See Powell, 'The Transmission and Circulation of the *Lay Folks' Catechism*' and Dutton, *Julian of Norwich*, for comparisons between *Book to a Mother*'s treatment of the Ten Commandments and those in *Life of Soul* within Bodl. Lib., MS Laud misc. 210, pp. 19–24. Moon also notes parallels between the treatment of the Ten Commandments in *Life of Soul* and *Pore Caitif*: *Þe Lyfe of Soule*, pp. lxxxi–lxxxv.

(where the dialogue is between a father and sister); and BL, MS Arundel 286 (where the dialogue is between a father and son).[18] This form is significant as it allows readers to envision themselves in the role of an interlocutor, questioning and learning from the authoritative teaching voice, which is consistently that of a priest or confessor.[19] The fact that the pupil's identity changes between layman and religious novice across the versions suggests that the text was adapted for a variety of audiences. Moreover, in Bodl. Lib., MS Laud misc. 210, Sir shows a sophisticated grasp of the Bible which suggests that the text was not intended for complete beginners but for readers with a certain degree of devotional literacy, hence its suitability for both monastic audiences (Huntington and Arundel) and the literate laity (Laud misc.).[20]

Life of Soul also employs a number of strategies to help its readers imitate Christ's example of self-sacrificing love. Particular themes that will be explored here include suffering and the ideal of patient love,[21] the necessity of tribulation and contrition, the possibility of a relationship with God in suffering, and love of God and neighbour. These themes are given literary form through *Life of Soul*'s chief characteristic: its self-conscious compilation of a vast amount of biblical material in apparently original translations, particularly the gospels and Pauline epistles. As Paul Schaffner observes, 'The Bible is cited frequently, at length, and to the exclusion of all other authorities, to the extent that over half of the book consists of biblical quotations'.[22]

---

[18] In addition to *Life of Soul*, Bodl, Lib., MS Laud misc. 210 also contains Rolle's *Form of Living*, *Book to a Mother*, various short treatises, *The Charter of the Abbey of the Holy Ghost* and *The Abbey of the Holy Ghost*. San Marino, Huntington Library, MS HM 502 contains Thomas of Wimbledon's sermon *Redde racionem villicacionis tue*, *The Form of Living*, a proverb (DIMEV 1867), *The Mirror of St Edmund*, a Pater Noster, and a short treatise beginning 'Pryde, wraþþe & envie'. MS Arundel 286 contains a *Treatise upon the Passion of Christ*, *Milicia Christi*, a prose prayer, two of Rolle's epistles, *The Book of Tribulation*, extracts from *The Mirror of St Edmund*, a treatise 'Of Maidenhood' (also extant in London, Westminster School, MS 3), *Ave Maris Stella*, *Benjamin Minor*, and a Wycliffite *Treatise on the Ten Commandments*. *Þe Lyfe of Soule*, ed. by Moon, reproduces the catalogue entries for each manuscript, pp. v–xii.

[19] Dutton, *Julian of Norwich*, p. 87. Dutton further discusses the function of dialogue in the compiling and teaching of doctrinal material in Julian's *Revelation*, pp. 86–122.

[20] Dutton, *Julian of Norwich*, pp. 89–90.

[21] Patience in the face of tribulation is a formative experience and tribulation a key term in Cassian's *Conferences* and *Institutes*: Appleford, *Learning to Die in London*, p. 102.

[22] *Life of Soul*, ed. by Schaffner, p. 121. Moon further notes its resemblance to a southern prose version of the Bible (*c*. 1388). The version referred to is *A Fourteenth-Century English Biblical Version*, ed. by Paues; see *Þe Lyfe of Soule*, pp. lxxiv–lxxvii.

Life of Soul is extremely interested in the Bible as a text that should saturate the reader's consciousness. In particular, it promotes a devotion to the *words* of the Bible in English. For example, in answer to the fundamental question, what causes the soul to live, the compiler has Friend ventriloquize a collection of quotations from the gospels:

> But sire, more harme is, I se ful fewe doon after Cristes techyng and his wordis, þof þei seen hem iwryten ouþer heren hem ispoken. And, neuerþeles, in his wordes is þe lyf of oure soule. For as he seiþ: þe wordes þat I haue of spoken ben spiriȝt and lif [John 6. 64]. And he seiþ also: He þat kepiþ my word schal neuer dye [John 8. 51].[23]

The imagery of words translated into actions permeates this passage. Christ's words teach the compiler, who in turn constructs a narrative that seeks to incorporate the words of everlasting life into the reader's lived experience. This is a theme that continues throughout *Life of Soul*. For example, drawing on the parable of the wise and foolish builders, Sir later petitions:

> tel me opunliche wordes þat I mow fulfillen hem in dede, þat I bylde me an hows on a fondement of ston to aȝeyn stonde wyndes and reynes and oþer stormes of þe deueles temptaciouns [Matthew 7. 24–25]. And wryte to me opunliche þe techyng of crist þat I mowe ben iheled þerby of þe sekenes of my soule.[24]

Words not only have the power to inspire actions, but they are an active protection against sin and temptation. In addition, in this example the spoken word is textualized as the in-text questioner of the Laud text, Sir, asks Friend to actively compile and expound biblical narrative, thereby mirroring the external actions of the compiler himself. Moreover, that the meaning of these words should be demanded 'openly' not only suggests that the teacher is at times rather vague (elsewhere termed 'ful schort and derk'),[25] but also that his full vernacular exposition would enable a degree of understanding that has hitherto been hidden. Indeed, *Life of Soul* regularly celebrates attaining a detailed and in-depth understanding of the words of the Bible, and the informed interlocutor uses his existing knowledge of scripture to demand more. For instance, drawing on the warning against hiding light under a bushel, Sir insists that Friend 'hyde not from me but telle openliche þat I axed raþer: Whyche is þe lyflode of oure

---

[23] *Þe Lyfe of Soule*, ed. by Moon, p. 15, ll. 6–12. This is followed by quotes from John 12. 49–50 and Luke 12. 47–48.

[24] *Þe Lyfe of Soule*, ed. by Moon, p. 20, ll. 10–15.

[25] *Þe Lyfe of Soule*, ed. by Moon, p. 18, l. 14.

soule'.²⁶ In this there exists a confident expectation of satisfaction, which the teacher then provides at length in his discussion of Christ as bread and as man. Thus even though the cleric holds the superior position, the literate layman has the power to insist on access to deeper understanding of biblical text.

Sir's insistence also serves to prefigure the text's central message, embodied in the most important words in the Bible, the Evangelical Precepts: love of God and neighbour. These are 'Cristes wordes as he tauȝte hem':

> þes wordes ben two wordes of loue þat enclosen alle þe ten hestis. Þe first word of þes is þe first & þe grettest comaundement of goddis lawe and þat is: Þou schalt loue þi Lord God abouen alle oþer þinges [Mark 12. 30; Matthew 22. 37; Luke 10. 27] [...]. Þe secunde grettest comaundement is ilyche to þis. Þou schalt loue þi broþer as þi seluen, and in þes two comaundementis hangeþ alle þe lawe and þe prophetes [Matthew 22. 39–40].²⁷

The compiler thus purposefully weaves translations of his biblical source into his own exposition to demand a redirection of the reader's experience of love towards the divine. He foreshadows the biblical terms in his own expression ('words', 'love', 'commandment' or 'hestis') to blur the line between exposition and source, thus saturating the reader in the language of the Bible. Moreover, these biblical words, insists the compiler, are textually embodied in the person of Christ, whose example we should read literally: 'Þis loue had oure Lord Iesu Crist to his Fader of heuene to ȝeuen vs ensample how we schulden loue oure Lord, fader of heuene, abouen alle oþer þinges'.²⁸ Thus the writer does not identify Christ as the object *of* love, rather as the textual exemplar of *how to* love.

Christ as exemplar, who directs rather than demands the reader's love, introduces the idea that an ascetic denial of all that is unrelated to the love of God is integral to the life of soul. Indeed, such love enables the reader to overcome temptation and achieve the life of soul 'whyles he is in þis world'.²⁹ Love, often a highly emotive and affective concept in devotional literature,³⁰ is here paired with an ascetic ideal of self-perfection through sacrifice, contrition, and renunciation of sin. It is both a way of enduring tribulation and the means by which tribulation becomes a transformative experience through contrition, for 'þe

---

[26] *Þe Lyfe of Soule*, ed. by Moon, p. 21, ll. 8–9.
[27] *Þe Lyfe of Soule*, ed. by Moon, p. 28, ll. 13–17; p. 37, ll. 7–10.
[28] *Þe Lyfe of Soule*, ed. by Moon, p. 30, ll. 9–11.
[29] *Þe Lyfe of Soule*, ed. by Moon, p. 4, l. 2.
[30] McNamer, *Affective Meditation*, pp. 49–52, discusses compassion as proof of love.

grettest herying of god is charite, as seynt poule seiþ [1 Corinthians 13. 13]'.
This loving praise can express itself through 'sacrifice', for God

> wilt not dispisen an herte þat is contrit and humulied to þe [Psalm 50. 19]. It is certeyn þat ȝif a man loueþ God wiþ al his herte and abouen alle oþer þinges, whan he knoweþ how he haþ displesyd God þoru synne he wil make miche sorowe in his herte for his synne, and humylien hymseluen ful lowe to God to haue forȝeuenes of his trespass.
>
> And in þis wyse Mary Maudeleyne hadde forȝeuenes of hire synnes. For Crist seiþ: Many synnes were forȝeuen hire for scho loued myche [Luke 7. 47].[31]

Thus *Life of Soul* does not focus on affectivity or penitence but on aiding its reader to establish an identity based on a continual state of ascetic contrition grounded in love of God through imitation of scriptural (that is, textual) example.

In the process of developing this state of contrition *Life of Soul* also encourages its reader to engage more overtly with text-based asceticism rather than image-based affectivity, a transition indicated by the sheer number of vernacular quotations from the Bible, which it employs as its only named authoritative source. *Life of Soul* is distinguished from the vast majority of devotional manuals (such as Edmund of Abingdon's *Speculum ecclesiae*, Richard Rolle's *Form of Living*, *The Book of Tribulation*, and *The Abbey of the Holy Ghost*, all of which are extant with *Life of Soul* in its three surviving manuscripts) by the way in which it promotes the language of the Bible and the fact that it is steeped in scriptural metaphors and allusions.[32] Biblical quotations were, of course, extremely common in devotional works; in *The Chastising of God's Children*, for instance, the compiler inserts a number of biblical quotations in English, in Latin, or both, taken variously from the Vulgate and other sources as well as original translations.[33] But, as in the quote above, *Life of Soul* does not offer citations of the Vulgate followed by translations in the form typical of many devotional works; it simply presents the text in English. In fact, *Life of Soul* is unusual for

---

[31] *Þe Lyfe of Soule*, ed. by Moon, p. 36, l. 10 – p. 37, l. 2.

[32] *Speculum Ecclesiae* and Rolle's *Form of Living* are found with *Life of Soul* in San Marino, Huntington Library, MS HM 502; *The Book of Tribulation* in MS Arundel 286; and *The Abbey of the Holy Ghost* in Bodl. Lib., MS Laud misc. 210.

[33] Sutherland, '*The Chastising of God's Children*', p. 361. In addition, the Wycliffite Bible was owned by a wide variety of readers, including religious houses: Hanna, 'English Biblical Texts', esp. p. 145. For access to the Bible, see Hudson, *The Premature Reformation*, pp. 231–38. There is also an acknowledged gap between Wycliffite Bibles and Lollardy ideology; see Poleg, 'Wycliffite Bibles as Orthodoxy'.

its complete exclusion of Latin. Helen Moon sees this as anticipating the extensive scriptural quotation used in devotional material of the fifteenth century.[34] Yet, as Michael Sargent observes, thinking of a text as 'premature' or 'out of time' is problematic, because it negates the significance of a piece of writing in its own period.[35] Moreover, James Simpson stresses 'that pre-Reformation, late medieval spirituality was already moving towards chastened, non-visual forms of spiritual experience', such as that advocated by the *Cloud*-author or expounded later in the English translations of Thomas à Kempis's *Imitation of Christ*.[36] Thus *Life of Soul* offers a significant insight into late medieval devotion to the *words* of scripture, and to the Bible both quoted and 'authoritatively expounded' in the vernacular.[37] The compilation strategy in *Life of Soul* is to assemble a huge amount of biblical material so as to create a work which is biblical in tone and lexis and where the authorial voice is almost indistinguishable from the translated material.[38] This act of compilation epitomizes the text's aim to seamlessly integrate the Bible into the mindset of the reader and ultimately promotes English as a language of biblical instruction.

As noted above, unlike many other devotional works, *Life of Soul* does not offer quotations from the Vulgate followed by translations. Instead it incorporates English translations so that 'the reader is scarcely aware of the ending of biblical quotation and the beginning of explanatory or linking sentences'.[39] This emphasis on vernacular biblical text, the desire to immerse readers in the language of the Bible, and the significance of text rather than image are features usually discussed in relation to Wycliffite writing.[40] Yet, unlike texts such as *The Cloud of Unknowing*, where the Latin text is the ultimate biblical authority, or *The Chastising of God's Children*, which ultimately expresses concerns over the

---

[34] *Þe Lyfe of Soule*, ed. by Moon, p. xlix.

[35] Sargent, 'Censorship or Cultural Change?', pp. 59–60.

[36] Simpson, '1543–1550s: Texts', pp. 253–54.

[37] Hanna, 'English Biblical Texts', p. 146, uses this phrase in relation to Cambridge, Magdalene College, MS Pepys 2498.

[38] While *Life of Soul* chiefly compiles its contents from the Bible, it does have parallels with material on the Ten Commandments in *Pore Caitif* and shares structural similarities with *Book to a Mother*. *Life of Soul*, ed. by Schaffner, pp. 121–22.

[39] *Þe Lyfe of Soule*, ed. by Moon, p. i.

[40] *Life of Soul* has been considered sympathetic to Lollardy for its vernacular biblical material. Other reasons include the fact that it dismisses oath-taking, invokes a memorial view of the Eucharist, and supports Wycliffe's concept of dominion. *Life of Soul*, ed. by Schaffner, pp. 122–23. However, it does not explicitly attack or question orthodox teaching.

suitability of English as a language of theological discourse, *Life of Soul* has no apparent anxieties about offering seemingly original vernacular Bible translations.[41] The effect of offering free scriptural translations is to explicitly locate biblical authority in the vernacular to the exclusion of other spiritual authorities. This occurs elsewhere in orthodox writings. Richard Rolle, for example, states that 'The comandement of God is þat we loue oure Lord in al our hert, in al oure soule, in al oure thoght', making no reference to the Vulgate or to the scriptural origins of the text (Luke 10. 27; Matthew 22. 37; and Mark 12. 30).[42] *Life of Soul* similarly provides a biblical foundation for its vision of love which does not acknowledge its sources; however, it does so repeatedly and to the complete rather than partial exclusion of Latin. For instance, when quoting the account of the agony in the garden from Matthew 26, the biblical text is edited and compiled so as to flow directly into the writer's commentary. Christ prays:

> Fader, if it mow be, late þis cuppe passe a wey from me. But neuereþeles, / nouȝt as I wde, but as þou wilt [Matthew 26. 39] and he seyde also: Fadir, ȝif þis cuppe ne mowe not passe awey fro me but I drynke hym, þi wille be fulfillid [Matthew 26. 42].[43] And þus Crist was buxum to his Fader of heuene to þe deþ, techyng vs to be boxom to our Fader and to louen hym in þe same wyse. And ȝif we louen so myche oure God þat we wulden for his loue sufferen þe deþ, þanne drynk we Cristes blood to sauacioun of oure soule and of þe same cuppe þat Crist drank [...]. Drynkeþ hereof euerychon [Matthew 26. 27].[44]

Through this commentary on the institution of the Eucharist, the compiler reorders the biblical text to qualify his central message that the kind of love modelled by Christ can be imitated by the reader. That the reader should aspire to overcome all selfish interest and sacrifice everything for love is made especially clear through the way in which Christ's actions in the biblical text authorize the reader to suffer an ascetic death of self for God. The biblical quotation and the author's message are also interwoven through their shared language; in particular, Christ's cup becomes the reader's, and the act of drinking is shared

---

[41] For biblical translation and the *Cloud* author, see Sutherland, 'Dating and Authorship in the *Cloud* Corpus', esp. p. 88, and for anxieties in *The Chastising*, see Sutherland, 'The Chastising of God's Children', p. 364.

[42] *The Commandment*, in Rolle, *Prose and Verse*, ed. by Ogilvie-Thomson, p. 34. See also Sutherland, 'The English Epistles of Richard Rolle', p. 699.

[43] The Vulgate reads 'Pater mi, si possibile est, transeat a me calix iste: verumtamen non sicut ego volo, sed sicut tu. [...] Pater mi, si non potest hic calix transire nisi bibam illum, fiat voluntas tua'.

[44] *Þe Lyfe of Soule*, ed. by Moon, p. 32, ll. 5–19.

with him. The continuation of the narrative with the connectives 'And þus Crist' and 'he seyde also' also ensures that the biblical words and the writer's exposition flow seamlessly into the reader's imagination. Finally, in this passage direct biblical quotation authorizes the refiguring of suffering into love.

This is a compilation strategy used throughout *Life of Soul*, and it is employed repeatedly in the promotion of Christ as biblical example of patient love, for readers should always aspire to 'fulfille cristes techynges in ȝoure lyuyng'.[45] For instance, the washing of the disciples' feet gives 'ȝow ensample þat ȝe doon as I haue doon to ȝow' [John 12. 13–15], 'ȝou' referring to both the in-text audience of disciples and to the reader.[46] Directives to readers continually seek to include them in the biblical narrative; for example, in the version of *Life of Soul* in MS Arundel 286 the text asserts that by turning the other cheek 'wee mow see how crist euer tauȝt vs pacience. And þerfore seynt Peter seiþ crist haþ suffurd for vs ȝefynge vs ensaumple þat we sewe his steppes' (fol. 126ʳ). Here, the collective pronouns and idea of following ('sewe') strongly imply a sense of discipleship on the part of the reader, an imitation of Christ exemplified and expounded by Peter in the Bible. Moreover, by equating suffering and patience, *Life of Soul* demonstrates by example that one's suffering can be active and purposeful, not merely a passive subjection to pain or tribulation; it reformulates suffering into spiritual sacrifice.[47]

In *Life of Soul*, Christ's endurance explicitly acts as a positive example of self-control in the face of adversity. It is out of love and as an example to all Christians that Christ 'suffered wilfullyche what disese men wolden do to hym boþe of word & of stroke & of deþ'.[48] Significantly, the text prioritizes the willing endurance of pain, not pain itself. It does not actively invite readers to contemplate or emulate Christ's physical suffering, his body, or his Passion; rather it invites them to imitate his patient fortitude. Even when it discusses the Crucifixion, the author points the reader not to the body in pain but to the example of love: 'we schulden haue mynde how Crist schede his blood for loue of his Fader and help of his breþeren'.[49] Likewise, the contemporary *Book of Tribulation*, which appears with *Life of Soul* in MS Arundel 286, offers Christ as an example of being 'esy & paciente to receyue mekeliche þe tormentis of

---

[45] *Þe Lyfe of Soule*, ed. by Moon, p. 16, ll. 12–13, italics mine.

[46] *Þe Lyfe of Soule*, ed. by Moon, p. 50, ll. 11–12, italics mine.

[47] Patience is overwhelmingly treated in conjunction with tribulation in late medieval treatises. Hanna, 'Some Commonplaces of Late Medieval *Patience* Discussions', p. 77.

[48] *Þe Lyfe of Soule*, ed. by Moon, p. 31, ll. 19–20.

[49] *Þe Lyfe of Soule*, ed. by Moon, p. 32, ll. 15–16.

tyrantes'.⁵⁰ The creation of exemplars for *imitatio* is central to asceticism, yet here Christ is not shown to exemplify the salvific nature of suffering, but rather as a model of how to act with forbearance in the face of physically or mentally painful experience.⁵¹

Patience is inseparable from love in *Life of Soul*, and Christ is the biblical exemplar and teacher of such patience, for 'Cristis lawe is charite, and pacience is a condicioun of charite, nedeliche, who þat wil kepe Goddis lawe mut be patient and sufferynge'.⁵² This echoes scholastic teaching on the relationship of patience and *caritas*. For instance, Thomas Aquinas asserts that 'patience, as a virtue, is caused by charity, according to 1 Corinthians 13. 4: "Charity is patient"'.⁵³ Indeed, patience in a medieval context is a self-conscious and carefully constructed undertaking, 'something other than Stoic fortitude or passive endurance; it was seen as an active virtue and a positive response to God's will in time of suffering'.⁵⁴ In this respect *Life of Soul* shares a common understanding of the term with texts such as *The Book of Tribulation*, which presents the patient endurance of tribulation as an ascetic ideal focused on love.

The Book of Tribulation aims to foster patience as an ascetic virtue and entreats its readers to 'suffer [tribulations] wiþ goode wille'.⁵⁵ Painting patience as an active and formative feature of religious experience, the *Book*'s overarching purpose is to provide a framework for transforming everyday suffering, including the problems of persecution, poverty, temptation, illness, and death, into profitable spiritual experiences that move the reader away from the external world and the body towards the interiority of the soul. It does this through an exposition of twelve profits of tribulation and an overarching insistence on overcoming one's dissatisfaction with the world by turning away from it mentally, if not physically: 'Lerne to comforde þe wiþinne in þi soule þat art discomforded wiþoute in þe world'.⁵⁶

---

⁵⁰ *Book of Tribulation*, ed. by Barratt, p. 137, l. 18.

⁵¹ This echoes strategies offered by Rolle in his *Commandment*. See Sutherland, 'The English Epistles of Richard Rolle', pp. 709–10.

⁵² *Þe Lyfe of Soule*, ed. by Moon, p. 47, l. 24 – p. 48, l. 2.

⁵³ *Summa Theologiae*, II, p. 136, l. 3, cited and translated in Kirk, 'Who Suffreth More than God', p. 95.

⁵⁴ Schiffhorst, *The Triumph of Patience*, p. 2.

⁵⁵ *Book of Tribulation*, ed. by Barratt, p. 134, l. 5. *The Book* is a translation of the Old French *Livre de tribulacion* (itself derived from the thirteenth-century *Tractatus de tribulacione*); see Barratt, pp. 18–27. Appleford, *Learning to Die in London*, p. 102, notes that 'tribulation belongs to the highest form of spiritual life'.

⁵⁶ *Book of Tribulation*, ed. by Barratt, p. 134, ll. 5–6.

Importantly, however, the text presents suffering not as punishment or even as penance, but as a way for the individual to foster a relationship with God.

One way of fostering this relationship with the divine in suffering is the mental purging of all that is unrelated to God. Suffering achieves a sharpening of the mind and a clear focus on the love of God, and tribulations connect the sufferer's mind directly to God's:

> þei putten þe into þe mynde & þe recorde of þi God, for whan he sendiþ þe tribulacions, he putteþ hymselfe into þi mynde, and þurȝ meke suffrynge of tribulacions þou puttes þee into his remembraunce, & þus tribulacions ioyneþ þe & hym togeder. Lerne þerfore to suffur paciently & in þi suffringe þenke upon him, & þou schalt constreyne hym for loue to þenke upon þee.[57]

Here, tribulation is a direct point of union between the human and the divine. It is a means of joining two minds. This example shows the patient endurance of tribulation to be a transformative experience. It seeks to focus the ascetic identity of the reader by making the commonplaces of everyday experience into vehicles of spiritual union. As Amy Appleford asserts, 'Patiently endured, tribulation becomes mortification,'[58] and the *Book* seeks to transform the reader's everyday experience of universal suffering associated with temptation, sickness, and age into a functional ascetic existence which facilitates loving union with God. Such mortification is not penitential; it is an ascetically inclined and continuing state of contrition, such as we find in *Life of Soul*.

This functional advocating of contrite asceticism is made even clearer through the way in which the *Book* incorporates direct biblical support for the mental union of its reader and God in suffering. However, unlike *Life of Soul* it makes recourse to the Latin:

> Cum ipso in tribulacione; eripiam eum, et glorificabo eum [Psalm 90. 15]; 'I am wiþ hym in tribulacion; I schal delyuer hym fro alle maner harme of his enemyes & for his meke suffraunce I schal glorifie hym wiþ þe croune of ioye'. Loo howe gladde þou may be þat art in tribulacion, siþ God makeþ hym felowe wiþ þe in all þat þou suffers [...]. And ȝif we be as we schuld be, þe presence of hym is more comfortable þan the heuynes of any tribulacion is greuous.[59]

The *Book* cites the Vulgate text as the authoritative source for its vision of the soul and God united in suffering, suggesting the possibility of an ongoing rela-

---

[57] *Book of Tribulation*, ed. by Barratt, p. 141, ll. 36–41.
[58] Appleford, *Learning to Die in London*, p. 203.
[59] *Book of Tribulation*, ed. by Barratt, p. 134, ll. 40–46.

tionship with the divine that is based on the active embrace of suffering. The state of patient endurance in tribulation literally brings the individual into the presence of God, and it does so in a straightforward manner that focuses the reader's mind on Christ's 'meke suffraunce'. There is thus a sense of joy (comfort and gladness) in the correct response to tribulation. This is echoed in *Life of Soul* which explicitly asserts that one should suffer if God wills it, for if a man is to achieve the life of soul, which is to be baptized in fire and the Holy Spirit,[60] he will become a disciple and so 'casten so brennyng a loue to God þat it was a solas and a mirþe to hem to suffre tribulacioun and persecucioun for loue of here god'.[61] The deep love and joy expressed here stem from knowledge that patient suffering fulfils God's wishes. Emphasis is not placed on the rewards that will come; rather individual desire is subsumed willingly to the control of the divine which makes the life of soul itself an ascetic undertaking.

Life of Soul takes this further still in the assertion that Christ's disciples 'wil gladeliche sufferen a gret disese to fulfillen his wille'.[62] It is precisely the patient endurance of suffering, indeed the joyful acceptance of it, which fosters and is fostered by a love of God. As opposed to focusing on temporary moments of penance, *Life of Soul* and *The Book of Tribulation* promote this state as one of continual contrition, an ascetic state of willing and continuous subjection to circumstances beyond one's control. Indeed, when *Life of Soul* does discuss the seven sacraments, penance is markedly absent. It is worth noting here the Wycliffite aversion to the term 'penance',[63] but also to assert that penance does not fit the text's concept of asceticism because it is a temporary state. Contrite love, by contrast, is an ongoing condition in which the individual is permanently transformed. Moreover, the very concept of life of soul is both contrite and ascetic, based on the stripping back of all resistance to tribulation, and emphasizing self-control through the relinquishing of all opposition to suffering through love, for he who inhabits the life of soul 'wil forsaken his owne lif, and putten himself to disese and to trauaile for help of his breþeren' in the service of the second commandment of love.[64]

The issue of asceticism in *Life of Soul* can be developed further still if we examine its manuscript context. Indeed, in the devotional miscellany MS

---

[60] *Þe Lyfe of Soule*, ed. by Moon, p. 12, ll. 19–20.

[61] *Þe Lyfe of Soule*, ed. by Moon, p. 13, ll. 2–3.

[62] *Þe Lyfe of Soule*, ed. by Moon, p. 13, ll. 14–15.

[63] Sargent, 'Censorship or Cultural Change?', p. 61; see also Hudson, *The Premature Reformation*, pp. 294–301.

[64] *Þe Lyfe of Soule*, ed. by Moon, p. 39, ll. 15–17.

Arundel 286 the text itself undergoes an ascetic transformation in which it is largely stripped of its affective imagery.[65] In MS Arundel 286 we encounter *Life of Soul* in its shortest and simplest form. This manuscript is a collection of devotional compilations, and it is important to note that other material in the book also exists here in its shortest known form. For instance, *The Book of Tribulation*, extant in three manuscripts, also appears in a severely edited version in the Arundel manuscript.[66] The extreme editing of both these texts not only reveals that the scribe had a taste for refining his sources, something that is evident in the other texts he transcribed in Arundel,[67] but is something that can be viewed as a form of textual asceticism, a point to which we will return. The manuscript is from Warwickshire, probably the Coventry area, and it includes a number of texts designed for personal devotion. *Life of Soul* and *The Book of Tribulation* were evidently intended to sit together in the manuscript as the *Book* begins on fol. 100^r and *Life of Soul* follows it immediately, continuing where the *Book* ends (fol. 115^r) and written in the same hand.

Even though the version of *Life of Soul* in MS Arundel 286 depicts a (spiritual) father and son, it is unclear who read the manuscript as its contents are suitable for both lay and religious audiences. The manuscript opens with a treatise on the Passion explicitly directed to a 'worschipful lady hauynge a symple spirit' (fol. 1^r) which seems to suggest a lay female reader. However, the word 'simple' echoes the way many authors and compilers appeal to their 'unlearned' audiences, both religious and secular.[68] It is also possible that the direct address could have been copied verbatim from its source. Indeed, Paul Schaffner suggests that Arundel was intended for a religious audience as the majority of its texts are instructional, and the subject of Christian perfection in *Life of Soul*, established by reference

---

[65] For a full outline of contents, see *Book of Tribulation*, ed. by Barratt, pp. 9–10, who expands Phyllis Hodgson's list in *Deonise Hid Diuinite*, ed. by Hodgson, p. xii.

[66] Bodl. Lib., MS Bodley 423; BL, MS Harley 1197; and MS Arundel 286. It is possible that the copies of *Life of Soul* and *The Book of Tribulation* from which the scribe of MS Arundel 286 worked were themselves abbreviated, but Ralph Hanna notes that 'this individual, rather than merely copying, constantly tailors the texts to their audience', largely through 'excisions and abridgement', through at times through paraphrasing. Hanna, *Pursuing History*, p. 40. See note 18 above for the other texts in MS Arundel 286.

[67] Hanna, *Pursuing History*, p. 40. Hanna further highlights the similarities between MS Arundel 286 and London, Westminster School, MS 3.

[68] For instance, *Contemplations of the Dread and Love of God* appeals to the 'simple knowyng' of its readers: *Contemplations*, ed. by Connolly, p. 5, l. 33. Michelle Karnes, 'Nicholas Love and Medieval Meditations on Christ', p. 385, also notes the monastic tradition in which novices were referred to as 'simple'.

to the Evangelical Counsels from the Sermon on the Mount, was 'the preserve of those with a calling to the monastic life'.[69] However, the text's invitation to its readers, 'be ʒe perfyʒt, as ʒoure heuenely fadre is perfiʒt' (Matthew 5. 48),[70] would suit those in the mixed life as well as religious, and as Schaffer notes, 'the counsels to perfection were embraced by many individuals and movements that were not monastic; and there is nothing specifically monastic about their interpretation here [...]. Even poverty and chastity are recommended in universal terms'.[71] Moreover, the Sermon on the Mount was an extremely popular subject for sermons and would have been familiar to a wide audience.[72] That said, Arundel severely edits material found in Laud on the subject of lechery and replaces it with a commentary on Christ's chastity and that of the Apostles, clearly advocating chastity based on Christ's example: 'forto ʒefe vs ensaumple of chastite crist cheese þis degre of lifynge for þe tyme of þis lyfe' (fol. 128^v).[73] This change might well reflect an intended monastic audience, although it could also be viewed as a paring back of the text in keeping with its scribe's interest in brevity.

Other changes are of greater relevance to the subjects of asceticism and compilation. Whilst *Life of Soul* is not averse to affective devotion it does not stress it particularly strongly. However, the Arundel text appears significantly less affective than the other versions. In Laud, which is considered the most complete text, one of few references to the Passion compares Christ's suffering directly to baptism. But rather than focusing on his suffering, his pain, or his body, the text redirects the significance of the Crucifixion to the reader's performance of good works and his keeping of faith, for 'Riʒt as a body is ded wiþouten spiriʒt, riʒt feiþ and beleue is ded wiþouten good werkes'.[74] However, Arundel contains a number of changes and omissions, as well as some additions not present in Laud, which downplay the other version's affective features. For instance, a long passage in Laud detailing the physical suffering of Christ and inviting readers to draw this image into their minds is omitted in Arundel. A short quotation will suffice to illustrate the Laud text:

---

[69] *Life of Soul*, ed. by Schaffner, p. 118. Ch. 58 of the Rule of St Benedict establishes the Evangelical Counsels' particular application to monastic life: St Benedict, *The Rule*, trans. by White, pp. 85–86.

[70] *Þe Lyfe of Soule*, ed. by Moon, p. 43, ll. 1–2.

[71] *Life of Soul*, ed. by Schaffner, p. 118.

[72] Poleg, *Approaching the Bible*, pp. 180–81; see also Somerset, *Clerical Discourse and Lay Audience*.

[73] Compare to *Þe Lyfe of Soule*, ed. by Moon, p. 62, l. 20 – p. 63, l. 12.

[74] *Þe Lyfe of Soule*, ed. by Moon, p. 8, ll. 7–8.

> Siþe / Crist haþ isuffered in flesch, be ʒe armed in þe same þouʒt. For he þat suffered in flesch laft synne, þat þe remenant þat lyueþ afterward in flesch ne lyuen not to þe desires of men, but to þe wille of god.[75]

Arundel omits this passage in its entirety and instead inserts a comment on how 'ʒoure conscience be waschen from alle filþe of synne, þurʒ virtue of þe passyon of ihesu crist' (fol. 119^v). It does not invite readers to imagine Christ's Passion; instead it reminds them of the meaning of the life of soul itself, that is 'lyfe oute of synne' (fol. 115^v) dedicated to Christ's words of love. The text is refined and trimmed of material that does not foster desire for the life of soul, and that includes invitations to affective meditation.

Arundel's *Life of Soul* is about half as long as Laud's, and this paring of the text down to its bare essentials is itself an ascetic act. The editing involves the exclusion of excessive imagery and excessive words, aiding the refinement of the reader's thoughts, but it also functions as an ascesis for the scribe who is performing his own ascetic act by focusing and refining the text, thereby distilling his own and the reader's experience of it. Even material related to mortification itself is omitted in Arundel. In this Arundel enacts an ascetic movement away from the physical to an emphasis on the textual of the very kind that *Life of Soul* itself advocates.

Life of Soul's promotion of ascetic transcendence of the physical can be seen in the practical advice it offers on the discipline of fasting. Seamlessly incorporating Matthew 6. 17–18, the Laud text advocates the development of an ascetic interiority:

> whan þat þou fastest, anoynte þin hed and wasche þi face þat þou seme not fastyng to men, but to þi fader in hydles. And þi fadre þat seþ it in hydles, wil ʒeue þe þi mede. In þis wyse, sire, Crist techeþ vs to doon oure werkes in mekenes, for elles we mowen lesen oure mede.[76]

This embodies the text's approach to spirituality. It asserts the inward and spiritual nature of acetic behaviour expected of those who would act in imitation of Christ, as opposed to the outward performative expression of piety. Removed from its liturgical context (where it is part of the gospel reading for Ash Wednesday), the expectation of interior asceticism becomes a part of everyday life and is underpinned by biblical citation. Using Matthew 6. 4 to emphasize charity done in secret ('hydles') and prayer performed behind closed doors,

---

[75] *Þe Lyfe of Soule*, ed. by Moon, p. 12, ll. 7–11.
[76] *Þe Lyfe of Soule*, ed. by Moon, p. 55, ll. 10–15.

the text further advocates the pursuit of an interior life, the rejection of one's outward-facing self, and a reconstitution of one's spiritual identity grounded in love. In Arundel, however, all these passages on alms-giving, fasting, and prayer are abbreviated to a simple statement on avoiding pride in one's good deeds: 'we schuld flee al mater of pride crist seiþ in the gospel. Whan þou dost þi goode dedys, doo hem priuyle, and þe fader of heuen þat seeþ alle priuey þinges schal quyte þe þi mede' (fol. 127ᵛ). This severe editing constitutes a form of textual asceticism, a negation of the unnecessary and the unfocused, and a movement away from bodily practices that even include mortification. It is a purging of the text in keeping with both its thematic interests and the scribe's desire for clarity. In fact it is closer to the biblical text than the version in Laud.

We can further observe Arundel's textual asceticism in its treatment of visual images. A reference to the Passion and shedding of Christ's blood is used in Arundel to assert the foolishness of humanity sinning again after the Crucifixion (fol. 118ᵛ), but otherwise there is very little recall to the reader's affective imagination. The text does not present subjects to contemplate in one's mind's eye nor does it advocate the use of devotional images; rather audiences of 'cristes techinge' are expected to have 'seene it writen oþur here it spoken' because in 'his wordis is þe liyf of soule' (fol. 120ʳ⁻ᵛ). As previously noted, words are particularly powerful, and now the importance of the written word is stressed even further when the compiler states that his dialogue is not in the form of a conversation but a written exchange. The father (writer) directly addresses the son (reader) saying he will 'write more opunly to þe of þe liyf of soule' (fol. 120ᵛ), and the son replies 'I prey þe fader þat þou wolt write to me' and thereby 'schewe to me þe techynge of Crist' (fols 121ᵛ–122ʳ). Moreover, the text comments on Luke 12. 47–48, stating:

> Who þat kepiþ my wordis schal neuer dye and who þat knoweþ and heriþ cristis wordis and dooþ not after hem schal haue more blame þan he þat neuer knew hem. For crist seiþ, he þat knoweþ þe wille of his lord and doþ it not schal haue many betynges and strokes, þat is many hard peynes. (fol. 120ᵛ)[77]

Life of Soul specifically stresses the importance of adhering to the words of Christian doctrine, to listening to what 'Crist seiþ in þe gospel' (fol. 120ᵛ) and following his example rather than seeking to conjure images of Christ's suffering in one's mind. Whilst both Laud and Arundel place emphasis on the written word as the source of transformation and salvation, the scribe of MS Arundel 286 enacts the text's own ascetic message in his scribal practice.

[77] Compare to *Þe Lyfe of Soule*, ed. by Moon, p. 15, l. 10 – p. 16, l. 4.

Ultimately, *Life of Soul* offers a series of ascetic exemplars intended to cultivate a state of ongoing contrition through the patient endurance of suffering in imitation of Christ's teaching in the scriptures. This is asserted explicitly through the activity of compiling an abundance of biblical passages in English which incorporate the language of the Bible into its readers' everyday experience, allowing them to 'fulfille cristes techynges in ȝoure lyuyng'.[78] Underlying the text is the sense that a refined ascetic identity can be achieved through the patient endurance of everyday suffering. Moreover, in the Arundel version we encounter asceticism in a specifically textual form: in the process of editing itself which seeks to downplay affective devotion to the physicality of Christ and which instead directs the reader towards a text-based imitation of Christ's love of God and neighbour. *Life of Soul* asserts that the words of scripture are paramount to the development of this mentality, more so than meditation on affective or penitential images, and points to the transformative potential of what 'crist seiþ' as the basis for converting one's experience of suffering into love.

---

[78] *Þe Lyfe of Soule*, ed. by Moon, p. 16, ll. 12–13.

Works Cited

Manuscripts

Cambridge, Magdalene College, MS Pepys 2498
London, British Library [BL], MS Arundel 286
London, British Library [BL], MS Harley 1197
London, Westminster School, MS 3
Oxford, Bodleian Library [Bodl. Lib.], MS Bodley 423
Oxford, Bodleian Library [Bodl. Lib.], MS Laud misc. 210
San Marino, Huntington Library, MS HM 502

Primary Sources

St Benedict, *The Rule of St Benedict*, trans. by Carolinne White (London: Penguin, 2008)
The Book of Tribulation, ed. from MS Bodley 423, ed. by Alexandra Barratt (Heidelberg: Winter, 1983)
Contemplations of the Dread and Love of God, ed. by Margaret Connolly, Early English Text Society, o.s., 303 (Oxford: Oxford University Press, 1993)
Deonise Hid Diuinite and Other Treatises on Contemplative Prayer, ed. by Phyllis Hodgson, Early English Text Society, o.s., 231 (London: Oxford University Press, 1955)
A Fourteenth-Century English Biblical Version, ed. by Anna C. Paues (Cambridge: Cambridge University Press, 1904)
Life of Soul, ed. by Paul F. Schaffner, in *Cultures of Piety: Medieval English Devotional Literature in Translation*, ed. by Anne Clark Bartlett and Thomas H. Bestul (Ithaca: Cornell University Press, 1999), pp. 118–40
Þe Lyfe of Soule: An Edition with Commentary, ed. by Helen M. Moon, Elizabethan and Renaissance Studies, 75 (Salzburg: Institut für englische Sprache und Literatur, 1978)
Rolle, Richard, *Richard Rolle: Prose and Verse* from MS. Longleat 29 and Related Manuscripts, ed. by S. J. Ogilvie-Thomson, Early English Text Society, o.s., 293 (Oxford: Oxford University Press, 1988)

Secondary Works

Appleford, Amy, *Learning to Die in London, 1380–1540* (Philadelphia: University of Pennsylvania Press, 2014)
——, 'The Sea Ground and the London Street: The Ascetic Self in Julian of Norwich and Thomas Hoccleve', *Chaucer Review*, 51.1 (2016), 49–67
Dutton, Elisabeth, *Julian of Norwich: The Influence of Late-Medieval Devotional Compilations* (Cambridge: D. S. Brewer, 2008)
Elchaninov, Alexander, *The Diary of a Russian Priest*, trans. by Helen Iswolsky (London: Faber and Faber, 1967)

Flood, Gavin. *The Ascetic Self: Subjectivity, Memory and Tradition* (Cambridge: Cambridge University Press, 2004)

Hanna, Ralph, 'English Biblical Texts before Lollardy and their Fate', in *Lollards and their Influence in Late Medieval England*, ed. by Fiona Somerset, Jill C. Havens, and Derrick G. Pitard (Woodbridge: Boydell, 2003), pp. 141–53

——, *Pursuing History: Middle English Manuscripts and their Texts* (Stanford: Stanford University Press, 1996)

——, 'Some Commonplaces of Late Medieval *Patience* Discussions: An Introduction', in *The Triumph of Patience: Medieval and Renaissance Studies*, ed. by Gerald Schiffhorst (Orlando: University Presses of Florida, 1978), pp. 65–87

Harpham, Geoffrey Galt, *The Ascetic Imperative in Culture and Criticism* (Chicago: University of Chicago Press, 1987)

Hudson, Anne, *The Premature Reformation: Wycliffite Texts and Lollard History* (Oxford: Clarendon Press, 1988)

Hughes-Edwards, Mari, *Reading Medieval Anchoritism: Ideology and Spiritual Practices* (Cardiff: University of Wales Press, 2012)

Humphries, Thomas L., *Ascetic Pneumatology from John Cassian to Gregory the Great* (Oxford: Oxford University Press, 2013)

Jasper, David, *The Sacred Body: Asceticism in Literature, Art, and Culture* (Waco: Baylor University Press, 2009)

Karnes, Michelle, 'Nicholas Love and Medieval Meditations on Christ: Interiority, Imagination and Meditations on the Life on Christ', *Speculum*, 82 (2007), 380–408

Kirk, Elizabeth D., 'Who Suffreth More than God: Narrative Redefinition of Patience in *Patience* and *Piers Plowman*', in *The Triumph of Patience: Medieval and Renaissance Studies*, ed. by Gerald Schiffhorst (Orlando: University Presses of Florida, 1978), pp. 88–104

Krueger, Derek, *Writing and Holiness: The Practice of Authorship in the Early Christian East* (Philadelphia: University of Pennsylvania Press, 2004)

McNamer, Sarah, *Affective Meditation and the Invention of Medieval Compassion* (Philadelphia: University of Pennsylvania Press, 2010)

Milhaven, J. Giles, 'Asceticism and the Moral Good: A Tale of Two Pleasures', in *Asceticism*, ed. by Vincent L. Wimbush and Richard Valantasis (New York: Oxford University Press, 1998), pp. 375–94

Poleg, Eyal, *Approaching the Bible in Medieval England* (Manchester: Manchester University Press, 2013)

——, 'Wycliffite Bibles as Orthodoxy', in *Cultures of Religious Reading in the Late Middle Ages: Instructing the Soul, Feeding the Spirit, and Awakening the Passion*, ed. by Sabrina Corbellini, Utrecht Studies in Medieval Literacy, 25 (Turnhout: Brepols, 2013), pp. 71–91

Powell, Sue, 'The Transmission and Circulation of the *Lay Folks' Catechism*', in *Late-Medieval Religious Texts and their Transmission: Essays in Honour of A. I. Doyle*, ed. by A. J. Minnis (Cambridge: D. S. Brewer, 1994), pp. 67–84

Sargent, Michael, 'Censorship or Cultural Change? Reformation and Renaissance in the Spirituality of Late Medieval England', in *After Arundel: Religious Writing in*

Fifteenth-Century England, ed. by Vincent Gillespie and Kantik Ghosh, Medieval Church Studies, 21 (Turnhout: Brepols, 2011), pp. 55–72

Schiffhorst, Gerald, ed., *The Triumph of Patience: Medieval and Renaissance Studies* (Orlando: University Presses of Florida, 1978)

Simpson, James, '1543–1550s: Texts', in *The Cambridge Companion to Medieval English Mysticism*, ed. by Samuel Fanous and Vincent Gillespie (Cambridge: Cambridge University Press, 2011), pp. 249–64

Somerset, Fiona, *Clerical Discourse and Lay Audience in Late Medieval England* (Cambridge: Cambridge University Press, 1998)

Sutherland, Annie, '*The Chastising of God's Children*: A Neglected Text', in *Text and Controversy from Wyclif to Bale: Essays in Honour of Anne Hudson*, ed. by Helen Barr and Ann M. Hutchison, Medieval Church Studies, 4 (Turnhout: Brepols, 2005), pp. 353–73

——, 'Dating and Authorship in the *Cloud* Corpus', *Medium Aevum*, 71 (2002), 82–100

——, 'The English Epistles of Richard Rolle', *Review of English Studies*, n.s., 56 (2005), 695–711

Ware, Kallistos, 'The Way of the Ascetics: Negative or Affirmative?', in *Asceticism*, ed. by Vincent L. Wimbush and Richard Valantasis (New York: Oxford University Press, 1998), pp. 3–15

Online Publications

The DIMEV: An Open-Access, Digital Edition of the 'Index of Middle English Verse', comp. by Linne R. Mooney, Daniel W. Mosser, and Elizabeth Solopova, <http://www.dimev.net>

Compilers' Voices in Cambridge, University Library, MS Ii.6.40

Marleen Cré

Cambridge, University Library, MS Ii.6.40 (C) is an intriguing anthology because it contains a number of compilations, each in a version unique to this manuscript. The transmission of texts in a manuscript culture is always subject to variation, whether as the result of deliberate editorial decisions or by chance. A manuscript culture, then, is effectively also a compilation culture, in which texts are most often transmitted with some kind of variation, and in which scribes and editors borrow from the texts they have available and adapt them, as in the case of C, freely and abundantly. In the manuscript transmission of texts, some scribes or editors make decisions that can be described as authorial, or as Malcolm Parkes aptly puts it: 'inside many a scribe there lurked a compiler struggling to get out'.[1]

In this essay, the acts that led to three compilations in C will be discussed. The anonymous agents of these processes of adaptation and transmission will be called compilers, as they responded creatively to the compilations they

---

[1] Parkes, 'The Influence of the Concepts of *Ordinatio* and *Compilatio*', p. 138. Though Parkes talks about the compiler here as someone who adds an apparatus to the text he copies, the statement is also applicable to compilers of texts and manuscripts.

Marleen Cré (cre.marleen@gmail.com) worked as a postdoctoral researcher on the Swiss National Science Foundation Project 'Late Medieval Religiosity in England: The Evidence of Late Fourteenth- and Fifteenth-Century Devotional Compilations' at the University of Lausanne from 2013 to 2017. She teaches at the Université Saint-Louis in Brussels and is an independent scholar affiliated with the Ruusbroec Institute, University of Antwerp.

transmitted in order to write a new, unique compilation with its own nuances of religious content and message.

C is a small volume measuring 120 × 75 mm, written in one hand on vellum.[2] It is dated to the mid-fifteenth century, and its dialect has been located on the north-east Cambridgeshire-Huntingdonshire border. The current binding of the volume is from the late sixteenth century, yet the uniform appearance of the script and layout suggest that it was produced in its present form. Only the Latin prayer that opens the volume has seemingly been added later, though apparently by the same scribe, on what initially were flyleaves:

a. fols 2ᵛ–3ᵛ: A prayer in Latin, 'Domine Iesus Criste qui videns Ierusalem pro peccatis civium lacrimatus es'

Booklet 1

1. fols 5ʳ–58ᵛ: *Contemplations of the Dread and Love of God*, 'Here bygynneþ holy mater þe which is clepid xii Chapiters'[3]

2. fols 58ᵛ–74ʳ: *An Information of the Contemplative Life and Active*, 'I fynd as I rede by doctors and holy mens lyues þat twey maner of lyuinge ben here in þis world most plesing to god'[4]

Booklet 2

1. fols 75ʳ–76ᵛ: *A Treatise of Perfect Love*, 'her folowiþ a tretis of parfyt loue'

2. fols 76ᵛ–95ʳ: *A Treatise of Tribulation*, 'her bygynniþ a tretis of tribulacion'[5]

3. fols 95ʳ–191ʳ: *Þe Pater Noster of Richard Ermyte*, 'here bigynniþ a tretis of pater noster'[6]

---

[2] The description of C is based on Hanna, *The English Manuscripts of Richard Rolle*, pp. 37–38. The titles in italics represent the accepted titles of these works. The incipits or titles of the texts as they occur in C are between single quotes. The titles as they occur in C will be used for 'A Tretis of Pater Noster' and 'A deuout meditacioun'.

[3] See *Contemplations*, ed. by Connolly. References to this edition are by chapter letters and line numbers.

[4] This is a translation of Birgitta of Sweden, *Revelaciones*, vi. 65. See Gilroy, 'English Adaptations of Revelations 6.65'.

[5] Healy Murphy, '*A Tretis of Tribulation*'. References to this edition are by line numbers.

[6] *The Pater Noster of Richard Ermyte*, ed. by Aarts. References to this edition are by page and line numbers.

4. fols 191ʳ–198ʳ: 'The Charter of Heaven' a tract from *Pore Caitif*, 'A charter of remissioun'⁷

5. fols 198ʳ–207ᵛ: *The Commandment*, with a passage from *The Form of Living*, 'In þis tretis we are tauȝt how we shul loue god on al wise'⁸

6. fols 207ᵛ–220ʳ: 'A deuout meditacioun of Ric' Hampole'; translated excerpts from Saint Edmund Rich, *Speculum ecclesie*, 'her byginniþ a deuout meditacioun of Richard Hampol'⁹

As is pointed out in all descriptions of this manuscript, it belonged to Johanne Mouresleygh, as can be seen from two inscriptions — one on fol. 2ʳ and one on fol. 4ᵛ, both erased, but visible under ultraviolet light, as reported by Ian Doyle in his 1954 thesis: 'Iste liber constat domine Johanne Mouresleygh'.¹⁰ Johanne Mouresleygh was recorded as a Benedictine nun at Shaftesbury Abbey (Dorset) in 1441 and 1460.¹¹ As her dates fit the period to which the manuscript is assigned, it is possible that she was the manuscript's first owner, though *Contemplations* and the other texts in the manuscript were

---

⁷ '*The Pore Caitif*', ed. by Brady, pp. 128–37.

⁸ Rolle, *Prose and Verse*, ed. by Ogilvie-Thomson, pp. 34–39 and p. 18. References to this edition are by line numbers. The same *Commandment-Form of Living* combination also occurs in Warminster, Longleat House, Marquess of Bath MS 32 (Hanna's MS 115), and in Bodl. Lib., MS Rawlinson A. 389 (Hanna's MS 93), though in this manuscript the fragment of the *Form* breaks off after the opening lines. See Hanna, *The English Manuscripts of Richard Rolle*, pp. 212–15 and pp. 171–74. The reference on p. 214 to 'another Norfolk Book' that shares Longleat House MS 32's item 5 ('A tretice of contemplacioun') should not be to MS 111 (Tokyo, Prof. Toshiyuki Takamiya, MS 66) in Hanna's catalogue, but to MS 19 (C), on pp. 37–38, as C has 'A deuout meditacioun', a rewriting of Edmund Rich's *Speculum ecclesie*, and Takamiya, MS 66 does not.

⁹ Robbins, 'An English Version of St. Edmund's *Speculum*'. References to this edition are by page and line numbers. As has been pointed out earlier, the same version also occurs in Longleat House MS 32. For a discussion of this version of the *Speculum ecclesie* extant in C and in Longleat House MS 32, see Goymer, 'A Parallel Text Edition of the Middle English Prose Version(s)', pp. 432–37.

¹⁰ Doyle, 'A Survey of the Origins and Circulation', pp. 90–91. Later owners were Thomas Worth (fol. 1ʳ) and Annys Dawns (fol. 222ʳ). Connolly, 'Mapping Manuscripts and Readers', pp. 273–75. Note that the wording of this ownership note is 'unexceptional and familiar' and 'common'. Wakelin, '"Thys ys my boke"', p. 13. The ownership note was probably erased when the manuscript changed hands.

¹¹ Joanne Mouresleygh must have been one of the fifty-five nuns who elected a new abbess in 1441, and one of fifty-one nuns who did so in 1460. Knowles and Hadcock, *Medieval Religious Houses*, pp. 255 and 265.

not necessarily revised and/or copied specifically for her. Indeed, the northeast Cambridgeshire-Huntingdonshire dialect of the manuscript makes this unlikely. In addition, the way *Contemplations* refers to its audience in C is inconclusive and does not suggest revision of the text for a female religious. Among the many minor omissions from the text, a striking one occurs at the very end, suggesting instead that the text was customized for a male religious:[12]

> And þan good broþer prey for me, whiche by þe teching of almiȝti god haue write to þe thes few wordys in helpe of þi soule. (fol. 58ᵛ)

> Goode broþer *or suster* preie þan for me, whiche bi þe techyng of almiȝti god haue write to þe þese fewe wordis in help of þi soule.[13]

However, earlier in the text, advice is given to 'eche man and woman' (fol. 9ᵛ, B 88), and in this phrase, the addition 'and woman' cancels the later omission.[14] Inconclusiveness about the intended audience can be seen throughout C. Though it has been argued that 'A Tretis of Pater Noster' was written for male lay readers,[15] the subheadings in 'A deuout meditacioun of Richard Hampole' point to an audience of religious, as they refer to the hours of the office.[16] Thus, inconclusiveness translates as inclusiveness: this kind of manuscript was open to a variety of readers, as was the religious life it supposes and supports. One can imagine a situation in which a female reader is one of the agents in the production of a volume such as C, as she may have voiced her wishes to the scribe about the volume she was to own. Yet in the case of C there is not enough evidence to name Johanne Mouresleygh, this one-time owner of the manuscript whose name was erased, as either the instigator or the intended

---

[12] Connolly, 'Mapping Manuscripts and Readers', p. 267.

[13] *Contemplations*, ed. by Connolly, Z 127–29; italics mine.

[14] The manuscript's tenor with regard to the position of women in the spiritual life would be worth further attention. Additions to Birgitta of Sweden's *Revelaciones*, VI. 65, in *An Information* seem to suggest that women are better suited to Martha's part (the active life) than Mary's (the contemplative life). In the description of Mary's part, all references are to men who will follow Mary (though women may have been subsumed under the general term 'men' as 'people'), whereas in the description of Martha's part, women are included explicitly and urged to folow Martha: 'I counceile neytheles *wifis and widows maydyns and oþer* to folow martha as miche as þei mow in wil and dede' (fol. 71ᵛ; italics mine).

[15] Vulić, '*þe Pater Noster of Richard Ermyte*', pp. 15–24.

[16] 'Contemplacioun afor matyns' (fol. 214ʳ), 'contemplacioun bifor pryme' (fol. 214ᵛ), 'contemplacioun byfor þe sixte oure' (fol. 215ʳ), 'Contemplacioun by fore vndern' (fol. 216ʳ), 'Contemplacioun bifor mydday' (fol. 216ᵛ), 'contemplacioun bifore none' (fol. 218ᵛ), and 'Contemplacioune bifore complyne' (fol. 219ᵛ).

first receiver of the compilatory activities that shaped the anthology. As in so many cases, we cannot put a name to compilatory agency in this anthology.

Instead, however, 'the whole book' that is MS C can be read as a good example of literary production in a compilation culture.[17] The scribe of C copied nine texts into the two booklets that make up this manuscript and decided to place the booklets in the order in which we have them now. This scribal agency is the surface level of agency; it operates at the level of the compilations and texts as we see them, and as Johanne Mouresleygh and later readers would have encountered them. Meaningful coherence in the manuscript as a whole can be found through an act of compilatory reading, which is the reading of texts within a manuscript 'so as to disclose an interpretably meaningful arrangement', even when the combination and ordering of its texts may be the result of ad hoc decisions.[18] Compilatory reading is a reading practice that scholars can be said to share with the earliest readers of the manuscript, who would also have approached the collection and combination of texts as meaningful.

Yet the coherence in C is not just the result of interpretation. There is thematic coherence in the anthology, so that 'a narrative of faith' can be found in the manuscript book.[19] All texts and compilations in C present and discuss guidelines to follow when living a life devoted to God: they list things readers have to keep in mind, and do not teach advanced contemplation — that is, they do not discuss or evoke mystical union between the believer and God — but they keep readers grounded in more concrete devotions directly related to catechetical instruction (such as the seven deadly sins, or how to prepare yourself to receive the Holy Ghost).[20] These devotions — it is implied — will enable readers to lead a life in God's service. The texts and compilations repeatedly invite readers to imitate Christ: they are invited to identify with the suffering Christ in the Latin opening prayer, in 'A tretis of tribulacion', and in 'A deuout meditacioun'.[21]

---

[17] The term derives from Nichols and Wenzel, *The Whole Book*.

[18] Bahr, *Fragments and Assemblages*, p. 3.

[19] Havens, 'A Narrative of Faith', pp. 68–70.

[20] See for instance how the subdivisions of the first degree of love in *Contemplations* are linked to the avoidance of the sins of gluttony, pride, and covetousness (fols 15^v to 18^r, cf. *Contemplations* E 1 to F 44), and the five ways in which to prepare for the coming of the Holy Ghost in 'A tretis of parfyt loue' (fols 75^r–76^v): to make oneself clean from sin, to be humble, to have love and charity, to be devout in prayer, to be discrete in abstinence.

[21] In the opening prayer in Latin, the speaker addresses Jesus, remembers how his eyes, ears, tongue, hands, feet, and heart were hurt during the Passion and Crucifixion, and prays that Jesus would heal the wounds in his own eyes, ears, tongue, etc., and would make sure that the speaker

Beneath the surface level of what has been called scribal agency, there is another, most likely prior level of agency at work in this manuscript. Indeed, C draws our attention because three of its nine texts — *Contemplations*, 'A Tretis of Pater Noster' and 'A deuout meditacioun' — are unique or rare, if not to say idiosyncratic versions, each differing in some way from their other attestations. These compilations as they occur in C make us aware of the compilers who left alterations in the texts that were then copied in their altered form by the scribe of C. They abbreviated *Contemplations* and incorporated *An Information of the Contemplative Life and Active* into it, paraphrased *Þe Pater Noster* into 'A Tretis of Pater Noster', and creatively translated (or added to a previous translation of) the *Speculum ecclesie* in 'A deuout meditacioun'. Scribes and compilers may have worked in close proximity.[22] That the shorter texts in C have not been revised to the same degree as the three compilations focused on here suggests that it is the longer texts that are most likely to be revised, which may mean that the size of the manuscript may have been one of the factors leading to revision prior to the copying of the manuscript.

Let us first turn to *Contemplations* and what is unique about the text version in C. In the 1993 EETS edition of *Contemplations*, Margaret Connolly points out that C was unsuitable as a base text for the edition, as it contains 'a heavily abbreviated version of the text'.[23] Indeed, C does not present the text in what Nicole Rice has called its 'monumental form':

> Literally organized to resemble a rule, [*Contemplations*] is divided into a series of chapters, with a table of contents preceding the main text. The text is prefaced with this advertisement: 'This schorte pistel þat folewith ys diuided in sundrei materes, eche mater bi himself in titlis as þis kalender scheweþ. And þat þou mowe sone finde what mater þe pleseþ, þese titles ben here and in þe pistil marked wiþ diuerse lettres in manere of a table'.[24]

uses the senses 'non [...] ad opera mala, sed ad opera bona, sancta et salutaria et tibi placenda' (not towards bad works, but towards good, holy, and beneficial works that please you) (fol. 3ʳ). 'A tretis of tribulacion' teaches the reader three degrees of patience in the face of tribulation, and elaborates on the last degree of patience so that it becomes an exhortation to the imitation of Christ (fols 94ᵛ–95ʳ, *Tribulation* 838–40). As we will see, in 'A deuout meditacioun' the compiler adds many passages that focus on Christ's Passion. The reader is invited to enter into Christ's suffering in these meditations, which evoke excessive pain (see, for instance, fol. 218ᵛ, 'A deuout meditacioun' 250/9–14).

[22] It is of course possible that the scribe is the same person as the compiler of one or all of these texts, but this cannot be proved.

[23] *Contemplations*, ed. by Connolly, p. xxxiv.

[24] Rice, *Lay Piety and Religious Discipline*, p. 32.

In C *Contemplations* lacks the table of contents, in which all chapters are identified by a letter of the alphabet, the chapter headings, and the marginal signposting that many full text manuscripts do have. Recapitulatory passages have also been left out. C adds *An Information*, the translation of Birgitta's *Revelationes*, Book VI, Chapter 65, as if it were another chapter of *Contemplations*. There is no *explicit* for *Contemplations*, nor is there a heading to mark *An Information* as a separate text. Like any other chapter of *Contemplations*, the beginning of *An Information* is marked by a coloured initial.

The abbreviation of *Contemplations* may have been a response to the small format of C, or may have been done exactly because the reader of C was not a 'busy reader in the world', and so did have 'the monastic or anchoritic *otium* necessary to read an entire text from start to finish',[25] and thus did not need headings to help him or her navigate the text. The abbreviation of the text is of the kind that could have been scribal, or the scribe could be following instructions in the copy text about what to leave out.[26] Alexandra Barratt has pointed out the occurrence of the same sequence *Contemplations – An Information* in Bodl. Lib., MSS Bodley 423 and Bodley 197. It seems likely, as Barratt suggests, that the scribe of C 'made his copy from a manuscript in which [both texts] were already closely associated'.[27] However, it is also possible that the C scribe's copy text presented both texts as separate, as is the case in MS Bodley 423,[28] and that the decision to copy *An Information* as if it were part of *Contemplations* was his. The decisions he would have made to incorporate *An Information* in this way mirror the decisions made when revising *Contemplations*. Incidentally (or not), Birgitta of Sweden's *Revelationes* is one of the source texts for *Contemplations*. If the scribe (or compiler) recognized *An Information* as being also by Birgitta, this might have been a reason for him to present the text as a constituent part of *Contemplations*.

[25] Rice, *Lay Piety and Religious Discipline*, p. 32.

[26] On manuscripts that have such instructions, see Jones, 'Jesus College Oxford, MS 39' and Cré, 'Spiritual Comfort and Reasonable Feeling'.

[27] Aelred of Rievaulx, *De Institutione Inclusarum*, ed. by Ayto and Barratt, p. xxix.

[28] On fol. 150ʳ of MS Bodley 423, *Contemplations* ends with an explicit: 'here endith þe tretyse that we clepen fferuor amoris'. The opening of *An Information* is signalled with a heading in red ink: 'These wordes and this matere whiche is folewynge is an Informacion of contemplatif lyf and actif. as it is drawe oute of the Revelacioun of seint Bride'. It needs to be pointed out here that the dialect of MS Bodley 423, dated to the fifteenth century, is south-east Cambridgeshire, not all that far removed from the Cambridgeshire-Huntingdonshire dialect of C. The argument that size matters in the revisions in C could be made here, too, as Part 2 of MS Bodley 423 (the part that has *Contemplations* and *An Information*) measures 270 by 200 mm. How the texts are laid out in MS Bodley 197 remains to be examined.

Contemplations does keep its subdivision in four sections according to the four degrees of love — a subdivision deriving from Birgitta of Sweden, *Revelationes*, Book III, Chapter 28[29] — 'ane ordeyne loue' (fol. 15ʳ, cf. *Contemplations* D 73), 'a clene loue' (fol. 20ʳ, cf. *Contemplations* I 27), 'a stedfast loue' (fol. 22ᵛ, cf. *Contemplations* M 31), and 'a parfite loue' (fol. 27ᵛ, cf. *Contemplations* S 1) — and signals subdivisions by two-line initials decorated by penwork.[30]

Yet *Contemplations* in C is not just an abbreviation. The text has also been altered in small ways in many places, and nearly all these alterations are unique to C. One type of change that occurs repeatedly is the inversion of doublets. C inverts the order in which the words in the doublet occur in the other manuscripts, the only rationale for which would seem to be the scribe showing his playful side:[31]

> Neuerþeles what euer þou be þat herest or redist þis. (fol. 8ᵛ)
> Neþeles whateuer þou be þat redist or herest þis.[32]

> if þou loue god þou schalt not loue ne desiren þe vanites of þe world. (fol. 16ᵛ)
> ȝif þou loue God þou schalt not desire ne loue vanites of þe world.[33]

> se þan how þei profer him to drynke eysil and galle. (fol. 55ᵛ)
> Se þan how þei profre him to drinke betir galle and eisel.[34]

---

[29] *Contemplations*, ed. by Connolly, p. 103.

[30] On the four degrees of love in *Contemplations* and how they are also linked to the treatment of the topic of the degrees of love in Rolle's *Form of Living* and *Ego dormio*, see Rice, *Lay Piety and Religious Discipline*, pp. 28–39. All medieval treatments of this topic are of course indebted to Richard of St Victor's *De quatuor gradibus violentae caritatis* (*On the four degrees of violent love*): wounding love, binding love, languishing love, and weakening love. For a recent translation and introduction to this text, see Kraebel, 'Richard of St Victor: *On the Four Degrees*'.

[31] The inversion of doublets also occurs in the C version of Richard Rolle's *The Commandment*. See fol. 200ᵛ: 'ordeyne þi wakynge and þi prayinge', cf. *Commandment* 62: 'ordeyn þi prayinge and þi wakynge'; fol. 200ᵛ: 'but loue is al wei þe best, wheþer þou do penance muche or litil', cf. *Commandment* 66–67: 'bot loue is euer þe best, wheþer þou do penaunce litel or mych'; fol. 202ᵛ: 'an hert þat is feire and clene in vertus', cf. *Commandment* 116–17: 'a hert þat is clene and faire in vertuȝ'; fol. 204ʳ: 'so þat þou miȝt haue sauoure and reste in his loue', cf. *Commandment* 147–48: 'so þat þou may haue reste and sauour in his loue'. This version is closely linked to the same *Commandment–Form of Living* combination in Bodl. Lib., MS Rawlinson A. 389 and Longleat House MS 32, with which C also shares 'A deuout meditacioun'. This rewriting activity was most likely carried out by the scribe. It could be explained as a way in which he stayed alert and avoided tedium.

[32] *Contemplations*, ed. by Connolly, B 56–57.

[33] *Contemplations*, ed. by Connolly, F 2.

[34] *Contemplations*, ed. by Connolly, AB 48–49.

Another change that stands out is the substitution of a second person singular address ('þou', 'þe') with a generalizing third person singular, 'a man' and 'he', especially in chapters B and C, and at the end of the text, in chapters V, X, and Z, as can be seen in the following examples.[35]

> þerfor I wil conceil *no man* for to leuen as þei diden for *men* mow by oþer maner of lyuing come to þe loue of god as 3e schullen here aftirward. (fols 6ᵛ–7ʳ, italics mine)
> I wol nat counsaile *þe* to liue as þei dude, for *þou* maist bi oþer maner liuinge come to þe loue of God, as þou schalt see afturward.[36]

> in þis maner eche man behouiþ to loue his god þat he wil be saued. Þerfore I conceile *al men and women* to kepe þis degre of loue er *þei* clymben to ony hi3er degre. (fol. 9ᵛ, italics mine)
> In þis manere eche man bihoueþ to loue his god þat wil be saued. Þerfore y counsele *þe* to haue and kepe þis loue or *þou* climbe to any hiere degre.[37]

> I say nat þat þou schalt fle bodyly frome þe world or from þi wordeli godis for þes be pryncipal occasions but I conseile þe in hert and in wil þou withstond þe lust of al suche vanytes for þou3e *a man* be a lord or a lady hosbond man or wyf *he* may haue as stable an hert and will and som religious þat sittiþ in þe cloistre. (fol. 52ʳ⁻ᵛ, italics mine)
> Y sey not þou schalt fle bodily from þe world or from þi wordeli goodis for þes ben principal occasiones, but I counsele þe in herte and in wil þat þou fle al suche vanites, for þay *þou* be a lord or a laidi, housbond-man or wif, *þou* maist haue as stable an herte and wil as some religious þat sitteþ in þe cloistre.[38]

It is unclear why the pronoun shift is happening at this precise point in the text and why the second person singular address is kept elsewhere. It is possible the compiler was thinking of his audience more consciously at the beginning and at the end of his editing work — provided he was working sequentially. The personal pronoun change may also derive from *An Information*, as it does not address the audience directly using a second person singular, but refers to 'he also þat wil folow mary' (fol. 59ᵛ) throughout this text.[39] The use of the third

---

[35] Other passages in which this shift occurs are fol. 11ʳ, 22 to fol. 11ᵛ, 23 (cf. *Contemplations*, ed. by Connolly, C 31–46); fol. 12ʳ, 2–23 (cf. *Contemplations* C 48–56); fol. 12ʳ, 23 to fol. 12ᵛ, 8 (cf. *Contemplations* C 60–65); fol. 40ʳ, 7–13 (cf. *Contemplations* V 107–10); and fol. 43ʳ, 8–15 (cf. *Contemplations* X 65–68).

[36] *Contemplations*, ed. by Connolly, B 8–10, italics mine.

[37] *Contemplations*, ed. by Connolly, B 68–70, italics mine.

[38] *Contemplations*, ed. by Connolly, Z 34–38, italics mine.

[39] In the Latin *Revelationes*, the phrase 'he þat wil folow mary' (e.g. fol. 59ᵛ) is lacking, as

person in these passages does have the effect of distancing, of shying away from teaching one's audience directly. It is possibly also an effect of caution and — perhaps — even diffidence. In the first two of the passages quoted above, the phrase 'I conceile / I wil conceil' occurs, and it seems that in these passages the compiler of *Contemplations* in C does shy away from addressing his audience directly when giving moral advice. In the passage on fol. 52^{r-v} (cf. Z 34–38), the pronoun change may have been made because the 'þou' in this passage addresses a layperson, and neither the compiler nor the intended reader of C may have been laypeople. Yet, as has been argued earlier, in the whole of the manuscript these passages are swept up in the general inconclusiveness of address, which alternates between direct second person singular, general third person singular, and inclusive first person plural.

It would appear that, in addition to the evidence of the pragmatic condensing of *Contemplations* and the incorporation of *An Information* in C, both possibly because of the small size of the manuscript, the compiler/scribe also shows a less functional and more creative side in the reversing of doublets and the ad hoc adjustment of personal pronouns.

'A Tretis of Pater Noster' also presents a text version of *Þe Pater Noster of Richard Ermyte* unique to the manuscript. Aarts, the editor of *Þe Pater Noster of Richard Ermyte*, points out throughout the edition 'how thoroughly C frequently differs from the other MSS'.[40] As in *Contemplations*, the compiler omits introductory enumerative passages, cuts quotations of biblical and patristic sources in Latin, and abbreviates and rephrases passages.[41] The compiler also adds two long passages, and in what follows the focus will be on these longer additions.

The first addition occurs in the introduction to the compilation, where, after the discussion of five impediments to prayer (the wicked life of the one who prays, that people at prayer do not ask what they should ask for, idle and foul thoughts, hardness of heart, and lack of real desire for the thing prayed for), C adds three more impediments: doubt, the unworthiness of the person prayed for, and the lack of perseverance in prayer.[42]

---

this text refers to 'Maria' throughout. Also, Birgitta is taught by Jesus rather than by 'doctors and holy mens lyues' (fol. 58^v), who teach the reader of the translated text. See *Revelaciones*, vi. 65.

[40] *The Pater Noster of Richard Ermyte*, ed. by Aarts, p. 70.

[41] A good example is the abbreviation of a story attributed to Jerome in *Vitae Patrum* about a knight, a lady, and a falcon as metaphors for the soul, God, and the world. The passage in C has been printed in the appendix to *The Pater Noster*, ed. by Aarts, p. 159 (equivalent to the longer story in the full text, *Pater Noster* 25/34 to 26/21).

[42] See fol. 100^r, cf. *Pater Noster* 7/5; fol. 100^v, cf. *Pater Noster* 7/26; fol. 102^v, cf. *Pater*

In a 1999 article, F. N. M. Diekstra points out the overlap of material between the fourteenth-century prose treatise *XII Lettyngis of Prayer*, *þe Holy Boke Gratia Dei* and *þe Pater Noster of Richard Ermyte* (C's 'A Tretis of Pater Noster').[43] Diekstra traces this material back to Peraldus's *Summa virtutum et vitiorum*, Book v, Chapter vii, Section 5 ('De impedimenta orationis') and concludes that not just this section, but a lot more material from Peraldus's *Summa* has been used by the compilers of *Holy Boke* and *Pater Noster*.[44] As such, he is the first to have identified Peraldus as an important source for these two compilations, as well as for the *Book for a Simple and Devout Woman*.[45] He also analyses how Peraldus's Latin is rendered in *Holy Boke* and *Pater Noster*, and concludes that the differences between the texts preclude the one having been copied from the other. The similarities between these compilations can only be explained by the existence of 'an adaptation of Peraldus's "De oratione" in English, either by itself or as part of a compilation, that served both compilers independently'.[46] Thus, in *Holy Boke* and *Pater Noster* compilers can be seen working creatively with a common source. In C's 'A Tretis of Pater Noster' the compiler creatively responds to *Pater Noster* as well, as he adds three more impediments to prayer, using the original source from which the impediments were selected in the first place.[47] This not only means that he recognized Peraldus's *Summa* as the source text, but also that he had access to a copy of this text and used it to write 'A Tretis'. The similarity of the compilation strategy used here to the incorporation of *An Information* into *Contemplations* is intriguing: material added or

Noster 9/14; fol. 103ᵛ, cf. *Pater Noster* 10/6; fol. 104ʳ, cf. *Pater Noster* 10/25 for the first five impediments. Impediments 6 to 8 in C follow on to *Pater Noster* 10/33 and can be found on fols 104ᵛ–106ʳ.

[43] *Holy Boke* presents six things that 'lettes prayere to be herde of God' as follows: the sins of those who pray (impediment 1 in C), the unworthiness of those for whom men pray (C 7), foul and idle thoughts (C 3), hardness of heart against the poor (C 4), little desire for the things men pray for and lack of perseverance (C 5 and 8), and foul and idle speech (not in C). *Þe Holy Boke Gratia Dei*, ed. by Arntz, pp. 52–57.

[44] For a concordance of this material in the *Summa Virtutum*, *The XII Lettyngis*, *Holy Boke*, and *Pater Noster*, see Diekstra, 'The XII Lettyngis of Prayer', pp. 130–45.

[45] Diekstra, 'The XII Lettyngis of Prayer', pp. 106–12. Also see *Book for a Simple and Devout Woman*, ed. by Diekstra. Arntz, the editor of *Holy Boke*, argued that *Pater Noster* may have been the compiler's source, just as Aarts, the editor of *Pater Noster*, thought *Holy Boke* was the source for *Pater Noster*.

[46] Diekstra, 'The XII Lettyngis of Prayer', p. 111.

[47] This revisiting of source material also occurs in other anthologies and compilations. See Denissen, 'Without the Multiplication of Many Books?', pp. 188–95.

appended is related to the material already used in the text. This suggests that scribes and compilers sometimes recognized a source of the compilation with which they were working and added more of the same. Thus, they seem to have been working in situations where collections of books were available to them.[48] The additions betray the compiler's interest in the content of the text and in the accretion of useful advice: the more impediments to prayer listed, the more of them the reader will be able to recognize and remedy.

The second long passage C adds occurs in the exposition of the verse 'Fiat voluntas tua sicut in celo et in terra' (*Pater Noster* 35/32–33). Where the *Pater Noster* treatise discusses two advantages of living according to God's will, by his grace, C adds a long discussion of banishing wrath from the heart as the first advantage (fols 150ʳ–159ʳ).[49]

> The first auantage is ȝif þou wolt feiþfulli be conformed to godes will, wilfully þou schalt put out of þine hert al enuye and wraþe, mevynge þe at no þinge þat may fall to þe saue only synne & most aȝene þine owne. Ffor of al þinge þat may fall contrarie to þe, þou schuldist ioy saue only for synne, seþen 'bi tribulacion vertu is preuyd', as poule seiþ. For wit þou wele: ȝife oþer in hert, mouþe, or werke þou schew any wraþe but onyly at syne, þou art proud and settist þi wil bifor godis wil. (fol. 150ʳ)

As Diekstra has shown, the passage translates and adapts material from pseudo-Chrysostom's *Opus imperfectum in Matthaeum*, Homilies X and XI, another source *Pater Noster* shares with *Book for a Simple and Devout Woman*, though in this case the compilers of these texts translate independently rather than borrow from an intervening English translation.[50] Again, the compiler of 'A Tretis

---

[48] Proof of the presence of collections of books where scribes and compilers were working can also be found in a copy of *The Prickynge of Love*, a translation of James of Milan's *Stimulus amoris* in New Haven, Yale University, Beinecke Library, MS Osborn fa46 (*olim* Taunton, Somerset Record Office, MS Heneage 3084 and, next, Oslo and London, Schøyen and London, MS 1701). The scribe of this manuscript, noticing that Chapter 33 of *The Prickynge* was missing, seems to have translated this chapter from the Latin to insert it into the text. This means that, while copying the English translation, the scribe also had access to a copy of the original Latin text. *The Prickynge of Love*, ed. by Kane, pp. xiii–xiv and pp. 573–76 (Appendix B, which offers a transcription of Chapter 33). In the compilations in C, however, books seem to have been consulted to add extra material to the compilation, not to remedy omissions from the text.

[49] In *Pater Noster*, the two advantages are (1) the absence of sorrow or wrath about anything that happens in the world except sin, and (2) being Lord of the world and all that is in it except sin.

[50] Diekstra, 'The XII Lettyngis of Prayer', pp. 122–24. For the Latin text of the *Opus Imperfectum*, see Pseudo-Chrysostomus, *Opus Imperfectum*, Homilia decima and Homilia undecima.

of Pater Noster' in C adds to *Pater Noster* using *Opus imperfectum*, from which the first compiler of this text selected as well. This means that the compiler recognized *Opus imperfectum* as a source and creatively expanded 'A Tretis' using fragments from *Opus* — most likely a work available to him at the time of writing — so that the readers would have at their disposal additional information that he deemed useful.

The third idiosyncratic compilation in C is its closing text, a translation of Edmund of Abingdon's *Speculum ecclesie*, which is, as Harry Wolcott Robbins puts it, 'noteworthy on account of the considerable additions which it includes'.[51] 'A deuout meditacioun of Richard Hampole' is a stage in the very complex transmission of the *Speculum*. It is commonly assumed that the *Speculum* was first written by Edmund of Abingdon in the thirteenth century as *Speculum religiosorum*, and afterwards translated into Anglo-Norman as *Le merure de seinte eglise*. When Anglo-Norman went into decline, the text was retranslated into Latin as *Speculum ecclesie*. This text survives in 'as many as six or seven different translations of the expanded text, drawn from the Anglo-Norman translation, or from the intermediate Latin version'.[52] 'A deuout meditacioun of Richard Hampole' is one of two copies of 'a heavily interpolated version, bearing an attribution to Richard Rolle'.[53]

'A deuout meditacioun' presents a severely abbreviated version of the text, as it leaves out Chapters 1, 8 to 19, and 27 to 30 of the *Speculum ecclesie*. This means that the text opens with a discussion of the Christian life in general (Chapters 2 to 5), selects the chapter discussing contemplation of God in his creatures (Chapter 6) and the first of eleven chapters addressing contemplation of God in the Scriptures (Chapter 7). The text skips Chapters 8 to 18, and does not select Chapter 19, which introduces the contemplation of God in his humanity. Borrowing resumes with the chapters detailing which episodes and aspects of Christ's humanity are appropriate for meditation during the hours

---

[51] Robbins, 'An English Version of St. Edmund's *Speculum*', p. 241. For editions of both *Speculum religiosorum* and *Speculum ecclesie*, see Edmund of Abingdon, *Speculum religiosorum*, ed. by Forshaw. All references to this edition are by page and line numbers.

[52] Lagorio and Sargent, 'English Mystical Writings', p. 3116. Also see *Vernacular Literary Theory*, ed. by Wogan-Browne, Fenster, and Russell, pp. 212–22.

[53] Lagorio and Sargent, 'English Mystical Writings', p. 3116. As pointed out above, the other copy of this text survives in Longleat House MS 32. On the basis of Hanna's description and dating of the Longleat copy to the middle or the third quarter of the fifteenth century, it is hard to say which is the later copy of the two. It needs to be noted here that, like C, Longleat House MS 32 is a small manuscript measuring 145 by 118 mm. Further research of this text will have to establish whether and in what way the two copies are related.

of the office (Chapters 20 to 26). All chapters on the contemplation of God in his divinity have been left untranslated, as have the first and last chapters, which frame the text in an opening and closing discussion of what it means to live honourably, amicably, and humbly. 'A deuout meditacioun' cuts material within the chapters it does translate, and though it is translated from the *Speculum ecclesie*, the second Latin version, it does share two readings with the *Speculum religiosorum*, which suggests that hybrid versions of both Latin translations may have circulated.[54]

Many of the additions to the *Speculum ecclesie* in 'A deuout meditacioun' are very graphic Passion meditations focusing on the gruesome aspects of Christ's suffering.[55] In addition, the compiler more narrowly refocuses statements about pure contemplation on to the readers as sinners, and on to the redemption of their sins through Christ's suffering on the cross.

> to knowynge of þi silfe þou miȝt come on þis maner: *to have compassioun and mynd of Ihesu Crist, what he sufferd for þe.* (fols 208[r–v])[56]

> Ad cognicionem tui ipsius potes venire *per frequentem meditacionem; ad cognicionem Dei per puram contemplacionem.*[57] (You can come to knowledge of yourself through frequent meditation; to knowledge of God through pure contemplation)

This focus is in keeping with the compiler's omissions as discussed earlier, which show that he decidedly favours devotion to the Passion over the more abstract and theology-based contemplation of God in his divinity, and text-based contemplation of God in the Scriptures. Where the phrase 'ad cognicionem Dei per puram contemplacionem' occurs in the *Speculum ecclesie* for a second time, however, it has been replaced in 'A deuout meditacioun' with a longer passage that stresses God's eternal greatness, wisdom, and justice without reference to the Passion. This passage is the closest the text — and the anthology — gets to

---

[54] '& seiden to him, "Heile, sir kynge of Iewis"' (fol. 216[r], 'Meditacioun' 248/16) is missing in the *Speculum ecclesie* 89/16 and would seem to derive from *Speculum religiosorum* 88/15, as does the exchange of the fourth and fifth of Christ's last words (fol. 219[r], 'Meditacioun' 250/22–26, cf. *Speculum religiosorum* 92/18–19 and *Speculum ecclesie* 93/22–24).

[55] A good illustration of this is in the 'Contemplation byfore undern', where the additions to the *Speculum* describe how a silk cloth is thrown over Christ's bleeding body. When the blood dries, the cloth sticks to the wounds. 'And when þei had þus scornid him þie drow of þat cloþe of sile, and it clevyd so fast to his body þat þei drew þerwiþ moche of his skynne and of his flesche also, and whanne þei saw þat blissid body so foule to here siȝt þei blerid on him and spitted in his face as þei wold have done on a tode' (fols 216[r–v], 'Meditacioun' 248/17–21).

[56] 'Meditacioun' 242/5–7, italics Robbins's.

[57] *Speculum ecclesie* 35/17–18.

evoking a form of contemplation that goes beyond meditation on the events of the Passion, though it keeps a focus on the readers' smallness and God's awareness of all their actions.

> by þis maner contemplacion þou schalt lerne to know þi silfe *and to love God and to serve him, for we schuld trow þat he is þe best þing þat may be, þe wisest and þe most iust þat any man may þinke on, and so he is ever wiþout bygining and without end. Knowynge al þinge he may not forȝet, ne no þing may aschappe him; but evermore he ordiniþ a þinge þat is gode.* (fols 211ᵛ–212ʳ)[58]

> Isto modo potes venire ad tui ipsius cognicionem *per sanctam meditacionem; venies ad cognicionem Dei per puram contemplacionem.*[59] (In this way can you come to knowledge of yourself through holy meditation; you will come to knowledge of God through pure contemplation)

'A deuout meditacioun' also adds to the story in the *Speculum* repeated references to 'þe fals Iewys' as the agents in the Passion story, reflecting a popular medieval anti-Semitic positioning of the Jews as the murderers of Christ.[60] The first of these instances is interesting, as it is a neutral reference that does not have the adjective 'false', but the compiler changes the Latin original to fit his agenda.[61] In the sentence 'hou Petir forsoke him sone after þre tymes for þe wiked wordis of þe Iewis' (fol. 215ʳ),[62] 'wordis of þe Iewis' translates the Latin 'verba cuiusdam ancille maledicte' (the words of a certain cursed servant).[63] This version of the *Speculum* may be rousing (for better or worse), but it is not exactly subtle.

In one instance, however, the compiler responds to the text in a subtly poetic way. Again, the compiler can be seen as a reader, who responds to the text he reads with additional text derived from his reading. Whereas in 'A Tretis' this additional text comes in the form of material from the original sources of the text, in the following fragment from 'A deuout meditacioun' the compiler's response is triggered by the very text that he is revising:

---

[58] 'Meditacioun' 244/29–35, italics Robbins's.

[59] *Speculum ecclesie* 43/30–32, italics mine.

[60] Levy, *Antisemitism*, p. 169.

[61] The other instances can be found on fol. 216ʳ, 'Meditacioun' 248/8; fol. 216ᵛ, 'Meditacioun' 248/29; fol. 218ᵛ, 'Meditacioun' 250/10; and fol. 219ʳ, 'Meditacioun' 250/22.

[62] 'Meditacioun' 247/19–20.

[63] *Speculum ecclesie* 85/24.

> Also bihold his moder, what sorow sche had *whan sche saw here swete son suffer al þat peyne, and for his sorow and wo sche becam blake and blo*, as sche seiþ of hersilf, 'Ne clepe ȝe me no more faire, lesse ne more, but clepiþ me fro hense forþ ward woman ful of sorow and wo, *and colore boþ blake and blo*.' (fol. 218ʳ)⁶⁴

The compiler's addition to this meditation is clearly triggered by the reference to Canticles 1. 5 included just after this passage: 'Ne merueile ȝe þat þouȝ I be broune and pale, for þe sunne haþ miscoloured me (fols 218ʳ⁻ᵛ).⁶⁵ The 'black and blue' expression is a common one and is also reminiscent of Julian of Norwich's description of Christ dying on the cross.⁶⁶ The compiler, in adding the colour reference to Mary's locution, might also be responding to the famous quatrain that follows in the *Speculum*:

> Now goþ de sonn under wode;
> Mary, me rewiþ þi faire rode.
> Now goþ þe sone under þe tre,
> Mari me reweþ þi sonne so fre. (fol. 218ᵛ)⁶⁷

The words that Mary speaks of herself can also be seen as verse, with the last two lines working especially well as a couplet.

> Ne clepe ȝe me no more faire, lesse ne more,
> but clepiþ me fro hense forþ ward
> woman ful of sorow and wo,
> *and colore boþ blake and blo*. (fol. 218ʳ)⁶⁸

The compiler may have been inspired by the 'Sunset on Calvary quatrain' to add a rhyming line. (In C, both poems are written as prose.)

The anthology found in C illustrates the operation of compilatory agency on various levels and at various times in the transmission of the compilations it presents. It remains difficult to pinpoint a clear agenda for the compiling activity in C, but we can see the effects of compilers' decisions in this manuscript.

---

⁶⁴ 'Meditacioun' 249/31–35.

⁶⁵ 'Meditacioun' 249/36–250/2.

⁶⁶ *A Vision Showed to a Devout Woman*, in Julian of Norwich, *The Writings*, ed. by Watson and Jenkins, p. 83.

⁶⁷ 'Meditacioun' 250/3–6. Most versions of this quatrain have 'Me rewiþ Marie þi son and þee' (*Speculum* 93/7). In a movement counter to the earlier addition, in which the compiler focuses on how Mary suffers like Christ, in this last line he moves his compassion away from her and settles it exclusively on Jesus.

⁶⁸ 'Meditacioun' 249/31–35.

The need to fit a long text into the first booklet of a small-size manuscript seems to have occasioned the condensing of *Contemplations*. The revisions in 'A Tretis of Pater Noster' and 'A deuout meditacioun' seem to result from the compilers' eagerness to make texts their own, and not just their audience's, in a process of transmission more creative than mere copying. In all three longer compilations, condensing and abbreviation have been counterbalanced by expansion of the text. The effect of these seemingly contradictory impulses on the part of the compiler is that *Contemplations* and 'A Tretis' in particular read like a list of spiritual guidelines to follow, expanded with subject matter which the compiler deemed important. When *An Information* is appended to *Contemplations*, the readers get more instruction on the active and contemplative life in the examples of Martha and Mary. In 'A Tretis' the compiler listed extra impediments to prayer and inserted the passage from the *Opus imperfectum* on how wrath can be avoided. In a similar way, the severe curtailing of the *Speculum ecclesie* has been counterbalanced by the addition of graphic Passion meditations. In the portrayal of the Jews as the perpetrators of the violence that causes Christ's pain, the compilation adds an anti-Semitic undertone absent from the original Latin text.

This essay has addressed various ways in which compilers and scribes played an active role in the reshaping of devotional compilations in transmission. They responded to the compilations by appending or inserting materials from the compilations' sources, or by creatively weaving material from the compilation itself into their additions. Though these compilers and scribes remain anonymous and elusive, and though we cannot say exactly where they worked, how many they were, what collections of books they had at their disposal, or how they collaborated, they can be seen openly making their mark in associative additions, in the playful reversal of doublets, and even in verse.

Works Cited

Manuscripts

Cambridge, University Library [CUL], MS Ii.6.40
New Haven, Yale University, Beinecke Library, MS Osborn fa46
Oxford, Bodleian Library [Bodl. Lib.], MS Bodley 197
Oxford, Bodleian Library [Bodl. Lib.], MS Bodley 423
Oxford, Bodleian Library [Bodl. Lib.], MS Rawlinson A. 389
Tokyo, Prof. Toshiyuki Takamiya, MS 66
Warminster, Longleat House, Marquess of Bath MS 32

Primary Sources

Aelred of Rievaulx, *Aelred of Rievaulx's De Institutione Inclusarum: Two English Versions*, ed. by John Ayto and Alexandra Barratt, Early English Text Society, o.s. 287 (Oxford: Oxford University Press, 1984)

Book for a Simple and Devout Woman: A Late Middle English Adaptation of Peraldus's 'Summa de Vitiis et Virtutibus' and Friar Laurent's 'Somme le Roi', Edited from British Library Mss Harley 6571 and Additional 30944, ed. by F. N. M. Diekstra, Mediaevalia Groningana, 24 (Groningen: Egbert Forsten, 1998)

Contemplations of the Dread and Love of God, ed. by Margaret Connolly, Early English Text Society, o.s. 303 (Oxford: Oxford University Press, 1993; repr. 2001)

Edmund of Abingdon, *Edmund of Abingdon: Speculum religiosorum and Speculum ecclesie*, ed. by Helen P. Forshaw, Auctores Brittanici Medii Aevi, 3 (Oxford: Oxford University Press for the British Academy, 1973)

Goymer, Clare Rosemary, 'A Parallel Text Edition of the Middle English Prose Version(s) of the *Mirror of St Edmund* Based on the Known Complete Manuscripts' (unpublished master's thesis, Royal Holloway, University of London, 1961)

Healy Murphy, Clodagh, '*A Tretis of Tribulation*: A Diplomatic Edition of the Text Contained in MS Cambridge University Library Ii. 6. 40' (unpublished master's thesis, University of Cork, 1991)

Julian of Norwich, *The Writings of Julian of Norwich: 'A Vision Showed to a Devout Woman' and 'A Revelation of Love'*, ed. by Nicholas Watson and Jacqueline Jenkins, Medieval Women: Texts and Contexts, 5 (Turnhout: Brepols, 2006)

Kraebel, Andrew, 'Richard of St Victor: *On the Four Degrees*', in *On Love: A Selection of Works of Hugh, Adam, Achard, Richard, and Godfrey of St Victor*, ed. by Hugh Feiss OSB, Victorine Texts in Translation, 2 (Turnhout: Brepols, 2011), pp. 260–300

The Pater Noster of Richard Ermyte: A Late Middle English Exposition of the Lord's Prayer, ed. by Florent Aarts (Nijmegen: Drukkerij Gebr. Janssen, 1967)

'*The Pore Caitif*: Edited from MS Harley 2336 with Introduction and Notes,' ed. by Mary Teresa Brady (unpublished doctoral dissertation, Fordham University, 1954)

The Prickynge of Love, ed. by Harold Kane, Salzburg Studies in English Literature: Elizabethan and Renaissance Studies, 92.10 (Salzburg: Institut für Anglistik und Amerikanistik, 1983)

Richard Rolle and Þe Holy Boke Gratia Dei: An Edition with Commentary, ed. by Mary Luke Arntz, Salzburg Studies in English Literature, Elizabethan and Renaissance Studies, 92.2 (Salzburg: Institut für Anglistik und Americanistik, 1981)

——, *Richard Rolle: Prose and Verse from MS. Longleat 29 and Related Manuscripts*, ed. by S. J. Ogilvie-Thomson, Early English Text Society, o.s. 293 (Oxford: Oxford University Press, 1988)

Robbins, Harry Wolcott, 'An English Version of St. Edmund's *Speculum*, Ascribed to Richard Rolle', *Publications of the Modern Language Association of America*, 40.2 (1925), 240–51

Vernacular Literary Theory from the French of Medieval England: Texts and Translations, ca. 1120–c. 1450, ed. by Jocelyn Wogan-Browne, Thelma Fenster, and Delbert W. Russell (Woodbridge: D. S. Brewer, 2016)

Secondary Works

Bahr, Arthur, *Fragments and Assemblages: Forming Compilations of Medieval London* (Chicago: University of Chicago Press, 2013)

Connolly, Margaret, 'Mapping Manuscripts and Readers of *Contemplations of the Dread and Love of God*', in *Design and Distribution of Late Medieval Manuscripts in England*, ed. by Margaret Connolly and Linne R. Mooney (York: York Medieval Press; Woodbridge: Boydell, 2008), pp. 261–78

Cré, Marleen, 'Spiritual Comfort and Reasonable Feeling: Annotating *The Chastising of God's Children* in Oxford, Bodleian Library, MS Rawlinson C 57', in *Emotion and Medieval Textual Media*, ed. by Mary C. Flannery (Turnhout: Brepols, 2018), pp. 149–76

Denissen, Diana, 'Without the Multiplication of Many Books? Compiling Styles and Strategies in *A Talkyng of the Love of God*, the *Pore Caitif* and *The Tretyse of Love*' (unpublished doctoral thesis, University of Lausanne, 2017)

Diekstra, F. N. M., '*The XII Lettyngis of Prayer*, Peraldus' *Summae virtutum ac vitiorum*, and the Relation between *Þe Holy Boke Gratia Dei*, *Þe Pater Noster of Richard Ermyte* and *Book for a Simple and Devout Woman*', *English Studies*, 80.2 (1999), 106–45

Doyle, A. I., 'A Survey of the Origins and Circulation of Theological Writings in English in the 14th, 15th and Early 16th Centuries with Special Consideration of the part of the Clergy Therein', 2 vols (unpublished doctoral dissertation, University of Cambridge, 1953)

Gilroy, Jane Hagan, 'English Adaptations of Revelations 6.65 in Manuscript and Early Print Editions', *Birgittiana*, 9 (2000), 3–16

Hanna, Ralph, *The English Manuscripts of Richard Rolle: A Descriptive Catalogue*, Exeter Medieval Texts and Studies (Exeter: University of Exeter Press, 2010)

Havens, Jill C., 'A Narrative of Faith: Middle English Devotional Anthologies and Religious Practice', *Journal of the Early Book Society*, 7 (2004), 67–84

Jones, E. A. 'Jesus College Oxford, MS 39: Signs of a Medieval Compiler at Work', in *English Manuscript Studies 1100–1700*, vol. VII, ed. by Peter Beal and Jeremy Griffiths (London: British Library, 1997), pp. 236–48

Knowles, David, and R. Neville Hadcock, *Medieval Religious Houses: England and Wales* (London: Longman, 1971)

Lagorio, Valerie M., and Michael G. Sargent (with Ritamary Bradley), 'English Mystical Writings', in *A Manual of the Writings in English, 1050–1500*, vol. IX, ed. by Albert E. Hartung (New Haven: Connecticut Academy of Arts and Sciences, 1993), pp. 3131–37

Levy, Richard S., ed., *Antisemitism: A Historical Encyclopedia of Prejudice and Persecution* (Santa Barbara, CA: ABC-CLIO, 2005)

Nichols, Stephen G., and Siegfried Wenzel, eds, *The Whole Book: Cultural Perspectives on the Medieval Miscellany* (Ann Arbor: University of Michigan Press, 1996)

Parkes, Malcolm B., 'The Influence of the Concepts of *Ordinatio* and *Compilatio* on the Development of the Book', in *Medieval Learning and Literature: Essays Presented to Richard William Hunt*, ed. by J. J. G. Alexander and M. T. Gibson (Oxford: Clarendon Press, 1976), pp. 115–44

Rice, Nicole, *Lay Piety and Religious Discipline in Middle English Literature*, Cambridge Studies in Medieval Literature (Cambridge: Cambridge University Press, 2008)

Vulić, Kathryn, '*Þe Pater Noster of Richard Ermyte* and the Topos of the Female Audience', *Mystics Quarterly*, 34.3–4 (2008), 1–43

Wakelin, Daniel, '"Thys ys my boke": Imagining the Owner in the Book', in *Spaces for Reading in Later Medieval England*, ed. by Mary C. Flannery and Carrie Griffin (Basingstoke: Palgrave Macmillan, 2016), pp. 13–33

Online Publications

St Birgitta of Sweden, *Revelaciones*, Book VI (Lübeck: Ghotan, 1492 Editio Princeps) <http://www.umilta.net/bk6.html> [accessed 20 January 2017]

Pseudo-Chrysostomus, *Opus Imperfectum in Mattheum*, from *Patrologia Graeca*, ed. by J. P. Migne, LVI, cols 611–946, <http://web.wlu.ca/history/cnighman/OpusImperfectum.pdf> [accessed 20 January 2017]

Part III

Compilation and Devotional Practice

A Hagiographic Compilation of Medieval Native Women in the *South English Legendaries*: Oxford, Bodleian Library, MS Bodley 779

Mami Kanno

The *South English Legendaries* (*SELS*) form one of the largest hagiographic works in Middle English. There are more than sixty manuscripts, compiled between the late thirteenth and fifteenth centuries, and each manuscript is known to form a unique anthology. Compilers of these manuscripts usually select texts from existing sources and arrange them in the contexts of their anthologies. Because of the way in which the manuscripts of the *SELS* have been compiled, examination of an individual manuscript provides us with insight into the intentions that the compiler might have had and contributes to unveiling the nature of this hagiographic work. One of the manuscripts of the *SELS*, Bodl. Lib., MS Bodley 779 (hereafter MS Bodley 779), compiled in the fifteenth century, deserves attention as a distinct anthology. It contains a number of unique *sanctorale* sermons (on saints' feast days) and *temporale* texts (for other feast days, such as Easter) that cannot be found in any other manuscripts. Moreover, MS Bodley 779 includes a group of *vitae* of five native female saints. All the native female saints included in this manuscript, namely Frideswide of Oxford, Æthelthryth of Ely, Mildred of Minster-in-Thanet, Edburga of Winchester, and Winifred of Gwytherin, were nuns and abbesses in England and Wales living between the seventh and tenth centuries.

Mami Kanno (mkanno@staff.kanazawa-u.ac.jp) is an Assistant Professor at Kanazawa University, Japan.

Although the inclusion of native saints, both male and female, is a distinct characteristic of the *SELS*, the focus on studies of native saints in the *SELS*, especially in the context of their contribution to a national identity, has been limited to such major English saints as Dunstan, Kenelm, Wulfstan, and Thomas Becket, who frequently appear in major manuscripts or in existing critical editions.[1] However, if we look at unpublished anthologies, such as MS Bodley 779, holy female saints also serve to map the nation through texts with diverse local backgrounds. Drawing upon hagiographic topoi in the *vitae* of classical female saints, the *vitae* of native women in MS Bodley 779 give models of saintly virtues to their contemporary audience in medieval England. A case study of this manuscript suggests that these women also play an important role in the making of a socio-religious map of medieval Britain.

Before moving on to discussing the *vitae* of native female saints in MS Bodley 779, it needs to be noted that all the manuscripts of the *SELS* vary in their contents and arrangement of texts. There are sixty-five extant manuscripts: twenty-six containing a more or less full cycle and thirty-nine fragments and miscellanies containing a single item from the *SELS*.[2] Despite their wide dissemination and reception throughout the Middle Ages, the *SELS* do not seem to have received the critical attention they deserve, especially from the perspectives of literary and cultural analysis. However, recent scholarship of the *SELS* has brought about a significant change, not only in opening up opportunities for wide-ranging discussions, but also in how we treat this hagiographic collection.[3] In early scholarship, the group of manuscripts was called the '*South English Legendary*' (*SEL*). However, since Thomas R. Liszka in 2001 pointed out the different characteristics of each manuscript in terms of content, arrangement, and intended audience, there has been a critical trend towards discussing them as a heterogeneous group referred to by the plural *SELS*.[4] This discussion came to fruition in *Rethinking the South English*

---

[1] Hamelinck, 'St. Kenelm and the Legends of the English Saints'; Jankofsky, 'National Characteristics'; Turville-Petre, *England the Nation*; Frederick, 'The *South English Legendary*'. One of the few exceptions which focus on native female saints is Kerryn Olsen's study on four Anglo-Saxon female saints in the *SELS*. See Olsen, 'Questions of Identity', pp. 172–82; Olsen, 'Women and Englishness'.

[2] See Görlach, *Textual Tradition of the 'South English Legendary'*, pp. viii–xi; Pickering and Görlach, 'A Newly-Discovered Manuscript of the *South English Legendary*'.

[3] On the critical history of the *SELS* up to 2000, see Scahill, *Middle English Saints' Legends*, pp. 39–75.

[4] Liszka, 'The *South English Legendaries*'.

Legendaries in 2012. Jocelyn Wogan-Browne and Heather Blurton claim that this hagiographic work should not be treated as a single literary work for the 'variety and flexibility' of 'contents, time and audience of these manuscripts'.[5] Kimberly K. Bell and Julie Nelson Couch's collection of essays, which was published in the same year, took a similar approach, focusing specifically on a manuscript of the *SELS*, Bodl. Lib., MS Laud. misc. 108.[6] The critical shift from the single *SEL* to the *SELS* reflects how scholars came to understand the nature of medieval works. The *SELS* most emphatically present characteristics of what Paul Zumthor calls *mouvance*, textual variations and fluidity produced in the course of textual transmission.[7]

Just as Zumthor's concept of *mouvance* raised the question of how to create critical editions of medieval works, the *SELS* themselves also reveal the limitations of producing a conventional critical edition by selecting one particular manuscript as its base text.[8] Of the two critical editions published by the Early English Text Society (EETS), Carl Horstmann's edition in 1887 is based on the earliest surviving manuscript, Bodl. Lib., MS Laud misc. 108. Horstmann nevertheless suggested that his edition, based on a single manuscript, was inadequate to understand the diverse nature of the work. In his introduction, he states that 'in publishing the great *South-English Legendary* [...], I begin with the version of Laud 108' and, as the volume number, 'I', appears on the title page, it seems that he intended to edit all the manuscripts of the *SELS* that he knew and to publish them as a series.[9] While Horstmann's edition presents one of the examples of diversified compilations, Charlotte D'Evelyn and Anna J. Mill's edition, published in 1956, is based on two major manuscripts (Cambridge, Corpus Christi College, MS 145 and BL, MS Harley 2277), emended and supplemented by two other manuscripts (Bodl. Lib., MS Ashmole 43 and BL,

---

[5] Blurton and Wogan-Browne, 'Rethinking the *South English Legendaries*', p. 10. Mills also points out that the modern title, the *South English Legendary*, is misleading because of the plurality of texts. See 'Violence, Community and the Materialisation of Belief', p. 87.

[6] Bell and Nelson Couch, *The Texts and Contexts of Oxford, Bodleian Library, MS Laud Misc. 108*. Bell and Nelson Couch discuss not only the *SEL*, but also its relationships with other vernacular works, such as the Middle English romances *King Horn* and *Havelock the Dane*, which appear in the same manuscript.

[7] Zumthor, *Toward a Medieval Poetics*, pp. 41–49; Millett, '*Mouvance* and the Medieval Author'.

[8] Millett, '*Mouvance* and the Medieval Author', pp. 12–13.

[9] *The Early South-English Legendary*, ed. by Horstmann, p. vii; Liszka, 'The *South English Legendaries*', p. 26.

MS Cotton Julius D IX).¹⁰ Although D'Evelyn and Mill's edition is often used as a standard critical edition of the *SELS*, the plurality and diversity of the manuscripts make it almost impossible for scholars to produce a single, definitive critical edition. For example, it is difficult to gain from this edition an overview of the saints included in the *SELS*. In particular, a certain group of saints that is not included in their chosen manuscripts can be overlooked easily unless we examine other compilations of the *SELS* at the manuscript level.

One such group of saints that could slip from our attention because of their exclusion from the existing critical editions are the native saints of the medieval British Isles. One of the distinct characteristics of the *SELS* is that they contain a number of local saints' lives as well as the lives of the so-called universal saints, most of whom were from the classical period and widely celebrated in medieval Europe.[11] Although the lives of many major male English saints, such as Saints Cuthbert, Kenelm, Edward the Martyr, Wulfstan, and Thomas Becket, are included in the earlier manuscripts, and consequently in either Horstmann's or D'Evelyn and Mill's critical editions, many more native saints' lives, both of male and female saints, were added to later manuscripts in the fourteenth and fifteenth centuries. Manfred Görlach identifies a group of such manuscripts which contain additional native saints' lives. These four manuscripts (BL, MS Egerton 1993; Bodl. Lib., MS Eng. poet. a. 1, known as the Vernon Manuscript; MS Bodley 779; and Cambridge, Trinity College, MS 605 (R.3.25)) are called the 'E' branch of manuscript stemma, which share the same textual tradition, taking the capital letter E from the oldest manuscript in this group, BL, MS Egerton 1993. This group of manuscripts includes the lives of a set of English saints, such as Æthelthryth, Birinus, Botulf, Edburga, Egwine, and Mildred.[12] The characteristic of compiling the *vitae* of local saints together with the *vitae* of universal saints in the *SELS* reflects tendencies seen in other hagiographic collections after the Conquest. Concerning the *Gilte Legende*, which contains supplementary lives of native saints in some manuscripts, and some of whose *vitae* draw on the *SELS* as their sources, Richard Hamer and Vida Russell state that supplementary texts often include new additions of saints' lives which were of interest to the institution, locality, or nation of the new compilers.[13] The same holds true for a particular group of later manuscripts of the *SELS*. Like the compilers of

---

[10] *The South English Legendary*, ed. by D'Evelyn and Mill.

[11] On the definition of universal and local saints, see Cubitt, 'Universal and Local Saints', p. 423.

[12] Görlach, *Textual Tradition of the 'South English Legendary'*, p. 17.

[13] *Supplementary Lives*, ed. by Hamer and Russell, p. xiv.

the supplementary *Gilte Legende*, the compilers of those later manuscripts of the *SELS* added a number of native English saints to their collections who were of interest to themselves or their intended readers. By composing and compiling the *vitae* of saints from Anglo-Saxon, British, Irish, or Celtic backgrounds, late medieval hagiographers present them as 'English' saints in their collections.

Compared to other hagiographic anthologies containing native saints' lives, it is one of the distinct characteristics that some anthologies of the *SELS* include more female saints of the medieval British Isles than other Middle English hagiographic collections. According to Katherine J. Lewis, the selection of native saints in late medieval English hagiographic collections, such as *Gilte Legende* and William Caxton's translation of the *Legenda aurea*, tends to be 'masculine'.[14] In contrast, in all manuscripts of the *SELS*, there are eight Anglo-Saxon and British female saints: Ursula, Helena, Bridget of Kildare, Winifred of Gwytherin, Frideswide of Oxford, Æthelthryth of Ely, Mildred of Minster-in-Thanet, and Edburga of Winchester. Among them, Frideswide, Æthelthryth, Mildred, Edburga, and Winifred form a group of medieval monastic women celebrated in specific, local areas of England and Wales. Of the manuscripts in which they commonly appear, MS Bodley 779 is the only one that contains all these female saints. Because of their exclusion from the EETS editions, the *vitae* of native monastic women have been edited and published individually, but each edition is based on a different manuscript: Æthelthryth, Mildred, and Edburga are edited from BL, MS Egerton 1993; Frideswide from Bodl. Lib., MS Ashmole 43 and Cambridge, Trinity College, MS 605; and Winifred from MS Bodley 779.[15] Except for that of Winifred, whose *vita* appears only in MS Bodley 779, their base manuscripts have been chosen based on the best preserved texts. Yet MS Bodley 779 deserves special attention as a collection that compiles the largest number of the native female saints' lives of all the *SEL* manuscripts and provides us with a significant corpus of the *vitae* of native female saints.[16]

MS Bodley 779 was compiled in the fifteenth century, containing 135 items of both *sanctorale* and *temporale* texts. Linguistic and dialectic features identify North Hampshire as its place of origin, but little is known of its prove-

---

[14] Lewis, 'Anglo-Saxon Saints' Lives, History and National Identity', p. 169.

[15] Editions of the five native female saints in the *SELS* are as follows: (Æthelthryth) Major, 'Saint Etheldreda'; (Mildred) Acker, 'St Mildred'; (Edburga) Braswell, 'Saint Edburga of Winchester'; (Frideswide) *Middle English Legends of Women Saints*, ed. by Reames, pp. 23–50; (Winifred) Horstmann, 'Des Ms. Bodl. 779', pp. 331–33.

[16] My discussion of the *vitae* of five native women in MS Bodley 779 is based on my transcriptions from the manuscript.

nance before the early seventeenth century when William Harwood, prebendary of Winchester, donated the manuscript to the Bodleian Library.[17] Also, MS Bodley 779 is idiosyncratic in terms of its *compilatio* and *ordinatio* of saints' lives.[18] Because of its inclusion of unique saints' lives, which cannot be seen in other *SEL* manuscripts, MS Bodley 779 is sometimes seen as a 'collector's copy' which is, according to Görlach, 'compiled from various sources, some at least fragmentary'.[19] In terms of native female saints, it contains not only the three from a group of additional English saints in the 'E' branch, but also Frideswide and Winifred.

One of the possible reasons that the compiler of MS Bodley 779 places the four Anglo-Saxon female saints together, as well as compiling the unique life of Winifred, is his attitude towards women. In MS Bodley 779, a text entitled 'Defence of Women' is inserted in the *Southern Passion* (fols 38^r–39^v). Of the nine manuscripts containing this work, the version in MS Bodley 779 is considered to be the most complete and original form.[20] In this text, the author criticizes the sexual double standards in medieval society by using metaphors of saints:

> And hou is hit þen of wommen, þat men blameþ hem so
> In songis and in rimis, and in bokis þerto,
> To segge þat hy fals beþ, and iuyl also to ileue,
> Vikel ek and leþir inou3, mony mon to greue?
> [...]
> Where wostou so stable mon, þat 3if a fayr woman come,
> Gent and hende, and hym bysou3t of folye ilome
> Þat he nolde torne his þou3t to folye at fyne?
> For 3if he ne dede me wold hym holde worþy to ligge in crine.
> And what is þan þe woman worþe, as þe meste del beþ,
> Þat ne beþ ouercome mid no biddyng, as we ofte iseþ?
> 3he ne chal be no seint iholde, as alle stille hit chal be;
> What reson is in þis manere? Day þat hit conne ise![21]

---

[17] Görlach, *Textual Tradition of the 'South English Legendary'*, pp. 76–77.

[18] On the concept of *compilatio* and *ordinatio* in medieval manuscripts, see Parkes, 'The Influence of the Concepts of *Ordinatio* and *Compilatio*' and Dutton, *Julian of Norwich*. Cynthia Turner Camp, furthermore, analyses a fifteenth-century collection of female saints of the East Anglian royal family (CUL, MS Additional 2604) in the light of *compilatio* and *ordinatio*. See her *Anglo-Saxon Saints' Lives as History Writing*, pp. 91–101.

[19] Görlach, *Textual Tradition of the 'South English Legendary'*, p. 76. On unique saints in MS Bodley 779, as well as their edited texts, see Horstmann, 'Des Ms. Bodl. 779', pp. 351–53.

[20] Pickering, 'The "Defence of Women" for the *Southern Passion*', pp. 160–61.

[21] Quotations from the 'Defence of Women' are taken from Pickering, 'The "Defence of

[How is it then that women are so criticized in verse and sayings and books, which claim that they are false, untrustworthy, fickle, and wicked, to many a man's cost? [...] Where would you find a man so steadfast, if a nice, attractive, charming woman were to come and keep on begging him for sex, that he would not change his tune and do it in the end? If he didn't, he'd be reckoned a saint fit to lie in a shrine! So, how should we rate a woman (and this includes most women) who does not give in to any amount of importuning, as can be seen every day? She won't be thought a saint — it will pass without notice. What logic is there in this attitude? Who on earth can see sense in it?][22]

Giving an example of sexual temptation, the author points out that men who defeat sexual temptation are often applauded as though they are worth to 'ligge in crine' ('lie in a shrine', l. 38), whereas women who overcome temptation are not called 'seint'. Then the author complains about the paucity of female saints, questioning why there are so few female saints, even though there are many who deserve to be so called. This query corresponds with the compiler's positive attitudes towards collecting more lives of female saints, especially those who are not included in contemporary hagiographic collections.

In hagiographic collections it is important to examine not only their *compilatio*, what the compilers collected, but also their *ordinatio*, how compilers arranged their material in context. In a conventional hagiographical structure, saints' lives are supposed to be arranged according to the saints' feast days in the order of the liturgical year, beginning from Advent, or in the order of the calendar. In the base manuscripts of D'Evelyn and Mill's critical edition all the items are compiled in calendar order, beginning from 'ȝeresday', or Christ's Circumcision, which falls on 1 January. However, the *SELS* are also known for the fact that each compilation has its own *ordinatio*, which does not always follow the conventional way of arranging saints' legends in hagiography. For example, Bodl. Lib., MS Laud misc. 108 consists of groups of saints' lives who are arranged in the order of the saints' feast days and those who are not. Liszka analyses a group of non-calendrically ordered saints which interrupts the group of calendrically ordered saints and suggests that those interrupting *vitae* of saints are grouped not only by their types, such as confessors and virgin martyrs, but also by their nationalities, such as English and Irish saints.[23] Thus, the liturgical calendar is not the only factor which determines the *ordinatio* of the

Women" from the *Southern Passion*', pp. 167–76, see p. 168, ll. 27–42.

[22] The Modern English translation of the 'Defence of Women' is taken from 'The Southern Passion', trans. by Blamires, p. 245.

[23] Liszka, 'Ms Laud. Misc. 108 and the Early History of the *South English Legendary*', p. 82.

compilations of the *SELS*. Saints' typologies, their nationalities and localities, and perhaps their gender also affect the compilers' *ordinatio* of saints' *vitae*.[24]

MS Bodley 779 is, as Liszka notes, an 'extreme example' of the 'largely disorderly' manuscripts of the *SELS*, which places saints' *vitae* by the compiler's peculiar sense of order, often interrupted and disrupted by the lives of other groups of saints.[25] Indeed, in MS Bodley 779, groups of randomly collected saints even appear in a random order, but a table of contents, written by a medieval hand (fol. 1), also suggests that MS Bodley 779 apparently has two principles of organizing saints' lives: one by the saints' feast days, the other by categories of saints. These two principles sometimes work together, but in most cases the *ordinatio* of the manuscript is determined by one of them. In one instance, the compiler places the items in calendar order, regardless of the saints' categories, and in another place, he gathers the lives of saints who have something in common, such as the time and places they lived, occupations, and gender. MS Bodley 779 not only collects various unique texts, but also attempts to categorize them into particular groups of saints according to their similarities, although not always consistently.

As Liszka notes, MS Bodley 779 begins with a group of the seven *sanctorale* texts of randomly collected saints, including two Irish saints, Brendan and Patrick (fols 2^r–17^r), and two Anglo-Saxon saints, Oswald (fol. 21) and Thomas Becket (fols 41^v–66^v), as well as the *temporale* texts, including the *Southern Passion* which contains the 'Defence of Women' (fols 38^r–39^v), arranged in random order.[26] It is followed by a group of lives of English saints (Oswald the Bishop, Edward the Martyr, Alphege, Dunstan, Aldhelm, Austin, Kenelm, and Swithun; fols 76^v–94^v), here arranged systematically according to their feast days between January and July. The contents in the middle of the manuscript show the most distinctive characteristic of this compilation: there is a group of saints' *vitae*, many of which are unique to MS Bodley 779. A unique *vita* of a Welsh female saint, Winifred (fol. 189), appears in this cluster of October saints (fols 177^r–201^v), although her feast day falls on 3 November. The second group of lives of English saints comes towards the end of the collection. While the first group of the *vitae* of English saints is exclusively male, this group does include three Anglo-Saxon female saints, Æthelthryth, Frideswide, and Edburga (fols 279^v–283^v), and after several *vitae* comes Mildred (fols 302^r–303^v). Those saints are not arranged in calendar order, but are apparently grouped for their shared themes, namely, their nationality, gender, and spiritual status.

[24] Robins, 'Modular Dynamics', p. 204.
[25] Liszka, 'The *South English Legendaries*', pp. 38–39.
[26] Liszka, 'The *South English Legendaries*', pp. 59–62 and p. 39.

All the native female saints included in MS Bodley 779, namely Winifred, Æthelthryth, Frideswide, Edburga, and Mildred, are holy nuns and abbesses in England and Wales, and their *vitae* share a similar theme of an exemplary life of holy female confessors. While the lives of classical martyrs, especially in terms of female saints, represent a major part of the hagiographic collections, such as *Legenda aurea*, holy confessors were also celebrated and compiled in medieval hagiography. Confessors, who completed their lives as bishops, abbots, nuns, and abbesses, or as pious kings and queens, are non-martyrs in a narrower sense, but they grew in importance in the Middle Ages, showing a different form of piety from classical martyrs, who were violently killed for their faith. This is particularly true of female saints in medieval England. While there were male martyrs in medieval England, such as Oswald, Edward the Martyr, Kenelm, and Thomas Becket, who were murdered for political reasons, all the monastic women in MS Bodley 779 are confessors who ended their lives as nuns or abbesses in their nunneries, except for the special case of Winifred, who was killed by her suitor but later resurrected by divine miracle. The *SEL vitae* of medieval monastic women present a new form of female sanctity, different from that of popular classical virgin martyrs.

The *vitae* of monastic women as confessors in MS Bodley 779, however, do not present a completely different narrative from those of classical virgin martyrs. In many ways, their narratives are based on those of their classical predecessors by drawing upon various hagiographic topoi. Above all, all the medieval monastic women in MS Bodley 779 are virgins, and the ways in which their virginity is constructed are similar to those of virgin martyrs. In the table of contents, native female saints are described as 'virgin' or 'holy maiden' (fol. 1ᵛ), and their *vitae* begin by referring to their virginity after their names, such as 'þe mayde' (Frideswide, fol. 280ᵛ), 'þe holy mayde' (Edburga, fol. 282ʳ), and 'gode mayde' (Æthelthryth, fol. 279ᵛ). In a sense, their virginity is more important than their identity as nuns. In MS Bodley 779, there are virgin martyrs, including Christina, Katherine, Agnes, Ursula, Lucy, Anastasia, and Cecilia. The power relationships in these virgin martyr legends usually centre on the religious conflict between Christian women and pagan male authorities. The legends of medieval holy nuns and abbesses retained the opposition between the sexes from the classical narratives, but this structure is developed within the Christian community featuring relationships between secular male authorities and celibate women. As is often the case with narratives of classical virgin martyrs, marriage is certainly one of the central themes in the narratives of medieval monastic women in MS Bodley 779. Barbara Yorke names this trope the 'virgin valiantly resisting marriage' motif in narratives of royal nuns, which was inherited from virgin saints' lives of Late Antiquity.[27] When conflicts over marriage structurally connect a secular man and a saintly woman, the narrative often produces patterns similar to the *passiones* of virgin martyrs, even though they are set in the medieval British Isles.

While the episodes of continuous trials and miracles suggest the saints' somewhat superhuman abilities, their quotidian activities, depicted as taking place in their cloistered lives, offer their audience important models of imitable virtues. In MS Bodley 779, the hagiographers often insert brief descriptions which give a glimpse of holy women's lives within the cloisters. The passage from the *vita* of Æthelthryth emphasizes cleanness and holiness in her daily life: 'Clennere lyf ne myȝte be þan Seint Etheldrede gan lede | of fasting & of orysones   & of almesdede' (fol. 280ʳ; Saint Æthelthryth began to lead the purest life of fasting, prayer, and alms-giving).[28] Æthelthryth's life, consisting of fasting, praying, and alms-giving, is presented as an ideal for cloistered women to imitate. Donald Weinstein and Rudolph M. Bell argue that the theme of the saints' acts of charity for the sick and the poor and asceticism (including private prayer), as well as their supernatural power (such as performance of miracles, visions, and mystical experience), are dominant in the *vitae* of female saints.[29] Among these virtues, in the *vitae* of monastic women in MS Bodley 779 their acts of praying are related to their ascetic practices and reading activities.

Praying ('oraison') plays a major part in their lives. In MS Bodley 779, the *vita* of Edburga depicts the saint observing a nightly vigil while her sister nuns are asleep:

> A nyȝt whan þe nonnes slep   Seint Edborw wold aryse
> & to chirche go wel stillelych   in Our Lords seruise
> to þe chapel of Seint Peter   gon ȝhe wold oft
> & ligge þer in her orisonys. (fol. 283ʳ)

[At night, when other nuns sleep, Saint Edburga would arise and secretly go to church to serve Our Lord. She would often go to the Chapel of Saint Peter and kneel down in prayer.]

---

[27] Yorke, *Nunneries and the Anglo-Saxon Royal Houses*, pp. 153–54.

[28] Capitalization and word-division are modernized, punctuation is editorial, and abbreviations are silently expanded. *Punctus elevatus* is reproduced by spacing. The translations are my own.

[29] Weinstein and Bell, *Saints and Society*, pp. 228–37.

This episode of the observation of vigils shows Edburga's asceticism. Furthermore, a life of prayer is shown through the saints' reading activities. As *Ancrene Wisse*, the thirteenth-century instructions for religious women, states that reading serves as a good prayer, reading is often associated with praying in a female monastic life.[30] The *vitae* of holy nuns in MS Bodley 779 also describe that they are educated and become acquainted with holy writings, such as the psalms and gospels, at a very early age: Edburga, who is given a gospel book at her request, learns how to read books from her abbess at a nunnery in Winchester (fol. 282^v), while Frideswide receives education at home from a female teacher called Ailgive (fol. 280^v). Mildred performs miracles through her experience of reading. Even when she is thrown into a heated oven by her evil abbess, she remains unhurt and sings the psalms (16. 3) 'þorw fer þou fondist me' (through fire you tried me) (fol. 302^v). These episodes not only suggest that female piety is often shown through the saints' affection for spiritual reading, but the hagiographers' frequent references to reading are also intended for their audience. They play an important role in building up an intimate relationship between the saints and their readers through their shared experience of reading.

In terms of raising sympathy, it is also important that the ideal life of cloistered women as presented in MS Bodley 779 is set in the English landscape. The legends of native women in MS Bodley 779 not only show an image of their nation through native saints, but also consciously map out the geographies surrounding their cult, depicting the various places where they lived, where they performed miracles, or where their relics were transferred after death. In MS Bodley 779, the *vitae* of Frideswide and Edburga begin with stating their English identity in a similar manner to male English saints, such as Swithun and Guthlac in the same manuscript:

> Seint Friswide þe mayde   was her of Ingelond.
> At Oxinforde ʒhe was ibore   as Ich ondirstond. (fol. 280^v)

[Saint Frideswide, the virgin, was from England. She was born in Oxford as I understand.]

Their Englishness, as well as their virginity, is a key element constructing the saints' identities. Furthermore, the *vitae* of native women in MS Bodley 779 not only present the saints collectively as national saints, but also depict the nation made up of various localities through native female saints. Despite their cloistered lives, monastic women in MS Bodley 779 travel for various reasons.

---

[30] *Ancrene Wisse*, ed. by Millett, IV. 1154.

For example, the *vita* of Frideswide depicts not only the city of Oxford but also Binsey and Bampton, small towns in Oxford where she takes eremitic retreat (fol. 281ᵛ). The *vita* of Edburga features Winchester, with references to other local Winchester saints, such as Swithun (fol. 283ʳ) and Æthelwold (fol. 283ᵛ), as well as Pershore (fol. 283ᵛ), where the hagiographer claims that she was posthumously translated to. Although the *vita* of Winifred does not contain her *translatio* from Wales to England as it does in John Mirk's *Festial*, it instead includes a miraculous episode of a watery conduit by which Winifred communicates from Wales with her spiritual master Beuno in an 'oþer contre' (fol. 189ᵛ).[31] The *vita* of Mildred goes beyond England to a 'straunge lond' (fol. 302ᵛ; foreign country), depicting her life in the monastery of Chelles in France (fols 302ᵛ–303ʳ). These references would have played an important role in situating narratives of saintly virtues in the English context. Given that the legends of most universal saints, which occupy a central position in most hagiographic compilations in medieval England, deal with holy women of distant places in ancient times, such as classical Rome, the *vitae* of medieval native female saints provide their contemporary English audience with more familiar narratives about female saints of their nation.

Because these texts would certainly have been of benefit to a female monastic audience, it is possible that the compiler of MS Bodley 779 considered them as part of his intended audience. The inclusion of the legends of nuns in the manuscripts of the *SELS* has led critics to assume later medieval nuns as readers. For example, the *SEL* in the Vernon manuscript contains three *vitae* of English nuns (Æthelthryth, Edburga, and Mildred). Since the manuscript also contains *Ancrene Wisse* and a Middle English translation of Aelred of Rievaulx's *De institutione inclusarum*, written for female religious, it is often considered as internal evidence of nuns' ownership of the manuscript.[32] Regarding MS Bodley 779, while manuscript evidence to demonstrate female monastic ownership is lacking, and it is difficult to determine the actual female ownership and readership from manuscript evidence, the *vitae* of native female saints in the manuscripts of the *SELS* including MS Bodley 779 characteristically feminize their audiences. In other words, the narrators intend their *vitae* not only for men but also for women of various social status, from nuns to married women, as their audi-

[31] On the *vita* of Winifred including her *translatio* in Mirk's *Festial*, see *John Mirk's 'Festial'*, ed. by Powell, I, 162–66, and *Chaste Passions*, ed. and trans. by Winstead, pp. 82–85.

[32] See Acker, 'St Mildred', p. 141; Blanton, 'Counting Noses and Assessing the Numbers', pp. 240–42. On the female audience of the Vernon manuscript, see Meale, 'The Miracles of Our Lady', p. 135, and Blake, 'Vernon Manuscript', p. 58.

ences. In the *vita* of Æthelthryth, when the saint pleads with her husband to divorce her, the narrator emphasizes her strong will by referring to other wives:

> ȝhe ber her so fayr to her lord & so gan on hym criȝe
> þat ȝhe was euer clene mayde witoute sin of folyȝe.
> So fare now alle our wyuis who so wol here wil dryȝe. (fol. 280ʳ)

[She endured a married life with her husband so well, and began to beg him, saying that she was a clean maiden without sins of folly. She behaved in the way all wives in our day who want to do as they please did.]

Through the reference to 'alle our wyuis', the narrator suggests a similarity between Æthelthryth, who is a married and widowed woman before entering a monastic life, and ordinary married women, who would have been part of the narrator's intended readers. This indicates that medieval women, including female religious, would possibly have formed an important part of the audience of MS Bodley 779.

It is possible that the collection of native female saints in MS Bodley 779 reflects the provenance of the manuscript or requests from the manuscript's commissioner. While there is no clear evidence to demonstrate a possibility for the latter, the inclusion of local saints' lives suggests that the manuscript has local characteristics. For example, Edburga, whose Middle English *vita* is unique to the three manuscripts of the *SELS* including MS Bodley 779, was celebrated as a local saint of Winchester, which is relatively close to the place where MS Bodley 779 originated. On the other hand, it is also true that the saints, such as Æthelthryth and Winifred, seem to have established their fame as national saints of England by the time MS Bodley 779 was compiled, given that a number of *vitae* both in Latin and vernaculars were compiled in the late Middle Ages.[33] Therefore, in terms of the selection of native female saints in MS Bodley 779, some saints are compiled for the compiler's interest in local saints, others are selected for the saints' established nationwide renown. Even though its *ordinatio* does not seem to have a consistent organizing policy, MS Bodley 779 shows the compiler's attitudes towards compiling as many lives of local saints as possible, especially of holy women who share their spiritual status. This makes this manuscript a unique anthology of saints' lives and provides its audiences with models of female piety through examples of medieval native women.

---

[33] For discussions of the *vitae* of Æthelthryth, see Blanton, *The Cult of St. Æthelthryth*. For the *vitae* of Winifred, see Gregory, 'A Welsh Saint in England'.

Works Cited

Manuscript

Cambridge, Corpus Christi College, MS 145
Cambridge, Trinity College, MS 605 (R.3.25)
Cambridge, University Library [CUL], MS Additional 2604
London, British Library [BL], MS Cotton Julius D IX
London, British Library [BL], MS Egerton 1993
London, British Library [BL], MS Harley 2277
Oxford, Bodleian Library [Bodl. Lib.], MS Ashmole 43
Oxford, Bodleian Library [Bodl. Lib.], MS Bodley 779
Oxford, Bodleian Library [Bodl. Lib.], MS Eng. poet. a. 1
Oxford, Bodleian Library [Bodl. Lib.], MS Laud. misc. 108

Primary Sources

Acker, Paul, 'St Mildred in the *South English Legendary*', in *The South English Legendary: A Critical Assessment*, ed. by Klaus P. Jankofsky (Tübingen: Francke, 1992), pp. 140–53

Ancrene Wisse: A Corrected Edition of the Text in Cambridge, Corpus Christi College, MS 402, with Variants from Other Manuscripts, ed. by Bella Millett, Early English Text Society, o.s., 325–26, 2 vols (Oxford: Oxford University Press, 2005–06)

Braswell, Laurel, 'Saint Edburga of Winchester: A Study of her Cult, AD 950–1500, with an Edition of the Fourteenth-Century Middle English and Latin Lives', *Mediaeval Studies*, 33 (1971), 292–333

Chaste Passions: Medieval English Virgin Martyr Legends, ed. and trans. by Karen A. Winstead (Ithaca: Cornell University Press, 2000)

The Early South-English Legendary, or Lives of Saints, vol. I: *MS. Laud, 108, in Bodleian Library*, ed. by Carl Horstmann, Early English Text Society, o.s., 87 (London: N. Trübner, 1887)

Horstmann, Carl, 'Des Ms. Bodl. 779 jüngere Zusatzlegenden zur südlichen Legendensammlung', *Archiv für das Studium der neueren Sprachen und Literaturen*, 82 (1889), 307–422

John Mirk's 'Festial': Edited from British Library MS Cotton Claudius A.II, ed. by Susan Powell, Early English Text Society, o.s. 334 and 335, 2 vols (Oxford: Oxford University Press, 2009–11)

Major, Tristan, 'Saint Etheldreda in the *South English Legendary*', *Anglia*, 128.1 (2010), 83–101

Middle English Legends of Women Saints, ed. by Sherry L. Reames (Kalamazoo: Medieval Institute Publications, 2003)

Pickering, O. S., 'The "Defence of Women" from the *Southern Passion*: A New Edition', in *The South English Legendary: A Critical Assessment*, ed. by Klaus P. Jankofsky (Tübingen: Francke, 1992), pp. 154–76

The South English Legendary, ed. by Charlotte D'Evelyn and Anna J. Mill, Early English Text Society, o.s., 235, 236, and 244, 3 vols (London: Oxford University Press, 1956–59)

'The Southern Passion', trans. by Alcuin Blamires, in *Woman Defamed and Woman Defended: An Anthology of Medieval Texts*, ed. by Alcuin Blamires, Karen Pratt, and C. W. Marx (Oxford: Clarendon Press, 1992), pp. 244–48

Supplementary Lives in Some Manuscripts of the 'Gilte Legende', ed. by Richard Hamer and Vida Russell, Early English Text Society, o.s., 315 (Oxford: Oxford University Press, 2000)

Secondary Works

Bell, Kimberly K., and Julie Nelson Couch, eds, *The Texts and Contexts of Oxford, Bodleian Library, MS Laud Misc. 108: The Shaping of English Vernacular Narrative* (Leiden: Brill, 2011)

Blake, N. F., 'Vernon Manuscript: Contents and Organisation', in *Studies in the Vernon Manuscript*, ed. by Derek Pearsall (Cambridge: D. S. Brewer, 1990) pp. 45–59

Blanton, Virginia, 'Counting Noses and Assessing the Numbers', in *Rethinking the South English Legendaries*, ed. by Heather Blurton and Jocelyn Wogan-Browne (Manchester: Manchester University Press, 2011), pp. 234–50

——, *The Cult of St. Æthelthryth in Medieval England, 695–1615* (University Park: Pennsylvania State University Press, 2007)

Blurton, Heather, and Jocelyn Wogan-Browne, 'Rethinking the *South English Legendaries*', in *Rethinking the South English Legendaries*, ed. by Heather Blurton and Jocelyn Wogan-Browne (Manchester: Manchester University Press, 2011), pp. 3–19

Camp, Cynthia Turner, *Anglo-Saxon Saints' Lives as History Writing in Late Medieval England* (Cambridge: D. S. Brewer, 2015)

Cubitt, Catherine, 'Universal and Local Saints in Anglo-Saxon England', in *Local Saints and Local Churches in the Early Medieval West*, ed. by Alan Thacker and Richard Sharpe (Oxford: Oxford University Press, 2002), pp. 423–53

Dutton, Elisabeth, *Julian of Norwich: The Influence of Late-Medieval Devotional Compilations* (Cambridge: D. S. Brewer, 2008)

Frederick, Jill, 'The *South English Legendary*: Anglo-Saxon Saints and National Identity', in *Literary Appropriations of the Anglo-Saxons from the Thirteenth to the Twentieth Century*, ed. by Donald Scragg and Carole Weinberg (Cambridge: Cambridge University Press, 2000), pp. 57–73

Görlach, Manfred, *The Textual Tradition of the 'South English Legendary'* (Leeds: University of Leeds School of English, 1974)

Gregory, James Ryan, 'A Welsh Saint in England: Translation, Orality, and National Identity in the Cult of St. Gwenfrewy, 1138–1512' (unpublished doctoral thesis, University of Georgia, Athens, 2012)

Hamelinck, Renee, 'St. Kenelm and the Legends of the English Saints in the *South English Legendary*', in *Companion to Middle English Literature*, ed. by N. H. G. E. Veldhoen and H. Aertson (Amsterdam: Free University Press, 1988), pp. 21–30

Jankofsky, Klaus P., 'National Characteristics in the Portrayal of English Saints in the *South English Legendary*', in *Images of Sainthood in Medieval Europe*, ed. by Renate Blumenfeld-Kosinski and Timea Szell (Ithaca: Cornell University Press, 1991), pp. 81–93

Lewis, Katherine J., 'Anglo-Saxon Saints' Lives, History and National Identity in Late Medieval England', in *History, Nationhood and the Question of Britain*, ed. by Helen Brocklehurst and Robert Phillips (Basingstoke: Palgrave, 2004), pp. 160–70

Liszka, Thomas R., 'Ms Laud. Misc. 108 and the Early History of the *South English Legendary*', *Manuscripta*, 33 (1989), 75–91

——, 'The South English Legendaries', in *The North Sea World in the Middle Ages: Studies in the Cultural History of North-Western Europe*, ed. by Thomas R. Liszka and Lorna E. M. Walker (Dublin: Four Courts Press, 2001), pp. 243–80; repr. in *Rethinking the South English Legendaries*, ed. by Heather Blurton and Jocelyn Wogan-Browne (Manchester: Manchester University Press, 2011), pp. 23–65

Meale, Carol M., 'The Miracles of Our Lady: Context and Interpretation', in *Studies in the Vernon Manuscript*, ed. by Derek Pearsall (Cambridge: D. S. Brewer, 1990), pp. 117–36

Millett, Bella, '*Mouvance* and the Medieval Author: Re-Editing *Ancrene Wisse*', in *Late-Medieval Religious Texts and their Transmission: Essays in Honour of A. I. Doyle*, ed. by A. J. Minnis (Cambridge: D. S. Brewer, 1994), pp. 9–20

Mills, Robert, 'Violence, Community and the Materialisation of Belief', in *A Companion to Middle English Hagiography*, ed. by Sarah Salih (Cambridge: D. S. Brewer, 2004), pp. 87–103

Olsen, Kerryn, 'Questions of Identity: Rewriting Anglo-Saxon Female Saints in Post-Conquest England, *c.* 1066–*c.* 1500' (unpublished doctoral thesis, University of Auckland, 2009)

——, 'Women and Englishness: Anglo-Saxon Female Saints in the *South English Legendary*', *Limina*, 19 (2013), 1–9

Parkes, M. B., 'The Influence of the Concepts of *Ordinatio* and *Compilatio* on the Development of the Book', in *Medieval Learning and Literature: Essays Presented to Richard William Hunt*, ed. by J. J. G. Alexander and M. T. Gibson (Oxford: Clarendon Press, 1976), pp. 115–41

Pickering, O. S., and Manfred Görlach, 'A Newly-Discovered Manuscript of the *South English Legendary*', *Anglia*, 100 (1982), 109–23

Robins, William, 'Modular Dynamics in the *South English Legendary*', in *Rethinking the South English Legendaries*, ed. by Heather Blurton and Jocelyn Wogan-Browne (Manchester: Manchester University Press, 2011), pp. 187–208

Scahill, John D., with the assistance of Margaret Rogerson, *Middle English Saints' Legends*, Annotated Bibliographies of Old and Middle English Literature, 8 (Cambridge: D. S. Brewer, 2005)

Turville-Petre, Thorlac, *England the Nation: Language, Literature, and National Identity, 1290–1340* (Oxford: Clarendon Press, 1996)

Weinstein, Donald, and Rudolph M. Bell, *Saints and Society: The Two Worlds of Western Christendom, 1000–1700* (Chicago: University of Chicago Press, 1982)

Yorke, Barbara, *Nunneries and the Anglo-Saxon Royal Houses* (London: Continuum, 2003)

Zumthor, Paul, *Toward a Medieval Poetics*, trans. by Philip Bennett (Minneapolis: University of Minnesota Press, 1992)

Devotional Compilations and Lollard Sanctity in a Fifteenth-Century Anthology*

Nicole R. Rice

In this essay I consider two important Middle English devotional compilations and how they were deployed to shape lollard spiritual identity during the fifteenth century.[1] My main object of study is BL, MS Additional 30897, a mid-fifteenth-century Midlands anthology featuring four Middle English texts: a lollard version of the compilation *Pore Caitif*, a brief lollard-inflected discussion of the Beatitudes, an extended lollard commentary on the Ave Maria, and a truncated copy of the compilation *Book to a Mother*.[2] The volume's codicology and combination of contents identify it as a lollard pro-

---

* I would like to thank the organizers and participants of the Lausanne conference on late medieval devotional compilations. I am very grateful to Marleen Cré, Diana Denissen, Denis Renevey, and the Brepols peer reviewer for helpful feedback on this essay.

[1] In this essay I use 'lollard' in accord with Fiona Somerset's definition of 'lollards' as 'writers and readers engaged in a textual culture that collaboratively produced writings about reformed forms of life and that attempted to make them a way of life. The production and spread of the books themselves, as well as evidence from heresy trials, suggests that some did make this attempt: *lollardy* is the way of life they attempted to pursue'. Somerset, *Feeling Like Saints*, p. 16. Like Somerset, I employ the lower-case form 'lollard' rather than 'Lollard' in order to maintain a relatively flexible, descriptive sense of the term, rather than 'implying that "Lollards" are a distinctive, cohesive social group' (Somerset, *Feeling like Saints*, p. 16).

[2] I use 'anthology' to refer to the entire volume and 'compilation' to denote the individual composite works contained within it. Recently Trivedi has dated BL, MS Add. 30897 to the mid-fifteenth century; see Trivedi, '"Trewe techyng and false heritikys"', p. 138. Adrian

---

Nicole R. Rice (ricen@stjohns.edu) is Professor of English at St John's University, New York.

duction, though its constituent texts have varying relationships to lollardy.[3] The late fourteenth-century compilation *Pore Caitif*, which incorporates many early Wycliffite texts as sources,[4] may have later been selectively interpolated by lollard readers. The late fourteenth- or early fifteenth-century *Book to a Mother* offers guidance in personal spiritual reform that overlaps with Wycliffite ideals in its strong resistance to external religious forms and ceremonies and its opposition to the professed religious life.[5]

My intention here is to try to understand the possible uses of these compilations within a mid-fifteenth-century lollard reading context. The contents of these compilations overlap in many respects with mainstream religious views, and the works travelled in variable contexts, manifesting some of the 'devotional cosmopolitanism' that Stephen Kelly and Ryan Perry have attributed to fifteenth-century compilations and anthologies.[6] While acknowledging these overlaps throughout my essay, I argue that BL, MS Add. 30897 is an intentional collection of complementary texts, an anthology designed for lollard readers, in which the two compilations are placed together to offer these readers textual avenues towards venerating the saints and pursuing their own forms of sanctity.[7] In the Additional manuscript's texts of *Pore Caitif* and *Book*

McCarthy identifies the dialect of *Book to a Mother* in BL, MS Add. 30897 as 'Midland, with some Southern characteristics, but there are no definite West Midland peculiarities' (*Book to a Mother*, ed. by McCarthy, p. xvii).

[3] The volume was copied by three scribes in succession and manifests the 'organized cooperative form of book-production' that Ralph Hanna III has attributed to some lollard volumes; see Hanna, 'Two Lollard Codices and Lollard Book Production', p. 57. Scribe A copied the first several tracts of *Pore Caitif*, until fol. 37ʳ, then Scribe B copied the rest of *Pore Caitif* as well as the Beatitudes commentary and Ave Maria commentary. Scribe C copied *Book to a Mother*, which begins on a new quire.

[4] See Brady, 'The Lollard Sources of the *Pore Caitif*'. These sources include the *Glossed Gospels* and the Early Version of the Wycliffite Bible.

[5] See below for more detailed discussion of these texts and their relations to lollardy.

[6] Kelly and Perry define 'devotional cosmopolitanism' as 'a radical openness to the suggestions of antithetical theologies which produces among readers a form of "hospitable reading" in which difference is tolerated, re-thought, adapted and appropriated in the interests of re-imagining Christian community in England'. Kelly and Perry, 'Devotional Cosmopolitanism', p. 365.

[7] I use 'lollard readers' to refer to an intended readership for this manuscript (as opposed to readers originally projected by, e.g., the *Pore Caitif*'s compiler). There is no evidence in the manuscript of contemporary ownership. Given the volume's dating, it was copied after the first, highly organized period of lollard book production (pre-1414) and during what Somerset

to a Mother, as well as in the intervening Ave Maria commentary, the Virgin Mary and the virgin martyrs appear as saints with particular relevance to lollard readers. I suggest that for such readers, these portraits work to reinforce a lollard ideology of sanctity that limited the canon to a small group of saints, rejected image veneration, and argued that prayers should be directed immediately towards God himself rather than to the saints.[8] Moving flexibly among the textual modes of pastoralia, meditation, and narrative, *Pore Caitif* and *Book to a Mother* describe saintly qualities of meekness and martyrdom that intersect in key ways with lollard sanctity.[9] As I will show, the Virgin Mary functions as an important example of meekness and source of comfort within all three compilations. In drawing out Mary's centrality to the Additional anthology, my analysis highlights her crucial role within lollard devotion.[10]

Sanctity is a good example of a lollard idea that overlaps with yet is also distinct in some particulars from the mainstream late medieval view. Some lollards went on record as rejecting the cult of the saints, particularly the veneration of saints' images and the practice of praying directly to them.[11] Yet rejection of some aspects of the cult did not mean wholesale rejection of all saints, their examples, or their lives.[12] Many lollard texts expressed scepticism about post-biblical saints, yet there was a select cadre whose sanctified status was never in doubt: this elite group included those saints 'expressid in holy writte' (explicitly mentioned in the Bible) and many of the early martyrs.[13] Lollard writers expressed devotion to the saints in various ways: a lollard biblical commentary references the saints as the foundation of 'holy chirche', and the lollard

has characterized as a period of more 'miscellaneous' production, a trend that might have evolved partially in response to Arundel's Constitutions of 1409. Although likely copied after Archbishop Chichele's 1428 restrictive legislation requiring suspected lollards to reveal any knowledge of books containing heretical material, the Additional volume testifies the continuing wide circulation of lollard works in the fifteenth century, 'an efflorescence in the copying of books of vernacular religion that cannot, on the face of it, be easily accommodated to claims of overarching repression'. Quotations from Somerset, 'Censorship', p. 251.

[8] See Von Nolcken, 'Another Kind of Saint', p. 433.

[9] See Somerset, *Feeling Like Saints*, p. 57 on meekness and p. 36 on martyrdom.

[10] See Rice, 'Forming Devotion' for a full analysis of the Ave Maria commentary in the Additional manuscript and a broader consideration of the Virgin's role in lollard devotion.

[11] See for example Lutton, *Lollardy and Orthodox Religion*, p. 152, pp. 160–61.

[12] Robyn Malo has persuasively argued that lollards did not reject the veneration of all relics, but rather objected (as Wyclif himself had) to the excessive ornamentation and commercialism associated with relic cults; see Malo, 'Behaving Paradoxically?'.

[13] Peikola, 'The Sanctorale, Thomas of Woodstock's English Bible', p. 154.

dissident William Thorpe uses hagiographic tropes in his autobiographical narrative.[14] Although we do not find fifteenth-century 'lollard texts that explicitly exhort their readers to read saints' lives', lollards may have owned such lives. For example, a group of sixteenth-century lollards in Coventry reportedly owned collections of saints lives and read them together.[15] Evidently lollard readers sought textual access to saints, even as they defined their devotion in a distinct way, as noted above.

With this particular approach to sanctity in mind, my discussion will unfold in three sections. Beginning with the *Pore Caitif*, the anthology's first compilation, I show how this lollard-interpolated text of the work uses pastoral instruction, meditation, and narrative to define proper devotion to the saints and imitation of the 'symple and meke lyuys and pacient suffryng of his seintes', a phrase that we first see mentioned in the work's Ten Commandments tract.[16] When we view the *Pore Caitif*, even those sections with no obvious lollard content, as part of a lollard devotional reading programme, we note how frequently in the various tracts emerge the particular values of meekness and self-sacrifice, and how often readers are urged to imitate the saints' 'pacient suffryng' in ways that would resonate with lollard views. In the second part of my paper I turn briefly to the volume's Ave Maria commentary to show how its focus on suffering the detractions of adversaries challenges lollard readers to strive towards sainthood. In the third and final section I show how the volume's truncated text of *Book to a Mother*, a compilation that begins with discussion of the Ten Commandments, likewise deploys pastoralia and narrative to teach lollard readers the intertwined values of meekness and martyrdom. *Book to a Mother* elaborates a form of sanctity that is grounded in the Ten Commandments and that draws its example from both the patient humility of the Virgin Mary and the defiant martyrdom of Saint Lucy. In my discussion of these three texts in this lollard manuscript context, I suggest that their repeated emphasis on the lived experience of saints, female saints in particular, solicits particular forms of devotion and participation from lollard readers.

---

[14] Anne Hudson notes: 'Thorpe's text appears to be in some senses a substitute saint's life — substitute, that is, for the hagiography of which the Lollards generally thoroughly disapproved'; see *The Testimony of William Thorpe*, ed. by Hudson, p. lvi.

[15] Somerset, *Feeling Like Saints*, p. 139. According to a heresy trial record of 1511, John Spon testified to having heard Roger Landesdale read saints' lives and the Pauline epistles; see *Lollards of Coventry*, ed. and trans. by McSheffrey and Tanner, p. 133.

[16] BL, MS Add. 30897, fol. 2^r.

The Lollard *Pore Caitif*: 'symple and meke lyuys and pacient suffryng of his seyntes'

The *Pore Caitif* is a late fourteenth-century devotional compilation that includes fourteen tracts in its complete form.[17] The work begins with syllabus material, including tracts on the Ten Commandments and Pater Noster; it includes discussions of patience and temptation, Christocentric meditations, and tracts on the active and the contemplative lives. It culminates with a tract on chastity.[18] As Mary Theresa Brady showed, thirteen extant copies of the *Pore Caitif* contain markedly lollard comments on topics including images, oaths, and preaching. BL, MS Add. 30897 is one such copy. Whether the lollard material was 'interpolated' into *Pore Caitif*, as Brady argued, or is 'original' to the work, which was later expurgated, as Kalpen Trivedi has recently contended, is hard to determine.[19] This vexing ambiguity signals the *Pore Caitif*'s importance, for in many ways the compilation connects mainstream to lollard concerns: the foregrounding of pastoral fundamentals, including the Creed and the Ten Commandments, and the emphasis on personal spiritual reform. I consider *Pore Caitif* to be a reformist work, composed during a period of religious ferment when Wycliffite and orthodox reformers shared many similar priorities, and before these categories had hardened under the pressure of legislation.[20] If the work was indeed interpolated by lollards, as I tend to believe, one can understand its appeal, for even the 'Mirror of Chastity' tract features reformist themes, such as an emphasis on biblical 'understanding' and

---

[17] The complete and most common order of tracts (present in twenty-three manuscripts) includes the following: Prolog; þe crede; Prolog of þe heestis; Prolog of þe pater noster; Counceil of crist; vertuous pacience; of temptacioun; Chartre of heuene; Of goostli bateile; þe name of ihesu; þe loue of ihesu; Of verri meekness; þe effect of wille; Actiif liif & contemplacioun; þe mirrour of chastite. List taken from '*The Pore Caitif*, ed. by Brady, p. xlvii.

[18] The *Pore Caitif* lacks a published critical edition. Karine Guibert's critical edition, based on BnF, MS Anglais 41, is forthcoming from Brepols. For an edition based on BL, MS Harley 2336, see '*The Pore Caitif*, ed. by Brady. For a recent study of fifteenth-century readers' uses of the *Pore Caitif*, focusing primarily on the appeal of catechetical contents, see Hill, 'Pedagogy, Devotion, and Marginalia'.

[19] For these two competing arguments, see Brady, 'Lollard Interpolations and Omissions', and Trivedi, '"Trewe techyng and false heritikys."' While Guibert has recently argued that the *Pore Caitif* compiler was sympathetic to lollardy, she disagrees with Trivedi that the 'Lollard interpolations' were originally part of the work and later excised; see Guibert, 'The "Mirrour of chastite"', p. 15. I am grateful to Dr. Guibert for sharing this unpublished paper with me.

[20] See Rice, 'Reformist Devotional Reading', especially pp. 178–80 and pp. 186–93.

a scepticism about images, that overlap with lollard concerns and rhetoric.[21] Although BL, MS Add. 30897 is one of the 'lollard' manuscripts of the *Pore Caitif* identified by Brady, the overwhelming majority of the work's contents, including whole tracts, such as the Chastity tract that I discuss below, are identical between the 'orthodox' and 'lollard' versions.[22] As I suggested above, any investigation into the *Pore Caitif*'s special appeal to lollard readers must be informed by the vast devotional ground shared by mainstream Christians and lollards alike.[23]

Within *Pore Caitif*, the basics of doctrine are persistently linked to the practices of devotion. When we view *Pore Caitif* in the context of the Additional anthology, we begin to see how pastoral instruction affords an early opportunity for defining an appropriate lollard approach to the saints. The Additional copy, which is missing some pages and hence lacks the general prologue and Creed sections, begins with the tract on the Ten Commandments, a particularly central element of lollard teaching. This tract has much to say about the saints, and its guidance on how to show them proper devotion and how to imitate them sets the tone for the entire compilation.

In expressing a circumspect view of images that becomes a more explicit critique in this lollard-interpolated text, the *Pore Caitif* repeatedly emphasizes, and gradually heightens, its emphasis on the value of saints' lives for devout readers. In the Additional manuscript, the *Pore Caitif* text begins abruptly amid discussion of the first commandment: not to worship strange gods nor make graven images. The first section features a passage on images as 'books for the unlearned', a Gregorian truism rendered here with a particular emphasis on saints' *lives*. It reads:

> Symylitudes oþer ymages scholden be as a kalender to lewede men; whanne hem lackeþ techenge þei scholde lerne bi ymages *whom þei scholde worschepe and folwe*

[21] On the overlap between 'orthodox' and lollard views on images, also see Simpson, 'Orthodoxy's Image Trouble'.

[22] Guibert contends on the basis of differences in style and source material that the 'Mirror of Chastity' tract was added later to the *Pore Caitif* compilation. She conjectures that the tract's traditional *speculum* form and apparently orthodox focus on chastity were designed to divert attention from the controversial claims made in the rest of *Pore Caitif* once Wycliffite positions had became subject to suspicion and censorship; see 'The "Mirrour of chastite"', p. 15.

[23] I seek to recover, with Somerset, 'a lollardy that consists not so much in opposition to contemporary mainstream religion […] but in a coherent set of ideas, feelings, and practices that shares much with the mainstream even as it works sharply to distinguish itself on some specific points'; see Somerset, 'Afterword', p. 319.

*in lyuynge.*²⁴ To do Godes worchep to ymages ech man is forfendid, but to lerne bi þe syȝte of hem *to folwe seyntes lyuynge good hit is to ech man.* Þis sentence seiþ Seynt Gregore to Serge [Sirenus] þe bischop, as þe lawe witnesseȝ.²⁵

Images are cast as particularly conducive not only to worshiping saints but to following saintly 'lyuynge', a term repeated twice. While the passage is traditional, the *Pore Caitif*'s emphasis on 'lyuynge' differs from one standard account of this wisdom as preserved in 'þe lawe' (i.e. canon law): 'Nam quod legentibus scriptura, hoc idiotis praestat pictura cernentibus, quia in ipsa etiam ignorantes uident quid sequi debeant' (a picture allows the unlearned to discern what may be read in scriptures, so that in it the ignorant may see what they ought to follow).²⁶ What 'they ought to follow' is rendered in *Pore Caitif* more precisely as 'seyntes lyuynge', an emphasis that deepens as the Commandments tract proceeds.

In a long passage on proper conduct in church, *Pore Caitif* again invokes images as a starting point for seeking out the holy *lives* of the saints. Advising readers on correct attitudes to strike before the Eucharist, crucifix, and statues of saints, the compiler appeals once more to the standard distinction between use and worship of an image, strongly emphasizing the internal, cognitive value of 'mynde' over the sensory 'siȝt' in order to establish saints as intercessors rather than as aesthetic objects of devotion. The passage, which is identical in both the orthodox and lollard textual traditions, reads:

> ȝef þei seen eny ymage oþer liknesse maad in mynde of eny oþer seynt, rere vp þe meynde of here soule to heuene, preiynge all þe seyntes þat ben þere to be meenes and preyours or bidders for hem to God, noȝt bileuynge oþer trestynge þat þilke ymage oþer licnesse myȝte brynge eny man or woman out of gostly oþer bodily meschef [...] þei schullen noȝt delyuere eny man fro deþ neþer restore a blynd man

---

²⁴ Also see Trivedi, '"Trewe techyng and false heritikys"', p. 142, for discussion of this passage, which is omitted in most of the early lollard copies. Unusually, this passage in BL, MS Add. 30897 omits part of the standard text, which makes reference to clerical teachers. Between 'kalenders to lewed men' and 'whanne hem lackiþ teching' most texts read, 'þat riȝt as clerkis seen bi her bookis what þei shulden do: so lewid folc'; cited from '*The Pore Caitif*, ed. by Brady, p. 31, where the rest of the above passage may be found.

²⁵ BL, MS Add. 30897, fol. 1ʳ⁻ᵛ, italics mine. When citing from the manuscript, I have retained original spellings, modernized punctuation and capitalization, and expanded abbreviations. Moira Fitzgibbons draws attention to this passage in her discussion of how *Dives and Pauper* adapts *Pore Caitif* in the context of fifteenth-century controversy over images; see Fitzgibbons, 'Women, Tales, and "Talking Back"', pp. 191–92.

²⁶ Brady notes this connection to canon law in '*The Pore Caitif*, p. 210. The Latin passage is taken from Gratian's *Decretum*, within the 'De Consecratione' section; see *Decretum Gratiani*, ed. by Richter, p. 1187.

to his siȝte, þus seiþ holy writ. *But only to teche men bi þe siȝte of hem to haue þe better mynde on hem þat ben in heuene, and to seche bisilyche þat lyf þei liueden in erþe þeruȝ þe whiche bi þe mercy of God þey ben now seyntes. And to folwe þilke lyf in al þat man may.*[27]

Moira Fitzgibbons has astutely noted the *Pore Caitif* compiler's focus, throughout many of the tracts, on bearing ideas and images 'in mynde', remarking that 'the most conspicuously recurrent phrase found in *Pore Caitif* is "haue in mynde"'.[28] Fitzgibbons connects this phrase to the work's overarching emphasis on the importance of 'internal reflection', and its view that 'only by steering one's mind in the proper direction can a person hope to achieve salvation'.[29] The *Pore Caitif*'s scepticism about images is consistent with this overall emphasis on internal reflection over external impression; thus it is revealing that the compiler moves in this passage from 'siȝte' to 'mynde' to 'lyf', ultimately directing readers to seek a verbal over a visual representation: either an oral recitation or a written *vita*. In so doing the reader may be moved 'to folwe þilke lyf', embodying the saint's example. If the reader wishes 'to seche bisilyche þat lyf þei liueden in erþe þeruȝ þe whiche bi þe mercy of God þey ben now seyntes. And to folwe þilke lyf in al þat man may', some sort of written guide is necessary: offering such a guide is one major purpose of the *Pore Caitif* itself.

In the Additional text of *Pore Caitif*, a lengthy lollard interpolation strongly heightens the *Pore Caitif*'s scepticism into a full-blown suspicion of images, all the while keeping the *lives* of the saints in the forefront. The interpolation expresses anxiety about over-reliance on images and a critique of improperly made images. Written in the margin of fol. 2ʳ, the passage reads:

> But certis þo folke ben ouer lewed and to beestly, þat kunne not haue in her mynde eiþer brynge into her mynde þe goodnes of her lord God and þe passyon þat he suffrede for saluacion of her soule, eiþer symple and meke lyuys and pacient suffryng of his seintes, wiþouten such grauen eiþer peyntede ymagis, þe whiche ben ful often grauen [...] and peynted amys and contrarie to our feyþe.[30]

---

[27] BL, MS Add. 30897, fols 1ᵛ–2ʳ, italics mine. For this passage, see '*The Pore Caitif*', ed. by Brady, pp. 31–32.

[28] Fitzgibbons, 'Poverty, Dignity, and Lay Spirituality', p. 227.

[29] Fitzgibbons, 'Poverty, Dignity, and Lay Spirituality', quoted phrases from p. 227 and p. 228.

[30] BL, MS Add. 30897, fol. 2ʳ. Since it is an interpolation, this passage is not in Brady's edition; see Brady, 'Lollard Interpolations and Omissions', p. 188, for discussion of the passage and a transcription from London, Lambeth Palace Library, MS 484.

Here again the devout subject's 'mynde' is all-important, for the text suggests that only people lacking mental resources, those 'ouer lewed and to beestly' in their intelligence, would require images to bring Christ's Passion or the 'symple and meke lyuys and pacient suffryng of his seintes' into their 'mynde'. The concern for images 'grauen [...] and peynted amys and contrarie to our feyþe' reflects an emphasis that Shannon Gayk has shown is commonplace in lollard writing about images: not an outright rejection but a persistent criticism of 'false images' and a 'call for reform' in their production and use.[31]

Most striking to me, in analysing this volume as a lollard devotional reading programme, is the fact that within this critique of image-reliance we find an emphasis on the *saints* as worthy objects for the devout mind's reflection. In the lollard interpolation, the saints are added to the text, placed next to Christ and his Passion as a focus for the reader's devotion. Recalling the encouragement just a few lines before 'to seche bisilyche þat lyf þei liueden in erþe', we see the lollard interpolator using this diatribe about images to enhance the visibility of the suffering saints, saints who will reappear numerous times within this compilation. Thus the lollard version of the *Pore Caitif*, even more strongly than the 'orthodox' version, seems to be suggesting a connection between a reader's following of the Ten Commandments and her own thoughtful devotion to the saints.

For the lollard reader, 'pacient suffryng' is not merely something to watch; it is also something to experience. As Somerset has argued, suffering and martyrdom are key elements of lollard self-conception and sense of religious distinction. She remarks, 'Postures of martyrdom are not unique to lollard writers in this period, but they are pervasive in their writings and integral to an ethical stance their writers urge readers to share, in a way not found elsewhere'.[32] That 'ethical stance' also involves a constant effort of love, which is a choice, and often

> a stark choice with dire consequences. Love is an act of will in tandem with properly disposed emotions, one that requires constant renewal [...] that places extraordinary burdens on the individual Christian, but also that permits (even requires) extraordinary freedoms. These freedoms might include sharply criticizing not only one's inferiors and one's peers but one's social superiors, and refusing to obey orders when they require one to commit sin.[33]

---

[31] Gayk, *Image, Text, and Religious Reform*, pp. 15–23. Gayk notes, 'Lollard iconology is fundamentally a call for reform' (p. 42). The critique of misleading images sounds similar to the lollard 'Thirty-Seven Conclusions'; see Gayk, *Image, Text, and Religious Reform*, pp. 19–20.

[32] Somerset, *Feeling Like Saints*, p. 36 n. 24.

[33] Somerset, *Feeling Like Saints*, p. 59.

This effort of love involves not only the endurance of suffering, but also the constant effort to remain meek under pressure. As one lollard sermon exhorts its hearers 'to reulen vs þus by mekenesse', the sermon writer invokes the example of Christ: 'Crist ȝaf ensaumple þus for to meken vs whenne he suffrede þe curside Jewes to buffeten hym and scorgen hym and to spitte in his face and coroune [crown] hym whit þornes and aftur nayle hym on þe cros bytwene twey þeues [two thieves], þat whit a word of his mouþ myȝthe [could] haue struyed [destroyed] hem alle'.[34] I wish to draw a connection between this typically lollard conjunction of meekness and martyrdom and the devotional strategies of the *Pore Caitif*. For when we read this text of the *Pore Caitif* as part of a lollard devotional reading programme, we become aware of how persistently the reformist compilation invites its readers to embrace a meek and suffering form of sanctity in the face of adversities: persecutions to which lollards had become accustomed by mid-fifteenth century.[35] But Christ is not the only model of sanctity in this manuscript: the Virgin Mary and early martyrs are equally important models of a sanctity combining meekness and martyrdom.

Pore Caitif contains a tract 'On Meekness', which stitches together extracts from biblical passages, Saint Bernard's homilies, and Richard Rolle's *Form of Living* to create a paradigm of sanctity that, I suggest, strongly solicits lollard readers of this particular manuscript.[36] While the tract is virtually identical between 'lollard' and 'orthodox' versions, in the context of this anthology, its combination of meekness and martyrdom has particular resonance. In this tract the Virgin provides the primary example of meekness for the reader. The tract begins by exhorting readers to imitate Mary:

> Meeknesse is þe modyr of Cryst, as Seyn Bernard seyth. Ffor þer þorw pryncypally þe blessede Virgyne Marye conceyuede þe swete chyld Ihesu. Ffor hadde sche nowȝth ben meeke al be it þat sche was virgine, ȝyt hadde sche noȝt conceyuyd Cryst. Þerfore ȝif þou wolt conseyue Ihesu, þat is saluacyoun oþir helpe of soule, bycome þou meke.[37]

---

[34] Cited from Somerset, *Feeling Like Saints*, p. 58. This is Sermon 44 in Cambridge, Sidney Sussex College, MS 74, fol. 119ʳ. This manuscript has connections to *Book to a Mother*: the scribe who copied BL, MS Egerton 826 (containing a partial copy of *Book to a Mother*) also copied the first part of SS, MS 74; see Fletcher, 'A Hive of Industry or a Hornet's Nest?', pp. 143–44.

[35] Consider, for example, the burning of the lollard priest William Taylor in 1423 in London, or the widely publicized Norwich heresy trials lasting from 1428 to 1431.

[36] Matti Peikola has remarked on the prominence of claims for meekness in fifteenth-century lollard writings, focusing on the use of the adverb 'mekely'; see Peikola, 'Individual Voice in Lollard Discourse', pp. 54–55.

[37] BL, MS Add. 30897, fol. 51ᵛ. For this passage, see '*The Pore Caitif*, ed. by Brady, p. 164.

The spiritually aspirant readers of the lollard *Pore Caitif*, though not necessarily expected to be virginal or even chaste, must strive to 'conseyue Ihesu' spiritually through the effort of meekness, in imitation of Mary. For as Bernard argues at length in the homily that forms the basis for this passage, Mary's meekness was more important than her virginity.[38] This equation of Mary and meekness is pithily expressed in the above passage's opening statement, 'Meeknesse is þe modyr of Cryst'. *Pore Caitif* readers must imitate Mary before they can go on to imitate Christ.

Meekness is, moreover, frequently bound up with 'pacient suffryng' in *Pore Caitif*. As the tract continues, the compiler combines gospel passages with extracts from Rolle to cast the work's readers as members of a committed spiritual community, a group of suffering saints. A few lines later the text asserts:

> al þat wolyn lyuen wel and plesyn Ihesu Cryst scholn suffryn persecucyouns. And by manye tribulacyouns it byhouyth to entryn into þe kyngdam of hefne. Ffor it is ȝouyn to swyche noȝt only þat þei byleuyn in Cryst, bote also þat þey suffryn for hym. Therfore þe meke louyere of Cryst byhouyth to faryn as a deed body, þat what some dooþ or seyth þerto answereþ noȝt.[39]

Where the first sections echo Paul's letters,[40] the final passage borrows from Rolle's *Form of Living* to define 'meke loue' in terms of suffering, in a portrait that looks much like Christ's own example as described in the lollard sermon from Sidney Sussex MS 74, cited above.[41] Exhorting a silence under pressure that emulates Christ's forbearance, this passage fashions a community of meekness: a group of readers who would act collectively as a 'deed body' even under the greatest physical or verbal persecution.[42]

This emphasis on silence, on refusal to answer one's persecutors, is particularly notable in the context of this lollard devotional anthology. When read in this manuscript context, silent forbearance of 'þe meke louyere of Cryst' under extreme pressure brings to mind the silence of the lollard dissident

---

[38] See Bernard of Clairvaux, *Opera: Sermones I*, ed. by Leclercq and Rochais, pp. 17–18, and for a translation, see *Homilies in Praise of the Blessed Virgin Mary*, trans. by Saïd, pp. 9–10.

[39] BL, MS Add. 30897, fol. 52ʳ. For this passage, see '*The Pore Caitif*', ed. by Brady, p. 165.

[40] See II Timothy 3. 12 and Philippians 1. 29.

[41] See Rolle, *The Form of Living*, ed. by Ogilvie-Thomson, p. 21; see note 34 above for the sermon reference.

[42] Nicholas Watson considers Rolle's treatment of persecution as a tribulation to be expected by the spiritually elect: 'All the elect must expect to suffer opprobrium, scandal-mongering and detraction (*Judica Me* 10.21–22); whoever wishes to rejoice with Christ must first be a partner with him in tribulation'; see Watson, *Richard Rolle and the Invention of Authority*, p. 64.

priest William Thorpe, who cultivated the tropes of hagiography in his Middle English 'Testimony', featuring silence as a key strategy for confronting persecution.[43] The anthologizer of this *Pore Caitif* text perhaps saw in its evocation of a love that eludes persecution, that remains undiminished by suffering, a confirmation of the lollards' own distinctive postures of sanctity.[44] Although few documentary references to Thorpe survive, at least two versions of his 'Testimony' had been copied by the first quarter of the fifteenth century, and a Latin copy was made circa 1430. A printed version was published in Antwerp *c.* 1530 and later incorporated in 1563 into John Foxe's *Acts and Monuments*.[45] Thus Thorpe seems to have had a continuous, if shadowy, existence through the fifteenth century and into the sixteenth: not quite as a martyr but as an example of lollard grace under pressure.

Thorpe frames his text with moments of pointed silence, both early in the process, as he contemplates a possible martyrdom, and later, after extensive questioning by Archbishop Arundel, when he persists in Christlike silence. In the first instance, Thorpe refuses to desist from preaching even as he is threatened with death by burning, as the archbishop shouts:

> 'eiþir now anoon consente to myn ordynaunce and submytte þee to stonde to myne decre, or bi seint Tomas þou schalt be schauen and sue þi felow into Smeþefelde'! *And at þis seiynge I stood stille and spak not. But in my herte I þouȝt þat God did to me a greet grace if he wolde of his greet mercy brynge me into such an eende, and in myn herte I was in no þing maad agast wiþ manassynge of þe Archebischop.*[46]

Here Thorpe's outward silence leads directly into inward contemplation of the 'grace' of martyrdom, as he claims to feel no fear in the face of dire threats.[47]

---

[43] On Thorpe's rhetorical strategies, see Schirmer, 'William Thorpe's Narrative Theology'; Somerset, *Feeling Like Saints*, pp. 152–54.

[44] While Thorpe's 'Testimony' recounts events of 1407, Rita Copeland dates the text to shortly after the promulgation of Arundel's 1409 *Constitutions*, arguing that Thorpe shows an awareness of the legislation and its dampening effect on Wycliffite community. She argues, 'the Thorpe identity is strangely disconnected from its putative historical moment (1407), and seems to be invested in a mythology of the dissident intellectual as survivor, remnant of a community lost to time, death, and the self-compromise that persecution produces'; Copeland, *Pedagogy, Intellectuals, and Dissent in the Later Middle Ages*, p. 197.

[45] The English versions survive in Bodl. Lib., MS Rawlinson C. 208 and Vienna, Österreichische Nationalbibliothek, MS 3936, the Latin in Prague, Metropolitan Library, MS O. 29; see *Two Wycliffite Texts*, ed. by Hudson, pp. xxvi–xxxiii.

[46] *The Testimony of William Thorpe*, ed. by Hudson, p. 36 (italics mine).

[47] Also see Katherine C. Little's discussion of this passage in *Confession and Resistance*,

The connection between silence under pressure and a joyful embrace of martyrdom is deepened close to the end of the 'Testimony', after Thorpe has undergone further 'manassynge'. Faced with the archbishop's demand to 'swere to ben obedient and to submitte hem to prelatis of holi chirche', his pledge to be obedient only according to his own definition of Holy Church 'as ferforþ as I can parseyue þat þese membris acorden wiþ her heed Crist', results in his being further 'rebukid and scorned and manassid on ech side. And ȝit after þis dyuerse persoones crieden vpon me to knele doun to submytte me. *But I stood stille and spak no word. And þanne þere were spoke of me and to me many greete wordis; and I stood and herede hem curse and manasse and scorne me, but I seide no þing*'.[48] As in the earlier scene, mounting scorn and 'manassing' lead Thorpe to further defiant silence. Elizabeth Schirmer notes, 'Thorpe, like Christ before Pilate, remains silent until he is returned to prison'.[49] Having evoked this parallel with Christ, once Thorpe hears the prison door shut, finding himself alone with his thoughts, he experiences relief and even joy:

> I, beyng þereinne bi mysilf, bisiede me to þenke on God and to þanke him of his goodnesse. And I was þanne gretli confortid in alle my wittis, not oonly forþi þat I was þan delyuered for a tyme [...] fro þe scornynge and fro þe manassinge of myn enemyes, but myche more I gladid in þe Lord forþi þoruȝ his grace he kepte me so boþe amonge þe flateryngis specialli, also amonge þe manassingis of myn aduersaries þat wiþouten heuynesse and agrigginge of my conscience I passid awei fro hem.[50]

Thorpe's ability to find refuge in his own thoughts, to rejoice not only in God's delivering him from danger, but also from any spiritual damage inflicted by his detractors, is a remarkable feature of his 'Testimony'. The notion that he manages to 'pass awei' not only physically unharmed, but without 'heuynesse and agrigginge [burdening] of my conscience', speaks to Thorpe's ability to maintain (and advertise) an inward, profound love of God even under duress.

In *Pore Caitif*, the combination of the Virgin Mary's fertile meekness with Christ's suffering meekness offers a powerful model for lollard devotional readers, a model exemplified in Thorpe's response to persecution. Joy amid suffering is one of the key signs, *Pore Caitif* argues, borrowing again from Rolle, of the devout soul's love of God:

pp. 71–73. Little argues that Thorpe uses traditional confessional discourse not to retreat inward but to keep his 'focus on the world outside' (p. 72).

[48] *The Testimony of William Thorpe*, ed. by Hudson, p. 90, p. 92, pp. 92–93 (italics mine).
[49] Schirmer, 'William Thorpe's Narrative Theology', p. 297.
[50] *The Testimony of William Thorpe*, ed. by Hudson, p. 93.

> The sefnþe [sign that a soul has love for Christ] is ioyfulnesse in sowle whan he is in tribulacyown, and þat he loue God and þanke hym in all his dissesis þat he suffryth. Þat is þe gretteste tokene þat he haþ þe loue of God, whan no wo, tribulacyoun, ne persecucyoun may bryngen hym doun fro þis loue.[51]

The incantatory repetition of the term 'loue' is Rolle's own touch, yet the emphasis on a defiant love that flourishes in the context of persecution is enhanced in the *Pore Caitif*, where the phrase 'no wo, tribulacyoun, ne persecucyoun' augments a line that included only 'wo' in Rolle's work.[52] This emphasis on love in the face of tribulation and persecution is strikingly congruent with Thorpe's account of being 'gladid' in the face of tribulation, and with Somerset's definition of love as 'an act of will in tandem with properly disposed emotions'. This is the embattled love that defines lollard sanctity.

One could multiply examples of such powerful meekness, exemplified in the *Pore Caitif* not only by the Virgin and Christ, but also by the virgin martyrs. I will point briefly to the narrative of Saint Cecilia, whose martyrdom involved meekness rather than rhetorical mastery. She appears in the *Pore Caitif*'s final 'Mirror of Chastity' tract. In the *Pore Caitif* Cecilia embodies a meek yet productive chastity resembling that of the Virgin Mary. Silently praying to God, Cecilia embodies a devotion both rebellious and fecund, as 'sche by took to owre lord hure chastyte. And by hure wern baptyȝed in hure hous mo þan fowre hundryd men and women'.[53] Her chaste evangelism is muted and domestic, and although her death by decapitation is elided in the *Pore Caitif* text, by virtue of her title 'Blessyd Cecilye mayden and martir', all the work's readers would have known that her life culminated in martyrdom. It is precisely the *Pore Caitif*'s form as a compilation — its strategic combination of sources and literary modes — that affords the opportunities to rearticulate the combination of 'meke lyuys and pacient suffryng', first mentioned at fol. 2ʳ, at various moments, and in different ways, across the whole length of the text. The placement of *Pore Caitif* within this particular volume invites lollard readers to identify these saints as models for their own devotional lives.

---

[51] BL, MS Add. 30897, fol. 52ᵛ. For this passage, see '*The Pore Caitif*, ed. by Brady, pp. 166–67.

[52] Rolle, *The Form of Living*, ed by Ogilvie-Thomson, p. 23, lines 812–13. For a recent examination of lollard attraction to Rolle, see Ian Johnson's discussion of the placement of an 'unadapted' *Form of Living* alongside lollard-leaning works in a fifteenth-century collection. Johnson, 'Vernacular Theology/Theological Vernacular', pp. 85–86.

[53] BL, MS Add. 30897, fol. 64ʳ. For this passage, see '*The Pore Caitif*, ed. by Brady, p. 195. For the Breviary source, of which this is a close translation, see *Breviarium*, ed. Procter and Wordsworth, col. 1088. Guibert adddresses the inclusion of St Cecilia in 'The "Mirrour of chastite"', p. 7.

Ave Maria and the 'assaylynge of aduersaryes'

The second major text in the BL, MS Add. 30897 volume is a lollard commentary on the Ave Maria salutation.⁵⁴ This unedited commentary, copied by the same scribe as the latter part of the *Pore Caitif* and the Beatitudes commentary, lies at the centre of the anthology. The work installs a loving yet circumspect devotion to the Virgin Mary as central to lollard practice, defining Mary as 'þe moodyr of alle trewe byleeuynge men'.⁵⁵ This commentary deploys various formal modes to shape readers in relation to saintly examples. I offer a short interlude between the two compilations to look briefly at a moment in the commentary's exposition of the phrase 'Ave Maria' to consider the work's own emphasis on suffering at the hands of detractors. I suggest that this text makes martyrdom part of its programme of lollard devotion to the Virgin Mary.

In teaching proper devotion to the Virgin Mary, this commentary functions, like the two long compilations framing it, to place lollard readers within a community of suffering saints. While Mary herself is not depicted as a martyr, she appears as a major source of comfort and assistance to those who greet her with the Ave. The commentary begins with textual explication of the Ave Maria salutation itself, encouraging devout readers to perform devotion in a careful, disciplined manner.⁵⁶ At the start the author exhorts readers to establish a mutual relationship with the Virgin, a relation based on a shared awareness of suffering. This section of the commentary explains at length how the reader should use the Ave to greet the Virgin 'duwely', 'trewely', 'oftyn', and 'wysly'. In the section on greeting her 'oftyn', the author notes, 'The secunde tyme y seye þat þou most greetyn hure oftyn, and as it were in costoume sche ofte and in þe same contynuaunce greete þe aȝeen. Wiþ help of hur ladyschyp consyderynge þe streyte nede of þyn oftyn assaylynge of aduersaryes'.⁵⁷ The commentary thus identifies readers as part of a community of those assailed by 'aduersaryes', offering the Virgin's 'help' as an aid to enduring them.

---

⁵⁴ For a detailed treatment of this work, see Rice, 'Forming Devotion'.

⁵⁵ BL, MS Add. 30897, fol. 71ʳ. The phrase 'trewe men' is a central lollard formulation; see Peikola, *Congregation of the Elect*, pp. 109–229, for an extensive, nuanced discussion of this term in various lollard texts.

⁵⁶ The commentary emphasizes that the *Ave* is a 'greeting', rather than a prayer, on the grounds that the word *Amen*, which transforms the salutation into a prayer, is not present in the biblical texts from which the salutation was compiled; see Rice, 'Forming Devotion', pp. 169–71, for a full discussion of this section.

⁵⁷ BL, MS Add. 30897, fol. 67ʳ.

In addition to textual explication, the formal strategy of narrative becomes a way to move from the 'riȝt rulynge of a mannys entent' into a performance of sanctity. In unfolding the proper way to 'hail' the Virgin Mary, the commentary considers how the practice of hailing appears in narratives of saintly persecution, exploring the sufferings of the protomartyr Saint Stephen, an undisputed saint within the lollard canon, under the rubric of the 'fullness of grace' that Mary possessed. Although Mary's grace is ultimately greater than Stephen's, his charity under pressure offers a graphic example of suffering 'perfection' for the reader:

> he hadde so mochel fulnesse in suffysaunce of grace and of charyte þat he preyde for hem þat stonyd hym to deþe. And he saw þe hefnys opyn, and Ihesu stondynge on Godys rygth syde. And for þis fulnes of suffisaunce it is seyd þus of hym in holy wryt (Actus Apostolorum 6): Stephanus plenus gratia, þat is, Steuene ful of grace. Þat is to seye by fulnesse of suffysaunce, for lasse scholde noȝt haue seruyd hym to þat perfeccyoun þat he was clepyd to.[58]

In this passage, which paraphrases and interprets Stephen's martyrdom from the Acts of the Apostles, Stephen shows perfect equanimity in his steadfast demonstration of 'charyte' for his persecutors even as he is being stoned to death.[59] By locating this moment of persecution within the larger frame of the Ave Maria, the commentary makes praise or hailing of the Virgin Mary into an avenue towards identification with saintly suffering, perhaps even a challenge to lollard readers to achieve something approaching Saint Stephen's level of 'perfeccyon' for the sake of a pure Christian belief.

Book to a Mother: From the 'ten hestes' to the 'hauen of heuene'

In this final section I consider how the devotional guide *Book to a Mother* exploits the strategy of compilation to teach a lollard 'ethical stance' combining meekness and martyrdom, a stance that complements the Additional anthology's larger focus on a suffering form of sanctity. *Book to a Mother* is a long devotional work ostensibly written by a priest for his mother, a devout widow. The compilation combines syllabus material, advice on spiritual formation, and anti-monastic polemic, among other textual modes, into a guide with an open-ended form that is difficult to characterize.[60] Although I have argued elsewhere

---

[58] BL, MS Add. 30897, fols 73ᵛ–74ʳ.

[59] See Acts 6. 8 for the description of Stephen as 'full of grace and fortitude'; Acts 7. 55 for his vision of the heavens opened, revealing God and Christ; Acts 7. 59 for his dying prayers on behalf of his persecutors.

[60] See Watson, 'Fashioning the Puritan Gentry-Woman', pp. 175–78 on the *Book*'s form,

that *Book to a Mother* is 'reformist' without being lollard,[61] I have been persuaded by Somerset's recent work, especially with the formal, linguistic, and thematic parallels drawn between the *Book* and other lollard works, that we should view *Book to a Mother* as 'a lollard form of living'.[62]

Book to a Mother survives as the last text in the Additional anthology, in a truncated copy missing the first bit (the introduction and brief discussion of Pater Noster, Ave Maria, and Creed). Thus the work begins at the end of the Ten Commandments section. (This copy also lacks the whole final section, which is largely a series of biblical paraphrases.)[63] As with the *Pore Caitif* text, the form in which we find *Book to a Mother* here foregrounds the Ten Commandments, the most central element of 'God's law' as the lollards understood it. The truncated form of the text also moves the narratives of the saints and Virgin Mary into a more prominent position, quite near the end of the work.

Like *Pore Caitif*, *Book to a Mother* employs pastoralia and narrative to link 'God's law' to the reader's personal effort at sanctity. As in the anthology's other two long texts, the Virgin Mary dwells at the core of this work: the author repeatedly encourages his addressee, ostensibly his mother, to understand her chaste widowhood as a valid mode of religious discipline, as an avenue towards spiritual perfection. The addressee's combination of piety and chastity connects her to the Virgin Mary and to the virgin saints, who in turn become models for the pious reader in their meekness and in their perfect forms of martyrdom.

Book to a Mother's emphasis on perfection is evident even in the catechetical sections that open the work. As I noted above, in the Additional volume, *Book to a Mother* is incomplete, beginning near the end of the discussion of

---

and pp. 170–72 on its movement between reformist and orthodox modes, as well as its presence in manuscripts containing orthodox and Wycliffite materials. On the work's complex form, see Rice, *Lay Piety and Religious Discipline*, pp. 55–59, and Dutton, *Julian of Norwich*, pp. 123–36.

[61] See Rice, *Lay Piety and Religious Discipline*, pp. 105–32.

[62] Somerset, *Feeling like Saints*, p. 239. For a close comparison of *Book to a Mother* with the lollard text *The Dialogue between Jon and Richard*, on the basis of their shared images of 'soul as cloister' and 'Christ as abbot', see Somerset, *Feeling Like Saints*, pp. 241–48 and pp. 253–56. Surveying aspects of the *Book*'s content that overlap with lollard ideas, including the tendency towards imagining 'material aspects of religious life in metaphorical terms that allow them to be imagined in new ways' (p. 262), Somerset considers the *Book*'s metaphorical treatment of the sacraments, its treatment of Christ as book, its distinctive emphasis on persecution, and its theories of salvation and predestination (pp. 262–72).

[63] See Dutton, 'Textual Disunities and Ambiguities'. Dutton argues that *Book to a Mother* is carefully truncated in BL, MS Add. 30897 at the start in order to avoid repetition of syllabus material (pp. 154–55).

the Ten Commandments. Incorporated into this Ten Commandments section is a lollard commentary on the seven works of mercy that circulated in varying forms in several manuscripts.[64] The commentary develops a 'metaphorical exposition' of the seven bodily works of mercy as based ultimately in the Ten Commandments, emphasizing every Christian's obligation to teach and minister to neighbours.[65] This treatise, interpolated early into the compilation, begins to offer a distinctively lollard vision of sanctity to its readers, a sanctity that values keeping the Commandments above all and from that basis elaborates the importance of embodying meekness and suffering martyrdom. From the start the treatise connects the works of mercy to the Ten Commandments. The section opens as follows:

> Of þe deedes of mercy God wol speke at þe day of doome to alle on hys ryȝt syde: com ȝee blessed chyldren of my fader, takeþ þe kyngdom þat is ordeynde to ȝow [...] I hungred, and ȝe ȝaue me mete. Þat is when þe leest of myne þat schal be saued was hungry for defaute of goostly foode, þat is to seye for to kepe Godes hestes, and ȝee tauȝte hym.[66]

Proceeding to connect the first work of mercy (feeding the sick), to devout *spiritual* acts of teaching, prayer, or doing penance, the author posits a continuum between those saints who performed these acts privately and those who did them publicly. As the text notes further,

> Moost blessid is he bifore God þat of moost feruent loue and moost humbulte, moost so releueþ of þe forsayde poore men, wheþer a man do so wiþ techynge of speche, as prechours or oþer þat can wel techen Goddes hestes, or wiþ deuout prayers sorwynge for her synnes, oþer wiþ penauns doynge: priuely as Oure Lady dide, and Seynt Joon Baptist and oþer sych, oþer opynlych as Crist and hys apostoles, martirs, confessoures and virgines diden al her besynes, and ȝeue her owne lyf to fulfille þis first deede of mercy.[67]

This passage not only offers a succinct summary of saints who truly count among the lollards, but it also draws a vivid picture of the two main pathways to lollard

---

[64] The commentary is present without significant variants in all copies of *Book to a Mother*. Somerset has edited the work as Appendix B to 'Textual Transmission, Variance, and Religious Identity', pp. 92–96.

[65] See Somerset, 'Textual Transmission, Variance, and Religious Identity', p. 83.

[66] BL, MS Add. 30897, fol. 78ʳ. For this passage, see *Book to a Mother*, ed. by McCarthy, p. 5.

[67] BL, MS Add. 30897, fol. 78ʳ⁻ᵛ. For this passage, see *Book to a Mother*, ed. by McCarthy, p. 5.

sanctity: private teaching, prayer, and suffering, or public teaching, prayer, and martyrdom. Thus we can see that from the start *Book to a Mother* places the saints in the forefront, offering these saintly models of conduct as complementary to each other and exemplary for the reader.

Book to a Mother's narratives about the saints function, in parallel with *Pore Caitif*, and in relation to this early passage, to define a suffering form of purity that remains grounded in the Ten Commandments. This form of sanctity combines the virgin martyr's 'open' rebellion with the Virgin Mary's 'private' humility and grace. I will look at one extended section of the text, in which a narrative about the virgin martyr Lucy shades into a discussion of the Virgin Mary. I suggest that in this extended passage we see how their forms of holiness complement each other, forming a complete picture of sanctity for a lollard reader. In the context of validating the addressee's chaste widowhood, *Book to a Mother* extensively narrates the story of Saint Lucy, a virgin martyr who refused to sacrifice to idols. Lucy's example involves precisely the giving to the poor that was exhorted in the first section, manifesting an effort of love that is sometimes painful.

Lucy's first major speech involves telling her mother to give away money while she is living rather than at her death: to give when it is painful, not when it is easy. Lucy exhorts:

> þat þou ȝeuest whan þou deyȝest, þou ȝeuest for þou mayst not haue hit wiþ þee. Ȝeue hit while þou lyuest, and þou shalt haue mede; for a ferþynge [yȝeue][68] by a mannes lyf is better þan al þe worldes good after.[69]

Crucially, it is revealed, as their household's money dwindles, that Lucy has been giving it all away to the poor: 'And when þe þynges were almoost sold, [her husband] parceyuede þat þei weren ȝeuen to pore men, and he pleynede to a tyraunt þat was clepede Pascasye, and seyde she was Cristene'.[70] In a lollard reading context, Lucy's exposure and punishment for being a Christian would resonate with membership in a persecuted minority of 'true' Christians. Lucy's giving to the poor, even until nothing is left, is an act rooted in the exhortations of Matthew (seen at fol. 78ʳ where the deeds of mercy were enumerated). In the text, this radical generosity identifies Lucy as a Christian and opens her up to

---

[68] This word is missing from BL, MS Add. 30897. I have supplied it from the printed edition in order to clarify the sense of the passage.

[69] BL, MS Add. 30897, fol. 115ʳ. For this passage and the following two quotations, see *Book to a Mother*, ed. by McCarthy, p. 95.

[70] BL, MS Add. 30897, fol. 115ᵛ.

martyrdom. After she has been handed to the tyrant Pascasius, Lucy's protest culminates with her redefinition of sacrifice as an act of charity rather than fealty to an idol. She argues:

> Clene sacrifice and unsoyled to þe Fader of heuene is to visite moderlees children and faderles, and widewes in here tribulacion. And y þis thre ȝeer ded no sacrifice but to God of lyf. Now y haue no more: y offre meself in sacrifice to God, do he wiþ his offrynge what he wole.[71]

There is nothing in this speech that would be controversial within the late medieval Christian context: indeed the entire narrative is translated from the standard Latin Breviary reading for Saint Lucy.[72] Yet the story has particular force within a lollard compilation, in which sanctity involves a combination of meek love, grounded in the works of mercy, leading to complete self-immolation, to self-sacrifice before God. Such an emphasis is heightened within the Additional anthology, with its larger focus on saintly suffering.

It is also striking that in *Book to a Mother*, Lucy's last stand leads, via a short intermediate story allegorizing the deadly sins as a dangerous sea, into praise of the Virgin Mary that makes Mary's example absolutely central to the reader's spiritual formation. Here we see that Lucy's fierce martyrdom is reinforced by the Virgin Mary's meekness. Referencing Mary's familiar title as 'stella maris' or 'star of the sea', *Book to a Mother* exhorts:

> When þou art in any tempestes of soule, byhold þe sterre and clepe in Mary. For she passede þis see al dryȝe foot: as God seyde to þe eddre þat she scholde, wiþ hyre feet, þat is with hire affecciouns, trede and defoule þe eddre heed, for he dispised pryde, þat is þe edder heed, wiþ hire mekenesse [...]. And so, wiþ her holy lyuynge, she shewed how foul and horrible was þe fendis pride. So ȝif we clepe in Marie, þat is, ȝif we make us liche to her lyuynge as þouȝ she were wiþinne vs, rulynge all oure werkes, we mowe trede and defoule wiþ oure fet þe deueles heed, þat is pryde, and knowe oure foule horrible lyuynge, and see by þe sterre to passe þe see to þe hauen of heuene.[73]

Casting Mary's meekness as the antidote to Eve's pride and an example to the lollard reader, working in parallel with the *Pore Caitif* and the Ave Maria commentary to install Mary as one's guiding light, making her life the source of a 'rule' within the reader, *Book to a Mother* offers both saintly martyrdom and

---

[71] BL, MS Add. 30897, fol. 115ᵛ.

[72] See *Breviarium*, ed. by Procter and Wordsworth, cols 54–55.

[73] BL, MS Add. 30897, fols 116ᵛ–117ʳ. For this passage, see *Book to a Mother*, ed. by McCarthy, p. 98.

Mary's benign example as paradigms for lollard devotion. Much of the above passage is paraphrased from Bernard of Clairvaux's second homily in praise of the Virgin Mary, but here Bernard's praise of Mary is augmented and put to the end of lollard sanctity.[74] While the general directive to follow Mary's example is found in Bernard, the notion that successful imitation of Mary will lead to perfection, and perhaps ultimately to arrival in heaven, is *Book to a Mother*'s own addition.[75] If lollard readers, intent upon the self-reformation and self-regulation that the work has promoted all along, succeed in 'lyuynge as þouȝ she were wiþinne vs, rulynge all oure werkes', they may ultimately 'see by þe sterre to passe þe see to þe hauen of heuene', joining the saints who have already reached that promised land. This explicit, hopeful anticipation of heaven is not present in Bernard's work. For lollard readers, that salvation is not an entitlement but an aspiration requiring a constant struggle of love against pride, whether through 'techynge of speche', 'deuout prayers', or 'penauns doynge': 'priuely' as the Virgin did, or 'opynlych as Crist and hys apostoles, martirs, confessoures and virgines diden', to recall the *Book*'s opening assertions.

In conclusion, I suggest that lollard devotion to the saints was very much alive in the mid-fifteenth century. In this unique anthology, devotional compilations were brought together to channel lollard devotion away from images and into texts. In combination, the *Pore Caitif* and *Book to a Mother*, together with the Ave Maria commentary, work to define a radically meek and suffering form of sanctity, one that lollard readers might both venerate and emulate.

---

[74] See Bernard of Clairvaux, *Opera: Sermones I*, ed. by Leclercq and Rochais, pp. 34–35. The opening line of *Book to a Mother*'s passage seems to be loosely translating the following from Bernard's Latin: 'Si iracundia, aut avaritia, aut carnis illecebra naviculam concusserit mentis, respice ad Mariam' (p. 35). A modern English translation reads, 'When rage or greed or fleshly desires are battering the skiff of your soul, gaze up at Mary' (*Homilies in Praise of the Blessed Virgin Mary*, trans. by Saïd, p. 30). The subsequent passage on the adder's head references Genesis 3. 15 (God's curse on the serpent) and, in the context of this particular volume, picks up on the Ave Maria commentary's discussion of how Mary reverses Eve's curse: 'Oure Ladyes meeknesse was contrarye to Eues pryde, and hure desyr of hiȝenesse. And þus for alle þese þre vertuous þynges þat weryn in Oure Lady aftyr þat Aue was seyd to hure of þe aungel contraryenge þese oþer þre wrecchydnessys þat weryn in Eua as it is seyd to fore' (BL, MS Add. 30897, fol. 71ᵛ).

[75] The sermon exhorts, 'Non recedat ab ore, non recedat a corde, et ut impetres eius orationis suffragium, non deseras conversationis exemplum. Ipsam sequens non devias, ipsam rogans non desperas, ipsam cogitans non erras' (Bernard of Clairvaux, *Opera: Sermones I*, ed. by Leclercq and Rochais, p. 35). The translation reads, 'Keep her in your mouth; keep her in your heart. Follow the example of her life and you will obtain the favor of her prayer. Following her, you will never go astray. Asking her help, you will never despair. Keeping her in your thoughts, you will never wander away' (*Homilies in Praise of the Blessed Virgin Mary*, trans. by Saïd, p. 30).

With their strategic combinations of explication and exhortation, meditation and narrative, these compilations offered a unique form of access to the saints, putting lollard readers in the right company, and perhaps even helping them to 'passe þe see to þe hauen of heuene'.

Works Cited

Manuscripts

London, British Library [BL], MS Additional 30897
London, British Library [BL], MS Egerton 826
London, British Library [BL], MS Harley 2336
London, Lambeth Palace Library, MS 484
Oxford, Bodleian Library [Bodl. Lib.], MS Rawlinson C. 208
Paris, Bibliothèque nationale de France [BnF], MS Anglais 41
Vienna, Österreichische Nationalbibliothek, MS 3936

Primary Sources

Bernard of Clairvaux, *Homilies in Praise of the Blessed Virgin Mary*, trans. by Marie-Bernard Saïd, Monastic Studies, 23 (Piscataway, NY: Gorgias Press, 2010)
—— , *Sancti Bernardi Opera: Sermones I*, ed. by J. Leclercq and H. Rochais (Roma: Editiones Cisterciences, 1966)
Book to a Mother: An Edition with Commentary, ed. by Adrian James McCarthy (Salzburg: Institut für Anglistik und Amerikanistik, 1981)
Breviarium ad usum Insignis Ecclesiae Sarum, ed. by Francis Procter and Christopher Wordsworth III (Cambridge: Cambridge University Press, 1886)
Decretum Gratiani emendatum et notationatibus illustratum, ed. by A. L. Richter (Leipzig: Bernhard Tauchnitz, 1839)
Lollards of Coventry, 1486–1522, ed. and trans. by Shannon McSheffrey and Norman Tanner, Camden Fifth Series, 23 (Cambridge: Cambridge University Press, 2003)
'*The Pore Caitif*: Edited from MS Harley 2336 with Introduction and Notes', ed. by Mary Teresa Brady (unpublished doctoral dissertation, Fordham University, 1954)
Rolle, Richard, *The Form of Living*, in *Richard Rolle: Prose and Verse from MS. Longleat 29 and Related Manuscripts*, ed. by S. J. Ogilvie-Thomson, Early English Text Society, o.s., 293 (Oxford: Oxford University Press, 1988), pp. 3–25
The Testimony of William Thorpe, in *Two Wycliffite Texts*, ed. by Anne Hudson, Early English Text Society, o.s., 301 (Oxford: Oxford University Press, 1993), pp. 24–93
Two Wycliffite Texts, ed. by Anne Hudson, Early English Text Society, o.s., 301 (Oxford: Oxford University Press, 1993)

Secondary Works

Brady, M. Teresa, 'Lollard Interpolations and Omissions in Manuscripts of *The Pore Caitif*', in *De Cella in Seculum: Religious and Secular Life and Devotion in Late Medieval England*, ed. by Michael G. Sargent (Cambridge: D. S. Brewer, 1988), pp. 183–203
——, 'The Lollard Sources of the *Pore Caitif*', *Traditio*, 44 (1988), 389–418
Copeland, Rita, *Pedagogy, Intellectuals, and Dissent in the Later Middle Ages: Lollardy and Ideas of Learning* (Cambridge: Cambridge University Press, 2001)
Dutton, Elisabeth, *Julian of Norwich: The Influence of Late-Medieval Devotional Compilations* (Cambridge: D. S. Brewer, 2008)
——, 'Textual Disunities and Ambiguities of *mise-en-page* in the Manuscripts Containing *Book to a Mother*', *Journal of the Early Book Society*, 6 (2003), 149–59
Fitzgibbons, Moira, 'Poverty, Dignity, and Lay Spirituality in *Pore Caitif* and *Jacob's Well*', *Medium Ævum*, 77 (2008), 222–40
——, 'Women, Tales, and "Talking Back" in *Pore Caitif* and *Dives and Pauper*', in *Middle English Religious Writing in Practice: Texts, Readers, and Transformations*, ed. by Nicole R. Rice, Late Medieval and Early Modern Studies, 21 (Turnhout: Brepols, 2013), pp. 181–214
Fletcher, Alan, 'A Hive of Industry or a Hornet's Next? MS Sidney Sussex 74 and its Scribes', in *Late-Medieval Religious Texts and their Transmission: Essays in Honour of A. I. Doyle*, ed. by A. J. Minnis (Cambridge: D. S. Brewer, 1994), pp. 131–55
Gayk, Shannon, *Image, Text, and Religious Reform in Fifteenth-Century England* (Cambridge: Cambridge University Press, 2010)
Guibert, Karine, 'The "Mirrour of chastite": Was the Last Chapter of the *Pore Caitif* a Later Addition?', unpublished paper
Hanna, Ralph, 'Two Lollard Codices and Lollard Book Production', *Studies in Bibliography*, 43 (1990), 49–62
Hill, Gabriel, 'Pedagogy, Devotion, and Marginalia: Using the *Pore Caitif* in Fifteenth-Century England', *Journal of Medieval Religious Cultures*, 41 (2015), 187–207
Johnson, Ian, 'Vernacular Theology/Theological Vernacular: A Game of Two Halves?' in *After Arundel: Religious Writing in Fifteenth-Century England*, ed. by Vincent Gillespie and Kantik Ghosh, Medieval Church Studies, 21 (Turnhout: Brepols, 2011), pp. 73–88
Kelly, Stephen, and Ryan Perry, 'Devotional Cosmopolitanism in Fifteenth-Century England', in *After Arundel: Religious Writing in Fifteenth-Century England*, ed. by Vincent Gillespie and Kantik Ghosh, Medieval Church Studies, 21 (Turnhout: Brepols, 2011), pp. 363–80
Little, Katherine C., *Confession and Resistance: Defining the Self in Late Medieval England* (Notre Dame: University of Notre Dame Press, 2006)
Lutton, Robert, *Lollardy and Orthodox Religion in Pre-Reformation England: Reconstructing Piety* (Woodbridge: Boydell, 2006)
Malo, Robyn, 'Behaving Paradoxically? Wycliffites, Shrines, and Relics', in *Wycliffite Controversies*, ed. by Mishtooni Bose and J. Patrick Hornbeck II, Medieval Church Studies, 23 (Turnhout: Brepols, 2011), pp. 193–210
Peikola, Matti, *Congregation of the Elect: Patterns of Self-Fashioning in English Lollard Writings*, Anglicana Turkuensa, 21 (Turku: University of Turku, 2000)

—— , 'Individual Voice in Lollard Discourse', in *Approaches to Style and Discourse in English*, ed. by Risto Hiltunen and Shinichiro Watanabe (Osaka: Osaka University Press, 2004), pp. 51–77

—— , 'The Sanctorale, Thomas of Woodstock's English Bible, and the Orthodox Appropriation of Wycliffite Tables of Lessons', in *Wycliffite Controversies*, ed. by Mishtooni Bose and J. Patrick Hornbeck II, Medieval Church Studies, 23 (Turnhout: Brepols, 2011), pp. 153–74

Rice, Nicole R., 'Forming Devotion in a Lollard Ave Maria Commentary', *Yearbook of Langland Studies*, 31 (2017), 163–81

—— , *Lay Piety and Religious Discipline in Middle English Literature*, Cambridge Studies in Medieval Literature (Cambridge: Cambridge University Press, 2008)

—— , 'Reformist Devotional Reading: The *Pore Caitif* in British Library, MS Harley 2322', in *The Medieval Mystical Tradition in England: Exeter Symposium VIII*, ed. by E. A. Jones (Cambridge: D. S. Brewer, 2013), pp. 177–93

Schirmer, Elizabeth, 'William Thorpe's Narrative Theology', *Studies in the Age of Chaucer*, 31 (2009), 267–99

Simpson, James, 'Orthodoxy's Image Trouble: Images in and After Arundel's Constitutions', in *After Arundel: Religious Writing in Fifteenth-Century England*, ed. by Vincent Gillespie and Kantik Ghosh, Medieval Church Studies, 21 (Turnhout: Brepols, 2011), pp. 91–113

Somerset, Fiona, 'Afterword', in *Wycliffite Controversies*, ed. by Mishtooni Bose and J. Patrick Hornbeck II, Medieval Church Studies, 23 (Turnhout: Brepols, 2011), pp. 319–33

—— , 'Censorship', in *The Production of Books in England, 1350–1500*, ed. by Alexandra Gillespie and Daniel Wakelin, Cambridge Studies in Codicology and Palaeography, 14 (Cambridge: Cambridge University Press, 2011), pp. 239–58

—— , *Feeling Like Saints: Lollard Writings after Wyclif* (Ithaca: Cornell University Press, 2014)

—— , 'Textual Transmission, Variance, and Religious Identity among Lollard Pastoralia', in *Religious Controversy in Europe, 1378–1536: Textual Transmission and Networks of Readership*, ed. by Michael Van Dussen and Pavel Soukup (Turnhout: Brepols, 2013), pp. 71–104

Trivedi, Kalpen, '"Trewe techyng and false heritikys": Some "Lollard" Manuscripts of the *Pore Caitif*', in *In Strange Countries: Middle English Literature and its Afterlife. Essays in Memory of J. J. Anderson*, ed. by David Matthews (Manchester: Manchester University Press, 2011), pp. 132–58

Von Nolcken, Christina, 'Another Kind of Saint: A Lollard Perception of John Wyclif', in *From Ockham to Wyclif*, ed. by Anne Hudson and Michael Wilks (Oxford: Blackwell, 1987), pp. 429–43

Watson, Nicholas, 'Fashioning the Puritan Gentry-Woman: Devotion and Dissent in *Book to a Mother*', in *Medieval Women: Texts and Contexts in Late Medieval Britain. Essays in Honour of Felicity Riddy*, ed. by Jocelyn Wogan-Browne and others, Medieval Women: Texts and Contexts, 3 (Turnhout: Brepols, 2000), pp. 169–84

—— , *Richard Rolle and the Invention of Authority* (Cambridge: Cambridge University Press, 1991)

'WHEN IS A MAN PROUDE. WHEN HE WOL NOT BEKNOWEN SUCHE AS HE IS': KNOWING ONESELF IN LONDON, BRITISH LIBRARY, MS ADDITIONAL 37787

Sheri Smith

London, British Library, MS Additional 37787, or John Northewode's prayer book, as the library catalogue designates the manuscript, is an eclectic miscellany of devotional texts in Latin, English, and French. Its categorization as a prayer book depends upon the prevalence of prayers amongst its varied contents and is also encouraged by the identification of the manuscript with its first owner, John Northewode, a Cistercian monk who entered the noviciate at St Mary's Abbey, Bordesley, near Worcester, in 1386.[1] The designation of the manuscript is not altogether stable, however, and the 'prayer book' title unused in the few scholarly works devoted to it. Its Middle English contents were edited and published in 1956 by Nita Scudder Baugh as *A Worcestershire Miscellany*. More recent work by Wendy Scase challenges the classification of the manuscript as a miscellany, alongside its association with book production in the West Midlands. She proposes instead understanding the manuscript as a composite created from distinct units which were very likely to have been copied and decorated in different locations before being assembled in its current form.[2] Yet the

---

[1] John Northewode's noviciate is recorded on fol. 182ᵛ of the manuscript.
[2] Scase, 'John Northwood's Miscellany Revisited', pp. 111–20.

Sheri Smith (smiths@uni-duesseldorf.de) is a Lecturer in Old and Middle English Language and Literature at Heinrich Heine Universität, Düsseldorf. Her research focuses on intersections between late medieval English devotional texts and poetry.

composite nature occasioned by the manuscript's production does not preclude conceiving of it as a miscellany, nor even a prayer book, and this essay will discuss it as both while acknowledging the questions raised about the book's format during the time between Northewode's noviciate and Goody Throckmorton's ownership of it around the end of the fifteenth century.[3]

My purpose in this essay is to examine correspondences across two vernacular collections of texts contained in BL, MS Add. 37787, focusing on the role played by the use of the English vernacular both to aid and to conceptualize the development of self-knowledge. A brief overview of the manuscript's various contents and the interrelation of its three languages in the first section provides the context in which to understand the two English texts to be considered in detail. The second section of this essay examines a key text chosen from each of the miscellany's two clusters of English texts, a form of confession and a petitionary prayer to the Trinity, tracing the relationship these texts present between the process of confession and the development of self-knowledge. The final section draws upon this analysis to argue that the language of confession made possible through the use of the variant forms of the Middle English verb 'knouen' enables a transition between the outward acknowledgement of sins and the inward knowing of the self as separate from sin.

The Vernacular Anthologies in a Composite, Trilingual Miscellany

The miscellany is both practical in purpose and to all appearances well used. It contains evidence of several hands and includes devotional material in Latin, English, and French, over one hundred items in total, with sermons, meditations, liturgies, visions, hymns, lyrics, and indulgences intermingled.[4] Latin

---

[3] See Scase, 'John Northwood's Miscellany Revisited', pp. 116–17.

[4] For the British Library catalogue description of MS Add. 37787, see *Catalogue of Additions*, pp. 140–50. Discussing the variation in scribal hands, Baugh quotes correspondence from Robin Flower, deputy keeper of manuscripts at the British Museum from 1929 to 1944, who suggests that the hands demonstrate the similarity of scribes working in the same scriptorium, but states that he cannot rule out the possibility that one of the hands might be Northewode's own. Baugh chooses to explain the difference in hands as naturally occurring over a period of time, suggesting that the entire compilation was written by Northewode. See *A Worcestershire Miscellany*, ed. by Baugh, pp. 36–37. In an unpublished doctoral thesis, Rebecca Farnham points to the limited nature of the material with which Baugh worked, distinguishing instead the work of four scribes. She assigns fols 3^r–17^v to Hand 1, 18^r–48^v and 161^r–182^v to Hand 2, fols 49^r–142^r to Hand 3, and 142^r–160^v to Hand 4. See Farnham, 'Producers and Readers', pp. 35–37. Hands 1 and 4 are responsible for the majority of the vernacular English texts.

texts account for the great majority of these items, comprising liturgical and devotional texts, including instructions for Mass, the Hours of the Cross, liturgies for saints' feasts, and litanies, in addition to hymns, meditations, visions, sermons, memorials, indulgences, charms, and prayers. Far outnumbered by those written in Latin, texts in the English vernacular show anthologizing tendencies on the part of the compiler which contrast with the more disparate nature of the Latin collections. English texts exceed twenty in number and appear in two distinct clusters, each of which represents an orderly approach to gathering related material into a short vernacular anthology.[5] Scase, arguing that the manuscript was compiled of three distinct units bound together, labels the first of these clusters (fols 3^r–17^v) unit one, proposing that the unit is likely to have been 'produced as a discrete little vernacular devotional resource'.[6] This first collection of English texts includes a form of confession (fols 3^r–11^v), the Hours of the Cross in verse (fols 12^v–14^r), a confession to Jesus (fols 14^r–16^r), and three prayers: a prayer to God (fol. 11^v–12^r), a prayer to be said at the Elevation (fol. 12^{r-v}), and a prayer to the Trinity (fols 16^r–17^v).[7]

The second cluster is located near the end of the manuscript (fols 142^r–160^v) and comprises the final section in the collection identified by Scase as unit three.[8] This collection of vernacular texts is taken up by a new hand mid-quire and consists primarily of prayers, religious lyrics, and *pastoralia* written in verse. It begins with two prayers addressed to the Trinity (fols 142^r–146^r), followed by two 'songs of love-longing' (fols 146^v–156^v), a prayer to the Virgin (fols 156^v–157^v), a condensed collection of *pastoralia*, titled in Latin and written in English verse, which includes the Seven Gifts of the Holy Spirit, the Seven Works of Mercy, and the Five Senses of Man (fols 157^v–159^r), the Ten Commandments (fols 159^r–160^r), and a levation prayer (fol. 160^{r-v}).[9] With the

---

[5] On the defining characteristics of a manuscript anthology, see Connolly, 'Understanding the Medieval Miscellany', pp. 4–5.

[6] Scase, 'John Northwood's Miscellany Revisited', pp. 103–04.

[7] See the following in *A Worcestershire Miscellany*, ed. by Baugh: 'A Form of Confession', pp. 87–95; 'A Prayer to God', p. 96; 'Prayer at the Elevation', p. 97; 'Hours of the Cross', pp. 98–100; 'A Confession to Jesus Christ', pp. 101–03; and 'A Prayer to the Trinity', pp. 104–05.

[8] Scase, 'John Northwood's Miscellany Revisited', pp. 109–11.

[9] See the following in *A Worcestershire Miscellany*, ed. by Baugh: 'A Prayer for the Three Boons', pp. 122–24; 'Oratio ad Trinitatem', pp. 125–28; 'Two Songs of Love-Longing', pp. 129–42; 'A Prayer to the Virgin', pp. 143–44; 'Septem dona spiritus sancti', 'Septem opera misericordie', and 'De quinque sensibus hominis', pp. 145–47; 'Decem precepta domini', p. 148; and 'Prayer at the Elevation', pp. 149–50.

exception of the first Trinitarian prayer, each of the items in this second cluster of vernacular texts is shared with the Vernon manuscript.[10]

One significant English text, 'The Disputation between the Body and the Soul', falls outside these two clusters, being located at fols 34^r–45^v amid an otherwise Latin collection, and provides an example of some of the irregularities to be found in the relationship between the manuscript's three languages.[11] This English verse is in fact titled in Latin, 'De disputacione noua inter corpus et animam'. The bilingual relationship between the Latin title and the English text supports John Scahill's observation that the use of Latin legitimizes vernacular texts. In his discussion of earlier trilingual manuscripts from England, Scahill identifies hierarchical linguistic features in which, he argues, Latin 'validates' the vernacular, with French taking precedence over English.[12] Many, although not all, of the English texts in Northewode's prayer book are given Latin titles or rubrics, including the subdivisions of the opening form of confession which is discussed in the next section.

A few examples from the miscellany, however, subvert any hierarchical expectation that Latin should lend authority to the vernacular, while French performs a similar function for English: these instances include the provision of a French title for a Latin prayer to say during the Mass of the Nativity (fol. 68^v); a Latin prayer to Mary preceded by a French title, French rubric, and invocation of Mary also in French (fol. 126^v); and a Latin litany of the names of God with an English rubric promising protection from hanging appended to it (fol. 174^v). 'De disputacione noua inter corpus et animam' is not only titled in Latin, but also given this explanation: 'q*uod* transpositu*m* est i*n* lingua anglicana. De lati*n*o q*uo*d dicitur sic noctis sub silencio te*m*pore &c' (translated into the English language from the Latin, which tells thus 'In the Silence of a Midwinter Night') (fol. 34^r).[13] The presumed audience understands Latin, but

---

[10] See 'Her biginneþ an orisun of þe trinite', 'Prayer for the Seven Gifts of the Holy Ghost', 'A Confessioun for Negligence of þe Dedes of Mercy', 'An Orisoun for the Sauynge of þe Fyue Wyttes', 'An Orysoun for Negligens of þe X. Commaundemens', and 'A Preyer at þe Leuacioun' in *Minor Poems*, ed. by Horstman and Furnivall, i, 16, 34–35, 36, and 24. The cataloguer of BL, MS Add. 37787 notes that the Prayer to the Virgin is only 'partly identical' with that of the Vernon manuscript ('A Preiere to vre Ladi', p. 22). For the Songs of Love-Longing, see *Minor Poems*, ed. by Horstman and Furnivall, ii, 449–62. For a description of the Vernon Manuscript, Bodl. Lib., MS Eng. poet. a. 1, see the Bodleian Library's *Medieval Manuscripts in Oxford Libraries*.

[11] See *A Worcestershire Miscellany*, ed. by Baugh, pp. 107–21.

[12] Scahill, 'Trilingualism in Early English Miscellanies', pp. 19–22.

[13] All quotations from BL, MS Add. 37787 are taken from my own transcriptions. The full texts of 'A Form of Confession' and 'A Prayer for the Three Boons' can be found in Baugh's

might not read English well enough to recognize the text, suggesting an awareness on the part of the scribe or compiler of the differing needs of different readers. A reader of Latin, such as a monk, might use the title and explanation to locate and choose an appropriate text for a reader of English.

Knowing Oneself and Knowing One's Sins through Confession and Prayer

A core concern evident in many of the miscellany's texts is to find the way to eternal bliss. The rubric to the manuscript's first text addresses this goal directly: 'Here is a goode confession. | That teches man to salvation' (fol. 3ʳ). The essential role played by penitence and the absolution of sins is highlighted by the text this rubric introduces, a form of confession written in the English vernacular which occupies a key place at the beginning of the manuscript (fols 3ʳ–11ᵛ).[14] The text, written in prose, is a first-person acknowledgement of a lifetime's burden of sin, beginning:

> I knowleche me gulti. and yelde me to god al myhti. And to his blessed moder marie. And to al þe cumpany of heuen. And to þe my gostly fader here in godes stude. Of al þe sinnes þat I haue greueslyche trespassed and synged in. from þe tyme þat I was bore in to þis day. (fol. 3ʳ)

In the presence of God, the penitent and the confessor share the revelation of the penitent's sinful inner state, a burden to be yielded up in trust. The term 'knowleche', as an active admission, the outward expression of a hidden inner landscape of sin, dominates the opening section of this confession (fols 3ʳ–5ʳ). The verb is repeated twice in claiming guilt and again repeated each time one of the seven deadly sins is confessed, being used to sum up the list of possible ways in which the sin might have been committed and to reaffirm the penitent's claim of guilt.[15] In employing the verb 'knowlechen' to signal the beginning of oral confession, this opening formula conforms to a typical confessional pattern.[16]

---

edition, for which the relevant page numbers are indicated above. The use of italics indicates expanded abbreviations.

[14] This form of confession is also included in the Vernon manuscript and is printed in *Yorkshire Writers*, ed. by Horstman, II, 340–45.

[15] See *A Worcestershire Miscellany*, ed. by Baugh, pp. 87–95, ll. 5, 14, 21, 22, 29, 38, 48–49, 57, 66, and 86. See also the final line of each paragraph of the confession in *Yorkshire Writers*, ed. by Horstman, II, 340–41.

[16] For examples, see 'I knoweliche to the god ful of mighte', a form of confession included in

This confession, like others, is structured in order to consider sin from several different angles, first examining the ways in which the penitent 'I' has committed the seven deadly sins, before considering the breaking of each of the Ten Commandments, the failure to carry out the seven works of mercy, and finally the involvement of the five senses in the commission of sin. The phrase 'I knowleche me' alternates with 'I ȝelde me' and 'I crie god merci', the prayer setting up a dynamic pattern based on the opening addresses of each line, shifting from the essential acknowledgement of sin through to the offering up of the helpless self to God's mercy ('I ȝelde') and the emotional plea for that mercy ('I crie'). By working systematically through the seven deadly sins, the Ten Commandments, the seven works of mercy, the five senses, and the Ten Commandments yet again, the form of confession given prominence as the opening text in BL, MS Add. 37787 also acts as a summary of *pastoralia* devoted to teaching these basic tenets of faith.[17] That the confession is itself a compilation is made clear by the compiler's *explicit*, which explains that the sins are not expected to be confessed in their totality, but have been compiled so that the penitent knows what ought to be confessed: 'Hec co*n*fessio p*re*scripta compilat*ur* no*n* ut q*u*ilibet ea*m* tota*m* dicat. S*ed* ut ea i*n* q*u*ib*u*s se reu*m* esse congnoscit co*n*fiteat*ur*' (This prescribed confession is compiled not in order that anyone should say it all, but so that he knows, from what is to be confessed, those sins of which he is guilty) (fol. 11ᵛ).

This form of confession displays both didactic aims appropriate to a confessor and features which tend towards the personal use of one undertaking the examination of the self necessary before confessing. The penitent who follows its guidance through a consideration of each of the seven deadly sins with which the form of confession begins will admit to failing to love God wholeheartedly, coveting fair women, and not praying for parents often enough. Divine mercy is also requested for a failure to keep holy days well by attending church to hear Mass and matins, among other transgressions:

---

the fifteenth-century London, Lambeth Palace Library, MS 559 (*DIMEV* 2207) and the opening lines, added in the fifteenth-century to a form of confession contained in the Bolton Hours, 'I knawe me gilty to God almyghty', in *Women's Books of Hours in Medieval England*, trans. by Scott-Stokes.

[17] In his unpublished doctoral dissertation, Michael E. Cornett has collected, catalogued, and analysed the form of confession as a genre. This feature of the genre is discussed in his second chapter. See Cornett, 'The Form of Confession', pp. 121–23.

Also I cry god mercy þat I haue not holden my haly dayes as I shulde do. I*n* goying to cherche. to here masse *and* matens. I prey god of forȝeuenes þ*at* on þe Sonday *and* on halidayes. I goo raþer to tau*er*ne *and* to ale houses fyhtynge flitting *and* backebiti*ng* my euen cristen. (fol. 5ᵛ)

Given that the presumed first owner of the miscellany was a Cistercian monk, certain of the acts potentially committed, including the failure to keep holy days well by attending church to hear Mass and matins and instead indulging the temptation to visit taverns, would perhaps seem less applicable to his personal use. Other sins to be confessed, such as not taking delight in preaching, are more evidently intended for the professed religious (fol. 4ʳ). Cistercians, like other regular clergy, had traditionally engaged in public confession, rather than private, as Henry Lea discusses.[18] In his study of the form of confession as a genre, however, Michael E. Cornett argues that late medieval regular clergy were required like other western Christians to engage in the annual confession stipulated by the reforms of Lateran IV.[19] Rebecca Farnham, on the other hand, suggests that the inclusion of sins which professed religious would have less opportunity to commit points to members of the laity as the form of confession's intended penitents.[20]

The rhetorical structure of the third part of the confession sets out a catechetical role for the confessor alongside the knowledge required by the penitent. Its paired questions and answers make evident its instructional aim. The imagined penitent is asked: 'How many comaundeme*ns* ben þer'; the response, 'ten', which is provided, is immediately followed with a further question: 'Wich ten' (fol. 7ʳ). Questions testing the penitent's knowledge concerning such details are followed in the text by the required answers, given in sentences using first-person pronouns. Thus the correct response to the question, 'Which ten?' begins 'God comau*n*deþ me to loue hi*m*. wiþ al my herte' (fol. 7ʳ). The instructional nature of this section of the confession points to its preservation for use by a confessor, rather than solely by a penitent. Openness and self-revelation on the

---

[18] Lea offers some evidence to support a change in monastic culture regarding confession, writing that by the late thirteenth century some Cistercian monks were making confession to their abbots in addition to continuing the practice of public confession to their brother religious. See Lea, *A History of Auricular Confession*, p. 201.

[19] Cornett, 'The Form of Confession', pp. 86–87, n. 87.

[20] Farnham argues that the two clusters of vernacular materials contained in the miscellany each represent a 'reading programme' intended for the use of Bordesley's corrodians, members of the laity possessing the right of residency and maintenance at the abbey in return for a grant of land. See Farnham, 'Producers and Readers', pp. 120–27.

part of the penitent underlies this text, although the exact method in which it was intended to be used in this particular context cannot be discerned from the manuscript alone. Whether the intended user might have been expected sometimes to fulfil the role of confessor and, at other times, the penitent, as seems likely from the evidence of its structure and content, or whether the text served as a manual of instruction for members of the laity, the comprehensive nature of the form of confession encourages both the development of a body of pastoral knowledge and also a thorough examination of the self.

The second vernacular cluster demonstrates a similar mingling of didactic and devotional materials as the first collection of English texts. All but one of these texts is shared with the Vernon manuscript, the single exception being a prayer of three petitions, written in tail-rhyme verse.[21] The importance of this prayer to the compiler is marked by its rubric: 'Incipit or*aci*o optima ad patre*m* et filiu*m* & spi*ritum* s*an*ctum. In qua continentur tres peticiones oportunitati a*nim*e maxime necessarie' (Here begins an excellent prayer to the Father and to the Son and to the Holy Spirit, in which is contained three petitions for an opportunity especially useful to the soul) (fol. 142ʳ). The designation *oracio optima* is otherwise reserved in this manuscript for prayers in Latin.[22] This prayer, titled the 'Prayer for the Three Boons' in *A Worcestershire Miscellany*, draws upon the fruits of self-examination through knowledge of sin and of the senses which participate in sin, pouring out pleas for mercy, for space and time to amend, and finally for salvation. In this prayer, sin and the person are carefully separated in order to allow a closer relationship between the Trinity and the supplicant:

>   Fader & sone & holygost,
>   To þe I clepe & calle most.
>   O god in trynyte.
>   To þe lord, I clepe & calle.
>   5   Ffor me synful, my frynd*us* alle.
>   Þ*o*u gra*u*nt me bon*us* þre.
>
>   My furst bo*n* þus I bygynne.

---

[21] The scribe has set the tail rhymes in the margins, with exceptions at the ends of the first and second stanzas, where the tail rhymes have been written in the verse column. The marking of stanza breaks is irregular.

[22] Some of these Latin prayers have subsequently been removed from the manuscript, such as the prayer to Saint Edmund (an 'oracio optima') which originally followed its rubric on fol. 49ᵛ.

> Haue mercy lord on my synne.
> Þat I haue don seþ I was born.
> 10 Wyt word, wyt wille, wyt herte þou3t.
> Wyt flesch wyt blod wyt hondes wrou3t
> Wyt mouþ spoken and þe forsworn
>
> In my 3ouþe & in my welde
> Mou3t I not my wyttes helde.
> 15 To synne þei were redy.
> Hedy þei were to don ful ille.
> Slou3 to worchen lord þy wille.
> I cri þe ihesu mercy.
>
> Don I haue synnes seuene.
> 20 Þat wolde reue me þe blis of heuene.
> And broken þe x commaundemens.
> Alle my synne I wol forsake.
> And to þe I wol me take.
> So don amendemens.
>
>   (fol. 142ʳ⁻ᵛ, ll. 1–24)

The prayer draws upon the self-knowledge promoted by such *pastoralia* as the instructive texts contained in the following folios, accounting for the role played by the senses and the active will of the supplicant in committing sin.

Yet the prayer also displays a determined separation of the person, the sinner, from the acts, or the sins. The fifth line brings the two together, pairing the supplicant with the designation 'synful', the only instance in the prayer where the speaker is characterized with an adjective. Yet the juxtaposition of 'me synful' is awkward, implying a slight pause after the pronoun, with the awkwardness increased by the stress falling on both syllables, 'me' and 'syn'. In the eighth line, mercy is asked on the sins themselves, rather than on the sinner. And as intimate as 'flesh', 'blood', 'hands', and 'mouth' are, these are presented as distinct from the self, each a medium through which the will acts (ll. 11–12). The supplicant 'I' has been unable to restrain the 'wits', which have been ever ready to engage in sin (ll. 13–16). In lines 8 and 18, this same 'I' pleads mercy and promises afterwards to forsake sin (ll. 22–24). In its structure and its language, the prayer presents a self at odds with, and at a remove from, the sins which the 'I' promises to forsake.

The second request features the concern with unshriven death expressed elsewhere in the manuscript, asking for strength and time to repent:

>   Myn oþer bone & my askyng.
>   Þat I þe biseche heuene kyng.
>   Þat I mot haue grace.
>   Þat I mot my synnus leeten.
> 35   Er deþ and I to geder meeten.
>   Lord sende me my3t and space.
>   (fol. 142ᵛ, ll. 31–36)

The voice of the supplicant becomes insistently self-referential here, with 'I' repeated in four sequential lines, finally varying from the repetitive formulation 'Þat I' to look towards the speaker's inevitable meeting with death. Such a focus on the self contrasts strikingly with those petitions which position Christ as the active subject and the supplicant as the recipient of grace, the typical grammatical relationship between Christ and the supplicant evident in line 36. The focus of this stanza begins on the penitent self before turning in its final line to the one whose aid is sought.

The third, and final, petition of the prayer asks the supplicant's safe arrival in heaven:

>   My þridde bone to þe I pray.
>   þat I mot to heuene þat riht way.
>   To blis on my deþ day.
>   Wel I wot my lif haþ ende.
> 65   When I schal out of þis world wende.
>   þat tyme witen I ne may.
>
>   Þerfore Ihesu þou graunt a þrowe.
>   Þat I mot my self i-knowe.
>   Clene me to schryue.
> 70   Of prestes hond houseled to be.
>   Bifore my deþ þou graunt hit me.
>   Ffor þi wondes fyue.
>   (fols 142ᵛ–143ʳ, ll. 61–72)

Here the prayer turns to the vital necessity of space and time for confession and for the penitent to be 'houseled', that is, to receive the consecrated host from a priest, before the moment of death. This gift asked from God corresponds to the object of the many late medieval protectionary prayers concerned with the moment of death, as well as instances where prayer rubrics promise that daily recital of a specific prayer will prevent an unshriven death.²³ Being shriven is essential in order to receive salvation and arrive by 'þat riht way | to blis'. Elsewhere the manuscript evinces concern with the possibility of unshriven death, as, for example, in the rubric to a list of angel's names, which promises: 'That day þat ʒe neomyth þes angel*es* namys ʒe schal not dye wi*th*ouʒte co*n*fessyon' (fol. 171ᵛ).

This prayer for the 'three boons' contains a striking difference to the only other known version of the prayer, edited in Carleton Brown's *Religious Lyrics of the XIVth Century* from a late fourteenth-century East Anglian book of hours.²⁴ The two versions of this prayer have a number of minor differences, which Baugh attributes to sharing a partially illegible parent text.²⁵ Her hypothesis is supported by the lack of a discernible thematic pattern to the discrepancies between the two. However, the prayer contained in BL, MS Add. 37787 differs from the version printed by Brown in one significant respect at the point where the supplicant requests time to confess. Whereas the prayer printed in *Religious Lyrics of the XIVth Century* asks 'þat i mowe my sinnes knawe', line 68 of the compiler's 'oracio optima' in BL, MS Add. 37787 asks 'þat I mot my self i-knowe'.²⁶ In the context of a miscellany which displays some interest in the idea of self-knowledge, the use of the word 'self' where 'sins' would be equally appropriate is potentially significant. Indeed, a closer look at the request for the third boon shows that confession itself is conceived as taking part in three acts: to know oneself, to 'shrive' oneself by partaking in the sacrament of confession, and to receive the consecrated host, in being 'houseled'.²⁷ Although the aim of the first of these acts is to begin the process which will allow the penitent to partake of salvation, the separation of 'knowing' the self from orally 'acknowledging' one's sins has taken place in these lines. Each of the two clusters of vernacular texts yields evidence of some interest in the encouragement of interiority, especially through the requirements and practice of confession.

---

²³ Marian prayers, for instance, often ask for mercy at the hour of death. Besides the Ave Maria, see 'O Maria piissima' for a good example of this theme: 'O Maria piissima', Malling Abbey Hours, Bodl. Lib., MS Gough liturg. 9, fols 233ᵛ–234ʳ, in *Women's Books of Hours in Medieval England*, trans. by Scott-Stokes, p. 104.

²⁴ The version printed by Carleton Brown is contained in Bodl. Lib., MS Rawlinson liturgical g. 2. Baugh comments on the unique nature of the 'Prayer for the Three Boons': 'The idea behind the poem seems not to have had a wide circulation, for I have not come across the idea either in verse or prose, English or Latin'. See *A Worcestershire Miscellany*, ed. by Baugh, p. 61.

²⁵ *A Worcestershire Miscellany*, ed. by Baugh, pp. 60–61.

²⁶ Compare 'A Prayer for Three Boons', ed. by Brown, pp. 219–22, l. 68.

²⁷ BL, MS Add. 37787, ll. 68–70.

'Knowlechen': From Oral Confession to the Inward Knowing of Oneself

The argument proposing the development of the medieval 'self' through the practice of confession has been set forth by John F. Benton and Katherine C. Little, among others. Writing of the modes of self-examination available to twelfth-century members of European societies, Benton focuses on the emphasis placed by penitential literature on the concept of intention. Intention, he argues, separates the conscious self and its desires from those acts which the self undertakes.[28] Little explores the role of confession in greater detail, especially its provision of a language of subjectivity.[29] She discusses the development of self-knowledge through confession in terms of coming to know oneself by the sins one commits, her argument drawing especially upon the language of pastoral instruction in the *Lay Folks' Catechism* and the penitential guidance of *Fasciculus morum*. By questioning whether one is plagued by, or drawn into, a particular sin, one comes to define oneself in its terms. Giving the example of penitential questioning on a propensity to engage in backbiting, Little writes, 'In either case, the subject is produced in relation to the language offered by the priest (or this text) as he or she "appropriates" the identity to him- or herself and defines the self in relation to "backbiting"'.[30] The confessing person, she argues, asks, 'Am I therefore, a backbiter?'.[31] Yet the evidence of Northewode's miscellany implies that the self and the sin are not interchangeable; the self is not defined by the sin. Rather than identifying as a backbiter, the supplicant envisaged in the 'Prayer for the Three Boons' might instead ask, 'How have I participated in back-biting?'.

By fulfilling the instructive aims of its *pastoralia*, in combination with the spiritual self-examination required of confession, a vernacular form of con-

---

[28] Benton, 'Consciousness of Self and Perceptions of Individuality', pp. 272–73.

[29] See Little, *Confession and Resistance*, p. 7. The particularly Cistercian contribution to the development of interiority, especially as a site in which to encounter God, but also as a focus on the self as individual, has been discussed by Ruth Smith. See Smith, 'Cistercian and Victorine Approaches to Contemplation'. For further exploration of medieval selfhood, see also Denis Renevey's work on self-fashioning in the commentary tradition in his *Language, Self and Love*. Peter Biller offers a general treatment of the issues surrounding confession in the Middle Ages; see his 'Confession in the Middle Ages'. For an alternate view, based on the incompatibility of prescribed categories of sins with the idea of the individual, see Arlinghaus, 'Conceptualising Pre-Modern and Modern Individuality', pp. 10–12.

[30] Little, *Confession and Resistance*, p. 7.

[31] Little, *Confession and Resistance*, p. 7.

fession, such as the text with which BL, MS Add. 37787 begins, provides an accessible framework for the development of self-knowledge. Little views such instructional texts as 'offering a number of different discourses for shaping the self'.[32] This formation, taking place through the interaction of the lay person with the instructional elements of *pastoralia*, envisages a self in outward relation to community as well as inward relation to its own interior. Little also emphasizes the importance of *pastoralia* in positing an ideal self in addition to fostering awareness of the existing self.[33] Instructional texts, she writes, teach penitents a discourse vital to the exploration of identity:

> We should think of the sins, as well as the other pastoral formulas, as a capacious psychological language given to penitents by the priest to think about their identity, identity understood both as an inner self and as a self in relation to the larger Christian community.[34]

Language shapes the identity, offering tools with which penitents can begin to understand themselves and also to explain themselves to a confessor.

In Middle English, the language of confession also works through a fluidity of expression which does not always distinguish between inner knowledge, perception, oral production, active subject, and passive recipient, all meanings which can be related through the verb, 'knouen'. BL, MS Add. 37787 preserves at least three differing forms related to the Middle English verb 'knouen', including 'knowleche', 'beknowen', and 'i-knowe'. 'Knowleche', an insistent presence in the form of confession, with its repeated formula, 'I knowleche me gulti', equates to 'acknowledge'. 'Knowleche', in this sense, means publically to own up to those aspects of one's behaviour which are transgressive, illegal, sinful, or shameful — all in order to be forgiven, thus maintaining the status of a communicant and gaining some protection from suffering after death.[35] In confession, the inner state is expressed outwardly to another person. 'Beknouen' also appears in the manuscript's first form of confession, marking the shift to the instructional section interrogating the penitent's understanding of the

---

[32] Little, *Confession and Resistance*, p. 7.

[33] Little, *Confession and Resistance*, p. 6.

[34] Little, *Confession and Resistance*, p. 53.

[35] Many of the senses listed in the *Middle English Dictionary* for 'knoulechen' share this element of knowledge transmitted beyond a single individual, including senses 1–5: to find out, to become familiar, to recognize; to make known, to declare, to say/speak/tell; to acknowledge, confess, or admit; to profess; to acknowledge a fact about another person. The senses offered for 'beknouen' and 'iknouen' are, predictably, almost identical.

deadly sins: 'When is a man proude. When he wol not beknowen suche as he is' (fol. 9ʳ). Pride, the penitent must be aware, this deadliest of all deadly sins, as well as the father and source of all other sins, results when a man will not 'beknowen' himself. This form of the verb draws subject and object together: the penitent undertakes the effort to become aware, to recognize, to know, and the focus of this activity is himself, exactly as he is. The English verb 'knouen' encompasses the meanings of the Latin 'noscere' and 'cognoscere', while also being pressed into service as 'confiteri'.[36] The fluidity of meaning possible when a single term must be employed to convey several different, albeit related, concepts plays a role in the conflation in Middle English between confessing sins and developing inner awareness.

The development of self-knowledge in John Northewode's prayer book is inextricably linked with confession, and because the texts with which the penitent may explore the self in order to prepare a confession are written in the English vernacular, the link between knowledge of self and the use of the vernacular is in itself unremarkable.[37] Yet an analysis of the 'Prayer for the Three Boons' suggests more than this simple connection. As instruction is best accomplished through the vernacular, so too is the most intimate of tasks, coming to know oneself, achieved through the medium of the mother tongue. The process of developing self-knowledge depends not merely on knowing oneself to be a sinner, and thus identifying the self with the sin, but, more importantly, on knowing oneself to be apart from one's sins. Conversely, refusing to engage in this process, choosing not to know oneself, might indeed lead to being identified with the sin: 'When is a man proude? When he wol not beknowen suche as he is' (fol. 9ʳ). The compiler's decision to place the vernacular form of confession and other material at the front of the miscellany, the scribal designation of the 'oracio optima' for the opening prayer of the second vernacular cluster, and the language of self-knowledge evident in the manuscript indicate the importance of nourishing interiority to the first users and owners of this book.

---

[36] 'Knouen' in each of its forms derives from the Old English 'cnāwan', defined in T. Northcote Toller's Supplement to Bosworth's Anglo-Saxon dictionary according to the two Latin terms 'noscere' and 'cognoscere'. See the entry for 'cnāwan', Toller and Bosworth, *An Anglo-Saxon Dictionary: Supplement*.

[37] Following Archbishop Pecham's Lambeth Constitutions of 1281, many texts aimed at the instruction of the laity were written in English.

Works Cited

Manuscripts

London, British Library [BL], MS Additional 37787
London, Lambeth Palace Library, MS 559
Oxford, Bodleian Library [Bodl. Lib.], MS Eng. poet. a. 1
Oxford, Bodleian Library [Bodl. Lib.], MS Gough liturg. 9
Oxford, Bodleian Library [Bodl. Lib.], MS Rawlinson liturgical g. 2

Primary Sources

The Minor Poems of the Vernon Manuscript, ed. by Carl Horstman and F. J. Furnivall, Early English Text Society, o.s., 98 and 117, 2 vols (London: Kegan Paul, Trench, Trübner, 1892–1901)
'A Prayer for Three Boons', in *Religious Lyrics of the XIVth Century*, ed. by Carleton Brown (Oxford: Clarendon Press, 1924), pp. 219–22
Women's Books of Hours in Medieval England: Selected Texts Translated from Latin, Anglo-Norman French and Middle English with Introduction and Interpretive Essay, trans. by Charity Scott-Stokes (Cambridge: D. S. Brewer, 2006)
A Worcestershire Miscellany, Compiled by John Northwood, c. 1400, Edited from British Museum MS. ADD. 37,787, ed. by Nita Scudder Baugh (Philadelphia: privately published, 1956)
Yorkshire Writers: Richard Rolle of Hampole, an English Father of the Church, and his Followers, ed. by Carl Horstman, 2 vols (London: Swan Sonnenschein, 1895–96)

Secondary Works

Arlinghaus, Franz-Josef, 'Conceptualising Pre-Modern and Modern Individuality: Some Theoretical Considerations', in *Forms of Individuality and Literacy in the Medieval and Early Modern Periods*, ed. by Franz-Josef Arlinghaus, Utrecht Studies in Medieval Literacy, 31 (Turnhout: Brepols, 2015), pp. 1–46
Benton, John F., 'Consciousness of Self and Perceptions of Individuality', in *Renaissance and Renewal in the Twelfth Century*, ed. by Robert L. Benson, Giles Constable, and Carol D. Lanham (Oxford: Clarendon Press, 1982), pp. 263–95
Biller, Peter, 'Confession in the Middle Ages: Introduction', in *Handling Sin: Confession in the Middle Ages*, ed. by Peter Biller and A. J. Minnis (Woodbridge: York Medieval Press, 1998), pp. 1–33
Catalogue of Additions to the Manuscripts in the British Museum in the Year MDCCCCVI–MDCCCCX (London: British Museum, 1912)
Connolly, Margaret, 'Understanding the Medieval Miscellany', in *Insular Books: Vernacular Manuscript Miscellanies in Late Medieval Britain*, ed. by Margaret Connolly and

Raluca Radulescu, Proceedings of the British Academy, 201 (Oxford: Oxford University Press for the British Academy, 2015), pp. 3–15

Cornett, Michael E., 'The Form of Confession: A Later Medieval Genre for Examining Conscience' (unpublished doctoral dissertation, University of North Carolina at Chapel Hill, 2011)

Farnham, Rebecca Michelle, 'The Producers and Readers of London, British Library, Additional MS 37787' (unpublished doctoral thesis, University of Birmingham, 2002)

Lea, Henry Charles, *A History of Auricular Confession and Indulgences in the Latin Churches* (Philadelphia: Lea Brothers, 1896)

Little, Katherine C., *Confession and Resistance: Defining the Self in Late Medieval England* (Notre Dame: University of Notre Dame Press, 2006)

Renevey, Denis, *Language, Self and Love: Hermeneutics in the Writings of Richard Rolle and the Commentaries on the Song of Songs* (Cardiff: University of Wales Press, 2001)

Scahill, John, 'Trilingualism in Early English Miscellanies: Languages and Literature', *Yearbook of English Studies*, 33 (2003), 18–32

Scase, Wendy, 'John Northwood's Miscellany Revisited', in *Insular Books: Vernacular Manuscript Miscellanies in Late Medieval Britain*, ed. by Margaret Connolly and Raluca Radulescu, Proceedings of the British Academy, 201 (Oxford: Oxford University Press for the British Academy, 2015), pp. 101–20

Smith, Ruth, 'Cistercian and Victorine Approaches to Contemplation: Understandings of Self in *A Rule of Life for a Recluse* and *The Twelve Patriarchs*', in *The Medieval Mystical Tradition in England, Ireland and Wales: Exeter Symposium VI*, ed. by Marion Glasscoe (Cambridge: D. S. Brewer, 1999), pp. 47–65

Toller, T. Northcote, and Joseph Bosworth, *An Anglo-Saxon Dictionary: Based on the Manuscript Collections of the Late Joseph Bosworth: Supplement* (Oxford: Clarendon Press, 1921)

Online Publications

Bodleian Library, University of Oxford, 'MS. Eng. poet. a. 1', *Medieval Manuscripts in Oxford Libraries*, <https://medieval.bodleian.ox.ac.uk/catalog/manuscript_4817> [accessed 18 May 2018]

The DIMEV: An Open-Access, Digital Edition of the 'Index of Middle English Verse', comp. by Linne R. Mooney, Daniel W. Mosser, and Elizabeth Solopova, <http://www.dimev.net> [accessed 18 May 2018]

Middle English Dictionary, ed. by Robert E. Lewis and others (Ann Arbor: University of Michigan Press, 1952–2001); online edition in *Middle English Compendium*, ed. by Frances McSparran and others (Ann Arbor: University of Michigan Library, 2000–18), <http://quod.lib.umich.edu/m/middle-english-dictionary>

Resignation or Rebuttal? Three Biblical *Exempla* in Richard Whitford's *Dyuers Holy Instrucyons and Teachynges*

Brandon Alakas

Following the turbulent years of Henry VIII's break from Rome, initial reform of the English Church, and dissolution of the monasteries — years which witnessed the dispossession of hundreds of religious as well as the execution of individuals who refused to accept royal supremacy — Richard Whitford's *Dyuers Holy Instrucyons and Teachynges Very Necessary for the Helth of Mannes Soule* was printed in London by William Middleton in 1541. Several details concerning the work's publication history attest to its distinctiveness. *Holy Instrucyons* is the last printed text written by a brother of the Birgittine community at Syon Abbey. *Holy Instrucyons* is also the first printed work to appear with a clear association to Syon after the dispersal of the community in 1539 and the first new text produced by one of the brothers since the martyrdom of Richard Reynolds, the only Birgittine executed for denying the supremacy in 1535.[1] At first glance, Whitford's anthology of four texts for Birgittine sisters and devout laity, which are bound by loose thematic linkages that remain implicit, seems nostalgic and even out of step with the times, especially as the

---

[1] Prior to the *Dyuers Holy Instrucyons*, the most recent Syon text to have been printed was Whitford's *A Daily Exercise of Death* and John Fewterer's *Mirror or Glass of Christ's Passion*, both of which were first issued in 1534. Of Whitford's several printed works, the last to be reissued were the *Preparation for Communion*, *A Work for Householders* — both in 1537 — and, finally, *A Daily Exercise of Death* in 1538.

Brandon Alakas (alakas@ualberta.ca) is Assistant Professor of English at the University of Alberta.

greater monasteries had all been dissolved two years previously.² Nevertheless, the decision to have *Holy Instrucyons* printed at this particular moment cannot be overlooked as it informs the way each text in the anthology would have been read and, moreover, bears witness to the continuously shifting contours of the reformed faith in England at the outset of the 1540s. Richard Whitford's *Holy Instrucyons* targets readers who had always sought printed texts associated with Syon; however, by 1541 the religious climate in England had changed, and this audience had become a beleaguered community. Whitford's pastoral guidance now provided direction on navigating changes in society and advice on coping with situations which would hitherto have been thought impossible.

An anthology of four texts ranging in length from twenty chapters to a short 'draught' of several hundred words,³ *Holy Instrucyons* contains two general prefaces, the *Boke of Pacience* (fols 1ʳ–48ᵛ), *A Worke of Dyuers Impediments and Lettes of Perfection* (fols 49ʳ–65ᵛ), a translation of the counsels of Saint Isidore based on the *Monita* or *Consilia Isadori* (fols 66ʳ–85ᵛ), and an excerpt from a sermon 'On Detraction' based on a translation of John Chrysostom (fols 86ʳ–90ᵛ). Although composed at different points during a twenty-year period beginning around 1516, all are thematically linked as each text reiterates appeals to abandon worldly concerns and anxieties and accept with patience and sanguinity the deprivations life brings. However, despite these works being associated by broad themes, the publication date of *Holy Instrucyons* raises several questions about its purpose as well as the specific events which led to its going to press. Mary C. Erler refers to Whitford's anthology as a text 'full of surprises' for the many ways it gives evidence of continuity — whether it be suggestions regarding the continuation of communal life or the author's recurring anxieties expressed in earlier works over anonymous publication.⁴ Her recent discussion further suggests a possible single identity for the anonymous Syon brother(s) to whom Whitford refers in the prefaces to three works in the anthology as urging

---

² In using the term 'anthology' to describe Whitford's volume, I follow Margaret Connolly's definition of the term as 'a collection of texts within which some organising principles can be observed' in Connolly, 'Understanding the Medieval Miscellany', p. 5. This usage departs from Erler's use of the term 'compilation' to describe the 'successful formula of presentation' Whitford or his publishers adopted in bringing together 'a group of several texts, more or less closely related'. See Erler, *Reading and Writing during the Dissolution*, p. 141. My reluctance to use the term 'compilation', however, stems from a reticence about overstressing the thematic unity of Whitford's volume.

³ Whitford describes his translation of Chrysostom's sermon as a 'draught' in the short preface which precedes it on fol. 86ʳ.

⁴ Erler, *Reading and Writing during the Dissolution*, p. 129, p. 132.

him to translate material: John Massey, a lay brother at Syon and contemporary of Whitford.[5] Yet, despite the unity implied by this person's conviction to see these works printed, Erler cautions against overstating any thematic linkages that bind the four texts as well as inferring any connection to the historical moment out of which they emerged. Erler also downplays Whitford's role as compiler by shifting emphasis instead onto Massey, who, she argues, 'both provided Whitford with new material and pointed out thematic correspondences between [his] older work and his current projects'.[6] Finally, Erler assumes a similar detachment on the part of Whitford when she states that *Pacience*, the first text in this collection, 'seems not to reflect the turbulence of the 1530s in which Syon was involved: the executions of Elizabeth Barton, Thomas More and John Fisher, the Carthusians, and Richard Reynolds, in 1534/5'.[7]

Certainly nothing in this anthology responds explicitly to events that occurred between 1534 and 1535 or to the subsequent efforts to have the Birgittines accept royal supremacy or surrender Syon. Yet, while Erler suggests that Whitford's final work demonstrates 'the continuation of some form of community life',[8] I suggest that *Dyuers Holy Instrucyons* is very much a work produced for religious and devout laypeople living in a post-Reformation England. The pastoral guidance Whitford provides throughout this anthology speaks to the needs of an audience with a strong attachment to religious life. And, taken together, the four texts in the collection, which he explicitly identifies as his own works chosen for this anthology,[9] all seek to bolster the resolve of a belea-

---

[5] In the prefaces to *A Worke of Dyuers Impediments* (fol. 49ʳ), the pseudo-Isidorian *Consilia* (fol. 66ʳ), and his sermon 'On Detraction' (fol. 86ʳ), Whitford recalls that each text was undertaken at the request of one of his Syon brothers. Erler assumes a single identity for the brother to whom Whitford alludes within the anthology and proposes John Massey as the most likely candidate. See Erler, *Reading and Writing during the Dissolution*, p. 139.

[6] Erler, *Reading and Writing during the Dissolution*, p. 132.

[7] Erler, *Reading and Writing during the Dissolution*, p. 134.

[8] Erler, *Reading and Writing during the Dissolution*, p. 132.

[9] Whitford, *Dyuers Holy Instrucyons*, sig. A. 1ᵛ. Locating any concrete evidence that Whitford himself carefully chose this specific group of texts for his anthology and then saw them through to press is difficult; however, Whitford's insistence on identifying himself as the author of the four works gathered together in *Dyuers Holy Instrucyons* suggests an involvement with its publication. Whitford's concern over 'fatherles bokes' (sig. A. 2ʳ) — anonymous texts written by Lutherans — is identified as the chief motivation for his carefully setting out details about the authorship and content of the work: 'I am compelled not onely to set forth my name, but also to ioyne therunto this catalogue and wryttynge of the contentes (by nomber) of this volume. And that I do: charitably to gyue you warnyng to serche well / and surely that none

guered readership while counselling them to avoid apostasy: a difficult task in 1541. Nevertheless, Whitford's anthology accomplishes this work by providing programmatic advice for maintaining one's Catholic faith while avoiding behaviours that would draw undue attention from spiritual (and political) authorities. As a whole, the guidance offered in *Dyuers Holy Instrucyons*, which reinforces tacit connections between each of the four texts in the anthology, consists largely of the following: be patient, do not speak ill of people, do not complain, and do not quarrel. Wise advice for Catholics seeking to weather what they prayed would be a short-term rift with Rome.

Unsurprisingly, each work in *Dyuers Holy Instrucyons* is densely laced with biblical citations and allusions; however, what is remarkable in Whitford's use of biblical texts is the way in which many may be read as responding directly to the recent trauma of dissolution and dispossession. Although Whitford's strategy for engaging with these concerns is to encode his discourse within superficially generic pastoral guidance, his careful use of biblical *exempla* provides tacit commentary on changes religious life had undergone in the last decade. In this context, his references to three Old Testament figures in the *Boke of Pacience* — Job, Susanna, and Naboth the Jezreelite — are especially resonant. Whitford's use of each narrative, which focuses either on material deprivation or false accusation against one's personal and spiritual integrity, evokes the process of dissolution. Furthermore, each narrative seeks to rally the spirits of a despondent and bewildered readership by tacitly inviting audiences to slot their contemporary experiences — for which no precedent existed — into familiar narrative paradigms which render comprehensible the rejection of Catholicism in England.

Of course, even to read the Bible in this way suggests a distinctively Catholic hermeneutic eschewed — ostensibly, at least — by radical reformers. To be sure, Whitford's use of the traditional fourfold approach to biblical interpretation runs throughout this anthology as he explicitly reads these narratives anagogically — that is, as pertaining to heavenly things such as the soul.[10] Job, for example, is

---

suche other workes, be put amonge them: that myght deceyue you'. See Whitford, *Dyuers Holy Instrucyons*, sig. A. 1ᵛ.

[10] The traditional fourfold manner of biblical reading consists of first a literal reading, which focuses on events in the narrative, second a typological reading, which draws connections between the Old and New Testaments, third a tropological reading, which interprets the text ethically, and fourth an anagogical reading, which focuses on the mystical or spiritual sense of the text. For an overview of the traditional manner of biblical interpretation, see Van Lier, 'Biblical Exegesis'.

described by Whitford as 'but a figure of the most excellent and chefe champion, the prynce of pacience, and the very selfe essenciall pacience'.[11] In other words, he is interpreted *allegorically*, as a type of Christ and as the virtue itself. Although Whitford is often explicit in directing readers towards such interpretations, he remains cautiously silent in pointing readers towards a moral, or tropological, reading of these biblical narratives.[12] This latter type of reading often links the biblical narrative to the lives of contemporaries which serve as models to be upheld or avoided by the community, and in this way they bestow a certain immediacy on the interpretation.[13] As Beryl Smalley pithily notes, such readings 'hold a mirror' to the present.[14]

Although polemical interpretations grounded in a moral reading of scripture crossed confessional lines, evangelicals remained ambivalent towards allegorical interpretation. Uneasiness about traditional multilevel exegesis is conveyed by William Tyndale. For him, such reading strategies have the potential to lead readers away from an understanding of the text rooted in the literal sense: 'beware of allegories, for there is not a more hansome or apt a thyng to bigyle wythall than an allegory'.[15] Whitford, however, forcefully positions his work against evangelical insistence on the literal, and his overt use of allegory accomplishes three tasks: first, his use of such interpretive strategies reinscribes a traditionally Catholic biblical hermeneutic; also, they align the text with the state of religious life in 1541; and finally, these same strategies simultaneously advance a number of polemical and theological aims that underwrite Catholic Christianity in England.

Whitford's multiple references to and citations of Job reinforce the virtue of forbearance in the face of dispossession.[16] His citing on several occasions the penultimate verse of the first chapter of that text — in Latin and English — sets the tone for much of what follows:

---

[11] Whitford, *Dyuers Holy Instrucyons*, fol. 35ʳ. A comprehensive discussion of anagogy is found in De Lubac, *Medieval Exegesis*, II, 179–226.

[12] A fulsome account of tropological exegesis may be found again in De Lubac, *Medieval Exegesis*, II, 127–77.

[13] Mayeski, 'Early Medieval Exegesis', esp. p. 92.

[14] Smalley, *Study of the Bible*, p. 245.

[15] Tyndale, *The Byble*, fol. 41ᵛ. Noting Tyndale's use of allegory — despite his disavowal of traditional exegesis — James Simpson comments on the reformer's conflicted relationship with traditional fourfold reading. See Simpson, *Burning to Read*, pp. 111–17, pp. 211–21.

[16] Direct references to Job abound throughout *Holy Instrucyons* as the anthology contains a total of twenty-one to the Old Testament figure.

Dominus dedit, dominus abstulit. Sicut domino placuit, ita factus est, sit nomen domini benedictus [...] Our lorde hath gyuen us all, and our lorde hath taken hyt a way, As it hathe pleased our lorde. So be it. Blessed be euer the name of god.[17]

Material deprivation, according to Whitford, must be accepted with resignation, even if the mind is 'troubled and gruged therwith'.[18] Such guidance, encoded within more general advice to accept misfortune, is consonant with the almost quietest position that he adopts in the general preface. From the outset of the text, Whitford positions himself as a defender of 'the kynges honour' against the 'worke of the archeheretyke Luter' and defers to regal authority — Henry VIII's 'noble worke' (the *Assertio septem sacramentorum*) that 'condempned [Luther] for an heretyke' — while himself simultaneously attacking the reformer's writing as 'poyson [...] couered with sugar'.[19] Whether out of prudence or genuine loyalty to the monarch, Whitford's position, as he states in the anthology's second preface, remains constant: 'thys virtue of pacyence is a noble vertu and muche necessarie for *euery faythfull Christiane*, as shall plainly appere vnto you'.[20] The 'faithful Christian', which for Whitford in 1541 would have invariably meant the Catholic Christian, is urged to emulate Job's patience in weathering the current deprivations.

Such glosses on Job's exemplary virtue are drawn out in a unique allegorical set-piece found in the *Boke of Pacience* which relies on imagery drawn from Prudentius's *Psychomachia*. In this episode, a personified Patience is threatened by Dame Ire who 'first [...] mocked her, and then rayled vpon her'.[21] In the face of Patience's remaining 'style stable', Ire proceeds to 'shoute and crye vpon her' before raising her sword to strike her 'vpon the mydle of the hed'.[22] Faced with increasingly aggressive attacks, Patience vanquishes her enemy through nonviolent resistance and admonishes the reader to note 'howe [...] we haue without bloudshed / or blemyshe, without hurte, or harme [...] vanquished, and ouer-

---

[17] Whitford, *Dyuers Holy Instrucyons*, fol. 18^{r-v}.

[18] Whitford, *Dyuers Holy Instrucyons*, fol. 14^v.

[19] Whitford, *Dyuers Holy Instrucyons*, sigs. A. 1^v, A. 2^r.

[20] Whitford, *Dyuers Holy Instrucyons*, sig. A. 2^{r-v}, italics mine.

[21] Whitford, *Dyuers Holy Instrucyons*, fol. 6^r. Whitford's narrative embellishes Prudentius's description of Ire's first encounter with Patience as she 'darts her eyes, all shot with blood and gall, and challenges her with weapon and with speech for taking no part in the fight'. See Prudentius, *Psychomachia*, ll. 114–16, trans. by Thomson, p. 287.

[22] Whitford, *Dyuers Holy Instrucyons*, fol. 6^r. This description of Ire's assault on Patience parallels Prudentius, *Psychomachia*, ll. 138–39, trans. by Thomson, p. 288.

comen' the enemy.²³ At the end of the episode, it is Job, the only figure in her retinue identified by name, who stands at Patience's side.²⁴

Whitford's narrative insert follows the *Psychomachia* closely, yet he draws attention to the sequence of Ire's increasingly hostile attacks on Patience. What is especially fascinating is that such verbal and physical assaults strongly resemble the ever more belligerent efforts of Thomas Cromwell's visitors who were sent first to examine and then to suppress the monasteries.²⁵ Retracing the process of visitations through the letters of Cromwell's agents such as John ap Rice and Richard Layton, David Knowles notes their evolving tenor: ap Rice 'began sympathetically but coarsened after a time', and Layton, who 'began in a spirit of coarse good-humour [..., developed] the qualities of a bully'.²⁶ Whitford himself experienced such intimidation from another of Cromwell's agents, Thomas Bedyll, who had begun visiting Syon in 1534 to secure the brothers' submission to the Acts of Succession and Supremacy.²⁷ Excerpts from two of Bedyll's letters illustrate an almost identical movement from verbal to physical violence as that displayed by Ire. The first is dated 21 July 1534 and was written shortly after Bedyll visited the abbey to ensure the brothers' submission to royal supremacy. The letter suggests Whitford's passive resistance during what must have been an increasingly tense interview:

> I handled Whitford [...] in the garden bothe with faire wordes and with foule, and shewed him that throughe his obstinacy he shuld be brought to the greate shame of the world for his irreligious life, and for using bawdy wordes to diverse ladys at the tymes of their confession [...] but he hath a braysyn forhead, whiche shameth at nothing.²⁸

---

²³ Whitford, *Dyuers Holy Instrucyons*, fol. 6ᵛ. In Prudentius, Patience, upon defeating her foe, makes the following declaration: 'We have overcome a proud Vice with our wonted virtue, with no danger to blood or life. This is the kind of warfare that is our rule, to wipe out the fiends of passion and all their army of evils and their savage strength by bearing their attack'. See *Psychomachia*, ll. 154–59, trans. by Thomson, p. 291.

²⁴ Job's presence also parallels the narrative in Prudentius, *Psychomachia*, l. 163, trans. by Thomson, p. 291.

²⁵ Knowles dispenses with the claim that visitors were sent early on with the more benign role of attempting to reform religion in *Religious Orders in England*, III, 269.

²⁶ Knowles, *Religious Orders in England*, III, 288.

²⁷ On Bedyll's surveillance of the preaching activities at Syon Abbey, see Gillespie, 'Hid Diuinity'.

²⁸ Wright, *Three Chapters of Letters*, p. 49.

Bedyll's accusations of shamelessness or misconduct against Whitford certainly recall the false accusations against which the brother counsels a strategy of non-engagement elsewhere in *Dyuers Holy Instrucyons*: to be sure, advice warning against confrontation and indiscrete criticism of others is present in each text within the anthology.[29] But these accusations also suggest the Birgittine's own patience and commitment to maintaining the sacraments of the old religion. Whitford's quiet obstinacy to the king continued even after Richard Reynolds was executed at Tyburn. Less than three months after the death of Reynolds, Bedyll wrote again to Cromwell about the state of the community, and his comments concerning Whitford's intransigence towards royal policy shed light on the extent to which members of the royal commission would go to silence opposition:

> Whitford, one of the most wilful of that house, preched and wolde speke no worde of the Kinges Grace said title; and this man hath but small lernyng, but is a greate rayler [...] if any such remedie shalbe put in execution, as towching the attachment, or putting in prison, of any of thaim, it shuld best be bestowed, in myne opinion, upon Frire Whitford and upon Lache, which bee the vaunperlers, and heddes of thair faction.[30]

In the end, these pockets of resistance within the community conceded to the pressure applied by Cromwell's agents and would have to adapt more innovative approaches to maintaining their community before resettling on the continent.[31] Bedyll's letters demonstrate, however, the close proximity of Whitford's

---

[29] Unsurprisingly, advice against confronting others over wrongs suffered or to reprove the conduct of others is found throughout the *Boke of Pacience*. See especially chapters 2–5, 7–9, 13, 16, and 19. Similar advice against such indiscretions is found in Whitford's discussion of the third and fourth *Impediments of Perfection* (see fols 53^r–55^v), and in the pseudo-Isidorian *Consilia* when Whitford explores the topics of constancy of mind, patience in adversity, the custody and keeping of the mouth, and detraction (see fols 70^{r-v}, 74^v–76^v). Finally, Whitford's own sermon 'On Detraction' counsels throughout against focusing on others' errors and urges readers instead to concern themselves primarily with reforming themselves.

[30] *Letters and Papers*, ed. by Gairdner, let. 1090, Bedyll to Cromwell, 28 August. Knowles notes that this letter is erroneously printed under the year 1534 rather than 1535. See *Religious Orders in England*, III, 218, n. 2.

[31] Richard Lache was eventually persuaded to side with the king, and soon after his conversion wrote to the brothers at the London Charterhouse urging them to submit to the Acts. William Copynger, who became confessor-general, met personally with Cromwell and was likewise persuaded to join the king's camp. For a more complete account of the capitulation of these Syon brothers, see Knowles, *Religious Orders in England*, III, 218–20. On the immediate strategies for survival employed by the Syon community in the 1540s, see Cunich, 'The Syon Household at Denham, 1539–1550'.

own experiences, and those of religious in general, to the successive assaults on Patience described in this episode from his *Boke of Pacience*. With such trauma so fresh in the reader's mind, it seems unlikely that the 'faythfull Christiane' reader to whom he appeals at the outset of the *Dyuers Holy Instrucyons* would not have drawn parallels between this allegorical episode and the process of dissolution that had recently unfolded.

Whitford also evokes an equally vivid and immediate illustration of Job's patience which is interwoven with domestic imagery drawn from the parable of the wise and foolish builders from Matthew's Gospel.[32] Citing Chrysostom's gloss on Job,[33] he associates the house built on stone with the patient soul, which is best exemplified by the Old Testament prophet. The house built on gravel, however, represents the impatient soul who is 'sone ouerthrowne with [...] aduersite'.[34] Rather suggestively, Whitford stresses that houses built on gravel fall because the 'foundacion, and grounde was not all one'.[35] Lack of unity and failing to do as Job did by building 'surely vpon *the* rocke' precipitates the ruin and collapse of the house.[36] Although Whitford identifies the soul as being represented figuratively by the house, his description of weak foundations in terms that imply discord are highly evocative of the lack of unity that existed in many monastic houses. As well, his statement that a sure foundation can only be built upon 'the rock' is a phrase reminiscent of the declaration by Christ concerning Peter's primacy that was used to underwrite papal authority.[37]

The importance Whitford places on unity for ensuring the survival of a house recalls the internal rifts within monasteries that facilitated many speedy surrenders. Martin Heale and Mary Erler have both commented on Cromwell's manoeuvring to exploit internal divisions within them — pithily summed up by an anonymous Elizabethan who observed that '[Cromwell] placed abbots and friars in divers great houses [... who] were ready to make surrender of their

---

[32] Matthew 7. 24–27.

[33] Whitford's citation of Chrysostom's 'Homily IV: On Fortitude and Patience' allows him to draw a clear association between the Old Testament text (Job 2. 9) and Christ's words in Matthew's Gospel. See Chrysostom, 'Homily IV: On Fortitude and Patience', pp. 80–81, and Whitford, *Dyuers Holy Instrucyons*, fol. 32ᵛ.

[34] Whitford, *Dyuers Holy Instrucyons*, fol. 33ʳ.

[35] Whitford, *Dyuers Holy Instrucyons*, fol. 33ᵛ.

[36] Whitford, *Dyuers Holy Instrucyons*, fol. 33ᵛ, my emphasis.

[37] On the use of the Mathew 16. 18 as a foundation of Papal Primacy, see Froehlich, 'Saint Peter, Papal Primacy, and the Exegetical Tradition, 1150–1300'.

houses at the king's commandment'.[38] In the case of Syon, tensions arose from within as John Fewterer, who served as confessor-general from 1523 until his death in 1536, attempted to navigate the Birgittines through a rapidly escalating spiritual and political tempest. Bedyll's description of him as a 'sad man, bothe tractable and comfortable to do everything according to his dutie' has left posterity an unflattering portrait.[39] Fewterer was pressured both to persuade members of his own community to accept royal supremacy and to sign a letter (written in fact by John Copynger) urging the neighbouring Carthusians at Sheen to do so as well.[40] Difficult to evaluate, his ambiguous actions during this period have left unresolvable questions concerning his true position on the king's supremacy.[41] Nevertheless, factions — to use Bedyll's own language — did exist within the abbey. Drawing together fragmentary evidence, Alexandra Da Costa delineates some of these divisions which formed over the course of Syon's evolving response to Henry's 'great matter' and which Cromwell's commissioners were able to exploit in their effort to contain support for the traditional faith within the abbey.[42]

When addressing concerns over false accusations, a subject that had become equally vital for Catholic faithful, Whitford on more than one occasion evokes the figure of Susanna. Excised from the Old Testament by reformers, Susanna's narrative focuses on a young wife who, when threatened with an ultimatum from two judges, must decide between surrendering herself to their desires

---

[38] Wright, *Three Chapters of Letters*, p. 114. Quoted in Erler, *Reading and Writing during the Dissolution*, p. 66. See also Heale, '"Not a Thing for a Stranger to Enter Upon"'.

[39] Bedyll's letter to Cromwell dated 28 August 1534 is reproduced in Aungier, *History and Antiquities of Syon Monastery*, pp. 435–38, p. 436.

[40] Cromwell would later choose Copynger as the next confessor-general of Syon upon Fewterer's death.

[41] Gillespie offers perhaps the most charitable description of Fewterer as one who had embraced a 'politics of survival' in order to navigate Syon through such turbulent political waters. See Gillespie, 'Hid Diuinity', p. 190. James Carley and Ann Hutchison comment on Fewterer's 'tactical illness' which prevented him from explaining his 'full mynde' in the postscript to the abovementioned letter in '1534–1550s: Culture and History', p. 234. Da Costa also comments on Fewterer's ambivalent efforts to support the supremacy in 'The King's Great Matter', pp. 18–19.

[42] Da Costa cites a letter from Robert Rygote in which he claims being labelled a 'wrecche [and heret]yke and thretynd to be cast in the fyre and byrnyd' for preaching royal supremacy. Da Costa also cites a letter from Bedyll in which the commissioner reports that as early as 1534, Fewterer confided being in 'fear and danger of his life' on account of his 'consent[ing] to the kinges said title', which exasperated the opposing faction within the community. See Da Costa, 'The King's Great Matter', p. 20.

or being accused of unfaithfulness with another man.[43] Whitford celebrates Susanna's endurance as exemplary of the patience needed when facing threats against one's possessions and one's body:

> As was in holy Susan, when she was in harde case and shamefully accused: but se what her maystres, my lady dame pacience dyd for her. For neuer accused her fals accusers, ne yet vnto her dere fryndes, dyd she excuse her selfe: but bydynge with her lady pacience: she remytted and cummytted her holle cause vnto our lorde.[44]

Refusing to yield to her assailants' cupidity, Susanna is brought to court where she stands silent while facing a series of false accusations which cast the virtuous wife as being driven to infidelity by carnal desire. Whitford uses Susanna as an *exemplum* of fortitude for contemporary readers who, like this virtuous wife, are 'shamefully accused' of beliefs they do not hold or actions they have not committed.[45] Once more urging a strategy of non-engagement, Whitford reminds his readers that Susanna did not actively defend herself: she 'neuer accused her fals accusers' nor sought to exculpate herself 'vnto her dere fryndes'.[46] Instead of pleading her innocence in the face of her enemies or rallying support among her friends, Susanna abandons and entrusts the facts of her case to God alone.[47] Evoking again Prudentian allegory further on in the *Boke of Pacience*, Whitford states that 'by the meane of [...] pacience [...] and of her mother mekenes' Susanna is in time delivered and her fame greatly multiplied.[48]

The figurative potential of Susanna's narrative to explain contemporary events was likely not lost on Whitford. To be sure, Hippolytus of Rome was the first to read Susanna as the persecuted Church, Joachim her husband as Christ, and the elders as enemies of Catholicism.[49] Whitford's use of Susanna also anticipates her subsequent use within Counter-Reformation polemic: excluded by Luther, Tyndale, and other early reformers from their Bible translations as

---

[43] Daniel 13. 19–21.

[44] Whitford, *Dyuers Holy Instrucyons*, fol. 15ʳ.

[45] Whitford, *Dyuers Holy Instrucyons*, fol. 15ʳ.

[46] Whitford, *Dyuers Holy Instrucyons*, fol. 15ʳ.

[47] Whitford, *Dyuers Holy Instrucyons*, fol. 15ʳ.

[48] Whitford, *Dyuers Holy Instrucyons*, fol. 15ʳ. Although Prudentius describes Patience as 'modesta' (meek) in *Psychomachia*, l. 109, trans. by Thomson, p. 287, this quality itself is not allegorized. Whitford's allegorizing of Patience and Meekness is nevertheless reminiscent of Prudentius's *Psychomachia*.

[49] Olszewski, 'Expanding the Litany', p. 42.

apocryphal, this narrative almost immediately becomes, as Edward Olszewski notes, a 'visual assertion of Catholic tradition'.[50] In this emerging early modern tradition, the elders are read as evangelical reformers who falsely accuse an institutional Church whose innocence and truth are indicated by her unblemished naked body.[51] Whitford's suggestive use of Susanna seems to anticipate such a multidimensional reading of this Old Testament figure.

Finally, Whitford's admonishments to accept deprivation should not be mistaken for defeatism. Another site in the text where Whitford maintains this pose of resignation while attacking spiritual enemies is in his retelling the story of Naboth the Jezreelite.[52] Returning to the need to resign oneself to 'the loss of worldly goods', Whitford recalls Naboth who 'by no meanes wolde departe from his inheritance that kyng Ahab wolde haue bought, and, bycause he sayde hym nay, hyt coste hym hys lyfe, although by wronge which wrong was after reuenged by almyghty god'.[53] In Whitford's telling, Naboth's obstinacy — his refusal to sell the land — costs him his life. This reading of the biblical narrative, however, runs counter to the message conveyed in the Old Testament. For, whereas Whitford foregrounds Naboth's resistance to the monarch, the biblical account places much greater emphasis on Ahab's sullenness. 1 Kings describes Naboth's vineyard as being located adjacent to Ahab's palace. Naboth refuses to sell his land to the king because he cannot: it is an ancestral inheritance and, under Hebrew law, he does not have the right to parcel out family property. Ahab returns home 'resentful and sullen', laying down in his bed and refusing to eat.[54] Seeing her husband sulking and aloof, Jezebel takes action by having Naboth falsely accused by the nobility of failing to serve God and the king.[55] Little imagination is required to map this narrative onto Syon's recent history. As early as Saint Birgitta's *Regula Salvatoris*, the Birgittine community had been described as 'a newe vyneʒerde'.[56] As well, Anne Boleyn's sponsorship of radical religious reform in England, summed up by E. W. Ives's claim that she 'played a major part in pushing Henry into asserting his headship of the church', would have aligned her in the minds of many contemporaries with the biblical

[50] Olszewski, 'Expanding the Litany', p. 46.
[51] Olszewski, 'Expanding the Litany', p. 46.
[52] The brief episode concerning Naboth the Jezreelite is found in 1 Kings 21. 1–16.
[53] Whitford, *Dyuers Holy Instrucyons*, fols. 14^v, 19^{r-v}.
[54] 1 Kings 21. 4.
[55] 1 Kings 21. 10.
[56] *Rewyll of Seynt Sauioure*, ed. by Hogg, II, 4.

figure of Jezebel who leads a passive king into heterodoxy.[57] Such a comparison, already made rather daringly by the Franciscan Observant William Peto in his 1532 Easter sermon delivered in the presence of Henry VIII,[58] would have been especially appropriate for readers attached to Syon as the queen took special pains in 1534 to bring the Birgittine nuns — her neighbours at Richmond Palace — over to the reformed faith.[59] These tacit references to Syon's contemporary history appear throughout the *Boke of Pacience* but are seemingly made explicit when Whitford reflects on his own deprivations near the end of *Pacience*: 'we conclude that our owne myserie and wrechednes may be an occasion of pacience'.[60]

The qualities of patience and non-violent engagement as well as injunctions against quarrelsome behaviour which Whitford's biblical narratives illustrate and reinforce are further enjoined at the end of *Pacience* by reference to contemporary events. Near the end of the first work in this anthology, Whitford reflects on the way in which monastic life requires a person to 'stand continually euery daye, and houre in the front of the batayle [...] as olde excercised and approued warriours'.[61] Whitford's martial metaphor portrays religious in a way that contrasts with popular anti-monastic stereotypes by placing them at the vanguard of the struggle against heterodoxy. While such a comment might seem anachronistic in 1541, Syon, as well as other communities, continued and practised some form of regular life after being dispossessed. Following their initial dispersal from the abbey, Syon brothers and sisters divided themselves to form a handful of smaller communities, and Peter Cunich has explored the efforts of Agnes Jordan to reconstruct an adapted form of conventual living for a group of Birgittines at Denham during the period when Whitford's anthol-

---

[57] Ives, *The Life and Death of Anne Boleyn*, p. 302. On Anne Boleyn's efforts to promote reformed Christianity, see also Dickens, *The English Reformation*, pp. 135–36, and Guy, *Tudor England*, pp. 116, 125, and 153.

[58] Mayer, 'Peto, William (*c.* 1485–1558)'. Carley and Hutchison discuss Peto's sermon against the king's divorce, and its consequences for the observant friar, in 'William Peto, O.F.M.Obs., and the 1556 Edition of The folowinge of Chryste', p. 98.

[59] William Latymer's *Cronickille of Anne Bulleyne* describes her visitation to Syon Abbey in 1534 and attempt to impose the use of English prayer books on the nuns in a brief vignette that aims to disparage the Birgittines. See 'William Latymer's Cronickille of Anne Bulleyne', ed. by Dowling. Da Costa reads the tacit resistance shown by the nuns in this same narrative in 'The King's Great Matter'.

[60] Whitford, *Dyuers Holy Instrucyons*, fol. 42^r.

[61] Whitford, *Dyuers Holy Instrucyons*, fol. 44^r.

ogy was published.[62] Whitford, who joined one of these communities which took up residence in lay households, appears to reflect rather poignantly on recent history when he acknowledges the losses incurred in such warfare: in addition to 'worldly goodse', there are also the 'kyn [and] frendes which we haue vtterly forsakyn already with al pleasures of them'.[63] In the scene Whitford paints, maintaining orthodox belief not only entails dispossession but also ostracism. Yet Whitford's text is even more frank in its depiction of the risks involved in remaining patient as he exhorts readers to steel their resolve:

> We must abyde and bere more and greater payne, prysonment, stockes, fethers, chenes, flayles, fyre, the rackynge, the swerde and all kyndes and maner of tourmentes, yee and also the losse of lyfe.[64]

Whitford's description of the possible consequences of such resolution vividly brings to mind the execution Reynolds had undergone.

Whitford's decision to have this anthology published in 1541 not only suggests a strong measure of tenacity but also sheds light on the shifting political and spiritual climate of the early 1540s. While we may be inclined to take Bedyll's comments about Whitford's 'braysyn forhead' with some scepticism, they do imply a personality that would not easily surrender when a principle was at stake. Whitford likely swore the oath of supremacy, yet he remained loyal to the Catholic faith. And at the start of the new decade it appeared that his patience was about to bear fruit. With the failure of Henry's marriage to Anne of Cleves and the unravelling of the nascent Protestant confederation about which many had hoped would result in a diplomatic thaw towards the Lutheran princes of Northern Europe,[65] Thomas Cromwell, whose administrative efficiency had helped pave the way for many reforms as well as the transfer of monastic lands to the Crown, had fallen out of favour. At the outset of this new decade Henry seemed to be softening his tone and looking towards some form of reconciliation with the Catholic Church. Such a turn towards conserv-

---

[62] Cunich, 'The Syon Household at Denham, 1539–1550', pp. 176, 179–81. More general discussions of female communities responding and adapting to the dissolution may be found in Erler, *Reading and Writing during the Dissolution* as well as Erler, 'Religious Women after the Dissolution'. Additional examples are discussed in Cooke, 'The English Nuns and the Dissolution'.

[63] Whitford, *Dyuers Holy Instrucyons*, fol. 44^r.

[64] Whitford, *Dyuers Holy Instrucyons*, fol. 44^{r-v}.

[65] On Cromwell's efforts to build a Protestant confederation by fostering diplomatic relations with Lutheran princes, see Dickens, *Thomas Cromwell and the English Reformation*, pp. 160–65.

atism may be seen even earlier with the king's active interest in and marginal contributions to the 1539 Act of Six Articles, which reasserted a doctrinal foundation for his church that closely aligned it with Catholicism.[66] Conservatives who had been waiting for an inevitable reaction on the part of the king to the reforms promoted by Thomas Cranmer and Cromwell must have also had their hopes buoyed by Henry's decision to marry Catherine Howard, the niece of Thomas Howard, Duke of Norfolk, who, with Stephen Gardiner, vigorously promoted a conservative religious policy at this point during the king's reign.[67] Each one of these events must have been viewed with optimism on the part of Catholic faithful who hoped that Henry's and the English Church's breach with Catholicism would be short-lived.[68]

Whitford's counsel to be patient and avoid quarrelling reads as general advice but equally well as specific guidance to dispersed members of religious communities and to devout laity who looked to them as models of Christian living. In this way, *Dyuers Holy Instrucyons* anticipates the way in which recusant literature sought to minister to a besieged Catholic community in need of spiritual fortification. Indeed, Whitford's anthology is the earliest printed text which provides guidance on coping with the current circumstances in which they found themselves as well as mistrusting prosperity and viewing material deprivation as a trial.[69] Contributing to this end is Whitford's use of the three figures of Job, Susanna, and Naboth, all of which highlight the way his guidance operates on two levels: on the one hand as general moral advice and on the other as specific *exempla* whose behaviours are perfectly appropriate to post-

---

[66] The Act of Six Articles, which incorporates each one of Henry's marginal additions, asserts, among other things, the veracity of transubstantiation, clerical celibacy, and the need for auricular confession. On Henry VIII's additions to the Six Articles, see Scarisbrick, *Henry VIII*, pp. 408–10.

[67] David Starkey comments on the hopes of conservatives that Catherine would become 'the figurehead for a revived anti-Reform policy' in *Six Wives*, p. 654.

[68] In addition to these signs hinting that a reconsideration of England's relationship with Rome was imminent, smaller-scale events were also afoot. Publication of *Dyuerse and Holy Instrucyons* with the formula 'cum privilegio ad imprimendum solum' printed on the frontispiece indicates that royal privilege had been granted for the publication of the work, and such a license would have bequeathed to it a further measure of status. On the significance of the formula *cum privilegio ad imprimendum solum*, see Albright, 'Ad imprimendum solum'.

[69] Thomas More's *Dialogue of Comfort* and John Fisher's *Spirituall Consolation*, both written in 1534 during their imprisonment in the Tower, may have been intended for a wider audience but did not reach an English Catholic readership until 1553 and 1735, respectively. On the development of these themes by recusant authors in the later sixteenth century, see Secker, 'Consolatory Literature of the English Recusants'.

Reformation England. When these examples of Old Testament narratives from Whitford's anthology are read through the immediate aftermath of the dissolution, they illustrate the way in which the brother encodes his less explicit 'holy instrucyons and teachynges' to pious readers in order to alleviate their concerns as they reel from such massive upheaval but still hope for an end to the king's rift with Rome.

Works Cited

Primary Sources

Chrysostom, John, 'Homily IV: On Fortitude and Patience', in *The Homilies of S John Chrysostom, Archbishop of Constantinople, On the Statutes, or To the People of Antioch*, trans. by Edward Budge (London, 1842), pp. 76–91

Letters and Papers, Foreign and Domestic, of the Reign of Henry VIII, ed. by James Gairdner, 21 vols (London: Longman, 1864–1924)

Prudentius, *Prudentius*, trans. by H. J. Thomson, Loeb Classical Library, 2 vols (London: William Heinemann, 1949), vol. I

The Rewyll of Seynt Sauioure, ed. by James Hogg, 2 vols (Salzburg: Institut fur Englische Sprache und Literatur, 1978)

Tyndale, William, *The Byble that is to say all the holy Scripture* (London: John Daye, 1549), *STC* 83:03

Whitford, Richard, *Dyuers Holy Instrucyons and Teachynges Very Necessary for the Helth of Mannes Soule* (London: William Middleton, 1541), *STC* 25420

'William Latymer's Cronickille of Anne Bulleyne', ed. by M. Dowling, in *Camden Miscellany*, vol. XXX, Camden Society, 4th series, 39 (London: Royal Historical Society, 1990), pp. 29–44

Secondary Works

Albright, E. M., 'Ad imprimendum solum', *Modern Language Notes*, 34.2 (1919), 97–104

Aungier, G. J., *The History and Antiquities of Syon Monastery, the Parish of Isleworth and the Chapelry of Hounslow* (London, 1840)

Carley, James P., and Ann M. Hutchison, '1534–1550s: Culture and History', in *The Cambridge Companion to Medieval English Mysticism*, ed. by Samuel Fanous and Vincent Gillespie (Cambridge: Cambridge University Press, 2011), pp. 225–48

——, 'William Peto, O.F.M.Obs., and the 1556 Edition of *The folowinge of Chryste*: Background and Context', *Journal of the Early Book Society*, 17 (2015), 94–118

Connolly, Margaret, 'Understanding the Medieval Miscellany', in *Insular Books: Vernacular Manuscript Miscellanies in Late Medieval Britain*, ed. by Margaret Connolly and

Raluca Radulescu, Proceedings of the British Academy, 201 (Oxford: Oxford University Press for the British Academy, 2015), pp. 3–15

Cooke, Kathleen, 'The English Nuns and the Dissolution', in *The Cloister and the World: Essays in Medieval History in Honour of Barbara Harvey*, ed. by J. Blair and Brian Golding (Oxford: Clarendon Press, 1996), pp. 287–301

Cunich, Peter, 'The Syon Household at Denham, 1539–1550', in *Religion and the Household: Papers Read at the 2012 Summer Meeting and the 2013 Winter Meeting of the Ecclesiastical History Society*, ed. by John Doran (†), Charlotte Methuen, and Alexandra Walsham (Woodbridge: Boydell, 2014), pp. 174–87

Da Costa, Alexandra, 'The King's Great Matter: Writing under Censure at Syon Abbey, 1532–1534', *Review of English Studies*, n.s., 62 (2011), 15–29

De Lubac, Henri, *Medieval Exegesis: The Four Senses of Scripture*, trans. by Mark Sebanc, 3 vols (Grand Rapids, MI: Eerdmans, 1998–2009)

Dickens, A. G., *The English Reformation*, 2nd edn (University Park: University of Pennsylvania Press, 1989)

——, *Thomas Cromwell and the English Reformation* (London: English Universities Press, 1959)

Erler, Mary C., *Reading and Writing during the Dissolution: Monks, Friars, and Nuns, 1530–1558* (Cambridge: Cambridge University Press, 2013)

——, 'Religious Women after the Dissolution', in *London and the Kingdom: Essays in Honour of Caroline M. Barron. Proceedings of the 2004 Harlaxton Symposium*, ed. by Matthew Davies and Andrew Prescott (Donington: Shaun Tyas, 2008), pp. 135–45

Froehlich, Karl, 'Saint Peter, Papal Primacy, and the Exegetical Tradition, 1150–1300', in *The Religious Roles of the Papacy: Ideals and Realities, 1150–1300*, ed. by Christopher Ryan (Toronto: Pontifical Institute for Mediaeval Studies, 1989), pp. 3–44

Gillespie, Vincent, 'Hid Diuinity: The Spirituality of the English Syon Brethren', in *The Medieval Mystical Tradition in England: Exeter Symposium VII*, ed. by E. A. Jones (Cambridge: D. S. Brewer, 2004), pp. 189–206

Guy, John, *Tudor England* (Oxford: Oxford University Press, 1988)

Heale, Martin, '"Not a Thing for a Stranger to Enter Upon": The Selection of Monastic Superiors in Late Medieval and Tudor England', in *Monasteries and Society in the British Isles in the Later Middle Ages*, ed. by Janet Burton and Karen Stover (Woodbridge: Boydell and Brewer, 2008), pp. 51–68

Ives, E. W., *The Life and Death of Anne Boleyn* (Oxford: Blackwell, 2004)

Knowles, David, *The Religious Orders in England*, 3 vols (Cambridge: Cambridge University Press, 1948–59; repr. 2004)

Mayer, T. F., 'Peto, William (*c*. 1485–1558)', in *Oxford Dictionary of National Biography*, ed. by H. C. G. Matthew and Brian Harrison (Oxford: Oxford University Press, 2004)

Mayeski, Mary A., 'Early Medieval Exegesis: Gregory I to the Twelfth Century', in *A History of Biblical Interpretation*, vol. II: *The Medieval through the Reformation Periods*, ed. by Alan J. Hauser and Duane F. Watson (Grand Rapids, MI: Eerdmans, 2008–09), pp. 86–112

Olszewski, Edward, 'Expanding the Litany for Susanna and the Elders', *Notes in the History of Art*, 26.3 (2007), 42–48

Scarisbrick, J. J., *Henry VIII* (Los Angeles: University of California Press, 1968)

Secker, Josephine Evetts, 'Consolatory Literature of the English Recusants', *Renaissance and Reformation*, 6.2 (1982), 122–41

Simpson, James, *Burning to Read: English Fundamentalism and its Reformation Opponents* (Cambridge, MA: Belknap, 2007)

Smalley, Beryl, *The Study of the Bible in the Middle Ages* (Notre Dame: Notre Dame Press, 1964)

Starkey, David, *Six Wives: The Queens of Henry VIII* (New York: Harper Perennial, 2003)

Van Lier, Frans, 'Biblical Exegesis through the Twelfth Century', in *The Practice of the Bible in the Middle Ages: Production, Reception, and Performance in Western Christianity*, ed. by Susan Boynton and Diane J. Reilly (New York: Columbia University Press, 2011), pp. 157–78

Wright, Thomas, ed., *Three Chapters of Letters Relating to the Suppression of the Monasteries*, Camden Society, 26 (London: AMS, 1968)

Part IV

Mystics Compiled

'DESYRABLE IS THI NAME':
FASHIONING THE NAME OF JESUS IN SOME DEVOTIONAL COMPILATIONS

Denis Renevey

The devotion to the Name of Jesus enjoyed significant popularity in England from the eleventh century onwards, as attested by Anselm's *Meditatio ad concitandum timorem*, some pseudo-Anselmian prayers, the sequence *Dulcis Iesu memoria*, John of Howden's Latin *Philomela* and Anglo-Norman *Li rossignos*, and countless anonymous Anglo-Norman and Middle English lyrics. These texts attest to the vitality of the devotion in the pre-Rollean period.[1] As part of an established tradition they played a major role in triggering Richard Rolle's interest in the devotion. Indeed, Rolle's commentary on the first verses of the Song of Songs, which is central to the development of his interest in the Name of Jesus, is highly influenced by this tradition, including of course Bernard of Clairvaux's sermon 15 totally devoted to the Name.[2] The devotion played a significant role in shaping his most significant

---

[1] See Anselm of Canterbury, *Opera omnia*, ed. by Schmitt, III, 76–79; Anselm of Canterbury, *The Prayers and Meditations*, ed. and trans. by Ward, pp. 221–24; *Le 'Jubilus'*, ed. by Wilmart; John of Howden, *Rossignos*, ed. by Hesketh; John of Howden, *Poems*, ed. by Raby; for a survey of the emergence of the devotion in the West, see Renevey, 'The Emergence of Devotion' and 'Anglo-Norman and Middle English Translations and Adaptations'.

[2] See Bernard of Clairvaux, *Opera*, vol. I, *Sermones super Cantica Canticorum 1–35*, ed. by Leclercq, Talbot, and Rochais, pp. 82–88; for an English translation, see Bernard of Clairvaux, *On the Song of Songs I: Sermons 1–20*, ed. by Walsh, pp. 105–13.

Denis Renevey (Denis.Renevey@unil.ch) is Professor of medieval English language and literature at the University of Lausanne, Switzerland.

spiritual characteristics, such as his typical *dulcor*, *calor*, and *canor*.³ *Expositio super primum versiculum Canticum Canticorum*, his own commentary on the first verses of the Song of Songs, and *Incendium amoris* provide powerful examples of the transformative power of the devotion: it triggered a change in Rolle which made possible the experience of hearing heavenly music and having it translated into the self as a perceptible sound within the mind.

Although the hearing of heavenly music may have been the highest experience of the devotion that Rolle claimed for himself, passages in *Expositio super primum versiculum Canticum Canticorum*, *Incendium amoris*, *Melos amoris*, *Emendatio vitae*, as well as the three Middle English epistles, attest to its multipurpose functions at all levels of the spiritual life.⁴ *Emendatio vitae*, *The Commandment*, *Ego dormio*, and *The Form of Living* all make reference to the practice of the devotion of the Name at different levels, and they regularly make use of Rolle's preceding Latin writings on the Name to achieve that.⁵ For instance, the description of the third and highest degree of love, called '*singularis*' in *Emendatio vitae*, borrows from previous discussions, as found for instance in *Expositio*, in order to express the highest degree of contemplative practice.⁶ Yet elsewhere the devotion to the Name is associated with lower stages of the contemplative life, such as the fight against the world, the devil, and the flesh.⁷ This essay looks first at Rolle's *Expositio super primum versiculum Canticum Canticorum* and the *Oleum effusum* compilation, which epitomizes the importance of the devotion to the Name as part of his spiritual practice. It then assesses the significance of these texts in the spread of the devotion in the first half of the fifteenth century by considering two devotional compilations, *The Chastising of God's Children* and *Disce mori*, both of which integrate the devotion to the Name as part of their larger devotional

---

³ For a discussion of these phenomena, see Watson, *Richard Rolle and the Invention of Authority*, pp. 113–91; see also Renevey, *Language, Self and Love*, pp. 38–40, 121–50; for a detailed account of *canor*, see Albin, 'Listening for *Canor*'.

⁴ These works are available in the following editions: Rolle, 'Comment on the Canticles', ed. by Murray; Hanna, *Editing Medieval Texts*, pp. 108–39; Rolle, *Incendium amoris*, ed. by Deanesly; Rolle, *The Melos amoris*, ed. by Arnould; Rolle, *Emendatio vitae*, ed. by Watson; for a discussion of this particular degree of love and the role played by Richard of St Victor, see Renevey, *Language, Self and Love*, pp. 39, 75, and 89.

⁵ For Rolle's Middle English writings, see Rolle, *Prose and Verse*, ed. by Ogilvie-Thomson, and Rolle, *Uncollected Prose and Verse*, ed. by Hanna.

⁶ See Rolle, *Emendatio vitae*, ed. by Watson, p. 59.

⁷ See for instance the reference of the Name of Jesus in the second degree of love mentioned in *Ego dormio*; Rolle, *Prose and Verse*, ed. by Ogilvie-Thomson, p. 29.

programme.[8] The chapter considers the extent to which Rolle's material on the Name of Jesus is incorporated in the compilations.

Rolle's *Expositio super primum versiculum Canticum Canticorum* and the Latin *Oleum effusum* compilation, which is mainly made up of passages from the *Expositio*, were copied and translated in fairly large numbers, thus attesting to an interest in the practice of the devotion.[9] The *Oleum effusum* compilation is made up of Part 4 of *Super canticum*, with a section of a letter by Saint Anselm, as well as Chapters 12, 15, and the opening paragraph of the eighth chapter of *Incendium amoris*. However, the core text for this compilation is made up of the fourth section of the *Super canticum* by Rolle, now available in Ralph Hanna's 2015 edition.[10] According to Hanna, Rolle's commentary appears in fourteen more or less full copies.[11] In addition, there are two discrete Latin traditions in which *Super canticum*, 4, appears as excerpts. Ten additional manuscripts contain a portion of *Super canticum*, 4. The same portion of text, with other portions of the commentary, appears within a compilation found in nine manuscripts that is systematically attached to a truncated version of Rolle's *Incendium amoris*.[12]

The way in which the 'I-voice' conveys its enthusiasm for the practice of the devotion may have had an impact on its popularity. It suffices to offer a brief passage here:

> Est autem nomen Ihesu in mente mea cantus iubileus, in aure mea sonus celicus, in ore meo dulcor mellifluus. Vnde non mirum, si illud diligam nomen quod michi in omni angustia prestat consolamen. Nescio orare, nescio meditari, nisi reso-

---

[8] Rob Lutton offers very useful information about the practice of the devotion in pre-Reformation England; see especially Lutton, '"Love this Name that is IHC"' and Lutton, 'The Name of Jesus'.

[9] Hanna lists fifteen manuscripts for the Latin *Super canticum* and Allen lists ten Latin copies of the *Oleum effusum*; see Hanna, *Editing Medieval Texts*, pp. 25–26; see Allen, *Writings Ascribed to Richard Rolle*, pp. 66–68.

[10] See Hanna, *Editing Medieval Texts*, pp. 108–39.

[11] Hanna provides a description of five manuscripts for which there is no formal published description; see Hanna, *Editing Medieval Texts*, pp. 141–60; for brief manuscript references, see Allen, *Writings Ascribed to Richard Rolle*, pp. 62–88. Hanna has discovered three additional manuscripts to the list compiled by Allen. Harvard, Houghton Library, MS Lat. 165 contains the last four segments of Rolle's commentary. Lincoln, College Library, MS 229 has *Super canticum*, 4, appended to *Emendatio vitae*. Oxford, Merton College, pb 58.c.8 contains the opening of *Super canticum*, 4, preceding an excerpt from the opening of Book II of James of Milan/ps.-Bonaventura's *Stimulus amoris*. See Hanna, *Editing Medieval Texts*, pp. 23–26.

[12] See Hanna, *Editing Medieval Texts*, pp. 21–22.

nante Ihesu nomine. Non sapio gaudium quod Ihesu non est mixtum. Quocunque fuero, vbicunque sedero, quicquid egero, memoria nominis Ihesu a mente mea non recedit. *Posui illud ut signaculum super cor meum, ut/ signaculum super brachium meum, quia fortis est ut mors dileccio.* Sicut mors omnes perimit, ita amor omnia vincit. Deuicit me eternus amor, non ut me occidat set ut viuificet. Attamen uulnerauit me ut mederetur; transfixit cor meum ut medullitus sanetur. Et iam victus succumbo; vix viuo pre gaudio. Pene morior, quia non sufficio in carne coruptibili tante maiestatis perferre tam affluentem suauitatem. Illabitur menti mee dulcedo deliciosissima et dum inebriat illam, cadit caro. Non potest non a sua uirtute deficere dum tantis gaudijs rapitur anima iubilare. Set vnde michi iste iubilus, nisi quia Ihesus? Nomen Ihesu me canere docuit, et feruore increate lucis mentem illustrauit.

[Moreover, the name of Jesus is a jubilee-song in my mind, a heavenly sound in my ear, a honey-flowing sweetness in my mouth. So it is no wonder if I love that name that offers me consolation in every hardship. I would not know how to pray or how to meditate, were the name of Jesus not resounding in me. I know no joy that is not mixed with Jesus. Anywhere I have been, wherever I have sat, whatever I have done, the memory of the name of Jesus does not withdraw from my mind. 'I have put it as a seal upon my heart, and as a seal upon my arm, for love is strong as death' (Cant. 8. 6). Just as death annihilates all men, so love conquers all things. Eternal love has conquered me, not so that it might kill me, but so that it might give me life. And what's more, it has wounded me so that it might heal me; it has pierced my heart so that it might be healed to its very depths. And now conquered, I succumb to it; I scarcely live because of my joy. I nearly die, because in my corruptible flesh I am not strong enough to sustain such abundant pleasure of so great a majesty. The most delightful sweetness glides into my mind and, so long as it makes it drunk, my flesh fails. My soul may not fail of its strength, so long as it is seized with such joys in rejoicing. But whence does this joy come to me, if not from Jesus? The name of Jesus taught me to sing, and it illuminated my mind with the heat of uncreated light.][13]

The passage clearly mentions the role played by the practice of the devotion in triggering the phenomena of *dulcor*, *calor*, and *canor*, which are perhaps idiosyncratic to Rolle, but which emerge from his extensive experimentation with the devotion to the Name. Indeed, several passages in his writings reveal how the practice of the devotion to the Name led him to experience sweetness, warmth and heavenly melodies. Rolle labelled these complex senso-spiritual experiences as *dulcor*, *canor*, and *melos*.

The degree of success in fashioning the Latin *Oleum effusum* compilations is attested by the large number of extant manuscripts, as well as three abbreviated

---

[13] Hanna, *Editing Medieval Texts*, pp. 120–21; Hanna's edition provides a modern English translation.

Middle English translations, found in the following manuscripts: BL, MS Harley 1022 (fol. 62a; dated 1350–1400); Lincoln, Cathedral Library, MS 91, called the Thornton manuscript (fol. 192a; dated 1425–50), and Dublin, Trinity College, MS 155 (C.5.7) (fols 60b–64a; dated *c.* 1400).[14] In addition, one fragment of the Middle English version is found appended to a copy of the *Pore Caitif*, which itself incorporates an English version of a section of the *Oleum effusum* commentary. This version is found in BL, MS Stowe 38 (fol. 161a; fifteenth fragment). There are at least forty copies of the *Pore Caitif* with the Middle English version 'Oleum effusum', which makes it the most popular version in terms of its circulation.[15] The possibility of presenting the devotion to the Name in compact or more extensive format, its impeccable orthodoxy and authority supported with references to Anselm and Bernard, and the multiplicity of its functions within catechetic, affective, or mystical programmes made it fashionable material for inclusion in larger devotional compilations.

The Chastising of God's Children is a good case in point. This compilation is found in twelve manuscripts, including MS Don. e. 247, acquired by the Bodleian Library in 2014. Half of *The Chastising*, including the twenty-fourth chapter on the Name, is part of another compilation, *Disce mori*, extant in two manuscripts.[16] Chapter twenty-four of *The Chastising* is found in one other manuscript, BL, MS Harley 2218, alongside Chapter 25. As pointed out by the editors, the compilation can be compared to a series of conferences or daily readings that would have been required in women's houses. The reading of a chapter a day would have offered reading for about a month.[17] The compilation is about temptations and how to deal with them. It also considers God's absence and presence, spiritual infirmities and how one can learn from them, the causes, remedies, and benefits of temptations.[18] *The Chastising*, whose date of composition is between 1391 and 1409,[19] was very popular in religious houses

---

[14] I follow Hanna in his assessment of the version in Trinity College, which, against Allen's initial statement based on the incipit only, he regards as a version similar to the Harley and Lincoln Cathedral versions; see Rolle, *Uncollected Prose and Verse*, ed. by Hanna, pp. lv–lvi.

[15] See Hanna, *Editing Medieval Texts*, pp. 21–22.

[16] See *The Chastising of God's Children*, ed. by Bazire and Colledge, p. 1.

[17] See *The Chastising of God's Children*, ed. by Bazire and Colledge. pp. 43–44.

[18] For a recent assessment of *The Chastising*, more particularly compiling strategies, see Marleen Cré's forthcoming article, 'Miscellaneity, Compiling Strategies, and the Transmission'; a more detailed discussion of the build-up of the text can be found in Cré, '"ȝe han desired to knowe in comfort of ȝoure soule"'.

[19] See Sutherland, '*The Chastising of God's Children*', pp. 355–57.

throughout the fifteenth century, with two nuns of the Augustinian house at Campsey and four nuns of the Bridgettine house of Syon owning printed copies.[20] Whether or not *The Chastising* was initially written at the instigation of a woman religious for whom the author acted as spiritual adviser, the fact is that the compilation found a regular audience among women religious.[21]

The passage devoted to the Name of Jesus, found in the twenty-fourth chapter on patience as remedy against temptations, offers a compact version of the devotion. *The Chastising* makes reference to the Name as a remedy against wicked spirits, and suggests a use that should be made alongside rumination on his Passion, with the gesture of crossing oneself upon forehead and breast. I offer the full passage here:

> Also anoþer remedie is and special aȝens wikid spirites to þenke on þe passion of crist, wiþ crossyng upon þe forhed and brest; and sum do principalli wiþ þe token of thau, and seien: In nomine iesu signo me thau. And wiþ oþer blissyngges sum seien a uerse that is in the ympne Cultor dei memento, in þis maner: O tortuose serpens, discede: *christus* hic est, *christus* hic est, liquesce: signum quod ipse nosti dampnat tuam cateruam. Sum sein: Iesus autem transiens per medium illorum ibat. In nomine patris et cetera. Per crucis hoc signum et cetera. Also þis hooli name iesus, whanne it is clepid to oure help, it is to us gracious liȝt to liȝtne us in derknesse of oure soule. It is also a mete fulfillyng us wiþ grete goostli sauours, and it is medicyne to us to hele al oure soores. Þerfor seiþ seint bernard up þe canticles: Noþing so refreyneþ the fiersnesse of malencolie or of ire as to clepe þe name of iesu: noþing so swagiþ þe lymes of pride as þat hooli name iesu: noþing so heliþ þat wounde of enuye as þe uertu of þat name iesu: noþing tempriþ so couetise as to þenke on þat name iesu: noþing restreyneþ so þe lust of lecherie as to þenke on þe uertu of þat name iesu: noþing voidiþ so soone sleuþ as þis name iesu; and so forþ of al oþer. And so þese and suche oþer bien siknesse and sooris of þe soule, but to clepe to þis name iesu, and to þenke on þe uertu, þat is souereyn medicyne to alle þese goostli feuers or sikenessis; and þat oure lord shewiþ us bi his owne techyng, whan he seide bi þe wordis of þe prophete: Clepe me in þe day of tribulacion, for I shal delyuer þe, and þou shalt worship me: for in al temptacion it is a remedie souereynli to vse and to clepe þis name iesu. Seint anselme þouȝt wel also þat (þer) was grete uertu and comfort in þis name, and þerfor he uside to seie it oft: Iesu, iesu, iesu, propter nomen tuum sanctum sis michi iesu.[22]

---

[20] Bazire and Colledge make reference to a lost manuscript formerly in the Harleian library, one in Göttingen University Library, and Cambridge, Sidney Sussex College, MS Bb. 2. 14, for the final text owned by two Syon nuns; see *The Chastising of God's Children*, ed. by Bazire and Colledge, p. 38.

[21] *The Chastising of God's Children*, ed. by Bazire and Colledge, p. 41.

[22] *The Chastising of God's Children*, ed. by Bazire and Colledge, pp. 202–03.

The reference to Anselm points to a certain use of the invocation of the Name that, quite appropriately in a compilation that presents remedies against tribulations, serves to fight off various forms of temptations linked to the seven deadly sins. The way in which moderate use is made of the devotion to the Name in this compilation supports the compiler's general tendency of abbreviating his sources, such as for instance the suppression of Books I and III of Jan van Ruusbroec's *The Spiritual Espousals*, as well as careful abbreviation of Book II.[23]

The relatively unassuming place given to the devotion to the Name in the compilation nonetheless gives it a specific role in the fight against temptations.[24] If the references to Anselm and Bernard of Clairvaux as choice authorities on the devotion to the Name are perfectly justified, they nonetheless also call attention to the blatant absence of reference to Rolle on the subject of the Name in particular, and in the whole of the compilation in general. Considering the extensive use of sources, some of them recently written, such as Ruusbroec's *Spiritual Espousals* and Alphonse of Pecha's *Epistola solitarii*, it is difficult to believe that Rolle's contribution to the general material of the compilation, and more specifically to the Name of Jesus, was unfamiliar to the compiler.[25] On the other hand, if, as Bazire and Colledge attest, *The Chastising* was written as a treatise that, among others, strove to repress 'enthusiasm', then the absence of Rollean passages should be read as a conscious late fourteenth-century/early fifteenth-century effort in erasing Rolle's affectively inflected writings from the late medieval devotional landscape.[26] That effort may have been part of a larger perception of the possible danger of Rolle's effusive spirituality, to which the defence of Thomas Basset against the detractors of Rolle contributes additional information. In the case of the *Defensorium*, the concern is directed at a learned Carthusian.[27] Whether *The Chastising* was produced in a Carthusian milieu or

---

[23] See *The Chastising of God's Children*, ed. by Bazire and Colledge, pp. 48–49; for a more careful and convincing assessment of the compiler's choices with regard to his sources, and Ruusbroec in particular, see Cré, '"We are United with God (and God with Us?)"'; also see Cré, 'Take a Walk on the Safe Side'.

[24] *The Chastising of God's Children*, ed. by Bazire and Colledge, p. 48.

[25] For a discussion of the sources, see *The Chastising of God's Children*, ed. by Bazire and Colledge, pp. 41–49.

[26] Bazire and Colledge mention four main concerns on the part of the author: the recognition and combat of heresy; the repression of 'enthusiasm'; the 'discerning of spirits'; and the claims of the liturgy against private devotions; *The Chastising of God's Children*, ed. by Bazire and Colledge, p. 47.

[27] For a transcription of Thomas Basset's *Defensorium*, see Allen, *Writings Ascribed to Richard Rolle*, pp. 527–37; see also Sargent, 'Contemporary Criticism of Richard Rolle'.

not, one can be quite confident that the absence of Rollean passages reflects concerns similar to those of the Carthusians.[28] *The Chastising*, like several other fifteenth-century religious treatises, shows that the devotion to the Name of Jesus in England relied on a long tradition based on the writings of established authorities and therefore, as is also the case in Eleanor Hull's meditation on the Name of Jesus, did not necessarily require reference to Rolle.[29]

Disce mori, written between 1453 and 1464, offers an altogether different perspective on authorial affiliations linked to the devotion to the Name. Indeed, and despite very heavy borrowings from *The Chastising*, 'Exhortacion', the final part of *Disce mori*, makes heavy use of Rollean material in a way that reflects a different attitude from *The Chastising*.[30] *Disce mori* belongs to the genre of the manual of religious instructions. It borrows extensively from a French thirteenth-century manual, the *Miroir du monde*, also called *Somme le roi*, which circulated in over a hundred manuscripts and which was translated in several vernacular languages.[31] But borrowings in *Disce mori* do not end here. Indeed, following the descriptions and subdivisions of sins as offered in *Miroir du monde*, the compiler has recourse to a fifteenth-century Latin compilation, *Speculum spiritualium*, to look for material that is going to be used as remedy against each sin.[32] This compilation, which contains material by Rolle, Walter Hilton, Bridget, and Henry Suso, plays a significant role disseminating their experiences and advice in the Middle English language.[33] *Disce mori* both borrows extensively from other compilations, thus demonstrating the respectable status compilations reached in the middle of the fifteenth century, and contributes material towards the composition of a sister compilation, *Ignorantia sacerdotum*, possibly written by the same author/compiler, or at least written

---

[28] Sutherland offers a good summary about the state of discussions on the authorship of *The Chastising*, with Carthusian authorship remaining a possibility; see Sutherland, 'The Chastising of God's Children', p. 358.

[29] Indeed, the devotion to the Name of Jesus by Eleanor Hull (*c.* 1390–1460) is another interesting case, which I discuss in my forthcoming book, *Name above Names*, ch. 5. The meditation by Eleanor Hull is unedited and available in two manuscripts, CUL, MS Kk.1.6, and Chicago, University of Illinois, MS 80. For more information on Hull, see *A Commentary on the Penitential Psalms*, ed. by Barratt.

[30] See *The 'Exhortacion'*, ed. by Jones.

[31] *The 'Exhortacion'*, ed. by Jones, pp. x–xi.

[32] See Doyle, 'The *Speculum spiritualium*'.

[33] *The 'Exhortacion'*, ed. by Jones, p. xi; for a discussion of *Speculum spiritualium*, see Jones, 'A Chapter from Richard Rolle'.

in the same milieu.³⁴ There is no information about the compiler in any of the manuscripts, but the presence of Oxford, Jesus College, MS 39 at Syon in the sixteenth century, as well as linguistic evidence pointing to the London area, suggest Syon and the Carthusian house of Sheen as possible origins for the composition of the compilations.³⁵ Suggestions have been made for an original readership made up of Syon nuns, although many passages suggest a more general readership.³⁶

The final part of *Disce mori*, called 'Exhortacion', which could be read as a treatise separate from *Disce mori*, addresses a certain 'suster' (who could possibly be 'Dame Alice' of the *Disce mori* prologue), with the use of feminine pronouns, but only in the first chapter. After that, a more general audience seems to be addressed again, with the use of generically masculine pronouns.³⁷ The 'Exhortacion' is divided into nine chapters. The sources used in the 'Exhortacion' are extensive, but Rolle's presence is particularly overwhelming, with explicit reference to 'Richard Hampol(e)' in section two of Chapter 1, and section four of Chapter 4, with two references.³⁸ If most references use 'Richard Hampol(e)' to introduce a particular passage from his corpus, the first reference in Chapter 1 adds to that aspect an invitation for the 'suster' to emotionally bond with Rolle: 'þe hooly heremite Richard Hampole wrote ful discretely in his dayes to suche a woman as yee be'.³⁹ This passage invites the recipient to feel part of the community of solitaries and enclosed men and women to whom Rolle devoted some of his writings. Chapter 6, called 'How deuocion

---

³⁴ *Disce mori* is available in only two manuscripts, Oxford, Jesus College, MS 39, written around 1453–64, and Bodl. Lib., MS Laud misc. 99, dated after 1470. *Ignorantia sacerdotum* is found in Bodl. Lib., MS Eng. th. c. 57, and is also dated around 1453–64. Jones provides a useful appendix showing the extent of borrowings from *Disce mori* into *Ignorancia*; see *The 'Exhortacion'*, ed. by Jones, pp. xxxvii–xlii; for a possible origin at the Bridgettine house of Syon, see Jones, 'Jesus College Oxford, MS 39', pp. 244–45.

³⁵ *The 'Exhortacion'*, ed. by Jones, p. xxviii.

³⁶ Syon Library contained important early manuscripts containing mystical and devotional texts, such as the writings of John of Howden, Richard Rolle, and Walter Hilton, as well as the Carthusian compilation on the spiritual life, the *Speculum spiritualium*; see Gillespie, 'The Mole in the Vineyard', p. 148.

³⁷ For a discussion of Syon origin and a Syon readership for *Disce mori*, see Jones, 'The Heresiarch'; see also Gillespie, 'The Mole in the Vineyard', p. 161 n. 78, who mentions the fact *Disce mori* may be the work of a Syon brother addressing a vowess postulant to the house.

³⁸ See *The 'Exhortacion'*, ed. by Jones, pp. 9, 32, 55; for an extensive discussion about the mode of composition of *Disce mori*, see Jones, 'The Compilation(s)', pp. 92–97.

³⁹ *The 'Exhortacion'*, ed. by Jones, p. 9.

lost shal be recouered', is almost entirely devoted to the Name of Jesus. It borrows from the Latin compilation mentioned previously, the *Speculum spiritualium*, whose ultimate sources on the Name of Jesus are Rolle's Latin *Oleum effusum* and Chapter 46 of Hilton's *Scale of Perfection*, Book I.[40] Yet another passage from the 'Exhortacion', the second part of Chapter 1, called 'A lessone of perfit lyuyng', borrows from *The Commandment* a passage in which Richard Hampole is mentioned alongside Saint Paul and Saint John. In that part, the practice of the name has the power to prevent any form of evil to dwell in the heart. Indeed, it chases away the devil, destroys temptations and puts away all vices and wicked deeds, purifies the soul and fills it with grace, so that the soul becomes a bed and resting place for the spouse Jesus Christ.[41] The compiler of *Disce mori* links the devotion to the Name with the imagery of the bed inspired by the *lectus noster floridus* from the Song of Songs (Cant. 1. 15), thus emphasizing further the strong link with the commentary tradition of this book, especially Bernard's sermon 15 on the *Oleum effusum* verse, for the emergence of the devotion.[42] The pervasive presence of Rolle and, more importantly, of his spiritual programme in the 'Exhortacion' is further emphasized with the reference to 'Richard Hampol' and the 'iii degrees of þis loue'.[43]

Borrowing from *Speculum spiritualium*, which is ultimately based on the Latin *Oleum effusum* compilation, the *Disce mori* compiler dutifully follows the Latin original in offering the same seven properties linked to the Name:[44]

> Þere is noþinge þat so destroieth euel þoughtes, vices and venenouses affeccions and occupasions as doth þis name 'Ihesu' truly holden in mynde; ne þat so planteth vertues, nurissheth charite, and þat so feedeth deuocioun with heuenly þoughtes, refourmeth pees in þe soule, and turneth alle erthly þinges into a manere spirituel abhominacioun, & filleth a louyng soule with spirituel ioye, as doth þis name 'Ihesus'.[45]

---

[40] See Hudson, 'A Chapter from Walter Hilton'; Hudson notes that Rolle is mentioned five times, Hilton four, but that no attribution to Hilton is made by the compiler with reference to the passage discussed by Hudson, which is found in a long section on the seven deadly sins (pages 53 to 177 of the Jesus manuscript).

[41] *The 'Exhortacion'*, ed. by Jones, p. 9.

[42] Considering the possible Bridgettine origin of Oxford, Jesus College, MS 39, it is worthwhile mentioning the presence in the Syon library of texts linked to the devotion to the Name, such as John of Howden's *Philomela*, some sermons by Bernardine of Siena, and other sermons on the Holy Name; see Gillespie, 'Syon and the New Learning', pp. 85–86.

[43] *The 'Exhortacion'*, ed. by Jones, pp. 32–33.

[44] *The 'Exhortacion'*, ed. by Jones, p. 95.

[45] *The 'Exhortacion'*, ed. by Jones, p. 55.

The *Disce mori* compiler does not fear saturating the 'Exhortacion' part with Rolle's presence. Indeed, in addition to the reference to 'Richard Hampole', and in contrast to some English versions of the *Oleum effusum* compilation that omit reference to the autobiographical passage originally found in *Incendium amoris*,[46] he chooses to contextualize it by offering an important complement to the version found in *Speculum spiritualium*:

> This Richard Hampole writeth of himself þat vpon a tyme þe deuel appered vnto him liyng in his bed in þe fourme of a faire woman, and leide hir in þe bed by him. Þe whiche, dredyng þe perile, wolde haue lifte vp his hande to blesse him, but he might neyther moeue ne speke. Wherfore he turned his hert to him þat suffred deth for to redeme hym fro þe power of þe enemye, and þought in mynde, 'O, my Lorde Ihesu, hou precious is þi blode!' And þat do, sodeinly al vanished away, and he þanked God. A lyke temptacioun had Seint Esmond of Pountey, and was delyuered oonly by þe þought of þis name, 'Ihesu', lyke as is contened in þe legende of his lyf.[47]

The passage that ends with Saint Edmund's own temptation is found neither in the Latin original, nor in the *Speculum spiritualium*.[48] As a result, what was initially conveyed in other versions as idiosyncratic to Rolle is presented here as pertaining to a tradition of saintly figures that go back to the desert fathers, but that also include the thirteenth-century Edmund Rich (*c.* 1180–1240), Archbishop of Canterbury and author of the *Speculum ecclesie*, who stands as an impeccably orthodox and highly institutional medieval figure — in contrast to Rolle being an unregulated hermit. The *Disce mori* compiler achieves an unparalleled act of authorization in placing Rolle as part of a line of prestigious practitioners of the devotion to the Name, going back, among others, to the Apostle Paul — with the passage on bowing to the Name of Jesus in his letter to the Philippians (2. 9–10), Saint Ignatius, Saint Edmund, and 'many oþere gloriouse seintes'.[49]

---

[46] See for instance the version in TCD, MS 155; Rolle, *Uncollected Prose and Verse*, ed. by Hanna, pp. 8–11.

[47] *The 'Exhortacion'*, ed. by Jones, p. 55. I am grateful to Ralph Hanna who first brought Edmund Rich to my attention. For a version of the Edmund story, see *Thesaurus novus anecdotorum*, ed. by Martène and Durand, III, 1783–84. For a discussion of demons taking the shape of women, with reference to desert hermits such as Antony, see Salisbury, 'When Sex Stopped Being a Social Disease', pp. 51–52; for an account of Edmund Rich fighting the devil disguised (or not) as a woman, see a Dominican book of exempla from around 1275: *Friars' Tales*, ed. by Jones, pp. 183–84.

[48] *The 'Exhortacion'*, ed. by Jones, p. 96.

[49] *The 'Exhortacion'*, ed. by Jones, p. 56.

The part 'How deuocion lost shal be recouered' gives a prominent place to Richard Hampole's take on the devotion to the Name of Jesus. It participates in aligning his practice with that of the above-mentioned authoritative figures that have equally profited from the use of the devotion. As significant as the borrowings from ancient authorities is the borrowing of a well-known passage on the Name of Jesus from Walter Hilton's *Scale*, which ends with '*Hec Walterus Hilton*'.[50] 'How deuocion lost shal be recouered', therefore, offers a comprehensive account on the Name, making ambitious claims for whoever practises the devotion, as it can lead one to experience the ravishment into the third heaven as recounted by Saint Paul, even if that experience does not completely match the real encounter with Jesus, 'for he passeþ al mannes knowleche in þis lyf, haue he neuere so spiritual felynge of him'.[51] The compiler nevertheless insists on the appropriate balance between spiritual feeling and reason for a thorough investigation of the work of contemplation. He borrows from Hilton in support of this point: 'For oure Lorde seith in þe Gospel, *Lucerna corporis tui est oculus tuus*. For, lyke as þe light of þi body is þin eigh, so it may be saide þat þe light of þi soule is reson, by whiche þi soule may se al spirituel þinges'.[52] The reference to Hilton is effective in showing that the use made by Rolle of the devotion is not its endpoint, but that it is part of an ongoing development, and that someone as moderate as Hilton praises its use as part of contemplative practice.[53] The creation of the devotion to the Holy Name as a feast in the late 1480s in England demonstrates even further its broad and orthodox appeal.[54]

An investigation of the use of the devotion to the Name of Jesus in two fifteenth-century devotional compilations demonstrates that it became part and parcel of the devotional tool-kit of lay and religious pious practitioners. The *Chastising* compiler must have been aware of the role played by the Rollean corpus for the spread of the devotion in some religious milieus; however, he seems to have consciously chosen not to flag him up as one of the authorities on the devotion. On the other hand, *Disce mori*'s double act is puzzling in many ways: firstly, it renders faithfully the Holy Name passage as found in

---

[50] The passage is also taken from *Speculum spiritualium*, but is ultimately from Hilton's *Scale* I, Chapters 46 to 48; see *The 'Exhortacion'*, ed. by Jones, pp. 53–54, 95; see also Hilton, *The Scale of Perfection*, ed. by Bestul, pp. 83–87.

[51] *The 'Exhortacion'*, ed. by Jones, p. 55.

[52] *The 'Exhortacion'*, ed. by Jones, p. 54.

[53] Renevey, 'Name above Names', pp. 113–21.

[54] For the feast to the Holy Name in England, see Duffy, *The Stripping of the Altars*, p. 45.

Chapter 24 of *The Chastising*, with no reference to Richard Rolle;[55] secondly, the 'Exhortacion' aligns Richard Rolle with a long line of practitioners of the devotion, giving to the latter a significant authoritative position. By making reference to Edmund Rich's own practice of chasing the devil disguised in the form of a woman by the use of the Holy Name, the *Disce mori* compiler also translates what could have been regarded as an idiosyncratic practice into a prayer followed by venerable saints. The attention given to Rolle, the alignment of his devotional practices to reputable religious figures in the 'Exhortacion', contrasts with his complete absence in the main body of the compilation. As stated by Jones, if the bulk of *Disce mori* follows the pattern of the manual of religious instruction in structure and content, the 'Exhortacion' stands as a manual on the contemplative life, which may have been written after the main body of the text.[56] Considering the role given to Rolle in his relationship to the Holy Name devotion in that final part, one should question whether the compiler of the 'Exhortacion' is the same as the compiler of the bulk of *Disce mori*. In the case of the same compiler at work in both *Disce mori* and the 'Exhortacion', one needs to assess the role he gives to Rolle in the final part of *Disce mori*. Perhaps he considered references to Rolle more appropriate to the contemplative practice that the 'Exhortacion' encourages, while the passage in *Disce mori*, which is a faithful rendering of *The Chastising* passage in Chapter 24, emphasizes its devotional tenor more. If *The Chastising*'s cautious encouragement towards the spiritual life is carried forward in the main body of *Disce mori*, its final treatise, 'Exhortacion', adopts a slightly more daring and ambitious attitude, which is marked in the case of the devotion to the Name of Jesus with the rehabilitation of Rolle as one of its authoritative exponents and practitioners.[57] Considering that Rolle was revered at Syon, and that the religious house was a strong agent in the creation of the feast of the Holy Name in the last quarter of the fifteenth century, the suggestion of a Syon brother (re)instating the role played by Rolle in the spread of the devotion is a persuasive one.[58]

The two case studies open an initial window into the complexity of the transmission of material and authorial voices linked to the devotion to the Name of

[55] *The Chastising*, Chapter 24, is found on pages 288–94 of Oxford, Jesus College, MS 39; see *The 'Exhortacion'*, ed. by Jones, p. xl.

[56] *The 'Exhortacion'*, ed. by Jones, p. xiv.

[57] For a careful reassessment of *The Chastising*, see Cré, 'Take a Walk on the Safe Side', p. 242.

[58] For more information on Rolle and the Holy Name at Syon, see Powell, 'Preaching at Syon Abbey', pp. 242–44.

Jesus in the fifteenth century.[59] Devotional compilations such as *Speculum spiritualium*, the Latin *Oleum effusum* compilation and its Middle English translations, *The Chastising*, *Disce mori*, but also *Pore Caitif*, testify to its importance in late medieval religious culture.[60]

---

[59] Lutton, 'The Name of Jesus' offers useful information about the way in which Nicholas Love in his *Mirror* of the Blessed Life of Jesus Christ makes reference to the Name, but fails to address the subject further, as he initially promised, thus demonstrating tensions with regard to the usefulness of the devotion within certain orthodox circles.

[60] See for instance the end of an Ave Maria commentary copied in BL, MS Additional 30897, which ends with a treatment on the Holy Name that is quite similar to that of the 'Exhortacion'. Information provided by Nicole Rice in a private communication; see also the chapter by Rice in this volume.

Works Cited

Manuscripts and Early Modern Printed Books

Cambridge, Sidney Sussex College, MS Bb. 2. 14
Cambridge, University Library [CUL], MS Kk.1.6
Chicago, University of Illinois, MS 80
Dublin, Trinity College, MS 155 (C.5.7)
Harvard, Houghton Library, MS Lat. 165
Lincoln College Library, MS 229
Lincoln, Cathedral Library, MS 91
London, British Library [BL], MS Additional 30897
London, British Library [BL], MS Harley 1022
London, British Library [BL], MS Harley 2218
London, British Library [BL], MS Stowe 38
Oxford, Bodleian Library [Bodl. Lib.], MS Don. e. 247
Oxford, Bodleian Library [Bodl. Lib.], MS Eng. th. c. 57
Oxford, Bodleian Library [Bodl. Lib.], MS Laud misc. 99
Oxford, Jesus College, MS 39
Oxford, Merton College, pb 58.c.8

Primary Sources

Anselm of Canterbury, *S. Anselmi Cantuariensis archiepiscopi opera omnia*, vol. III, ed. by Franciscus Salesius Schmitt (Edinburgh: Apud Thomam Nelson et Filios, 1946)
——, *The Prayers and Meditations of St Anselm, with the Proslogion*, ed. and trans. by Benedicta Ward (London: Penguin, 1973)
Bernard of Clairvaux, *On the Song of Songs I: Sermons 1–20*, vol. II, ed. by K. Walsh (Kalamazoo: Cistercian Publications, 1971)
——, *S. Bernardi Opera*, vol. I, *Sermones super Cantica Canticorum 1–35*, ed. by J. Leclercq, C. H. Talbot, and H. M. Rochais (Roma: Editiones Cistercienses, 1957)
The Chastising of God's Children and the Treatise of Perfection of the Sons of God, ed. by Joyce Bazire and Eric Colledge (Oxford: Basil Blackwell, 1957)
A Commentary on the Penitential Psalms Translated by Dame Eleanor Hull, ed. by Alexandra Barratt, Early English Text Society, 307 (Oxford: Oxford University Press, 1995)
The 'Exhortacion' from Disce mori: Edited from Oxford, Jesus College, MS 39, ed. by E. A. Jones, Middle English Texts, 36 (Heidelberg: Winter, 2006)
Hilton, Walter, *Walter Hilton: The Scale of Perfection*, ed. by Thomas H. Bestul, TEAMS, Middle English Texts (Kalamazoo: Medieval Institute Publications, 2000)
John of Howden, *Poems of John of Howden*, ed. by F. J. E. Raby, Surtees Society, 154 (London: Bernard Quaritch, 1939)

—— , *Rossignos by John of Howden*, ed. by Glynn Hesketh, Anglo-Norman Texts, 63 (London: Anglo-Norman Texts Society, 2006)

Le 'Jubilus' dit de Saint Bernard: Etude avec Textes, ed. by André Wilmart, Storia e Letteratura, 2 (Roma: Edizion di Storia e Letteratura, 1944)

Rolle, Richard, 'Richard Rolle's Comment on the Canticles: Edited from MS. Trinity College, Dublin, 153', ed. by E. M. Murray (unpublished doctoral thesis, Fordham University, 1958)

—— , *Emendatio vitae. Orationes ad honorem nominis Ihesu*, ed. by Nicholas Watson, Toronto Medieval Latin Texts, 21 (Toronto: Pontifical Institute of Mediaeval Studies, 1995)

—— , *The Incendium amoris*, ed. by Margaret Deanesly (Manchester: University of Manchester Press, 1915)

—— , *The Melos amoris*, ed. by E. J. F. Arnould (Oxford: Blackwell, 1957)

—— , *Richard Rolle: Prose and Verse from MS. Longleat 29 and Related Manuscripts*, ed. by S. J. Ogilvie-Thomson, Early English Text Society, o.s., 293 (Oxford: Oxford University Press, 1988)

—— , *Richard Rolle: Uncollected Prose and Verse, with Related Northern Texts*, ed. by Ralph Hanna, Early English Text Society, o.s., 329 (Oxford: Oxford University Press, 2007)

Thesaurus novus anecdotorum, ed. by Edmond Martène and Ursin Durand, 5 vols (Paris: Lutetiae Parisiorum, 1717)

Secondary Works

Albin, Andrew, 'Listening for *Canor* in Richard Rolle's *Melos amoris*', in *Voice and Voicelessness in Medieval Europe*, ed. by Irit Ruth Kleiman (New York: Palgrave Macmillan, 2015), pp. 177–98

Allen, Hope Emily, *Writings Ascribed to Richard Rolle and Materials for his Biography* (New York: D. C. Heath; London: Oxford University Press, 1927)

Cré, Marleen, 'Miscellaneity, Compiling Strategies and the Transmission of *The Chastising of God's Children* and *The Holy Boke Gratia Dei*', in *Late Medieval Personal Miscellanies*, ed. by S. Corbellini, G. Murano, and G. Signore, Bibliologia (Turnhout: Brepols, forthcoming)

—— , 'Take a Walk on the Safe Side: Reading the Fragments from Ruusbroec's *Die geestelike brulocht* in *The Chastising of God's Children*', in *De letter levend maken: Opstellen aangeboden aan Guido de Baere bij zijn zeventigste verjaardag*, ed. by Kees Schepers and Frans Hendrickx, Miscellanea Neerlandica, 39 (Leuven: Peeters, 2010), pp. 233–46

—— , '"3e han desired to knowe in comfort of 3oure soule": Female Agency in *The Chastising of God's Children*', *Journal of Medieval Religious Cultures*, 42 (2016), 164–80

—— , '"We Are United with God (and God with Us?)": Adapting Ruusbroec in *The Treatise of Perfection of the Sons of God* and *The Chastising of God's Children*', in *The Medieval Mystical Tradition in England: Exeter Symposium VII*, ed. by E. A. Jones (Cambridge: D. S. Brewer, 2004), pp. 21–36

Doyle, A. I, 'The *Speculum spiritualium* from Manuscript to Print', *Journal of the Early Book Society*, 11 (2008), 145–53

Duffy, Eamon, *The Stripping of the Altars: Traditional Religion in England, 1400–1580* (New Haven: Yale University Press, 1992)

Gillespie, Vincent, 'The Mole in the Vineyard: Wyclif at Syon in the Fifteenth Century', in *Text and Controversy from Wyclif to Bale: Essays in Honour of Anne Hudson*, ed. by Helen Barr and Ann H. Hutchison, Medieval Church Studies, 4 (Turnhout: Brepols, 2005), pp. 131–62

——, 'Syon and the New Learning', in *The Religious Orders in Pre-Reformation England*, ed. by James G. Clark (Woodbridge: Boydell, 2002), pp. 75–95

Hanna, Ralph, *Editing Medieval Texts: An Introduction, Using Exemplary Materials Derived from Richard Rolle, 'Super canticum' 4*, Exeter Medieval Texts and Studies (Liverpool: Liverpool University Press, 2015)

Hudson, Anne, 'A Chapter from Walter Hilton in Two Middle English Compilations', *Neophilologus*, 52 (1968), 416–21

Jones, David, *Friars' Tales: Sermon Exempla from the British Isles* (Manchester: University of Manchester Press, 2011)

Jones, E. A., 'A Chapter from Richard Rolle in Two Fifteenth-Century Compilations', *Leeds Studies in English*, n.s., 27 (1996), 139–62

——, 'The Compilation(s) of Two Late Medieval Devotional Manuscripts', in *Text and Controversy from Wyclif to Bale: Essays in Honour of Anne Hudson*, ed. by Helen Barr and Ann H. Hutchison, Medieval Church Studies, 4 (Turnhout: Brepols, 2005), pp. 79–97

——, 'The Heresiarch, the Virgin, the Recluse, the Vowess, the Priest: Some Medieval Audiences for Pelagius's *Epistle to Demetrias*', *Leeds Studies in English*, n.s., 31 (2000), 205–27

——, 'Jesus College Oxford, MS 39: Signs of a Medieval Compiler at Work', in *English Manuscript Studies 1100–1700*, vol. VII, ed. by Peter Beal and Jeremy Griffiths (London: British Library, 1997), pp. 236–48

Lutton, Rob, '"Love this Name that Is IHC": Vernacular Prayers, Hymns and Lyrics to the Holy Name of Jesus in Pre-Reformation England', in *Vernacularity in England and Wales, c. 1300–1550*, ed. by Elisabeth Salter and Helen Wicker, Utrecht Studies in Medieval Literacy, 17 (Turnhout: Brepols, 2011), pp. 119–45

——, 'The Name of Jesus, Nicholas Love's *Mirror*, and Christocentric Devotion in Late Medieval England', in *The Pseudo-Bonaventuran Lives of Christ: Exploring the Middle English Tradition*, ed. by Ian Johnson and Allan F. Westphall, Medieval Church Studies, 24 (Turnout: Brepols, 2013), pp. 19–53

Powell, Susan, 'Preaching at Syon Abbey', *Leeds Studies in English*, n.s., 31 (2000), 229–67

Renevey, Denis, 'Anglo-Norman and Middle-English Translations and Adaptations of the Hymn *Dulcis Iesu Memoria*', in *The Medieval Translator / Traduire au Moyen Age 5*, ed. by R. Ellis and R. Tixier (Turnhout: Brepols, 1996), pp. 264–83

——, 'The Emergence of Devotion to the Name of Jesus in the West', in *Aspects of Knowledge: Preserving and Reinventing Traditions of Learning in the Middle Ages*, ed. by Marilina Cesario and Hugh Magennis (Manchester: Manchester University Press, 2018), pp. 142–62

—— 'Name above Names: The Devotion to the Name of Jesus from Richard Rolle to Walter Hilton's *Scale of Perfection I*', in *The Medieval Mystical Tradition in England, Ireland and Wales: Exeter Symposium VI*, ed. by Marion Glasscoe (Cambridge: D. S. Brewer, 1999), pp. 103–21

——, *Language, Self and Love: Hermeneutics in the Writings of Richard Rolle and the Commentaries on the Song of Songs* (Cardiff: University of Wales Press, 2001)

Salisbury, Joyce E., 'When Sex Stopped Being a Social Disease: Sex and the Desert Fathers and Mothers', in *Medieval Sexuality: A Casebook*, ed. by April Harper and Caroline Proctor (London: Routledge, 2007), pp. 47–58

Sargent, Michael, 'Contemporary Criticism of Richard Rolle', in *Kartäusermystik und -mystiker*, vol. I, Analecta Cartusiana, 55.1 (Salzburg: Institut für Anglistik und Amerikanistik, Universität Salzburg, 1981), pp. 160–87

Sutherland, Annie, '*The Chastising of God's Children*: A Neglected Text', in *Text and Controversy from Wyclif to Bale: Essays in Honour of Anne Hudson*, ed. by Helen Barr and Ann M. Hutchison, Medieval Church Studies, 4 (Turnhout: Brepols, 2005), pp. 353–73

Watson, Nicholas, *Richard Rolle and the Invention of Authority* (Cambridge: Cambridge University Press, 1991)

THE SCALE OF PERFECTION IN DEVOTIONAL COMPILATIONS

Michael G. Sargent

My aim here is, first, to clear away the long-standing modern critical limitation of the consideration of affect in late medieval devotional writing to discussion of compassionate meditation on the life, and particularly the Passion, of Christ. Second, I will describe the use of certain terms in the discourse of affect — particularly the terms 'affect', 'affection', and 'devotion' — in late medieval English and document the prominence of the term 'feeling' (particularly in the key phrase 'reformation in faith and in feeling') in the second book of Walter Hilton's *Scale of Perfection*. This in turn raises the question of what manner of affect Hilton is describing in the latter part of this work. Finally, with these matters clarified, I will describe the textuality of Hilton's 'affective turn': the embodiment of the *Scale*, and particularly of the text of *Scale* II in surviving late medieval English devotional compilations.

Affect Theory and Late Medieval English Devotional Literature

It might seem incongruous to speak of Walter Hilton in the context of late medieval English devotional compilations, since Hilton is usually thought of as a writer in the 'cognitive' tradition, representative of the 'institutional and the pedagogic' rather than the affective impulse in mystical writing.[1] I would

---

[1] See Ellis and Fanous, '1349–1412: Texts', p. 145.

Michael G. Sargent (michael.sargent@qc.cuny.edu) is Professor of English at Queen's College, City University of New York, and a member of the Graduate Center.

argue rather that the history of the use of several key terms, particularly 'affect', 'affective', and 'affection', 'devout' and 'devotion', has privileged and continues to privilege certain kinds of affect in our consideration, and has occluded others. In the fourteenth and fifteenth centuries, the consideration of the affective tended to be concentrated on contrition, compunction, and compassion; modern discussion has tended to focus on compassion. The rise of affect theory and affect studies in recent years, on the other hand, and the change in the meaning of the concept of affect that this has entailed, enables a reading of Hilton as an affective writer in a way that has not been possible in the recent past.

The characterization of 'affective', as opposed to 'cognitive', spirituality dates back at least as far as Pierre Pourrat's grand historical account of *La Spiritualité chrétienne*.[2] As Mary Agnes Edsall has pointed out,[3] the prominence of the term 'affective piety' among English-speaking scholars to describe 'a style of highly emotional devotion to the humanity of Jesus, particularly in his infancy and his death', derives from R. W. Southern's influential discussion of the works of Saint Anselm of Canterbury.[4] Southern argues that Anselm's discussion of the necessity of the sacrifice of the God-man Christ in reparation for the infinite crime of *lèse-majesté* in the disobedience of Adam and Eve led to a focus on the human suffering of Christ of which the emotionalism of Anselm's own meditations and prayers and those of others was a result. Southern does not himself use the term 'affect' or 'affective', speaking rather of 'a new note of personal passion, of elaboration and emotional extravagance, which anticipated some of the chief features of later medieval piety [...] an unusual combination of intensity of feeling and clarity of thought and expression'.[5] The 'Southern thesis', as Edsall terms it, traces the transmission of this new form of piety through the Cistercians (especially Saint Bernard of Clairvaux) and the Franciscans (especially Saint Bonaventure) and on into the vernacular lyric and devotional literature. Early versions of this critical tradition argued the respective claims of Cistercian and Franciscan affectivity to predominance in late medieval spirituality; more recent iterations have stressed the claims of the vernacular and of the feminine.[6] Present-day scholar-

---

[2] Pourrat, *Christian Spirituality*, trans. by Mitchell and Jacques; originally published as *La Spiritualité chrétienne*.

[3] 'Affective Piety', *Wikipedia*.

[4] Southern, *The Making of the Middle Ages*, pp. 226–40, and *Saint Anselm and his Biographer*, pp. 34–47.

[5] Southern, *Saint Anselm and his Biographer*, p. 47.

[6] See particularly Amsler, *Affective Literacies*; McNamer, *Affective Meditation*. The dependence of McNamer on Bynum, *Jesus as Mother* should also be noted.

ship on affectivity in late medieval English spirituality has tended to focus on Passion meditation, on the characteristic experiences of 'calor', 'canor', and 'dulcor' — 'heat', 'sweetness', and 'song' — of Richard Rolle, and on the roaring and the tears of Margery Kempe.[7] The Southern thesis, however, and the use of the term 'affective' to describe one aspect of late medieval devotional spirituality and literature, is still with us.[8]

But there is a problem with that, which is that the word 'affect' is coming less and less often in critical discussion outside of our particular research area to refer to the outward, social aspect of emotions that well up from within the autonomous human(ist) subject, and more to describe various conceptualizations of the embodiedness of emotion. These conceptualizations call into question the priority of emotion to affect and raise questions concerning the social aspect of the construction of emotion. The most influential strand in this rethinking of affect in North America has occurred under the influence of the psychologist Silvan Tomkins,[9] who uses the term 'affect' to refer to a set of innate, precognitive biological responses (startle, fear, interest, distress, anger, joy, contempt, disgust, and shame) that he describes as 'the biological portion of emotion'.[10] This form of affect theory has not gained particularly widespread recognition in psychology or psychotherapy (outside of couples therapy) but, particularly in the work of gender theorist Eve Kosofsky Sedgwick, sociologist Patricia Clough, political philosopher and social theorist Brian Massumi, and others,[11] it has demonstrated considerable explanatory force in a variety of other areas. Discussions of affect in the English-speaking European critical context have been influenced particularly by the work of the cognitive linguist Zoltán Kövacses and the psychologist-philosopher Claire Amon-Jones.[12] In this growing field, affect is conceived as relational, as a matter of forces and intensities both between human subjects and between the human and the universe of non-human actants that surround and interact with human subjects. As the introduction to *The Affect Theory Reader* puts it:

---

[7] See, for example, Gillespie, 'Strange Images of Death' and 'Mystic's Foot', both published in revised versions in Gillespie, *Looking in Holy Books*; Beckwith, *Christ's Body*; Renevey, *Language, Self and Love*.

[8] See, for example, Bestul, 'Meditatio/Meditation'.

[9] Tomkins, *Affect Imagery Consciousness*.

[10] Nathanson, *Shame and Pride*, ch. 2.

[11] Sedgwick, *Touching Feeling*; Clough and Halley, *The Affective Turn*; Massumi, *Parables for the Virtual*; see also Gregg and Seigworth, *The Affect Theory Reader* and Sedgwick and Frank, *Shame and its Sisters*.

[12] Kövacses, *Metaphor and Emotion*; Amon-Jones, *Varieties of Affect*.

Affect, at its most anthropomorphic, is the name we give to those forces — visceral forces beneath, alongside, or generally *other than* conscious knowing, vital forces insisting beyond emotion — that can serve to drive us toward movement, toward thought and extension, that can likewise suspend us (as if in neutral) across a barely registering accretion of force-relations, or that can even leave us overwhelmed by the world's apparent intractability.[13]

Affect theory has made several appearances in recent studies of late medieval religious literature. In Sarah McNamer's *Affective Meditation and the Invention of Medieval Compassion*, we should note that the term 'intimate scripts' derives from Tomkins's conceptualization of 'script theory', a later working out of the implications of 'affect theory', although McNamer cites William Reddy's concept of 'emotive' illocutionary acts as her primary model.[14] The markers for Reddy's 'emotive' illocutions, McNamer notes, are that they are 'first-person, present-tense utterances, designed to be enacted by the reader'. She describes these 'intimate scripts' as 'quite literally scripts for the performance of feeling — scripts that often explicitly aspire to performative efficacy'.[15]

McNamer's discussion is very much a rewriting of the 'Southern thesis' in the Franciscan key — quite specifically, Franciscan writing done by women. Another analysis that emphasizes the influence of the Franciscan tradition is Michelle Karnes's *Imagination, Meditation and Cognition in the Middle Ages*. According to Karnes, the imagination played a role in higher cognitive function in the blend of Aristotelian and Augustinian psychology that she attributes to Saint Bonaventure, and did not act merely as the mediator between the sensuality and the cognitive faculties, as it did in traditional medieval Aristotelian-scholastic psychology. In such a view, imaginative meditation on the life and Passion of Christ was a higher form of contemplative activity than the exercise for novices and the corporeally minded that it was usually taken to be. But she notes that the two primary Middle English translations of (pseudo-)Bonaventuran meditative literature, Nicholas Love's *Mirror of the Blessed Life of Jesus Christ* and the translation of the *Stimulus Amoris* attributed to Walter

---

[13] Gregg and Seigworth, *The Affect Theory Reader*, p. 1.

[14] McNamer, *Affective Meditation*, p. 213 n. 46, acknowledges Tomkins's 'Script Theory', but further down the page of text on which that reference occurs, describes her 'intimate scripts' as 'emotives' according to Reddy's description in *The Navigation of Feeling*, pp. 104–05. I will set aside without further remark here McNamer's essentializing gendering of the practice of compassion as 'feeling like a woman': it simply does not correspond to life as I experience it.

[15] See McNamer, *Affective Meditation*, p. 12.

Hilton, 'scale back the purpose and the potency of imaginative meditation by limiting the scope of imagination proper to sensible, earthly things'.[16]

Another strand in the history of emotion in the medieval period, one that stresses the communal nature of feeling, derives from Barbara Rosenwein's ongoing exploration of the history of medieval western European emotional communities.[17] Drawing on McNamer, Kövacses, Amsler, and Rosenwein's *Emotional Communities in the Early Middle Ages*, Ayoush Lazikani has shown how several twelfth- and thirteenth-century English and Anglo-Norman devotional texts, including the lyric, as well as church art, inspire and stimulate 'affective pain' in the reader/hearer. 'Reading is a nurturance of affective literacy', Lazikani observes,

> but it is also itself enhanced by the affective-literate behaviours brought to it. As such, emotional communities can be strengthened by the congregational bonds imagined in homiletics, and emotional communities can also reach a level of intensity where participants do not only value the same feeling, but also co-feel.[18]

As Amsler states in *Affective Literacies*, his discourse analysis of the crossing-points of Latin and vernacular, clerical and lay literacies:

> I use the term 'affective literacy' here to describe how we develop physical, somatic, and/or activity-based relationships with texts as part of our reading experiences. We touch, sense, or perceive the text or vocalize it with our eyes, hands, and mouths. Affective literacy also involves the emotive, noncognitive, paralinguistic things we do with texts or to texts during the act of reading.[19]

What affect theory provides is way of thinking about a non-cognitive, non-intentional, embodied emotional interaction with times, with places, with things, with practices, with repetitions, with memories, with sounds, with silences, and of observing the affective force of texts that traditional discussion may fail to recognize as affective.

---

[16] Karnes, *Imagination, Meditation and Cognition*, p. 207.

[17] Rosenwein, *Anger's Past*, *Emotional Communities*, and *Generations of Feeling*. I would add here that Monique Scheer's conceptualization of emotional practices in terms of Bourdieuan *habitus* adds a particularly rich explanatory depth that is worth exploring in further discussion of late medieval devotional and contemplative literature. See Scheer, 'Are Emotions a Kind of Practice?'.

[18] Lazikani, *Cultivating the Heart*, p. 4.

[19] Amsler, *Affective Literacies*, p. 102.

Walter Hilton's Affective Turn

The word *affect*, from the Latin *affectus*, 'a state or mind or body produced by some influence' (derived from *afficio*, 'to do something to one: to exert an influence on mind or [rarely] body, so as to bring it into a particular state'),[20] only entered the English vocabulary late in the fourteenth century. The *MED* distinguishes two lexemes, one for the capacity to be affected emotionally, and the other for emotion itself or emotional disposition (although one may disagree with their distribution of the various occurrences). The form 'affect' in John Trevisa's translation of Bartholomeus's *De proprietatibus rerum* is a direct translation of Latin *affectus*; those in *The Romance of the Rose* and Geoffrey Chaucer's *Troilus and Criseyde* are probably both translations as well. The term 'affect' occurs independently in the *Speculum christiani*, and remarkably often, in both of the senses distinguished by the *MED*, in the mid-fifteenth century writings of Bishop Reginald Pecock. The form 'affective' ('affectif') also occurs in Pecock, but not again in English, according to the *OED*, until the seventeenth century.

The *MED* also distinguishes two lexemes for the word *affection*: The first describes 'the faculty of soul concerned with emotion and volition; the emotional (as opposed to the intellectual) side of human nature, capacity for feeling or emotion'; or 'the capacity for desiring or willing'. The second, in parallel with the distinction between the two lexemes of *affect*, describes emotion itself; this lexeme is further distinguished according to whether it refers to emotion in general, or to that particular emotion that we now know by the name of *affection*. As Lazikani has pointed out,[21] a remarkably early use of the word *affectiun* occurs in *Ancrene Wisse* to refer to the capacity of the soul to be attracted to sin (as Lazikani points out, 'there can be no simplified taxonomy of feeling' for the texts that we are dealing with). The underlying text of Saint Bernard uses the word 'affectio'. The *Ayenbite of Inwit* also uses the word 'affeccioun', allying it as a mental faculty with 'wyl' as distinguished from 'skele', which is allied with 'onderstandinge'. The *MED* records further usages of the word *affeccioun* in all senses from the late fourteenth century onward.

---

[20] Definitions in the following discussion, unless otherwise identified, derive from the entries in Lewis and Short, *A Latin Dictionary*, the online *Middle English Dictionary* (*MED*), and the online *Oxford English Dictionary*. Citations of particular occurrences of the words discussed, unless otherwise identified, derive from the same sources.

[21] Lazikani, *Cultivating the Heart*, pp. 19–21; the citation is from *Ancrene Wisse*, ed. by Millett, IV. 1572–80 and notes.

Walter Hilton uses the word *affection* six times in his letter *On Mixed Life*,[22] written to a layman of means who felt himself drawn to the life of contemplation, probably before the mid-1380s (like the first book of *The Scale of Perfection*). Three of these occurrences refer to the faculty of emotion and volition in the phrases 'affeccioun of hire soule' or 'affeccioun wiþinne' in the discussion of the bishops and pious laymen for whom the mixed life is appropriate (ll. 212, 215, and 220); a fourth refers to 'deuocion [...] in affeccioun' (l. 755). A fifth occurrence, a count form occurring in the plural, must refer to an emotion, 'to stire þyne affecciouns more to þe loue of him' (l. 626); and the sixth to the emotion, 'tendre affeccioun of loue' (l. 71).

The first book of Hilton's *Scale of Perfection* is nearly four times the length of *Mixed Life* and refers to *affeccioun* thirty-six times.[23] Twenty-one of these occurrences refer to the faculty of soul concerned with emotion; particular clusters of examples occur in the discussion of the higher and lower parts of contemplation in Chapters 4–8 (ll. 92, 98, 134, and 147),[24] in the reformation of the virtues (particularly meekness) in affection in Chapters 14, 19, and 20 (ll. 315, 321, 323, 328, 462, 464, 474, 482, 488, and 489). Fifteen occurrences of the word *affeccioun* refer to the emotions or attractions themselves; eight refer to 'earthly', 'fleshly', 'worldly', 'evil', 'clene', and 'unclene' affections (ll. 150, 660, 709, 1331, 1403, 1450, 2495, 2499).

The second book of *The Scale*, probably completed shortly before Hilton's death on the eve of the feast of the Annunciation, 24 March 1395/96, is a third again as long as *Scale* i. The word *affeccion(s)* occurs fifty-five times in *Scale* ii,[25] approximately evenly distributed between occurrences referring to the faculty of emotion, and emotion itself (or the emotions themselves). Thirteen of the latter usages occur in the phrase 'fleschly affeccyon', or in the verbal context of the word 'fleschly'; nine of these are occurrences of the plural form 'affeccyons'. Six occurrences of 'affeccion' or 'affeccions' in conjunction with 'fleschly' are in the discussion of how the contemplative soul is 'hyd fro noyse and dynne of fleschly affeccyons, werdly desires and vnclene þoghtes' in Chapter 24.[26]

---

[22] Cited from Hilton, *Mixed Life*, ed. by Ogilvie-Thomson. Line references in the following discussion are to this edition. The rate of occurrence of forms of *affection* in the *Mixed Life* is approximately once every 1500 words.

[23] A rate of occurrence of approximately once every 1250 words.

[24] Hilton, *The Scale of Perfection*, ed. by Bestul. Line references to *Scale* i in the following discussion are to this edition.

[25] A rate of occurrence of approximately once every thousand words.

[26] Chapter and line references to *Scale* ii in the following discussion are to Hilton, *The*

The largest cluster of occurrences of the word *affeccion* (fifteen occurrences) is in the discussion of '[h]ow sum soules lufen Jesu by bodily feruours and by þer owne manly affeccions þat are stered by grace and by resone, and sum lufe Jesu more restfully by gostly affeccyons only stered inward þurgh speciale grace of þe Holy Gost' in Chapter 35.[27] This distinction is first made in Chapter 34, and the discussion continues into Chapter 36; but the core of Hilton's distinction between the 'manly' — what we may call 'devotional' — affect, which arises out of a person by his or her own efforts (although blessed with the common grace by which all believers are saved), and the 'gostly' affect infused through special grace by the Holy Ghost (the created form of the love of which the Holy Ghost is himself the uncreated form, Hilton adds) lies in Chapter 35:

> Oþer soules þat kunnen not luf þus, bot trauellen hemself by here owne affeccyons, and steren hemself þurgh thenkynge of God and bodily exercyse for to drawen owte of hemself by maystrie þe felynge of lufe by feruours and oþer bodily sygnes, lufe not so gostly. Þey done wele and medefully, by so þat þei wille knowen mekely þat here werkyng is not kendly þe gracious feleng of lufe bot it is manly, don be a soule atte þe biddynge of resone. And neuerþeles þurgh [þe] godenesse of God, bycause þat þe soule doth þat in it is, þese manly affeccyons of þe soule stered into God by mans werkyng are turned into gostly affeccyons, and are made medful as if þey had ben don gostly in þe first bygynnynge. And þis is a grete curtaysye of oure Lord schewed vnto meke soules, þat turneth al þese manly affeccyons of kendly lufe into þe affeccyon and into þe mede of his owne lufe, as if he had wroght hem alle fully by himself. And so þese affeccyons so turned moun ben called affeccyons of gostly lufe þurgh purchace, noȝt þurgh kendly brynggynge forth of þe Holy Gost.[28]

The object of Hilton's comparison here is not a devotion to the experiences of 'calor', 'canor', and 'dulcor' characteristic of the spirituality of Richard Rolle — experiences that he discusses in the letter *Of Angels' Song*, and several chapters earlier in *Scale* II, where he describes such experiences as characteristic of

---

Scale of Perfection, Book II, ed. by Hussey and Sargent, and are given in the format chapter/line number(s). The phrase 'fleschly affeccyon' (or 'affeccyon' in near conjunction with 'fleschly') occurs at 11/26, 24/69, 24/144, and 40/107; the plural form 'fleschly affeccyons' occurs at 24/77, 24/91, 24/123, 24/149, 25/27, 34/105, 40/103, 41/91, and 41/132 (ll. 483, 1389, 1455, and 2943; 1396, 1408, 1436, 1459, 1490, 2389, 2939, 3085, and 3119, respectively, in the Bestul edition).

[27] Hilton, *The Scale of Perfection, Book II*, ed. by Hussey and Sargent, 35/2, 3, 48, 55, 56, 58, 59, 60, 61, 63, 72, 77, 78, 79, and 83 (ll. 2420, 2421, 2458, 2464, 2465, 2467, 2468, 2469, 2471, 2479, 2482, 2483, 2484, and 2487 in Bestul).

[28] Hilton, *The Scale of Perfection, Book II*, ed. by Hussey and Sargent, 35/47–62 (ll. 2458–70 in Bestul).

beginners in the contemplative life. What he is speaking of here is the 'manly affeccyons of the soul' aroused by devotional exercises, caused (as, in Hilton's Augustinian theology, every good movement of the soul must be caused) by the common grace by which all who believe — all who are reformed to the image of God in faith, in the terminology characteristic of *Scale* II — are saved. This is contrasted with the 'gostly affeccyons' that the soul feels by the 'special grace' of the Holy Ghost:

> Bot I sey þat swilk affeccyons arn of God, made by þe mene of a soule after þe general grace þat he ȝifeth to alle his chosen soules, not of speciale grace made gostly by towchynge of his gracious presence, as he werketh in his parfyte lufers, as I hafe before seyd. For in inperfyte lufers of God lufe werketh al ferly by þe affeccyons of man; bot in perfyte lufers lufe werketh neerly by his owne gostly affeccyons, and sleth for þe tyme in a soule al oþer affeccyons, boþe fleschly, kendly and manly. And þat is proprely þe werkynge of lufe by himself. Þis lufe may ben had a litel in party here in a clene soule þurgh gostly syght of Jesu, bot in þe blisse of heuene it is fulfilled by clere syght of him in his godhed; for þer schal non affeccyon be felt in a soule, bot al godly and gostly.[29]

Hilton thus distinguishes between 'kendly' (natural), devotional affect and a second kind of affect that is directly inspired by the Holy Ghost:

> And þat lufe, as I haue befor seyd, is not þe affeccyon of lufe þat is formed in a soule, bot it is þe Holy Gost himself, þat is lufe vnformed þat saueth a soule. For he ȝifeth himself to a soule first or þe soule lufe him, and he formeth affeccyon in þe soule and makeþ þe soule for to lufen him only for himself.[30]

This, it is the aim of *Scale* II to teach, is the reformation of the soul to the image of God 'in faith and in feeling'.

But before we proceed to look at this second reformation in *Scale* II, let us consider Hilton's use of the word *devotion*. The root of the word *devotion* is the Latin *voveo* — 'to vow' or 'consecrate', from an Indo-European etymon meaning 'to praise, worship, pray: to speak formally'. In poetic usage in late classical Latin, *devoveo* could also mean 'to curse' (to consecrate something to the infernal gods) or 'to enchant'. *Devotus* meant 'devoted', 'attached', or 'faithful' to someone or something; among Christian writers of the patristic period, it could mean specifically 'pious' or 'devout'. *Devotio* had the abstract, non-count

---

[29] Hilton, *The Scale of Perfection, Book II*, ed. by Hussey and Sargent, 35/72–83 (ll. 2478–88 in Bestul).

[30] Hilton, *The Scale of Perfection, Book II*, ed. by Hussey and Sargent, 36/19–23 (ll. 2503–07 in Bestul).

meaning of 'a devoting', 'a consecration', but also 'a cursing' or 'an enchantment: sorcery'; among patristic Christian writers, 'piety' or 'devoutness' — an attitude (an affect), not an action or set of actions. It is in this sense that the word *devotion*, borrowed from French, first occurs in English in the *Ancrene Wisse*.[31]

Late in the fourteenth century, however, a count lexeme of the word *devotion* makes its first appearance, referring, according to the *MED*, to 'a religious ceremony of worship, or an instance of it; a service or prayer'.[32] The earliest citation is from Trevisa's translation of Ralph Higden's *Polychronicon*, referring to 'places [...] þat were couenable for contemplacioun, for bedes, and deuocioun': an activity, but not necessarily a count noun. The guild returns for 1389 record that the Guild of the Holy Trinity in Norwich ordained '[y]at alle ye bretheren and sisteren of yis fraternite shul kepen [...] her deuocioun on ye euen of ye feste of ye Trinite': the name of an activity, with a determiner ('her deuocioun'). Chaucer's 'Retraction' refers to 'bookes of legendes of seintes, and omelies and moralitee, and deuocioun'. John Lydgate's *Troy Book* states that 'Priam [...] ordeyned [...] prestis for to dwelle in þe temple, in her deuociouns': an activity, in the plural form. This is the first recorded instance of the plural English word *devotions*.

Walter Hilton's use of the word *devotion* fits into this pattern. In the *Mixed Life*, the word occurs relatively often: twenty-eight times.[33] Of these, all but two refer to an attitude rather than an activity: the two exceptions are a reference to 'þi praieres and þi deuociouns' (ll. 324–25) and the phrase 'in what deuocioun þat þou be' (l. 790). Devotion is usually referred to in conjunction with other contemplative attitudes and activities: 'deuocion and [...] contemplacion in praieres and in meditacioun' (ll. 194–95); 'deuocioun and contemplacion' (ll. 351–52); 'deuocioun [...] praiere or [...] meditacioun' (ll. 388–89); 'deuocioun and [...] praier' (ll. 285, 754, and 759); 'deuocioun and meditacioun' (l. 280); 'reeste in deuocion' (l. 355), 'grace of deuocioun and reste in conscience' (ll. 360–61); 'grace of deuocioun' (ll. 159 and 397); 'deuocioun' and 'feruour' (ll. 124, 628, and 758); and 'fier of deuocioun' (ll. 435–36). Devotion and meditation are once specifically referred to the 'mynde of [the] passion [of Christ], and of his oþere werkes in his manheed' (l. 279), the 'deuocion and goosteli praier' that are the 'kisse [of Jesus's] mouþ' (l. 285), contrasted with the care for 'his feet þat aren þyn children, þi seruauntes, þi tenauntes, and alle þyn euene–Cristen' (l. 280). The greatest concentration of references to devotion is

---

[31] *Ancrene Wisse*, ed. by Millett, II. 239 and VI. 288.

[32] Citations from works other than Hilton's, here and in the following discussion, are taken from the online *OED* and *MED*, for which see above, note 20.

[33] A rate of occurrence of approximately three times per one thousand words.

in the allegorization of the patriarch Jacob's desire for Rachel (ll. 350–61, 383, 389, and 397), whose name is interpreted as 'reeste in deuocion' (l. 355). The conjunction of 'rest' and 'devotion' does not occur elsewhere; and two of the three occurrences of the conjunction of 'grace' and 'devotion' occur in the same passage. In the *Mixed Life*, then, Hilton uses the word *devotion* to describe the contemplative life generally for his secular addressee.

Despite the fact that *Scale* I is nearly four times the length of the *Mixed Life*, the word *devotion* occurs approximately the same number of times (thirty times, to be exact).[34] In *Scale* I it is also more restricted in reference, used to speak of the 'unlettrid men which gyven hem hooli to deuocion' (l. 94); or to describe the lower, second part of contemplation, 'brennande love in devotion', as opposed to the higher 'brennande love in contemplacion' (l. 163). The greatest concentration of occurrences (twelve) is in the series of short chapters on prayer (Chapters 24–29 and 33), particularly the prayer of those who have been recently converted to the spiritual life — 'hem that gyven hem newli to devocion' (ll. 81, 651, 672, 676, 681, 689, 692, 718, 734, 736, 737, 833, and 839). A number of the same conjunctions of *devotion* with other terms mentioned above (some of which are reminiscent of Richard Rolle's sensory experiences) occur again here: 'devotion' and 'love' twice (ll. 163, 281); 'devotion' and 'fervor', 'comfort', and 'savor' twice each (ll. 601 and 2229, 718 and 1036, 822 and 839); 'devotion' and 'rest' once (l. 822), with 'graces and giftes' once (l. 1102), and with 'grace' and 'gift' once each (ll. 736, 1070). Even closer to the language of Rolle's spirituality are the phrases 'brennande love in devotion' (l. 163), 'her hertis melten in devocion' (l. 941), and 'savour and swettnesse with devocioun' (l. 839). Two occurrences of the word *devotion* refer to the 'bodili [...] presence' and the 'bodili likness' of Jesus (ll. 737 and 902); one refers to 'grete devocioun of his passioun' (l. 885); and another to 'devocion in praier or in the passion of Christ' (l. 1070). The word *devotion* does not occur at all, however, in the introspective meditation on the image of sin in the soul and the destruction of that image that occupies the latter half of *Scale* I.[35]

Hilton's *Scale* II refers to devotion only sixteen times,[36] all but two of these in chapters dealing with the beginning stages of the spiritual life. Five occurrences are in the discussion in Chapter 10 of how those who are reformed to

---

[34] A rate of occurrence of approximately once every 1500 words.

[35] The word *devotion* does occur twice in the latter half of *Scale* I: once in a discussion of the physical impediments to spiritual activity (l. 2229), and once in a reference to the anchoress's being interrupted 'in preiere or in devocioun' by someone who wishes to speak to her (l. 2388).

[36] A rate of occurrence of approximately once in every 3500 words.

the image of God in faith through the sacraments may not 'felen þe special ȝifte of deuocion or of gostli felynge' (10/3–4, ll. 390–91 in Bestul); that they are saved even though they never have 'gostli felynge ne inly sauour ne special grace of deuocion in al her lyfe tyme' (10/20–21, ll. 404–05 in Bestul); those who may 'felen deuocion and gostli sauour in God, as sum soules done þurgh speciale grace' (10/22–24, l. 407 in Bestul) are not the only ones saved, but also those 'þe qwhilke felen not þe gifte of speciale deuocion ne gostli knowyng of God as sum gostly men don' (10/53–55, ll. 432–34 in Bestul), that 'kun not speken perfitely to God be feruour of deuocion ne brennend loue in contemplacion' (10/82–83, ll. 456–57 in Bestul).

The next nine occurrences of the word *devotion* occur in the discussion of the gifts of spiritual beginners in Chapters 28 and 29: 'For in begynnynge of turnynge, swilk a man þat is disposed to mykel grace is so qwykly and so felendly inspyred and feleþ often so grete swetnes in deuocyon, and haþ so many terys in compunccyon' (28/29–32, ll. 1799–1801 in Bestul). 'Sum han grete compunccions for here synnes, and sum han grete deuocyons and feruours in preyers' (29/6–8, ll. 1855–6 in Bestul); but that these gifts, although they seem greater than the gifts of others who have travailed longer and further in the spiritual life, 'þese gostly felynges, where þei standen in compunccyon or in deuocyon or in gostly ymaginacyon, are not þe gostly felynges whilk a soule schal hafe and fele in þe grace of contemplacyon' (29/15–18, ll. 1863–5 in Bestul).[37] The theme continues in the discussion of the meditation on Christ as man, and as God in man, in Chapter 30: 'many soules bygynnend and profytend haue grete feruour and mikel swetnes in deuocyon and, as it semeþ, brennen al in lufe' (30/50–52, ll. 1973–74 in Bestul). But 'þe lufe þat þe soule felyth in þenkynge and beholdynge of God in man, whan it is graciously schewed, is wurthyere, gostlyere and more medful þan al feruour of deuocyon þat þe soule feleþ by ymagynacyon only of þe manhed' (30/98–101, ll. 2013–15 in Bestul).[38] Devotion is only referred to twice in the latter part of *Scale* II, both times in the context of prayer.[39] The allegories of the pilgrimage to Jerusalem, the city on the plain, the good night and the bad day, the midday fiend, and the three men standing in the sun — all of the descriptions of the higher part of the contemplative life in *Scale* II — lack any reference to 'devotion'. In *Scale* II, even more than in *Scale* I and the *Mixed Life*, devotion is a gift, an affect, and an activity appropriate to

---

[37] Other occurrences of *devotion* in this chapter are at 29/28, 77, and 80 (ll. 1875, 1914, and 1916 in Bestul).

[38] There is one other occurrence of *devotion* at 30/106 (l. 2020 in Bestul).

[39] At 42/64 and 43/86 (ll. 3205 and 3343 in Bestul).

spiritual beginners whose meditation is on the manhood of Christ, and whose reward is a 'manly', a sensual, rather than a 'godly', a 'gostly', a spiritual, fervour. As Hilton puts it at the end of *Of Angels' Song*, his critique of a spirituality modelled on the experiences of Richard Rolle, 'It sufficith to me for to lyffe in trouthe principally and noghte in felynge'.[40]

And yet. There seems to be an affective turn here, because *Scale* II is about nothing but feeling. To backtrack a moment: the word *feeling* occurs six times in the letter *On Mixed Life*.[41] Two of these refer to physical sensation (ll. 22, 484), and three occur in the comparisons of knowing in understanding and feeling in love (ll. 22, 798, and 801). One expresses a sentiment like that just cited from *Of Angels' Song*: in an explication of 1 Cor. 5. 6, 'while we are at home in the body we are away from the Lord', Hilton observes, 'We goo bi trouþe, not bi siȝt; þat is we lyuen in trouþe, not in bodili feelynge' (ll. 527–29).

There are forty-two occurrences of the word *feeling* in *Scale* I,[42] approximately evenly divided between references to 'bodily' and to 'ghostly' feeling.[43] The largest concentration of references to bodily feeling (fourteen references) occur in Chapters 9–12, in the discussion of

> visiones or revelaciouns of ony maner spirite, bodily apperynge or in ymagynynge, slepand or wakand, or ellis ony othere feelinge in the bodili wittes maad as it were goosteli; either in sownynge of the eere, or saverynge in the mouth, or smellynge in the nose or ellis ony felable heete as it were fier glowand and warmand the breest, or ony othere partie of the bodi, or onythinge that mai be feelyd bi bodili wit, though it be never so comfortable and lykande.[44]

These, Hilton says, 'aren not verili contemplacion; ne thei aren but symple and secundarie though thei be good, in regard of goostli vertues and in goosteli knowynge and loovyng of God'.[45]

The greatest concentration of references to 'gostli' feeling occur in the discussion of the reformation of the soul 'bi fulheed of vertues turnyd into affec-

---

[40] Hilton, *Of Angels' Song*, ed. by Horstman, I, 175–82.

[41] A rate of occurrence of once every 1500 words.

[42] A rate of occurrence of once every 1100 words.

[43] References to bodily feeling occur in Bestul, at ll. 165, 181, 184, 198, 202, 209, 212, 217, 223, 230, 237, 239, 247, 251, 280, 469, 470, and 601; references to ghostly feeling occur at ll. 165, 287, 288, 345, 360, 386, 389, 399, 400, 475, 498, 606, 771, 773, 803, 804, 1597, 2191, 2192, and 2613.

[44] Bestul, ll. 200–205.

[45] Bestul, ll. 205–07.

cion' in the following chapters,[46] and particularly in the discussion of the virtue of meekness in Chapters 16 and 19–20.

Scale II, on the other hand, refers to 'feeling' a remarkable 213 times.[47] The reason for the emphasis on feeling is that there has been a major shift in the way that Hilton describes — and, to an extent, conceptualizes — the contemplative life. Treating the gift — the grace — of contemplation as a second stage in the reformation of the human soul from the image of sin to which it was corrupted by the sin of Adam and Eve to the image of God in which it was first created, Hilton describes a process of reformation in faith alone and of reformation in faith and in feeling. The first nine chapters of *Scale* II discuss the reformation of the soul in faith, by the redemptive sacrifice of the God-man (drawing on Anselm of Canterbury's *Cur Deus homo*), through the sacraments of baptism and penance. The tenth raises the question why those who are saved through faith might 'not felen þe special ȝifte of deuocion or of gostli felynge'.[48] The next six chapters deal with the difference in feeling, made explicit in Chapter 13, among those who are not reformed, those who are reformed in faith alone, and those who are reformed in faith and in feeling. The seventeenth through twentieth chapters make the transition between the discussion of reformation in faith alone and reformation in faith and in feeling. At Chapter 21, entitled 'An entre how þou schalt come to þis reformyng'[49] (the Carmelite friar Thomas Fishlake's contemporary Latin translation calls it an 'Introduccio'), the focus of *Scale* II changes: from here on, it will deal almost entirely with the reformation in faith and in feeling. What Hilton does from here on is to rewrite every major theme of his earlier works — from his discussion of the extirpation of the vices and the cultivation of the virtues to imaginative and sensory devotion — in terms of a contemplative grace of love, the gift of a derivative, created version of that love the uncreated version of which is the Holy Spirit, the third person of the Trinity. What this grace causes, Hilton says, is a complete conversion of feeling.[50]

[46] Quotation from Bestul, l. 315.

[47] A rate of occurrence of nearly four times in every thousand words.

[48] Hilton, *The Scale of Perfection, Book II*, ed. by Hussey and Sargent, 10/3–4 (ll. 391 in Bestul).

[49] Hilton, *The Scale of Perfection, Book II*, ed. by Hussey and Sargent, 21/1–2. This chapter has a different title in Lambeth Palace Library, MS 472, on which the Bestul edition is based.

[50] It should be noted that Thomas Fishlake appears to have mistaken Hilton's meaning here: he invariably translates 'feeling' as 'sensacio'. This is, I believe, of a piece of his tendency to include Christo-centric and Passion-centric meditational additions throughout the text: his version is much more 'devotional' in the conventional sense than Hilton's original. See Sargent,

In Chapter 31, he defends his formulation, 'reformation in faith and in feeling' on the basis of several Pauline texts, beginning with 'nolite conformari huic sæculo, sed reformamini in novitate sensus vestri' (Romans 12. 2), a text that present-day translations render as 'be not conformed to this world; but be reformed in the newness of your mind' — the Wycliffite version is 'of ȝoure wit' — but which Hilton translates as:

> Ȝe þat are þurgh grace reformed in feiþ, conforme ȝow not henforward to maners of þe werd, in pride, in coueytyse, and oþer synnes, bot be ȝe reformed in newhed of felynge. Lo, here þou maight se þat Seyn Poule spekeþ of reformynge in felynge, and what þat new felynge is he expouneþ in anoþer place þus: *Vt impleamini in agnicione voluntatis eius, in omni intellectu et sapiencia spirituali.* Þat is: We preye God þat ȝe moun be fulfilled in knowynge of Goddis wille, in al vndirstondynge and in al maner gostly wysdom. Þis is reformynge in felynge. For þou schalt vnderstondyn þat þe soule haþ two maner of felynges: one withouten of þe fyfe bodily wittes, anoþer withinne of þe gostly wyttes þe whilk are properly þe myȝtes of þe soule: mende, reson and wille. Whan þese myȝtes are þurgh grace fulfilled in al vnderstondynge of þe wil of God and in gostly wysdom, þan haþ þe soule new gracyous felynges. (31/18–28)

Hilton goes on to describe the reformation in feeling of these three powers of the soul, mind (or memory), reason, and will — the created image of the uncreated Trinity — in ever more rhapsodic terms: in Chapter 40 in particular, the 'opnyng of þe gostly eye', the 'lyghtty mirkenes', the 'ry[che] noȝt',

> purete of spirit and gostly rest, inward stilnes and pees of conscience, heyghnes or depnes of thoght and onlynes of soule, a lyuely felyng of grace and pryuete of herte, þe wakere slepe of þe spouse and a tastyng of heuenly sauour, brennyng in lufe and schynyng in lyght, entre of contemplacyon and reformyng in felynge. (40/3, 9–13)

His language here verges on that of the Song of Songs, the tradition of commentary on which underlies much of the latter chapters of *Scale* II, which describes the inspirations and revelations received by the contemplative soul as 'bot swete lettre-sendyngys made atwix a louynge soule and Jesu loued; or ellys if I schal sey sothlyer atwix Jesu þe trewe lufere and soules lufed of him' (46/96–8), as the 'pryuey rownynge of Jesu in þe ere of a clene soule' (46/51–2). And, in a phrase used three times in the last two chapters of *Scale* II (a phrase with which the text may originally have ended): 'Þis is þe voyce of Jesu' (46/54: see also 40/36, 44/3, 44/14).

This is the affective turn of Walter Hilton.

'Patterns of Circulation and Variation in the English and Latin Texts'.

Book II *of The Scale of Perfection in Late Medieval English Devotional Compilations*

Hilton describes such emotional practices as tears of compunction and contrition for one's sins, the *incendium* and the *melos amoris* that warmed the breast of Richard Rolle, and the sympathetic suffering of compassion for the Passion of Christ as aspects of the experience of spiritual novices and *proficientes*, categorically different from the 'reformation in faith and in feeling' of the *perfecti*. As he describes it in the passages cited just above and elsewhere in the latter half of *Scale* II, this feeling consists in a complete conversion of intellect (understanding) and will by grace that creates a *habitus* of love for God that gives shape and reason to all the acts and feelings of the contemplative's life. As Barbara Rosenwein has pointed out, this *habitus* of charity was articulated particularly within the physical limitations in which the emotional communities of the reformed monastic orders of the twelfth century spent their lives (she uses the Cistercian Aelred of Rievaulx as her exemplar);[51] but as Hilton and other late fourteenth- and fifteenth-century writers taught, emotional communities moved and governed by the same (or similar) *habitus* could equally be constituted out of the readership of their books. Hilton was particularly aware that the monastic life was not a universal ideal, writing in several of his Latin letters to encourage or discourage his readers in their choice of vocation, and questioning his own reticence to enter a religious order;[52] he wrote the first book of *The Scale of Perfection* for a woman enclosed as an anchoress who was unable (probably for lack of Latinity) to carry out the normal monastic contemplative practice of reading, meditation, and prayer; and he famously wrote his English letter *On Mixed Life* for a layman of means who wished to devote himself to a life of contemplation, but could not leave aside his worldly obligations. Not only was Hilton himself actively engaged in the construction of the *habitus* of the contemplative life outside of religious orders, but in the affective circuit of writing and reading, copying, and compiling, those who transmitted his text constituted themselves as not just a reading community, but an affective community as well. It is thus not inappropriate that *The Scale of Perfection* should occur in late medieval English devotional compilations, and it is to the consideration of some of these compilations that we turn at this point.

[51] See 'Love and Treachery', in Rosenwein, *Generations of Feeling*, pp. 88–143.

[52] Hilton wrote his Latin letter *De Utilitate et prerogativis religionis* to encourage his friend Adam Horsley to join the Carthusian order; his *Epistola ad Quemdam seculo renunciare volentem* argues the opposite; both comment on the fact that he has not joined a religious order himself. See Hilton, *Latin Writings*, ed. by Clark and Taylor, 119–72, 249–98.

There are two senses in which the *Scale* may be spoken of as occurring in devotional compilations: the complete text of the *Scale*, or of one or the other book of the *Scale*, may be one of the contents of a devotional anthology; or sentences or passages drawn from the *Scale* may be included in a compilation.[53] It should be noted further that compilations may have a strong identity as works in themselves like *The Chastising of God's Children*, or their constituent parts may be loosely connected in variable manuscript attestation like the *Pore Caitif*. Such compilations may also be the only contents of a given manuscript or included with other works in an anthology.

To deal with devotional anthologies first: we should note that the complete text of *The Scale of Perfection* occurs in surviving medieval manuscripts together with other contents eleven times out of twenty-two originally complete examples.[54] One surviving affiliational group of four manuscripts, the London group, comprises three anthologies of Hilton's English writings: Lambeth Palace Library, MS 472; Inner Temple, MS Petyt 524; BL, MS Harley 2397; and Bodl. Lib., MS Bodley 592.[55] The best-known of these, Lambeth MS 472,

---

[53] I will distinguish in this discussion between 'compilations' — individual works composed of materials drawn from various sources — and 'anthologies' — manuscripts comprising various contents. The distinction between anthologies, the contents of which have an observable organizing principle, and miscellanies, which do not, is made in the Introduction to this volume. Because the manuscripts in which Hilton material occurs tend to have organizing principles (they are collections of contemplative materials), they are generally to be thought of as anthologies.

[54] Large Middle English texts seldom occur in manuscripts with many other contents, although large single manuscript collections do have their place, like the Vernon and Simeon manuscripts or the thick paper anthologies of monastic materials in which a number of copies of Thomas Fishlake's Latin version of the *Scale* occur. See, e.g., Monica Hedlund's description of Uppsala, Universitetsbiblioteket, MS C 159, in her '*Liber Clementis Maydeston*'.

[55] The use of the term 'London group' to designate this affiliational group of manuscripts of *Scale* II is a more precise usage than that in Sargent, 'Walter Hilton's *Scale of Perfection*', which also included manuscripts that are now recognized to belong to the 'Carthusian-Brigittine' group that (with the exception of CUL, MS Ee.4.30, to be discussed below) is not textually or codicologically connected with the 'London group'. The Carthusian-Brigittine group comprises Brussels, Bibl. Royale, MSS 2544–45; Cambridge, Trinity College, MS B.15.18 (James 354); the unnumbered, uncatalogued Chatsworth manuscript; San Marino, Huntington Library, MS HM 266; BL, MSS Harley 2387 and 6579, and London, Westminster School, MS 4; Bodl. Lib., MS Bodley 100 and MS Laud misc. 602; New Haven, Yale University, Beinecke Library, MS Takamiya 3, and the 1494 Wynkyn de Worde print (*STC* 14042) and all subsequent incunable printings of the *Scale*. Oxford, All Souls' Library, MS 25 is affiliated with this group for the first half of the text of *Scale* II. For fuller details of all of these manuscripts and manuscript groups, see the Introduction to Hilton, *The Scale of Perfection, Book II*, ed. by Hussey and Sargent.

is the 'common-profit' book made from the goods of John Killum, a London grocer whose will was attested in 1416; this manuscript has both books of the *Scale*, the *Mixed Life*, the *Eight Chapters of Perfection*, and the commentaries on 'Qui habitat', 'Bonum est', and the 'Benedictus'.[56]

The Petyt manuscript belonged to the London organmaker Henry Langford (by his name, apparently a man of Northern origin), 'dwelling in the Minories' — that is, near the house of Franciscan nuns (the Poor Claires — the 'minoresses') without Aldgate. This manuscript is a direct copy of Lambeth MS 472, even including, in the hand of the scribe, the marginal corrections and annotations added by others in the margins of the Lambeth manuscript. The Petyt manuscript comprises the two books of the *Scale* preceded by a fragment of the end of the *Mixed Life*, and the *Eight Chapters of Perfection*.

BL, MS Harley 2397 was given by Elizabeth Horwood, abbess of the Poor Claires, to that house in memory of herself, her father and mother, and one Robert Alderton. It comprises the text of *Scale* II,[57] the *Mixed Life*, and the 'Bonum est' commentary. There is some variation in format between the text of the *Scale* and the other Hilton materials.

Bodl. Lib., MS Bodley 592 is closely affiliated in text to the Lambeth and Petyt manuscripts; in fact, some of its readings appear to reflect corrections made to the text of Lambeth MS 472 by one of its correctors. Bodl. Lib., MS Bodley 592 is written in a textura hand and central midland standard dialect that obscure its origin.[58] It contains nothing but the complete text of the *Scale*, written in the same page format (including headers) as the Lambeth Palace manuscript.

It should also be noted that CUL, MS Ee.4.30, a fair copy of a thorough conflation of the London and Carthusian-Brigittine forms of the text of *Scale* II, comprises, like all other manuscripts of the latter group, the complete text of both books of the *Scale* alone.

Two other manuscripts comprising both books of the *Scale* also contain other works by Walter Hilton. One manuscript of the 'Carthusian-Brigittine' affiliational group of manuscripts of *Scale* II, MS Takamiya 3 in the Yale University, Beinecke Library (*olim* Luttrell Wynne), comprises Hilton's *Angels' Song* as well.

---

[56] As is often noted, the lost manuscript corresponding to item M.26 in the catalogue of the library of the brethren at Syon Abbey had the same contents as the Lambeth Palace manuscript. See *Syon Abbey*, ed. by Gillespie, pp. 469–70.

[57] The *ex libris* occurs on fol. 94ᵛ. This manuscript does not contain *Scale* I, but the *incipit* of *Scale* II (fol. 1ʳ) describes it as, 'þe secunde part of þe reformyng of mannys soule drawyn of Maistir Watir Hiltone hermyte'.

[58] Samuels, 'Some Applications of Middle English Dialectology', p. 79 n. 5.

Textually, it is the closest surviving copy to the 1494 Wynkyn de Worde editio princeps of the *Scale* (to which Hilton's *Mixed Life* was added as a 'Third Book', apparently at the request of Lady Margaret Beaufort). Another manuscript, New York, Columbia University Library, MS Plimpton 271, which was originally part of the same manuscript as MS Plimpton 257 of the *Scale* (probably separated in the nineteenth century, and acquired separately by Plimpton), comprises Hilton's *Mixed Life*. The connections of this manuscript will be described below.

Three manuscripts of *Scale* II that may be members of another affiliational group all share the characteristic that they read 'God' over one hundred times where the other manuscripts read 'Jesus' — a 'theocentric' (as opposed to 'Christocentric') tendency also found in the text of *Scale* I in the same manuscripts.[59] The earliest of these manuscripts is Bodl. Lib., MS Rawlinson C. 285, which Ralph Hanna has demonstrated to be the source of two other surviving manuscripts, CUL, MSS Dd.5.55 and Ff.5.40.[60] As originally written at the end of the fourteenth century, the Rawlinson manuscript comprised four separate booklets written by two scribes: the first booklet, made up of four gatherings written by the first scribe, contained a copy of *Scale* I that lacked the 'Christocentric' additions, the 'Holy Name' passage at the end of Chapter 44, and the 'Charity' passage in Chapter 78,[61] dialectally localizable to northern Yorkshire.[62] A second scribe added an extract from *The Prick of Conscience*, written in a scribal dialectally localizable to north-western Yorkshire, on the last sheet. The second booklet, now missing, would probably have been written by the same second scribe, and comprised Rolle's *The Commandment*, the short tract 'Proper Will', Hilton's *Angels' Song*, and a tract on 'Deadly Sin' (*IPMEP* 660, 551, 146, and 149, respectively) in one gathering.[63] The third booklet (the second surviving booklet), written by the same scribe, was made up of two gath-

---

[59] MSS Bodl. Lib., Rawlinson C.285, BL Add. 11748, and Plimpton 257. These manuscripts are at the core of the group that Evelyn Underhill and Helen Gardner noted as lacking the 'Christo-centric additions' to Book I of the *Scale* found in BL, MS Harley 6579. This was one of the major criteria of their textual analysis. See Hilton, *The Scale of Perfection*, ed. by Underhill, pp. xliii–l, and Gardner, 'The Text of *The Scale of Perfection*'.

[60] Hanna, *The English Manuscripts of Richard Rolle*, items 94, 12, and 15; see also Hanna, 'The History of a Book'. The following discussion follows Hanna's construction.

[61] A member, thus, of Rosemary Dorward's textual Group **N**, A. J. Bliss's Group **Z**. See Sargent, 'Editing Walter Hilton's Scale of Perfection'.

[62] Booklets 1–3 are described by McIntosh, Samuels, and Benskin, *A Linguistic Atlas of Late Mediaeval English* (hereafter *LALME*), LP 22, as Northern, probably Yorkshire; for the characterization of the *Prick of Conscience* fragment, see Hanna, *The English Manuscripts of Richard Rolle*, item 94.

[63] *IPMEP* is Lewis and others, *Index of Printed Middle English Prose*.

erings containing Rolle's *Form of Living* followed by a set of nine extracts from Hilton's *Scale* I, other extracts from Rolle, and other contemplative writings. The fourth booklet (the third surviving) comprises a single gathering begun by the second scribe, who copied the *Meditation on the Passion* often ascribed to Rolle (*IPMEP* 480), to which a third northern Yorkshire scribe has added *The Epistle of St John the Hermit* and a set of English extracts from the 'Sayings of the Fathers' (*IPMEP* 274 and 546, respectively).

CUL, MS Dd.5.55, written in a single hand dialectally localizable to northwest Yorkshire (*LALME*, I, 254), comprises *Scale* I, Rolle's *Commandment*, the short tract 'Proper Will', Hilton's *Angels' Song*, and the tract on 'Deadly Sin', all closely affiliated to Bodl. Lib., MS Rawlinson C. 285 textually, followed by the same extract from *The Prick of Conscience* as occurs in the Rawlinson manuscript. It also contains a number of shorter pieces that may have been added into the Rawlinson manuscript as gathering- and booklet-filler. CUL, MS Ff.5.40, written by three scribes in hands dialectally localizable to northeastern Norfolk (*LALME*, LP 4663: adjacent to the border of Ely and southern Lincolnshire), opens with a copy of Hilton's *Mixed Life* and one of the English versions of Rolle's *Ego Dormio*, followed by *Scale* I, Rolle's *Commandment*, the short tract 'Proper Will', Hilton's *Angels' Song*, and the tract on 'Deadly Sin', then the extract from *The Prick of Conscience* and the materials that follow it in the third and fourth booklets of the Rawlinson manuscript.

These three manuscripts were anthologies of materials on the contemplative life drawn primarily from Hilton and Rolle, and apparently originating in Yorkshire, where both the Rawlinson manuscript and CUL, MS Dd.5.55 were written. The Rawlinson manuscript seems to have been returned to an area of Norfolk near the point of origin of Hilton's early writings in Cambridge and Ely, where a fourth hand, dialectally localizable to western Norfolk,[64] added a copy of a 'theocentric' version of *Scale* II that matched the 'theocentric' text of *Scale* I. Both of the Cambridge manuscripts were presumably copied before this addition was made.

Closely affiliated with these three manuscripts textually are two other manuscripts of *Scale* I, Oxford, University College, MS 28, written late in the fifteenth century in a dialect localizable to the West Riding of Yorkshire (*LALME*, LP 358), and BL, MS Harley 1022, in a dialect localizable to north-west Yorkshire (*LALME*, LP 115). BL, MS Harley 1022 also comprises a small anthology of other contemplative works that includes copies of an English version of Rolle's *Oleum effusum*, *The Rule of Life of Our Lady*, and Gaytrygge's *Catechism* juxta-

---

[64] See Hanna, *The English Manuscripts of Richard Rolle*, item 94.

posed just as in BL, MS Additional 11748, a manuscript written in the first half of the fifteenth century in a scribal dialect displaying overlaid southern (Dorset) and West Midland features.[65] BL, MS Add. 11748 also contains a copy of the same 'theocentric' form of *Scale* II as Bodl. Lib., MS Rawlinson C. 285.[66]

One other manuscript has both *Scale* I and *Scale* II in 'theocentric' form like Bodl. Lib., MS Rawlinson C. 285 and BL, MS Add. 11748: New York, Columbia University Library, MS Plimpton 257. As mentioned above, this manuscript and MS Plimpton 271 were originally a single large volume, written in the later fifteenth century in a dialect localizable to Surrey (*LALME*, LP 5620). MS Plimpton 257 contains a copy of *Scale* I closely affiliated with the text in the Vernon and Simeon manuscripts; MS Plimpton 271 contains Hilton's *Mixed Life* equally closely affiliated with the copies of that text in Vernon and Simeon.[67] Vernon and Simeon do not have *Scale* II: a copy of the 'theocentric' form of that text like that in the Rawlinson manuscript has been added in MS Plimpton 257.

The 'theocentric' form of *Scale* I thus circulated in the north and west of England (although it does occur elsewhere) at the end of the fourteenth century in manuscripts in which it is compiled with other contemplative works, particularly those of Richard Rolle. The 'theocentric' form of *Scale* II occurs only in manuscripts already containing the 'theocentric' form of *Scale* I, to which it was added in the fifteenth century, in copies with more southerly connections.

There are two other devotional anthologies that comprise both books of the *Scale*: neither is affiliated with any textually or codicologically identifiable group of manuscripts for *Scale* II; both Dorward and Bliss describe them as related for *Scale* I.[68] The earlier of the two, Philadelphia, University of Pennsylvania Library, codex 218, was written in two hands in the first quarter of the fifteenth century, all but the last item in a dialect localizable to Ely (*LALME*, LP 559); the scribal dialect of the final item is localizable to the adjacent area of southeast Lincolnshire.[69] The late fifteenth-century blind-stamped binding is by the

---

[65] Angus McIntosh, in private correspondence with A. J. Bliss, *c.* 1964.

[66] For BL, MS Harley 1022, see Hanna, *The English Manuscripts of Richard Rolle*, item 48. *Scale* I and the compilation in BL, MS Harley 1022 occupy the middle two of four 'originally separate (although linked) books' that comprise this manuscript. Hanna notes the similarity of this compilation to that in Bodl Lib., MS Rawlinson C. 285 and its descendants CUL, MSS Dd.5.55 and Ff.5.40 in 'The History of a Book', pp. 79–80.

[67] See Hilton, *Mixed Life*, ed. by Ogilvie-Thomson, p. xxxv.

[68] Both are members of Dorward's and Bliss's textual Group **Q**.

[69] Lewis and McIntosh, *A Descriptive Guide*, item MV 92.

'Virgin and Child' binder, active in the Winchester area.[70] Besides the *Scale*, this manuscript comprises a copy of *The Prickyng of Love* with an ascription to Hilton,[71] and a complete text of the *Contemplations of the Dread and Love of God*.[72] The second hand has added a one-gathering fragment of the beginning of *The Prick of Conscience* at the end.

The second independent devotional anthology containing a complete copy of the *Scale* is Cambridge, Corpus Christi College, MS R.5 (James 268), written in the mid- to late fifteenth century in a dialect localizable to Suffolk (*LALME*, LP 8390). There is a note of gift by Elizabeth Wylby, a nun of the Augustinian priory of Campsey in the early sixteenth century; Elizabeth Wyllowby is also recorded as giving a printed copy of *The Chastising of God's Children* to Catherine Symond of the same house.[73] *Scale* I in the Corpus Christi College manuscript is preceded by a unique one-gathering 'confortable tretyes to strengthyn and confortyn creaturys in the feyth specialy hem that arn symple and disposyd to fallyn in desperacyon'.[74] Immediately following *Scale* I in the Corpus manuscript is a copy of the *Seven Points of True Love and Everlasting Wisdom*,[75] the last verso of the final gathering of which is blank; *Scale* II begins a new gathering.

All of the devotional anthologies containing copies of *Scale* II, and the other manuscripts with which they are connected, are thus collections of similar contemplative materials. The small number of compilations comprising material drawn from the *Scale* also occurs in manuscript anthologies of contemplative writings. Probably the best known of these is the 'Westminster Compilation' (London, Westminster Cathedral Treasury, MS 4), which has been edited by Marleen Cré.[76] Although, as Cré notes, this compilation can be read as a coherent work in itself (and thus not an 'anthology' per se),[77] it has usually been dis-

---

[70] Zacour and Hirsch, *Catalogue of Manuscripts*, p. 50; Krochalis, '*Contemplations of the Dread and Love of God*'.

[71] See Sargent, 'A New Manuscript of *The Chastising of God's Children*' and *The Prickynge of Love*, ed. by Kane, p. viii.

[72] *Contemplations*, ed. by Connolly.

[73] Erler, *Women, Reading, and Piety*, p. 125.

[74] Jolliffe, *Check-List*, K.13.

[75] This is the compilation drawn from Henry Suso's *Horologium sapientiae*. See Suso, *Horologium sapientiae*, ed. by Künzle, pp. 267–74, and Lovatt, 'Henry Suso and the Medieval Mystical Tradition in England'.

[76] Cré, 'London, Westminster Cathedral Treasury, MS 4'.

[77] Cré, 'Authority and the Compiler in Westminster Cathedral Treasury MS 4' and '"This Blessed Beholdyng"'.

cussed because one of its component sections is a set of extracts from the Long Text of the *Revelations* of Julian of Norwich — the only medieval witness to the Long Text.[78] The compilation comprises sets of extracts from Hilton's commentaries on 'Qui habitat' and 'Bonum est', both books of Hilton's *Scale*, and Julian's *Revelations*, in that order. The extracts from the two commentaries and from Julian follow the order of their original texts; those from the *Scale* are interwoven into a more sophisticated tract entitled, in a sixteenth-century header, 'Of the Knowledge of Ourselves and of God'. The text of *Scale* II in the Westminster Compilation is most closely affiliated with that of the Carthusian-Brigittine group of manuscripts, although it also shares the tendency to replace the name 'Jesus' with 'God' with the 'theocentric' group of manuscripts described above — although the 'theocentric' tendency of the Westminster Compilation may be idiosyncratic, since it reads 'God' for 'Jesus' even where the manuscripts of the 'theocentric' group agree with all others in reading 'Jesus'.

The *Scale* is also drawn upon in a pair of related short compilations, 'Of Actyfe Lyfe and Contemplatyfe Declaracion' in the northern English devotional anthology, BL, MS Additional 37049, and 'Via ad Contemplacionem' in BL, MS Additional 37790.[79] Both compilations comprise extracts from *The Cloud of Unknowing* and two other works of the *Cloud*-corpus, the *Benjamin Minor* and the *Pistle of Discrecioun of Stirings*, from Hugh of Balma's *Mystica theologia*, Rolle's *Form of Living*, and both books of the *Scale*, interwoven into a tract on the contemplative life. The extracts from *Scale* II, all of a sentence or less, are taken in order from Chapters 21 through 23.

Finally, there is a collection of passages from Chapters 21–25 and 41–46 of *Scale* II added in a two-gathering booklet at the end of Dublin, Trinity College, MS A.5.7, a manuscript of *The Cloud of Unknowing* and *The Book of Privy Counselling* copied c. 1500,[80] and a six-folio set of extracts from both books of the *Scale* in Dublin, Trinity College, MS C.5.20, a commonplace book kept by Edmund Horde. Horde was a Carthusian first of London, then of Hinton Charterhouse, where he was prior 1529–39; he joined the Marian refounda-

---

[78] See Julian of Norwich, *A Book of Showings*, ed. by Colledge and Walsh, I, 9–10; Julian of Norwich, 'The Westminster Revelation (with Hugh Kempster)', ed. by Watson and Jenkins.

[79] See Jolliffe, 'Two Middle English Tracts'; Marleen Cré discusses the second of these in *Vernacular Mysticism in the Charterhouse*, pp. 239–45.

[80] See *The Cloud of Unknowing*, ed. by Hodgson, p. xvii. Unfortunately, as Hodgson notes (p. xx), the Dublin manuscript was discovered only when the edition was already at press (in the midst of World War II), and it was not possible to incorporate it into the edition beyond the observation of its agreement with CUL, MS Kk.6.26 and BL, MS Harley 2373 in a small group of textually significant readings.

tion of Sheen and was exiled with the community of Sheen Anglorum, among whom he died in Louvain in 1578.

* * *

What has been offered here is only a partial view of the ways in which Walter Hilton's *Scale of Perfection* is textually embedded in late medieval English devotional anthologies and compilations: it has dealt only with manuscripts comprising the text — or parts of the text, at least — of *Scale* II. The complex textual situation of *Scale* I will have to be described when work on the critical edition allows for a more accurate determination than is possible at this point of the textual relations of copies in which Hilton's first book circulated alone. Some of that complexity has spilled over into the discussion of the 'theocentric' group of texts of *Scale* II: three of the manuscripts of this group — Bodl. Lib., MS Rawlinson C. 285, New York, Columbia University Library, MS Plimpton 257, and BL, MS Add. 11748 — also include versions of *Scale* I that occur in related manuscripts alongside of compilations drawn from the works of Richard Rolle and others. Three of the four manuscripts of the London group comprise collections of Hilton's works.

There are also four surviving manuscripts that are not related to any of these affiliational groups. Two of these, Cambridge, Corpus Christi College, MS R.5 (James 268) and University of Pennsylvania Library, codex 218, are anthologies that also comprise works not by Hilton. Another independent manuscript, BL, MS Harley 6573, comprises a copy of both books of the *Scale* alone, with no other contents. The fourth independent copy, Cambridge, Magdalene College, Old Library MS F.4.17, has a copy of *Scale* II alone with a unique opening that suggests it was adapted to stand without *Scale* I.

The largest group of manuscripts comprising both books of *The Scale of Perfection*, the eleven medieval manuscripts of the Carthusian-Brigittine group,[81] contain the *Scale* alone. On the other hand, the 1494 Wynkyn de Worde editio princeps,[82] which is textually a member of the Carthusian-Brigittine group, and the seventeenth-century Brussels manuscript that was copied from a printed exemplar also contain Hilton's *Mixed Life* as an additional 'Third Book' of the

---

[81] Including Oxford, All Souls' Library, MS 25 and CUL, MS Ee.4.30, which are partially affiliated with the Carthusian-Brigittine group. The Yale (*olim* Luttrell-Wynne, *olim* Takamiya) manuscript is an exception to the generalization stated above: it also comprises a copy of Hilton's *Angels' Song*.

[82] *STC* 14042.

Scale. As I have noted elsewhere,[83] the addition of the *Mixed Life* appears to have been made at the desire of Margaret Beaufort, who sponsored the printing of the *Scale*. The *Mixed Life* is codicologically independent of the text of the *Scale* in the 1494 print, having a different set of signatures and page layout; and the *Mixed Life* occurs only in five of sixteen surviving copies. When Julian Notary reprinted the *Scale* in 1507,[84] he seems to have been working from a copy of the de Worde print without the *Mixed Life*, for he adds it to the end of the *Scale* not as a 'Third Book', but as a separate work, and copies it from a different exemplar. De Worde's three subsequent incunable prints,[85] and Brussels, Bibliothèque Royale, MSS 2544–45 as well, follow Notary. It is in this form that most sixteenth-century readers of Walter Hilton, like Thomas More,[86] probably encountered the *Scale*. From its first circulation at the end of the fourteenth century until the Reformation of the sixteenth century, Walter Hilton's *Scale of Perfection* often travelled in the company of the great devotional literature of the age.

---

[83] Sargent, 'Walter Hilton's *Scale of Perfection*', pp. 206–08.

[84] *STC* 14043.

[85] Wynkyn de Worde 1519, 1525, and 1533 (*STC* nos. 14043.5–14045).

[86] More famously suggests in the Preface to his *Confutation of Tyndale's Answer* that people would do better to read 'Bonauenture of the lyfe of Cryste, Gerson of the folowynge of Cryste, and the deuoute contemplatyue booke of Scala perfectionis with suche other lyke' (see More, *The Confutation of Tyndale's Answer*, ed. by Schuster and others, p. 37). All three of these are books readily available in incunable printings: Nicholas Love's *The Mirror of the Blessed Life of Jesus Christ*, the English version of the pseudo-Bonaventuran *Meditationes vitae Christi*, was printed by William Caxton in 1484 and 1490, Richard Pynson in 1494 and 1506, and de Worde in 1494, 1506, 1517, 1525, and 1530 (*STC* 3259–67); *The Imitation of Christ*, attributed to Jean Gerson, by Pynson in 1503, 1504, and 1517, and de Worde in 1515, 1522, and 1525 (*STC* 23954–60). See Love, *The Mirror*, ed. by Sargent, intro pp. 95–96.

Works Cited

Manuscripts

Brussels, Bibliothèque Royale, MSS 2544–45
Cambridge, Corpus Christi College, MS R.5 (James 268)
Cambridge, Magdalene College, Old Library MS F.4.17
Cambridge, Trinity College, MS B.15.18 (James 354)
Cambridge, University Library [CUL], MS Dd.5.55
Cambridge, University Library [CUL], MS Ee.4.30
Cambridge, University Library [CUL], MS Ff.5.40
Cambridge, University Library [CUL], MS Kk.6.26
Chatsworth MS
Dublin, Trinity College, MS A.5.7
Dublin, Trinity College, MS C.5.20
London, British Library [BL], MS Additional 11748
London, British Library [BL], MS Additional 37049
London, British Library [BL], MS Additional 37790
London, British Library [BL], MS Harley 1022
London, British Library [BL], MS Harley 2373
London, British Library [BL], MS Harley 2387
London, British Library [BL], MS Harley 2397
London, British Library [BL], MS Harley 6573
London, British Library [BL], MS Harley 6579
London, Inner Temple, MS Petyt 524
London, Lambeth Palace Library, MS 472
London, Westminster Cathedral Treasury, MS 4
London, Westminster School, MS 4
New Haven, Yale University, Beinecke Library, MS Takamiya 3
New York, Columbia University Library, MS Plimpton 257
New York, Columbia University Library, MS Plimpton 271
Oxford, All Souls' Library, MS 25
Oxford, Bodleian Library [Bodl. Lib.], MS Bodley 100
Oxford, Bodleian Library [Bodl. Lib.], MS Bodley 592
Oxford, Bodleian Library [Bodl. Lib.], MS Laud misc. 602
Oxford, Bodleian Library [Bodl. Lib.], MS Rawlinson C.285
Oxford, University College, MS 28
Philadelphia, University of Pennsylvania Library, codex 218
San Marino, California, Huntington Library, MS HM 266
Uppsala, Universitetsbiblioteket, MS C 159

Primary Sources

Ancrene Wisse: A Corrected Edition of the Text in Cambridge, Corpus Christi College, MS 402, with Variants from Other Manuscripts, ed. by Bella Millett, Early English Text Society, o.s., 325–26, 2 vols (Oxford: Oxford University Press, 2005–06)

The Cloud of Unknowing and the Book of Privy Counselling, ed. by Phyllis Hodgson, Early English Text Society, o.s., 218 (Oxford: Oxford University Press, 1944, for 1943; repr. 1981)

Contemplations of the Dread and Love of God, ed. by Margaret Connolly, Early English Text Society, o.s., 303 (Oxford: Oxford University Press, 1994)

Cré, Marleen, 'London, Westminster Cathedral Treasury, MS 4: An Edition of the Westminster Compilation', *Journal of Medieval Religious Cultures*, 37 (2011), 1–59

Hilton, Walter, *Walter Hilton's Latin Writings*, ed. by John P. H. Clark and Cheryl Taylor, Analecta Cartusiana, 124 (Salzburg: James Hogg, as by the Institut für Anglistik und Amerikanistik, Universität Salzburg, 1987)

——, *Walter Hilton's Mixed Life, Edited from Lambeth Palace MS 472*, ed. by S. J. Ogilvie-Thomson, Salzburg Studies in English Literature: Elizabethan & Renaissance Studies, 92:15 (Salzburg: James Hogg, as by the Institut für Anglistik und Amerikanistik, Universität Salzburg, 1986)

——, *Of Angels' Song*, in *Yorkshire Writers: Richard Rolle of Hampole, an English Father of the Church, and his Followers*, ed. by C. Horstman, 2 vols (London: Swan Sonnenschein, 1895–96; repr. in one volume with a new preface by Anne Clark Bartlett, Woodbridge, Suffolk, 1999), I, 175–82

——, *Walter Hilton: The Scale of Perfection*, ed. by Thomas H. Bestul, TEAMS Middle English Text (Kalamazoo: Medieval Institute Publications, 2000), available at <http://d.lib.rochester.edu/teams/publication/bestul-hilton-scale-of-perfection> [accessed 12 March, 2016]

——, *Walter Hilton: The Scale of Perfection, Book II: An Edition based on British Library MSS Harley 6573 and 6579*, begun by S. S. Hussey; completed by Michael G. Sargent, Early English Text Society, o.s., 348 (Oxford: Oxford University Press, 2017)

——, *The Scale of Perfection, by Walter Hilton, Canon of Thurgarton*, ed. by Evelyn Underhill (London: Watkins, 1923)

Jolliffe, P. S., 'Two Middle English Tracts on the Contemplative Life', *Mediæval Studies*, 37 (1975), 85–121

Julian of Norwich, *A Book of Showings to the Anchoress Julian of Norwich*, ed. by Edmund Colledge and James Walsh, 2 vols (Toronto: Pontifical Institute of Mediaeval Studies, 1978)

——, 'The Westminster Revelation (with Hugh Kempster)', in *The Writings of Julian of Norwich: 'A Vision Showed to a Devout Woman' and 'A Revelation of Love'*, ed. by Nicholas Watson and Jacqueline Jenkins (University Park: Pennsylvania State University Press, 2006), pp. 417–31

Love, Nicholas, *The Mirror of the Blessed Life of Jesus Christ: A Full Critical Edition*, ed. by Michael G. Sargent (Exeter: University of Exeter Press, 2005)

More, Thomas, *The Confutation of Tyndale's Answer*, ed. by Louis A. Schuster, Richard C. Marius, James P. Lusardi, and Richard J. Schoeck, The Yale Edition of the Complete Works of Thomas More, 8 (New Haven: Yale University Press, 1973)

The Prickynge of Love, ed. by Harold Kane, Salzburg Studies in English Literature: Elizabethan & Renaissance Studies 92.10 (Salzburg: James Hogg, as by the Institut für Anglistik und Amerikanistik, Universität Salzburg, 1983)

Suso, Henry, *Heinrich Seuses Horologium Sapientiae: erste kritische Ausgabe*, ed. by Pius Künzle (Freiburg: Universitätsverlag Freiburg, 1977)

Syon Abbey, with the Libraries of the Carthusians, ed. by Vincent Gillespie, Corpus of British Medieval Library Catalogues, 9 (London: British Library, 2001)

Secondary Works

Amon-Jones, Claire, *Varieties of Affect* (New York: Harvester Wheatsheaf, 1991)

Amsler, Mark, *Affective Literacies: Writing and Multilingualism in the Late Middle Ages* (Turnhout: Brepols, 2011)

Beckwith, Sarah, *Christ's Body: Identity, Culture and Society in Late Medieval Writings* (London: Routledge, 1993)

Bestul, Thomas, 'Meditatio/Meditation', in *The Cambridge Companion to Christian Mysticism*, ed. by Amy Hollywood and Patricia Z. Beckman (Cambridge: Cambridge University Press, 2012), pp. 157–66

Bynum, Caroline Walker, *Jesus as Mother: Studies in the Spirituality of the High Middle Ages* (Berkeley: University of California Press, 1982)

Clough, Patricia, and Jean Halley, eds, *The Affective Turn: Theorizing the Social* (Durham, NC: Duke University Press, 2007)

Cré, Marleen, 'Authority and the Compiler in Westminster Cathedral Treasury MS 4: Writing a Text in Someone Else's Words', in *Authority and Community in the Middle Ages*, ed. by Donald Mowbray, Rhiannon Purdie, and Ian P. Wei (Stroud: Sutton, 1999), pp. 153–76

——, '"This Blessed Beholdyng": Reading the Fragments from Julian of Norwich's *A Revelation of Divine Love* in London, Westminster Cathedral Treasury, MS 4', in *A Companion to Julian of Norwich*, ed. by Liz Herbert McAvoy (Cambridge: D. S. Brewer, 2008), pp. 116–26

——, *Vernacular Mysticism in the Charterhouse: A Study of London, British Library, MS Additional 37790*, The Medieval Translator/Traduire au Moyen Age, 9 (Turnhout: Brepols, 2006)

Ellis, Roger, and Samuel Fanous, '1349–1412: Texts', in *The Cambridge Companion to Medieval English Mysticism*, ed. by Samuel Fanous and Vincent Gillespie (Cambridge: Cambridge University Press, 2011), pp. 133–61

Erler, Mary C., *Women, Reading, and Piety in Late Medieval England* (Cambridge: Cambridge University Press, 2002)

Gardner, Helen, 'The Text of *The Scale of Perfection*', *Medium Ævum*, 5 (1936), 11–30

Gillespie, Vincent, *Looking in Holy Books: Essays on Late Medieval Religious Writing in England*, Brepols Collected Essays in European Culture, 3 (Turnhout: Brepols, 2011)

——, 'Mystic's Foot: Rolle and Affectivity', in *The Medieval Mystical Tradition in England: Exeter Symposium II*, ed. by Marion Glasscoe (Exeter: University of Exeter, 1982), pp. 199–230

——, 'Strange Images of Death: The Passion in Later Medieval English Devotional and Mystical Writing', in *Zeit, Tod and Ewigkeit in der Renaissance-Literatur*, ed. by James Hogg, Analecta Cartusiana, 117 (Salzburg: James Hogg, as by the Institut für Anglistik und Amerikanistik, Universität Salzburg, 1987), pp. 111–59

Gregg, Melissa, and Gregory J. Seigworth, eds, *The Affect Theory Reader* (Durham, NC: Duke University Press, 2010)

Hanna, Ralph, *The English Manuscripts of Richard Rolle: A Descriptive Catalogue*, Exeter Medieval Texts and Studies (Exeter: University of Exeter Press, 2010)

——, 'The History of a Book: Bodleian Library, MS Rawlinson C.285', in Ralph Hanna, *Introducing English Medieval Book History: Manuscripts, their Producers and their Readers* (Liverpool: Liverpool University Press, 2013), pp. 59–95

Hedlund, Monica, '*Liber Clementis Maydeston*, Some Remarks on Cod. Ups. C 159', in *English Manuscript Studies 1100–1700*, vol. III, ed. by Peter Beal and Jeremy Griffiths (London: British Library; Toronto: University of Toronto Press, 1992), pp. 73–101

Jolliffe, P. S., *A Check-List of Middle English Prose Writings of Spiritual Guidance*, Subsidia mediaevalia, 2 (Toronto: Pontifical Institute of Mediaeval Studies, 1974)

Karnes, Michelle, *Imagination, Meditation and Cognition in the Middle Ages* (Chicago: University of Chicago Press, 2011)

Kövacses, Zoltán, *Metaphor and Emotion: Language, Culture, and Body in Human Feeling* (Cambridge: Cambridge University Press, 2000)

Krochalis, Jeanne Elizabeth, '*Contemplations of the Dread and Love of God*: Two Newly Identified Pennsylvania Manuscripts', *The Library Chronicle*, 42 (1977), 3–22

Lazikani, Ayoush Sarmada, *Cultivating the Heart: Feeling and Emotion in Twelfth- and Thirteenth-Century Religious Texts* (Cardiff: University of Wales Press, 2015)

Lewis, Charlton T., and Charles Short, *A Latin Dictionary* (Oxford: Clarendon Press, 1879)

Lewis, Robert E., and Angus McIntosh, *A Descriptive Guide to the Manuscripts of the Prick of Conscience*, Medium Ævum Monographs, 12 (Oxford: Society for the Study of Mediaeval Languages and Literature, 1982)

Lewis, R. E., and others, *Index of Printed Middle English Prose* (New York: Garland, 1985)

Lovatt, Roger, 'Henry Suso and the Medieval Mystical Tradition in England', in *The Medieval Mystical Tradition in England: Exeter Symposium II*, ed. by Marion Glasscoe (Exeter: University of Exeter Press, 1982), pp. 47–62

Massumi, Brian, *Parables for the Virtual: Movement, Affect, Sensation*, Post-Contemporary Interventions (Durham, NC: Duke University Press, 2002)

McIntosh, Angus, M. L. Samuels, and Michael Benskin, *A Linguistic Atlas of Late Mediaeval English*, 4 vols (Aberdeen: Aberdeen University Press, 1986)

McNamer, Sarah, *Affective Meditation and the Invention of Medieval Compassion* (Philadelphia: University of Pennsylvania Press, 2010)

Nathanson, Donald L., *Shame and Pride: Affect, Sex, and the Birth of the Self* (New York: Norton, 1992)

Pourrat, P., *Christian Spirituality*, trans. by W. H. Mitchell and S. P. Jacques, vol. II (London: Burns, Oates and Washbourne, 1922)

——, *La Spiritualité chrétienne*, 2 vols (Paris: Gabalda, 1918–21)

Reddy, William M., *The Navigation of Feeling: A Framework for the History of Emotion* (Cambridge: Cambridge University Press, 2001)

Renevey, Denis, *Language, Self and Love: Hermeneutics in the Writings of Richard Rolle and the Commentaries on the Song of Songs* (Cardiff: University of Wales Press, 2001)

Rosenwein, Barbara H., *Anger's Past: The Social Uses of an Emotion in the Middle Ages* (Ithaca: Cornell University Press, 1998)

——, *Emotional Communities in the Early Middle Ages* (Ithaca: Cornell University Press, 2006)

——, *Generations of Feeling: A History of Emotions, 600–1700* (Cambridge: Cambridge University Press, 2015)

Samuels, M. L., 'Some Applications of Middle English Dialectology', in *Middle English Dialectology: Essays on Some Principles and Problems*, ed. by Margaret Laing (Aberdeen: Aberdeen University Press, 1989), pp. 64–80

Sargent, Michael G., 'Editing Walter Hilton's Scale of Perfection: The Case for a Rhizomorphic Historical Edition', in *Probable Truth: Editing Medieval Texts from Britain in the Twenty-First Century*, ed. by Vincent Gillespie and Anne Hudson (Turnhout: Brepols, 2013), pp. 509–34

——, 'A New Manuscript of *The Chastising of God's Children* with an Ascription to Walter Hilton', *Medium Ævum*, 46 (1977), 49–65

——, 'Patterns of Circulation and Variation in the English and Latin Texts of Books I and II of Walter Hilton's *Scale of Perfection*', in *Medieval and Early Modern Religious Cultures: Essays Honouring Vincent Gillespie on his Sixty-Fifth Birthday*, ed. by Laura Ashe and Ralph Hanna (Cambridge: D. S. Brewer, 2019), pp. 83–99

——, 'Walter Hilton's *Scale of Perfection*: The London Manuscript Group Reconsidered', *Medium Ævum*, 52 (1983), 189–216

Scheer, Monique, 'Are Emotions a Kind of Practice (And Is that What Makes Them Have a History)? A Bourdieuian Approach to Understanding Emotion', *History and Theory*, 51 (2012), 193–220

Sedgwick, Eve Kosofsky, *Touching Feeling: Affect, Performativity, Pedagogy* (Durham, NC: Duke University Press, 2003)

Sedgwick, Eve Kosofsky, and Adam Frank, eds, *Shame and its Sisters: A Silvan Tomkins Reader* (Durham, NC: Duke University Press, 1995)

Southern, R. W., *The Making of the Middle Ages* (New Haven: Yale University Press, 1953)

——, *Saint Anselm and his Biographer: A Study of Monastic Life and Thought, 1059–c. 1130* (Cambridge: Cambridge University Press, 1963)

Tomkins, Silvan, *Affect Imagery Consciousness*, 4 vols (New York: Springer, 1963–92; complete edition 2008)

——, 'Script Theory: Differential Magnification of Affects', in *Nebraska Symposium on Motivation 1978*, ed. by H. E. Howe and R. A. Dienstbier (Lincoln: University of Nebraska Press, 1979), pp. 201–36

Zacour, Norman, and Rudolph Hirsch, *Catalogue of Manuscripts in the Libraries of the University of Pennsylvania to 1800* (Philadelphia: University of Pennsylvania Press, 1965)

Online Publications

'Affective Piety', *Wikipedia*, <http://wikipedia.com> [accessed 6 March 2016]

Middle English Dictionary, ed. by Robert E. Lewis and others (Ann Arbor: University of Michigan Press, 1952–2001); online edition in *Middle English Compendium*, ed. by Frances McSparran and others (Ann Arbor: University of Michigan Library, 2000–18), <http://quod.lib.umich.edu/m/middle-english-dictionary> [accessed 8 April 2016]

Oxford English Dictionary, <http://oed.com> (cited as *OED*) [accessed 8 April 2016]

STC = *Universal Short Title Catalogue*, <https://www.ustc.ac.uk/>

The *Liber specialis gratiae* in a Devotional Anthology: London, British Library, MS Harley 494

Naoë Kukita Yoshikawa

The *Liber specialis gratiae* (*Liber*) contains the revelations of Mechtild of Hackeborn (1240–1298), a German mystic and chantress at the Benedictine/Cistercian convent of Helfta. The *Liber* is thought to have been compiled by Gertrude the Great and another unknown nun during the last decade of the thirteenth century, but it was soon abridged by an anonymous editor and disseminated widely in Europe. The popularity of the *Liber* is seen not only in the Latin and vernacular manuscripts but also in printed books, such as an anthology printed by Jacques Lefèvre d'Étaples in 1513, which transmits the revelations of Hildegard of Bingen, Elisabeth of Schönau, and Mechtild of Hackeborn.[1] The abridged version of the *Liber* was circulating in England by the end of the first quarter of the fifteenth century, and was translated into Middle English in due course in a Carthusian or Birgittine milieu, entitled *The Booke of Gostlye Grace* (*Booke*).[2] The *Liber* was one of a number of

---

[1] *Liber trium virorum et trium spiritualium virginum*, ed. by Lefèvre d'Étaples. For the extant Latin and vernacular manuscripts, see Bromberg, *Het Boek*, and Hellgardt, 'Latin and the Vernacular', among others.

[2] *Revelationes Gertrudianae ac Mechtildianae*, ed. by Paquelin (hereafter *Revelationes*); *The Booke of Gostlye Grace*, ed. by Halligan (hereafter *Booke*). All references to *Liber Specialis Gratiae* and *The Booke of Gostlye Grace* are from these editions and will be followed by part, chapter, and page numbers. The Syon library once held seven copies of Mechtild's revelations in Latin. See

---

Naoë Kukita Yoshikawa (kukita.naoe@shizuoka.ac.jp) is Professor of English at Shizuoka University, Japan.

older texts with 'an impeccably orthodox pedigree or an unimpeachable authorial reputation',[3] translated into Middle English most probably at Syon in the wake of Arundel's decrees of 1409 and during the episcopate (1414–43) of Arundel's successor, Henry Chichele. Representing an orthodox authority at a time of spiritual upheaval and renewal, the *Liber* was translated into Middle English along with the texts of other authoritative continental women mystics.[4] The Middle English translation survives in two fifteenth-century manuscripts, BL, MS Egerton 2006 (upon which Halligan's edition is based),[5] and Bodl. Lib., MS Bodley 220,[6] which are similar except that the former contains rubrics preceding the chapters.

Like other contemporary English translations of devotional texts, the *Booke* was originally prepared for professional religious. However, like many of the textual productions by or for the nuns of Syon, it found its way, by accident or design, to readers outside the enclosure,[7] although the readership was largely restricted to a limited group of wealthy, female aristocrats. As such, by the second quarter of the fifteenth century, Mechtild's revelations were circulating in English at Syon Abbey and among the female nobility. In her will of 1438, Alianora Roos of York bequeathed to Dame Johanna Courtenay 'unum librum vocatum Maulde buke',[8] and Cecily Neville, Duchess of York, among others, was an avid reader of Mechtild's *Booke*. Cecily's piety is well documented in her household ordinance.[9] This document attests to her pious life and her collection of devotional texts. Her daily devotional reading included the revelations of Saint Birgitta and Mechtild of Hackeborn, and a life of Saint Catherine of Siena.[10] In 1495 she left her granddaughter Brigitte (a daughter of Edward IV

Booke, ed. by Halligan, 'Introduction', pp. 8–10. During this same period Bridget of Sweden's *Liber Celestis* and Catherine of Siena's *Dialogo* were also translated into English for Syon nuns.

[3] Gillespie, '1412–1534: Culture and History', p. 174.

[4] An extract of Mechtild's *Booke* is incorporated into the *Speculum Devotorum*, written by a Carthusian at Sheen, who calls Mechtild, Elizabeth of Töss, Catherine of Siena, and Birgitta of Sweden 'approuyd wymmen': see *A Mirror to Devout People*, ed. by Patterson, pp. 6, 141; *The Idea of the Vernacular*, ed. by Wogan-Browne and others, p. 76; Gillespie, '1412–1534: Culture and History', p. 184.

[5] This manuscript was owned by Richard III and his wife Anne Neville. See Sutton and Visser-Fuchs, *Richard III's Books*, p. 279 and passim.

[6] *The Boke of Gostely Grace*, ed. by Mouron and Yoshikawa.

[7] Gillespie, '1412–1534: Culture and History', p. 173.

[8] *Testamenta Eboracensia*, pp. 65–66.

[9] *A Collection of Ordinances*, pp. 37–39; Armstrong, 'The Piety of Cicely', pp. 140–42.

[10] Cecily's copy could be any of these texts: Raymond of Capua's *Legenda major* (1395),

and Elizabeth Woodville), who was a nun at the Dominican house at Dartford, her 'boke of St Matilde', along with a copy of the *Legenda aurea* in vellum and a copy of the Life of Catherine of Siena.[11]

In addition to complete manuscript copies of the *Liber* and the *Booke*, there are a number of compilations and anthologies which contain passages of Mechtild's revelations in Latin and/or English. The extracts from the *Liber* were circulating in manuscripts immediately after the foundation of Syon Abbey.[12] BL, MS Harley 494 (hereafter MS Harley 494) is one of the compiled books in which Mechtild's revelations are among the sources.[13] This manuscript, dated

---

a Middle English version of a letter about Catherine's life written by the Carthusian Stefano Maconi (d. 1424) to support her canonization (see Brown, 'From the Charterhouse to the Printing House', pp. 21–28), or *The Lyf of Saint Katherin of Senis*, an English version printed by Wynkyn de Worde in 1492, based on Raymond's *vita* (*STC* 24766).

[11] *Wills from Doctors' Commons*, ed. by Nichols and Bruce, pp. 2–3.

[12] Among numerous devotional compilations which contain Mechtildian passages, BL, MS Harley 4012 was owned by Anne Harling, a Norfolk woman. As we shall see, Mechtildian fragments are also contained in Cambridge, Trinity College, MS O.1.74, a small book owned by a nun.

[13] I call MS Harley 494 an anthology. The manuscript has the features of a devotional miscellany, yet it was very probably planned as a prayer book, interspersed by didactic, devotional materials in prose that would nurture the spiritual growth of its readers. MS Harley 494 has recently been the focus of Alexandra Barratt's exemplary study, *Anne Bulkeley and her Book*. All quotations from this manuscript and the translation of its Latin texts are from Barratt's edition in the Appendix of *Anne Bulkeley and her Book*.

A select list of the contents of MS Harley 494: (1) English elevation prayer; (2) Five Latin prayers on the Five Joys of the Resurrection; (3) Eight Latin prayers for the Gifts of the Holy Spirit; (4) Latin prayer invoking St Onuphrius; (5) Latin prayer to the Virgin; (6) English treatise on daily living, an adaptation of the anonymous *Dyurnall* (printed 1532?, 1542?); (7) Latin Office of the Virgin; (8) Eight English prayers; (9) English treatise on preparation for Communion; (10) 'A short meditacion and informacyon of oure lord Jhesu schewyd to seynt Mawde by reuelacion', English treatise on morning devotions; (12) Instructions on intercessory prayer from Richard Whitford's translation of the pseudo-Bernadian *Godlen Pystle* (1531, 1537); (13) Four English intercessory prayers, three adapted from William Bonde, *Pilgrymage of perfeccyon* (1531); (14) English treatise on preparation for Communion, made up extracts from Whitford's *Due preparacion unto houselynge* (1531, 1537); (15) 'Certane prayers shewyd vnto a devote person callyd Mary Ostrewyk'; (22) English translation of chapter from Saint Birgit, *Revelationes*; (28) (i) 'Here folo[wi]th þe bedis of pardon in englyshe of saynt gregorrys pytye'; (ii) three pairs of prayers alternately in Latin and English; (33) Short English prayer. For the complete list, see Barratt, *Anne Bulkeley and her Book*, pp. 11–13.

MS Harley 494 contains several texts that derive from the works of Richard Whitford and William Bonde as well as Bridget's revelations: for the strong Birgittine influences on MS Harley 494, see Barratt, *Anne Bulkeley and her Book*, especially chs 3, 4.

between 1532 and 1535, is an anthology of devotional texts written in a variety of late fifteenth- or early sixteenth-century hands and owned by Anne Bulkeley, a Hampshire widow, and possibly later by her daughter Anne, a nun at Amesbury Priory.[14] As a little book comprised of English and Latin prayers and English devotional treatises, MS Harley 494 illuminates the owner's and/or compiler(s)' devotional taste and aspirations. One might speculate that the owner of the book may have understood some Latin, although it is often the case that many prayers and common brief quotations are left in Latin in vernacular texts even when the recipient of the volume did not read Latin.[15]

Significantly, Alexandra Barratt's meticulous textual analysis has revealed that MS Harley 494 contains more materials from the *Liber* than hitherto believed.[16] In addition to short extracts, there are three substantial extracts from the *Liber* among the manuscript's thirty-one items:[17] Item 2 (prayers entirely in Latin), Item 10 (a series of meditation and prayers in a mixture of English and Latin), and Item 28 (prayers in a mixture of Latin and English), and each of them is written by a different hand.[18]

As Barratt indicates, MS Harley 494 was written at least by seventeen scribes.[19] Item 10 was written by a scribe, identified as Robert Taylor, who has written sixteen items, including all the longer devotional texts and is thought to have

---

[14] The ownership inscription is written on the flyleaf (verso): 'Domine Anne Bvlkeley / Attinet Liber iste'. Anne Bulkeley was wife of Robert Bulkeley of Fordingbridge. Barratt speculates that the hand on the flyleaf belongs to Anne's daughter, Anne. See *Anne Bulkeley and her Book*, pp. 8, 22–33, especially pp. 27–29.

[15] The main hand in MS Harley 494 is that of Robert Taylor (see below). Comparing MS Harley 494 with Taylor's other known manuscripts, Barratt suggests from internal evidence (i.e. the comparative plainness of MS Harley 494 in terms of the use of red ink, underlining, etc.) that Anne Bulkeley was presumably 'an experienced reader who did not need much assistance with her reading' (*Anne Bulkeley and her Book*, pp. 17–18). Yet, a question remains whether it is reasonable to assume that Anne Bulkeley or any other reader knew some Latin since there are Latin texts in her prayer book. In connection with this, Barratt also argues that 'Anne Bulkeley was less highly educated (although not wholly without skills in Latin, presumably) but fully literate in the vernacular and in the spiritual life' (p. 126).

[16] Barratt corrected Voaden's assessment (in 'The Company She Keeps', pp. 59–60) about extant compilations that contain Mechtildian passage(s).

[17] Mechtild's influence on MS Harley 494 seems pervasive, especially in terms of a daily devotional exercise and its themes, such as devotions to Passion and the Virgin (Barratt, *Anne Bulkeley and her Book*, ch. 5), but it is beyond the scope of this essay to deal with it exhaustively.

[18] Mechtildian extracts in Item 2 and Item 28 are not, however, attributed to her in the text.

[19] Syon nuns may well have served as subsidiary scribes. See Barratt, *Anne Bulkeley and her Book*, p. 43.

acted as the principal scribe,[20] while Item 2 and Item 28 are written by two of sixteen other hands.[21] Taylor was Clerk of the Works at Syon Abbey, who was 'in control of Syon's extensive building operations, which were continuing'.[22] A very prolific scribe, Taylor is known to have written and signed the only manuscript of the *Myroure of oure Ladye*, which contains two excerpts with some modifications from 'Mawdes boke'.[23] He was literate at least in English, but there is no reason that he would have had the spiritual awareness to oversee the compilation of MS Harley 494.[24] Nevertheless, 'there is a very distinctive discrimination at work in MS Harley 494'.[25] Anne Bulkeley must have been close to the clergy and 'reliant on them for most if not all of the material in her book, as well as for the sacraments and for spiritual advice and direction'.[26] One could speculate that Richard Whitford (d. 1543?),[27] a Syon monk, a writer, and a spiritual director, might have supervised the compilation and brought 'a controlling intelligence' to this anthology.[28] Whitford, a learned father, must have been very knowledgeable about Mechtild's revelations and her influence on the Birgittines and beyond. He himself was probably attracted by Mechtild's authenticated visionary experience and borrowed the Mechtildian extracts for the devotional use of the laity who were keen to model themselves on holy women and female religious.[29]

Such a practice of modelling one's spiritual way of life on fashionable, holy texts is illuminated by an example of Margaret, Lady Hungerford (d. 1478), a

---

[20] This does not, however, exclude the possibility that another scribe or more scribes were involved in the compiling activity. Therefore, in this essay the term compiler(s) will be used where it is relevant.

[21] Barratt, *Anne Bulkeley and her Book*, pp. 11–15.

[22] Barratt, *Anne Bulkeley and her Book*, p. 15.

[23] *The Myroure of oure Ladye*, ed. by Blunt, pp. 38–39, 276–77. The manuscript is now split between Aberdeen, University Library, MS 134 and Bodl. Lib., MS Rawlinson C. 941.

[24] It is also unlikely that he was a translator as well as a scribe. Mechtild's Latin is not easy for a Clerk of the Works to work on.

[25] Barratt, *Anne Bulkeley and her Book*, p. 42.

[26] Barratt, *Anne Bulkeley and her Book*, p. 69.

[27] See Rhodes, 'Whitford, Richard (d. 1543?)'. I would like to thank Professor Barratt for sharing her ideas about Taylor and Whitford with me. On Whitford, also see Brandon Alakas's paper in this volume.

[28] Barratt, *Anne Bulkeley and her Book*, p. 4.

[29] Barratt argues that originally narrative and visionary material is 'mined for prayers and devotional practices' by the compiler(s) to give divine authentication through the association with Saint Maud: see *Anne Bulkeley and her Book*, p. 31.

wealthy dowager, known to have owned a book of Syon use, presumably the *Myroure*.[30] Through her sojourn in Syon Abbey, following the insurrection known as the Lincolnshire Rebellion of March/May 1470,[31] she seems to have acquired considerable knowledge of the Syon use by participating in the sisters' services. As a result, the Syon use features in the statutes of the Hungerford chantry chapel in Salisbury Cathedral, concerning the vestments, texts, and prayers. It is a similar culture of piety that Anne Bulkeley seems to have participated in.

Unique to this anthology is that it presents Mechtild as a familiar figure of orthodox piety and an expert on prayers who will offer a good example of holy living to its readers.[32] But it is also the case that Mechtildian passages are often radically abbreviated and modified from the original Latin texts, becoming what Barratt calls 'innocuous'.[33] This essay will focus on the three substantial extracts from the *Liber* embedded in MS Harley 494, and compare the modified texts with the Latin original text and the complete Middle English translation in order to illuminate the way Mechtild's text was transformed and reshaped by her translator(s)/compiler(s) to satisfy the various audiences of the text in late medieval England.[34]

* * *

Item 2 (fols 2^r–4^r, *inc*. 'laudo, amo, adoro') of MS Harley 494 contains a rendition of five Latin Mechtildian prayers about the five joys of the risen Christ borrowed from the *Liber*, Pars i Cap. 19, beginning:

> Laudo, amo, adoro, magnifico, glorifico, gracias ago et benedico te, Jhesu bone, in illo ineffabili gaudio quod habuisti, quando tua beatissima humanitas in resurreccione glorificacionem suscepit a Patre diuine clarificacionis [...]. Per illud ineffabile

---

[30] Hicks, 'The Piety of Margaret', pp. 23–24. See also Harris, 'A New Look at the Reformation'. I would like to thank Professor Vincent Gillespie for drawing my attention to these sources.

[31] For the historical background during the War of Roses, see Holland, 'The Lincolnshire Rebellion'.

[32] Another visionary woman included in this manuscript is Maria van Oisterwijk (*c*. 1470–1547), a Brabant beguine. A short extract of her translated prayers (Item 15) is centred on the five wounds of Christ: see Barratt, *Anne Bulkeley and her Book*, p. 218.

[33] Barratt, *Anne Bulkeley and her Book*, p. 97.

[34] Several copies of the *Liber* and the *Booke* were in the London area at the end of the fifteenth century: see Blake, 'Review of *The Booke*, ed. by Halligan', pp. 387–88; *Syon Abbey*, ed. by Gillespie, pp. 236, 239.

gaudium rogo te, o amantissime Dei et hominum mediator, vt eandem quam michi tunc dedisti claritatem, tua gracia conserues illesam, in die iudicij cum gaudio assumendam.

[I praise, love, adore, magnify, glorify, give thanks, and bless thee, good Jesu, in that unspeakable joy which thou didst have when thy most blessed human nature received glorification at the Resurrection from the divine brightness of the Father [...]. By that unspeakable joy I ask thee, O most loving mediator of God and men, that thou shouldest keep unharmed the same brightness which thou then gavest me, to be taken up with joy on the day of judgement.][35]

In this set of prayers, 'laudo, amo, adoro, magnifico, glorifico, gracias ago et benedico te, Jhesu bone' ('I praise, love, adore, magnify, glorify, give thanks, and bless thee, good Jesu') is repeated five times, followed each time by a prayer on one of the five joys of the Resurrection. The prayers are almost identical with the relevant texts in the original *Liber*,[36] except that in MS Harley 494 they are followed by Christ's promise of special graces made to those who recite them before, during, and after death, material which, in the *Liber*, comes before these prayers:

Si quis horum gaudiorum me meminit, pro primo dabo ei, si desiderauerit, ante mortem eius gustum mee diuinitatis. Secundo, dabo ei intellectum cognicionis [...]. Quinto, jocundam sanctorum ei societatem dabo.

[If anyone reminds me of these joys, for the first I shall give her, if she has desired it, taste of my divinity before death. For the second I shall give her knowledge of understanding [...]. For the fifth I shall grant her the joyful company of the saints.][37]

The *Booke*, on the other hand, retains the order of the *Liber*, although the scribe added an introduction to Mechtild's prayers which explains how Mechtild made the five prayers through the inspiration of the Holy Spirit:

[B]e the inspyracion of þe Holye Goste sche gaffe worscheppys ande thankkynges to oure lorde for his ioyes [...] ande sayde: 'O god Ihesu, y gyffe the praysynge ande thankkynge; I worschepe ande magnyfye þe; y gloryfye ande blesse the in þat grete ioye þat maye now3t be schewede be speche, whiche ioye þou hadde when þyne blyssede humanyte in thy resureccioun toke of þe fadere gloryficacion of the deuyne claryficacion.'[38]

---

[35] MS Harley 494, fol. 2ʳ; Barratt, *Anne Bulkeley and her Book*, pp. 173–74.
[36] See *Revelationes*, ed. by Paquelin, Pars i Cap. 19, pp. 65–67.
[37] MS Harley 494, fols 3ᵛ–4ʳ; Barratt, *Anne Bulkeley and her Book*, pp. 174–75.
[38] *Booke*, ed. by Halligan, I. 41. 191.

Interestingly, this devotion is supposed to be 'la lauda di donna Matelda' ('the laud of Lady Matelda'), mentioned by a rich weaver in Boccaccio's *Decameron*, VII. 1.[39] Indeed, it was popular throughout Europe in the later Middle Ages. A version of this devotion appears in a popular devotional anthology, *Anthidotarius animae* (Antidote for the soul), compiled by Nicolas Salicetus, a Cistercian monk.[40] Furthermore, as Barratt argues, Item 1 in MS Harley 494, an elevation prayer, is very likely a later addition to the manuscript.[41] If so, Item 2 was originally the opening item of this anthology. This suggests that the Latin devotions taken from Mechtild's revelations were intended to enhance the divine authentication of the anthology, the role which Mechtildian materials often play in later medieval compilations. The compiler (if not Whitford) may well have consciously chosen this devotional prayer to accommodate his readership with the highly renowned prayer attributed to an approved woman mystic.

Item 10, entitled 'A short meditacion and informacyon of our lorde Jhesu schewyd to Seynt Mawde by reuelacion' (fols 26ʳ–30ʳ),[42] contains four sections, written predominantly in English although prayers are occasionally supplied in Latin. The material is taken from the *Liber*, but the Mechtildian passages are rendered less discernible as they were extensively abbreviated and modified. The first extract is a passage spoken by Christ concerning the seven canonical hours:

> In the nyght or in the mournyng: when þou rysest, commende the, both bodye and soule, vn-to me, thankyng me for þi rest and for oþer benefettes þat þou hast receyued of me, hauynge in mynde how for þi loue I suffered my-self to be betrayed in-to the handes of wyckede men and to be bounde of them. I was obedyent to my fader vn-to the deth.[43]

This translates a passage from Pars iii Cap. 29 of the *Liber*, 'De septem horis canonicis' (Of seven canonical hours).[44] It is, in fact, Christ's answer to a question impregnated with imagery of bridal mysticism: 'Sposa solet fructificare

---

[39] Gardner, *Dante and the Mystics*, p. 284; Paquelin's note in *Revelationes*, p. 65 n. 1. As captain of the laud-singers (*laudesi*) at Santa Maria Novella in Florence, the weaver learns a few prayers which include the laud of Lady Matelda, who could certainly have been Mechtild of Hackeborn. Barbara Newman argues that 'the Florentine *lauda* was one of many compositions that circulated orally or independently': see 'Seven-Storey Mountain', p. 70.

[40] Rhodes, 'The Body of Christ', p. 414 n. 74.

[41] Barratt, *Anne Bulkeley and her Book*, p. 35.

[42] Barratt, *Anne Bulkeley and her Book*, pp. 195–98.

[43] MS Harley 494, fol. 26ʳ; Barratt, *Anne Bulkeley and her Book*, p. 195.

[44] *Revelationes*, ed. by Paquelin, Pars iii Cap. 29, p. 233.

sponso suo; quem ergo fructum, o floride sponse, tibi proferam?' ('A bride is accustomed to bear fruit to her spouse: what fruit, o spouse, am I to offer to you?').⁴⁵ In the *Liber*, this question is preceded by a passage also saturated in bridal mysticism, in which Christ promises:

> <<Nunc Cor meum tuum est, et cor tuum meum est.>> Dulcissimoque amplexu et tota virtute sua divina sic animam illam sibi intraxit, ut unus cum eo spiritus effici videretur.
>
> [Now my heart is yours, and your heart is mine. With sweet embrace and all the might of his divine majesty, he drew her soul into himself, so she seemed to become one with the Spirit.]⁴⁶

In contrast to the mystical thrust of the Latin original, the response in Anne Bulkeley's book lacks in mystical expressiveness. But this process of reducing the mystical tone had already begun in the *Booke*, where the mystical context of the revelations was occasionally disregarded by the translator. Like the translator(s) of the Mechtildian texts in MS Harley 494, the translator of the *Booke* excised the passage that begins, 'Now my heart is yours, and your heart is mine' and omits the provocative question, 'what fruit, o spouse, am I to offer to you?'⁴⁷ Moreover, as mentioned earlier, he occasionally repeats this practice throughout the translation. For example, in responding to Mechtild's question, '"whate es thy moste ioye in þame [virgins]?", Owre lorde God awnswerede: "My fadere loves so moche eche virgynne ande abydeth the comynge of here with more ioye þan euere anye kynge aboyde hys awne spowse offe whom he hopys sone to haffe a grete eyre."'⁴⁸ But, while retaining the question and its answer, the translator of the *Booke* omits the rest of the passage steeped in bridal mysticism:

> Dehinc amantissimo amplexu me illi imprimo, in quo me cum tota divinitate sic illi infundo et pertranseo, ut in omnibus membris ejus, quocumque se vertat, totus esse videar; eamque vicissim mihi sic intraho, ut etiam ipsa intra me in omnibus membris appareat gloriose. Insuper ex me ipso facio ei coronam, unde eam velut sponsam meam legitimam dignissime coronabo.

---

⁴⁵ *Revelationes*, ed. by Paquelin, Pars iii Cap. 29, p. 233; Barratt, *Anne Bulkeley and her Book*, p. 97.

⁴⁶ *Revelationes*, ed. by Paquelin, Pars iii Cap. 29, p. 233. Translation mine.

⁴⁷ *Booke*, ed. by Halligan, III. 28. 469–71. The *Booke*, however, faithfully translates how Christ taught her to spend the seven canonical hours.

⁴⁸ See *Booke*, ed. by Halligan, II. 36. 396.

[Then with the most loving embrace I clasp myself to her. In so doing, I pour myself into her and infuse her with all my divinity, so that I am seen in all her limbs wherever she turns; and I draw her close to me and into me, that she may appear within me glorified in all her limbs. Moreover I make a crown out of myself so that I may crown her most worthily as my lawful bride.][49]

The translator of the *Booke* also made drastic changes to the original Latin text in terms of the scribe's relationship with Mechtild. The *Liber* was produced by the two nun scribes at Helfta to whom Mechtild confided about her visions, but the Middle English translator transformed the *Liber* into a narrative in which Mechtild composed her text with the assistance of a male confessor, conforming to contemporary preference for clerically approved devotional works.[50] Moreover, although Mechtild's revelations were generally received as orthodox and free from theological innovations and daring imagery, the Middle English translator occasionally, according to his judgement, eliminated revelations saturated with bridal mysticism, turning the text into a more moderate, less challenging one.

In fact, bridal mysticism never enjoyed full-blown popularity in England, and such practice of excision, in an attempt to sanitize bridal mysticism, is in line with a general movement from the more sophisticated mystical materials found in Latin manuscripts to the less challenging, devotional exercises found in vernacular manuscripts, although some members of the gentle and noble laity read visionary texts in Middle English and developed a taste for theologically challenging texts.[51] Indeed, editorial intervention is not unusual in late medieval translation culture. As Roger Lovatt argues, 'integration as dilution — absorption as emasculation —'[52] is noticeable in, for instance, *The Treatise of the Seven Points of True Love*, the Middle English translation of Henry Suso's *Horologium sapientiae*. Here the translator 'reduced his work to the level of a conventional, weakly affective, almost anodyne piety',[53] to make it suitable for a wider and less sophisticated readership. This attitude is also seen in *The Chastising of God's Children*, written for female religious, probably not long before the promulgation of Arundel's Constitutions.[54] Although drawing on such highly affec-

---

[49] *Revelationes*, ed. by Paquelin, Pars ii Cap. 36, p. 185. Translation mine.

[50] See Rydel, 'Inventing a Male Writer', especially p. 211.

[51] Grisé, 'Continental Holy Women', p. 167. As stated above, Cecily Neville read Bridget's and Mechtild's visionary texts as well as the life of Catherine of Siena in English.

[52] Lovatt, 'Henry Suso and the Medieval Mystical Tradition in England', p. 57.

[53] Lovatt, 'Henry Suso and the Medieval Mystical Tradition in England', p. 57.

[54] *The Chastising of God's Children*, ed. by Bazire and Colledge. See Sutherland, '*The Chastising of God's Children*', p. 358, which contains the most recent views on the dating of the

tive texts as Suso's *Horologium sapientiae* and Jan van Ruusbroec's *Spiritual Espousals*, the *Chastising* author is preoccupied with 'the suppression of religious fervour, the dangers of seeking "sweetness of devotion" during the performance of the canonical hours'.[55] These examples illuminate the way the translator eliminated the imagery of bridal mysticism in favour of rather straightforward instructions that would profit the laity's devotional and spiritual needs.

The next section in Item 10 of MS Harley 494 translates the *Liber*, Pars iii Cap. 17, 'Qualiter homo cor dei salutet, et cor suum deo offerat, et sensus suos commendet' ('How a person should greet the divine Heart and offer his own heart to God, and commend his senses'),[56] but the translated extract consists only of the morning offering of the heart, and leaves out the passage steeped in bridal mysticism:

> Also in þe mornynge
> Offre thy hart to me, prayng that þou neuer do ne speke, think ne desyre that thing whiche myȝtt displease me, commyttyng all thy gouernance to me and say thus. Say this blessing att euery werke that thou shalt begynne: *Pater sancte, in vnione amantissimi filij tui, commendo tibi spiritum meum* (Holy Father, in union with thy most loving Son I commend my spirit to thee).[57]

Compared with the Latin original,[58] the Middle English version in Anne Bulkeley's book is again much abbreviated and the tone of bridal mysticism is tempered. The translator excises a passage on a rose and a pomegranate, as well as the imagery of flowers and fruits associated with the Song of Songs,[59] and keeps those passages that exclude Mechtild's outpouring mystical expressiveness.

This treatment is, however, different from that of the *Booke* which translates the Latin source faithfully, retaining the imagery of the rose and pomegranate, and foregrounding the flourishing image of the divine heart. The vivid image

---

Chastising as well as a suggestion that it 'was composed somewhat intermittently, and that it was only eventually gathered together and circulated as a complete treatise'. See also Bridget of Sweden, *The Liber Celestis*, ed. by Ellis, pp. xii–xiii.

[55] Ellis and Fanous, '1349–1412: Texts', p. 153. Marleen Cré argues that *The Chastising* evidences 'a liking for texts that combine staunchly orthodox attitudes with more daring vistas of fulfilling personal encounter with God': 'Take a Walk on the Safe Side', p. 243.

[56] *Revelationes*, ed. by Paquelin, Pars iii Cap. 17, p. 217; Barratt, *Anne Bulkeley and her Book*, p. 98.

[57] MS Harley 494, fol. 26ʳ; Barratt, *Anne Bulkeley and her Book*, pp. 195–96, 198.

[58] See *Revelationes*, ed. by Paquelin, Pars iii Cap. 17, p. 217, and its Middle English translation quoted in my discussion below.

[59] *Revelationes*, ed. by Paquelin, Pars iii Cap. 17, pp. 217–18.

of divine love that flows out from the heart of the divine lover emphasizes the close relationship between Christ and Mechtild:

> Owre lorde tawȝt þis maydene to worschepe his herte in this fourme of wordes ande sayde: 'Furste whene þowe ryseste erlye greet ande doo reuerence to the floryschynge and to the luffynge herte of þyne luffere [...] ande saye thus: I loue, I blysse, I glorifie, I grete þe delycious herte of Ihesu, my trewe luffe, ȝeldynge þonkkynges to þe, my lorde Ihesu, for the trewe kepynge wharewith þowe haffes defendede me this nyght [...]. I offre m[ye] herte to the als a schynynge roose þat þe gladnesse þareof maye drawe þy eyen to lykynge [...]. Moreouere I offre to the my herte as a pomegarnete of a fulle goode sauour [...] þat when þowe eetes þareof þowe drawe itt so into the þat fro þis tyme forwarde my herte maye fele hym graciouslye praye withyn the so that eche thoght, spekynge, ande wyrkynge, ande my wille maye be gouernede þis daye efter the pleysauncz of þyne benigne wille [...]. I commende my spyritte to the in the vnyon of luffe of þy luffynge sonne, whiche wordes þowe schalte reheerse atte alle þyne werkes'.⁶⁰

Though radically abbreviated, Anne Bulkeley's Mechtildian extract, nevertheless, bears witness to the popularity of this particular revelation. Clearly, it derives from one of the distinctively Mechtildian revelations that focus on 'the materialization of the Sacred Heart, the cult which developed at Helfta'.⁶¹ Given Syon's preoccupation with Christ's five wounds, blood, and the heart, Mechtild's currency within the Carthusians and Birgittines is understandable.⁶² Moreover, this predilection extends outside these two religious orders. There is an independent English version of this extract contained in Cambridge, Trinity College, MS O.1.74 (hereafter MS O.1.74), fols 77ᵛ–80ʳ.⁶³ This manuscript is a small book of treatises, devotions, and prose meditation on the Passion that belonged to a nun.⁶⁴ The Mechtildian excerpts in this book begin with the devotion of the triple Ave, followed by a prayer to the heart of Jesus and prayers for the senses.⁶⁵ Like the translator of MS Harley 494, the translator of the Trinity manuscript excises the imagery of the rose and pomegranate from the

---

⁶⁰ *Booke*, ed. by Halligan, III. 15. 444–46.

⁶¹ Voaden, 'Mechtild of Hackeborn', p. 431.

⁶² The Birgittine habit includes the white linen crown placed on the black veil. On the crown are sewn five pieces of red cloth to represent the five wounds of Christ. See Ellis, *Syon Abbey*, pp. 14–15, p. 14 n. 19 for the description of the crown in the Rule.

⁶³ Barratt, *Anne Bulkeley and her Book*, p. 198.

⁶⁴ *Women's Writing in Middle English*, ed. by Barratt, p. 52.

⁶⁵ *Revelationes*, ed. by Paquelin, Pars i Cap. 47, p. 133; Pars iv Cap. 23, p. 280; Pars iii Cap. 17, p. 218.

prayer to the divine heart, yet he retains the flourishing image of the heart with an emphasis on the intimate relationship between Christ and the visionary:

> Firste whanne thou risiste eerly at morwe, grete and do reverence to the florisching and the loving hert of thi lovere Jesu, from whom al goodnesse flowid oute, flowith, and schal flowe withoute ende. Therfore with a good herte thou schalt seie thus: I loue, Y blisse, Y glorifie, Y grete that delycious herte of Jesu, my trewe love, yelding thangingis to thee [...] for the trewe keping wherewith thou hast defendit me this nyght [...] and al thingis wiche Y scholde have do, thou hast parformed for me.
>
> And now, my only love, Y offre my herte to thee with al maner reverence, besechinge thee that thou drawe it to thee and accept it to thee, so that from this tyme forward it may fele itsilf graciously thine withynne so that eche thought, speche and worching and my wil mowe be governyd this day after the pleasaunce of thi benygne wil.[66] (MS O.1.74, fols 77^v–80^r)

The treatments of the Trinity version and the *Booke* underscore the extensive excision that the translator of MS Harley 494 made in the Mechtildian passage, by reducing the impact of the mystical, and individual, passionate relationship with Christ.

Yet the Latin prayers that follow the prayer to the divine heart in MS Harley 494 are a more or less faithful copy of the Latin text.[67] These are the Latin prayers for the sanctification of the senses of sight and hearing, and of the suppliant's mouth, voice, hands, and heart, and each of them is introduced in English:

> For kepyng of þi siy3t say thus
> Domine Jhesu Christe, tue diuine sapientie commendo visum meum interiorem & exteriorem vt lumen cognicionis mei dones, quo voluntatem tuam et omnia beneplacita tibi agnoscere valeam.
>
> [Lord Jesu Christ, I commend my sight, both inward and outward, to thy divine wisdom that thou grant me light of knowledge by which I may recognize thy will and all that is pleasing to thee.][68]

On the other hand, both the *Booke* and the prayer in MS O.1.74 faithfully translate these passages into English:

---

[66] *Women's Writing in Middle English*, ed. by Barratt, p. 63.
[67] See *Revelationes*, ed. by Paquelin, Pars iii Cap. 17, p. 218.
[68] MS Harley 494, fol. 26^{r-v}; Barratt, *Anne Bulkeley and her Book*, pp. 196, 198.

Also commende thy syght, as wele þyne inwarde syght as þyne outewarde syght, to the deuyne wysdome ande praye þat he gyffe þe the lyght of knawynge wharewith þowe maye knawe his wille ande alle thynges pleysynge to hym.[69]

Lord Jesu, I comende my syght, as wel myn ynward sight as outward sight, to thi devyne wisdom, byseching thee, Lord, that thou yeve me knowyng wherwith Y mowe knowe thi wil and al thingis that be plesing to the this daye.[70] (MS O.1.74, fols 77ᵛ–80ʳ)

Compared with MS O.1.74, MS Harley 494 is uniquely bilingual. It is difficult to know what expectations scribes and compilers had of their audiences when direct addresses and prologues are lacking in the manuscripts. But the Trinity College compilation is less 'innocuous' in that it translates important passages, making them available to all readers. The audience of MS Harley 494 might have been bilingual, or one might speculate that the translator did not want his audience to understand the content of the Latin text.[71] Yet, even if some members of the audience did not understand the Latin, they could still have a phonetic literacy without necessarily understanding the text's full meaning, especially knowing that it concerned the familiar senses such as sight, hearing, etc., rather than complicated, theological expositions, and they could presumably have a sense of the text.[72] Furthermore, in addition to the question of literacy, we could speculate that the Latin prayers in Mechtildian extracts assumed authority and power like a talisman.[73] As C. Annette Grisé points out, non-Latinate audiences accepted the Latin as a power language for prayer, and this led to 'the incorporation of Latin prayers into vernacular devotions'.[74] By participating in the vocalization of bilingual Mechtildian prayers, the reader was able to embrace the sacred power they impart.

---

[69] *Booke*, ed. by Halligan, III. 15. 446.

[70] *Women's Writing in Middle English*, ed. by Barratt, p. 63.

[71] Building on Sutherland's discussion, Cré argues that the *Chastising* author shows an impulse of restriction, by 'barring the reader's access to material that may endanger her humility' ('Take a Walk on the Safe Side', pp. 237–38): see Sutherland, 'The *Chastising of God's Children*', pp. 372–73. I would like to thank Professor Catherine Innes-Parker for discussing this with me.

[72] For phonetic literacy, see Saenger, 'Books of Hours and the Reading Habits', pp. 240–41; Yoshikawa, *Margery Kempe's Meditations*, p. 27.

[73] Voaden noticed the same point: see 'The Company She Keeps', p. 60. See also *The Chastising of God's Children*, ed. by Bazire and Colledge, pp. 220–22, where the author says that the words are sufficient without understanding.

[74] Grisé, 'Continental Holy Women', p. 167.

In MS Harley 494, this set of Latin prayers for commendation of the senses is followed by another set of brief meditations on the Hours of the Passion, borrowed from the *Liber*, Pars iii Cap. 29, and rendered freely, this time, in English. Yet, again, the final prayer in Item 10, borrowed from the *Liber*, Pars iv Cap. 23, is in Latin and also introduced in English:

> Whan thou woldest praise me, lawd or thanke me, or loue me [...] than say thus: *Jhesu bone, laudo te & quicquid minus est in me, rogo vt te supleas pro me. Jhesu bone, amo te et si quid minus est in me, rogo ut cordis tui amorem Patri offeras pro me.* [Good Jesu, I praise thee and wherever I fall short I ask that thou make it good on my behalf. Good Jesu, I love thee and wherever I fall short I ask that thou offer thy heart's love to the Father on my behalf.]
> And as ofte as þou praiest thus, I schall offre my-self to my father for the.[75]

These bilingual passages again suggest that the translator produced the translation for a bilingual readership, or perhaps for a mixed audience.

The third substantial borrowing from Mechtild's *Liber* is placed towards the end of MS Harley 494 (Item 28, fols 105ʳ–106ᵛ). Written by one of the sixteen hands, this item is entitled 'þe bedis of pardon in Englyshe of Saynt Gregorrys pytye',[76] a version of the pardon Beads of Syon. It begins with a popular devotion, 'O swete blessyd Jhesu, for thy holy name & thy byttere passion, save vs from synne [...] Amen', which appears in early printed books of hours and late medieval devotional manuscripts.[77] This prayer is repeated on every bead, alternating with five different prayers to be pronounced when touching other beads. It is then followed by 'a set of three Latin prayers, based on the triple recitation of the Ave Maria, each of which is followed by a similar but not identical prayer in English'.[78] The exercise of the Triple Aves derives from the *Liber*, Pars i Caps 11 and 47:[79] in the former Mechtild is instructed, during the feast of Saint Agnes, to say three Aves, celebrating the Virgin in terms of the attributes of the Trinity, while in the latter (the last chapter of Pars i) Mechtild implores for the Virgin's intercession to ensure her deathbed assistance. The Virgin then gives her detailed instructions including the recitation of the Triple

---

[75] MS Harley 494, fol. 30ʳ; Barratt, *Anne Bulkeley and her Book*, p. 198.

[76] Barratt, *Anne Bulkeley and her Book*, p. 114.

[77] MS Harley 494, fol. 105ʳ⁻ᵛ; Barratt, *Anne Bulkeley and her Book*, p. 256. For the Pardon of Syon, see Hirsh, 'A Fifteenth-Century Commentary on "Ihesu for thy holy name"'.

[78] Barratt, *Anne Bulkeley and her Book*, p. 99.

[79] For the Middle English translation, see *Booke*, ed. by Halligan, I. 23 and 87. The *Liber* promotes the recitation of Ave Maria.

Aves. In MS Harley 494, the third Ave (in invoking the Holy Spirit) is followed by the request of the Virgin's presence at the hour of death: 'O glorious lady [...] I beseche the so be present, & greet me love & grace, & kepe me in my ryght naturall wyttes, and temper the passiones of my deth.'[80] Placed towards the end of Anne Bulkeley's book, Mechtildian materials in Item 28 highlight the Virgin's role as a *mediatrix* within Marian devotions for the laity.

***

Anne Bulkeley's prayer book illuminates how mystical texts were translated from their original context for devotional use of the laity. In producing MS Harley 494, the supervisor/compiler seems to have instructed the translators/scribes to follow a common practice of extracting episodic versions for compilation, rather than copying an entire revelation. But we may also deduce that he was very familiar with the Latin *Liber* and probably also with the *Booke*, which was translated in a Carthusian/Birgittine milieu and the copies of which were circulating among the religious and devout laity in England: as the one in charge of planning and compilation, the supervisor/compiler thus embedded the Mechtildian material in this anthology and appropriated Mechtild's revelations for the devotional purposes of the female laity.

In fifteenth-century England, the reduction of mystical texts to collections of prayers was often 'an attempt to change them from being Latin texts with a prophetic edge of clerical admonition and correction to more overtly devotional, vernacular materials',[81] but Mechtildian materials contained in MS Harley 494 reveal that the supervisor (and other translators) rather concentrated on reducing the mystical material to the level of less affective piety and selecting devotional prayers from the renowned, approved mystic's revelations, thereby responding to the devout but amateur audience. Yet, this appropriation is already seen in the making of the complete Middle English text. When the *Booke* was originally prepared for a religious audience, its male translator/scribe filtered Mechtild's revelations, dictated and edited by her fellow nuns at Helfta, through his idea of representing Mechtild as a model of devotional practice and appropriated her revelations for the English readership by weakening the intensity of bridal mysticism.

As a result, whilst the *Liber* (and, to a certain extent, the *Booke*) records at much greater length and in much greater detail the accounts of Mechtild's

---

[80] MS Harley 494, fol. 106ᵛ; Barratt, *Anne Bulkeley and her Book*, p. 257.

[81] Private correspondence with Professor Vincent Gillespie (24 May 2016), to whom I am very grateful.

dynamic and developing relationship with Christ, MS Harley 494 might undermine the uniqueness of her revelatory experience by extensive excisions, making the Mechtildian spirituality less affective. Nevertheless, in assembling pieces of Mechtildian prayers and meditations, MS Harley 494 contributed to the dissemination of Mechtild's name and the growth of devotional exercises, and made Mechtild an approachable, devotional model for a wider readership. Compilations, miscellanies, and anthologies are not merely substitutes for the original texts: they are carefully selected and appropriated sets of works for amateur readership. As they cater for different readerships, they do illuminate the diversity of literary form and of spiritual content appreciated by diverse audiences in late medieval England. The Mechtildian extracts in MS Harley 494 prove this aspect of anthologies as an important literary genre. The passages (along with other items) both provide its readership with a model for emulation and spiritual authority and help them construct devotional self-identity through prayerful dialogue with the Mechtildian texts uniquely assembled for their own anthology.

Works Cited

Manuscripts

Aberdeen, University Library, MS 134
Cambridge, Trinity College, MS O.1.74
London, British Library [BL], MS Egerton 2006
London, British Library [BL], MS Harley 494
London, British Library [BL], MS Harley 4012
Oxford, Bodleian Library [Bodl. Lib.], MS Bodley 220
Oxford, Bodleian Library [Bodl. Lib.], MS Rawlinson C. 941

Primary Sources

The Boke of Gostely Grace, edited from Oxford, MS Bodley 220 with Introduction and Commentary, ed. by Anne Mouron and Naoë Kukita Yoshikawa with the assistance of Mark Atherton, Exeter Medieval Texts (Liverpool: Liverpool University Press, forthcoming)

The Booke of Gostlye Grace of Mechtild of Hackeborn, ed. by Theresa A. Halligan (Toronto: Pontifical Institute of Medieval Studies, 1979)

Bridget of Sweden, *The Liber Celestis of St Bridget of Sweden: The Middle English Version in British Library MS Claudius B I, Together with a Life of the Saint from the Same Manuscript*, ed. by Roger Ellis, Early English Text Society, o.s., 291 (Oxford: Oxford University Press, 1987)

The Chastising of God's Children and the Treatise of Perfection of the Sons of God, ed. by Joyce Bazire and Eric Colledge (Oxford: Basil Blackwell, 1957)

A Collection of Ordinances and Regulations for the Government of the Royal Household (London: John Nichols for the Society of Antiquaries, 1790)

The Idea of the Vernacular: An Anthology of Middle English Literary Theory, 1280–1520, ed. by Jocelyn Wogan-Browne, Nicholas Watson, Andrew Taylor, and Ruth Evans, Exeter Medieval Texts and Studies (Exeter: University of Exeter Press, 1999)

Liber trium virorum et trium spiritualium virginum, ed. by Jacques Lefèvre d'Étaples (Paris: Henri Estienne, 1513)

A Mirror to Devout People (Speculum Devotorum), ed. by Paul J. Patterson, Early English Text Society, o.s., 346 (Oxford: Oxford University Press, 2016)

The Myroure of oure Ladye, ed. by John Henry Blunt, Early English Text Society, e.s., 19 (London: N. Trübner, 1973)

Revelationes Gertrudianae ac Mechtildianae, ed. by Ludwig Paquelin, 2 vols (Paris: H. Oudin, 1875–77)

Syon Abbey, with the Libraries of the Carthusians, ed. by Vincent Gillespie, Corpus of British Medieval Library Catalogues, 9 (London: British Library, 2001)

Testamenta Eboracensia: A Selection of Wills from the Registry at York, Part 2, Surtees Society, 30 (London: J. B. Nichols, 1855)

Wills from Doctors' Commons: A Selection from the Wills of Eminent Persons, ed. by John Gough Nichols and John Bruce (London: John Bowyer Nichols and Sons, 1863)

Women's Writing in Middle English, ed. by Alexandra Barratt, 2nd edn (Harlow: Longman, 2010)

Secondary Works

Armstrong, C. A. J., 'The Piety of Cicely, Duchess of York: A Study in Late Mediaeval Culture', in *England, France and Burgundy in the Fifteenth Century* (London: Hambledon, 1983), pp. 135–56

Barratt, Alexandra, *Anne Bulkeley and her Book: Fashioning Female Piety in Early Tudor England*, Texts and Transitions, 2 (Turnhout: Brepols, 2009)

Blake, N. F., 'Review of *The Booke of Gostlye Grace of Mechtild of Hackeborn*, ed. by Theresa A. Halligan', *Speculum*, 56 (1981), 386–89

Bromberg, R. L. J., *Het Boek der Bijzondere Genade van Mechtild van Hackeborn*, 2 vols (Zwolle: Tjeenk Willink, 1965)

Brown, Jennifer, 'From the Charterhouse to the Printing House: Catherine of Siena in Medieval England', in *Middle English Religious Writing in Practice: Texts, Readers, and Transformations*, ed. by Nicole R. Rice, Late Medieval and Early Modern Studies, 21 (Turnhout: Brepols, 2013), pp. 17–45

Cré, Marleen, 'Take a Walk on the Safe Side: Reading the Fragments from Ruusbroec's *Die geestelike brulocht* in *The Chastising of God's Children*', in *De letter levend maken: Opstellen aangeboden aan Guido de Baere bij zijn zeventigste verjaardag*, ed. by Kees Schepers and F. Hendrickx, Miscellanea Neerlandica, 39 (Leuven: Peeters, 2010), pp. 233–46

Ellis, Roger, *Syon Abbey: The Spirituality of the English Bridgettines*, Analecta Cartusiana, 68.2 (Salzburg: Institut für Anglistik und Amerikanistik, Universität Salzburg, 1984)

Ellis, Roger, and Samuel Fanous, '1349–1412: Texts', in *The Cambridge Companion to Medieval English Mysticism*, ed. by Samuel Fanous and Vincent Gillespie (Cambridge: Cambridge University Press, 2011), pp. 133–62

Gardner, Edmund G., *Dante and the Mystics* (New York: Octagon, 1968)

Gillespie, Vincent, '1412–1534: Culture and History', in *The Cambridge Companion to Medieval English Mysticism*, ed. by Samuel Fanous and Vincent Gillespie (Cambridge: Cambridge University Press, 2011), pp. 163–93

Grisé, C. Annette, 'Continental Holy Women and the Textual Relics of Prayers in Late-Medieval England', in *The Medieval Translator / Traduire au Moyen Age 10*, ed. by Jacqueline Jenkins and Olivier Bertrand (Turnhout: Brepols, 2007), pp. 165–78

Harris, Barbara J., 'A New Look at the Reformation: Aristocratic Women and Nunneries, 1450–1540', *Journal of British Studies*, 32 (1993), 89–113

Hellgardt, Ernst, 'Latin and the Vernacular: Mechthild of Magdeburg — Mechthild of Hackeborn — Gertrude of Helfta', in *A Companion to Mysticism and Devotion in Northern Germany in the Late Middle Ages*, ed. by Elizabeth Andersen, Henrike Lähnemann, and Anne Simon (Leiden: Brill, 2014), pp. 131–45

Hicks, M. A., 'The Piety of Margaret, Lady Hungerford (d. 1478)', *Journal of Ecclesiastical History*, 38 (1987), 19–38

Hirsh, John, 'A Fifteenth-Century Commentary on "Ihesu for thy holy name"', in *New Index of Middle English Verse*, ed. by Julia Boffey and A. S. G. Edwards (London: British Library, 2005), no. 1703

Holland, P., 'The Lincolnshire Rebellion of March 1470', *English Historical Review*, 103 (1988), 849–69

Lovatt, Roger, 'Henry Suso and Medieval Mystical Tradition in England', in *The Medieval Mystical Tradition in England: Exeter Symposium II*, ed. by Marion Glasscoe (Exeter: University of Exeter Press, 1982), pp. 47–62

Newman, Barbara, 'The Seven-Storey Mountain: Mechthild of Hackeborn and Dante's Matelda', *Dante Studies*, 136 (2018), 62–92

Rhodes, J. T., 'The Body of Christ in English Eucharistic Devotion, *c*. 1500–*c*. 1620', in *New Science out of Old Books: Studies in Manuscripts and Early Printed Books in Honour of A. I. Doyle*, ed. by Richard Beadle and A. J. Piper (Aldershot: Scolar, 1995), pp. 388–419

Rydel, Courtney E., 'Inventing a Male Writer in Mechtild of Hackeborn's *Booke of Gostly Grace*', *Journal of Medieval Religious Cultures*, 40 (2014), 192–216

Saenger, Paul, 'Books of Hours and the Reading Habits of the Later Middle Ages', *Scrittura e civiltà*, 9 (1985), 239–69

Sutherland, Annie, '*The Chastising of God's Children*: A Neglected Text', in *Text and Controversy from Wyclif to Bale: Essays in Honour of Anne Hudson*, ed. by Helen Barr and Ann M. Hutchison, Medieval Church Studies, 4 (Turnhout: Brepols, 2005), pp. 353–73

Sutton, Anne F., and Livia Visser-Fuchs, *Richard III's Books: Ideals and Reality in the Life and Library of a Medieval Prince* (Stroud: Sutton, 1997)

Voaden, Rosalynn, 'The Company She Keeps: Mechtild of Hackeborn in Late-Medieval Devotional Compilations', in *Prophets Abroad: The Reception of Continental Holy Women in Late Medieval England*, ed. by Rosalynn Voaden (Cambridge: D. S. Brewer, 1996), pp. 51–69

—— , 'Mechtild of Hackeborn', in *Medieval Holy Women in the Christian Tradition, c. 1100–c. 1500*, ed. by Alastair Minnis and Rosalynn Voaden, Brepols Collected Essays in European Culture, 1 (Turnhout: Brepols, 2010), pp. 431–51

Yoshikawa, Naoë Kukita, *Margery Kempe's Meditations: The Context of Medieval Devotional Literature, Liturgy, and Iconography* (Cardiff: University of Wales Press, 2007)

Online Publications

Rhodes, J. T., 'Whitford, Richard (d. 1543?)', in *Oxford Dictionary of National Biography*, <http://www.oxforddnb.com/view/article/29308> [accessed 21 May 2019]

STC = *Universal Short Title Catalogue*, <https://www.ustc.ac.uk/>

Part V

Texts, Images, and Affect

The Living Book of Cambridge, Trinity College, MS B.15.42: Compilation, Meditation, and Vision

Laura Saetveit Miles

Compilations demonstrate how medieval literary traditions acutely challenge any modern notions of homogeneity or consistently hierarchized canon formation. As a medieval religious prose genre wherein 'extracts from a source or sources are woven together into a text which is presented as a single, distinct work', compilations resist the idea of a single 'major author' by both explicitly and implicitly incorporating the work of many authors, and then usually leaving the compiler himself anonymous.[1] When we consider compilations within their manuscript context, the profundity of 'the medieval book's fundamentally anthologistic or miscellaneous character' becomes even more evident.[2] Compilations very often survive in miscellanies (codices containing multiple works which may be unrelated, or somewhat related) or in anthologies (codices containing works that do seem to be related or put together by design) — though of course manuscripts often resist these somewhat subjective categories. Thus in this situation the *composite* nature of medieval literature presents itself at all levels, both text and context; to appropriate Roland Barthes's words in his famous essay 'The Death of the Author', the compilation and miscellany/

---

[1] Dutton, *Julian of Norwich*, p. 3.

[2] Lerer, 'Medieval English Literature', p. 1253. See also the seminal essay by Malcolm Parkes, 'The Influence of the Concepts of *Ordinatio* and *Compilatio*'.

Laura Saetveit Miles (laura.miles@uib.no) is Associate Professor of English literature in the Department of Foreign Languages at the University of Bergen, Norway.

anthology each operate as a 'multi-dimensional space in which a variety of writings, none of them original, blend and clash'.³

The compilation genre in particular offers a provocative demonstration of Barthes's claim that 'the text is a tissue of quotations drawn from the innumerable centers of culture'.⁴ While it can be difficult to discern the level of planning that went into the creation of a codex, compilations present a more apparent unity, a cohesion from the conception of their composition, because by nature they are 'always created in the mind of the compiler'.⁵ In other words, as he writes it, the compiler likely holds in his mind the overall narrative and its various 'tissues of quotations' that he weaves together for the text — recalling the etymology of *texta* as 'something woven', something not homogeneous but textured in a way that can be felt through reading as a kind of touching.

This essay focuses on the textual and textural juxtapositions captured in the miscellany manuscript Cambridge, Trinity College, MS B.15.42 (hereafter MS B.15.42) and especially focusing on one of its contents, a little-studied Middle English compilation usually called the *Meditaciones domini nostri*. *Meditaciones domini nostri* can be seen as part of a 'core' of longer texts in MS B.15.42 which together consistently draw attention to the interconnectedness of body, contemplation, and vision, and the necessity of their juxtaposition for moral living and salvation. This core consists of first vernacular and then Latin works: Richard Rolle's *The Commandment*, the anonymous compilations *Meditaciones domini nostri* and *Contemplations of the Dread and Love of God*, and the Latin visionary accounts of the Monk of Eynsham and Tnugdal. When considered holistically, this unique combination of texts teaches how reading, prayer, and vision offer different modes of accessing other worlds, whether the past of Christ's life or the eternity of purgatory. The codex emphasizes the conflation of book and body to demonstrate how an understanding of the salvific power of Christ's body can also be preserved in our own body as a kind of corporeal text — enabled by the Word made flesh.

Such an exploration stops short of claiming any insight into the *intentio* behind the *compilatio* of the manuscript; nor do I aim to perform some kind of authentic medieval reading. Rather I agree with Jessica Brantley when she articulates that

---

³ Barthes, 'The Death of the Author', p. 223.
⁴ Barthes, 'The Death of the Author', p. 223.
⁵ Dutton, *Julian of Norwich*, p. 4.

the kinds of sustained scrutiny that modern scholars can turn toward such medieval books can reveal, if not replicate, the kinds of literary and visionary attention paid by fifteenth-century readers. A miscellany is most meaningful, not because it was *designed* to work in a particular way, but simply because it *does*.[6]

As a miscellany MS B.15.42 *does* work, and in complex ways. So I hope to listen for the resonances that emerge organically from this combination of works in the manuscript, and from the combination of sources in the compilations, to hear how these 'tissues of quotations' reverberate off each other. While it may be that 'miscellany manuscripts are frequently governed by an inscrutable internal logic',[7] it is also true that 'a combination of happenstance acquisition and variously motivated selection is quite typical of a large range of Middle English manuscript books'.[8] Whether entirely or partly purposefully planned, the arrangement of items in MS B.15.42 nonetheless produces a sense of the vital importance of visionary activity as a way of understanding the common corporeality shared by both humans and Christ — and vice versa, the relevance of the body and the senses to any kind of visionary or transcendent experience of God.

The Manuscript

MS B.15.42 dates from the early to mid-fifteenth century, and its medieval provenance is unknown beyond the ownership inscription of a brother ('frater') William Caston dated 1468 on the back flyleaf.[9] The 110 parchment folios are pricked and ruled in double columns of forty-four lines. A first scribe is responsible for fols 1–103, the part of the manuscript this essay will focus on, and a second scribe for fols 104–09. The clear Anglicana main hand beginning on fol. 1ʳ is combined with rubricated textura headings, in the same hand as occasional rubricated textura marginal notations. Blue and red three-line initials appear intermittently, sometimes at the beginning of new texts and some-

---

[6] Brantley, *Reading in the Wilderness*, p. 11.

[7] Gillespie, *Looking in Holy Books*, p. 159.

[8] Hanna, 'Miscellaneity and Vernacularity', p. 47.

[9] The inscription is on fol. 110ʳ, the last flyleaf, which shows considerable wear. Nearly illegible in parts, the first part reads 'anno d[omi]ni cccc° sexagesim° viii° seruiuit fr[ater] Will[ieu]m[u]s Caston sub egidio' (In the year of our lord 1468 served Brother William Caston under(?) [St.] Giles). St Giles might provide a clue to a monastery or priory dedicated to that saint. William Caston has not yet been identified. My thanks to Vincent Gillespie and Ralph Hanna for insights on the inscription.

times in the middle, and are missing after fol. 78ʳ. A brief list of the contents by the first scribe:[10]

1. fol. 1ʳ A tract on the sacraments, beginning and ending imperfectly (Middle English)

2. fol. 2ʳ Richard Rolle, *The Commandment* (Middle English)

3. fol. 5ʳ *Meditaciones domini nostri* (Middle English)

4. fol. 43ʳ *Contemplations of the Dread and Love of God* (Middle English)

5. fol. 62ʳ *Visio monachi de Eynsham* (Latin)

6. fol. 86ᵛ *Speculum peccatoris et regula moriendi* (Latin)

7. fol. 91ᵛ Excerpt from *Visio Tnugdali* (Latin)

8. fol. 93ʳ Miscellaneous extracts from the Sentences (Latin)

9. fol. 96ᵛ Exposition of the Lord's Prayer (Latin)

10. fol. 98ᵛ On the Conception of the Virgin (Latin)

11. fol. 101ʳ On the seven deadly sins (Latin, with Middle English quatrains)

The combination of vernacular and Latin texts suggests clerical or monastic use, as do items one, six, and nine, which all offer guidance related to a priestly purview. Caston's ownership inscription reinforces this tie to a professed religious audience.

A later likely sixteenth-century hand has added a table of contents on the verso of the front flyleaf, and below in the same ink appears a remarkable portrait of a man with a beard and pointed hood, open in front and similar to a slightly wilted-looking Phrygian cap, in eleventh- or twelfth-century fashion.[11]

---

[10] For the original contents listing, see James, *The Western Manuscripts*, MSS 376 (previously 374, 375, 376, now rebound), pp. 510–13. The vernacular items are also detailed in Mooney, *The Index of Middle English Prose Handlist 11*, pp. 19–20. The entire manuscript has been scanned and is available online at the Wren Digital Library of Trinity College, Cambridge, <http://trin-sites-pub.trin.cam.ac.uk/james/viewpage.php?index=244> [accessed 18 May 2018].

[11] Under the portrait is written the named 'Grvnson' and '1196 floruit' (lived 1196). The year 1196 is when the Monk of Eynsham experienced his visions, as noted at the top of that text on fol. 62ʳ, in an early modern hand: 'Tractatus de Purgatori scriptus AD 1196'. Based on the

Sporadically throughout the manuscript, a sixteenth-century hand (possibly the same as the portrait artist) makes marginal annotations, alongside occasional medieval corrections and brief annotations in several hands. The only medieval illustrations of any kind can be found in the margins of fols 2^r, 2^v, and 3^r, and match the red ink of the rubricated headings, suggesting they were added by the original rubricator of the manuscript as part of its initial production. Over these folios seven black ink wounds seem to slice open the pages, with copious red blood drops dripping down (Figure 1).

Blood, Book, and Meditation on the Body of Christ

These graphic images, representing Christ's side wounds, accompany the text of *The Commandment* of Richard Rolle (fols 2^r–5^r). This didactic letter seems to have been originally written for a nun of Hampole, perhaps Margaret of Kirkby, though its practical instruction on spiritual living and prayer is general enough to be relevant to a range of religious readers. Like most of the other manuscript witnesses, Rolle's name is not mentioned in MS B.15.42.[12] However, the bloody gashes help to link the anonymous text to Rolle's characteristically corporeal affective piety, acting as a kind of calling card. For example, another one of Rolle's texts, *Meditation B*, explicitly links Christ's crucified body to the rubricated parchment page:

> O Christ, thy body is like a boke written al with rede ynke: so is thy body al written with rede woundes. Now, swete Ihesu, graunt me to rede vpon thy boke, and somwhate to vnderstond the swetnes of that writing, and to have likynge in studious abydyne of that redynge, and yeve me grace to conceyve somwhate of the perles love of Jesus Christ, and to lerne by that ensample to loue God agaynward as I should.[13]

Not only does such a metaphor recall for the reader Christ's suffering and love, but it also gives the reader a mode of reading the body as a text and an image

---

number forms and ink color, the portrait and its inscription on the front flyleaf could be by the same later hand as the title inscription on fol. 62^r. For a similar-looking hat, see Amphlett, *Hat*, p. 18, fig. 16.

[12] *The Commandment* is edited in Rolle, *Prose and Verse*, ed. by Ogilvie-Thomson, pp. 34–39; list of manuscripts, pp. xlv–xlvi; on manuscript relationships and Margaret of Kirkby as original recipient, pp. lxxvi–lxxx. Only three of the fifteen surviving manuscript witnesses identify Rolle as the author, and one identifies a sister of Hampole as original recipient.

[13] Rolle, *Prose and Verse*, ed. by Ogilvie-Thomson, p. 75, ll. 236–41.

simultaneously. Thus the marginal wounds in MS B.15.42 make the manuscript page come alive as the body of Christ on the cross, freshly wounded by the spear, and the text on the page transforms into Christ's body as well. By adding these visual reminders of Christ's body so early in the manuscript, the scribe of these marginalia in MS B.15.42 sets up the parallel between book and Christ's body as a fundamental framework for approaching the rest of the codex.

Generally speaking, MS B.15.42's inky wounds exemplify 'the distinctly somatic turn of late medieval spirituality' that developed blood piety into a complex part of theology and devotion in this period, most strikingly manifested in manuscripts such as BL, MS Egerton 1821, made in England *c.* 1480–90 and likely a Carthusian production from Sheen.[14] This manuscript contains solid red pages painted as Christ's blood, and marks of wear strongly suggest that its medieval reader(s) 'most fervently and repeatedly touched, scratched, rubbed, and/or kissed' the paint.[15] In her examination of BL, MS Egerton 1821, Nancy Thebaut argues that 'blood is not revered as a mere indicator or sign, but as a quasi-sacramental rupture in the flesh, inviting access to Christ'.[16] MS B.15.42 invites access to Christ through visual and tactile engagement of the painted blood simultaneous with the reading of the main text, a meditative move also found throughout another remarkable Carthusian manuscript, BL, MS Additional 37049. Among many examples of blood, word, and image coming together on the page, fol. 24ʳ of BL, MS Add. 37049 depicts a large heart with a bloody gash, a bleeding Christ beside it, and a praying Carthusian monk below. On the same page is a lyric often associated with Rolle. Brantley interprets the combination to suggest that the 'Carthusian figure uses these Rollean words to respond to Christ's call to meditate on the Passion'.[17] With its side wound marginalia, MS B.15.42 likewise pairs Rolle's *Commandment* with visual aids to draw readers towards a more multimedia, and evidently thus more effective, mode of meditating on Christ's body. Though blood piety was widespread, perhaps MS B.15.42's combination of Rollean text and image specifically geared towards shaping the reader's meditative practice as a way of reading

---

[14] As Dyan Elliott articulates it in 'True Presence/False Christ', p. 241. On blood in medieval culture, see, most notably, Bynum, *Wonderful Blood*; Bildhauer, *Medieval Blood*; Hennessy, 'Aspects of Blood Piety in a Late Medieval English Manuscript'.

[15] See Thebaut, 'Bleeding Pages, Bleeding Bodies', p. 180. Rudy, 'Kissing Images, Unfurling Rolls', also examines manuscript evidence from signs of wear that suggest ritual touching and kissing of some English medieval prayer books.

[16] Thebaut, 'Bleeding Pages, Bleeding Bodies', p. 178.

[17] Brantley, *Reading in the Wilderness*, p. 219; see fig. 6.2 for this folio.

Christ's body suggests a connection to the Carthusian traditions found in BL, MS Add. 37049 and BL, MS Egerton 1821.

If it was the rubricator who was responsible for the wounds, as is likely considering the matching ink colour and style, he seems acutely aware of several complementary aspects of Rolle's spirituality: not only the blood piety, but also the overlapping reverence of the Holy Name with which Rolle was strongly associated and which briefly appears in this text. Towards the end of *The Commandment* on fol. 5ʳ, when the text reads 'Ther for set thy loue in this name Ihesu', the scribe has marked with a box the abbreviated name of Jesus ('ihū'), and then called it out by writing the 'ihc' monogram version of the Holy Name in the margin (Figure 2). This marginalia echoes the insistent dedication to the Holy Name found in the margins of several other manuscripts dedicated to Rolle's works.[18] In Bodl. Lib., MS Bodley 861, for instance, the monogram 'IHU' appears at the top of every single folio, while in Warminster, Longleat House, Marquess of Bath MS 29, the name 'Ihesu' appears ten times in the margin of *The Commandment* — along with dozens of other occurrences in Rolle's two other English epistles, *Ego dormio* and *Form of Living*.[19] All of these extra-textual expressions demonstrate the late medieval devotion to the name of Jesus or the Holy Name, wherein 'the pictorial word becomes the divine person himself, embodying in one symbol the narrative of his life and even replicating emblematically his miraculous performance of redemptive sacrifice'.[20] Already in the first few folios, the human body of Christ, unable to be bounded by the text and its narrow columns, emerges as a powerful force in Cambridge, Trinity College, MS B.15.42.

---

[18] Such as Bodl. Lib., MS Bodley 861; Warminster, Longleat House, Marquess of Bath MS 29; Bodl. Lib., MS Douce 322; Bodl. Lib., MS Rawlinson C. 285; and in a unique way, BL, MS Add. 37049; see Brantley, *Reading in the Wilderness*, p. 187 n. 65.

[19] Renevey, 'The Name Poured Out', p. 133; Rolle, *Prose and Verse*, ed. by Ogilvie-Thomson, lists the occurrences. McIlroy also discusses this scribal phenomenon in her book, *The English Prose Treatises*, pp. 177–80.

[20] Brantley, *Reading in the Wilderness*, p. 179; Brantley discusses at length the equivalencies between the Holy Name and the physical holy body of Christ, especially the charter of Christ, pp. 180–95. Considerations of the Holy Name devotion include Lutton, 'The Name of Jesus' and Carsley, 'Devotion to the Holy Name'.

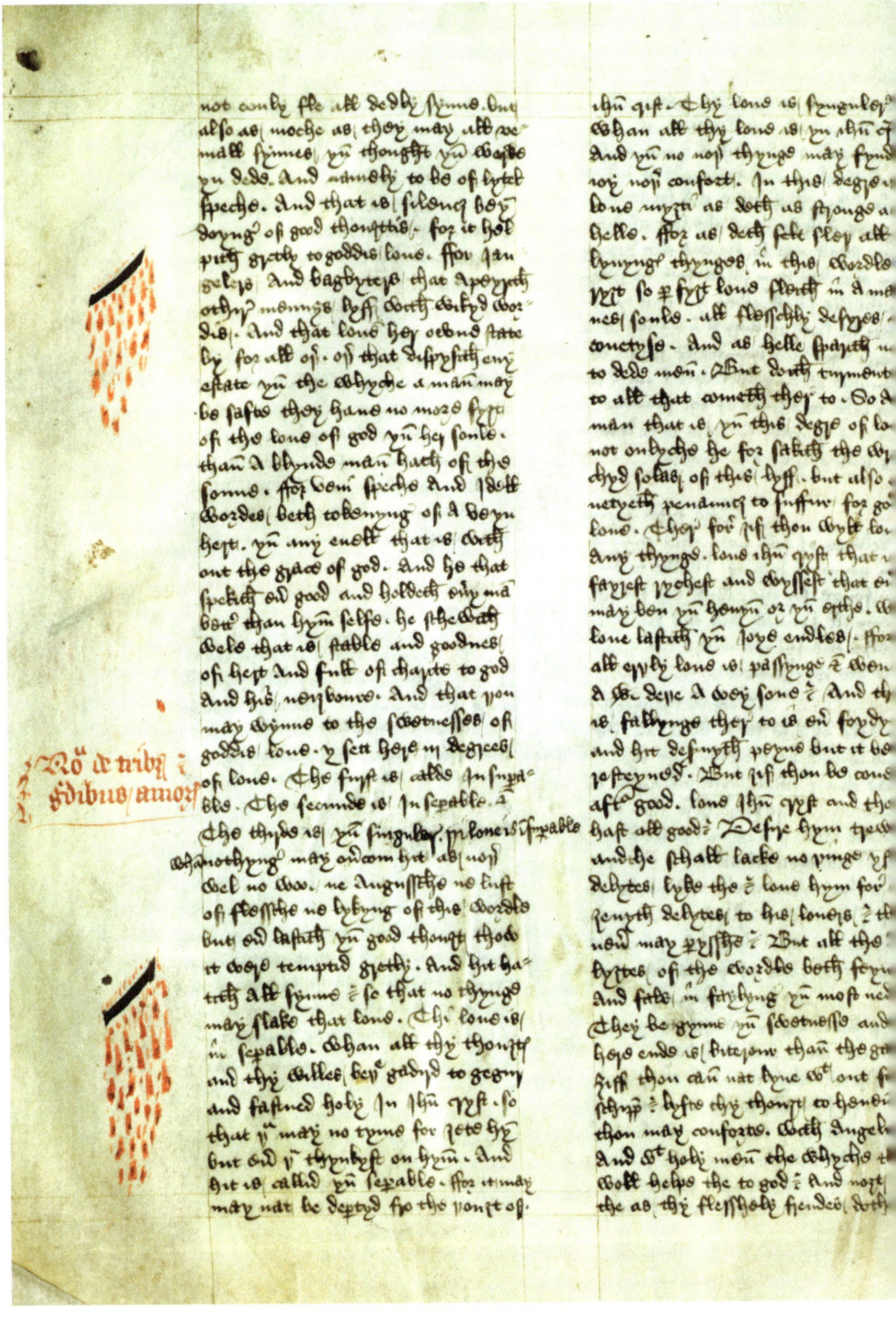

Figure 1. Richard Rolle, *The Commandment*, with side wounds marginalia (six total over page spread). Cambridge, Trinity College, MS B.15.42, fols 2ᵛ–3ʳ. Early to mid-fifteenth century. Reproduced with permission of the Master and Fellows of Trinity College Cambridge.

[Middle English manuscript, left column partially cut off at left margin]

...rne thy wytt a whyle thy lust /
...hyngys of synne & thou schalt
...o afterwardis alle thyn wyll for to
...enfyd of synne & make so
...at he schall lust nothyng but
...at is plesyng to almyghty god /
...the lust to speke for hope all ye
...mynge for goddis loue & aftyr
...en thy hert felyth delyght in
...e thou wolt not speke no
...e to speke but of ihū cryst ȝif
... may not suffyr to sytte or to
... thy selfe / vse the myȝth
... cryst Ihu · And he wolt so sta
...che sette the · that alle thi solace
...e wordis schall not nombe ye
...or ye wote not lusty thoȝ off
...an ewse ay by thi selfe be all
...o that slepe come on yu þer
...n good meditacion & ordyr
... walkynge And thy prayingys
... thy fastyng that it be in dis...
...tt on moche & noȝt on lytell
... thynke on that of alle thyngys
...e plesyth god loue of mankus
... And therefor seke more to
...hym than to do eny pena...
... for vnskylfull penaunce
...eth worthy or noȝt · cryste
...od that wil ȝeue ye that ȝe
...yst þe of skylfully / skylfull
...yer is that a cristen sowle
... and aske nyȝt and day
...loue of ihū cryste · that he
...loue hym verely felyngly
...fort and delyte yn hym out
...ynge all worldly thoȝtys /
...enell bysynesse · And sykyr
...on ȝif thou conceyt his loue
...y in þat lastynyth so þe no
...of thi flesshe ne angres of ye
...li ne specche ne haȝed of men

nou bil

...space the a ȝon And not the nob in
busynesse of bodelyche thyngys · thou
schalt haue his loue and fynde it
felt that hit is delectablior · yn
on odyr than all the welthe that
the se here · may be to domes day /
And yf ȝu fayle or falle for tempta
cons or for angrys or for mochell
loue off thi frendis · hit is no won
dy yf he holde hem the that thy
ȝe that thou couetyst not · ffor thy
he seyth he louyth hem that louyth
hym · And tho yt eyrly wake to hym þay schalt fynde hȳ
Thu oyt erly wakynge ofte syro why
than fyndest thou hym noȝt · I say
yf thou seke hym ryghtfullyche þ
schalt fynde hym · But whyhst yt
sekost erthly ioy yon yt wake now so
erly thou mayst not fynde erthly
for he is not founde in her loue /
that loue flesschly lustos / the /
medyr whan he fy ther sche souȝt
hym ful erly and sate a mongys
her kynredon and his / but sche fon
de hym not · for all her sekynge
it at the laste sche come yn to the
temppull and they sche founde hȳ
syttynge a mongys the maystres herde
and answerynge · So behowyth ye
to do yf thou wolte fynde hym
seke hym y̎ yn wordly tyowthe
and yn hopes and yn chapyto · vt
holichyche castynge out of synne
and hate hit yn all thyn hert &
ffor oonly synne holdyth hym fro ye
And lettith that thu may not fynde
hym · Tho kyndes that souȝt hȳ
fonde hym syttyng yn a cherche bi
twen two bestes by tokenynge þt
that thou wolte seke hym verly ye
behowth to go in þe wey of rede .

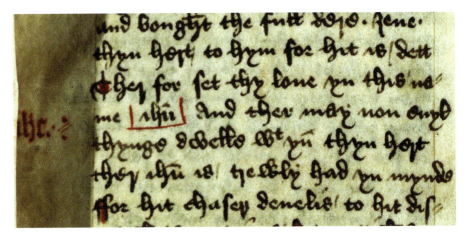

Figure 2. Richard Rolle, *The Commandment*, with red marginal 'ihc' monogram noting the 'ihu' monogram with a red box around it in the text, for the Holy Name. Cambridge, Trinity College, MS B.15.42, fol. 5ʳ. Early to mid-fifteenth century. Reproduced with permission of the Master and Fellows of Trinity College Cambridge.

Figure 3. *Meditaciones domini nostri* with parchment holes, through which the rubricated table of contents of *Contemplations of the Dread and Love of God* can be seen. Cambridge, Trinity College, MS B.15.42, fol. 42ʳ. Early to mid-fifteenth century. Reproduced with permission of the Master and Fellows of Trinity College Cambridge.

Holy Bodies Meditating; Meditating on Holy Bodies

In a closely related kind of participatory piety, Christ's body comes alive again as part of the reader's imaginative journey through his life, death, and Resurrection led by the next text, an anonymous vernacular compilation gospel meditation usually known as *Meditaciones domini nostri*. The only other witness being Bodl. Lib., MS Bodley 578, this little-studied text probably dates from the early to mid-fifteenth century — that is, closely contemporary with MS B.15.42's own creation — and begins in MS B.15.42 after a rubricated *explicit* and without any title.[21] As a compilation, it is woven together with about half of the material deriving from the pseudo-Bonaventuran *Meditationes vitae Christi*, and the other half a combination of verses from the Vulgate, some apocryphal gospels, various patristic sources such as Jerome, excerpts from Bernard of Clairvaux's sermons, Nicholas of Lyra's *Postilla*, and perhaps most noticeably, two female visionaries: of the twelve total marginal attributions, nine notes mention the *Revelations* or *Sermo angelicus* of Saint Bridget of Sweden as a source, and one note the *Revelations* of Saint Elizabeth of Hungary. A single marginal note claims a borrowing from Richard of St Victor (fol. 8ʳ).

These passages identified with Bridget, Elizabeth, and Richard of St Victor all concern the Virgin Mary and help give the *Meditaciones domini nostri* a strong emphasis on Mary's role in Christ's life. While the previous text in the manuscript, *The Commandment*, almost exclusively focuses on Christ as an exemplary inspiration for living and praying, this longer gospel narrative introduces Mary as an important model. The Richard of St Victor attribution marks an extended meditation on the moments leading up to the Annunciation, when the Virgin Mary is reading and meditating on the prophecies foretelling the Incarnation (Isaiah 7. 14) just before the angel Gabriel's arrival. This material is closely copied from another understudied Middle English devotional treatise known as *Of Three Workings of Man's Soul*, a late fourteenth-century devotional

---

[21] This text is edited as a doctoral dissertation, 'The Lyf of Oure Lord', ed. by Blom-Smith. Blom-Smith's extensive work includes a linguistic profile and dialectal analysis for the witness in this manuscript, where she links the language to the Norfolk or Suffolk area, pp. xlviii–liii. Salter, *Nicholas Love's 'Myrrour'*, briefly mentions this text as part of group D, pp. 55–56, p. 106. In the *Manual of Writings in Middle English*, vol. IX, specifically Lagorio and Sargent, 'English Mystical Writings', only this witness of the text is listed under '[76] The Revelations of St Birgitta of Sweden', MS 8, where it is identified as 'Trinity Camb B.15.39 (James 374, 375, 376)', because it had not yet been rebound apart from 374 and 375; the text is not mentioned under the other possible heading of '[62] Non-Love Versions of the *Meditationes vitae Christi*'. The text is not listed in Jolliffe, *Check-List*.

text beginning with a translation of Richard of St Victor's *Benjamin major*, and surviving in four manuscripts.[22] Its author is unknown, though Ralph Hanna has recently argued in favour of Richard Rolle's authorship of the text.[23]

However, the compiler here does not borrow anything from the entire first half of *Of Three Workings*, the part containing Richard of St Victor's *Benjamin major* and its consideration of the hierarchy of thinking, meditation, and contemplation. Rather, he retains much of the second half of the treatise, the part most likely an original Rollean composition: an unusual visualization of Mary's mind and body while rapt in a contemplative ecstasy initiated by the scriptural reading. The section describes her in corporeal terms:

> Byholde besyly vnto this blessid lady how that scheo settith hure vpryght yn body lenynge, lokynge yn the boke and lokynge vp to heuen. Byholde that blessid lowly visage of this lady how deuoute it is, the swete mowthe close and the hyen closid and therwith noone euell brethe passynge out of hure mouthe ne nose. And byholde therwith how pale scheo is. And no blood ne rede yn hure vysage. And þe clerkes seith this is the skyll: what tyme that a mannes sowle is fully reuesschid yn desyre of enythynge þan all the bloode of hym is igadurd ynto on place of hym ther the soule moste regneþ, and that is in þe hert.[24]

Physiological details highlight the proper bodily symptoms of contemplation, verified by expert 'clerkes', as signs the readers should take note of, presumably with reference to their own contemplative practice or those around them. This static moment of deep concentration on the body in stillness, with the text's long description enforcing the reader's slow contemplation of the ravished body, is a striking contrast to the continuous action of the rest of the life of Christ — an otherwise unstoppably unfolding linear narrative. Not only do readers learn proper reading, meditation, and contemplation through Mary's example, by concentrating on Mary's flesh and blood readers are also reminded of how she shares these with Christ at the (imminent) Incarnation, the same flesh and blood featured in the graphic side wounds on the earlier folios. As she

---

[22] I set forth the identification of this borrowing in 'An Unnoticed Borrowing' and further discuss these two texts in my forthcoming book, *The Virgin Mary's Book at the Annunciation*. *Of Three Workings* has most recently been edited in Rolle, *Uncollected Prose and Verse*, ed. by Hanna, pp. 84–88, and lxviii–lxix where he discusses its affinities with Rolle's oeuvre and the strong possibility that Rolle is the author; and previously edited in 'Of Three Workings in Man's Soul', ed. by Hayes.

[23] Rolle, *Uncollected Prose and Verse*, ed. by Hanna, p. lxix.

[24] *Meditaciones domini nostri*, MS B.15.42, fol. 8ᵛ ('The Lyf of Oure Lord', ed. by Blom-Smith, pp. 13–14). Transcriptions are my own.

reads the Old Testament book — the Word of God — she channels the divine presence into both her soul and her body, conceiving the Word as Christ. Body and soul, book and body, are inextricably woven together. For the reader, meditation on Mary's ravished body, like meditation on Christ's suffering body, could produce certain physiological changes in their body that would signal genuine mystical, ecstatic experience. The body functions as a fully necessary part of ascent to the divine.

The profound connection between Christ's suffering body and Mary's mothering body comes up again later on in the *Meditaciones domini nostri*. After the Ascension Mary stays in Jerusalem, frequently visiting the site of the Crucifixion; 'And his passyon was so inwardly preyntid in her hert, that wherever sche ete or dranke, or wrouʒte, hit was ever fressche and new in her mynde'.[25] Mary's body becomes her memory — the story of her son's death impressed like a wax seal upon the flesh deep inside her.[26] Specifically mentioning her heart here connects this moment to the earlier description of Mary as an advanced contemplative, exhibiting the bodily response of ravishment wherein 'the bloode of hym is igadurd ynto on place of hym ther the soule moste regneþ, and that is in þe hert'. Thus in both her ecstatic contemplative state and in her everyday actions, Mary's body enables her spiritual and mental engagement with Christ.

The metaphor of writing on the heart as a means of recalling the passion with the mind is an important trope in late medieval devotion that recurs in a widely popular fifteenth-century English devotional text, *The Fifteen Oes*, a series of prayers attributed to Saint Bridget but whose author is unknown. Coming from the same literary devotional world as MS B.15.42, they circulated among both lay and religious readers in England and appear to have been closely connected to Syon Abbey, but also to the 'devotional world of the Yorkshire hermitages associated with figures like Richard Rolle and his disciples'.[27] Here the reader implores Christ to use his own blood for the inscription: 'for the mynde of this passion, wryte al thy woundes in myn herte wyth thy precyous blode that I may bothe rede in theym thy drede and thy love'.[28] Christ's wounds are now transposed as text on the interior body of the devotee; they can be read like an inward book, one that is also reflected in the wound images painted on manu-

---

[25] *Meditaciones domini nostri*, MS B.15.42, fol. 41ʳ ('The Lyf of Oure Lord', ed. by Blom-Smith, p. 152).

[26] On the medieval tradition of writing on the heart, see Jager, *The Book of the Heart*.

[27] Duffy, *The Stripping of the Altars*, p. 249; also on authorship and audience, see Rogers, 'About the 15 Oes'; and '*The Fifteen Oes*', ed. by Krug.

[28] '*The Fifteen Oes*', ed. by Krug, p. 215.

script pages. Christ's body becomes the codex; the codex becomes the reader's body; and finally Christ's body becomes the reader's body. In the *Meditaciones domini nostri*, Mary offers the ultimate example of such corporeal conflation, since through the Incarnation — described some folios before — she actually shares in Christ's body; now she can relive his death through the memory of that same flesh.

The fleshy materiality of the book as an object presents itself quite vividly towards the end of the compilation *Meditaciones domini nostri*, on fol. 42ʳ of MS B.15.42 (Figure 3). Two gaping holes in the parchment page forced the scribe to write around them, while some red text shines through like freshly spilt blood. Either resulting from wounds suffered by the animal before or after its death, or possibly created during the parchment preparation process, the holes preserve the memory of the page's first life as part of a living creature, and its 'eternal' life now as a text enabled by that creature's death.[29] In both their story and their presence these gapes recall Christ's wounds signified through ink many folios earlier. Perhaps medieval readers might have felt the edges of these wounds, a touching in echo of Thomas's probing of Christ's side.

Material texture resonates with the text itself: the words surrounding the parchment wounds describe how the Virgin possessed a special understanding of the Incarnation of Christ, which the compilation has already connected to her mothering body as well as her inscribed heart. The compilation explains Mary's role with the Apostles after the Ascension, how she

> spake and comenyd of the incarnation of ihesu criste; moche more kunnyngly and trewly than any other. For in the bygynnynge sche lerned alle thynges more fully by the holy goste. And clerly saw alle thynges as we rede that an angell seide to Seynt Brigitte. As we find in her revelacions these words that followen.[30]

While earlier Mary was represented as the expert contemplative, here she is the expert theologian who knows 'moche more kunnyngly and trewly than any other', pointedly raising her above the male Apostles. This is because, 'in the bygynnynge', that is, at the Annunciation, the Holy Ghost overshadowed her and conceived in her womb the God made man. However, these insights into Mary's status are revealed to us by another authoritative female figure, Saint

---

[29] Although, as Holsinger argues, there is little evidence medieval readers may have felt any ethical conflict about the suffering or death of animals in order to make manuscripts, or connected their suffering to Christ's suffering; see 'Of Pigs and Parchment', p. 621.

[30] *Meditaciones domini nostri*, MS B.15.42, fol. 42ʳ ('The Lyf of Oure Lord', ed. by Blom-Smith, p. 155).

Bridget of Sweden. 'These words that followen' comprise a long excerpt from the *Sermo Angelicus* that comprises nearly half of the remaining compilation text, all focused on the Virgin's authority and how she helps various groups of people.[31] Like Mary, as a visionary Bridget channelled divine power from the Holy Ghost, through the gift of prophecy. Mary, Bridget, Elizabeth, and other visionary women possessed a vital privileged access to God and sacred truth that gospel meditations like this one often explicitly promoted. Mary's model of conceiving Christ, the *logos*, while reading the Word should be understood in the light of the *Meditaciones*'s frequent excerpting from Bridget's *Revelations* as well as those of Elizabeth of Hungary: holy women channel God in powerful ways, this text emphasizes, and can facilitate the reader's own spiritual conception of Christ by means of text-based meditation. Far from being a source of sin, the female body can engender Christ and channel sacred knowledge.

Reforming the Self in Christ's Image through Prayer

The red writing of fol. 43ʳ visible through the parchment holes is a special table of contents or calendar for another compilation, known as *Contemplations of the Dread and Love of God* or *Fervor amoris*, concerning how to fear and love God, and the four degrees of love.[32] Like Margaret Connolly, the modern editor, who considers this text still anonymous and not by Rolle, this version does not ascribe it to any specific author. Yet there are frequent borrowings from Rolle's works, including *Form of Living* and *Ego dormio*. Among those can be found another unacknowledged source: Bridget's *Revelationes* (III. 28), most noticeably the description of the fourth city of joy that lends its four forms of charity to the structure of the entire text, among other quotations and echoes.[33] Her visions silently permeate the whole work; there are none of the marginal references that draw explicit attention to the saint's contributions like in the previous life of Christ text. Rather the *auctors* Rolle and Bridget are woven seamlessly into this compilation, without the more obviously textured (i.e. signalled) borrowings found in *Meditaciones domini nostri*.

---

[31] See 'The Lyf of Oure Lord', ed. by Blom-Smith, p. 240.

[32] *Contemplations*, ed. by Connolly. Gillespie remarks that the sophisticated apparatus of alphabetized chapters and coordinating calendar constitute 'one of the major innovations in vernacular works of this type' (*Looking in Holy Books*, p. 141).

[33] On the borrowings from and association with Rolle, see *Contemplations*, ed. by Connolly, pp. xvi–xvii; and in more detail on both Rolle and Bridget, pp. 262–64 of Connolly, 'Mapping Manuscripts and Readers'.

However, while visions provide raw material for this compilation, visionary activity or even high contemplation plays no part in its agenda. Much like *The Commandment* earlier in the manuscript, *Contemplations of the Dread and Love of God* is a practical guide to living in virtue and charity, how to avoid sin, how to pray, how to live like Christ and end up in heaven instead of hell. This text brings the reader out of the distant past of Christ's life captured in the previous gospel meditation and back again to the immediate present where everyday actions, both major and trivial, impact one's chance at salvation. While in *Meditaciones*, Mary appeared as a lesson of advanced, ecstatic contemplation, here readers are presented with the basics of beginning prayer, both in Chapter V and in Chapter AB, which is titled 'What maner men or women of simple conning mowe þenke or preie in here bigynning'.[34] The practice meditation readers are presented with, however, brings readers full circle to the preceding text of *Meditaciones domini nostri*: it concludes with a short meditation on the Passion, a sort of sample of the longer types of the life of Christ genre represented by *Meditaciones*. This final Passion meditation begins with an emphatic reminder of one of the *Contemplations*' key points: 'þer is no more sinful þan þou art' and God 'abide þe til þou woldest leue sinne and turne to godnes'; thus 'he bycam mad and bore was of a maide'.[35] With the personal connection between one's own sin and the Crucifixion in mind, the reader launches into the Passion meditation.

What is at stake in leaving sin, loving God, and praying and meditating on Christ's sacrifice? So far the second text of MS B.15.42, *The Commandment*, and the fourth text, *Contemplations*, have been quite clear that there are two types of people: those who love the world and those who love God. As Rolle asks in *The Commandment*,

> whare þe worldes louers ben now, and whar þe louers of ben of God [...]. Certes, þei wer men and wommen as we ben, and ete and dranke and laghet; and þe wreches þat loued þis world toke ese to har body, and lyued as ham lust in lykynge of har wicked wille [...] and in a poynt þai fel in to helle.[36]

The next two longer texts in MS B.15.42 show very clearly what happens to those lovers of the world who do not follow the practical advice of treatises like *Contemplations* and *The Commandment*, or who do not meditate on Christ's

---

[34] *Contemplations*, ed. by Connolly, p. 41; MS B.15.42, fol. 59ᵛ, where the chapter title is written in by a later hand.

[35] *Contemplations*, ed. by Connolly, p. 41, l. 10 – p. 42, ll. 14, 16–17; MS B.15.42, fols 59ᵛ–60ʳ.

[36] Rolle, *Prose and Verse*, ed. by Ogilvie-Thomson, p. 39, ll. 198–211; MS B.15.42, fol. 4ᵛ.

Passion like with *Meditaciones domini nostri* or the end of *Contemplations*. Indeed, there is another place besides hell where lovers of the world may go: purgatory, that place in between life and death where souls pay for having taken 'ese to har body' and living 'as ham lust in lykynge of har wicked wille'. Like with Christ's life, visionary experience affords special access to these other worlds outside the reader's.

Purgatory Visions and the Fragmented Body

Purgatory's pains come to life starting on fol. 62ʳ of MS B.15.42, where it shifts to Latin with *Visio monachi de Eynsham*, or *The Revelation of the Monk of Eynsham*.[37] While the previous vernacular texts would have been appropriate for a broader audience of both lay and religious readers, the shift to Latin signals a more clerical audience as the intended readership for the manuscript. *Visio monachi de Eynsham*, produced at the end of the twelfth century, presents a vision of the afterlife in the long tradition of *katabasis* literature, or descents to the underworld, featuring some combination of heaven, hell, and purgatory. Visions of the otherworld was a very popular genre of visionary literature in eleventh- and twelfth-century England, and only increased in popularity through the fifteenth century, when this and the *Vision of Tnugdal* were translated into Middle English and reached a wider lay audience. What inspired the scribe to include this three-hundred-year-old Latin text in MS B.15.42 perhaps reflects the continued interest in 'visions of the other world and the advice and teaching they provided about one's conduct in this life and the mutually beneficial relations that could and should exist between the living and the dead'.[38] In this particular manuscript context, the two purgatory visions sustain the validity of visionary activity as a crucial component of religious knowledge and spiritual development, and the centrality of the human body to the fate of the soul.

Visio opens by describing how in Easter 1196, a Benedictine monk, Edmund, fell into a kind of trance state and experienced two days of visions in which he

---

[37] This Latin version is the C text, the same text edited (though not from this manuscript) in *The Revelation*, ed. by Easting. It is untitled by the main scribe, but with a later hand labelling it in the top margin, '*Tractatus de Purgatoris scriptus A: D. 1196*'. Just between *The Commandment* and the *Visio*, an originally blank folio now bears two sixteenth- and seventeenth-century tables of Sunday letters, for calculating when Easter falls; the table on fol. 61ʳ runs from 1539 to 2017, and the table on fol. 61ᵛ runs from 1616 to 2074. They are among the many interesting signs of use of this manuscript from those post-medieval centuries, unfortunately outside the scope of this paper.

[38] *The Revelation*, ed. by Easting, pp. xix–xx.

was led down into purgatory with Saint Nicholas as his guide. In purgatory he meets many souls there for a variety of reasons; these tortured souls now provide lengthy speeches of advice and teaching that offer valuable lessons to the living on how to avoid such an unpleasant fate. As Robert Easting points out, the visionary Edmund seems less interested in purgatorial pains than in 'the spiritual process of souls' purification, the progress of their salvation, and the efficacy of alms and suffrages performed by the living for the benefit of souls in purgatory'.[39] Such a constructive approach should be seen as paralleling the practical advice found earlier in MS B.15.42, in *The Commandment* and *Contemplations*.

Employing a more graphic approach, all the possible gore and pain missing from the first purgatory account can be found in the second account, starting on fol. 91[r]: *Visio Tnugdali*, or *The Vision of Tnugdal*. Also from the twelfth century, this was a very popular text about a dissolute Irish knight who dies but not quite entirely, and returns to life three days later with a vivid story of his tour through purgatory as a spectating soul.[40] Here, unlike *Visio monachi de Eynsham*, Tnugdal witnesses the very graphic penance each soul pays for their worldly sins. Souls are tortured in innumerable gruesome ways. Rather than letting Tnugdal's narrative stand alone as a kind of sadomasochistic, somewhat traumatizing reading experience, MS B.15.42's combination of texts demonstrates how, for medieval readers, there was rather more at stake than mere gratuitous violence: the fate of the soul, in which Christ has a vested interest. These two purgatory visions provide the kind of consequences to make the spiritual guidance texts in this manuscript seem particularly urgent. In purgatory and hell bodies that are torn apart, only to come back together, only to be torn apart again, offer a kind of subversion of Christ's fragmented body — whose wounds heal all wounds, and whose blood gives life. In earlier folios, the gospel meditation *Meditaciones domini nostri* offers readers the torture and death of Christ with equally vivid description, but concludes with the salvific promise of Christ's Resurrection and the ultimate wholeness of his and each repentant believer's body. This hope lingers beyond the seemingly hopeless fates of sinners.

In this brief initial exploration of MS B.15.42, unfortunately I have not had space to touch on the other texts found in the manuscript. Yet such an intermittent experience in a way replicates how some medieval readers might have

---

[39] *The Revelation*, ed. by Easting, p. lxxxiv.

[40] A modern English translation of the Latin *Visio Tnugali* can be found in *Visions of Heaven and Hell*, ed. and trans. by Gardiner, pp. 149–96; and of the Monk of Eynsham's vision, pp. 197–218.

interacted with the codex: not reading from beginning to end in a linear fashion, but ranging over the texts, consulting different items as desired. The chapter apparatus and tables of contents found with *Contemplations of the Dread and Love of God* suggest precisely such a non-linear approach to the book, as it allows readers to find various sections at will; the same with the added table of contents at the beginning of the manuscript.[41] Thus the different themes of the texts interweave in entirely fresh ways each time a reader chooses a new combination of readings.

The wound illustrations on the early folios of the manuscript remind us how vital it is to consider medieval texts in their original manuscript context, how medieval readers would have encountered them. Such material details as the rubricated gashes and the holy name monograms tighten this codex's connection to Carthusian circles interested in mystical and visionary traditions centring here on Richard Rolle and Bridget of Sweden. *The Commandment* and borrowings from Rolle in *Contemplations* make sure that Rolle's presence is felt, while *Meditaciones domini nostri* prioritizes the power of holy women with its dramatic representation of the contemplating Mary in rapture and the insistence on Bridget as *auctor* in both the text and marginal notations.

Far from being 'merely' a tissue of quotations, the compilations in MS B.15.42 demonstrate the complex textures of authorship, authority, and prayer in late medieval devotional culture. They facilitate a layered interlacing of vision and body within each text and throughout the whole codex. Together, the visionary voices of Cambridge, Trinity College, MS B.15.42 — Tnugdal, the monk of Eynsham, Bridget, Elizabeth — reinforce the conviction that there was a constant traffic of souls in both directions, between worlds, between the past of Christ's life, the now of our material world, and the future yet always already present worlds of heaven, hell, and purgatory: those spaces that exist outside of time and thus all the time (as far as we can understand it). This codex shows how thin the barriers between these worlds could be for medieval readers — and how, by reading, praying, meditating, and contemplating, one could experience other worlds either vicariously or first-hand. The repeating visual motif of Christ's side wound reminds readers that just as skin can be pierced, so can the invisible veils between the living and dead, between the present and the past. Flesh is not only a metaphor, or something to be cast aside in exchange for the purely spiritual, but actually a conduit for accessing divinity, something

---

[41] While the chapter headings up to K have been included by the medieval scribe (the rest being added in the appropriate blank lines by a post-medieval annotator), still the chapter organization remained apparent and at least somewhat useful to medieval readers.

important and indeed necessary for the spirit: exemplified with Mary, who both bears Christ in her womb and then writes Christ onto her heart. At the same time, most crucially, the body must be regulated: with *The Commandment* and *Contemplations* and other practical texts, this manuscript reminds readers to reform the self in the image of Christ — and reminds them that the smallest actions, day in and day out, are intrinsically linked to salvation.

Works Cited

Manuscripts

Cambridge, Trinity College, MS B.15.42
London, British Library [BL], MS Additional 37049
London, British Library [BL], MS Egerton 1821
Oxford, Bodleian Library [Bodl. Lib.], MS Bodley 578
Oxford, Bodleian Library [Bodl. Lib.], MS Bodley 861
Oxford, Bodleian Library [Bodl. Lib.], MS Douce 322
Oxford, Bodleian Library [Bodl. Lib.], MS Rawlinson C. 285
Warminster, Longleat House, Marquess of Bath MS 29

Primary Sources

Contemplations of the Dread and Love of God, ed. by Margaret Connolly, Early English Text Society, o.s., 303 (Oxford: Oxford University Press, 1993)
'The Fifteen Oes', ed. by Rebecca Krug, in *Cultures of Piety: Medieval English Devotional Literature in Translation*, ed. by Anne Clark Bartlett and Thomas H. Bestul (Ithaca: Cornell University Press, 1999), pp. 212–16
'The Lyf of Oure Lord and the Virgyn Mary: Edited from MS Trinity College Cambridge B.15.42 and MS Bodley 578', ed. by Elisabeth Blom-Smith (unpublished doctoral dissertation, King's College, London, 1992)
The Revelation of the Monk of Eynsham, ed. by Robert Easting, Early English Text Society, o.s., 318 (Oxford: Oxford University Press, 2002)
Rolle, Richard, *Richard Rolle: Prose and Verse from MS. Longleat 29 and Related Manuscripts*, ed. by S. J. Ogilvie-Thomson, Early English Text Society, o.s., 293 (Oxford: Oxford University Press, 1988)
——, *Richard Rolle: Uncollected Prose and Verse, with Related Northern Texts*, ed. by Ralph Hanna, Early English Text Society, o.s., 329 (Oxford: Oxford University Press, 2007)
Visions of Heaven and Hell before Dante, ed. and trans. by Eileen Gardiner (New York: Italica Press, 1989)

Secondary Works

Amphlett, Hilda, *Hat: A History of Fashion in Headwear* (Chalfont St. Giles: Richard Sadley, 1974)
Barthes, Roland, 'The Death of the Author', in *The Book History Reader*, ed. by David Finkelstein and Alistair McCleery (London: Routledge, 2002), pp. 221–24
Bildhauer, Bettina, *Medieval Blood* (Cardiff: University of Wales Press, 2006)
Brantley, Jessica, *Reading in the Wilderness: Private Devotion and Public Performance in Late Medieval England* (Chicago: University of Chicago Press, 2007)
Bynum, Caroline Walker, *Wonderful Blood: Theology and Practice in Late Medieval Northern Germany and Beyond* (Philadelphia: University of Pennsylvania Press, 2007)
Carsley, Catherine A., 'Devotion to the Holy Name: Late Medieval Piety in England', *Princeton University Library Chronicle*, 53 (1992), 156–72
Connolly, Margaret, 'Mapping Manuscripts and Readers of *Contemplations of the Dread and Love of God*', in *Design and Distribution of Late Medieval Manuscripts in England*, ed. by Margaret Connolly and Linne R. Mooney (York: York Medieval Press; Woodbridge: Boydell, 2008), pp. 261–78
Duffy, Eamon, *The Stripping of the Altars: Traditional Religion in England, 1400–1580*, 2nd edn (New Haven: Yale University Press, 2005)
Dutton, Elisabeth, *Julian of Norwich: The Influence of Late-Medieval Devotional Compilations* (Cambridge: D. S. Brewer, 2008)
Elliott, Dyan, 'True Presence/False Christ: The Antinomies of Embodiment in Medieval Spirituality', *Mediaeval Studies*, 64 (2002), 241–65
Gillespie, Vincent, *Looking in Holy Books: Essays on Late Medieval Religious Writing in England*, Brepols Collected Essays in European Culture, 3 (Turnhout: Brepols, 2011)
Hanna, Ralph, 'Miscellaneity and Vernacularity: Conditions of Literary Production in Late Medieval England', in *The Whole Book: Cultural Perspectives on the Medieval Miscellany*, ed. by Stephen G. Nichols and Sigfried Wenzel (Ann Arbor: University of Michigan Press, 1996), pp. 37–52
Hayes, Stephen B., 'Of Three Workings in Man's Soul: A Middle English Prose Meditation on the Annunciation', in *Vox Mystica: Essays for Valerie M. Lagorio*, ed. by Anne Clark Bartlett and others (Cambridge: D. S. Brewer, 1995), pp. 177–99
Hennessy, Marlene Villalobos, 'Aspects of Blood Piety in a Late Medieval English Manuscript: London, British Library Additional 37049', in *History in the Comic Mode: Medieval Communities and the Matter of Person*, ed. by Rachel Fulton and Bruce W. Holsinger (New York: Columbia University Press, 2007), pp. 182–91
Holsinger, Bruce, 'Of Pigs and Parchment: Medieval Studies and the Coming of the Animal', *PMLA*, 124.2 (2009), 616–23
Jager, Eric, *The Book of the Heart* (Chicago: University of Chicago Press, 2000)
James, M. R., *The Western Manuscripts in the Library of Trinity College, Cambridge: A Descriptive Catalogue* (Cambridge: Cambridge University Press, 1904)
Jolliffe, P. S., *A Check-List of Middle English Prose Writings of Spiritual Guidance*, Subsidia mediaevalia, 2 (Toronto: Pontifical Institute of Mediaeval Studies, 1974)

Lagorio, Valerie M., and Michael G. Sargent (with Ritamary Bradley), 'English Mystical Writings', in *A Manual of Writings in Middle English, 1050–1500*, vol. IX, ed. by Albert E. Hartung (New Haven: Connecticut Academy of Arts of Sciences, 1993), pp. 3049–36, 3405–71

Lerer, Seth, 'Medieval English Literature and the Idea of the Anthology', *PMLA*, 118.5 (2003), 1251–67

Lutton, Rob, 'The Name of Jesus, Nicholas Love's *Mirror*, and Christocentric Devotion in Late Medieval England', in *The Pseudo-Bonaventuran Lives of Christ: Exploring the Middle English Tradition*, ed. by Ian Johnson and Allen F. Westphall, Medieval Church Studies, 24 (Turnhout: Brepols, 2013), pp. 19–53

McIlroy, Claire Elizabeth, *The English Prose Treatises of Richard Rolle* (Cambridge: D. S. Brewer, 2004)

Miles, Laura Saetveit, 'An Unnoticed Borrowing from the Treatise of Three Workings in Man's Soul in the Gospel Meditation *Meditaciones Domini Nostri*', *Journal of the Early Book Society*, 20 (2017), 277–84

——, *The Virgin Mary's Book at the Annunciation: Reading, Interpretation, and Devotion in Medieval England* (Woodbridge: Boydell & Brewer, forthcoming)

Mooney, L. R., *The Index of Middle English Prose Handlist 11: Manuscripts in the Library of Trinity College, Cambridge* (Cambridge: Cambridge University Press, 1995)

Parkes, Malcolm B., 'The Influence of the Concepts of *Ordinatio* and *Compilatio* on the Development of the Book', in M. B. Parkes, *Scribes, Scripts and Readers: Studies in the Communication, Presentation and Dissemination of Medieval Texts* (London: Hambledon, 1991), pp. 35–69

Renevey, Denis, 'The Name Poured Out: Margins, Illuminations and Miniatures as Evidence for the Practice of Devotions to the Name of Jesus in Late Medieval England', in *The Mystical Tradition and the Carthusians*, vol. IX, ed. by James Hogg, Analecta Cartusiana, 130.9 (Salzburg: Institut für Anglistik und Amerikanistik, Universität Salzburg, 1996), pp. 127–47

Rogers, Nicholas, 'About the 15 Oes, the Brigittines and Syon Abbey', *St. Ansgar's Bulletin*, 80 (1984), 29–30

Salter, Elizabeth, *Nicholas Love's 'Myrrour of the Blessed Lyf of Jesu Christ'*, Analecta Cartusiana, 10 (Salzburg: Institut fur Englische Sprache und literatur, 1974)

Thebaut, Nancy, 'Bleeding Pages, Bleeding Bodies: A Gendered Reading of British Library MS Egerton 1821', *Medieval Feminist Forum*, 45.2 (2009), 175–200

Online Publications

Rudy, Kathryn, 'Kissing Images, Unfurling Rolls, Measuring Wounds, Sewing Badges and Carrying Talismans: Considering Some Harley Manuscripts through the Physical Rituals they Reveal', *The Electronic British Library Journal* (2011), <http://www.bl.uk/eblj/2011articles/article5.html> [accessed 22 October 2018]

THE DESERT OF RELIGION:
A TEXTUAL AND VISUAL COMPILATION*

Anne Mouron

At the end of *The Desert of Religion*, a Middle English devotional text of the first half of the fifteenth-century, the reader is told that 'þis tretis [...] is taken of bokes sere'.[1] If one agrees with Elisabeth Dutton's definition, that in a compilation 'extracts from a source or sources are woven together into a text which is presented as a single, distinct work, and the sources are rarely acknowledged',[2] one would be justified in seeing *The Desert of Religion* as an example of a devotional compilation and its instigator as a compiler. In other ways too, *The Desert of Religion* complies with our understanding of what a compilation is. It has been shown that texts of this kind 'are not written by named authors, but by anonymous compilers'.[3] Hence it is not surprising that *The Desert of Religion* does not name the person responsible for the 'tretis', but

---

* I wish to thank Ronald Richenburg for his many stylistic suggestions for this paper.

[1] Please note that 'reader' is used in this paper in the traditional way and means both men *and* women. *The Desert of Religion*, ed. by Mouron, l. 922. Unless otherwise stated all references to the *Desert of Religion* will be made to this edition. This edition is based on BL, MS Additional 37049, which offers the best text. Note that line numbers refer to the main text of the poem, folio numbers refer to the two series of illustrations. *The Desert of Religion* survives in two other manuscripts both held by the British Library: MS Cotton Faustina B VI, pars ii and MS Stowe 39. See below.

[2] Dutton, *Julian of Norwich*, p. 3.

[3] Cré and Denissen, '"Multiplication of Many Bokes"', p. 3. I thank Dr. Marleen Cré for sending me a copy of this paper.

Anne Mouron (anne.mouron@bodleian.ox.ac.uk) is a member of Regent's Park College and teaches Old and Middle English for Wycliffe Hall, Oxford University. She is also a member of staff at the Bodleian Library.

says at most, according to its version in BL, MS Cotton Faustina B VI, pars ii, 'Kepis wele þis dere presande (gift), | Þat firste was written with hali man hande',[4] with BL, MSS Add. 37049 and Stowe 39 saying no more than 'A haly man sent itt to his frende',[5] in which phrase the 'haly man' could simply mean an intermediary. Similarly, we do not know who the 'frende' are. The text continues:

> To haue itt to þair lyfes ende,
> And þan to lefe (leave) itt in som place,
> Whar gederyng of pepull wase (Where there was a gathering of people).[6]

It would seem, therefore, that *The Desert of Religion* is aimed at a community. As the editorial title, *The Desert of Religion*, already intimates, the concept of 'desert' or 'wilderness' is at the centre of the text.[7] In this regard, it is interesting to note that the French *Compileison de la vie de gent de religion*, which is a translation and adaptation of the *Ancrene Wisse*, clearly states: 'Desert si est uie solitarie de la mansion de moine. ou de frere. de nonein. ou de recluse. ou de autre homme ou femme de quel religion ke ceo soit' (The word 'desert' refers to the solitary life in a house of monks or of friars or of nuns or of recluses or of men or women of whatever order they might be).[8]

Although the original manuscript has not survived, it is still possible to hazard a guess as to which religious order may have been responsible for *The Desert of Religion*. Indeed the first line of the poem, 'Ecce elongavi fugiens, et mansi in

---

[4] Mouron, 'An Edition of *The Desert of Religion*', II, 315, ll. 920–21. This edition is based on a different manuscript, BL, MS Cotton Faustina B VI, pars ii. Although this manuscript has more defective lines than BL, MS Add. 37049 (but still very few), it is nevertheless well known for its exquisite illustrations. See Scott, *Later Gothic Manuscripts, 1390–1490*, II, cat. 63, pp. 192–93. It could be argued, therefore, that in BL, MS Cotton Faustina B VI, pars ii all three parts of the poem, the text, and its two series of illustrations fit together more harmoniously than in BL, MS Add. 37049 and in MS Stowe 39. For the same line, BL, MS Add. 37049 reads: 'Take gude kepe to þis tretis, | Þat here is written on englis' (see *The Desert of Religion*, ed. by Mouron, ll. 920–21); and BL, MS Stowe 39: 'Take now N þis presande | Þat I wryte þe with my hand', fol. 31^v. The first person singular in BL, MS Stowe 39 refers most likely to the scribe. There is no suggestion of authorship in this manuscript.

[5] *The Desert of Religion*, ed. by Mouron, l. 928. Note that BL, MSS Cotton Faustina B VI, pars ii and Stowe 39 also include this line. See Mouron, 'An Edition of *The Desert of Religion*', II, 315, l. 928; BL, MS Stowe 39, fol. 31^v.

[6] *The Desert of Religion*, ed. by Mouron, ll. 929–31.

[7] In all manuscripts, the poem is without a title. The text of *The Desert of Religion* was first edited by Walter Hübner who chose this title for his edition. See 'The Desert of Religion', ed. by Hübner.

[8] *The French Text of the 'Ancrene Riwle'*, ed. by Trethewey, p. 270.

solitudine', seems to be especially appropriate to the Carthusian Order.⁹ It has often been noted that the twelfth-century renaissance generally emphasized a return to the life of the Desert Fathers, but it was 'the Carthusians who really succeeded in translating the ideal of the desert into a fortress of stone'.¹⁰ The Cistercian William of St Thierry, for example, bears witness to this claim at the beginning of the *Golden Epistle* which he addressed to the Carthusians of Mont-Dieu:

> Fratribus de Monte Dei, orientale lumen et antiquum illum in religione Aegyptium feruorem tenebris occiduis et gallicanis frigoribus inferentibus, uitae scilicet solitariae exemplar et caelestis formam conuersationis ...
>
> [As the Brethren of Mont-Dieu introduce to our Western darkness and French cold the light of the East and that ancient fervor of Egypt for religious observance — the pattern of solitary life and the model of heavenly conduct ...]¹¹

It is perhaps not surprising, then, that when Adam of Dryburgh (or Adam Scotus, twelfth-century monk and author) leaves the Premonstratensian Order in order to enter the Charterhouse of Witham and is asked to preach a sermon to his new brethren, he chooses as his theme the very same biblical verse, 'Ecce elongavi fugiens, et mansi in solitudine'.¹² The insistence on the concept of 'desert' or 'wilderness' throughout *The Desert of Religion* itself also seems to point to a Carthusian origin.¹³ Another recurrent theme of the poem, the rejection of the world and the necessity for asceticism through a life of penance, has also been recognized as a Carthusian characteristic. Although it remains a matter of speculation, it would seem, therefore, that a Carthusian origin for *The Desert of Religion* is likely.¹⁴

When looking at other and perhaps better-known devotional compilations, such as *The Chastising of God's Children*, *Þe Holy Boke Gratia Dei*, the

---

⁹ Psalm 54. 8 (Vulgate). 'Lo, then would I wander far off, and remain in the wilderness', Psalm 55. 7 (King James).

¹⁰ Lawrence, *Medieval Monasticism*, p. 159.

¹¹ Respectively, William of St Thierry, 'Epistola ad fratres de Monte Dei', ed. by Verdeyen and Ceglar, p. 228; William of St Thierry, *The Golden Epistle*, trans. by Berkeley, p. 9.

¹² See Wilmart, 'Maître Adam, chanoine prémontré devenu chartreux à Witham', p. 221.

¹³ In the poem's Prologue of forty-eight lines alone there are twelve references to the 'desert' or 'wilderness'. See *The Desert of Religion*, ed. by Mouron, respectively ll. 1, 5, 6, 9, 18, 20, 21, 24, 25, 27, 28, 37.

¹⁴ This claim appears to be strengthened further by the probable origin of one of the surviving manuscripts. See below. For a longer discusssion on the possible Carthusian origin of *The Desert of Religion*, see Mouron, 'An Edition of *The Desert of Religion*', I, 19–29.

Pore Caitif, and *Disce mori*, to mention just a few, one cannot fail to notice that *The Desert of Religion* is very different from any of these works. These are all prose texts of substantial length which are usually unillustrated, whereas *The Desert of Religion* is a poem of rhymed couplets; it is only 943 lines long, and it is heavily illustrated in all its surviving manuscripts. Can it, then, still be regarded as a compilation? This paper will argue not only that it can, but that it also represents what devotional compilations can offer at their most sophisticated level.

Flourishing in the Wilderness: The Desert of Religion, a Treatise of Trees

The Desert of Religion survives in three fifteenth-century British Library manuscripts: MS Additional 37049, MS Cotton Faustina B VI, pars ii, and MS Stowe 39, all of which are generally believed to have come from monastic houses in the north of England.[15] Indeed MS Add. 37049 (which contains over seventy pieces and has been described as 'An Illustrated Yorkshire Carthusian Religious Miscellany')[16] probably comes from a Carthusian house, possibly Mount Grace; MS Cotton Faustina B VI, pars ii, perhaps from a Benedictine monastery in the North Riding; and MS Stowe 39 from a 'nunnery (probably Benedictine), perhaps in one neighbourhood of the North Riding'.[17] Two illustrated texts accompany *The Desert of Religion* in all of its three surviving manuscripts. The first is most commonly known as *Vado mori* where three characters, a king, a bishop, and a knight, tell of their encounters with Death.[18] The second illustrated text is usually entitled *A Debate for the Soul*, in which a dying soul is praying for help to Christ and is fought over by an angel and a demon.[19] These two additional texts confront the reader with the immediate reality of death and may be seen, therefore, as a further incitement for him to avoid sins and espouse virtues, in other

---

[15] For a description of the *Desert of Religion* in all three manuscripts, see Mouron, 'An Edition of the *Desert of Religion*', I, 6–10.

[16] See Hogg, 'An Illustrated Yorkshire Carthusian Religious Miscellany'.

[17] See Doyle, 'A Survey of the Origins and Circulation', pp. 191–93.

[18] See BL, MS Add. 37049, fol. 36^r; BL, MS Cotton Faustina B VI, pars ii, fol. 1^v; BL, MS Stowe 39, fol. 32^r. See also Brantley, *Reading in the Wilderness*, pp. 86–95.

[19] BL, MS Add. 37049, fol. 19^r; BL, MS Cotton Faustina B VI, pars ii, fol. 2^r; BL, MS Stowe 39, fol. 32^v. See Brantley, *Reading in Wilderness*, pp. 87–95. For another example of these two texts travelling together, see Brantley, *Reading in the Wilderness*, p. 87 and p. 357, n. 26.

words: to 'study and see | Vertus to folow and vices to flee', which will lead him 'withouten ende in heuen hee (high)'.[20]

As noted above, the poem begins with a quotation from the Psalms encouraging the reader to flee the world and the flesh to live in the 'wyldernes', which is glossed not simply as 'penaunce', but as '*herd* penaunce', which (as has been mentioned previously) appears as a leitmotif throughout *The Desert of Religion*.[21] Indeed, there is a second biblical quotation in the Prologue (Matthew 4. 1) which also urges the reader to penance, as this Gospel verse was often chosen for the theme of Lenten sermons.[22] With this insistence on asceticism, it will come as no surprise, then, that *The Desert of Religion* emphasizes the catechetical Christian doctrine which became standard after the Fourth Lateran Council of 1215: the seven virtues, the seven deadly sins, the Ten Commandments, and so on.

Since many texts from the thirteenth century onwards repeat this basic doctrine, it is perhaps to be expected that a fifteenth-century poem, in the vernacular and dealing with vices and virtues, would be 'taken of bokes sere (many)', but the text does not say what these 'bokes' are, although at some point it mentions 'Austyn (Augustine) in his sermouns' and 'þe lyfe of Saynt Thomas of Ynde'.[23] Indeed, the poem's contents are taken from, in order of importance: the *Speculum vitae*, a prose text written in Middle English and originally in French in spite of its Latin title (for the majority of the poem); *The Prick of Conscience* (for three sections of the text); Richard Rolle's *Emendatio vitae* (for one section); Bernard of Clairvaux's *De gradibus humilitatis et superbiae* (for part of two sections); *De claustro animae*, attributed to Hugh of Folieto (for part of one section); *De duodecim abusionibus saeculi*, a seventh-century text usually attributed to Saint Cyprian or Saint Augustine (for part of one section); and the 'Legend of St Thomas the Apostle' (for one section of the poem).[24]

---

[20] *The Desert of Religion*, ed. by Mouron, respectively, ll. 924–25, 896.

[21] *The Desert of Religion*, ed. by Mouron, l. 7, italics mine. In this instance 'penaunce' refers first and foremost to the 'practice of asceticism and self-mortification as a penitential discipline; a life of renunciation and asceticism'. See *Middle English Dictionary* (*MED*) online. One way religious espoused this ascetic life was by going into the wilderness as hermits or moving to a stricter order such as the Carthusian Order.

[22] 'Ductus est Jesus in desertum a Spiritu, ut tentaretur', Matthew 4. 1 (Vulgate). 'Then was Jesus led up of the Spirit into the wilderness to be tempted of the devil' (King James). For a Lent sermon on this verse, see, for example, Gregory, 'Homilia XVI, Liber Primum', ed. by Migne, cols 1134D–1138C.

[23] *The Desert of Religion*, ed. by Mouron, respectively, ll. 289, 792.

[24] See, respectively, *Speculum vitae*, ed. by Hanna; Morris, *Prick of Conscience*, ed. by Hanna

Bernard Guenée points out that compilations are made in two stages — first, material is extracted from a number of texts, and secondly, rearranged together — and that this gathering of extracts is often portrayed metaphorically.[25] He quotes Sicardus, Bishop of Cremona (d. 1215), endorsing in his prologue to his own chronicle a concept already expressed in Rufinus's translation of Eusebius: 'velut ex racionabilibus campis flosculos verborum decerpens in unum corpus coaugmentare satago, decerpta in serti fasiculum redigendo' (I gathered in the fields of the mind flowers of words and now I am doing my best to unite them all in one body, weaving what I had gathered into a little garland).[26] Other texts use the words 'deflorare', 'efflorare', and 'colligere', that is to say horticultural metaphors, and one may also think of the number of Florilegia that have survived.[27] It may be coincidental but nevertheless quite appropriate, therefore, that *The Desert of Religion* not only tells its reader that 'þis tretis is "taken of bokes sere"', but also that this material, if not strictly speaking 'flowers of words', still is

> made groveand in *treys* (trees) here,
> Bath þat þou may study and see
> Vertus to folow and vices to flee.[28]

Of course, *The Desert of Religion* is not the only devotional treatise to mention trees. To take some examples, the Middle English translation of Catherine of Siena's *Dialogue* considers the revelations gathered in this volume as a 'fruyt-

and Wood; Rolle, *De emendatione vitae*, ed. by Spahl; Bernard of Clairvaux, *De gradibus humilitatis et superbiae*, ed. by Leclercq and Rochais; Hugh of Folieto, *De claustro animae*, ed. by Migne; Auctor incertus, *De duodecim abusivis gradibus*, ed. by Migne; Ælfric, *Two Aelfric Texts*, ed. and trans. by Clayton. The Introduction to the forthcoming edition of *The Desert of Religion* specifies the source text of each section of the poem when it is known, and the Commentary gives more specific references.

[25] Guenée, 'L'Historien et la compilation au XIIIe siècle', pp. 120–21. See also Petitjean, 'Compiler', pp. 18–20.

[26] Guenée, 'L'Historien et la compilation au XIIIe siècle', p. 120. My translation is based on Guenée's rendering of the Latin into French. In the *Gemma ecclesiastica*, Gerald of Wales also chooses a horticultural metaphor to describe his role as a compiler. See Goddu and Rouse, 'Gerald of Wales and the *Florilegium angelicum*', p. 489.

[27] See Guenée, 'L'Historien et la compilation au XIIIe siècle', pp. 120–21. For the reference to Florilegia, see Hathaway, 'Compilatio', p. 40. One of the most often used Florilegia of the Middle Ages, aptly entitled *Manipulus florum*, for example, was compiled in the fourteenth century by Thomas of Ireland. It survives in 180 manuscripts. See Rouse and Rouse, *Preachers, Florilegia and Sermons*, Introduction, p. x. See also *The Electronic Manipulus florum Project*. On the use and multiplication of *Flores*, see Guenée, 'L'Historien et la compilation au XIIIe siècle', p. 129.

[28] *The Desert of Religion*, ed. by Mouron, ll. 923–25, italics mine.

ful orcherd' or a 'goostli orcherd'.²⁹ One may also think of the Tree of Charity in *Piers Plowman*, or of 'Penitence, that may be likned into a tree' in Geoffrey Chaucer's Parson's Tale.³⁰ In most of these texts, however, the image of the tree is alluded to succinctly. It is perhaps a trait of genius from the compiler of *The Desert of Religion*, then, to gather the usual doctrine on the virtues, the vices, the Ten Commandments, the Creed, etc. into the allegory of a forest which gives the poem its very shape.

From its very first line *The Desert of Religion* incites its reader to go to the wilderness, which may allude to geographic deserts in the *Sayings of the Desert Fathers*, but in north-western Europe, wilderness would usually refer to large inhabited forests. The Prologue to *The Desert of Religion* states:

> In þis gastely foreste groves (grow)
> Trees with braunches and boghes:
> Sum groves to heuen and sum to hell,
> Sum to stande and sum to fell,
> Svm to grove in gastely garthe (an enclosed yard),
> And sum to grub awai with þe swarth (turf).³¹

Each subsequent section (except for the last one which is a kind of Epilogue) is referred to as a 'tre', and together these are described as 'spryngand', 'floryschand', 'grov[ing]', and 'ber[ing] froyte'.³²

But *The Desert of Religion*'s compiler does not simply choose the concept of the 'tre' to refer to its internal subdivisions: the concept is used further to include the reader. Saint Bernard of Clairvaux, in his second series of *Sentences*, wrote that

> Ligna sunt omnes iusti, qui plantati in medio ecclesiae temporaliter, facere debent fructus vitae qui manent. Videat autem ubi eligat sibi *locum irriguum, in quo fructificans ferat in tempore suo vitae fructum.*

> [The trees are all the just who have been temporally planted in the middle of the Church. As long as they remain there, they ought to produce the fruits of life. Let each of them see to it, therefore, that he chooses for himself *a well-watered spot, in which in his season he can be productive and bear the fruit of life.*]³³

---

²⁹ *The Orchard of Syon*, ed. by Hodgson and Liegey, p. 1.

³⁰ Respectively, Langland, *The Vision of Piers Plowman*, ed. by Schmidt, Passus XVI, pp. 198–203; Chaucer, 'The Parson's Tale', ed. by Benson, p. 289.

³¹ *The Desert of Religion*, ed. by Mouron, ll. 43–48.

³² *The Desert of Religion*, ed. by Mouron, respectively ll. 134, 165, 43, 137.

³³ Bernard of Clairvaux, 'Sententiae series secunda', ed. by Leclercq, Talbot, and Rochais, p. 30; *The Sentences*, trans. by Casey and Swietek, pp. 145–46, italics mine.

Bernard's text echoes Psalm 1. 3, which is itself mentioned at the end of the First Tree of *The Desert of Religion*:

> Þis is þe tre of whylk we here
> Þat Dauyd of spekes in þe sawtere (Psalter):
> 'Þe ryghtwys (righteous) is als a tre þat standes
> Besyde þe course of þe water strandes (streams),
> And gyfes his froyte in conabill (appropriate) tyme;
> His lefe sall nother fade ne dwyne (wither)'.[34]

Thus, the image of the tree in *The Desert of Religion* not only alludes to the form of the text, referring to its various sections, but also to its content, which allows the reader to interiorize the doctrine provided, as he is invited to see himself as the tree. This inward movement is underlined throughout the poem by its emphasis on the reader's 'hert', with the word occurring over forty times in the poem, and is perhaps best represented by the following verses:

> Criste in þe trouth ay duelles,
> Ande þe trouth is in þe thoght,
> And thoght is in þe hert broght.[35]

The First Tree of the poem may serve as an example and demonstrate how brilliantly and simply the compiler has put together his material.[36] The forest allegory is used to introduce the theme of this section, the Seven Virtues:

> Þe fyrste tre of þis forest schene (beautiful)
> Is þe tre of vertus þat ay is clene,
> Þat in mekenes festis his rotes (roots).
> Of hym vertus vpwarde schotes,
> And sprynges, and spredes his leues, and gro[v]es,
> And buriones (sprouts) bath with braunches and boghes.[37]

---

[34] *The Desert of Religion*, ed. by Mouron, ll. 83–88. Gertrud of Helfta also uses a paraphrase of Psalm 1. 3 to refer to the religious. See Gertrud the Great of Helfta, *The Herald of God's Loving-Kindness*, trans. by Barratt, pp. 59–60. For the Latin original, see Gertrude d'Helfta, *Oeuvres spirituelles: Le Héraut*, ed. and trans. by Doyère, pp. 156–58.

[35] *The Desert of Religion*, ed. by Mouron, ll. 306–08.

[36] For the text and illustrations of the First Tree, see *The Desert of Religion*, ed. by Mouron, ll. 49–88, fol. 47ʳ.

[37] *The Desert of Religion*, ed. by Mouron, ll. 49–54.

The next lines (55–58) are taken from the *Speculum vitae*,[38] with the first line of the passage ('thai suld become bathe meeke and mylde') changed by the compiler in *The Desert* to fit its new allegorical context: '*Þis tre betakenes* men þat ar mylde'.[39] Lines 59 to 74 in *The Desert* are also taken from the *Speculum vitae*, but from a later passage in the work.[40] The next two lines (75–76) appear to be the compiler's, and the first section of *The Desert of Religion* then ends with a return to the tree allegory and the paraphrase of Psalm 1. 3 noted earlier (lines 77–88). The compiler thus seamlessly embeds his material taken from different parts of the *Speculum vitae* (or the other texts in question) into the allegory of the forest which is referred to at the beginning and end of most sections of the poem.

The Desert of Religion is made up of twenty such trees. Although it does not have a table of contents at the beginning, nonetheless it embraces fully the concept of 'utilitas' often referred to in compilations,[41] in that its material is clearly set out to enable the reader to navigate through the text easily.[42] Each section of the poem covers a verso and a recto, as will be shown later, in a layout which features in all three surviving manuscripts.[43] When one considers that *The Desert of Religion*'s principal source is the *Speculum vitae*, a poem of 16,096 lines, *The Desert* with its 943 lines also espouses another regular characteristic of compilations, brevity.[44] Although *The Desert of Religion* does not include everything that is explored in the *Speculum vitae*, nevertheless it offers a comprehensive programme for its reader, as will be outlined below.[45]

---

[38] *Speculum vitae*, ed. by Hanna, I, 9, ll. 137–40.

[39] *The Desert of Religion*, ed. by Mouron, l. 55, italics mine.

[40] Lines 59–64 and 65–74 in *The Desert* are excerpted from the *Speculum vitae*, ed. by Hanna, respectively, I, 55, ll. 1565–70, 1573–82.

[41] For the concept of 'utilitas', see Hathaway, 'Compilatio', pp. 27–29; Coste, 'Poétique et éthique de la compilation médiévale', pp. 306–07.

[42] Each section's subject matter is clearly stated at the beginning of each tree.

[43] This clear and user-friendly presentation is especially striking in BL, MS Add. 37049, which contains many texts and images. That these texts and images are often arranged in a haphazard way contrasts with the repetitive order of *The Desert of Religion*.

[44] See Guenée, 'L'Historien et la compilation au XIIIᵉ siècle', pp. 125–26.

[45] 'The Desert of Religion: A Guide to the Religious Life', pp. 396–400. One of the characteristics of *The Desert of Religion* is to allow its reader to develop his own reflection. See Mouron, '*The Desert of Religion*: A Voice and Images in the Wilderness', pp. 169–70, 174–77.

The First Series of Illustrations: Tree-Diagrams

The allegory of the forest, as brilliant as it is as a stylistic means to unify different sources into a single text, is also given a more literal interpretation in that each section of the poem is accompanied by the illustration of a tree. Indeed, the compiler has added to the text a series of tree-diagrams which visually complement the text.[46] Sometimes these tree-diagrams simply repeat the information given in the text in an easily memorable form; sometimes they provide extra information that is absent from the text.[47] The First Tree text, as we have seen, mentions 'vertus' and 'in mekenes festis his rotes', but the text does not list what these virtues are.[48] The accompanying tree-diagram, on the recto folio, does just that, as it has seven branches: on top, the three theological virtues, that is, Faith, Hope, and Charity; followed in the lower branches by the four cardinal virtues, that is, Righteousness, Methfulnes (or Temperance), Qwayntnes (or Prudence), and Strength.[49] Note that in all three manuscripts the branch of Charity is placed at the centre at the top, subtly demonstrating its pre-eminence, in the words of *The Manere of Good Lyvyng*, another devotional text, that the 'vertue of charite ys so grete þat wher it lackyth, oþere vertues be hadde in vayne',[50] but it is for the reader to recognize the pre-eminence of Charity in the tree-diagram, as the poem does not mention it. This First Tree-diagram also enables the reader to extend his reflection further by subdividing each virtue, or branch of the tree, into seven sub-virtues or leaves. The branch of Charity, for example, has the following leaves: 'Forgifnes', 'Concorde', 'Pees' (Peace), 'Pyte', 'Compassion', 'Mercy', and 'Grace'. But again the precise thoughts that would come to the reader meditating on any of these terms are left up to him.[51]

---

[46] It seems clear that one person is responsible for devising the poem and its illustrations which I understand to be the compiler. However, it is entirely possible that the execution of the poem was done by two different people, scribe and illustrator, but Jessica Brantley believes that in BL, MS Add. 37049 scribe and illustrator may have been one and the same person. See Brantley, *Reading in the Wilderness*, p. 10, n. 64. The manuscript is available online: <http://www.bl.uk/manuscripts/FullDisplay.aspx?ref=Add_MS_37049> [accessed 24 April 2016].

[47] Michael Camille, for example, notes: 'for [...] reasons of clarity, immediacy and the avoidance of ontological problems, diagrammatic layout became an aesthetic basis [...] teaching in the cloister or schools [...] in the Gothic period'. Camille, 'The Book of Signs', p. 137. See also Yates, *The Art of Memory*, p. 55; Carruthers, *The Book of Memory*, pp. 248–57.

[48] *The Desert of Religion*, ed. by Mouron, ll. 50–51.

[49] See *The Desert of Religion*, ed. by Mouron, fol. 47ʳ.

[50] *The Manere of Good Lyvyng*, ed. by Mouron, p. 53.

[51] 'Him' is here used in the traditional way and may refer either to a monk or to a nun. The

Although one finds diagrams of catechetical material, including trees of vices and virtues, elsewhere (one obvious example would be the diagrams of the De Lisle Psalter), it is unlikely that the compiler simply found all these diagrams readily available in one manuscript and excerpted them for inclusion in *The Desert of Religion*.[52] It is more likely, then, that the compiler may have been inspired by other manuscripts but designed the tree-diagrams in *The Desert of Religion* himself, all the more so because other diagrammatic trees are usually in Latin. It is also noticeable that the tree-diagrams not only feature in all three surviving manuscripts of *The Desert of Religion*, but that they do so with very little variation.

The Second Series of Illustrations: Saints and Hermits

The compiler's input does not stop here, as *The Desert of Religion* offers its reader a second series of illustrations, mostly of saints and hermits.[53] A saint or hermit is usually depicted alone praying or meditating in a bare background and surrounded by two trees in a way which reminds one of praying saints in illustrated books of hours.[54] If the text of the poem alludes to the tree-diagrams, it does not refer to this second series of illustrations, but these illustrations provide the reader with two things. First, as every saint's life would point out, saints are examples to imitate, and *The Desert* espouses this idea when it states:

> þe relygiouse þat loues his saule (soul)
> Suld take ensampell at Saynt Paule,

original audience of the poem was probably Carthusian, but the audiences of the manuscripts which have survived possibly included Benedictine nuns. See above.

[52] For the diagrammatic trees in the De Lisle Psalter, see BL, MS Arundel 83, fols 128ᵛ–29ʳ. The manuscript is available online: <http://www.bl.uk/manuscripts/FullDisplay.aspx?ref=Arundel_MS_83> [accessed 2 May 2016]. For trees in other works, see *Speculum virginum*, ed. by Bernards, plates 2–3, between pp. 24 and 25; Lambert, *Liber floridus*, ed. by Derolez, II, fols 231ᵛ–232ʳ; Katzenellenbogen, *Allegories of the Virtues and Vices in Medieval Art*, pp. 63–67; Saxl, 'A Spiritual Encyclopaedia of the Later Middle Ages', pp. 107–15.

[53] For the hermit accompanying the First Tree, for example, see *The Desert of Religion*, ed. by Mouron, fol. 46ᵛ.

[54] Interestingly, the only two occurrences of the word 'saint' in the text itself are in references to Saint Paul and Saint Thomas. Although there may be doubt whether the first is represented in the illustrations, as Paul the First Hermit is but not Saint Paul the Apostle, the second certainly is not. The allusion to 'Saynt Paule' in *The Desert of Religion* is quoted below. For examples of book of hours illustrations similar to the representations of saints in *The Desert of Religion*, see Mouron, '*The Desert of Religion*: A Voice and Images in the Wilderness', p. 173.

> And, als he dyd, þe werld forgett
> And all þat may relygioune lett (hinder).[55]

Secondly, these illustrations allow the reader to empathize with the depicted saint or hermit and thus to enter the forest himself.[56] The use of the first person singular in the little texts attached to this second series of illustrations makes this clear. Paul the First Hermit, for example, says:

> Fourty ȝer in wyldernes
> I dwelled in a caue,
> Whare God of his gret godenes
> Graunted me forto haue,
> And ilk (each) day to me gun dres (did send)
> With a raven halfe a lafe (loaf of bread).[57]

Most compilations bring together a number of texts, and *The Desert of Religion* does this, but the poem, as has been seen, also gathers into one harmonious entity two series of illustrations: one of tree-diagrams and one of saints and hermits, both of which assist the reader in his *lectio divina*, that is in reading, meditating, and praying. The resulting poem, of this threefold verbal and visual compilation, is much more than the sum of its parts (another feature of compilations)[58] and is unique among Middle English devotional compilations. But the extraordinary achievement of the compiler is even more manifest when the contents of the poem are considered more closely.

The Desert of Religion: A Guide to the Religious Life

It has been recognized that the 'preponderance of structures such as *scalae celi* demonstrates that medieval piety was conceptually hierarchical and progressive'.[59] It will not come as a surprise, then, that there is just such a *scala*

---

[55] *The Desert of Religion*, ed. by Mouron, ll. 243–46.

[56] It is interesting to note that the *Desert of Religion* in BL, MS Stowe 39 is preceded by the *Abbey of the Holy Ghost* in a version which has a unique illustration of the abbey at the end of the text. Boyda Johnstone notes that its reader is also meant to enter the Abbey: 'the viewer's eye might escape the devil's advocates, ascend the stairs to the left, and find shelter amongst the welcoming nuns in the top floor'. See Johnstone, 'Reading Images, Drawing Texts', p. 36.

[57] *The Desert of Religion*, ed. by Mouron, fol. 46ᵛ.

[58] See Bahr, *Fragments and Assemblages*, p. 3.

[59] Brantley, *Reading in the Wilderness*, p. 13.

celi in *The Desert of Religion*.[60] Additionally, when one looks more closely at *The Desert of Religion*'s twenty trees, it becomes clear that the poem is also progressive and can be divided into three parts (without taking into account the Prologue and Epilogue). The first eleven trees offer the reader basic catechetical doctrine: the seven virtues, the seven vices, humility, pride, and so on.[61] Such topics are often encountered in one form or another in many other devotional texts of the period as, for example, in Dan Gaytryge's sermon.[62] Having examined these concepts, the reader is then led to the Twelfth Tree or Tree of Confession which, the text explains,

> sprynges of a mannes hert,
> Þat vnto God is convert
> Fra all wikkednes and his synnes.[63]

Dan Gaytryge's sermon and similar manuals would stop here, but *The Desert of Religion* then embarks on a second course of doctrine of a more specific nature: *accidia* or sloth, chastity, the sins of the tongue, prowess or fortitude, perfection, and the twelve virtues of Thomas of India.[64] This last tree aptly ends the second part thus:

> For he þat will vndertake
> A gode way for God[es] sake,
> So fast *his hert sall be sett*
>
> *On his purpose, þat noght itt lett* (obstructs),
> And for nathyng to be abayste (afraid),
> Bot in God ay seker trayste (truly trust).[65]

---

[60] The ladder has nine rungs, with 'Humiliacione' being the lowest and 'Contemplacion' the highest rung. See *The Desert of Religion*, ed. by Mouron, fol. 49ᵛ.

[61] I.e. the Seven Virtues (First Tree), the Seven Vices (Second Tree), Humility (Third Tree), Pride (Fourth Tree), 'Þe twelfe abucions | þat growes emange religiounes' (Fifth Tree), 'Þe twelfe abucyons hard | þat ar growyng in þe warlde' (Sixth Tree), the Creed (Seventh Tree), the Tree of the Seven Sacraments and the Seven Virtues (Eighth Tree), the Seven Works of Mercy (Ninth Tree), the Ten Commandments (Tenth Tree), and the Five Witts (Eleventh Tree).

[62] 'Dan Jon Gaytryge's Sermon', ed. by Perry, pp. 1–14.

[63] *The Desert of Religion*, ed. by Mouron, ll. 549–51.

[64] I.e. Accidia or Sloth (Thirteenth Tree), Chastity (Fourteenth Tree), the Sins of the Tongue (Fifteenth Tree), Prowess or Fortitude (Sixteenth Tree), Perfection (Seventeenth Tree), and the Twelve Virtues of Thomas of India (Eighteenth Tree).

[65] *The Desert of Religion*, ed. by Mouron, ll. 799–804, italics mine.

In other words, if after the first part of the text the reader's heart was 'vnto God [...] convert', after this second part it is now 'sett on his purpose, þat noght itt lett'.

The last part of the poem comprises only two trees, 'þe tre of confusion' or of the Pains of Hell (Nineteenth Tree), and lastly 'þe last tre of price' of the 'ioyes and þe blissehedes' that 'florysh in heuen ryke (the kingdom of heaven)' (Twentieth Tree),[66] this ultimate destination being the aim of all the poem's readers, as the text makes clear:

> Now pray we bath day and nyght,
> Þat God graunt vs grace and myght
> To taste þe suete (sweet) froyte of þis tree,
> Withouten ende in heuen hee (high).[67]

In BL, MS Add. 37049, this last tree is also illustrated by a ladder, appropriately called 'þe leddyr of heuen' with three rungs consisting of (from lowest to highest) the three theological virtues, 'Fayth', 'Hope', and 'Charite'.[68] The poem then ends with an Epilogue.

On the one hand, then, as illustrated by the use of the *scala celi*, *The Desert of Religion* can be viewed as 'conceptually hierarchical and progressive', with a first set of instructions followed by more specific teachings.[69] This may invite the reader to read the poem consecutively, as it is laid out in the manuscript, that is from Prologue to Epilogue. On the other hand, the poem emphasizes that the fight against sin and the acquisition of virtue is a never-ending struggle and thus encourages a different mode of reading. Indeed, like trees in a forest which are not arranged hierarchically, the reader can go from one tree of *The Desert of Religion* to another and back as he wishes, and decide in which order he reads the poem's twenty trees.[70] This continual battle against sin is portrayed in two ways: firstly by using throughout *The Desert of Religion* a number of perhaps

---

[66] *The Desert of Religion*, ed. by Mouron, respectively, fol. 65ʳ; ll. 853, 857, 891.

[67] *The Desert of Religion*, ed. by Mouron, ll. 893–96.

[68] *The Desert of Religion*, ed. by Mouron, fol. 65ᵛ. The progressive aspect of the poem discussed here is reinforced throughout the poem by the concept of Perseverance which already features in the First Tree-diagram as a sub-virtue of Strength, and is mentioned later in the Seventeenth Tree as the 'vertu of þe contynuande' and at the end of the Eighteenth Tree in those who 'fullfill with all [their] might | þat [they] ha[ve] begunnen ryght'. *The Desert of Religion*, ed. by Mouron, respectively, fol. 47ʳ; ll. 752, 805–06.

[69] Brantley, *Reading in the Wilderness*, p. 13.

[70] *The Orchard of Syon* points out: 'I wole þat ȝe disporte ȝou & walke aboute where ȝe wolen wiþ ȝoure mynde & resoun, in what aleye ȝou like, [and] hamely þere ȝe sauuouren best, as ȝe ben disposid'. *The Orchard of Syon*, ed. by Hodgson and Liegey, p. 1.

more active images (the concept of military warfare, of the heart as a castle or city, and the image of the wind, all of which would be familiar to the reader as they are often encountered in devotional texts); and secondly by revisiting the same concepts again and again.

Firstly, then, from its very inception, *The Desert of Religion* uses the image of military warfare, developed by the Desert Fathers as illustrated by Athanasius's *Life of St Anthony* (Saint Anthony who, incidentally, features in the Second Tree of *The Desert of Religion*).[71] The Prologue remarks that the religious is 'als man þat suld wende | Into þe felde to fyght with þe fende'.[72] The reader is later referred to as 'Goddes knyght',[73] and in the Fifteenth Tree the saint and hermit illustration includes an angel presenting a shield with the *arma Christi* to a praying monk with a scroll saying: 'Arme me Ihesu with þis schelde, | My faas [foes] þat I may fell in felde'.[74] This image of military warfare culminates in the next section in the 'Tree of Prowess' which lists 'Seuen victories þat here awayles | Of seuen manere of batayles'.[75]

The concept of continual fighting is also interiorized by the poem with the use of another commonly encountered image, that of the heart as a castle or city.[76] When examining the five senses, for example, *The Desert of Religion* explains:

> A castell, mannes hert here is called,
> Þat with vertuse wele is walled,
> Or els a cite þat hase gates.

---

[71] See *The Desert of Religion*, ed. by Mouron, fol. 47ᵛ.

[72] *The Desert of Religion*, ed. by Mouron, ll. 14–15.

[73] *The Desert of Religion*, ed. by Mouron, l. 194.

[74] *The Desert of Religion*, ed. by Mouron, fol. 60ᵛ. In all three manuscripts, the Fifteenth Tree is accompanied by an illustration of a shield presenting the *arma Christi*. See BL, MS Cotton Faustina B VI, pars ii, fol. 17ᵛ; BL, MS Stowe 39, fol. 25ᵛ.

[75] *The Desert of Religion*, ed. by Mouron, ll. 703–04. The accompanying saint and hermit illustration also has a shield (with the five wounds of Christ). See *The Desert of Religion*, ed. by Mouron, fol. 61ᵛ.

[76] 'The Castle of the Soul', for example, specifies: 'The kastel of þe sowle haþ four spiritual walles wyþynne, þe whyche hue schold be closed, and þey beþ four cardinal vertws, as ryʒtwysnesse, and prudence, temperaunce, and gostlyche strenkþe'. Bodl. Lib., MS Bodley 110, fol. 154ʳ. This short text survives in a single manuscript and is described by Robert Raymo as 'a short text of West Midland origin deriving from the *Ancrene Riwle*'. Raymo, 'Works of Religious and Philosophical Instruction', no. 178, pp. 2335, 2542. For other examples of the castle image, see Wheatley, *The Idea of the Castle in Medieval England*, pp. 78–111; Whitehead, *Castles of the Mind*.

> Þir fyue (i.e. the five senses) betakens þe ȝates (gates),
> Be þe whilk (which) men gase (go) oute or jn,
> Or (before) þai þe cite lose or wyn.⁷⁷

In addition to this, the poem alludes to the image of the wind, which William Langland, for example, also used in *Piers Plowman*.⁷⁸ *The Desert of Religion*, when exploring the virtue of humility, warns its reader against the 'wynd of pryde' that it

> dryfe itt [that is the Tree of Humility] not doune,
> Ne stele þe froyte þat on itt groves,
> Ne breke þe braunches ne boghes.⁷⁹

Secondly, *The Desert of Religion* revisits a number of concepts time and time again. As was seen earlier, the First Tree lists the seven virtues,⁸⁰ but this is not the only place in the poem where these seven virtues are encountered. They recur in the Eighth Tree, 'þe tre of þe sacramentes | And þe vertuse'.⁸¹ The same is true of individual virtues: 'Faith', or 'Trouth', for example, recurs later in the poem a number of times. The Seventh Tree is entirely devoted to the Creed which is said to be '[þe] ground of þe *trouth* to se | Þat founded is in þe trynite' and it 'behoues be rotede wele | In our *faith*'.⁸² The Eighth Tree lists the seven sacraments which 'in our *trouth* suld hynge [grow]'.⁸³ The Eighteenth Tree consists of 'tuelfe degrese of vertus', the first one being 'verray *trouth* of Criste',⁸⁴ and the accompanying hermit and saint illustration presents the reader with a 'shield of faith' or '*scutum fidei*'.⁸⁵ This recurrence of Faith or Trouth, and of many other sins and virtues, reminds the reader that whether he is a novice or has been a monk for many years, he should constantly re-examine himself.

---

⁷⁷ *The Desert of Religion*, ed. by Mouron, ll. 505–10. The use of a castle or a city for the allegory of the heart is strengthened in BL, MS Stowe 39 with its illustrated copy of *The Abbey of Holy Ghost*. See BL, MS Stowe 39, fols 8ᵛ–9ʳ.

⁷⁸ See Langland, *The Vision of Piers Plowman*, ed. by Schmidt, Passus XVI, pp. 198–99.

⁷⁹ *The Desert of Religion*, ed. by Mouron, ll. 174–76. For other occurrences of the image of the wind in the poem, see ll. 467–68, 635–38.

⁸⁰ See above, pp. 392, 394.

⁸¹ *The Desert of Religion*, ed. by Mouron, ll. 383–84. For the Eighth Tree, see ll. 341–86.

⁸² *The Desert of Religion*, ed. by Mouron, respectively, ll. 303–04, 337–38, italics mine.

⁸³ *The Desert of Religion*, ed. by Mouron, l. 362, italics mine.

⁸⁴ *The Desert of Religion*, ed. by Mouron, l. 779, italics mine.

⁸⁵ *The Desert of Religion*, ed. by Mouron, fol. 63ᵛ.

The Desert of Religion: A Horticultural Treatise?

It is hoped that this article has shown that *The Desert of Religion* is an extraordinary and unique compilation. But to conclude with a final twist, one needs to consider briefly the compiler's own voice which is heard at the beginning and end of most sections of the text, and which may include advice familiar from an altogether different quarter. Every monastery had a garden where herbs were planted and used for medicinal purposes, and usually also an orchard or *pomarius* to grow fruit trees. Latin treatises, such as the *Opus agriculturae* by Palladius, were translated in the fifteenth century, and horticultural treatises, like *The Feate of Gardeninge* by Mayster Jon Gardener, were already written in the vernacular in the fourteenth century.[86] When *The Desert of Religion* tells its reader about the Tree of Pride:

> Grub and graue als gode gardynere (dig up)
> Abowt þe rote bath day and ȝere (year),
> And fell itt doune into þe fyre,[87]

or about 'þe tre of mekenes gode' that it is

> Spryngand full fayr [...],
> Wyth leues on ilka (each) syde bedene (indeed),
> Þat wynter and somer is ay grene,
> And beres froyte þat is ay rype,

and '[...] beres þe froyte þat ay is swete, | And delycyous forto ette' so that 'Þis [tree] suld men sett in þair orthȝarde (orchard)', such advice may be reminiscent of garden treatises.[88] The gardener of the Middle English version of Palladius's treatise, or *Palladius on Husbondrie* is told in the section for September,

---

[86] Willy Braekman notes in fourteenth-century England the 'existence [...] of a highly developed horticultural science'. See Braekman, 'Bollard's Middle English Book', p. 26. See also Palladius, *Palladius on Husbondrie*, ed. by Lodge; 'A Middle English Treatise on Horticulture', ed. by Cylkowski; Mayster Ion Gardener, 'A Fifteenth Century Treatise on Gardening', ed. by Amherst; Harvey, 'The First English Garden Book'; Harvey, 'Henry Daniel'; Harvey, 'Daniel, Henry (fl. 1379)'; Keiser, 'Through a Fourteenth-Century Gardener's Eyes'; Keiser, 'A Middle English Rosemary Treatise'.

[87] *The Desert of Religion*, ed. by Mouron, ll. 209–11. The poem also says about the Tree of Vices: 'grub itt vp be þe rotes, | And all þe braunches þat of hym schotes'. *The Desert of Religion*, ed. by Mouron, ll. 131–32.

[88] *The Desert of Religion*, ed. by Mouron, respectively, ll. 134–37, 169–71.

> This tyme is to be stocked [trimmed] every tree
> Away with herbes brode, eke root and bough,
> And iche impediment oute taken be.[89]

At other times, like the reader of *The Desert of Religion*, the *Palladius* gardener is told to be aware of the wind. Vines, for example should

> [...] in playne [be] sette that may endure
> Eke (also) myst and frost, but sette in hilles hie (high)
> That wyndes may endure and dayes drie.[90]

If he does what is necessary, his trees also will be 'saf for *vice*'.[91]

But medieval treatises on horticulture are not entirely restricted to such practical advice. At the beginning of *Palladius on Husbondrie*, for example, the reader is also warned against pride:

> And take on hande in husbonding thi lande
> As thowe may bere in maner and mesure;
> War arrogaunce in takyng thing in hande;
> For after pride in scorne thou maist assure.[92]

The Middle English version, moreover, includes addresses to God which, like *The Desert of Religion*, refers to protection against sin and hell fire. At the end of the chapter on September, for example, *Palladius on Husbondrie* adds the following verses:

> September is anende (come to an end). Honoure, empire (supreme power),
> Laude, Ympne, and Bliss ascende [un]to oure Eterne
> Almighty Lorde, that wolde us alle enspire
> In werk his worde to holde, if galle (excrescence, evil) interne,
> Yf synne in oure entente hèm nolde externe (alienate).
> O Jesse floure (flower), so hent and bold us heer (hear)
> To fle fro synne and derk (dark) fire sempiterne,
> As me to gynne (begin, undertake) a werk atte Octobeer.[93]

---

[89] Palladius, *Palladius on Husbondrie*, ed. by Lodge, p. 182.

[90] Palladius, *Palladius on Husbondrie*, ed. by Lodge, p. 63.

[91] Palladius, *Palladius on Husbondrie*, ed. by Lodge, p. 95, italics mine. Of course 'vice' here is meant for tree diseases, but the use of the same word may not be a coincidence.

[92] Palladius, *Palladius on Husbondrie*, ed. by Lodge, p. 9.

[93] Palladius, *Palladius on Husbondrie*, ed. by Lodge, p. 186.

Although there is no direct influence from Palladius on *The Desert of Religion*, the similarities between both texts suggest that *The Desert of Religion* could be seen as a spiritual horticultural treatise. From garden treatises, to herbals, which describe not the virtues which help the soul as *The Desert of Religion* does, but the 'vertu'[94] of trees and plants or their medicinal powers to heal the body, it is only one short step. Illustrated herbals, with depictions of plants on every folio, although not identical, certainly share a resemblance with *The Desert of Religion* with its trees on every recto folio.[95] The therapeutic benefit of gardens had also long been recognized as illustrated by an anonymous twelfth-century description of Clairvaux's orchard and garden:

> Intra hujus septa multae et variae arbores variis fecundae fructibus instar nemoris pomarium faciunt: quod infirmorum cellae contiguum, infirmitates fratrum non mediocri levat solatio, dum spatiosum spatiantibus praebet deambulatorium, aestuantibus quoque suave reclinatorium. Sedet aegrotus cespite in viridi [...] et ad doloris sui solatium, naribus suis gramineae redolent species. Pascit oculos herbarum et arborum amoena viriditas, et pendentes ante se, atque crescentes immensae ejus deliciae, ut non immerito dicat: *Sub umbra arboris illius, quam desideraveram, sedi, et fructus ejus dulcis gutturi meo* (*Canticum canticorum*, 2. 3) [...]. Ubi pomarium desinit, incipit hortus [...]. Pulchrum et hic infirmis fratribus praebetur spectaculum, dum super viridem puri gurgitis marginem sedent.

> [Within this cincture [i.e. the monastery's wall] many fruit-bearing trees of various species make a veritable grove of orchards, which by their nearness to the infirmary afford no small solace to the brothers in their sickness: a spacious promenade for those able to walk, an easeful resting-place for the feverish. The sick man sits on the green turf [...] his discomfort further eased by the drifting scent of the grasses. While he feeds his gaze on the pleasing green of grass and trees, fruits, to further his delight, hang swelling before his eyes, so that he can not inaptly say: '*I sat in the shadow of his tree, which I had desired, and its fruit was sweet to my taste*' (Song of

---

[94] The *MED* includes the following in its definition of 'vertu': 'the quickening power of a flower or root' and 'a medicinal property; also fig.; a specific efficacious quality or restorative property'.

[95] See, for example, Manfredus de Monte Imperiali, *Liber de herbis et plantis*, BnF, MS Latin 6823, fol. 10ʳ; Bartholomaei Mini de Senis, Platearius, and Nicolaus of Salerno, *Tractatus de herbis*, Melegueta Pepper, and Nux Vomica, BL, MS Egerton 747, fol. 68ᵛ. Both manuscripts are available online. Respectively, <http://gallica.bnf.fr/ark:/12148/btv1b6000517 p./f. 27.image.r=Liber%20de%20herbis%20et%20plantis%206823> [accessed 31 May 2016]; <http://www.bl.uk/catalogues/illuminatedmanuscripts/record.asp?MSID=8319> [accessed 31 May 2016]. It is hardly surprising, then, that medical books would be given titles as *Rosa medicinae* or *Lilium medicinae*. See Rawcliffe, '"Delectable Sightes and Fragrant Smelles"', p. 10.

Songs 2. 3) [...]. Where the orchard ends the garden begins [...]. Here too a pretty spectacle is afforded to the sick, who can sit on the grassy banks.]⁹⁶

Even if there is no suggestion of physical illness in *The Desert of Religion*, the very verse from the Song of Songs quoted in this passage could also apply to the majority of its saints or hermits, usually depicted sitting between two trees.

Conclusion

The compiler's richness of vision in *The Desert of Religion* and its realization in words as well as in two sets of images (saints and hermits and tree-diagrams), not to mention the presence of horticultural treatises in the background, is quite extraordinary and deserves recognition. Whoever he was, the compiler of *The Desert of Religion* did not merely weave 'together into a text which [he] presented as a single, distinct work' 'extracts from [a number of] sources'.⁹⁷ He selected them, arranged them, and added to them in a new and unique way: indeed the concept, combination, and layout of the text and its two sets of illustrations, brought together by the forest allegory at the beginning and end of every section, are entirely his own. *The Desert of Religion*, therefore, offers its reader not simply a devotional compilation, but one par excellence.

---

⁹⁶ Respectively, Auctor incertus, *Descriptio positionis seu situationis monasterii Claraevallensis*, ed. by Migne, cols 569B–70A, italics mine. *A Description of Clairvaux*, trans. by Matarasso, pp. 287–88, italics mine.

⁹⁷ Dutton, *Julian of Norwich*, p. 3.

Works Cited

Manuscripts

London, British Library [BL], MS Additional 37049, <http://www.bl.uk/manuscripts/ FullDisplay.aspx?ref=Add_MS_37049> [accessed 24 April 2016]
London, British Library [BL], MS Arundel 83, <http://www.bl.uk/manuscripts/ FullDisplay.aspx?ref=Arundel_MS_83> [accessed 2 May 2016]
London, British Library [BL], MS Cotton Faustina B VI, pars ii
London, British Library [BL], MS Egerton 747, <http://www.bl.uk/catalogues/illumina tedmanuscripts/record.asp?MSID=8319> [accessed 31 May 2016]
London, British Library [BL], MS Stowe 39
Oxford, Bodleian Library [Bodl. Lib.], MS Bodley 110
Paris, Bibliothèque nationale de France [BnF], MS Latin 6823, <http://gallica.bnf.fr/ ark:/12148/btv1b6000517p/.f.27.image.r=Liber%20de%20herbis%20et%20plantis%206823> [accessed 31 May 2016]

Primary Sources

Ælfric, *Two Aelfric Texts: The Twelve Abuses and the Vices and Virtues*, ed. and trans. by Mary Clayton (Cambridge: D. S. Brewer, 2013)
Auctor incertus, *Descriptio positionis seu situationis monasterii Claraevallensis*, in *Patrologiae cursus completes: series latina*, ed. by Jacques-Paul Migne, 221 vols (Paris: Garnier, 1844–65), CLXXXV, cols 569A–74B
Auctor incertus (Augustinus Hipponensis?), *De duodecim abusionum gradibus liber unus*, in *Patrologiae cursus completus: series Latina*, ed. by J.-P. Migne, 221 vols (Paris: Migne, 1844––65), XL (1861), cols 1079–88
Bernard of Clairvaux, *De gradibus humilitatis et superbiae*, in *Tractatus et opuscula*, in *Bernardi opera*, ed. by Jean Leclercq and Henri M. Rochais, 8 vols (Roma: Editiones Cistercienses, 1957–77), III (1963), 1–59
——, *The Sentences*, in *The Parables & The Sentences*, trans. by Michael Casey and Francis R. Swietek, ed. by Maureen M. O'Brien, Cistercian Father Series, 55 (Kalamazoo: Cistercian Publications, 2000), pp. 101–458
——, 'Sententiae series secunda', in *Liber sententiarum*, in *Bernardi opera*, ed. by Jean Leclercq, Charles H. Talbot, and Henri M. Rochais, 8 vols (Roma: Editiones Cistercienses, 1957–77), VI.2 (1972), 23–58
Chaucer, Geoffrey, 'The Parson's Tale', in *The Canterbury Tales*, in *The Riverside Chaucer*, 3rd edn, ed. by Larry D. Benson (Oxford: Oxford University Press, 1987; repr. 1990), pp. 288–328
'Dan Jon Gaytryge's Sermon', in *Religious Pieces in Prose and Verse*, ed. by George G. Perry, Early English Text Society, o.s., 26 (London: N. Trübner, 1868), pp. 1–14
A Description of Clairvaux, in *The Cistercian World: Monastic Writings of the Twelfth Century*, trans. by Pauline Matarasso (London: Penguin, 1993), pp. 285–92

'The Desert of Religion', ed. by Walter Hübner, *Archiv für das Studium der neueren Sprachen und Literaturen*, 126 (1911), 55–74, 360–64

The Desert of Religion: An Edition based on London, British Library, MS Add. 37049, ed. by Anne Mouron, forthcoming

The French Text of the 'Ancrene Riwle': Edited from Trinity College Cambridge, MS. R. 14. 7, with Variants from Bibliothèque Nationale, MS. F. FR. 6276 and MS Bodley 90, ed. by William Hilliard Trethewey, Early English Text Society, o.s., 240 (London: Oxford University Press, 1958; repr. 1971)

Gertrud the Great of Helfta, *The Herald of God's Loving-Kindness*, trans. by Alexandra Barratt, Cistercian Fathers Series, 35 (Kalamazoo: Cistercian Publications, 1991)

Gertrude d'Helfta, *Oeuvres spirituelles: Le Héraut (Livres I et II)*, ed. and trans. into French by Pierre Doyère, Sources chrétiennes, 139 (Paris: Les Editions du Cerf, 1968)

Gregory, 'Homilia XVI, Liber Primum', in *XL Homiliarum in evangelia libri duo*, in *Patrologiae cursus completes: series latina*, ed. by Jacques-Paul Migne, 221 vols (Paris: Garnier, 1844–65), LXXVI, cols 1134D–1138C

Hugh of Folieto, *De claustro animae*, in *Patrologiae cursus completes: series latina*, ed. by Jacques-Paul Migne, 221 vols (Paris: Garnier, 1844–65), CLXXVI, cols 1058–86

Lambert, le chanoine, *Lamberti S. Audomari Canonici Liber floridus. Codex authographus bibliothecae universitatis Gandavensis. Auspiciis eiusdem universitatis in commemorationem diei natalis*, ed. by Albert Derolez (Ghent: In aedibus Story-Scientia, 1968)

Langland, William, *The Vision of Piers Plowman: A Complete Edition of the B-Text*, ed. by Aubrey Vincent Carlyle Schmidt, new edn, Everyman's Library (London: Dent, 1987)

The Manere of Good Lyvyng: A Middle English Translation of Pseudo-Bernard's 'Liber de modo bene vivendi ad sororem', ed. by Anne Mouron, Medieval Women: Texts and Contexts, 30 (Turnhout: Brepols, 2014)

Mayster Ion Gardener, 'A Fifteenth Century Treatise on Gardening', ed. by Alicia M. Tyssen Amherst, *Archaeologia*, 2nd ser., 54 (1894), 157–72

'A Middle English Treatise on Horticulture: *Godfridus super Palladium*', ed. by David G. Cylkowski, in *Popular and Practical Science of Medieval England*, ed. by Lister M. Matheson, Medieval Texts and Studies, 11 (East Lansing: Colleagues Press, 1994), pp. 301–29

Morris, Richard, *Richard Morris's Prick of Conscience: A Corrected and Amplified Reading Text*, ed. by Ralph Hanna and Sarah Wood, Early English Text Society, o.s., 342 (Oxford: Oxford University Press, 2013)

Mouron [as McGovern-Mouron], Anne, 'An Edition of *The Desert of Religion* and its Theological Background', 2 vols (unpublished doctoral thesis, University of Oxford, 1996)

The Orcherd of Syon, ed. by Phyllis Hodgson and Gabriel M. Liegey, Early English Text Society, o.s., 258 (London: Oxford University Press, 1966)

Palladius, Rutilius Taurus Aemilianus, *Palladius on Husbondrie*, ed. by Rev. Barton Lodge, Early English Text Society, o.s., 52 (London: N. Trübner, 1873–79)

Rolle, Richard, *De emendatione vitae: eine kritische Ausgabe des lateinischen Textes von Richard Rolle: mit einer Übersetzung ins Deutsche und Untersuchungen zu den lateinischen und englischen Handschriften*, ed. by Rüdiger Spahl (Bonn: Bonn University Press, 2009)

Speculum virginum: Geistigkeit und Seelenleben der Frau im Hochmittelalter, ed. by Matthäus Bernards (Köln: Böhlau Verlag, 1955; repr. 1982)

Speculum vitae: A Reading Edition, ed. by Ralph Hanna, Early English Text Society, o.s., 331–32, 2 vols (Oxford: Oxford University Press, 2008)

William of St Thierry, 'Epistola ad fratres de Monte Dei', in *Opera didactica et spiritualia*, ed. by Paul Verdeyen and Stanislaus Ceglar, Corpus Christianorum Continuatio Mediaevalis, 83 (Turnhout: Brepols, 2003), pp. 223–89

——, *The Golden Epistle*, trans. by Theodore Berkeley, Cistercian Fathers Series, 12 (Kalamazoo: Cistercian Publications, 1980)

Secondary Works

Bahr, Arthur, *Fragments and Assemblages: Forming Compilations of Medieval London* (Chicago: University of Chicago Press, 2013)

Braekman, Willy Louis, 'Bollard's Middle English Book of Planting and Grafting and its Background', *Studia Neophilologica*, 57.1 (1985), 19–39

Brantley, Jessica, *Reading in the Wilderness: Private Devotion and Public Performance in Late Medieval England* (Chicago: University of Chicago Press, 2007)

Camille, Michael, 'The Book of Signs: Writing and Visual Difference in Gothic Manuscript Illumination', *Word and Image*, 1 (1985), 133–48

Carruthers, Mary J., *The Book of Memory: A Study of Memory in Medieval Culture*, Cambridge Studies in Medieval Literature, 10 (Cambridge: Cambridge University Press, 1990; repr. 1993)

Coste, Florent, 'Poétique et éthique de la compilation médiévale', *French Studies*, 65 (2011), 306–14

Cré, Marleen, and Diana Denissen, '"Multiplication of Many Bokes": Devotional Compilations and Religiosity in Late-Fourteenth and Fifteenth Century England', unpublished paper given at the Oxford Medieval Research Seminar, English Faculty, 18 November 2015

Doyle, A. I., 'A Survey of the Origins and Circulation of Theological Writings in English in the 14th, 15th and Early 16th Centuries with Special Consideration of the part of the Clergy Therein', 2 vols (unpublished doctoral thesis, University of Cambridge, 1953)

Dutton, Elisabeth, *Julian of Norwich: The Influence of Late-Medieval Devotional Compilations* (Cambridge: D. S. Brewer, 2008)

Goddu, André A., and Richard H. Rouse, 'Gerald of Wales and the *Florilegium angelicum*', *Speculum*, 52 (1977), 488–521

Guenée, Bernard, 'L'Historien et la compilation au XIIIe siècle', *Journal des Savants*, 1 (1985), 119–35

Harvey, John H., 'The First English Garden Book: Mayster Jon Gardener's Treatise and its Background, *Garden History*, 13.2 (1985), 83–101

——, 'Henry Daniel: A Scientific Gardner of the Fourteenth Century', *Garden History*, 15.2 (1987), 81–93

Hathaway, Neil, 'Compilatio: From Plagiarism to Compiling', *Viator*, 20 (1989), 19–44

Hogg, James, *An Illustrated Yorkshire Carthusian Religious Miscellany, British Library London Additional MS 37049*, 3 vols, Analecta Cartusiana, 95 (Salzburg: Institut für Anglistik und Amerikanistik, Universität Salzburg, 1981)

Johnstone, Boyda, 'Reading Images, Drawing Texts: The Illustrated *Abbey of the Holy Ghost* in British Library MS Stowe 39', in *Editing, Performance, Texts: New Practices in Medieval and Early Modern English Drama*, ed. by Jacqueline Jenkins and Julie Sanders (Basingstoke: Palgrave Macmillan, 2014), pp. 27–48

Katzenellenbogen, Adolf, *Allegories of the Virtues and Vices in Mediaeval Art from Early Christian Times to the Thirteenth Century*, Studies of the Warburg Institute, 10 (London: Warburg Institute, 1939)

Keiser, George R., 'A Middle English Rosemary Treatise in Verse and Prose', *ANQ: A Quarterly Journal of Short Articles, Notes and Reviews*, 18.1 (2005), 9–19

——, 'Through a Fourteenth-Century Gardener's Eyes: Henry Daniel's Herbal', *Chaucer Review*, 31.1 (1996), 58–75

Lawrence, Clifford Hugh, *Medieval Monasticism: Forms of Religious Life in Western Europe in the Middle Ages*, 2nd edn (London: Longman, 1989; repr. 1993)

Minnis, Alastair, '*Nolens auctor sed compilator reputari*: The Late-Medieval Discourse of Compilation', in *La Méthode critique au Moyen Âge*, ed. by Mireille Chazan and Gilbert Dahan, Bibliothèque d'histoire culturelle du Moyen Âge, 3 (Turnhout: Brepols, 2006), pp. 47–63

Mouron, Anne, 'The *Desert of Religion*: A Voice and Images in the Wilderness', in *Art and Mysticism: Interfaces in the Medieval and Modern Periods*, ed. by Helen Appleton and Louise Nelstrop (Abingdon: Routledge, 2018), pp. 165–85

Rawcliffe, Carole, '"Delectable Sightes and Fragrant Smelles": Gardens and Health in Late Medieval and Early Modern England', *Garden History*, 36.1 (2008), 3–21

Raymo, Robert R., 'Works of Religious and Philosophical Instruction', in *A Manual of the Writings in Middle English, 1050–1500*, vol. VII, ed. by Albert E. Hartung (New Haven: Connecticut Academy of Arts and Sciences, 1986), pp. 2255–378 and 2467–582

Rouse, Richard H., and Mary A. Rouse, *Preachers, Florilegia and Sermons: Studies on the 'Manipulus florum' of Thomas of Ireland*, Studies and Texts, 47 (Toronto: Pontifical Institute of Mediaeval Studies, 1979)

Saxl, Fritz, 'A Spiritual Encyclopaedia of the Later Middle Ages', *Journal of the Warburg and Courtauld Institutes*, 5 (1942), 82–142

Scott, Kathleen L., *Later Gothic Manuscripts, 1390–1490*, A Survey of Manuscripts Illuminated in the British Isles, 6, 2 vols (London: Harvey Miller, 1996)

Wheatley, Abigail, *The Idea of the Castle in Medieval England* (York: York Medieval Press, 2015)

Whitehead, Christiania, *Castles of the Mind: A Study of Medieval Architectural Allegory*, Religion & Culture in the Middle Ages (Cardiff: University of Wales Press, 2003)

Wilmart, André, 'Maître Adam, chanoine prémontré devenu chartreux à Witham', *Analecta Praemonstratensia*, 9 (1933), 209–32

Yates, Frances Amelia, *The Art of Memory* (London: Routledge & Kegan Paul, 1966)

Online Publications

The Electronic Manipulus florum Project, <http://web.wlu.ca/history/cnighman/index.html> [accessed 2 May 2016]

Harvey, John H., 'Daniel, Henry (fl. 1379)', *Oxford Dictionary of National Biography*, Oxford University Press, 2004 <http://ezproxy-prd.bodleian.ox.ac.uk:2167/view/article/7116> [accessed 2 May 2016]

Middle English Dictionary, ed. by Robert E. Lewis and others (Ann Arbor: University of Michigan Press, 1952–2001); online edition in *Middle English Compendium*, ed. by Frances McSparran and others (Ann Arbor: University of Michigan Library, 2000–18), <http://quod.lib.umich.edu/m/middle-english-dictionary> [accessed 29 May 2016]

Petitjean, Johann, 'Compiler: Formes, usages et pratiques', *Hypothèses*, 13 (2010), 15–25, <http://www.cairn.info/revue-hypotheses-2010-1-page-15.htm> [accessed 24 April 2016]

What Grace in Presence: Affective Literacies in *The Chastising of God's Children*

A. S. Lazikani

The grace found in God's presence — and the anguish felt in his absence — is central to the semiotics of *The Chastising of God's Children*.[1] This 'translation-compilation', to use Marleen Cré's term, was possibly written by a Carthusian compiler in the late fourteenth century.[2] As a treatise on temptation, it was originally composed for one 'religious sister', although it later circulated among both female and male religious and the literate laity.[3] Indeed, it benefited from wide acclaim in the Middle Ages. In her essay on *The Chastising* as a 'neglected text', and again in her recent book on the Psalms, Annie Sutherland deduces the compilation's popularity through its dense manuscript tradition.[4] Nicholas Watson also defines it as one of 'the vernacular theologies most widely read in the fifteenth century' and one of the 'classics from

---

[1] On the semiotic presence/absence of Jesus in devotional text and image, see Amsler, *Affective Literacies*, p. 147.

[2] See Cré, 'Contexts and Comments', p. 127. On Carthusian authorship, see Sutherland, *English Psalms in the Middle Ages*, p. 32.

[3] *The Chastising of God's Children*, ed. by Bazire and Colledge, 195/1; all subsequent references are to this edition, to page and line numbers respectively. See Bryan, *Looking Inward*, p. 28; see also Sutherland, *English Psalms in the Middle Ages*, p. 32.

[4] Sutherland, '*The Chastising of God's Children*', p. 353; and Sutherland, *English Psalms in the Middle Ages*, p. 32.

A. S. Lazikani (ayoush.lazikani@ell.ox.ac.uk) is a Lecturer in Old and Middle English at the University of Oxford. She specializes in devotional writing of the High Middle Ages.

the years before 1410'.⁵ But despite such status among medieval readers, *The Chastising* has not enjoyed the same level of modern scrutiny.

Situated in research on its readers' literacy, the present essay examines affective reading practices in this text — focusing on one possible way in which it may have been read. It contends that, among many possible modes of reading, *The Chastising* responds and contributes to the advanced 'affective literacies' of its readers. As Mark Amsler defines the term, affective literacies 'denote a range of emotional, spiritual, physiological, somatic responses readers have when reading or perceiving a text, such as crying, laughing, imagining, or becoming aroused'.⁶ Such responses do not run contrary to the nature of *The Chastising* as a knowledge-based text. There is an inescapable cognitive component to affective response, and, furthermore, 'emotion' and 'reason' cannot be polarized in this pre-Enlightenment text.⁷ As the *Chastising* compiler might put it, affections can be 'reasonable'; in a recent essay, Marleen Cré demonstrates that 'reason and reasonable feeling' are 'stabilising factors in the spiritual life' in this text.⁸ Affective literacy is not devoid of cognitive activity, nor does it demand a suspension of reason.⁹ This chapter focuses on the hide-and-seek game of intimacy with the Lord — the basis of understanding temptation. It first investigates relevant parts of *The Chastising*, and then turns to three church wall paintings. In doing so, it seeks to handle both text and image as inseparable components of devotional semiotics.

Literacy in *The Chastising of God's Children*

Scholarship has revealed the active role of this compilation's readers — most recently in an essay by Marleen Cré, who illustrates that the religious sister has agency through the instruction she receives.¹⁰ Work on the readers' agency has formed part of the vast research into productive vernacular readerships in the later Middle Ages.¹¹ Most germane to the present article are 'vernacular

---

⁵ Watson, 'The Middle English Mystics', pp. 560–61.

⁶ Amsler, *Affective Literacies*, p. 103.

⁷ See further *Ancrene Wisse*, ed. by Shepherd, p. liii.

⁸ *The Chastising*, 192/25; Cré, 'Spiritual Comfort and Reasonable Feeling', p. 151.

⁹ Reason can be defined as the 'intellectual faculty', related to Latin *ratio*. See 'resoun (n.(2))', in the *Middle English Dictionary*.

¹⁰ Cré, '"ȝe han desired to knowe in comfort of ȝoure soule"'.

¹¹ See Salter and Wicker, *Vernacularity in England and Wales*; and Machan, *English in the Middle Ages* (especially pp. 1–20).

theologies'. 'Vernacular theologies' have been probed by Watson as 'a huge cultural experiment involving the translation of Latin and Anglo-Norman texts, images, conceptual structures [...] into what contemporary commentators termed the "barbarous" mother tongue, English'.[12] As noted earlier, he identifies *The Chastising*, with its dense manuscript tradition, as one of 'the most widely read' of these texts in the fifteenth century.

For both medieval and modern analysts, 'vernacular' is a term which 'carries as much affective as intellectual freight'.[13] Such affective baggage is inevitable, given its myriad associations with enslavement, vulgarity, nationalism, commonality, and revolt.[14] If the terms 'vernacular' and 'affective' are combined in an alternative way, however, it is also clear that employment of a vernacular language had a powerful impact on affective reading practices. This has been highlighted by Fiona Somerset in her work on 'excitative speech' in Margery Kempe's (*c.* 1373) *Book*. This fourteenth-century visionary, argues Somerset, 'envisages a way in which lay devotional emotion may be socially beneficial'; Margery thus embraces an 'integrative vernacular theory' where lay devotional 'excitation' is charged with positive potential.[15]

The *Chastising* compiler cannot be seen as a straightforwardly 'integrative vernacular theorist' in the way that Margery can. Sutherland unearths the compiler's complex response to the translation debate. As she affirms, he vacillates between 'democratic and despotic impulses' in his management of biblical citation: 'As the treatise progresses, so its biblical voice becomes increasingly fraught in its attempts to negotiate an orthodox alliance between the Vulgate and the vernacular'.[16] The readers of *The Chastising* are thus endowed with agency. They are not force-fed meaningless Latin sentences; instead, they ruminate on the Word in their own language.

This is not to say that any encounter with Latin strips the readers of their independence, however. In her monograph on literacy and liturgy in late medieval England, Katherine Zieman has shown 'the value of illiterate liturgical recitation' in *The Chastising*, with Latin prayer based on an 'entent' rather than an unthinking repetition:

---

[12] Watson, 'The Middle English Mystics', p. 544.

[13] Somerset and Watson, 'Preface', p. x.

[14] See especially Somerset and Watson, 'Preface', p. ix.

[15] Somerset, 'Excitative Speech', p. 73.

[16] Sutherland, '*The Chastising of God's Children*', p. 373. See also her *English Psalms in the Middle Ages*, pp. 32–34.

the Latin words of the service are capable of bearing an 'entent', even if that 'entent' is a 'feruent desire upward to god' that is not directly related to the grammatical meaning of the words.[17]

Even when voicing Latin prayer, then, the readers of *The Chastising* maintain a level of agency in their literacy, with an 'intention' that informs prayer in a foreign tongue.

In this vein, the readers' 'affective literacy' is rigorous and discerning. Readers of *The Chastising* are far from automatons, reproducing affective responses unthinkingly; as mentioned earlier, affective literacy is not antithetical to cognitive or reason-based processes. The present chapter investigates only one possible — and ideal — way that *The Chastising* may have been read. This form of reading, one that encourages advanced affective literacies, is not necessarily reflective of how the text was read in practice, nor of the compiler's expectations of his readers' capacities. It should also be noted that whilst the text may have been read sequentially — with the reader's affective sensitivity developing as the text progresses, reaching its apex in Chapter 23 — it may have been read alternatively in discrete sections in varying order, testified by the numerous cross-references throughout.[18]

In the words of Cré, *The Chastising* seeks to 'teach the reader how to react to temptations in order to become closer to God'.[19] Temptation is a profoundly painful struggle for the devotee — partly because it demands constant self-examination and vigilance, as encapsulated in the Matthew 26. 41 refrain: 'Uigilate et orate, ut non intretis in temptacionem: wakeþ and preieþ, þat ȝe entre nat into temptacion'.[20] But even more than this, temptation is painful because it is bound up with a soul's fluctuating intimacy with the Lord. As such, a sensitive and sophisticated affective literacy is ideal for its reading. The process of *compilatio* is crucial in fostering this literacy: the compiler discriminates and employs his material to achieve a coherent affective practice for his readers. These readers are invited to embrace an affective literacy rooted in the 'eyes of the heart', in turn guided by both text and image.[21] Through these semiotic practices, the readers play a game of hide-and-seek, searching for a Lord at once present and absent.

---

[17] Sutherland, '*The Chastising of God's Children*', p. 373; Zieman, *Singing the New Song*, pp. 122–24.

[18] See further Cré, '"ȝe han desired to knowe in comfort of ȝoure soule"'.

[19] See Cré, 'Contexts and Comments', p. 127.

[20] *The Chastising*, 96/12. See the 'Appendix' at the end of this chapter for all biblical quotations; citations are to the Douay-Rheims version.

[21] On the tradition of the 'eyes of the heart', see Carruthers, *The Book of Memory*, p. 31.

Semiotic Games in *The Chastising*

Seeking a Lord who is both present and absent is the perennial labour of the contemplative. This 'game of hide-and-seek' encapsulates the dialectic tension between intimacy and detachment, absence and presence, faced by a soul dwelling on Earth yet devoted to God. In an essay on Julian of Norwich (b. 1343), Vincent Gillespie and Maggie Ross write on 'the game of mystical hide and seek acted out over centuries'. And in his monograph on Richard Rolle (*c.* 1290–1349) and related exegesis, Denis Renevey has commented on this game between bridegroom and beloved in the work of William of St Thierry (*c.* 1075–1147/48).[22]

In a well-known passage adapted from a Latin version of *Ancrene Wisse*, the *Chastising* compiler recounts this game. Notably, in *The Chastising*, the game is played not between lovers, but between a mother and her child:

> whanne oure lord suffrith us to be tempted in oure bigynnynge, he pleiþ wiþ us as þe modir with hir child, whiche sumtyme fleeth awei and hideþ hir, and suffreþ þe child to wepe and crie and besili to seke hir wiþ sobbynge and wepynge. But þanne comeþe þe modir sodeinli wiþ mery chier and lauȝhynge, biclippynge hir child and kissynge, and wipeþ awei þe teeris: þus fariþ our lord wiþ us, as for a tyme he wiþdraweþ his grace and his comfort from us.[23]

The mother's presence/absence is understood explicitly as the enactment or withdrawal of the Lord's grace and comfort. Indeed, as observed by Jennifer Bryan in her monograph on shaping the self in devotional reading, 'the idea of the absent mother proves a powerful explanatory and structuring device' in *The Chastising*.[24] This analogy of the motherly game is also witnessed in other fourteenth-century English texts, including the devotional compilation the *Pore Caitif*. Like *The Chastising*, the *Pore Caitif* bases its passage on a Latin version of *Ancrene Wisse* similar to that preserved in the fragmentary Bodl. Lib., MS Laud misc. 111: the *Quandoque tribularis* compilation.[25]

On 'devotional literacy' which takes both text and image into its remit, see Aston, *Lollards and Reformers*, pp. 101–33 (especially p. 118).

[22] Gillespie and Ross, 'The Apophatic Image', p. 278; Renevey, *Language, Self and Love*, p. 58.

[23] *The Chastising*, 98/3–10.

[24] Bryan, *Looking Inward*, p. 166.

[25] On the *Quandoque tribularis*, see further Cré, '"ȝe han desired to knowe in comfort of ȝoure soule"'. For discussion of the source text, see *The Chastising of God's Children*, ed. by Bazire

The ludic nature of the encounter is crucial: it suggests vitality rather than inertia, variation rather than stasis, and potential rather than complacency. Through this game, the readers are invited into the complex hide-and-seek dynamic of the Lord's love. The description in *The Chastising* vivifies the play between Lord and humanity, following *Ancrene Wisse* to do so. The corresponding passage in the *Quandoque tribularis* reads:

> Item cum dominus permittit vos temptari, ludit vobiscum sicut mater cum caro filio suo, que surgit ab eo et abscondit se, dimittit eum solum clamare: Dame, dame: et diligenter circumspicere et flere ad tempus. Et tunc ipsa expansis manibus prosilit, ridens, amplexans et osculans eum, et oculos abstergit. Sic nos dominus dimittit ad horam, et subtrahit gratiam suam, consolamen et solacium a nobis.[26]

> [Also when the Lord allows you to be tempted, he plays with you as a mother with her dear child; she flees from him and hides herself, and leaves him alone crying out 'Mother, mother', carefully looking around, and weeping for a while. Then, with arms spread out she leaps forth, laughing; she embraces and kisses him, and wipes his eyes. Thus our Lord withdraws from us for a time, and takes away his grace, consolation, and solace from us.]

As is evident from comparison of the quotations, the *Chastising* compiler retains the evocative detail of the child weeping and the mother wiping away its tears — a clear attempt at affective stimulation. However, the *Chastising* compiler does not include the voice of the child crying out to its mother, whereas the compiler of the *Pore Caitif* does: 'suffriþ him to crie: Dame, dame'.[27] In *The Chastising*, this silencing of the child is perhaps an attempt to maintain an unbroken authorial voice, in keeping with the compiler's self-perception as a 'teacher'.[28]

The use of this passage in *The Chastising* germinates from a deep-rooted tradition on the Lord's motherhood.[29] The biblical origins of this tradition are found in Isaiah 49. 1, Isaiah 49. 15, Isaiah 66. 11–13, Ecclesiasticus 24. 24–26, and the key New Testament reference, Matthew 23. 37. At Isaiah 49. 1 and Isaiah

---

and Colledge, pp. 259–60; see also p. 263 n. 98.4. For discussion of the adaptation of *Ancrene Wisse* in *The Chastising* and the *Pore Caitif*, see Innes-Parker, 'The Legacy of *Ancrene Wisse*'.

[26] *Quandoque tribularis* in *The Chastising of God's Children*, ed. by Bazire and Colledge, p. 260.

[27] For the relevant quotation from the *Pore Caitif*, see *The Chastising of God's Children*, ed. by Bazire and Colledge, p. 262.

[28] On the compiler's role as teacher, see further Sutherland, '*The Chastising of God's Children*', p. 373.

[29] See Bynum, *Jesus as Mother*, pp. 110–69.

49. 15, humanity is returned to a foetal state, in turn inspiring God's remembrance. Isaiah 66. 11–13 and Ecclesiasticus 24. 24–26 reveal the Mother-God/Christ as the supreme feeder and carer. The Matthew reference, in turn, displays the Lord as maternal protector. In *The Chastising*, the readers are invited to employ their affective literacy to apprehend this playful yet scripturally founded interaction between Lord and soul, Mother and child.[30]

Having invoked this tradition of the Lord's motherhood, the *Chastising* compiler generates for the reader the affective-somatic response to this Mother's painful absence. This passage is based on Henry Suso's *Horologium sapientiae* (Book I, Chapter viii):[31]

> in his absence we bien al cold and drie, swetnesse haue we noon ne sauoure in deuocion, slouȝ we bien to preie or to trauaile (þe wreched saule sodanly is chaungeð) and made ful heue and ful of sorwe and care.[32]

This description resembles typical accounts of *acedia* — or spiritual 'depression' — and states associated with it, prior to the compiler's discussion of despair in Chapter 14.[33] These are states to which those living a harsh eremitic or even coenobitic life would have been acutely vulnerable.[34] The conditions observed here in Chapter 1 are lukewarmth (even approaching a spiritual iciness), dryness, and a lack of spiritual sweetness, all induced by deprivation of the Lord. As remarked by Gillespie, dryness encompasses 'a thirst for release from time and language into unmediated presence'.[35] It is a presence still unattainable for the readers of *Chastising* at this stage in the text — they remain entrenched in the play of perpetual concealment and pursuit.

As Chapter 1 progresses, the *Chastising* compiler demonstrates the 'wirchynge' of presence and the 'withdrawynge' of absence in richer detail, still continuing to base his work on Suso (Book I, Chapter viii).[36] The aim is to

---

[30] For a list of biblical references in *The Chastising*, see Sutherland, '*The Chastising of God's Children*', p. 367. On the lack of direct biblical citation in *The Chastising*, see Dutton, *Julian of Norwich*, pp. 56–59.

[31] For an explanation of the Suso text and its divisions in the manuscript tradition, see *The Chastising of God's Children*, ed. by Bazire and Colledge, p. 263 n. 98.9.

[32] *The Chastising*, 98/11–14.

[33] *The Chastising*, 151/15–155/25.

[34] For an overview of these states, see Wenzel, *The Sin of Sloth*, p. 60; for the association of *acedia* with hermits and anchorites, see Toohey, *Melancholy, Love, and Time*, p. 138.

[35] Gillespie, *Looking in Holy Books*, p. 330.

[36] *The Chastising*, 99/3–4; see also p. 264 n. 99.3 and n. 99.19.

immerse the readers in the affective-somatic sensation of the Lord's presence and absence, rendering the heart pliable to this painful game. A recurrent concern for the *Chastising* compiler is this need for the devotee to make her heart soft, receptive to the Lord's working/withdrawing. The heart's malleability is an image found in earlier Latin and English writings; it may have ultimate roots in Psalm 22. 14 (21. 15) and Isaiah 13. 7.[37] This process of softening the heart is given significant attention later in *The Chastising*, in Chapters 13 and 23.

Chapter 13 takes as its focus the profit of temptation, a discussion rooted in Isidorian and Gregorian sources.[38] It contains a passage on God wounding his children, based on Gregory the Great's (*c.* 540–604) *Moralia* (Book VI. 25).[39] The heart is softened through such incision: 'god woundiþ his chosen children, whan he wondiþ þe soule inward and cesith of his betyng outward. For þanne he smyteþ þe hardenesse of oure herte wiþ his desire'.[40] As God shifts from outer to inner beating, the heart is made receptive, its hardness broken. Employing the paradoxical motif common in penitential writings of 'injury as healing', the compiler affirms: 'whanne he smyteþ he heeliþ, for he clepiþ us aʒen to þe feelyng of riʒtwisnesse'.[41] A parallel may be drawn here with the penitential 'thorns' in Part VI of *Ancrene Wisse*, which tear the penitent yet also protect her soul from the prowling devil.[42] As the compiler of *The Chastising* explains, hearts cannot be healed without such wounding:

> Oure hertis bien ful yuel heelid whanne þei bien nat wounded wiþ no loue of god, whan þei feele nat þe harm and þe perel of oure lyueng, whanne þei langour nat bi compassioun ne bi noon affeccions, ne for infirmytees ne disease of oure neiʒbore.[43]

This softness precipitates feeling. Without tenderness, the heart is insentient — poorly made for the Lord's entrance. Although wounding is an act of division, a dealing out of flesh, God's wound forms a unified, healed being: 'oure lord sum tyme woundeþ oure hertis for þei schulden be hoole'.[44]

---

[37] On affective 'malleability', see further Lazikani, *Cultivating the Heart*, pp. 13–14.
[38] See *The Chastising of God's Children*, ed. by Bazire and Colledge, p. 45.
[39] See *The Chastising of God's Children*, ed. by Bazire and Colledge, p. 278 n. 146.8.
[40] *The Chastising*, 146/8–10.
[41] *The Chastising*, 146/11–12.
[42] *Ancrene Wisse*, ed. by Millett, I, 143, ll. 436–40.
[43] *The Chastising*, 146/13–17.
[44] *The Chastising*, 146/17–18.

Pliability is again expounded in Chapter 23 of *The Chastising*, where the compiler focuses on the nature of 'affection' — its types and workings in the soul. The material for this chapter is based on Aelred of Rievaulx's (1110–1167) *Speculum caritatis*, with Aelred named directly by the compiler as '[a]n hooli clerk, alred, þe abbot of reuaws'.[45] Affection, the *Chastising* compiler says, is 'a wilful lowynge or inclyneng of a mans hert wiþ loue to anoþer man'.[46] He affirms that he will focus on 'goostli and resonable affeccion', of which 'compunction' forms a part. Notably, this compunction is understood as a softening and melting of the heart:

> for þe herte or þe wil of a man is stired, what tyme þe soule bi compunccion is made soft and liȝt (and is moltyn) in swetnesse and loue of god, or into a tendirnesse of charite in brethirhed, wiþ a priuey and a sodeyn visitacion of þe hooli goost.[47]

The phrase 'soft and liȝt (and is moltyn) in swetnesse' is an especially resonant echo of Psalm 22. 14 (21. 15).

Affection of this nature 'comeþ of an inwarde biholdynge of anoþer mans uertu'.[48] Through such beholding, a devotee can feel a 'tender softness of love': 'whan a uertu or an hoolynesse knowen of any man or womman bi comon fame or bi redyng of any mans liif moueþ oure soule into a tendir softnesse of loue'.[49] This reference to the movement of the soul is a classic definition of the *affectus*.[50] The movement facilitates a 'soft compunction', and with it an important mindfulness:

> Þis affeccion stiriþ a man to a softe compunccion, and makiþ hym haue mynde, wiþ a likynge goostli ioie of meditacion, of uertuouse dedis þat bien do bifore: as whanne he heriþ of þe gloriouse passion of martirs and of oþer seintis lyues.[51]

This mindfulness ('makiþ hym haue mynde') gestures towards the careful cognitive manoeuvres involved in meditation on past saints. Softness thus activates the devotee's meditative capacities.

---

[45] *The Chastising*, 193/10. See further Cré, 'Spiritual Comfort and Reasonable Feeling'; and *The Chastising of God's Children*, ed. by Bazire and Colledge, p. 46.
[46] *The Chastising*, 193/4–5.
[47] *The Chastising*, 193/12–16.
[48] *The Chastising*, 194/1–2.
[49] *The Chastising*, 194/2–4.
[50] See Pourrat, 'Affections', p. 235; and Renevey, *Language, Self and Love*, pp. 36–37.
[51] *The Chastising*, 194/4–8.

These later accounts of affective pliability inform the motherly game of Chapter 1. To return to this first chapter: in a close translation of the *Horologium sapientiae*, the compiler provides a highly immersive account of the Lord's presence. His presence is a revitalizing force and a generator of possibility:

> al þing þat was hard and sharp and impossible to semynge, anon thei wex softe and swete, and al maner excercises, in fastynge and in wakyge and alle goode werkis, suche excercises bien turned into mirþ.⁵²

This transformation renders the heart 'softe and swete' — in other words, suitably pliant for the Lord's working within it. As would be expected, the affective foundation of this softening of the heart is true Christian *caritas*: 'for grete desire and loue þe soule is fulfilled wiþ charite, and al maner clennesse'.⁵³ The soul is nourished by spiritual sweetness, resonating with the Lord's role as nurturing mother.

Devotional activity is facilitated by this nourishment, whether through 'visitations' ('uisitaciouns') or tears: 'Þanne comen so many mery meditacions, wiþ plente of teeris: teeris of contricion, teeris of compunccion, teeris of compassioun, teris of loue and deuocion'.⁵⁴ Each tear is given an affective essence, following Bonaventure's *Commentary on the Gospel of Saint Luke* (Chapter 10, verse 39): contrition, compunction, compassion, and finally 'love and devotion' as an affective duo.⁵⁵ The compiler distinguishes contrition from compunction here. He presumably understands 'contrition' precisely as the remorse that enables remission of sin; by 'compunction' he seems to mean the broader *compunctio cordis* that, in Gregorian terms, involves love for God and sorrow for sin in equal measure.⁵⁶ The readers are not expected to effect this change with only rudimentary tears: they are offered the possibility to pursue a rich affective response and activity.

This explication of tears is expanded further in a key passage later in the treatise, in Chapter 21; it is another quotation from the *Horologium sapientiae* (II. v).⁵⁷ In Chapter 21, the compiler discloses the affective constitution of tears: they are formed from feeling 'gladnessse or ioie in þi soule of ony suche

---

⁵² *The Chastising*, 99/22–100/3.

⁵³ *The Chastising*, 100/3–4.

⁵⁴ *The Chastising*, 100/6–10.

⁵⁵ For the source, see Bonaventure, *Commentarius in Euangelium sancti Lucae*, ch. 10, verse 39.

⁵⁶ See Adnès, 'Pénitence', p. 971; and Leclercq, *The Love of Learning*, pp. 38–39.

⁵⁷ See *The Chastising of God's Children*, ed. by Bazire and Colledge, p. 294 n. 186. 6.

sweetnesse of teeris', and as such are related to the unspecified 'oþer tokenes of comfort'.[58] To attain the grace of the Lord's presence, the complex and painful process of weeping must be enacted, supported by a reference to Abel's sacrifice (based on Genesis 4. 1–8). In both Chapters 1 and 21 of *The Chastising*, tears are sources of comfort and sacrifice; the weeper offers up tears, and in turn they bring God's succour, his reassuring presence.

From its basis in Chapter 1, Chapter 2 of *The Chastising* continues the subject of the 'wirchynge' of the Lord's presence and the 'withdrawynge' of his absence. The compiler achieves this by adaptation of passages from Latin versions of *Ancrene Wisse* and *The Spiritual Espousals* of Jan van Ruusbroec (d. 1381).[59] The latter's transmission in England has been investigated thoroughly by Michael Sargent and Marleen Cré.[60] Through his *compilatio* in this chapter, the *Chastising* compiler enriches the readers' affective literacy by encouraging an immersion in the Lord's withdrawal and working. The readers must become familiar with the nature of both, embracing an affective literacy that can discern presence and absence.

After a list of reasons for the Lord's withdrawal based on *Ancrene Wisse*, the chapter follows Ruusbroec closely to explain how the Lord makes himself present in the hearts of contemplatives at an early stage in their ascent.[61] The compiler progresses in detail through sweetness, 'likynge' (desire), comforts, and drunkenness as signs of the Lord's working in nascent contemplative hearts. This is bolstered by invocation of the biblical epistles:

> Suche maner wirchynges god wrou3t oft siþes to man and to womman in her first begynnyng, whan þei drowen to goostli luyenge, and whan þei turned hem al hooli to god, þat is to sei whan þei forsaken al worldli comfort and put her hope fulli in god; and 3it for al þis, þei ben ri3t tendre, as children þat nede milke and softe mete and swete. For harde metis and soure þei mowen nat suffir, þat is to sey þei may not suffir stronge temptacions, for þei mowen not ne kynne nat suffre esili þe absence of oure lord.[62]

In this 'first begynnyng', the soul is in a fragile, infant state unable to withstand the Lord's absence 'esili'. The Lord, ever a sensitive Mother, refrains from harsh

---

[58] *The Chastising*, 186/13–14.

[59] See further *The Chastising of God's Children*, ed. by Bazire and Colledge, p. 45.

[60] Cré, 'We are United with God'; Sargent, 'Ruusbroec in England'.

[61] *The Chastising*, 101/1–102/1. See further *The Chastising of God's Children*, ed. by Bazire and Colledge, p. 266 n. 102.3.

[62] *The Chastising*, 103/19–104/5.

treatment of this nestling soul. Through this account, the readers are asked to apprehend the Lord as a nurturing and educative mother by broader association with 1 Corinthians 3. 1–2, Hebrews 5. 12, and 1 Peter 2. 2.[63] This biblical forage is then balanced through an exposition on 'unkyndenesse' — a hallmark of the knowledge-based nature of this text. By the term 'unkyndenesse', the compiler refers to the unnatural absence of affection that arises in fledgling souls during the Lord's absence; they consequently become negligent in their devotional duties, further alienating God.[64] The compiler perceives this unnatural lack of feeling to stem from deficient knowledge: 'unkyndenesse is cause of unkonnynge', he affirms; less developed souls have a 'defaute of knowynge hou thei shul haue hem in his presence'.[65] His work thus provides guidance on 'hou we shul haue us in his presence, þat for vnkyndenesse we cause nat his absence'.[66] Through these opening chapters, the compiler has deepened the readers' discernment of the Lord as present/absent mother, the core of this text's concern with temptation.

In order to put forward a cohesive affective practice, the compiler also reveals the later stage in the soul's development — the point at which a rougher chastising becomes possible. This comes in Chapter 5 of the work, on the Lord as a parent disciplining a child; it is one of the few chapters of *The Chastising* for which no source has been found.[67] The compiler refers back to the discussion on children earlier in the text, the play of the Lord with his ghostly little ones, and thus reiterates the compilation's coherence.[68] Now, the soul is ready for sterner handling:

> He binemeþ hem þe reste of herte and suffreþ hem be troubled to preue wele hir pacience, esili first wiþ outward þinges, as bacbityng, scornes, repreues, wronges and worldli diseases; he spekiþ aftieward sharpli, and bringeþ hem in grete drede, and sumtyme he þreteneþ hem and bringeþ hem in dredeful doutis.[69]

The list of easier temptations provides straightforward instruction for readers. The harsher chastising is a concept less easily understood, with the description

---

[63] On the employment of Hebrews 5. 12 in *The Chastising*, see further Sutherland, '"Oure Feyth Is Groundyd in Goddes Worde"', p. 11.

[64] See entry 'unkindenes(se (n.)' in the *Middle English Dictionary*.

[65] *The Chastising*, 104/8–9, 13.

[66] *The Chastising*, 104/13–15.

[67] See further *The Chastising of God's Children*, ed. by Bazire and Colledge, p. 46.

[68] *The Chastising*, 113/6–11.

[69] *The Chastising*, 114/ 9–14.

becoming increasingly abstract; it is nonetheless clarified for the readers by the intensifying adjectives of 'grete' and 'dredeful'. As the compiler asserts unequivocally, 'þe strenger þe soule is to þe loue of god bi mekenesse and suffraunce, þe sharper rodde oure lord takiþ'.[70] In a stronger soul, the Lord can inflict a rod-based 'beating' through absence — a notable paradox.

Another parallel can be drawn here with a paradox of absent beating in *Ancrene Wisse*, found in one of this text's puissant Crucifixion scenes featuring a Mother-Christ. God beats his Son pitilessly, for 'he ber flesch ilich ure, þet is ful of sunne' (he bore flesh like ours, which is full of sin). In turn, the compassionate Christ shields humanity from this enraged Father, 'ase moder þet is reowðful' (as a mother who is full of pity). As he feels the blows of the Father, the Mother-Christ cries out in pain. Mark 15. 34 is then expanded to evoke his vulnerability: 'Mi Godd, mi Godd, mi deorewurðe feader, hauest tu al forwarpe me, þin anlepi sune, þe beatest me se hearde?' (My God, my God, my precious father, have you forsaken me completely, your only son, you who beat me so hard?).[71] And thus, this becomes a beating enacted within an absence: part of the torment stems from the absence of the attacking Father. In *Ancrene Wisse*, which more frequently distinguishes Christ and God than *The Chastising* does, the Mother-Christ is present, absorbing the violence of the Father who attacks through absence; the child remains protected. In *The Chastising*, on the other hand, it is the Lord-as-Mother who hurts his own child through absence, to strengthen its soul. This paradox of 'affliction through absence of the afflicter' is testament to the potentially advanced affective literacies of its readers.

Semiotic Games in Wall Paintings

The act of becoming immersed in the game of the Lord's absence and presence is enriched for the medieval reader by an affective literacy that encompasses both text and image: as such, examining one without the other gives modern scholars a restricted view of devotional semiotics. The later male Carthusian readership of at least one of the manuscripts of *The Chastising* (Bodl. Lib., MS Bodley 505) is a case in point: in the words of Jessica Brantley, 'performative reading of devotional imagetexts was a fundamental part of medieval Carthusian life'.[72] As such, this essay will now turn to three relevant wall paintings, as examples

---

[70] *The Chastising*, 114/19–21.

[71] *Ancrene Wisse*, ed. by Millett, I, 138, ll. 245, 261–63, 252–53, 255–57.

[72] Brantley, *Reading in the Wilderness*, p. 28; see also p. 79. On the Carthusian readership of Bodl. Lib., MS Bodley 505, see Cré, 'Contexts and Comments', especially p. 132.

of the kind of images that may have been available to professional religious or lay readers of *The Chastising*. Wall paintings were widespread in fourteenth-century churches, and there is evidence that viewers were offered guidance on reading them.[73] Sophisticated reading of wall paintings may have also been encouraged by homilists, as Miriam Gill has shown.[74]

As has become increasingly clear through scholarship by Roger Rosewell and others, church wall paintings facilitate an affective literacy as sophisticated as that enabled by texts. The potentially rich affective response inspired by wall paintings is testified by none other than John Lydgate (*c*. 1370–1450) himself. In his *Testament*, the Benedictine monk of Bury St Edmunds Abbey remembers a wall painting and inscription from his childhood: 'Myd of a cloyster, depicte vpon a wall, | I savgh a crucifyx, whos woundes were not smalle, | With this [word] "vide" wrete there besyde, | "Behold my mekenesse, O child, and leve thy pryde"'.[75] The Latin command 'vide' (see) beside the painting refers to a visual-affective absorption of the crucifix, a command for the viewer to meditate upon Christ's vulnerability. The impact of this wall painting on the monk is profound, leading in his later life to a rich 'remembraunce of Crystes passioun'.[76] Wall paintings can immerse viewers in the Lord's presence whilst also heightening awareness of their remoteness from him. A viewer of a wall painting, like a reader of *The Chastising*, must see and feel her mutable relationship with the Lord.[77]

On the wall of St Mary's Church in Belchamp Walter, Essex, is a fourteenth-century *Virgo lactans* image.[78] This painting uses facial expression to indicate the familiarity and relaxed receptiveness between mother and child — a quality more famously evident in the earlier, thirteenth-century roundel at the Bishop's Palace in Chichester Cathedral.[79] The Belchamp Walter image exudes maternal

---

[73] See further Rosewell, *Medieval Wall Paintings*, p. 184.

[74] Gill, 'Preaching and Image'.

[75] Lydgate's *The Testament*, in *The Minor Poems*, ed. by Maccracken, part 1: verse 99, p. 356, ll. 640–746.

[76] Lydgate's *The Testament*, in *The Minor Poems*, ed. by Maccracken, part 1: verse 100, p. 357, l. 752.

[77] On affective reading of wall paintings, see further Lazikani, *Cultivating the Heart*, pp. 21–24.

[78] An image of this painting in Belchamp Walter is available in Rosewell, *Medieval Wall Paintings*, p. 59.

[79] For a discussion of the Chichester roundel, see Caiger-Smith, *English Medieval Mural Paintings*, pp. 12 and 68; see also p. 15 for a comment comparing the Chichester roundel with the Belchamp Walter scene.

connection, with the Virgin's breast visible as an adult-like Christ suckles on it; the tradition of Christ's own Motherhood was constantly buttressed in medieval text and image by his close relationship with Mary. According to Anne Marshall, it is possible that this painting in Belchamp Walter originally had altars underneath.[80] Such a layout would have intensified a devotee's engagement with the maternal fleshliness of this image. The Body and Blood of the Lord would have been present beneath an image of him as an infant receiving his own maternal nurturance.

In the case of a fourteenth-century Doom scene at the Church of St Botolph in North Cove, Suffolk, the image cultivates a mobile, unfixed dynamic of absence and presence.[81] In this painting the Virgin, Christ, and John the Baptist are at an affective remove from the audience: they are elevated to the point of being unreachable and have facial expressions that are resolutely impassive. The large, imposing Christ with his raised hands invites meditation on his glory rather than his anguish. His hand gesture also appears to bar the viewer from drawing any closer, as it is reminiscent of surviving wall paintings of the 'Noli me tangere' biblical episode (in John 20. 17). Like him, the Virgin and John the Baptist have outstretched arms with open palms — in their case, indicating intercession and thereby reminding viewers of their lowliness and wickedness. The figures remain 'absent', detached affectively from the viewer.

Yet, the erect Mary on this North Cove wall also has exposed breasts. The image of a bare-breasted Mary interceding for humanity in the Last Judgement was inspired in Christian Europe by the writings of Benedictine Arnold of Bonneval (d. after 1156), though it also has pre-Christian, classical origins.[82] On the North Cove wall, Mary draws attention to her maternal capacity for nourishment, in turn reflecting on Christ's own. The wounding at Christ's heart-point is clear in this painting, with a definite trickle of blood invoking for viewers the place at which the Church was born. As asserted by Augustine (354–430), 'mortuo Christo, lancea perforatur latus, ut profluant Sacramenta, quibus formetur Ecclesia' (the side of the dead Christ is pierced so that the sacraments may flow forth, from which the Church is formed).[83] The glori-

---

[80] See Marshall, 'Medieval Wall Painting in the English Parish Church'. See also Rosewell, *Medieval Wall Paintings*, pp. 74–75.

[81] An image of this painting in North Cove is available in Rosewell, *Medieval Wall Paintings*, p. 75.

[82] Ryan, 'The Persuasive Power of a Mother's Breast', pp. 63, 70–71, 74.

[83] Augustine, *In Iohannis Evangelium tractatus* IX. 10, ed. by Migne, col. 1463. For parallels made between Christ's side wound and Mary's breast, see further Bynum, *Fragmentation and*

fied Mother and Son thus remain present as nurturers, each labouring for and feeding humanity. With disrobed chests, Mary and Christ become vulnerable through their role as present nourishers.

A similar affective dynamic is stimulated by a fourteenth-century Last Judgment painting at St Mary Magdalene's church in Ickleton, Cambridgeshire, which hosts a bare-breasted Virgin in the same pose. Her plain dress displays her bosom, while her large, open palm reaches towards Christ and meets the equally large hand of an angel. Mary and the angel are interlocutors on behalf of humanity, their hands joined in an act of mediation for the dissipated sinner. She thus remains a distant mediator, but, bare-breasted in mercy, she also permits and generates closeness. She is a mother both present and absent for the believers, her children, as is the Mother-Christ by her side. Their children are at once blessed with grace and tormented by its lack.

With percipient affective literacies, readers of *The Chastising of God's Children* can discern the maternal hide-and-seek game between the Lord and the human soul — the lifeblood of a contemplative existence. The readers are immersed in the presence and absence of the Lord, his 'wirchynge' and 'withdrawynge'; it is an essential skill in coping with temptation. This affective literacy is nurtured by both text and image: the affective strategies of *The Chastising* can be mapped onto wall paintings, and vice-versa. This essay has given particular attention to the *Virgo lactans* image in Belchamp Walter and the Doom scenes in North Cove and Ickleford, which draw viewers into a dialectic of intimacy and distance. Inscribed in *The Chastising* and on the painted walls, the game of absence/presence with the Lord is vivified for devotees, readying them for an incessant strain against temptation. Along with Mathew 26. 41, again and again they must intone:

> A, goode god, what grace is in thi presence, hou precious is þi loue, whan al loue and grace faileþ in þin absence![84]

Redemption, pp. 102–08, 113. On this theme of 'double intercession' observed by art historians, see especially p. 106.

[84] *The Chastising*, 110/24–25.

Appendix: Biblical Quotations Cited

Old Testament

Genesis 4. 4	Abel quoque obtulit de primogenitis gregis sui, et de adipibus eorum: et respexit Dominus ad Abel, et ad munera ejus.
	Abel also offered of the firstlings of his flock, and of their fat: and the Lord had respect to Abel, and to his offerings.
Psalm 22. 14 (21. 15)	Sicut aqua effusus sum; et dispersa sunt omnia ossa mea. Factum est cor meum tamquam cera liquescens in medio ventris mei.
	I am poured out like water; and all my bones are scattered. My heart is become like wax melting in the midst of my bowels.
Ecclesiasticus 24. 24–26	Ego mater pulchrae dilectionis, et timoris, et agnitionis, et sanctae spei. In me gratia omnis viae et veritatis: in me omnis spes vitae et virtutis. Transite ad me, omnes qui concupiscitis me, et a generationibus meis implemini.
	I am the mother of fair love, and of fear, and of knowledge, and of holy hope. In me is all grace of the way and of the truth, in me is all hope of life and of virtue. Come over to me, all ye that desire me, and be filled with my fruits.
Isaiah 13. 7–8	Propter hoc omnes manus dissolventur, et omne cor hominis contabescet, et conteretur.
	Therefore shall all hands be faint, and every heart of man shall melt, And shall be broken.
Isaiah 49. 1	Audite, insulae; et attendite, populi de longe; Dominus ab utero vocavit me, de ventre matris meae recordatus est nominis mei.
	Give ear, ye islands, and hearken, ye people from afar. The Lord hath called me from the womb, from the bowels of my mother he hath been mindful of my name.
Isaiah 49. 15	Numquid oblivisci potest mulier infantem suum, ut non misereatur filio uteri sui? Et si illa oblita fuerit, ego tamen non obliviscar tui.
	Can a woman forget her infant, so as not to have pity on the son of her womb? and if she should forget, yet will not I forget thee.

Isaiah 66. 11–13	Ut sugatis et repleamini ab ubere consolationis ejus, ut mulgeatis et deliciis affluatis ab omnimoda gloria ejus. Quia haec dicit Dominus: Ecce ego declinabo super eam quasi fluvium pacis, et quasi torrentem inundantem gloriam gentium, quam sugetis; ad ubera portabimini, et super genua blandientur vobis. Quomodo si cui mater blandiatur, ita ego consolabor vos, et in Jerusalem consolabimini.
	That you may suck, and be filled with the breasts of her consolations: that you may milk out, and flow with delights, from the abundance of her glory. For thus saith the Lord: Behold I will bring upon her as it were a river of peace, and as an overflowing torrent the glory of the Gentiles, which you shall suck; you shall be carried at the breasts, and upon the knees they shall caress you. As one whom the mother caresseth, so will I comfort you, and you shall be comforted in Jerusalem.

New Testament

Matthew 23. 37	Jerusalem, Jerusalem, quae occidis prophetas, et lapidas eos, qui ad te missi sunt, quoties volui congregare filios tuos, quemadmodum gallina congregat pullos suos sub alas, et noluisti?
	Jerusalem, Jerusalem, thou that killest the prophets, and stonest them that are sent unto thee, how often would I have gathered together thy children, as the hen doth gather her chickens under her wings, and thou wouldest not?
Matthew 26. 41	Vigilate, et orate ut non intretis in tentationem. Spiritus quidem promptus est, caro autem infirma.
	Watch ye, and pray that ye enter not into temptation. The spirit indeed is willing, but the flesh weak.
Mark 15. 34	Et hora nona exclamavit Jesus voce magna, dicens: Eloi, eloi, lamma sabacthani? quod est interpretatum: Deus meus, Deus meus, ut quid dereliquisti me?
	And at the ninth hour, Jesus cried out with a loud voice, saying: Eloi, Eloi, lamma sabacthani? Which is, being interpreted, My God, my God, why hast thou forsaken me?
John 20.17	Dicit ei Jesus: Noli me tangere, nondum enim ascendi ad Patrem meum : vade autem ad fratres meos, et dic eis : Ascendo ad Patrem meum, et Patrem vestrum, Deum meum, et Deum vestrum.
	Jesus saith to her: 'Do not touch me, for I am not yet ascended to my Father. But go to my brethren, and say to them: I ascend to my Father and to your Father, to my God and your God.'

1 Corinthians 3. 1–2	Et ego, fratres, non potui vobis loqui quasi spiritualibus, sed quasi carnalibus. Tamquam parvulis in Christo, Lac vobis potum dedi, non escam: nondum enim poteratis: sed nec nunc quidem potestis: adhuc enim carnales estis.
	And I, brethren, could not speak to you as unto spiritual, but as unto carnal. As unto little ones in Christ. I gave you milk to drink, not meat; for you were not able as yet. But neither indeed are you now able; for you are yet carnal.
Hebrews 5. 12	Etenim cum deberetis magistri esse propter tempus, rursum indigetis ut vos doceamini quae sint elementa exordii sermonum Dei: et facti estis quibus lacte opus sit, non solido cibo.
	For whereas for the time you ought to be masters, you have need to be taught again what are the first elements of the words of God: and you are become such as have need of milk, and not of strong meat.
1 Peter 2. 2	Sicut modo geniti infantes, rationabile, sine dolo lac concupiscite: ut in eo crescatis in salutem.
	As newborn babes, desire the rational milk without guile, that thereby you may grow unto salvation.

Works Cited

Manuscripts

Oxford, Bodleian Library [Bodl. Lib.], MS Bodley 505
Oxford, Bodleian Library [Bodl. Lib.], MS Laud misc. 111

Primary Sources

Ancrene Wisse: A Corrected Edition of the Text in Cambridge, Corpus Christi College, MS 402, with Variants from Other Manuscripts, ed. by Bella Millett, Early English Text Society, o.s., 325–26, 2 vols (Oxford: Oxford University Press, 2005–06)

Ancrene Wisse: Parts Six and Seven, ed. by Geoffrey Shepherd (Manchester: Manchester University Press, 1972)

Augustine, *In Iohannis Evangelium tractatus*, in *Patrologiae cursus completus: series Latina*, ed. by J. P. Migne, 221 vols (Paris: Migne, 1844–65), XXXV, cols 1379–1976; *Patrologia Latina Database* (1996) <http://pld.chadwyck.co.uk/>

The Chastising of God's Children and the Treatise of Perfection of the Sons of God, ed. by Joyce Bazire and Eric Colledge (Oxford: Basil Blackwell, 1957)

Lydgate, John, *The Minor Poems of John Lydgate*, ed. by Henry Noble Maccracken, Early English Text Society, e.s., 107 (London: Kegan Paul, 1911 for 1910)

Secondary Works

Adnès, Pierre, 'Pénitence', in *Dictionnaire de spiritualité: Ascétique et mystique, doctrine et histoire*, ed. by Marcel Viller and others, 17 vols (Paris: G. Beauchesne, 1937; repr. 1962), XII, 943–1010

Amsler, Mark, *Affective Literacies: Writing and Multilingualism in the Late Middle Ages* (Turnhout: Brepols, 2011)

Aston, Margaret, *Lollards and Reformers: Images and Literacy in Late Medieval Religion* (London: Hambledon Press, 1984)

Brantley, Jessica, *Reading in the Wilderness: Private Devotion and Public Performance in Late Medieval England* (Chicago: University of Chicago Press, 2007)

Bryan, Jennifer, *Looking Inward: Devotional Reading and the Private Self in Late Medieval England* (Philadelphia: University of Pennsylvania Press, 2008)

Bynum, Caroline Walker, *Fragmentation and Redemption: Essays on Gender and the Human Body in Medieval Religion* (New York: Zone Books, 1991)

—— , *Jesus as Mother: Studies in the Spirituality of the High Middle Ages* (Berkeley: University of California Press, 1982)

Caiger-Smith, Alan, *English Medieval Mural Paintings* (Oxford: Clarendon Press, 1963)

Carruthers, Mary J., *The Book of Memory: A Study of Memory in Medieval Culture*, Cambridge Studies in Medieval Literature, 10 (Cambridge: Cambridge University Press, 1990)

Cré, Marleen, 'Contexts and Comments: *The Chastising of God's Children* and *The Mirror of Simple Souls* in MS Bodley 505', in *Medieval Texts in Context*, ed. by Denis Renevey and Graham D. Caie (London: Routledge, 2008), pp. 122–35

——, 'Spiritual Comfort and Reasonable Feeling: Annotating *The Chastising of God's Children* in Oxford, Bodleian Library, MS Rawlinson C 57', in *Emotion and Medieval Textual Media*, ed. by Mary C. Flannery (Turnhout: Brepols, 2018), pp. 149–76

——, '"We Are United with God (and God with Us?)": Adapting Ruusbroec in *The Treatise of Perfection of the Sons of God* and *The Chastising of God's Children*', in *The Medieval Mystical Tradition in England: Exeter Symposium VII*, ed. by E. A. Jones (Cambridge: D. S. Brewer, 2004), pp. 21–36

——, '"ȝe han desired to knowe in comfort of ȝoure soule": Female Agency in *The Chastising of God's Children*', *Journal of Medieval Religious Cultures*, 42 (2016), 164–80

Dutton, Elisabeth, *Julian of Norwich: The Influence of Late-Medieval Devotional Compilations* (Cambridge: D. S. Brewer, 2008)

Gill, Miriam, 'Preaching and Image: Sermons and Wall Paintings in Later Medieval England', in *Preacher, Sermon and Audience in the Middle Ages*, ed. by Carolyn Muessig (Leiden: Brill, 2002), pp. 155–80

Gillespie, Vincent, *Looking in Holy Books: Essays on Late Medieval Religious Writing in England*, Brepols Collected Essays in European Culture, 3 (Turnhout: Brepols, 2011)

Gillespie, Vincent, and Maggie Ross, 'The Apophatic Image: The Poetics of Effacement in Julian of Norwich', in *Looking in Holy Books: Essays on Late Medieval Religious Writing in England*, Brepols Collected Essays in European Culture, 3 (Turnhout: Brepols, 2011), pp. 277–305

Innes-Parker, Catherine, 'The Legacy of *Ancrene Wisse*: Translations, Adaptations, Influences and Audience, with Special Attention to Women Readers', in *A Companion to Ancrene Wisse*, ed. by Yoko Wada (Cambridge: D. S Brewer, 2003), pp. 145–73

Lazikani, Ayoush Sarmada, *Cultivating the Heart: Feeling and Emotion in Twelfth- and Thirteenth-Century Religious Texts* (Cardiff: University of Wales Press, 2015)

Leclercq, Jean, *The Love of Learning and the Desire for God*, trans. by Catharine Misrahi (New York: Fordham University Press, 1961)

Machan, Tim William, *English in the Middle Ages* (Oxford: Oxford University Press, 2003)

Marshall, Anne, 'Medieval Wall Painting in the English Parish Church: A Developing Catalogue', <www.paintedchurch.org/> [accessed 1 August 2016, currently unavailable]

Pourrat, Pierre, 'Affections', in *Dictionnaire de spiritualité: Ascétique et mystique, doctrine et histoire*, ed. by Marcel Viller and others, 17 vols (Paris: G. Beauchesne, 1937; repr. 1962), I, 235–40

Renevey, Denis, *Language, Self and Love: Hermeneutics in the Writings of Richard Rolle and the Commentaries on the Song of Songs* (Cardiff: University of Wales Press, 2001)

Rosewell, Roger, *Medieval Wall Paintings in English and Welsh Churches* (Woodbridge: Boydell, 2008)

Ryan, Salvador, 'The Persuasive Power of a Mother's Breast: The Most Desperate Act of the Virgin Mary's Advocacy', *Studia Hibernica*, 32 (2002/03), 59–74

Salter, Elisabeth, and Helen Wicker, eds, *Vernacularity in England and Wales, c. 1300–1550*, Utrecht Studies in Medieval Literacy, 17 (Turnhout: Brepols, 2011)

Sargent, Michael G., 'Ruusbroec in England: *The Chastising of God's Children* and Related Works', in *Historia et Spiritualitas Cartusiensis: Colloquii Quarti Internationalis Acta*, ed. by J. de Grauwe (Ghent: De Grauwe, 1983), pp. 303–12

Somerset, Fiona, 'Excitative Speech: Theories of Emotive Response from Richard Fitzralph to Margery Kempe', in *The Vernacular Spirit: Essays on Medieval Religious Literature*, ed. by Renate Blumenfeld-Kosinski, Duncan Robertson, and Nancy Bradley Warren (New York: Palgrave, 2002), pp. 59–79

Somerset, Fiona, and Nicholas Watson, 'Preface: On "Vernacular"', in *The Vulgar Tongue: Medieval and Post-Medieval Vernacularity*, ed. by Fiona Somerset and Nicholas Watson (University Park: Pennsylvania State University Press, 2003), pp. ix–xiii

Sutherland, Annie, '*The Chastising of God's Children*: A Neglected Text', in *Text and Controversy from Wyclif to Bale: Essays in Honour of Anne Hudson*, ed. by Helen Barr and A. M. Hutchison, Medieval Church Studies, 4 (Turnhout: Brepols, 2005), pp. 353–73

——, *English Psalms in the Middle Ages, 1300–1450* (Oxford: Oxford University Press, 2015)

——, '"Oure Feyth Is Groundyd in Goddes Worde": Julian of Norwich and the Bible', *The Medieval Mystical Tradition in England: Exeter Symposium VII*, ed. by E. A. Jones (Cambridge: Cambridge University Press, 2004), pp. 1–20

Toohey, Peter, *Melancholy, Love, and Time: Boundaries of the Self in Ancient Literature* (Ann Arbor: University of Michigan Press, 2007)

Watson, Nicholas, 'The Middle English Mystics', in *The Cambridge History of Medieval English Literature*, ed. by David Wallace (Cambridge: Cambridge University Press, 1999; repr. 2005), pp. 539–65

Wenzel, Siegfried, *The Sin of Sloth: Acedia in Medieval Thought and Literature* (Chapel Hill: University of North Carolina Press, 1967)

Zieman, Katherine, *Singing the New Song: Literacy and Liturgy in Late Medieval England* (Philadelphia: University of Pennsylvania Press, 2008)

Online Publications

Bonaventure, *Commentarius in Euangelium sancti Lucae*, Library of Latin Texts: Series B (Turnhout: Brepols, 2015), <http://apps.brepolis.net/BrepolisPortal/>

The Holy Bible, Douay Version: Translated from the Latin Vulgate (Douay, A. D. 1609: Rheims, AD 1582) (London: Catholic Truth Society, 1956), <http://www.drbo.org/>

Middle English Dictionary, ed. by Robert E. Lewis and others (Ann Arbor: University of Michigan Press, 1952–2001); online edition in *Middle English Compendium*, ed. by Frances McSparran and others (Ann Arbor: University of Michigan Library, 2000–18), <https://quod.lib.umich.edu/m/middle-english-dictionary> [accessed 20 May 2018]

Afterword

The Terminology and Ethos of Vernacular *Compilatio*

Nicholas Watson

As the important collection of essays gathered in this volume attests, in recent years *compilation* has become both an indispensable term of art and a major topic of research in its own right, and nowhere more so than in the study of the religious literature of fifteenth-century England. There is a great deal to reflect on here, not only for scholars of religious compilations as such but for anyone interested in the diverse and interconnected ways in which late medieval English Christians from a range of backgrounds and educational levels read, thought, and felt about their faith, and in the equally diverse and rapidly changing textual and institutional environment in which they did so.

Nor is the topic of devotional compilations significant only for those interested in late medieval religion. The textual practices of collation and recombination that constitute compilation as medieval readers and writers understood it were as basic to the fifteenth-century information revolution in all its manifestations as the practice of translation or the introduction of moveable type themselves, underlying the entire range of corpora — imaginative, historical, ethical, legal, medical, and utilitarian as well as religious — that proliferated across the century in ways that have yet to be fully theorized and explored. The study of fifteenth-century English religious writing is still haunted by the violent interruption of the textual tradition that took place after the 1530s, to the extent that learning to navigate the stiff ideological headwinds generated by the Henrician reformation and its aftermath remains among the field's most serious

---

Nicholas Watson (nwatson@fas.harvard.edu) is Henry B. and Anne M. Cabot Professor of English literature at Harvard University.

scholarly challenges: a point to which I shall return at the end of these remarks. It needs stressing at the outset, however, that while the working lifetimes of most of the texts and books considered here had ended by the mid-sixteenth century, to study them is not to study a mere textual, religious, or cultural cul-de-sac. On the contrary, just as the devotional culture of post-Reformation England was in many ways continuous with the late medieval past, so the assumptions about textuality that underlay these compilations, the techniques used in their making, and their stances towards their target audiences continued to inform how writers, copyists, printers, and readers alike went about their business well into the early modern era.

In this response to a volume that not only moves the topic of religious compilations a clear stage further but notices many possible directions for future research, I take the opportunity to reconsider some basic matters of terminology and definition, building on the exceptionally rich accounts of *compilatio* in action presented in these essays in general, rather than particular, terms. Part of my purpose — weaving my own path through issues raised in other ways in Ian Johnson's suggestive essay on the term *heterarchy* and its utility in thinking about the shapeless and anxiety-provoking concept of *miscellaneity* — is simply to reflect upon why compilation is the messy topic it is, especially, perhaps, in vernacular and pastoral contexts. But I also have some thoughts of my own about how we approach the challenges raised by the topic, arising from reflection on two originally distinct historical stories and their changing relationship: that of compilation as a textual *term* and that of compilation as a textual *practice*. While all would agree in principle that the continuities between late medieval religious compilations and literary history more broadly extend backward as well as forward, most scholars of Middle English rarely consider much earlier materials, vernacular or Latin, unless their influence on the later period was direct and ascertainable. My more general suggestion here is that, as least so far as *compilatio* as term and practice are concerned, this habit is unhelpful. The contributions of late medieval compilations to the religious culture of the period can best be appreciated if we read them in light of their long past. My more particular suggestion is that the obstinate informality of compilation as an easily available means of generating useful texts and books for a variety of audiences helps account both for its prominence in late medieval England and for its special significance during a period of wide but diffused religious disagreement within the expanding community of the literate devout. In the century before the Reformation, the essentially conservative practice of textual compilation was also effectively a means of religious *accommodation*.

* * *

Although they become increasingly common in texts from the ninth century on, *compilatio*, *compilare*, and *compilator* seem to have become established as wide-ranging literary terms only during the course of the twelfth century, as they slowly lost the negative connotations they derived from their original association with violent plunder. In classical and patristic Latin, the primary meaning of *compilare* is to *rake together* or to *pillage*, and to accuse someone of textual compilation — as Jerome's opponents are said to have done of him in relation to the writings of Origen — is to accuse them of mere theft.[1] These associations are still uppermost when the Carolingian theologian Hincmar of Rheims (d. 882) refers repeatedly to his adversary Gottschalk as a *compilator* in the sense *plagiarist*, and their etymological grounding means that they remain perpetually available for revival.[2] By the thirteenth century, however, they had apparently become distant enough in most situations that the terms could be put to changed use by the scholastic theorists whose importance to the history of later medieval texts and books was first pointed out to Anglophone scholars by Malcolm Parkes.[3]

The ethically laden older sense of *compilator* still flickers in the rhetorical apology with which Bonaventure opens the second book of his commentary on Peter Lombard's *Sententiae*, where he calls himself no creator ('fabricator') but merely a 'pauper et tenuis compilator', striking a note of humility we often find in later compilations.[4] But in the important fourfold distinction between

---

[1] Jerome, *Commentarii in prophetas minores*, ed. by Adriaen, I, 473.226–27: 'nam quod dicunt, Origenis me uolumina compilare, et contaminari non decere ueterum scripta' (for some say that I have pilfered the volumes of Origen, and contaminated, not graced, the writings of the ancients). Note the paralleling of *compilare* and *contaminari*. A still earlier use of *compilare* in a textual sense is by Cicero, *Epistulae ad familiares*, referring contemptuously to 'Chresti compilationem' (the pilferings of Chrestus); see Cicero, *Letters to Friends*, ed. by Shackleton Bailey, letter 80, I, 354. A comprehensive sense of classical and patristic uses of the word, as well as much later ones, can be gathered from the Brepolis databases, using the Cross Database Searchtool, which I have gratefully used here. Earlier lexical aids such as the invaluable Niermeyer, *Mediae Latinitatis Lexicon Minus*, which draw their examples largely from later periods, tend to miss the longevity of negative senses of the language of compilation.

[2] Hincmar of Rheims, *De praedestinatione contra Godeschalcum*, ed. by Migne, where *compilator* and *compilatio* occur dozens of times: see e.g., cap. 6 (col. 92): 'Quod *furatus* iste *compilator* de medio!' (What sort of a thief is this common pilferer!) (italics mine).

[3] Parkes, 'The Influence of the Concepts of *Ordinatio* and *Compilatio*'. For a reappraisal that contains elements of critique, see Rouse and Rouse, '*Ordinatio* and *Compilatio* Revisited'.

[4] Bonaventura, *Commentaria in quattuor libros Sententiarum Magistri Petri Lombardi*,

auctor, *commentator*, *compilator*, and *scriptor* he makes in the first book of this work — as he sets out to represent the *Sententiae* itself as the work of an *auctor*, despite its extensive reliance on patristic source materials — *compilator* is represented in a more neutral way, denoting simply one kind of writing practice among others, described and distinguished according to a hierarchy of attributed intellectual ownership, with the *auctor* at its summit. In the process, *compilator* also comes to be defined around a new verb, one that historically lacked the negative connotations of *compilare*: *addere*, to associate, join together, or augment. In contrast to the *auctor* and *commentator*, both of whom write different kinds of words of their own as well as those of others, and to the *scriptor*, who copies what is in front of him, the *compilator* thus now simply becomes any figure who 'writes the words of others, putting them together without including his own' ('scribit aliena, addendo, sed non de suo'), whether this practice is systematic or casual, beneficial or harmful, open or concealed.[5]

Ever since it was made famous by Alastair Minnis during the 1980s, Bonaventure's account of compilation has brought shape to a field at once vast and bafflingly hard to map, just as a *distinctio* should.[6] Like so much scholastic argumentation, the account is quietly dependent on the ease with which Latin verbs can generate two different categories of noun: the verbal noun *compilatio*, the writing practice defined by 'scribit aliena […] non de suo', as well as its textual outcome, a *compilation*, which serves as the verb's implied direct object; and the common noun *compilator*, which still carries traces of the fluid activities and processes delineated by the verb but now hardens them into an *agent*, an entity susceptible of stable definition, which serves as its implied subject. Because Bonaventure's *distinctio* can only do its work if it is understood to define not only *compilator* but its two colleagues, to define a *compilator* as one who 'scribit aliena, addendo, sed non de suo' is in one sense to commit mere tautology: a compiler is one who compiles compilations; compilations are writings compiled by a compiler. Yet the very minimalism and circularity of this definition also serves both to purify the *terminology* of compilation of most of the traces of its earlier, pejorative meanings and to protect compilation as a *practice* from confusion with the three writerly categories from which it is being distinguished. Only in this carefully dehistoricized form can compilation gain

---

11. 10: 'Nec quisquam aestimet, quod novi scripti velim esse fabricator; hoc enim sentio et fateor, quod sum pauper et tenuis compilator' (Nor should anyone imagine that I aspire to be considered a maker; for I know and acknowledge this, that I am a poor and feeble compiler).

[5] Bonaventura, *Commentaria in quattuor libros Sententiarum Magistri Petri Lombardi*, I. 15.

[6] Minnis, *Medieval Theory of Authorship*.

its secure place within the hierarchy of writing practices Bonaventure is isolating and, in the process, creating.

We can see the effects of the neutralization of *compilatio* undertaken by twelfth- and thirteenth-century scholars in the proliferation of references to compilers, compiling, and compilation in a wide range of later medieval texts and genres, both Latin and vernacular. The best-known theological compilation of the later Middle Ages — Hugh Ripelin of Strasbourg's *Compendium theologicae veritatis*, likely written in 1268, some fifteen years after Bonaventure's commentary on Lombard's *Sententiae* — interestingly prefers a different term.[7] But the lexis of compilation, now used in a broadly positive sense to indicate any assemblage of *auctoritates*, became increasingly important to chroniclers, as a way to describe their gathering of mixed materials from various sources. By the early thirteenth century, it was also already beginning to take a vital place in the specialized textual context of canon law, where *compilatio* became the normative term used to identify and differentiate collections of legal texts in an array of genres, especially decretals. Although the negative sense of *compilatio* still sometimes hovers in the background, we begin to hear of first, second, and third compilations, old compilations and new, compilations identified by incipit, and so on. Certain *compilationes*, notably Raymond of Peñafort's *Nova compilatio decretalium*, written by combining the best elements of the so-called *Quinque compilationes antiquae* with the new decretals of Gregory IX, acquired a high degree of *auctoritas* of their own.[8]

The learned resonances of *compilator* in particular are apparent even when the word is used as vaguely as in its first known English appearance, in Henry Daniel's *Liber uricrisiarum* (*c.* 1379) — a pioneering work of vernacular medical prose by a London contemporary of Geoffrey Chaucer — which begs every future 'writer or compiler of þis' to preserve its language exactly, since 'trewe

---

[7] For this work, its author, its date, its historical context, and its remarkable popularity in manuscript and print, see Steer, *Hugo Ripelin von Strassburg*.

[8] Kuttner, 'Raymond of Penafort as Editor'. Characteristic of *compilatio* in this legal sense is that newer *compilationes* displace older ones: in 1234, Gregory IX decreed that Peñafort's *Nova compilatio*, which he had commissioned himself, rendered the authority of copies of the *Quinque compilationes* null and void. See *Corpus Iuris Canonici, Pars Secunda*, ed. by Richter and Friedberg, 9. The particular textual model legal *compilatio* enables, in which new texts displace old ones by assuming their authority, is also found in the visionary context of John of Morigny's *Liber florum* (1301–15), the second version of which, the 'nova compilacio', updates and displaces the 'antiqua compilacio', finished only four years earlier, as a result of new instructions from God and the Virgin. Here, there is nothing negative about the term. See John of Morigny, *Liber florum celestis doctrine*, ed. by Fanger and Watson, pp. 98–101 and Nova compilatio, III.i.14.

& perfite craft of ortographie is taugh in þis bok'. Although this passage precisely collapses Bonaventure's distinction between *scriptor* and *compilator* — as the reference to 'ortographie' suggests, both 'writer' and 'compiler' here mean simply *scribe* — it shows Daniel's sense of 'compiler' as a clerical term, suitable to a vernacular prose replete with scholarly neologisms such as the one he is developing.[9]

Occasionally, moreover, we appear to see Bonaventure's hierarchy of textual authority in direct action in vernacular compilatory contexts, whether or not the text in question refers to itself as a 'compilacioun'. When the writer of *The Chastising of God's Children* confesses 'drede' in dealing with the 'hiȝe matiers' contained in his book, the proper treatment of which would require of him an 'inwarde felinge' of 'goostlie science' he lacks, his rhetorical declaration of bafflement before what 'doctours wolden mene in her hooli writynges' locates primary authority for his material elsewhere, in his sources, very much like Bonaventure's compiler. This is so despite the fact that, as a 'short pistle' to a 'religious sister' in the form of a 'tretis', the work might most naturally be associated with authorship, albeit not precisely in the scholastic sense of this term. To press his point home, this exceptionally ambitious writer (whose work receives well-merited notice in this volume in essays by A. S. Lazikani and others) also conforms to the convention of anonymity that often signals deployment of the compilatory mode in vernacular contexts. Had he presented himself as a *translator*, contemporary practice suggests that there would have been significantly more generic pressure to name himself, as well as to cite the theological 'doctours' who wrote his source texts, most of whom (with the exception of the Church fathers) similarly go unnamed. In late medieval England, *translators* — excluded from Bonaventure's typically monolingual account of the modes of writing — often present both themselves and their sources in some detail and with self-conscious, even elaborate care. Likely writing from the safe space of a monastery and directing his words to a religious sister, perhaps at Barking Abbey, it is unlikely that the *Chastising* author is hoping to conceal his identity from his anticipated readers in practice. Although anonymity can have many motives, including spiritual ones, at least one of his

---

[9] Daniel, *Liber uricrisiarum*, ed. by Harvey, Tavormina, and Star, pp. 54–55. Thanks to Sarah Star, one of the editors, for this passage and reference, which appears to anticipate the earliest English instances of 'compiler' cited in the *Oxford English Dictionary* and the *Middle English Dictionary* (*MED*) by almost a decade. For Daniel and the *Liber*, see Jasin, 'The Transmission of Learned Medical Literature'. For Daniel's many apparent neologisms, see Star, 'MS HM 505'.

goals appears to be to situate his work near the middle of a scale of *auctoritas*, diffusing responsibility for the text and the rarified and recent materials it gathers, in accordance with the cautionary verse that serves as his *thema*: '*Uigilate et orate, ut non intretis in temptacionem*: wakeþ and preieþ, þat ȝe entre nat into temptacion' (Mt 26. 41).[10]

Reading these essays, however, I am struck once again by how seldom calibrations of authority of this kind are the point at issue for vernacular compilers such as the *Chastising* author. Certainly, vernacular compilers, like Latin ones, locate authority in the materials they collect, rather than claim direct responsibility for their efforts, going to elaborate efforts to avoid 'addendo [...] de suo', despite what can be their restless tendency to keep the process of adaptation moving that is detailed in Ralph Hanna's essay on the many versions of *The Three Arrows on Doomsday*. But for the most part Bonaventure's elegant formulation — designed for the scholarly setting of the university, where *auctoritas* is a formal term requiring a standard definition — seems to capture the fluid dynamics of the compilations discussed here even more poorly than the figures in a personification allegory, created out of verbs in the same way as the nouns *compilatio* and *compilator*, capture the full range of activities that fall under their purview. Some of these compilations, from *Speculum christiani* in the early fifteenth century to Richard Whitford's *Dyuers Holy Instrucyons and Teachynges* a hundred years later, take great care in the choice of their materials and teachings, anxiously aware of the theological and political pressures surrounding them, as Vincent Gillespie and Brandon Alakas respectively note in their essays on these texts. But *auctoritas* as such is no more the central concern of such works as it is for the composers of *A Talkyng of the Love of God, Pore Caitif, Contemplations of the Dread and Love of God, The Life of Soul*, or *The Desert of Religion*, the subjects of essays by Annie Sutherland, Margaret Connolly, Sarah MacMillan, and Anne Mouron; or for those who excerpted them in ways explored by Diana Denissen and others; or for those who compiled them along with other works into the large mixed compilations discussed by Marleen Cré, Laura Saetveit Miles, Nicole Rice, Michael Sargent, and Sheri

---

[10] *The Chastising of God's Children*, ed. by Bazire and Colledge, pp. 95–96. The work's anonymity is consistent with other major vernacular compilations of the period, such as *Pore Caitif, Fervor amoris*, and *Dives and Pauper*, but sets it apart from many works that claim some measure of *auctoritas*, such as Walter Hilton's *Scale of Perfection*, or from works that represent themselves as translations from a single source, such as many of the works of Osbern Bokenham, John Capgrave, and John Lydgate. On compilation and anonymity, see Dutton, *Julian of Norwich*, especially at p. 13. On the character of late medieval vernacular translation, see Watson, 'Theories of Translation'.

Smith. This is because vernacular compilation, like vernacular translation, is not at root a strategy for negotiating authority at all, deflected or otherwise, but a strategy of mediation.

Compilation mediates between what is available and what is understood to be useful through the activities of selection, arrangement, copying, and dissemination. The activity of selection of course involves discrimination between potential source materials, according to any number of criteria. Here, these include both the nationalist motivations that may have influenced the compiler of the *South English Legendaries* manuscript discussed by Mami Kanno and the devotional impulses that underlie the unique compilation of excerpts from Mechtild of Hackeborn's *Liber specialis gratiae* discussed by Naoë Kukita Yoshikawa and the Holy Name materials collected by Denis Renevey. Authority is centrally at stake in this process in Latin legal compilations, whose materials, duly cited, must be chosen from only the best-authenticated sources if the new collection is to succeed. It can be almost as important for writers of histories and chronicles. But in vernacular religious contexts the authority of specific potential sources is usually a less significant factor in inclusion or exclusion than simply their perceived relevance to the task or tasks in hand — whether these are general or particular, and whether they relate primarily to more or less imagined communities or to specific commissioning individuals. Especially in the majority of anonymous vernacular texts that follow *The Chastising* in leaving the materials they gather unnamed and unattributed, compilation simply *presupposes* the authority of its sources. Indeed, to generalize what is of course a complex situation, anonymous vernacular compilations both require and seek to instil an ethos of trust in the soundness of textuality itself. In some respects, therefore, Bonaventure's discriminations may be exactly inapposite. As the equation of the roles of *compilator* and the *scriptor* in Daniel's *Liber uricrisiarum* suggests, often enough, compilation unsystematically but purposefully confuses the very categories that scholastic literary theory methodically worked to distinguish.

* * *

Frequent scholarly recourse to Bonaventure's *distinctio* on authorship over the past thirty-five years has brought many benefits, including the recognition that *compilatio* is, indeed, a peculiarly medieval mode, one that offers a conceptual bridge between what we have traditionally thought of as the largely distinct activities of authors and scribes. Simply by asking us to consider the literary self-consciousness that inheres in texts and books most of which had previously been assumed resistant to any kind of coherent analysis, the concept of *compi-*

latio has had a powerfully constructive influence on the study of late medieval writing. Yet if we have indeed exaggerated both the explicit influence of the Bonaventuran writerly model on late medieval vernacular textual practice and its explanatory power, as begins to seem likely, it is worth reflecting on what we may perhaps be distorting or merely missing as a result.

Three suggestions seem worth making in this regard. The first again bears on the matter of terminology, but now with an emphasis on how the terminology of *compilation* is used in specifically vernacular contexts. The other two aim to take us further into what I am calling the *ethos* of compilation in the anonymous mode in which it often operates in vernacular and homiletic contexts: that is, its encoded assumptions about the nature of the texts and books from which compilations select materials, their rationale in making such selections, and the relationship they seek to create with readerships. These topics prove to have little directly to do with the emergence of the term *compilatio* itself in its late medieval guise. Rather, they belong to the deep history of compilation as a premodern textual *practice*.

The first suggestion: it is worth considering the possibility that the term's meanings in its French and English forms, however diverse and vague, might be a surer guide to the workings of vernacular compilations than how the terms are defined and used in scholastic Latin. The word *compilatio* seems to have made its first leap from Latin to a vernacular language during Bonaventure's lifetime, in the titles of the five books that constitute the huge Franciscan expansion of *Ancrene Wisse* and other works known simply as the *Compileison*, written between 1255 and 1274: *Compileison de set morteus pecches, Compileison de seinte penance, Compileison de purgatorie, Compileison des dis commandemenz,* and *Compileison de la vie de gent de religion*.[11] Although some of these books have only one or two proximate sources, and although these sources again go largely unspecified, the word's basic function here is to flag the composite nature of the work, as organized collections of relevant materials under separate textual roofs and categorizing heads: the sins, the Commandments, the qualities of true penance, the range of fates enjoyed or endured by souls and bodies in the afterlife. So far, so Bonaventuran. Yet the effect of the word in this vernacular context is already not to delimit the text's authority but to emphasize it, flagging the work's encyclopaedic scope, learning, and awareness of recent trends in scholarship in a writing situation where formal *authorship* is taken to be out of the question. Assuring us that the *Compileison* originates in a clerical

---

[11] For this ambitious work of Anglo-Norman prose, most of which remains unedited, see Watson and Wogan-Browne, 'The French of England'.

milieu with comprehensive access to potential source materials, the word asks us to trust both the authority of the materials selected and the integrity of the process of selection itself so that its readers and hearers may focus on what matters: to receive, learn, deploy, and share the life-giving spiritual instruction the work presents for their edification.

Following Daniel's example, Middle English *compilen* and its colleagues are also often meant to be received as learned in ways that emphasize the authority of the works they name rather than otherwise. This is true whether the context is once again self-consciously scholarly, as in Chaucer's *Treatise on the Astrolabe*, which contains our first recorded instances of English *compilatour*; or determinedly plain-style, as in the anonymous *Pore Caitif*, a 'tretis compilid of a pore caitif', which represents *compilatio* as a way to avoid the 'multiplicacioun of manye bookis', but again silently assures us of the probity of its unnamed sources.[12] The striking thing about the lexis of compilation in Middle English, however, is the sheer range of situations to which it applies. *Compilen* can be used of a scribe or writer gathering texts or information for a treatise, anthology, or encyclopaedia; of a historian collating sources, such as Ranulph Higden who 'compiled and made' the *Polychronicon*, or Virgil, who 'compiled' a book 'in worschip of Enee'; and of assemblies of authoritative legal materials such as those of interest to the writers of the *Rotuli parliamentorum* in the late fourteenth century. But it can also signify other compositional activities, from simple story-telling to the production of a saint's life to prophesying the future. According to Henry Parker's translation of Boccaccio's *De claris mulieribus*, the Erythaen Sibyl was of such 'wytt' that 'what she dydd compyle of ony nacion [...] all hir seyynge provyd allwey true'. While *compilacioun* is often applied to large textual projects, it can also refer to much smaller acts of assemblage, down to the writing of short passages of summary. Again doubling *compilen* with *maken*, and no doubt thinking of the prayer's famous combination of scope and brevity, John Lydgate describes the Pater Noster itself as 'Maad and compiled of our lord Iesu'. Although stylistic factors are clearly in play in several of these examples, the generality of this vernacular usage suggests more than elegant

---

[12] The examples that follow are from the *Middle English Dictionary*, with the exception of *Pore Caitif*, for which see *The Idea of the Vernacular*, ed. by Wogan-Browne, Watson, Taylor, and Evans, item 3.6, 239–40. *MED* gives one clear instance of ME *compilatour* in the sense *plagiarist*, in John Trevisa's translation of Higden's *Polychronicon*, in reference to the classical story that Virgil was called *compilator* for having stolen his poem from Homer. The other instance of the word in this sense that *MED* suggests, from the prologue to *The Treatise on the Astrolabe* ('I ne am but a lewid compilatour of the labour of olde astrologiens') is doubtful, though see Bonaventure's 'pauper et tenuis compilator' cited above.

variation or a striving for aureate language. Rather, the Middle English lexis of compilation reflects the way vernacular writing itself asks to be understood as secondary, reliably mediating bodies of authoritative and useful knowledge that have received their first formulations elsewhere. Vernacular writing is compilatory of its very nature.

My second suggestion: despite the major shift in meaning that *compilatio* undergoes half way through its medieval history, we might do well to keep in mind that compilation as a crucial writerly mode was already many centuries old when the term took on its scholastic role as the descriptor of a distinct set of genres, connected to a newly calibrated understanding of the nature of authorship and authority. The early medieval terminology of compilation tends to the informal, seldom treating it as a separate compositional practice and employing a range of terms when it does.[13] In the prologue to his *Liber scintillarum* (*c.* 700), a work whose very title announces its florilegial character, the monk Defensor represents himself as having collected ('collegi') brilliant *sententiae* with the avidity of a jeweller and his book itself as gathering ('congregans') the witness of many books — all drops from a single fountain of truth — for the convenience of the reader.[14] Although his pride in the breadth of the sources available to him and the skill with which he has arranged them is obvious, it is less so how far Defensor sees himself as engaged in a particular *mode* of composition, rather than participating at a high level in a textual culture in which compilation of earlier authorities was assumed to be the primary means by which writers worked or at least described their workings. Besides the language of sparks and fountains, the *Liber scintillarum* nonetheless gives us two new verbs to describe the activity of compilation, *collegere* and especially *congregare*, to collect or assemble, whose informal sense is neutral or benign (*collegere* also means to harvest, *congregare* to congregate or flock) and versions of which were used in Latin and vernacular contexts throughout the medieval period.

---

[13] For a recent discussion of miscellaneity and the terminological difficulties it creates for scholars of early medieval 'compilations', see Dorofeeva, 'Miscellanies, Christian Reform and Early Medieval Encyclopaedism'.

[14] 'Jussioni et doctrinae obtemperare volens, paginae quasque scrutans, sententiam fulgentem, sicuti inventam quasi margaritam aut gemmam avidius collegi. Quemadmodum guttae multae fontem efficiunt, sic de diversorum voluminibus congregans testimonia, hunc libellum condere tentavi' (wishing to submit to their commandments and teachings and poring over their writings, I the more eagerly gathered together each glittering saying as though I was finding a pearl or a jewel. In the same way as a fountain collects many drops, so this little book attempts to preserve the collected testimonials of many books.) See Defensor, *Liber Scintillarum*, ed. by Migne, cols 597–98. Thanks to Sean Gilsdorf for pointing me towards this prologue.

Possibly imitating Defensor, whose work was so much appreciated that it acquired canonical status of its own, Old English writers thus fairly regularly work outwards from one or other of these two verbs by representing the search for source materials as a process of *gathering*.[15] Returning laden but rejoicing from his latest successful visit to the forest of letters, the indomitably cheerful narrator of the tenth-century Alfredian *Old English Soliloquies* describes how he has 'gaderode' the different woods needed to build the little house that is his book, finding something he needed in every tree he saw ('On ælcum treowo ic geseah hwæthwugu þæs þe ic æt ham beþorfte').[16] Around the turn of the eleventh century, Ælfric more sombrely represents his calendrical *De temporibus anni* as the product of two distinct phases of gathering, as he 'dorste gadrian' materials from Bede that the saint himself 'gaderode of manegra wisra lareowa bocum' long before, situating himself in a lineage of selective borrowing in which the distinction between *auctor* and *compilator* is nowhere in sight and which might in principle extend back to the earliest Christian texts and beyond.[17] The textual sense of *gather* persists into insular French (usually as *assembler*) as it does into Middle English, where it regularly functions as one of several alternatives to *compile*. Introducing his *Abbreviacion of Chronicles*, John Capgrave writes that 'I have [...] be occupied [...] to gader eld exposiciones upon Scripture into o colleccion' — the only instance of *colleccion* in this textual sense offered by the *Middle English Dictionary* — while the writer of *The Mirror of Our Lady* uses 'gadrest' interchangeably with both 'compyled' and 'make' to describe the activities of a scholarly 'worthy clarke' who 'made many bokes out of holy scripture', but was nonetheless punished thereafter in the fires of purgatory for having neglected his liturgical duties.[18]

Although most senses of Latin *colligere*, *congregare*, and their vernacular equivalents have little to do with texts or writing — the terms are too broad to have attracted Bonaventure's eagerly classifying eye — *gathering* is far from a casual activity, requiring the same process of scrupulous selection and discrimina-

---

[15] For the work's popularity in tenth-century England, see *Defensor's Liber scintillarum*, ed. by Rhodes, from BL, MS Royal 7 C IV, which now lacks the folio that once contained Defensor's preface. For a study, see Bremmer, 'The Reception of Defensor's *Liber Scintillarum*'.

[16] *King Alfred's Version of St. Augustine's Soliloquies*, ed. by Hargrove, 2.

[17] Ælfric, *De Temporibus Anni*, ed. and trans. by Blake, chap. 1.1.

[18] Examples from *MED*, s.v. *gaderen* 2.a.2. The underlying Latin verbs across the citations listed here also include *capere*, to seize or pluck, but the influence of *collegere* and *congregare* (perhaps via French *assembler*) is clear from the frequency with which *gaderen* appears with *togidere*, as in the early fifteenth-century translation of Vegetius's *De re militari*: 'ȝe bede me [...] to gedere to-gider and write in book. [...] out of olde auctours [...] þilke þinges þat nedful ben to ben lerned.'

tion as *compiling*. After all, as the *Orrmulum* reminds us (alluding to Mt 3. 12), Christ himself in his predestining wisdom 'gaddresst [Lat. *congregabit*] [...] þe clene corn | All fra þe chaff togeddre', burning the latter with unquenchable fire ('igni inextinguibili').[19] Hence the care with which Ælfric, a dedicated opponent of anything he takes to be religious error, turns to the *gatherer* Bede to steer his own practice as a *gatherer* in a field in which he did not feel himself a specialist. Multipurpose though they are, the continuous histories of *collectio*, *congregatio*, and *gathering*, used in a consistent textual sense, nonetheless remind us that what we now call compilation was an ancient and consciously conservative practice — a practice of conservation by mediating transmission — whose natural bent was to revere *all* source materials except in shocking cases like that of the *compilator* Gottschalk, and which had little sense of the scholastic discriminations that grew up around the word *compilatio* late in the medieval period. These histories also suggest the possibility that the compositional habits and assumptions associated with the compilatory or *gathering* mode were highly durable, capable of surviving even in conditions that seemed to favour a more cautiously systematic and suspicious approach, such as those that pertained in the thirteen decades between Arundel's Constitutions and the Henrician reformation.

The third, more elaborate suggestion, which follows from its predecessors and with which I end: as *compilatio* has come into prominence across the past few decades, there has been a tendency not only to focus welcome attention on highly organized compilations such as *The Chastising of God's Children* and *Pore Caitif*, which refer to themselves with such generic labels as *treatise*, but also to look for controlling intelligence, formal or thematic cogency, or nameable agenda in less visibly organized texts and books. In Anglophone scholarship, this tendency has by now indeed acquired the status of a critical tradition, which grew up in opposition to earlier work that emphasized the miscellaneous character of medieval books and consciously traces its lineage back to Stephen G. Nichols and Siegfried Wenzel's *The Whole Book*, published in 1996. Examples from the past fifteen years include Andrew Taylor's *Textual Situations*, Marleen Cré's *Vernacular Mysticism in the Charterhouse*, Jessica Brantley's *Reading in the Wilderness*, Fiona Somerset's *Feeling Like Saints*, and Amy Appleford's *Learning to Die in London*.[20] All these fine monographs are

---

[19] *MED*, s.v. *gaderen* 2a.1.

[20] Nichols and Wenzel, *The Whole Book*; Taylor, *Textual Situations*; Cré, *Vernacular Mysticism in the Charterhouse*; Brantley, *Reading in the Wilderness*; Somerset, *Feeling Like Saints*; Appleford, *Learning to Die in London*. Also related is Bahr, *Fragments and Assemblages*. For a restatement of the position against which many of these books are in reaction — that late

studies of books, not texts. While of course they differ in crucial ways, all are also joined either in finding thematic coherence in books that have previously been treated as miscellanies or in using the seeming heterogeneity of these books to rethink the character of late medieval religious culture or the relationship between books and the institutions that produced them. In the interests of making late medieval vernacular textual culture lucid, all, that is, take the form, content, and thematic emphases of the books they consider as signs, at one level or another, of what scholastic literary theory called *intentio* and Middle English writers *entente*.

Although in theory I agree with critics of this scholarly tradition that it is *always* possible to find coherence of purpose if one looks out for it, however heterogeneous the material to hand, in practice it seems to me that we have no option but to pattern spot as these scholars of the 'whole book' have been doing, while taking due account of the difficulties involved, including the danger that the patterns spotted are discernible only from the perspective of the modern beholder. Indeed, I believe that thematic or formal patterns, even those that demand sustained attention to detail to recover, can constitute compelling evidence of design and sometimes intention. Compilation offers a special challenge to the pattern spotter, in that the coherence of a compiled text or book may depend on factors and purposes it does not express directly, but has to be reconstructed via a mode of contextual study in which the apparent randomness of a book's contents is understood as evidence of the variety of purposes it was designed to serve for its first readers. But the difficulties involved in this apparently circular process can be well worth it and the results convincing, indeed revelatory, especially in studies that take a range of mutually reinforcing approaches to the problem, rather than build a single, perilously pyramidal hypothesis on the evidence. A brilliant relatively recent case in point is Ralph Hanna's *London Literature, 1300–1380*, which recreates an entire vernacular textual culture of which we previously knew little in very much this way.[21] What is more, scholars of vernacular textuality, which often circulated at some distance from the major religious and secular institutions from which most of our records derive, have no choice but to work like this if they are to make progress. Most of our evidence survives within the books and texts themselves.

---

medieval manuscript compilations are too randomized to be read as integrated wholes — see Pearsall, 'The Whole Book'. For an example of the more cautious approach to the 'manuscript matrix' of the kind Pearsall advocates, see Boffey and Thompson, 'Anthologies and Miscellanies'.

[21] Hanna, *London Literature*.

Nonetheless, to come at last to my suggestion, there is also a sense in which those of us who study late medieval vernacular religious compilations have reason to *resist* the hermeneutic pressure to seek unity of theme, design, or purpose exerted by our training. Or at least, to put the same point the opposite way, we have reason to register a countervailing pressure towards the multiplicity of materials and methods of assembling them expressed by the practice of compilation from the early medieval centuries on. This is because the study of late medieval religion even now remains strongly influenced by the narrative about the period we inherit from the sixteenth century, in which the coming Reformation looms so large that the vernacular textual culture of the period appears to us already prospectively divided into opposing groups or attitudes. Much of the most celebrated scholarship on late medieval religion has approached it in this way. Indeed the search for the 'causes of the Reformation' has been almost as ubiquitous a topic in Church history as the 'quest for the historical Jesus' once was among biblical scholars.[22] To make things worse, there are at least reasonably good historical reasons for this. After all, the story Reformation historians told about the late Middle Ages was itself rooted in late medieval polemic and the fierce arguments and oppositions that underlay it, with the nonce-word *Lollard* doing especially important political and ideological work, albeit of a varied and sometimes inchoate kind, in writings from the 1380s onwards.

Scholars of Middle English religious writing have responded to this predicament in various ways across the years. Most recently, they have done so by worrying the terminology, so that *heretics* or *Wycliffites* are recast as small-l *lollards*, and the *orthodox* become *traditionalists*, *conservatives*, *mainstream*, and so on.[23] Yet to use any paired set of terms to characterize the religious attitudes and ideas typical of the period is ultimately to return ourselves to the historiographic status quo, reading Middle English religious writing through the eyes either of the post-Reformation future or of the small groups of medieval clerics, scholars, and bishops from whom this terminology derives. Even the useful emphasis on the common ground or *grey area* between the proponents of *radical reform* and *orthodox reform* found in a good deal of this scholarship does

---

[22] Among many examples, see Hamm, *The Reformation of Faith*, which works within an especially well-defined tradition of German 'causes of the Reformation' scholarship. For an overview of Reformation historiography, see Koslofsky, 'Explaining Change'.

[23] Small-l *lollard* is Fiona Somerset's coinage, used for a remarkably expansive range of texts, and is adopted in Nicole Rice's essay in this volume. On the changing and historically specific uses of the term *Lollard* across the period, see Cole, *Literature and Heresy in the Age of Chaucer*.

less to interrupt this tendency than it first appears.[24] Even as it seeks to provide us with a measure of analytic wiggle room, the term *grey area* indeed admits as much by imagining the texts, themes, and books it delineates as a mingling of black with white, heretical with orthodox, as though the final differences between these positions were already relatively clear on all sides during the late fourteenth and fifteenth centuries themselves: a possible conclusion about the period that the term illegitimately presses into service as a premise.

Scholars of heresy sometimes argue that, for those who work on the history or literature produced during periods of strong religious difference and tension, there is no way around this sort of difficulty over nomenclature — that however we seek to build away from the orthodox/heresy opposition and its more recent avatars, and whatever attitudes we take towards it, we are effectively stuck with versions of the ecclesiastical language used in our sources.[25] My own view has come to be that this terminological fatalism condemns us to the restatement of old positions in new guises, eventually making advances in the study of late medieval religious thought and writing impossible. Indeed, I believe the time may come for an all-out assault on our own, by now perhaps somewhat tired, use of the terminology of orthodoxy and heresy and their more recent substitutes, except in discussing a limited number of specific situations in which issues of doctrine and ecclesiology are in direct question. As things stand, our accounts both of the religious positions taken by late medieval vernacular texts and their readers and of their interaction may already run the risk of merely restating old arguments, rather than investigating the ideologically mixed religious landscape from which they emerged and which they continue to obscure from our view.[26]

And it is here, perhaps, that the obscure, proliferating, trustingly anonymous, obstinately heterogeneous, textually and often doctrinally fluid phenomenon that is the late medieval vernacular compilation can be of use to us. After all, many religious compilations are not only irreducibly plural in themselves; as much recent work on Middle English compilations has shown — and as a number of essays in this volume show once again — they collate materials that are themselves irreducibly plural, mixing instruction and devo-

---

[24] See, e.g., Havens, 'Shading the Grey Area'. Hudson popularized the term in ch. 9 of *The Premature Reformation*. *Orthodox reform* is Vincent Gillespie's preferred term for texts and books that acknowledge the moral critiques of the contemporary Church identified with Wyclif and his associates but repudiate their ecclesiology and theology. See his 'Chichele's Church'. See also Gillespie's essay in this volume.

[25] See, e.g., Swanson, 'Literacy, Heresy, History, and Orthodoxy'.

[26] I develop this line of argument in detail in Chapter 8 of the second volume of my *Balaam's Ass: Vernacular Theology before the English Reformation*.

tion, materials meant for audiences of different levels of religious literacy, and apparently inconsistent theological or ecclesiastical attitudes, all in ways that have so far proved resistant to detailed parsing. This is perhaps most clearly true of the important group of late fourteenth- and fifteenth-century 'miscellaneous manuals' aimed at literate lay owners first isolated by Robert R. Raymo in his superb chapter on 'Works of Religious and Philosophical Instruction' in *The Manual of Writings in Middle English*. Much discussed in recent years, whether as 'devotional compilations', 'pastoral manuals', or 'household books', these books were the product of a new development in late medieval religious culture, the devolution of spiritual responsibility to male heads of households, who had always been asked to think of themselves as moral guardians of their subordinates but now took on more extensive roles in the spiritual direction of their families, subjects, and even tenants. Resolutely miscellaneous, mixing demanding lay-oriented texts written from different perspectives during the late fourteenth-century Wycliffite crisis such as *Pore Caitif* or *Memoriale credencium* with a strikingly varied range of texts aimed at basic religious instruction, this group of books — the most famous of which among specialists is London, Westminster School, MS 3 — have increasingly been pressed into the service of fascinatingly different views of the period.[27]

Does the inclusion in many of these books of materials apparently connected to Wyclif's Oxford make them *Lollard* or *lollard*: the products of a devotional culture consciously in reaction to the *mainstream*, and in some way related to the groups persecuted as *Lollardi* by English bishops? Or, to put the opposite possibility, does their habit of working outwards from the topics listed in Pecham's Syllabus of 1281, whose centrality to Christian instruction was reaffirmed in Arundel's Constitutions of 1409, conversely render them expressions of *conservative orthodoxy* or *orthodox reform*? Are these books, to follow up with a compromise position, perhaps examples of the late medieval theological *grey area* between those seemingly irrepressible categories, *orthodoxy* and *heresy*? Or are they rather, to restate this latest possibility in a different way, instantiations of the 'cosmopolitan' nature of fifteenth-century English religious culture, its Broad Church interest in bringing different religious perspectives between the covers of one book, or under the roof of one household?[28]

---

[27] Raymo, 'Works of Religious and Philosophical Instruction', p. 2273. For the social and religious role played by these books, see Appleford, *Learning to Die in London*, especially ch. 1. For a recent discussion, see Perry, 'An Introduction to Devotional Anthologies'. For the Westminster manuscript, see Hanna, 'The Origins and Production of Westminster School MS 3'. My thoughts here are especially indebted to Kelly and Perry, 'Devotional Cosmopolitanism'.

[28] The first, third, and fourth of these readings of the 'miscellaneous manuals' are related

I have listed these questions on an ascending scale of agreement, from 'provisionally, no' to 'probably, yes', according to my present reading of the late medieval English religious scene on the one hand, the extent of their dependence on versions of the *orthodox/heretic* dichotomy on the other. What matters most, here, however, is that there are grounds for assent and dissent in all four cases, because of the striking combination of consistency of format and inconsistency of content that characterizes these lay-oriented vernacular books, as it does other types of compilation.

Once they have been fully investigated, these compilations may turn out to run the gamut of positions on a number of contemporary theological issues, including some that in certain contexts had become ecclesiastical litmus tests of Catholic orthodoxy — whether or not any individual book or group of books prove to take a recognizably coherent stance across a range of such issues in ways that suggest the construction of a systematic religious position, framed in opposition to others. On a collective level, however, it is almost as if the variety-within-uniformity of these books, each of which appears to take its own decisions about how to work through a repeating series of devotional, instructional, theological, paraliturgical, and occasionally controversial topics, were rather an attempt to *limit* such disagreement, in response to the serious long-term problems of maintaining Christian community among the privileged lay devout created by the theological crises of the period.

Perhaps we may use these books, in their heterogeneity and evident reluctance to distinguish themselves from one another along party lines, as a guide to our own thinking about late medieval vernacular religious culture. Perhaps the fluid processes by which such books come into being, the degree of *mouvance* they exhibit, and their *heterarchic* tendency towards ordered miscellany and miscellaneous order, might render these anonymous compilations invaluable allies in what will no doubt continue to be our struggle to break fully free of confessional historiography. Perhaps, then, the ancient, unostentatious, and largely untheorized genre that had only relatively recently come to be called *compilation* will thus ultimately prove to have been among the most revealing, significant, and characteristic religious genres of the final medieval century.

to positions advanced by Somerset, Havens (among others), and Kelly and Perry respectively. I have not seen the second reading advanced directly, although it might be taken as implicit in the account of the supposed conservatism of fifteenth-century religious culture laid out in Watson, 'Censorship and Cultural Change in Late-Medieval England'. For many further reflections, see Chapter 13 of Volume II of Balaam's Ass.

Works Cited

Manuscripts

London, British Library [BL], MS Royal 7 C IV
London, Westminster School, MS 3

Primary Sources

Ælfric, *De Temporibus Anni*, ed. and trans. by Martin Blake, Anglo-Saxon Texts, 6 (Cambridge: D. S. Brewer, 2009)
Bonaventura, *Commentaria in quattuor libros Sententiarum Magistri Petri Lombardi*, 2 vols, ed. by P. P. Collegii a S. Bonaventura (Roma: Ad Claras Aquas, 1885)
The Chastising of God's Children and the Treatise of Perfection of the Sons of God, ed. by Joyce Bazire and Eric Colledge (Oxford: Basil Blackwell, 1957)
Cicero, *Letters to Friends*, ed. by D. R. Shackleton Bailey, Loeb Classical Library, 216, 3 vols (Cambridge, MA: Harvard University Press, 1988)
Corpus Iuris Canonici, Pars Secunda: Decretalium Collectiones Decretales Gregorii, ed. by Emil Ludwig Richter and Emil Friedberg (Leipzig, 1881)
Daniel, Henry, *Liber Uricrisiarum: A Reading Edition*, ed. by E. Ruth Harvey, M. Teresa Tavormina, and Sarah Star (Toronto: University of Toronto Press, forthcoming)
Defensor, *Liber Scintillarum*, in *Patrologia Latina*, ed. by Jean-Paul Migne, 221 vols (Paris: Garnier, 1844–65), LXXXVIII, cols 597–98
Defensor's Liber scintillarum, with an Interlinear Anglo-Saxon Version, ed. by E. W. Rhodes, Early English Text Society, o.s., 93 (London: Trübner, 1889)
Hincmar of Rheims, *De praedestinatione contra Godeschalcum*, in *Patrologia Latina*, ed. by Jean-Paul Migne, 221 vols (Paris: Garnier, 1844–65), CXXV, cols 55–474
The Idea of the Vernacular: An Anthology of Middle English Literary Theory, 1280–1520, ed. by Jocelyn Wogan-Browne, Nicholas Watson, Andrew Taylor, and Ruth Evans, Exeter Medieval Texts and Studies (University Park: Pennsylvania State University Press; Exeter: Exeter University Press, 1999)
Jerome, *Commentarii in prophetas minores*, ed. by M. Adriaen, Corpus Christianorum Series Latina, 76–76A (Turnhout: Brepols, 1969–70)
John of Morigny, *Liber florum celestis doctrine / The Flowers of Heavenly Teaching*, ed. by Claire Fanger and Nicholas Watson, Studies and Texts, 199 (Toronto: Pontifical Institute of Mediaeval Studies, 2015)
King Alfred's Version of St. Augustine's Soliloquies, ed. by Henry Lee Hargrove, Yale Studies in English, 13 (New York: Henry Holt, 1908)
Niermeyer, J. F., *Mediae Latinitatis Lexicon Minus* (Brill: Leiden, 1997)

Secondary Works

Appleford, Amy, *Learning to Die in London, 1380–1540* (Philadelphia: University of Pennsylvania Press, 2014)

Bahr, Arthur, *Fragments and Assemblages: Forming Compilations of Medieval London* (Chicago: University of Chicago Press, 2013)

Boffey, Julia, and J. J. Thompson, 'Anthologies and Miscellanies: Production and Choice of Texts', in *Book Production and Publishing in Britain, 1375–1475*, ed. by Jeremy Griffiths and Derek Pearsall, Cambridge Studies in Publishing and Printing History (Cambridge: Cambridge University Press, 1989)

Brantley, Jessica, *Reading in the Wilderness: Private Devotion and Public Performance in Late Medieval England* (Chicago: University of Chicago Press, 2007)

Bremmer, Rolf H., Jr, 'The Reception of Defensor's *Liber Scintillarum* in Anglo-Saxon England', in *… un tuo serto di fiori in man decando: Scritti in onore di Maria Amalia D'Aronco*, ed. by Patrizia Lendinara (Udine: Udine University Press, 2008), pp. 75–89

Cole, Andrew, *Literature and Heresy in the Age of Chaucer*, Cambridge Studies in Medieval Literature, 71 (Cambridge: Cambridge University Press, 2008)

Cré, Marleen, *Vernacular Mysticism in the Charterhouse: A Study of London, British Library, MS Additional 37790*, The Medieval Translator/Traduire au Moyen Age, 9 (Turnhout: Brepols, 2006)

Dorofeeva, Anna, 'Miscellanies, Christian Reform and Early Medieval Encyclopaedism: A Reconsideration of the Pre-bestiary Latin *Physiologus* Manuscripts', *Historical Research*, 90 (2017), 1–16

Dutton, Elisabeth, *Julian of Norwich: The Influence of Late-Medieval Devotional Compilations* (Cambridge: D. S. Brewer, 2008)

Gillespie, Vincent, 'Chichele's Church: Vernacular Theology in England after Thomas Arundel', in *After Arundel: Religious Writing in Fifteenth-Century England*, ed. by Vincent Gillespie and Kantik Ghosh, Medieval Church Studies, 21 (Turnhout: Brepols, 2011), pp. 3–42

Hamm, Berndt, *The Reformation of Faith in the Context of Late Medieval Theology and Piety* (Leiden: Brill, 2004)

Hanna, Ralph, *London Literature, 1300–1380*, Cambridge Studies in Medieval Literature, 57 (Cambridge: Cambridge University Press, 2005)

—— , 'The Origins and Production of Westminster School MS 3', in *Pursuing History: Middle English Manuscripts and Their Texts* (Stanford: Stanford University Press, 1996), pp. 33–47

Havens, Jill C., 'Shading the Grey Area: Determining Heresy in Middle English Texts', in *Text and Controversy from Wyclif to Bale: Essays in Honour of Anne Hudson*, ed. by Helen Barr and Ann M. Hutchison, Medieval Church Studies, 4 (Turnhout: Brepols, 2005), pp. 337–52

Hudson, Anne, *The Premature Reformation: Wycliffite Texts and Lollard History* (Oxford: Clarendon Press, 1988)

Jasin, Joanne, 'The Transmission of Learned Medical Literature in the Middle English *Liber Uricrisiarum*', *Medical History*, 37 (1993), 313–29

Kelly, Stephen, and Ryan Perry, 'Devotional Cosmopolitanism in Fifteenth-Century England', in *After Arundel: Religious Writing in Fifteenth-Century England*, ed. by Vincent Gillespie and Kantik Ghosh, Medieval Church Studies, 21 (Turnhout: Brepols, 2011), pp. 363–80

Koslofsky, Craig, 'Explaining Change', in *The Oxford Handbook of the Protestant Reformations*, ed. by Ulinka Rublack (Oxford: Oxford University Press, 2017), pp. 586–600

Kuttner, Stephen, 'Raymond of Penafort as Editor: The *Decretales* and *Constitutiones* of Gregory IX', *Bulletin of Medieval Canon Law*, 12 (1982), 65–80

Minnis, A. J., *Medieval Theory of Authorship: Scholastic Literary Attitudes in the Later Middle Ages* (1984; repr. Philadelphia: University of Pennsylvania Press, 2012)

Nichols, Stephen G., and Siegfried Wenzel, eds, *The Whole Book: Cultural Perspectives on the Medieval Miscellany* (Ann Arbor: University of Michigan Press, 1996)

Parkes, Malcolm, 'The Influence of the Concepts of *Ordinatio* and *Compilatio* on the Development of the Book', in *Medieval Learning and Literature: Essays Presented to Richard William Hunt*, ed. by J. J. G. Alexander and M. T. Gibson (Oxford: Clarendon Press, 1976), pp. 115–41

Pearsall, Derek, 'The Whole Book: Late Medieval English Manuscript Miscellanies and their Modern Interpreters', in *Imagining the Book*, ed. by Stephen Kelly and John J. Thompson, Medieval Texts and Cultures of Northern Europe, 7 (Turnhout: Brepols, 2005), pp. 17–29

Perry, Ryan, 'An Introduction to Devotional Anthologies: One-Volume "Collections" and their Contexts', *Queeste: Journal of Medieval Literature in the Low Countries*, 20.2 (2013), 119–33

Raymo, Robert R., 'Works of Religious and Philosophical Instruction', in *The Manual of Writings in Middle English*, vol. VII, ed. Albert E. Hartung (New Haven: Connecticut Academy of Arts and Sciences, 1986), pp. 2255–2378 and pp. 2467–2582

Rouse, Richard H., and Mary A. Rouse, '*Ordinatio* and *Compilatio* Revisited', in *Ad litteram: Authoritative Texts and their Medieval Readers*, ed. by Mark D. Jordan and Kent Emery (Notre Dame: University of Notre Dame Press, 1992), pp. 113–34

Somerset, Fiona, *Feeling Like Saints: Lollard Writing after Wyclif* (Ithaca: Cornell University Press, 2014)

Star, Sarah, 'MS HM 505: Henry Daniel, Medieval English Medicine and Linguistic Innovation', *Huntington Library Quarterly*, 81 (2018), 63–105

Steer, Georg, *Hugo Ripelin von Strassburg: zur Rezeptions, und Wirkungsgeschichte des Compendium theologicae veritatis im deutschen Spätmittelalter* (Tübingen: Max Niemeyer, 1981)

Swanson, R. N., 'Literacy, Heresy, History, and Orthodoxy: Perspectives and Permutations for the Later Middle Ages', in *Heresy and Literacy, 1000–1530*, ed. by Peter Biller and Anne Hudson, Cambridge Studies in English Literature, 23 (Cambridge: Cambridge University Press, 1994), pp. 279–93

Taylor, Andrew, *Textual Situations: Three Medieval Manuscripts and their Readers* (Philadelphia: University of Pennsylvania Press, 2002)

Watson, Nicholas, *Balaam's Ass: Vernacular Theology before the English Reformation, Volume II* (Philadelphia: University of Pennsylvania Press, forthcoming)

——, 'Censorship and Cultural Change in Late-Medieval England: Vernacular Theology, the Oxford Translation Debate, and Arundel's Constitutions of 1409', *Speculum*, 70 (1995), 822–64

——, 'Theories of Translation', in *The Oxford History of Literary Translation in English*, vol. I: *To 1550*, ed. by Roger Ellis (Oxford: Oxford University Press, 2008), pp. 71–92

Watson, Nicholas, and Jocelyn Wogan-Browne, 'The French of England: The *Compileison*, *Ancrene Wisse*, and the Idea of Anglo-Norman', in *Cultural Traffic in the Medieval Romance World*, ed. by Simon Gaunt and Julian Weiss, special issue, *Journal of Romance Studies*, 4.3 (2004), 35–58

Online Publications

Middle English Dictionary, ed. by Robert E. Lewis and others (Ann Arbor: University of Michigan Press, 1952–2001); online edition in *Middle English Compendium*, ed. by Frances McSparran and others (Ann Arbor: University of Michigan Library, 2000–18), <http://quod.lib.umich.edu/m/middle-english-dictionary>

Index of Manuscripts

Brussels, Bibliothèque Royale, MS 2544–45: 333

Cambridge, Corpus Christi College, MS 145: 217
——, MS R.5: 330, 332
Cambridge, St John's College, MS G. 28: 135
Cambridge, Trinity College, MS 605 (R.3.25): 218–19
——, MS B.15.42 (MS B. 15.42): 18, 19, 364–65, 367–68, 372–73, 375–76, 378–81
Cambridge, Trinity Hall, MS 16: 40, 45
Cambridge, Cambridge University Library, MS Dd.5.55: 328
——, MS Dd.14.26: 45
——, MS Ee.4.30: 326
——, MS Ff.5.40: 327–28
——, MS Hh.1.12: 138, 146
——, MS Ii.6.2: 134, 143
——, MS Ii.6.40: 12, 138, 193–209

Dublin, Trinity College, MS A.5.7: 331
——, MS C.5.20: 331
——, MS 155: 295
Durham, University Library, MS Additional: 754 146

Glasgow, University Library, MS Hunter 520: 7, 10, 69–70, 74, 136, 138, 144–46, 148

Lincoln, Lincoln Cathedral, MS 91 (Thornton Manuscript): 3
London, British Library, MS Additional 11748: 329, 332
——, MS Additional 22283 (Simeon Manuscript): 85, 109
——, MS Additional 30897: 13–14, 231–52
——, MS Additional 37049: 17, 19, 331, 368–69, 386, 388, 398
——, MS Additional 37787: 14, 255–56, 260, 265, 267
——, MS Additional 37790: 11, 17, 331
——, MS Arundel 286: 12, 175, 181, 184–89
——, MS Cotton Faustina B VI: 19, 386, 388
——, MS Cotton Julius D IX: 217–18
——, MS Cotton Nero A XIV: 109
——, MS Cotton Titus D XVIII: 109
——, MS Egerton 1821: 368–69
——, MS Egerton 1993: 218–19
——, MS Egerton 2006: 342
——, MS Harley 494: 17–18, 343–57
——, MS Harley 1022: 295, 328
——, MS Harley 1076: 138, 146
——, MS Harley 2218: 295
——, MS Harley 2277: 217
——, MS Harley 2322: 9, 132–34, 145
——, MS Harley 2336: 135
——, MS Harley 2397: 325–26
——, MS Harley 6580: 37

———, MS Landsdowne 344: 37
———, MS Royal 5 A VI: 41
———, MS Stowe 38: 295
———, MS Stowe 39: 19, 386, 388
London, Inner Temple, MS Petyt 524: 325–26
London, Lambeth Palace Library, MS 460: 40
———, MS 472: 325–26
———, MS 487: 109
———, MS 541: 135
———, MS 3597 (The Coughton Court MS): 78
London, Westminster Cathedral Treasury, MS 4: 17, 330
———, MS 3: 136, 451

Manchester, John Rylands Library, MS English: 85 138
———, MS Latin 341: 40, 45

New Haven, Yale University, Beinecke Library, MS Takamiya 3: 326
———, MS Takamiya 96: 43, 45
———, MS Takamiya: 110 146
New York, Columbia University Library, MS Plimpton 257: 327, 329, 332
———, MS Plimpton 271: 327, 329

Oxford, Balliol College, MS 239: 45
Oxford, Bodleian Library, MS Ashmole 43: 217, 219
———, MS Ashmole 1286: 138–40, 142–43, 146, 148
———, MS Bodley 197: 199
———, MS Bodley 220: 342
———, MS Bodley 423: 10–11, 138, 143, 146, 157, 161–64, 168, 199
———, MS Bodley 505: 423
———, MS Bodley 578: 373
———, MS Bodley 592: 325–26
———, MS Bodley 779: 13, 215–27
———, MS Bodley 806: 64, 66
———, MS Bodley 861: 369
———, MS Bodley 938: 10–11, 164–68
———, MS Don. e. 247: 295
———, MS Douce 322: 73, 138, 146
———, MS Eng. Poet. A. 1 (Vernon manuscript): 85, 109–10, 218
———, MS Laud misc. 111: 415
———, MS Laud misc. 108: 217, 221
———, MS Laud misc. 210: 89, 172, 174–75, 186–88
———, MS Rawlinson C. 285: 327–29, 332
———, MS Rawlinson C. 299: 133
———, MS Rawlinson C. 894: 145
———, MS Tanner 336: 7, 70, 74
Oxford, Corpus Christi College, MS 132: 42
Oxford, Jesus College, MS 39: 299
Oxford, University College, MS 28: 328

Philadelphia, University of Pennsylvania Library, codex 218: 329, 332

San Marino, Huntington Library, MS HM 148: 3
———, MS HM 502: 174–75
Shrewsbury School, MS 3: 73

Warminster, Longleat House, Marquess of Bath MS 29: 369

General Index

Act of Six Articles (1539): 285
Adam of Dryburgh (Adam Scotus): 387
A Debate for the Soul: 388
'A deuout meditacioun of Richard Hampole': 12, 195–98, 205–07, 209
Ælfric: 447
  De temporibus anni: 446
Aelred of Rievaulx: 324
  De institutione inclusarum: 226
  Speculum caritatis: 419
Æthelthryth of Ely (Saint): 215, 218–19, 222–24, 226–27
Æthelwold (Saint): 226
Agnes (Saint): 223
Ailgive: 225
Alan of Lille: 32
Aldhelm (Saint): 222
Alin Kyes: 143–44
Alphege (Saint): 222
Alphonse of Pecha
  Epistola solitarii: 297
Amesbury Priory: 344
Anastasia (Saint): 223
Ancrene Wisse: 225–26, 314, 318, 386, 415–16, 418, 421, 423, 443
An Information of the Contemplative Life and Active: 194, 198–99, 201–03, 209
Anselm, Archbishop of Canterbury: 16, 109, 110–11, 122, 123–26, 127, 291, 293, 295–97, 310
  Cur Deus homo: 322

Liber meditationum et orationum: 109, 123–26
  Meditatio ad concitandum timorem: 292
Aquinas, Thomas: 182
Arnold of Bonneval: 425
Arundel, Thomas, Archbishop of Canterbury: 36, 38, 47, 87, 242, 342, 350, 447, 451
A Talkyng of the Love of God: 1, 8–9, 18, 109–28, 441
Athanasius
  Life of St Anthony: 399
A Treatise of Ghostly Battle: 7, 73–75, 78, 145
A Treatise of Perfect Love: 194
A Treatise of Tribulation: 194, 197
'A tretise of Pater Noster': 12, 194, 196, 198, 202, 204–05, 207, 209
Augustine: 75, 389, 425
  De doctrina christiana: 101
Austin (Saint): 222
A Worcestershire Miscellany: 255, 262
A Worke of Dyuers Impediments and Lettes of Perfection: 272
Axholme (Carthusian house): 46
Ayenbite of Inwit: 314

Barking Abbey: 440
Bartholomeus
  De proprietatibus rerum: 314
Barton, Elizabeth: 273
Basset, Thomas: 297

Beaufort, Margaret: 147, 327, 333
Beauvale (Carthusian house): 46
Becket, Thomas (Saint): 216, 218, 222–23
Bede: 446–47
Bedyll, Thomas: 277
Bernard of Clairvaux: 16, 240–41, 251, 291, 297, 310, 373
    De gradibus humilitatis et superbiae: 389
    Sententiae: 391
Beuno: 226
Bevis of Hamtoun: 78
Birgitta (or Bridget) of Sweden: 30, 31, 50, 51, 158, 373, 377, 381
    Revelationes: 12, 158, 199–200, 373, 377
    Sermo angelicus: 373, 377
Birinus (Saint): 218
Bishop's Palace, Chichester Cathedral: 424
Boccaccio
    Decameron: 348
    De claris mulieribus: 444
Boke of Pacience: 272, 274, 276, 279, 281, 283
Boleyn, Anne: 282
Book for a Simple and Devout Woman: 203–04
Book to a Mother: 1, 14, 174, 231–34, 240, 246, 247, 249–51
Bonaventure: 87, 310, 312, 437–43, 446
    Breviloquium: 92
    Commentary on the Gospel of Saint Luke: 420
Bordesley, St. Mary's Abbey: 14, 255
Botulf (Saint): 218
Bowet, Henry, Archbishop of York: 5, 28, 31, 33, 35, 38
Brendan (Saint): 222
Bridget of Kildare (Saint): 219
Bulkely, Anne: 17, 344–46, 349, 351–52, 356
Bury St Edmunds (Benedictine house): 424
Byng, Thomas: 149

Capgrave, John
    Abbreviacion of Chronicles: 446
Carpenter, Alexander: 72
    Destructorium viciorum: 7, 64
Cassian, John: 174
Caston, William: 365
Caxton, William: 219

Catherine of Siena (Saint): 30, 31, 342–43
    Dialogue: 390
Cecilia (Saint): 87, 223, 244
Chaucer, Geoffrey: 48, 439
    Canterbury Tales: 63, 84, 103, 105
    'Parson's Tale': 49, 391
    'Retraction': 318
    Treatise on the Astrolabe: 444
    Troilus and Criseyde: 314
Chelles Monastery: 226
Chichele, Henry, Archbishop of Canterbury: 36, 47, 342
Christina (Saint): 223
Chrysostom, John: 272
Cibus anime: 6, 30, 39–48, 50, 52, 90
Clairvaux (Cistercian house): 403
Cloos, Richard: 136
Cobham, Henry: 10, 136
Commentary on the *Ave Maria*: 14
Compileison de la vie de gent de religion: 386, 443
Compileison de purgatorie: 443
Compileison de seinte penance: 443
Compileison des dis commandemenz: 443
Compileison de set morteus pecches: 443
Contemplations of the Dread and Love of God (Fervor amoris): 3, 9, 10–12, 18–19, 85, 137–41, 143–50, 157–68, 194–96, 198–203, 209, 330, 364, 366, 372, 377–78, 381, 441
Council of Basel: 35
Council of Constance: 35
Council of Pavia-Siena: 35
Council of Pisa: 35
Council of Lateran (Fourth): 389
Cromwell, Thomas: 15, 277, 284
Cuthbert (Saint): 218
Cuttynge, Robert: 143
Cyprian: 389

Daniel, Henry: 444
    Liber uricrisiarum: 439–40, 442
Dartford (Dominican house): 343
De duodecim abusionibus saeculi: 389
Defence of Women: 13
Defensor: 446
    Liber scintillarum: 445
De Lisle Psalter: 395
Disce mori: 1, 3, 4, 9, 16, 131, 292, 295, 298, 300, 301–04, 388

GENERAL INDEX

Doctrinae Iesuiticae praecipua capita: 149
Dodesham, Stephen: 11, 161
Dulcis Iesu memoria: 291
Dunstan (Saint): 216, 222

Eborall, Thomas: 135
Edburga of Winchester (Saint): 215, 218–19, 222–27
Edmund of Abingdon (Edmund Rich): 1, 12, 195, 301, 303
  Speculum ecclesie: 1, 12, 178, 195, 198, 205–07, 209, 301
  Speculum religiosorum (earlier version of the *Speculim ecclesie*): 205–06
Edward the Martyr (Saint): 218, 222–23
Edward IV: 132, 147
Egwine (Saint): 218
Eight Points on Charity: 163
Elizabeth I: 132
Elizabeth of Hungary: 373
Elisabeth of Schönau: 341

Fasciculus morum: 266
Fisher, John: 273
Foxe, John: 137
  Acts and Monuments: 242
Friar Laurent
  Somme le Roi: 72
Frideswide of Oxford (Saint): 215, 219, 222–23, 225–26

Gamalin, John: 135
Gallicanus, Eusebius: 65, 66
Gardener, Jon
  The Feate of Gardeninge: 401
Gaytryge, Dan: 397
Gertrude the Great: 341
Gilte Legende: 218, 219
Gottschalk: 437, 447
Gower, John
  Confessio amantis: 84
Graunge, John: 135
Gregory the Great
  Homilies on Ezechiel: 66–67
  Moralia: 418
Gregory IX: 439
Grosseteste, Robert: 48–49
  Templum Dei (*Templum Domini*): 49

Guthlac (Saint): 225
Guy of Warwick: 78

Hackney Church (Middlesex): 149
Harwood, William: 220
Helena (Saint): 219
Helfta (Benedictine/Cistercian convent): 341, 350, 352, 356
Henry VIII: 132, 147
Higden, Ranulph
  Polychronicon: 444
Hildegard of Bingen: 30, 341
Hilton, Walter: 1, 16, 17, 114, 309–33
  Angels' Song: 316, 321, 326–28
  Eight Chapters of Perfection: 326
  Scale of Perfection: 16–17, 19, 42, 147, 300, 302, 309–33
  On Mixed Life: 315, 321, 324
Hincmar of Rheims: 437
Hoccleve, Thomas: 52, 171
Horde, Edmund: 331
Horwood, Elizabeth: 326
Hugh of Balma
  Mystica theologia: 331
Hugh of Folieto
  De claustro animae: 389
Hugh of Ripelin of Strasbourg
  Compendium theologicae veritatis: 439
Hull, Eleanor: 298

Jan van Ruusbroec: 421
  Spiritual Espousals: 297, 351, 421
Jerome: 373, 437
John of Howden: 291
Julian Notary: 333
Julian of Norwich: 1, 31, 101, 103, 171, 208, 331, 415
  Short Text (*A Vision Showed to a Devout Woman*): 31
  Long Text (*A Revelation of Love*): 331

Katherine (Saint): 223

Margery Kempe: 1, 28, 30, 31, 33–34, 36–37, 46, 48, 51, 413
  The Book of Margery Kempe: 5, 6 n. 25, 30, 33 n. 24, 35, 37, 103, 413
Kenelm (Saint): 216, 218, 222–23

Killum, John: 326
Kirkby, Margaret: 367

Langford, Henry: 326
Langland, William: 47, 101
   Piers Plowman: 84, 391, 400
Lay Folks' Catechism: 174, 266
Legenda aurea: 219, 223, 343
Legend of St Thomas the Apostle: 389
Le merure de Seinte Eglise: 205
Life of Soul: 1, 11, 12, 14, 18, 171–89, 441
Lincolnshire Rebellion (March/May: 1470): 346
Li rossignos: 291
Lombard, Peter
   Sententiae: 437–39
Love, Nicholas
   Mirror of the Blessed Life of Jesus Christ: 87, 147, 312
Lucy (Saint): 223, 234, 249–50
Luther: 267, 281
Lydgate, John: 444
   Testament: 424
   Troy Book: 318

Margaret, Lady Hungerford: 345
Mary Rose (ship): 143
Massey, John: 275
Matilda, Countess of Tuscany: 126
Mechtild of Hackeborn: 17, 341
   Liber specialis gratiae: 17, 18, 341–44, 346–51, 355–56, 442
Meditaciones Domini nostri: 18, 364, 366, 372–73, 375–81
Meditationes vitae Christi: 373
Memoriale credencium: 451
Middleton, William: 271
Mildred of Minster-in-Thanet (Saint): 215, 218–19, 222–23, 225–26
Mirk, John
   Festial: 226
Miroir du monde: 298
Mont-Dieu (Carthusian house): 387
More, Thomas: 273, 333
Morice, James: 147
Mount Grace (Carthusian house): 388
Mouresleygh, Johanne: 12, 195–97
Myroure of oure Ladye: 345

Neville, Cecily: 342
Nicholas of Lyra: 93
   Postilla: 373
Northewode, John: 14, 255–56, 258, 266, 268

Of Actyfe Lyfe and Contemplatyfe Declaracion: 17, 331
Of Three Workings of Man's Soul: 373–74
Old English Soliloquies: 446
Oleum effusum compilation: 16, 292–94, 300–01, 304
On Wel Swuðe Ureisun of God: 9, 109–16, 118–19, 122, 126
Origen: 437
Oswald (Saint): 22–23
Oswald the Bishop (Saint): 222

Palladius: 401
   Palladius on Husbondrie: 401–02
   Opus agriculturae: 401
Patrick (Saint): 222
Pecham, John: 47, 78, 174
   1282 Lambeth decree *Ignorantia sacerdotum*: 38, 40, 298
   Syllabus: 174, 451
Pecock, Reginald: 91–92, 103, 314
Peraldus, William
   Summa aurea (*Summa virtutum et vitiorum*): 64, 72, 203
Pershore Abbey: 226
Peter of Limoges
   De oculo morali: 72
Peter Pomegranate (ship): 143
Peto, William: 283
Pigna, Giovanni Battista
   Poetica Horatiana: 149
Pistle of Discrecioun of Stirings: 331
Pore Caitif: 1, 3, 3 n. 7, 4, 4 n. 17, 7, 9–11, 14, 44, 74, 76– 78, 132–40, 142–50, 157–68, 195, 231–45, 247, 249–50, 252, 295, 304, 325, 388, 415–16, 441, 444, 447, 451
Prudentius
   Psychomachia: 276
Pseudo-Bonaventura: 87
Pseudo-Chrysostom
   Opus imperfectum in Matthaeum: 204, 205, 209
Pupilla oculi (John de Burgh): 6, 40, 41, 45–47

Quandoque tribularis: 415–16
Quinque compilationes antiquae: 439

Raymond of Peñafort
   Nova compilatio decretalium: 439
Repingdon, Philip, Bishop of Lincoln: 39
Richard of St Victor: 373
   Benjamin major: 374
Richmond, William: 143
Reynolds, Richard: 271, 273, 278
Robert of Basevorn: 33, 68
   Forma praedicandi: 7, 33 n. 21, 67
Roberts, Edmund: 145
Roberts, Thomas: 9, 132, 133, 134, 145, 149
Rolle, Richard: 1, 15–17, 19, 39, 46, 65, 70, 95, 97, 148, 150, 180, 195, 205, 241, 244, 291, 303, 311–12, 316, 319, 324, 329, 332, 367–69, 374–75, 377, 381, 415
   Ego dormio: 200, 292, 328, 369, 377
   Emendatio vitae: 157, 292, 389
   Expositio super primum versiculum Canticum Canticorum: 15–16, 292–93
   Incendium amoris: 6, 16, 292–93, 301
   Judica me Deus: 47
   Meditation B: 367
   Melos amoris: 292, 324
   Psalm Commentaries: 65, 68, 95, 97
   The Commandment: 18, 195, 292, 300, 327, 364, 366–70, 372–73, 378, 380–82
   The Form of Living: 39, 157, 161, 165, 178, 195, 240–41, 292, 328, 331, 369, 377
Rotuli parliamentorum: 444
Rufinus: 390

Sayings of the Desert Fathers: 391
Seven Points of True Love and Everlasting Wisdom: 330
Shaftesbury Abbey: 12, 195
Sheen (Carthusian house): 280, 299, 332, 368
Shirburn Castle (Earls of Macclesfield): 149
Sicardus, Bishop of Cremona: 390
Somme le roi: 72, 298
Song of Songs: 292, 300, 323, 351, 404
South English Legendaries: 13, 215–27, 442

Speculum christiani: 1, 5, 6, 32–34, 37–52, 91, 314, 441
Speculum devotorum: 31
Speculum peccatoris: 75, 366
Speculum spiritualium: 298, 300-01, 304
Speculum vitae: 46, 389, 393
Stephen (Saint): 246
Stimulus amoris: 6, 312
St Botolph's church, North Cove: 425
St Mary at Hill, London: 136
St Mary's church, Belchamp Walter: 424
St Mary Magdalene's church, Ickleton: 426
Suso, Henry: 417
   Horologium sapientiae: 350, 417, 420
Swithun (Saint): 222, 225–26
Syon Abbey: 15, 17, 84, 271, 342–43, 345–46, 375

The Abbey of the Holy Ghost: 178
The Booke of Gostlye Grace: 18, 341
The Book of Privy Counselling: 331
The Book of Tribulation: 173, 178, 181–85
The Chastising of God's Children: 1, 3, 4, 16, 18–20, 178–79, 292, 295, 325, 330, 350, 387, 411–19, 421–24, 426, 440–42, 447
The Cloud of Unknowing: 1, 126, 179, 331
The *Cloud*-author: 1, 114, 179
The Desert of Religion: 1, 19, 385–93, 395–404, 441
The Epistle of St. John the Hermit: 328
The Fifteen Oes: 375
The Manere of Good Lyvyng: 394
The Mirror of our Lady: 446
The Mirror of Sinners: 7, 75–78
The Monk of Eynsham: 18, 364, 381
   Visio monachi de Eynsham: 366, 379–80
The Orcherd of Syon: 84
The Orrmulum: 447
The *Pearl*-poet: 102
The Prick of Conscience: 7, 39, 46, 74, 327–28, 330, 389
The Prickyng of Love: 330
The Rule of Life of Our Lady: 328
The Southern Passion: 220
The Three Arrows on Doomsday: 1, 6–9, 63–65, 67–70, 73–78, 441
The Treatise of the Seven Points of True Love: 350

Thomas à Kempis
  Imitation of Christ: 179
Thomas of Ireland
  Manipulus florum: 72
Thoresby, John, Archbishop of York: 38, 47, 174
Thornton, Robert: 3
Thorpe, William: 234, 242–44
Trevisa, John: 314
Tnugdal: 18, 364
  Visio Tnugdali: 366, 379–80
Tudor, Mary: 132, 147
Tyndale, William: 275

Ursula (Saint): 219, 223
Usk, Thomas: 101, 103
  Testament of Love: 104

Vado mori: 388
Vettori, Pietro
  Commentarii in librum Demetrii Phalerei de elocutione: 149
Vincent of Beauvais
  Speculum maius: 91
Virgil: 444
Vulgate: 89, 118, 134, 178, 180, 373

Whitford, Richard: 15, 17, 18, 345

Dyuers Holy Instrucyons and Teachynges: 15, 271–72, 441
William de Montibus: 66
William of Pagula
  Oculus sacerdotis: 40, 47
William of St Thierry: 415
  Golden Epistle: 387
Winifred of Gwytherin (Saint): 215, 219–20, 222–23, 226–27
Witham (Carthusian house): 387
Wulfstan (Saint): 216, 218
Wycliffite Bible: 94–95, 98
Wycliffite Psalms: 89
Wylby, Elizabeth: 330
Wynkyn de Worde: 147, 148, 150, 327, 332

XII Lettynges of Prayer: 203

York Minster: 46

Þe Holy Boke Gratia Dei: 3, 7, 67–68, 70, 203, 387
Þe Pater Noster of Richard Ermyte: 1, 194, 198, 202–05
Þe Wohunge of Ure Lauerd: 9, 109, 110, 111, 114–22

Medieval Church Studies

All volumes in this series are evaluated by an Editorial Board, strictly on academic grounds, based on reports prepared by referees who have been commissioned by virtue of their specialism in the appropriate field. The Board ensures that the screening is done independently and without conflicts of interest. The definitive texts supplied by authors are also subject to review by the Board before being approved for publication. Further, the volumes are copyedited to conform to the publisher's stylebook and to the best international academic standards in the field.

Titles in Series

Megan Cassidy-Welch, *Monastic Spaces and their Meanings: Thirteenth-Century English Cistercian Monasteries* (2001)

Elizabeth Freeman, *Narratives of a New Order: Cistercian Historical Writing in England, 1150–1220* (2002)

The Study of the Bible in the Carolingian Era, ed. by Celia Chazelle and Burton Van Name Edwards (2003)

Text and Controversy from Wyclif to Bale: Essays in Honour of Anne Hudson, ed. by Helen Barr and Ann M. Hutchison (2005)

Lena Roos, *'God Wants It!': The Ideology of Martyrdom in the Hebrew Crusade Chronicles and its Jewish and Christian Background* (2006)

Emilia Jamroziak, *Rievaulx Abbey and its Social Context, 1132–1300: Memory, Locality, and Networks* (2004)

The Voice of Silence: Women's Literacy in a Men's Church, ed. by Thérèse de Hemptinne and María Eugenia Góngora (2004)

Perspectives for an Architecture of Solitude: Essays on Cistercians, Art and Architecture in Honour of Peter Fergusson, ed. by Terryl N. Kinder (2004)

Saints, Scholars, and Politicians: Gender as a Tool in Medieval Studies, ed. by Mathilde van Dijk and Renée Nip (2005)

Manuscripts and Monastic Culture: Reform and Renewal in Twelfth-Century Germany, ed. by Alison I. Beach (2007)

Weaving, Veiling, and Dressing: Textiles and their Metaphors in the Late Middle Ages, ed. by Kathryn M. Rudy and Barbara Baert (2007)

James J. Boyce, *Carmelite Liturgy and Spiritual Identity: The Choir Books of Kraków* (2008)

Studies in Carthusian Monasticism in the Late Middle Ages, ed. by Julian M. Luxford (2009)

Kevin J. Alban, *The Teaching and Impact of the 'Doctrinale' of Thomas Netter of Walden (c. 1374–1430)* (2010)

Gunilla Iversen, *Laus angelica: Poetry in the Medieval Mass*, ed. by Jane Flynn, trans. by William Flynn (2010)

Kriston R. Rennie, *Law and Practice in the Age of Reform: The Legatine Work of Hugh of Die (1073–1106)* (2010)

After Arundel: Religious Writing in Fifteenth-Century England, ed. by Vincent Gillespie and Kantik Ghosh (2011)

Federico Botana, *The Works of Mercy in Italian Medieval Art (c. 1050–c. 1400)* (2011)

The Regular Canons in the Medieval British Isles, ed. by Janet Burton and Karen Stöber (2011)

Wycliffite Controversies, ed. by Mishtooni Bose and J. Patrick Hornbeck II (2011)

Nickiphoros I. Tsougarakis, *The Latin Religious Orders in Medieval Greece, 1204–1500* (2012)

Nikolaos G. Chrissis, *Crusading in Frankish Greece: A Study of Byzantine-Western Relations and Attitudes, 1204–1282* (2012)

Demetrio S. Yocum, *Petrarch's Humanist Writing and Carthusian Monasticism: The Secret Language of the Self* (2013)

The Pseudo-Bonaventuran Lives of Christ: Exploring the Middle English Tradition, ed. by Ian Johnson and Allan F. Westphall (2013)

Alice Chapman, *Sacred Authority and Temporal Power in the Writings of Bernard of Clairvaux* (2013)

Religious Controversy in Europe, 1378–1536: Textual Transmission and Networks of Readership, ed. by Michael Van Dussen and Pavel Soukup (2013)

Ian Johnson, *The Middle English Life of Christ: Academic Discourse, Translation, and Vernacular Theology* (2013)

Monasteries on the Borders of Medieval Europe: Conflict and Cultural Interaction, ed. by Emilia Jamroziak and Karen Stöber (2014)

M. J. Toswell, *The Anglo-Saxon Psalter* (2014)

Envisioning the Bishop: Images and the Episcopacy in the Middle Ages, ed. by Sigrid Danielson and Evan A. Gatti (2014)

Kathleen E. Kennedy, *The Courtly and Commercial Art of the Wycliffite Bible* (2014)

David N. Bell, *The Library of the Abbey of La Trappe: A Study of its History from the Twelfth Century to the French Revolution, with an Annotated Edition of the 1752 Catalogue* (2014)

Patronage, Production, and Transmission of Texts in Medieval and Early Modern Jewish Cultures, ed. by Esperanza Alfonso and Jonathan Decter (2014)

Devotional Culture in Late Medieval England and Europe: Diverse Imaginations of Christ's Life, edited by Stephen Kelly and Ryan Perry (2014)

Matthew Cheung Salisbury, *The Secular Liturgical Office in Late Medieval England* (2015)

From Hus to Luther: Visual Culture in the Bohemian Reformation (1380–1620), ed. by Kateřina Horníčková and Michal Šroněk (2016)

Medieval Liège at the Crossroads of Europe: Monastic Society and Culture, 1000–1300, ed. by Steven Vanderputten, Tjamke Snijders, and Jay Diehl (2017)

Episcopal Power and Local Society in Medieval Europe, 900–1400, ed. by Peter Coss, Chris Dennis, Melissa Julian-Jones, and Angelo Silvestri (2017)

Saints of North-East England, 600–1500, ed. by Margaret Coombe, Anne Mouron, and Christiania Whitehead (2017)

Tamás Karáth, *Richard Rolle: The Fifteenth-Century Translations* (2017)

In Preparation

Episcopal Power and Personality in Medieval Europe, 900–1480, ed. by Peter Coss, Chris Dennis, Melissa Julian-Jones, and Angelo Silvestri

Inwardness, Individualization, and Religious Agency in the Late Medieval Low Countries: The Devotio Moderna and Beyond, ed. by Rijcklof Hofman, Charles Caspers, Peter Nissen, Mathilde van Dijk, and Johan Oosterman

Bishops' Identities, Careers, and Networks in Medieval Europe, ed. by Sarah E. Thomas